Augmentative and
Alternative Communication

Augmentative and Alternative Communication

Management of Severe Communication Disorders in Children and Adults

Second Edition

by

David R. Beukelman, Ph.D.
University of Nebraska
Lincoln, Nebraska

Pat Mirenda, Ph.D.
University of British Columbia
Vancouver, Canada

·P A U L·H·
BROOKES
PUBLISHING C⁰

Baltimore • London • Toronto • Sydney

Paul H. Brookes Publishing Co.
Post Office Box 10624
Baltimore, Maryland 21285-0624

www.pbrookes.com

Typeset by Brushwood Graphics, Inc., Baltimore, Maryland.
Manufactured in the United States of America by
The Maple Press Co., York, Pennsylvania.

With the exception of Katie, the individuals described in this book are composites of various people, and pseudonyms have been used. Any similarity to actual individuals is coincidental, and no implications should be inferred.

Permission to reprint the poem appearing on p. 125 is gratefully acknowledged.

From Silverstein, S. (1974). *Where the sidewalk ends* (p. 101). New York: Harper & Row. Copyright © 1974 by Evil Eye Music, Inc. Reprinted by permission of HarperCollins.

Second printing, March 1999.

Library of Congress Cataloging-in-Publication Data

Beukelman, David R., 1943–
    Augmentative and alternative communication : management of severe communication
    disorders in children and adults / by David R. Beukelman and Pat Mirenda.—2nd ed.
        p.   cm.
    Includes bibliographical references and index.
    ISBN 1-55766-333-5
    1. Handicapped—Means of communication.   2. Communication devices for the disabled.
I. Mirenda, Pat.   II. Title.   [DNLM: 1. Communicative Disorders—rehabilitation.
2. Communication Aids for Disabled.   WL 340.2 B566a 1998]
RC423.B477   1998
616.85'503—dc21
DNLM/DLC
for Library of Congress   97-42827
                                                                                                                            CIP

British Library Cataloguing in Publication data are available from the British Library.

Contents

About the Authors

David R. Beukelman, Ph.D., Professor, Department of Special Education and Communication Disorders, University of Nebraska–Lincoln, 202F Barkley Memorial Center, Lincoln, NE 68583-0732

Dr. Beukelman is a speech-language pathologist with considerable experience in providing augmentative and alternative communication services. He is the Barkley Professor of Communication Disorders at the University of Nebraska–Lincoln and Director of Research and Education of the Speech and Language Pathology Division of the Munroe-Meyer Institute of Genetics and Rehabilitation, Omaha, Nebraska. Previously, Dr. Beukelman was Director of the Augmentative Communication Program, University of Washington Hospital, and Associate Professor in the Department of Rehabilitation Medicine of the University of Washington–Seattle.

Dr. Beukelman concluded a 4-year term in 1997 as Editor of the journal *Augmentative and Alternative Communication* and has published extensively in books and journals. Dr. Beukelman is a co-author of the book *Clinical Management of Dysarthric Speakers* (College-Hill, 1988) and is a co-editor of *Clinical Management of Communication and Swallowing Disorders in Persons with Traumatic Brain Injury* (PRO-ED, 1990) as well as numerous books in the area of motor speech disorders. In addition, Dr. Beukelman has co-authored several computer software programs for people with severe communication disorders, including the Sentence Intelligibility Test, Pacer/Tally, and Cue-Write.

Pat Mirenda, Ph.D., Associate Professor, Faculty of Education, University of British Columbia, 2125 Main Mall, Vancouver, British Columbia V6T 1Z4, CANADA

Dr. Mirenda earned her doctorate in behavioral disabilities from the University of Wisconsin–Madison and specializes in the education of people with severe and profound disabilities. For 8 years, she was a faculty member in the Department of Special Education and Communication Disorders, University of Nebraska–Lincoln. From 1992 to 1996, she provided a variety of training, research, and support services to individuals with severe disabilities through CBI Consultants, Ltd., in Vancouver, British Columbia. She is Associate Professor in the Department of Educational Psychology and Special Education at the University of British Columbia. Through the years, Dr. Mirenda has concentrated on augmentative and alternative communication for people with developmental disabilities. In addition, she has focused on the integration and inclusion of augmented communicators in general education classrooms.

Dr. Mirenda is the author of book chapters and extensive research publications concerning severe disabilities and augmentative communication. She is currently Editor of the journal *Augmentative and Alternative Communication*.

ABOUT THE CONTRIBUTORS

Kathryn L. Garrett, Ph.D., CCC-SLP, Assistant Professor, Department of Speech-Language Pathology, Duquesne University, 600 Forbes Avenue, Pittsburgh, PA 15282-2231

Dr. Garrett received her doctorate at the University of Nebraska–Lincoln. She has served as Director of AAC Services at the Madonna Rehabilitation Hospital, as Clinical Supervisor in the Barkley Speech and Hearing Clinic at the University of Nebraska–Lincoln, and as Director of Clinical Training in the Department of Communication at the University of Pittsburgh. Currently, she is an assistant professor in the Department of Speech-Language Pathology at Duquesne University, Pittsburgh. She has published extensively in the areas of aphasia and augmentative and alternative communication.

Janet Sturm, Ph.D., CCC-SLP, Assistant Professor, Division of Speech and Hearing Sciences, Department of Medical Allied Health Professions, the School of Medicine, CB# 7190 Wing D Medical School, University of North Carolina–Chapel Hill, Chapel Hill, NC 27599-7190

Dr. Sturm received her doctorate at the University of Nebraska–Lincoln and completed a postdoctoral fellowship at the Munroe-Meyer Institute of Genetics and Rehabilitation in Omaha, Nebraska. Dr. Sturm's professional interests include communication in classroom environments and literacy development.

Preface

Augmentative and Alternative Communication: Management of Severe Communication Disorders in Children and Adults, Second Edition, is an introductory text written for practicing professionals, preprofessional students, and facilitators who are interested in learning more about communication options for people who are unable to meet their daily communication needs through natural modes such as speech, gestures, or handwriting. Because severe communication disorders can result from a variety of conditions, diseases, and syndromes that affect people of all ages, many individuals may be interested in these approaches. Several characteristics of the augmentative and alternative communication (AAC) field have shaped the format, content, and organization of this book.

First, AAC is a multidisciplinary field in which users and their families, along with computer programmers, educators, engineers, linguists, occupational therapists, physical therapists, psychologists, speech-language pathologists, and many other professionals have contributed to the knowledge and practice base. We have attempted to be sensitive to these people's multiple perspectives and contributions by directly citing pertinent information from a wide variety of sources and by guiding the reader to appropriate additional sources when necessary.

Second, the AAC field has developed in many countries over the past five decades. For example, in 1998, individuals from 44 countries were members of the International Society for Augmentative and Alternative Communication (ISAAC). Although we are both from North America, we have made an effort to offer an international perspective in this book by including information about the contributions of AAC users, researchers, and clinicians from around the world. Unfortunately, within the constraints of an introductory textbook, only a limited number of these contributions can be cited specifically. Thus, we acknowledge that our primary sources of material have come from North America and hope that our AAC colleagues in other countries will tolerate our inability to represent multinational efforts more comprehensively.

Third, AAC interventions involve both electronic and nonelectronic systems. AAC technology changes very rapidly—products are being upgraded continually, and new products are always being introduced. Such product information presented in book form would be outdated very quickly. Therefore, we refer our readers to technical information resources that are updated on a regular schedule. These four resources provide assistive technology information in a variety of formats to meet the needs of individuals, agencies, universities, and resource centers:

1. *The Guide to Augmentative and Alternative Communication Devices* is a flipchart that provides information regarding device characteristics of AAC systems, voice amplifiers, and artificial electronic larynges, as well as a glossary and current information about manufacturers. This chart is available from the Rehabilitation Engineering Research Center on Augmentative and Alternative Communication, Applied Science and Engineering Laboratories, University of Delaware/Alfred I. DuPont Institute, 1600 Rockland Road, Post Office Box 269, Wilmington, DE 19899 (302-651-6830).

2. *Trace Resourcebook: Assistive Technologies for Communication, Control, and Computer Access, 1996–97 Edition* (Borden, Lubich, & Vanderheiden, 1995) lists products designed specifically to meet the needs of people with disabilities. It addresses "the full range of technologies for communication, control, and computer access" (p. vii). The *Trace Resourcebook* is available from the Trace Research and Development Center, University of Wisconsin–Madison, S-151 Waisman Center, 1500 Highland Avenue, Madison, WI 53705 (608-263-5788).

3. Co-Net is an electronic resource that contains Hyper-ABLEDATA and Hyper-Tracebase for Macintosh computers and DOS-ABLEDATA and DOS-Tracebase for IBM-compatible computers. Co-Net is available in CD-ROM form and also at the Trace Research and Development Center World Wide Web site (http://trace.wisc.edu/tcel/).

4. The AAC World Wide Web site hosted by the Barkley AAC Center at the University of Nebraska–Lincoln (http://aac.unl.edu) provides links to the World Wide Web sites of manufacturers and publishers in the AAC field. Information in the AAC World Wide Web site is updated regularly.

In addition, readers may refer to the Resource List in the Appendix for more information about the companies providing the AAC products and services that are mentioned in this book. Readers may also refer to the World Wide Web site associated with this book (http://www.pbrookes.com/aac/) for an online version of the references list and a glossary of AAC terminology.

A fourth characteristic of the AAC field is that it incorporates three general areas of information. The first area relates to the processes of AAC: messages, symbols, alternative access, assessment, and intervention planning. The second area describes procedures that have been developed to serve individuals with developmental disabilities who require AAC services. The third area focuses on people with disabilities acquired later in life. In an effort to cover these areas, we have divided the book into three sections.

Specifically, the eight chapters in Part I are organized to introduce readers to AAC processes. Chapter 1 introduces the reader to AAC in general and to people with severe communication disorders in particular. Often using these individuals' own words, we attempt to convey what it means to be unable to speak and to use AAC systems to interact. Chapter 2 reviews the message types that are frequently communicated by AAC users and, therefore, are often stored in their systems. Chapter 3 is a detailed presentation of the most common aided and unaided symbol systems used to represent messages, as well as message encoding and rate enhancement strategies used in AAC applications. Chapter 4 discusses a range of alternative access options to accommodate a variety of motor, language, and cognitive impairments. Chapter 5 focuses on team building to support AAC assessment and intervention. Chapters 6 and 7 discuss assessment, and Chapter 8 considers AAC intervention decision making. The latter three chapters also discuss in detail the interaction, participation, and consensus management frameworks that we have utilized extensively.

Part II contains six chapters that review AAC interventions for users with developmental disabilities. Specifically, Chapter 9 introduces AAC concerns unique to people with developmental disabilities. Chapter 10 describes AAC for beginning communicators who use nonsymbolic communication strategies. Chapter 11 focuses on beginning communicators who use symbolic approaches. Chapter 12 deals with the language development of AAC users; and Chapter 13, written with Janet Sturm, focuses on the literacy development of AAC users. Chapter 14, also written with Janet Sturm, describes a framework for the educational integration and inclusion of students with AAC systems.

Part III, composed of the last four chapters of the book, focuses on AAC users with acquired communication disorders. Chapter 15 reviews AAC interventions for adults with acquired physical disabilities, including amyotrophic lateral sclerosis, multiple sclerosis, Parkinson's disease, spinal cord injury, and brain-stem stroke. Chapter 16, written with Kathryn L. Garrett, describes a functional classification scheme for people with severe aphasia and contains related intervention strategies and techniques. Chapter 17 addresses AAC assessments and interventions according to the cognitive levels of people with traumatic brain injury. Finally, Chapter 18 reviews a wide range of AAC interventions for people in intensive and acute care medical settings. Particular attention is focused on individuals who are unable to communicate because of respiratory impairments.

REFERENCES

Borden, P., Lubich, J., & Vanderheiden, G. (1995). *Trace Resourcebook: Assistive technologies for communication, control, and computer access, 1996–97 edition.* Madison, WI: Trace Research and Development Center.

Trace Research and Development Center. (1997, April). *Co-Net* [CD-ROM]. Madison, WI: Author.

Rehabilitation Engineering Research Center on Augmentative and Alternative Communication. (1996). *The guide to augmentative and alternative communication devices* [Flipchart]. Wilmington: University of Delaware.

Acknowledgments

As we revised this book, we remained keenly aware of our dependence on those who have documented their experiences in the augmentative and alternative communication field. In order to tell the "AAC story," we expected to cite traditional documents— professional research papers, scholarly books, and manuals. What we found is that we also made extensive use of the perspectives of AAC users, as documented in a variety of magazines, videotapes, and other popular sources. AAC facilitators have also contributed to this book by giving their conclusions about the AAC experience through formal and informal case studies. Thus, we wish to thank those publishers, editors, associations, manufacturers, and institutions who supported the newsletters, bulletins, books, videotapes, magazines, and journals that now contain the historical record of the AAC field. Without these resources, we simply would have been unable to compile our book. We also want to acknowledge the role of the Barkley Trust in supporting AAC efforts at the University of Nebraska–Lincoln through the years. While we were revising this book, David R. Beukelman also served as Director of Research and Education of the Speech and Language Pathology Division of the Munroe-Meyer Institute of Genetics and Rehabilitation. Janet Sturm was a postdoctoral fellow at the Institute and was supported by Grant No. MCJ-319152, awarded to the Institute by the Bureau of Maternal and Child Health Services. In addition, we have appreciated the support, encouragement, and assistance from the people at Paul H. Brookes Publishing Co., especially Melissa Behm, Elaine Niefeld, Mika Sam, and Lisa Rapisarda.

Special appreciation is also due to a number of individuals with whom we have been fortunate to work before and during the production of this book. These include the students, families, staff, and administrators of the public school system in Lincoln, Nebraska; Madonna Rehabilitation Hospital; the Munroe-Meyer Institute of Genetics and Rehabilitation; the Educational Center for Students with Disabilities at the University of Nebraska–Lincoln; CBI Consultants, Ltd.; Sunny Hill Health Centre for Children; and Richmond School District #38 in British Columbia. These individuals have collaborated with us through the years and have thus greatly contributed to our AAC experiences and knowledge. Scott Cotton assisted us with photography, Cliff Hollestelle provided some illustrations, and Dyann Rupp and Michelle Dombrovskis managed the composite reference list. The "unsinkable" Nancy Brown was invaluably helpful as we organized, typed, proofed, checked, and rechecked the manuscript, and we are truly grateful for her support throughout the years. Finally, we thank the AAC users and their families who, through the years, have taught us about the AAC field and who have allowed us to use their stories. May their voices grow ever stronger.

Both the first edition and the second edition of this book were collaborative efforts, with both of us completing those tasks that fit our areas of expertise and skills. Because we shared these tasks so completely, it was difficult to order the authorship for the first edition, and we had hoped to reverse the order for the second edition. We have not done so, however, in order not to confuse the status of this book as a second edition.

To my wife, Helen, and my children, Julie, Jeffrey, and Jonathan, who understand and support my commitments to persons with severe communication disabilities

To my father, Verne, who showed me what it meant to live successfully with a disability and to my mother, Cora, who made certain that I learned to read and write during those years when I struggled

—David Beukelman

To those who have yet to receive effective AAC services, and especially to those who have lost their lives through acts of neglect or violence because they were unable to communicate

—Pat Mirenda

Augmentative and
Alternative Communication

Part I

Augmentative and Alternative Communication Processes

1

Introduction

What Is Augmentative and Alternative Communication?

Before answering the question "What is augmentative and alternative communication (AAC)?" we must first ask "What is communication?" A document produced by the National Joint Committee for the Communicative Needs of Persons with Severe Disabilities defined communication as

> Any act by which one person gives to or receives from another person information about that person's needs, desires, perceptions, knowledge, or affective states. Communication may be intentional or unintentional, may involve conventional or unconventional signals, may take linguistic or nonlinguistic forms, and may occur through spoken or other modes. (1992, p. 2)

The "other modes" in this definition refer directly to AAC, which the American Speech-Language-Hearing Association (ASHA) defined as

> An area of clinical practice that attempts to compensate (either temporarily or permanently) for the impairment and disability patterns of individuals with severe expressive communication disorders (i.e., the severely speech-language and writing impaired). (1989, p. 107)

In accordance with an ASHA position paper published in 1991, it is important to emphasize that AAC interventions should always be multimodal in nature; that is, they should utilize "the individual's full communication capabilities, including any residual speech or vocalizations, gestures, signs, and aided communication" (ASHA, 1991, p. 10). This document also introduced and defined several terms commonly used in the AAC field. An *AAC system* is "an integrated group of components, including the symbols, aids, strategies, and techniques used by individuals to enhance communication" (ASHA, 1991, p. 10). This definition of a system also emphasizes the use of multiple components or modes for communication. As used in this definition, the term *symbol* refers to the methods used for "visual, auditory, and/or tactile representation of conventional concepts (e.g., gestures, photographs, manual sign sets/systems, picto-ideographs, printed words, objects, spoken words, Braille)" (ASHA, 1991, p. 10). It is important to note that according to this definition, the use of gestural communication (including, for example, facial expressions, eye gazing, and body postures, in addition to hand gestures) falls within the overall definition of AAC. This means that interventions designed to increase the ability of individuals with the most severe intellectual disabilities (e.g., mental retardation requiring pervasive support) to communicate through gestures and other natural modes fall within the domain of the AAC specialist. This contrasts with other definitions that consider the use of such gestures to be AAC "prerequisites" rather than legitimate targets for AAC efforts (Shane & Bashir, 1980; see also Chapter 6).

The term *aid* refers to "a physical object or device used to transmit or receive messages (e.g., communication book, board, chart, mechanical or electronic device, computer)" (ASHA, 1991, p. 10). In this text, we use the terms *aid* and *device* interchangeably. A *strategy*, as defined by ASHA, is a "specific way of using [AAC] aids, symbols, and/or techniques more effectively for enhanced communication. A strategy, whether taught to an individual or self-discovered, is a plan that can facilitate one's performance" (ASHA, 1991, p. 10). Thus, role playing, graduated prompting/fading, and attending a college class to learn a word processing program are all strategies that are applicable to AAC interventions. Finally, the term *technique* refers to "a method of transmitting messages (e.g., linear scanning, row–column scanning, encoding, signing, and natural gesturing)" (ASHA, 1991, p. 10). These four components—symbol, aid, strategy, and technique—are the critical elements that compose all AAC interventions.

WHO USES AUGMENTATIVE AND ALTERNATIVE COMMUNICATION?

There is no typical AAC user. People who use or need to have access to AAC come from all age groups, socioeconomic groups, and ethnic and racial backgrounds. Their only unifying characteristic is the fact that, for whatever reason, they require adaptive assistance for speaking and/or writing. In North America, ASHA put forth the most commonly used definition of this population in 1991:

> Individuals with severe communication disorders are those who may benefit from AAC—those for whom gestural, speech, and/or written communication is temporarily or permanently inadequate to meet all of their communication needs. For those individuals, hearing impairment is not the primary cause for the communication impairment. Although some individuals may be able to produce a limited amount of speech, it is inadequate to meet their varied communication needs. Numerous terms that were initially used in the field but are now rarely mentioned include speechless, nonoral, nonvocal, nonverbal, and aphonic. (p. 10)

A variety of congenital or acquired impairments can cause the inability to speak or write without adaptive assistance. The most common congenital causes of such severe communication disorders include mental retardation, cerebral palsy, autism, and developmental apraxia of speech (Mirenda & Mathy-Laikko, 1989). Acquired impairments that most often result in the need for AAC assistance include amyotrophic lateral sclerosis, multiple sclerosis (MS), traumatic brain injury, stroke, and spinal cord injury (Beukelman & Yorkston, 1989; see also Parts II and III for prevalence figures and demographic information related to each of these impairments).

Published prevalence estimates of the number of people with severe speech and/or writing impairments vary widely, depending on the country, age group, and type(s) of disability surveyed. Beukelman and Ansel (1995) summarized the existing demographic data and suggested that 8–12 individuals per 1,000 in the general population (0.8%–1.2%) experience severe communication impairments that require AAC. For example, in the United States, 2,521,000 Americans older than the age of 15 experience difficulty having their speech understood by others; this represents 1.3% of the entire U.S. population in this age group (Census Bureau, 1996). However, this figure probably includes people with communication impairments that are usually unrelated to AAC, such as severe stuttering and lack of speech due to deafness (Fay, 1993). In addition, approximately 529,000 American children younger than the age of 15 experience a severe disability, although whether this includes a communication impairment is not clear (Census Bureau, 1996). The incidence of individuals with severe writing impairments in the United States is not known. In total, these figures represent a substantial increase over ASHA's 1991 estimate that 2 million Americans have severe communication impairments.

Lindsay, Cambria, McNaughton, and Warrick (1986) estimated that in Canada in the early 1980s, 200,000 children and adults had congenital, acquired, and progressive disabilities and severe speaking and writing impairments. Data extrapolated from the 1991 Health and Activity Limitation Survey (HALS) suggested that approximately 243,000 Canadians older than the age of 15 have difficulty speaking and being understood (Health and Welfare Canada, 1988); this represents approximately 0.9% of the total population in that age group. Approximately 20,000 of these Canadians also reported that they needed or actually used a "technical aid" for speaking (Health and Welfare Canada, 1988). These figures are undoubtedly conservative in that they include neither children younger than 15 nor individuals with severe writing impairments.

Outside North America, demographic estimates of the AAC population are more variable. Paralleling the North American estimates, a study by Enderby and Philipp (1986) suggested that 800,000 individuals (1.4% of the total population) in the United Kingdom have a severe communication disorder that makes it difficult for them to be understood by anyone outside their immediate family. An Australian survey of the province of Victoria, which has more than 4 million residents, however, identified approximately 5,000 individuals who were unable to speak adequately for communication; this represents only 0.12% of the population (Bloomberg & Johnson, 1990). Similarly, a nationwide survey in Hungary conducted from 1988 to 1989 suggested that 0.06% of the population had severe speech disorders; however, this did not include people with autism or with acquired disorders such as aphasia (Kalman & Pajor, 1996). The wide variations found in these studies are probably due more to the definitions and sampling techniques used than to actual differences in prevalence rates.

The prevalence of severe communication disorders also appears to vary considerably with age. Based on the results of several studies, Blackstone (1990) suggested that 0.2%–0.6% of the total school-age population worldwide has a severe speech impairment. A Canadian study suggested that the prevalence rate increases to 0.8% of individuals from 45 to 54 years of age and reaches a high of 4.2% for people 85 years of age and older (Hirdes, Ellis-Hale, & Pearson Hirdes, 1993).

WHAT IS IT LIKE TO HAVE A SEVERE COMMUNICATION DISORDER?

Perhaps more relevant (certainly, more interesting) than demographic figures are the stories and experiences of people who are unable to speak and write. A number of these individuals, using their various communication devices, have written firsthand accounts of their experiences; from these, we can sense what it is like to be unable to communicate. Rick Creech, a young man with cerebral palsy, wrote the following:

> If you want to know what it is like to be unable to speak, there is a way. Go to a party and don't talk. Play mute. Use your hands if you wish but don't use paper and pencil. Paper and pencil are not always handy for a mute person. Here is what you will find:

people talking; talking behind, beside, around, over, under, through, and even for you. But never with you. You are ignored until finally you feel like a piece of furniture. (Musselwhite & St. Louis, 1988, p. 104)

Being unable to communicate also has a dramatic impact on an individual's ability to control even the most mundane aspects of life, as noted by Sara Brothers:

I know what it is like to be fed potatoes all my life. After all, potatoes are a good basic food for everyday, easy to fix in many different ways. I hate potatoes! But then, who knew that but me? I know what it is like to be dressed in red and blues when my favorite colors are mint greens, lemon yellows, and pinks. I mean really, can you imagine? (1991, p. 59)

Other writers with disabilities have emphasized the importance of attentive and responsive communication partners. Christopher Nolan, in his first book of poetry and short stories that speaks of his own experiences through the character of Joseph Meehan, wrote of his character's gratitude for teachers and others who took the time to understand his gestural communication:

Such were Joseph's teachers and such was their imagination that the mute boy became constantly amazed at the almost telepathic degree of certainty with which they read his facial expression, eye movements, and body language. Many a good laugh was had by teacher and pupil as they deciphered his code. It was at moments such as these that Joseph recognized the face of God in human form. It glimmered in their kindness to him, it glowed in their keenness, it hinted in their caring, indeed it caressed in their gaze. (1981, p. 11)

Creech's and Nolan's accounts are among many that have been written by individuals with congenital disabilities (in particular, cerebral palsy) who use AAC (see Huer & Lloyd, 1988, 1990, for additional sources). The experiences of these individuals differ from those with acquired disabilities because, as Creech noted,

I would like to walk, run, play the piano, talk with as little effort as most people, and everything other people do. I would like to be able to, but I don't miss not doing them, because I never have. So I have not had the trauma of accepting physical limitations which were the result of an accident or illness, which [would have] left me "handicapped." (1981, p. 550)

As this passage shows, people with acquired disabilities seem to experience the loss of communication skills as more traumatic than do people who grew up with such impairments. Easton described the thoughts of a woman with motor neuron disease (a progressive disorder) as she wrote about what it was like for her and her family in the initial stages of impairment:

Our lives were being turned upside down; frustration, anger, exasperation, and exhaustion were very evident. No one knew what to do for the best and the family felt helpless. . . .I have tried—and to some extent succeeded—to keep calm, because with the amount of communicating I have to do to cope each day, I would be in a permanent state of frustration. If, however, I do show some signs of frustration, I am told repeatedly to keep calm! (1989, pp. 16–17)

Brian Pamplin, a man with MS who lived in a chronic care facility for several months before he died in 1996, echoed Easton's thoughts and added his own about the degenerative nature of his disability:

I understand why we are called "patients" because "patience" is a required virtue of people who are so dependent on others to help with the functions that through most of their lives, they took for granted. (1996b, p. 16)

Pamplin also said,

> I have not been able to share all my reasons and my feelings about [MS and the changes it has caused in my family]. This is where my communication limitations intensify the difficulties caused by my MS. My wife and son don't realize how much more I would like to say to them. (1996a, p. 18)

The experience of the individual whose inability to speak is sudden rather than progressive is perhaps even more devastating. Doreen Joseph, who lost her speech following an accident, and Sue Simpson, who lost the ability to speak after a stroke at age 36, wrote the following about their experiences:

> I woke up one morning and I wasn't me. . . .
> There was somebody else in my bed.
> And all I had left was my head. . . .
>
> Speech is the most important thing we have. It makes us a person and not a thing. No one should ever have to be a "thing." (Joseph, 1986, p. 8)

> So you can't talk, and it's boring and frustrating and nobody quite understands how bad it really is. If you sit around and think about all the things you used to be able to do, that you can't do now, you'll be a miserable wreck and no one will want to hang around you long. (Simpson, 1988, p. 11)

Clearly, someone who has not "been there" cannot understand the experience of having a severe communication disorder. Similarly, it is impossible for most people to imagine what it must be like to be able to talk or write with an adaptive device after months or years of silence. Christy Brown, who first communicated by writing with chalk held in his left foot, recounted the day when he printed his first letter:

> I drew it—the letter "A." There it was on the floor before me. . . . I looked up. I saw my mother's face for a moment, tears on her cheeks. . . . I had done it! It had started—the thing that was to give my mind its chance of expressing itself. . . . That one letter, scrawled on the floor with a broken bit of yellow chalk gripped between my toes, was my road to a new world, my key to mental freedom. (1954, p. 17)

Similarly, Nolan wrote eloquently of the power of communication:

> Joseph continued to write. He recounted his experiences, his escried creeds and his crested benediction in typewritten words selected especially to describe a glorious bountiful nightmare. He saw life recoil before him, and using the third person he rescued poor sad boyhood and casting himself inside the frame of crippled Joseph Meehan he pranked himself as a storyteller, thereby casting renown on himself and casting disability before the reader. Look, he begged, look deep down; feel, he begged, sense life's limitations; cry, he begged, cry the tears of cruel frustration; but above all he begged laughter, laugh, he pleaded, for lovely laughter vanquishes raw wounded pride. (1987, p. 28)

Sadly, the "magic" of AAC is not readily available to all who need it. James Viggiano, a man with multiple disabilities who uses AAC, reminds us of the many individuals who cannot tell their stories, either because of language and literacy barriers or because they lack access to appropriate interventions:

> With technological advances, a new day is dawning in the lives of many nonspeaking individuals. . . but what about the thousands of . . . consumers who live silent, isolated existences in an archipelago of institutions where the advances you see today never reach the potential user. It is unconscionable that thousands of nonspeaking individuals have not had the opportunity. . .to access state of the art technology and optimistic professionals. (1981, p. 552)

Anne McDonald, who spent 10 years in an institution for people with mental retardation requiring extensive to pervasive supports before she was provided with access to a simple communication system, echoed Viggiano's sentiments in even more straightforward terms:

> Crushing the personalities of speechless individuals is very easy: just make it impossible for them to communicate freely. (Crossley & McDonald, 1984, p. 142)

Professionals and AAC users alike remind us that along with technology come costs, both financial and personal (Beukelman, 1991). In the following excerpt, McDonald wrote about the cost of technology from a consumer's perspective:

> I am not a fan of high technology. . . . The more severely disabled one is, the greater the effort involved in learning to use technology and the smaller the gains. I'm reluctant to make the effort until I'm certain the results will make the effort worthwhile. (Harrington, 1988, p. 7)

Even when technology is available, and even when AAC users incorporate it in their communication systems, the outcomes are not always as we might hope, especially in the area of employment. Rick Creech commented on this following the first annual Pittsburgh Employment Conference for Augmented Communicators (PEC@):

> Once, it might have been enough to focus on getting technology, both light and high, to people with significant speech and multiple impairments (SSMI). Though this struggle is nowhere near complete, other struggles must take place as well. Training people to communicate with technology is an important focus. . . . However, . . . the field of augmentative communication must now focus on getting successful augmented speakers employed and keeping a person employed who is developing SSMI. I am an augmentative communicator, and . . . I believe it is my right as a citizen to be employed if I honestly and sincerely seek employment. (1993, p. 3)

Like Creech, many people who use AAC have experienced it as opening doors for them and allowing them to dream in ways previously impossible. Two years before his untimely death in 1994, Andrew Murphy wrote,

> We all hope and plan for a better life. What that means to each of us will vary. I am no different and spend a lot of time thinking about my future. Thinking about finishing my education so I can get a job. Thinking about developing the skills so I can live on my own, with help of course. Thinking about making new friends and staying in touch with my old friends. Thinking about seeing more of the world and how I can make it a better place. (1994, p. 6)

As is evident from the foregoing accounts, the experience of having a severe communication disorder defies simple categorization. Similarly, the attitudes and priorities of these individuals and their communication partners are as important to the success of an intervention as are their abilities and the available options. It is only through consideration of all of these factors that interventions result in communicative competence.

PURPOSES OF COMMUNICATION INTERACTIONS

Perspective of the Person Using an AAC System

The work of Nolan, McDonald, and others who use low-technology (i.e., nonelectronic) systems reminds us that the ultimate goal of an AAC intervention is not to find a technological solution to the communication problem but to enable the individual to efficiently and effectively engage in a variety of interactions. Light (1988), in an extensive review of AAC interaction research, identified four agendas or purposes that communicative interactions fulfill: 1) communication of needs/wants, 2) information transfer,

3) social closeness, and 4) social etiquette (see Table 1.1). As shown in Table 1.1, the goal of expressing one's needs and wants is to regulate the behavior of the listener toward an action-oriented response. Examples include asking for help or ordering food in a restaurant. Here, the content of the message is important, the vocabulary is relatively predictable, and the accuracy and rate of message production are critical. It is likely that the high degree of predictability and concreteness inherent in these messages explains why needs/wants vocabulary often tends to predominate in many communication systems. In fact, it is not unusual to see communication books or boards that consist almost entirely of such vocabulary, regardless of how motivating or relevant the person using the AAC system finds the messages.

The second area of interaction, information transfer, involves messages that are much more complex and difficult to convey because the goal is to share information rather than to regulate behavior. Examples of people engaging in this kind of interaction include a child telling his or her teacher what he or she did over the weekend, an adolescent talking with friends about the upcoming senior prom, and an adult answer-

Table 1.1.   Characteristics of interactions intended to meet various social purposes

| Characteristics | Social purpose of the interaction | | | |
	Expression of needs/wants	Information transfer	Social closeness	Social etiquette
Goal of the interaction	To regulate the behavior of another as a means to fulfill needs/wants	To share information	To establish, maintain, and/or develop personal relationships	To conform to social conventions of politeness
Focus of the interaction	Desired object or action	Information	Interpersonal relationship	Social convention
Duration of the interaction	Limited. Emphasis is on initiating interaction.	May be lengthy. Emphasis is on developing interaction.	May be lengthy. Emphasis is on maintaining interaction.	Limited. Emphasis is on fulfilling designated turns.
Content of communication	Important	Important	Not important	Not important
Predictability of communication	Highly predictable	Not predictable	May be somewhat predictable	Highly predictable
Scope of communication	Limited scope	Wide scope	Wide scope	Very limited scope
Rate of communication	Important	Important	May not be important	Important
Tolerance for communication breakdown	Little tolerance	Little tolerance	Some tolerance	Little tolerance
Number of participants	Usually dyadic	Dyadic, small or large group	Usually dyadic or small group	Dyadic, small or large group
Independence of the communicator	Important	Important	Not important	Important
Partner	Familiar or unfamiliar	Familiar or unfamiliar	Usually familiar	Familiar or unfamiliar

From Light, J. (1988). Interaction involving individuals using augmentative and alternative communication systems: State of the art and future directions. *Augmentative and Alternative Communication, 4,* 76; reprinted by permission.

ing questions during a job interview. As is the case with needs/wants, the content of the message is quite important. Information transfer messages, however, are likely to be composed of novel (rather than predictable) words and sentences that allow the speaker to communicate about a wide variety of topics. Accuracy and rate of message production again remain paramount.

Communication related to social closeness greatly differs from the expression of needs and wants or the transfer of information. The goal of this type of interaction relates to establishing, maintaining, or developing personal relationships. Thus, the content of the message is less important than the interaction itself, and such messages are not usually predictable. Examples of people interacting in this way include a child telling a joke to classmates, a group of teenagers cheering for their team at a basketball game, and a woman expressing her feelings of sympathy to a friend whose mother recently died. In such interactions, the rate, accuracy, and content of the message, as well as the independence of the person communicating, are secondary to the feelings achieved through the interaction, which are connectedness and, to a greater or lesser extent, intimacy.

The goal of the fourth type of interaction listed in Table 1.1, social etiquette, is to conform to social conventions of politeness through interactions that are often brief and contain predictable vocabulary. Examples of people practicing social etiquette include a child saying "please" and "thank you" to his or her grandmother and an adult responding appropriately to a co-worker's comment about the weather. These messages closely resemble messages that express needs and wants because rate, accuracy, and communicative independence all are important factors for success.

Most of the research and technical developments in the field of AAC have focused on strategies for enhancing communication of needs and wants and, to a lesser extent, information transfer (Light, 1988, 1996). The lack of attention to interactions of social closeness reflects both a narrow clinical perspective and the very real difficulties inherent in achieving the goals of social closeness interactions. Nevertheless, from the perspectives of many AAC users and their significant communication partners, this type of interaction may be more important than any other. It is likely that the majority of interactions that most people typically have in the course of a week primarily fulfill a social closeness agenda even though they masquerade as information transfer, social etiquette, or expression of needs and wants. When two friends chat over lunch about the problems in their offices or when a group of people talk about their summer vacations at a cocktail party, the ostensible goal is information exchange, but is this really their primary agenda? Is the content of these communicative interactions really more important than the feeling of connection the messages allow the partners to experience?

In many cases, there are multiple goals involved in any single interaction; in the context of AAC interventions, the team must identify these goals for each person who uses AAC so that team members can make appropriate systems and vocabulary available to the user. One wonders how many times communication interventions have "failed" (e.g., "She has a wonderful communication system but refuses to use it") because of a discrepancy between the communication agenda of an AAC user and an AAC specialist. For example, some people who use AAC prefer to use low-technology systems that require ongoing interaction and turn taking with their communication partners (e.g., alphabet boards with messages spelled out) because they enjoy the social closeness achieved through such approaches (see Haaf, 1994, for an example). Anne McDonald, who uses such a system, noted that "if using the computer means I . . . [have] less personal contact then it [is not] worthwhile. I don't like using a machine if there's a person available to help me. . . . The message, not the medium, is what matters for people who cannot use their own voices" (McDonald, 1994, p. 15). Similarly, when an individual using an AAC system wants to achieve social closeness but the available vocabulary of the communication system is primarily related to needs/wants and social etiquette, problems are bound to occur. Careful attention to the needs and priorities of people who use AAC and their partners is critically important in order to maximize competence.

Perspective of the Communication Partner

Communicative competence from the perspective of the person who uses AAC involves the ability to efficiently and effectively transmit messages in all four of the interaction categories, based on individual interests, circumstances, and abilities. Communication partners report that AAC users who are judged to be competent communicators also possess an additional set of skills. The research of Light (1988) and Light and Binger (1997) suggested that competent communicators are able to do the following:

- Portray a positive self-image to their communication partners
- Show interest in others and draw others into interactions
- Actively participate and take turns in a symmetrical fashion
- Be responsive to their communication partners by, for example, making relevant comments, asking partner-focused questions, and negotiating shared topics
- Put their partners at ease with the AAC system through the use of, for example, an introductory strategy (e.g., a card that says, HI, MY NAME IS GORDON; I USE THIS MACHINE TO COMMUNICATE. I WILL TOUCH THE PICTURES OF WHAT I WANT TO SAY); humor and predictable, readable signals might also serve this purpose.

Professionals should be aware of the fact that different types of partners might perceive the importance of various strategies related to communicative competence differently. For example, Light et al. (1997) found evidence that for both adults *without* prior AAC experience and professionals *with* prior AAC experience, nonverbal feedback from AAC users during conversational interactions was positively related to their perceptions of communicative competence. However, adolescents without experience did not find this factor to be critical. Clearly, part of every AAC intervention should involve 1) identification of critical skills for communicative competence from the perspective of relevant listeners and 2) strategic instruction to support the highest level of communicative competence possible. Such strategies are described in detail in Chapter 11.

OVERVIEW OF CHAPTERS

The organization of this book reflects our experiences while teaching AAC classes together at the University of Nebraska–Lincoln and at the Nebraska Summer AAC Institute. We realize that individuals from a wide range of disciplines will be introduced to AAC through this text; therefore, the chapters contained in Part I provide specific information about the concepts, strategies, and techniques that are unique to the AAC field. In Part II we shift our focus to the AAC needs of people with developmental disabilities by emphasizing nonsymbolic and symbolic strategies for beginning communicators, language learning, literacy, and inclusion in school. In Part III, we deal with individuals who were at one time able to speak and write but now require AAC systems because of an acquired injury, disease, or condition.

2

Messaging

Vocabulary, Small Talk, and Storytelling

What do you think?

How would it feel to be restricted to the words, phrases, and stories selected for you by someone else? Even if you could spell out all of your messages at a rate of about five to seven words per minute, you would still need complete phrases to communicate urgent messages, break into a conversation, engage in small talk, or tell a lengthy story. Obviously, the appropriateness of the messages stored in your augmentative and alternative communication (AAC) system would be very important to you. If you could pick a few people to select your messages for you, who would they be—people who know a lot about *language* or people who know a lot about *you*? *What do you think?*

AAC is about helping individuals who cannot speak to interact with others. To that end, this book contains extensive information about symbols, communication boards, switches, displays, and speech output. However, because the central goal of AAC is to provide individuals with the opportunity and capability 1) to communicate messages so that they can interact in conversations; 2) to participate at home, in school, at work, and during recreational activities; 3) to learn their native language; 4) to establish and maintain their social roles (e.g., friend, student, spouse); and 5) to meet their personal needs, we designed this chapter to introduce the factors that influence message selection in AAC in such contexts. Because the message selection process in AAC is unique and is influenced by such a wide range of factors, this chapter provides an overview to supplement information that is included in Chapters 9–18, which cover specific interventions.

The Barkley AAC Center's World Wide Web site (http://aac.unl.edu) provides extensive messaging resources for AAC users across the age span.

FACTORS THAT INFLUENCE AAC MESSAGE SELECTION

The process of selecting the messages to be included in a communication system is unique to the AAC field. Because word selection and message formulation are such efficient processes for most typical speakers, people usually enter communication situations without giving much consideration beforehand to the words, phrases, and stories they will use. Indeed, message selection during natural speech interaction and written communication is so automatic that most AAC specialists themselves have little experience selecting vocabulary items in advance of the acts of speaking or writing. Even professionals who have regular contact with individuals who experience communication disorders such as stuttering, voice problems, articulation problems, and cleft palate rarely need to preselect messages to support conversational or written communication.

In addition to the lack of experience with which most AAC facilitators (i.e., people who assume or are assigned responsibility for supporting an individual's communicative efforts) approach message selection, a variety of other factors influence the types of messages used by different communicators. Differences in age, gender, and social role exert powerful influences on both natural speakers and AAC users. Children use different messages than adults. Older adults speak about different topics and use different small-talk phrases than younger adults. Men and women tend to talk about different topics. When AAC users and AAC facilitators represent different age, gender, and social cohorts, message selection becomes complicated.

In addition to generic differences in message use, individuals vary in their message needs and preferences. The environments in which they live influence the ways in which they wish to communicate. Communication at home is different than that in nursing centers, community living facilities, schools, and hospitals. The type of disability experienced influences peoples' interactions with caregivers, medical staff, education personnel, and family. The messages included in AAC systems must reflect individual differences related to the names of family members, streets, stores, pets, and interests. Finally, differing life experiences leave individuals with different stories to tell.

Fortunately, the futures of individuals with lifelong disabilities are not nearly as limited as they once were (Mirenda, 1993). At one time, people with lifelong disabilities lived segregated lives at home or in institutions; thus, their communication needs were quite restricted and predictable. Societal involvement of people with disabilities since the early 1970s, however, has increased dramatically. As people with disabilities are included more successfully in the educational, social, religious, recreational, and vocational realms of our communities, their communication needs change dramatically. As their opportunities and choices continue to increase, their communication needs will continue to grow.

Changes in technology have also had an extensive impact on the communication patterns of individuals with severe communication disorders. Early in the development of the AAC field, the memory and display capabilities of AAC systems were so limited that these devices could store only relatively small message sets. With new elec-

We cannot help but reflect on some of our experiences related to messaging and AAC. We saw Bob and Michael Williams both use their AAC systems to address hundreds of listeners in large auditoriums at the International Society for Augmentative and Alternative Communication (ISAAC) '96 conference without the aid of interpreters or printed texts. Scott stopped Dave in a crowded hallway at ISAAC and engaged him in an extended conversation through the skillful use of small talk. He also conveyed a long story narrative about the development of his personal World Wide Web site. Randy and his wife danced and sang during the ISAAC party to the tune of "Satisfaction." After ISAAC, Bill made numerous telephone calls to Dave to discuss his various concerns, and Jim accompanied Dave on a site visit of an AAC research facility. Roxi participated in a general junior high school curriculum, and Pat escorted Bev to her high school prom with her boyfriend Tomas, both of whom use AAC. Mark wrote, talked on the telephone, told jokes, and sent frequent e-mail messages until his death from amyotrophic lateral sclerosis. Sharon and Allen made a videotape about their lives as two people with AAC systems—married, living in the community, traveling by bus, doing their banking and shopping, living extraordinarily ordinary lives. Would any of this have been possible 10 or 20 years ago?

tronic designs and inexpensive computer memory, the storage and computing capacity of electronic communication devices has expanded dramatically; many now have a nearly limitless capacity for message storage. Thus, AAC devices can now include an unrestricted number of messages including those related to small talk, scripts, and stories that earlier systems could not manage. In addition, with the advent of dynamic display devices (computer screens that change like the pages of a book and use lights to signal available message options), AAC facilitators can organize and symbolize huge message pools using strategies that do not rely solely on the memory capabilities of users (see Chapter 3). Finally, the most common voice-output options are intelligible enough to allow most AAC users to talk in a wide range of contexts. Together, these technological advances permit the use of message sets by AAC users who wish to communicate with strangers as well as with friends and before large or small groups as well as on a one-to-one basis.

THE MESSAGES OF CONVERSATION

Conversations have a rather predictable structure. Usually, a person initiates a conversation with a greeting followed by a segment of small talk. Some conversations then progress to an information-sharing segment, whereas others do not. The shared information can take a variety of forms, including stories (i.e., narratives), procedural descriptions, or content-specific conversations. Most conversations close with some wrap-up remarks and a final farewell. To provide AAC users with the messages needed to support conversation, it is useful to select and organize messages with this conversational contour in mind.

Greetings

Greetings are essential to initiating social interactions. Greetings can be rather generic in that they do not usually convey specific information. Rather, they signal awareness of someone's presence, communicate the speaker's intention to be friendly, and often include a bid to start a conversation. Despite the apparent simplicity of greetings, however, AAC teams must have some awareness of the social status or ages of the individuals involved when selecting appropriate greetings. This awareness is generally communicated by the degree of formality used for the greeting. Usually, a younger person does not greet an older person or a person of higher status (e.g., a boss, a teacher) with an excessively informal or familiar message. However, at least in middle-class North American culture, it is permissible to use informal messages that may contain personal references (e.g., "Yo! Big guy!") or even mild profanity (e.g., "How ya doing, you old *&#?") with close friends or peers. Although specific greeting conventions may change from culture to culture, there is always a need for variety in this type of message. Thus, greeting messages selected for AAC users should include a range of message options that are culturally sensitive so that individuals are able to signal their awareness of social conventions. In addition, the availability of a range of different messages discourages the overuse of the same greetings.

This week, when you go to work or to religious services, pay attention to how you greet others. Notice that you use a variety of different greetings. Try to determine whether you understand the social rules that you use. Pay careful attention to those around you, and note the age and gender of individuals who say things such as "Well, hello, deary!" "Hi there!" "Goodness gracious, it's been a long time!" "Yo!" "Good morning!" and "Gimme five!"

Small Talk

Small talk is a type of conversational exchange used for initiating and maintaining conversational interactions. Small-talk scripts provide for the incremental sequence of social engagement and disengagement messages that seem necessary when people attempt to interact in a social setting. Some conversations may never progress past the small-talk stage, such as often occurs at cocktail parties. Often, however, it seems as though small talk is used as a transition between the greeting and the information-sharing stage, especially when the communication partners do not know each other well or do not possess a lot of shared information.

Adult AAC users frequently report that social situations are very difficult for them. The following are remarks we have collected through the years:

"Dinner parties with my spouse kill me. Eating, talking, smiling, and small talk—it is too much to handle."

"My fiancée told me that she wouldn't go to a party with me again until I learned something about small talk!"

"I didn't get serious about learning small talk until I was 45 years old. I thought it was a total waste of time. Why should I work so hard to say nothing of content? But I was wrong."

One type of small talk in particular is useful for AAC users. We call it *generic small talk* or small talk that people can use with a variety of different conversational partners because it does not refer to specific shared information. Table 2.1 contains some examples of generic and specific small talk. In an effort to determine the relative frequency and types of generic small talk used by speakers of various ages without disabilities, several groups of researchers at the University of Nebraska–Lincoln recorded everyday conversations using portable, voice-activated tape recorders. Table 2.2 reports the results of these studies. Nearly half of the utterances of preschool children (3–5 years of age) in both home and school settings were classified as generic small talk. For young adults (20–30 years of age), 39% of all utterances were generic small talk (Ball, Marvin, Beukelman, Lasker, & Rupp, 1997; King, Spoeneman, Stuart, & Beukelman, 1995; Lasker, Ball, Bringewatt, Stuart, & Marvin, 1996). Both older men and women used somewhat less small talk than the young adults; 31% of the utterances of 65- to 74-year-olds and 26% of the utterances of 75- to 85-year-olds were small talk. These results confirm the extensive role of small talk in everyday communicative interactions for individuals across the age range. In order for AAC users to interact in integrated social contexts, access to small talk and the ability to use it seems essential.

Overall, preschool children produced more utterances classified as confirmation/negation (26%) than any other type of small talk. They used continuers and environmental control utterances with similar frequencies. This high level of use of environmental control phrases is highly unique to preschool children, as none of the adult groups used these phrases more than 1% of the time. The young children also commented quite frequently about internal and external evaluations. For all of the adult groups reported in Table 2.2, continuers were the most commonly used type of generic small-talk utterance. Individual AAC users should have opportunities to select the messages that they prefer from detailed resource lists and other sources. As an example, detailed information about small-talk use patterns is now available on the Barkley AAC Center's World Wide Web site (http://aac.unl.edu).

Table 2.1.   Examples of generic and specific small talk

Generic	Specific
How is your family?	How is your wife?
What's happening?	What are you doing?
Isn't that beautiful!	That is a beautiful flower!
Good story!!	Good story about your vacation.
She is great.	She is a great teacher.

Table 2.2.   Classification of generic small-talk utterances across the age span

Small-talk category	Age (years)			
	3–5 %	20–30 %	65–74 %	75–84 %
Confirm/negative	25.9	15.8	19.1	27.3
Continuers	16.8	23.7	28.6	23.5
Environmental control	17.7	<1.0	<1.0	<1.0
Evaluations: Internal	10.5	25.7	18.4	14.7
Evaluations: External	12.0	13.1	15.3	16.0
Other	17.0	12.5	9.6	18.5

The messages used during small talk vary somewhat across the age span. Table 2.3 summarizes the most frequently occurring small-talk utterances for each age group, as compiled from the studies cited previously.

Storytelling

For adults, storytelling is a rather common communication form. Older adults in particular use stories to entertain, teach, and establish social closeness with their peers. Storytelling remains an important communication form even for adults who are unable to speak. This is particularly true as older adults begin to focus more and more of their social time on acquaintances and friends rather than on families. As these individuals lose their spouses and move to retirement or care facilities, the need to socially connect with individuals their own age becomes important, and storytelling provides a vehicle for this.

In his very interesting book *Tell Me a Story: A New Look at Real and Artificial Memory*, Schank (1990) discussed story formulation, refinement, and storage in detail. He pointed out that we use stories from a variety of sources. *First-person stories* are those that have occurred to the speaker personally. *Second-person stories* are those that a speaker has learned from others through listening or reading. It is permissible to tell a second-person story, as long as we give credit to the source. *Official stories* are those that are used to teach a lesson or explain a phenomenon and are frequently used by families, schools, and religious groups. Finally, *fantasy stories* are those that are "made up." Marvin and her colleagues studied the communication patterns of typically developing preschool children and found that, on average, 9% of what they talked about at home and 11% of their conversations at school involved some type of fantasy (Marvin, Beukelman, & Bilyeu, 1994).

As the memory capacity of electronic AAC devices has increased and the intelligibility of speech synthesis has improved, storytelling with AAC systems has become

Table 2.3.   Frequently occurring small-talk utterances for four age groups

Preschoolers		Adults ages 20–30 years	Adults ages 65–74 years	Adults ages 75–85 years
At school	At home			
Ah (19)	Ah (14)	All right (16)	All right (22)	Boy (2)
Come on (16)	Bye/Bye-bye (9)	Are you serious/sure/kidding (6)	Boy (11)	Do you (2)
Don't (10)	Come here (19)	Bye guys/kids (10)	Come on (5)	Don't you (2)
Get me (7)	Come on (19)	Come on man/honey (5)	Did you (7)	Fine (2)
Good (9)	Don't (9)	Gees (11)	Good (8)	God (2)
Here (17)	Give me a five/Give me five (9)	Go ahead (6)	Gosh (5)	Good (7)
Hey (89)	Good (9)	Good (11)	He did (3)	Good for you (2)
Hi/Hello (29)	Here (23)	Hello (6)	Hello (4)	Good God (2)
Ha ha ha (7)	Hey (60)	Hi (18)	Hmm (10)	Good Lord (2)
I know (21)	Hi/Hello (24)	Hold on (5)	Huh (26)	Gosh (2)
Look (18)	Huh (19)	Huh (18)	I don't know (13)	Hello (4)
Lookit (28)	I don't know (7)	I don't know (34)	I know (3)	Hi how are you (2)
Mmm (7)	I know (20)	I don't think so (5)	I know it (3)	Hmm (7)
No/Nope/Nah (170)	Mmm (12)	I know (23)	I'll be darned (5)	Huh (9)
Now (28)	No/Nope (150)	My God (5)	Is that right (3)	I don't know (5)
Nuh-uh (34)	Now (14)	My gosh (7)	Mhmm (56)	I see (5)
Oh (58)	Nuh-uh (47)	No/Nope (41)	Mmm (8)	Mhmm (29)
Oh no (12)	Oh (95)	Oh (45)	My goodness (4)	Mmm (3)
Oh yeah (10)	Oh no (15)	Okay (105)	No (17)	My (2)
Okay (116)	Oh-oh (8)	Ouch (6)	Oh (44)	No (27)
Ooh (12)	Oh yeah (15)	Really (40)	Okay (72)	Oh (34)
Ouch/Ow (9)	Okay (119)	Right (11)	Really (8)	Okay (17)
Please (12)	Ooh (18)	So (14)	So (8)	Pardon (3)
Pow (9)	Please (9)	Thank you/Thanks (15)	Sure (11)	Really (7)
Quit it (16)	Right (7)	That's good (7)	Thank you (6)	Right here (2)
Right here (7)	See (28)	Uh huh (11)	That's good (7)	Right (13)
See (23)	Thanks/Thank you (10)	Well (10)	That's right (11)	So (5)

(continued)

19

Table 2.3. (continued)

Preschoolers		Adults ages 20–30 years	Adults ages 65–74 years	Adults ages 75–85 years
At school	At home			
Sit down (7)	There (23)	What are you doing (5)	Uhhuh (16)	Sure (7)
So (8)	There you go (7)	What (26)	Wait a minute (3)	Thank you (4)
So what (8)	Uh (15)	What's that (7)	Well (10)	That's a good one (2)
Stop (7)	Uh-huh (86)	Why (6)	What (5)	That's it (2)
Thanks/Thank you (8)	Um (29)	Wow (5)	What's that (5)	That's right (5)
There (23)	Wait (8)	Yes/Yep/Yeah (229)	Where (3)	That's true (2)
There you go (7)	Watch this (7)	You did (10)	Whoo (5)	They're good (4)
This way (8)	Well (31)	You know (11)	Yes/Yep/Yeah (178)	Those are good (2)
Ugh (8)	What (59)	You're kidding (5)	You do (3)	Uh (4)
Uh-huh (187)	Whoa (13)			Uhhuh (8)
Um (31)	Why (20)			Was she (2)
Watch this (8)	Yeah/Yes/Yep (216)			Well (2)
Well (27)	You know what (9)			Yes/Yep/Yeah (148)
What (33)	Yummy (9)			
Whoa (47)				
Yeah/Yes/Yep (241)				

20

much more practical. AAC facilitators play an important role in storytelling by assisting AAC users to capture stories for this type of communication. First, the facilitator must understand the story that the user wishes to include in his or her AAC system. This is critical because storytelling is very personal and must be individualized to reflect the experiences (e.g., through first-person stories), the interests (e.g., through second-person stories), and the affiliations (e.g., through official stories) of the AAC user. Next, the facilitator can help to program the AAC device by dividing the story into segments (usually of sentence length) that the device can release (i.e., spoken with synthetic speech) sequentially to tell the story, one sentence at a time. Finally, the AAC user should receive opportunities to practice telling the story. As the number of stories included in an AAC system increases, AAC facilitators also need to assist users to index them according to the main topics, key participants, or major life events they represent so that users can retrieve the stories efficiently. Of course, facilitators can also use non-electronic AAC strategies to store and retrieve stories. For example, a man with aphasia due to stroke used to tell the story of how he got his unusual name, Roderick, by guiding his communication partner through his communication book one segment at a time, indicating the line of the story that the partner should read aloud. Other individuals may tell stories using line-drawing symbols arranged in sequential order with the written story underneath each symbol.

Procedural Descriptions

Procedural descriptions provide detailed information about processes or procedures. Usually, they 1) are rich in detail, 2) contain information that must be related sequentially, and 3) require communication that is both timely and efficient. Examples include giving someone directions about how to drive to your house for the first time or telling someone your recipe for a favorite cake. In addition to the kinds of procedures that most speakers may need to describe, many individuals with disabilities need to instruct family members and attendants about the procedures required for personal care and other specific needs. Typically, these descriptions are unique to the individual communicator.

Content-Specific Conversations

Content-specific conversations contain the informational give-and-take with which we all are familiar. Typically, these conversations are not scripted and the vocabulary in them varies widely depending on many different factors, including the communication partners themselves, the topic, the context, and so forth. To participate successfully in such conversations, AAC users usually need to be able to generate unique and novel utterances. Most individuals do so by constructing messages on a letter-by-letter or word-by-word basis.

Wrap-Up Remarks and Farewell Statements

Most communicators use wrap-up remarks to signal their desire or intent to end an interaction. Then they terminate conversations with farewell statements. Phrases such as "Nice to talk with you," "We need to talk again some time," "I have to go now," "I have work to do," "The kids need me," and "The phone is ringing" are typical wrap-up remarks in conversations. Phrases such as "See ya," "Good-bye," "So long," and "See you later" are typically used as farewell statements, at least in North America. The Barkley AAC Center's World Wide Web site (http://aac.unl.edu) contains extensive information about wrap-up remarks and farewell statements that people of different ages use.

VOCABULARY NEEDS FOR DIFFERENT COMMUNICATION MODES AND CONTEXTS

The words with which we communicate are greatly influenced by different communication contexts and modalities. For example, we speak more colloquially and casually when conversing with friends than we do when presenting a formal report to a class, business meeting, or professional group. When adults speak to young children, they use different words and grammatical structures than when they speak to other adults. Furthermore, written communication is somewhat different from spoken communication. It is important for the AAC team to have a general knowledge of these different vocabulary-use patterns when selecting vocabulary items for AAC systems.

Spoken and Written Communication

Although speaking and writing may seem to be different but equivalent ways of communicating, there are actually inherent differences between these two modes of communication that may not be immediately apparent (Barritt & Kroll, 1978). In general, spoken communication involves the use of more personal references and more first- and second-person pronouns (e.g., *I, we, you*) than does written communication. Less lexical (i.e., vocabulary) diversity is present in speech than in writing because speakers tend to repeat words more often. Speech also tends to contain shorter thought units, more monosyllabic and familiar words, and more subordinate ideas than writing.

In a study that compared spoken and written language in the classroom, McGinnis (1991) collected 1,000-word spoken and written samples from 34 third-grade students in a general education setting. She found that the students' written vocabulary was considerably more diverse than their spoken vocabulary. For example, the type-to-token ratio (TTR, the number of different words divided by the total number of words in a sample) was lower for spoken (TTR = 0.30) than for written language samples (TTR = 0.46). This indicates that the children repeated more spoken words than written words because fewer spoken words represented a greater proportion of the total language sample than did a similar sample of written words.

School Talk and Home Talk

Vocabulary use also varies for spoken communication depending on the communication context. For example, "school talk" can be quite different from "home talk." Children do not use language in school for the same purposes, such as to meet immediate needs and achieve social closeness with familiar partners, as they do at home. Instead, children talk primarily with relatively unfamiliar adults in school in order to build a theory of reality, share their understanding of actions and situations, and acquire knowledge (Westby, 1985). In doing so, they must "shift away from the expectation of shared assumptions (implicit meaning) to interpreting overtly lexicalized intentions (explicit meaning)" (1985, p. 187).

Few investigations have documented in detail the vocabulary-use patterns of children or adults at home and in school. One exception is the work of Marvin et al. (1994), which recorded the vocabulary spoken by five typically developing preschool-age children at home and in school. Approximately one third of the words produced by these children were spoken only at school, one third were spoken only at home, and one third were spoken both at home and at school. Beukelman, Jones, and Rowan (1989) reported that 100 words accounted for 60% of those produced at school by six typically developing children (3–4 years of age) when 3,000-word samples from each child were analyzed. In addition, in a related study, Fried-Oken and More (1982) reported a vocabulary core list for preschoolers based on development and environmental language sources. Table 2.4 provides summary information regarding preschool vocabulary use from these related studies.

Differences across specific school environments might also be expected to have dramatic effects on the words that children communicate in classrooms. The content of elementary and secondary school curricula in various subject areas requires students to have access to vocabulary items that may change daily or weekly. For example, as the topics in a student's science unit shift from plants, to planets, to prehistoric animals, to rocks, the extent to which he or she can communicate successfully in the classroom will depend largely on the availability of appropriate vocabulary. The vocabulary set designed to support a student's conversational interactions, which are relatively stable and predictable, is unlikely to be useful in meeting frequently changing curricular communication needs. (For a more complete discussion of communication patterns in school settings, see Chapter 14.)

Age Variables

Research reports suggest that age, gender, and cultural (e.g., ethnic) differences may affect the topics and vocabulary words that an individual uses during interactions. For example, researchers have investigated the communication patterns of older adults from at least two different perspectives. One perspective has been to study and document the language differences between older adults and younger people in order to describe the language impairments that people experience as they grow older. Studies from this perspective have suggested that people produce fewer proper nouns, more general nouns, and more ambiguous references as they age. In addition, the lexical variety of their nominal and syntactic structures decreases (Kemper, 1988; Kynette & Kemper, 1986; Ulatowska, Cannito, Hayashi, & Fleming, 1985). Goodglass (1980) reported that the size of individuals' active expressive vocabularies decreases quite markedly during their 70s.

A second perspective has been to view aging in terms of a model of human cognitive development, in which the performance of older adults is seen as a legitimate, adaptive stage of development (Mergler & Goldstein, 1983). Viewed from this perspective, older adults appear to tailor their communicative interactions to the unique task of "telling," that is, information sharing. In their role as "tellers," older adults relate to the past as a resource for assigning meaning to the present (Boden & Bielby, 1983). For example, Stuart, Vanderhoof, and Beukelman (1993) examined the topical references that five older women, ranging in age from 63 to 79 years, made during conversational exchanges. The younger women made more "present-oriented" comments and referred much more frequently to topics related to family life than did the older women. In con-

Table 2.4. Composite initial vocabulary list for preschoolers

Word	School (Beukelman, Jones, & Rowan, 1989)	Parent/SLP language samples (Fried-Oken & More, 1992)	School (Marvin, Beukelman, & Bilyeu, 1994)	Home (Marvin, Beukelman, & Bilyeu, 1994)
A	×	×	×	×
Again				×
All	×	×	×	×
Am	×			
And	×	×	×	×
Are	×	×	×	×
At	×		×	×
Back		×	×	
Be	×	×	×	×
Because	×	×	×	×
Bed		×		
Big	×			
Boo	×			
Boy		×		
But	×		×	×
By			×	
Can	×	×	×	×
Car		×		
Chair	×	×		
Come	×	×		×
Could				×
Dad		×		×
Did	×	×	×	×
Do	×	×	×	×
Does	×			
Dog	×	×		
Done	×			
Door		×		
Down	×	×	×	×
Duck			×	
Eat	×	×		
For	×	×	×	×
Get	×	×	×	×
Girl		×		
Go	×	×	×	×
Going	×	×	×	×
Gonna		×	×	×
Good	×			
Got	×	×	×	×
Grandma		×		
Had			×	
Has	×			
Have	×	×	×	×
He	×	×	×	×

(continued)

Table 2.4. (*continued*)

Word	School (Beukelman, Jones, & Rowan, 1989)	Parent/SLP language samples (Fried-Oken & More, 1992)	School (Marvin, Beukelman, & Bilyeu, 1994)	Home (Marvin, Beukelman, & Bilyeu, 1994)
Her		×		
Here	×	×	×	×
Hey	×		×	×
Him		×		
His		×		
Home	×	×		
House	×	×		
How	×	×	×	×
Huh			×	×
I	×	×	×	×
If			×	×
I'll	×		×	×
I'm		×	×	×
In	×	×	×	×
Is	×	×	×	×
It	×	×	×	×
Just	×	×	×	×
Kind				×
Know	×	×	×	×
Let	×	×		×
Like	×	×	×	×
Little	×	×	×	×
Look	×	×	×	
Long			×	
Make	×		×	×
Man			×	
Me	×	×	×	×
Mine	×		×	×
Mom		×		×
Mommy				×
More	×	×	×	
My	×	×	×	×
Muffin			×	
Name	×			
Named				×
Need	×	×	×	×
No	×	×	×	×
Not	×	×	×	×
Now	×	×	×	×
-n't		×	×	×
Of	×	×	×	×
Off	×		×	
Oh	×		×	×
Okay	×	×	×	×

(*continued*)

Table 2.4.   (*continued*)

Word	School (Beukelman, Jones, & Rowan, 1989)	Parent/SLP language samples (Fried-Oken & More, 1992)	School (Marvin, Beukelman, & Bilyeu, 1994)	Home (Marvin, Beukelman, & Bilyeu, 1994)
On	×	×	×	×
One	×	×	×	×
Out	×	×	×	×
Over	×	×		
Paint	×			
Person #1	×		×	×
Person #2			×	×
Person #3				×
Person #4				×
Person #5				×
Play	×	×		×
Please	×			
Pop				×
Put	×	×	×	×
-'re		×	×	
Red			×	
Right	×	×	×	×
-s, 's		×	×	×
Said			×	
Say			×	
See	×	×	×	×
She	×	×		
Show	×			
Sleep		×		
Sit	×	×		
Snake			×	
So	×	×	×	×
Some	×	×	×	×
Something				×
Take	×	×	×	×
That	×	×	×	×
The	×	×	×	×
Them	×	×	×	×
Then		×	×	×
There	×	×	×	×
These	×	×	×	×
They	×	×	×	×
Thing			×	
This	×	×	×	×
Those	×			
Three	×			
Through			×	
Time		×		
To	×	×	×	×

(*continued*)

Table 2.4. *(continued)*

Word	School (Beukelman, Jones, & Rowan, 1989)	Parent/SLP language samples (Fried-Oken & More, 1992)	School (Marvin, Beukelman, & Bileyu, 1994)	Home (Marvin, Beukelman, & Bilyeu, 1994)
Too	×	×	×	
Try				×
Two	×	×	×	×
Uh			×	×
Um			×	×
Up	×	×	×	×
Us	×			
Wanna		×		
Want	×	×	×	×
Was		×	×	×
Watch		×		
We	×	×	×	×
What	×	×	×	×
When			×	×
Where	×	×		×
Who	×			
Why				×
Will	×	×	×	×
With	×	×	×	×
Yeah			×	×
Yes	×	×		
You	×	×	×	×
Your	×		×	×

This composite list is composed of the 100 most frequently occurring words from each list.

Note: SLP = speech language pathologist.

Greg's friends came to me one day and said, "You need to put some cool stuff in Greg's machine (an electronic communication device). He sounds weird now."

"What do you mean?" I asked, "What's wrong with what's in there?"

"Well, you know how he says 'Hello, how are you?' when he comes into the class in the morning?" his friends replied. "No one talks like that. We say 'How you doin', dudes?' or 'Hey, guys, what's happening?' or something." (P. Daharsh, Greg's teacher, personal communication, March 1991)

---

trast, the older women referred to their social networks outside the family much more often than did their younger counterparts.

Gender Variables

A number of researchers have written about the influence of gender on language and word use. For example, men and women appear to use parts of speech differently. Men use fewer pronouns and more adjectives, unusual adverbs, and prepositions than do women. Women use more auxiliary words and negations than do men (Gleser, Gottschalk, & John, 1959; Poole, 1979). Men also appear to speak about different topics than women. Gleser et al. (1959) found that women refer to motivations, feelings, emotions, and themselves more often than do men. Men tend to refer to time, space, quantity, and destructive actions more often than do women.

Stuart summarized the work of a number of different researchers who examined the differences between "male talk" and "female talk" as follows:

> The studies were conducted in a Spanish village; in a traditional working-class family in England; among !Kung bushmen in Africa; during sidewalk conversations in New York City; Columbus, Ohio; and London; among women working in a telephone company in Somerville, Massachusetts; between blue-collar couples in New York; and among participants in the draft resistance movement in the United States. The results were impressively similar and can be reported collectively. Female topics were found to be people (themselves, other women, men), personal lives/interpersonal matters (age, lifestyles, life's troubles), household needs, books, food, clothes, and decorations. Male topics were found to be work (land, crops, weather, animals, prices, business, money, wages, machinery, and carpentry), legal matters, taxes, army experience, and sports or amusements (baseball, motorcycles, sailing, hunting, mountain climbing, and cockfighting). (1991, pp. 43–44)

Information about the vocabulary-use patterns of AAC users of different genders and ages is still very limited. Until such information is available, AAC specialists must be sensitive to how these factors and others (e.g., cultural differences) may affect the vocabulary selection process. Peer informants are perhaps the best source of knowledge about an individual's specific vocabulary needs, and AAC teams should use their insights as a resource to guard against the selection of inappropriate vocabulary. We have found that the summary list provided on the Barkley AAC Center's World Wide Web site (http://aac.unl.edu) provides excellent resource material from which AAC users, their facilitators, caregivers, family members, and peers can select to create personalized vocabulary lists for various communication situations.

VOCABULARY NEEDS OF PEOPLE WITH DIFFERENT COMMUNICATION CAPABILITIES

The overall communication capability of individuals who use an AAC system is another important factor that AAC teams should consider as they select vocabulary. This section discusses three types of individuals: 1) those who are preliterate, such as young children who have not yet learned to write and read; 2) those who are nonliterate, such as individuals who are not able to learn to read or write and people who have lost these abilities because of their impairments; and 3) those who are literate.

They (people who use AAC) are unable to create spontaneously their own lexicon and must operate with a vocabulary selected by someone else or preselected, not spontaneously chosen by themselves. (Carlson, 1981, p. 140)

Vocabulary Selection for Preliterate Individuals

Individuals who are preliterate have not yet developed reading and writing skills. These individuals are often young children, but they may also be older individuals or even adults who never received the instruction needed to become literate. Thus, their AAC systems represent vocabulary items with one or more of the symbols or codes discussed in Chapter 3. Generally, the vocabulary requirements of preliterate individuals can be divided into two categories: vocabulary that is needed to communicate essential messages and vocabulary that is needed to develop their language skills.

Coverage Vocabulary

Vanderheiden and Kelso (1987) referred to vocabulary that is needed to communicate essential messages as *coverage vocabulary* because it contains messages that are necessary to cover an individual's basic communication needs. Because preliterate individuals are unable to spell out unique messages on a letter-by-letter basis, AAC teams must take care to include as many such messages as these individuals will require, regardless of how frequently they will use the messages. For example, a person may use a message such as I AM HAVING TROUBLE BREATHING very rarely, but if this could be even an occasional occurrence, it should be included in the coverage vocabulary.

The objective of this type of word set (coverage vocabulary) is to try to provide the individual with the ability to communicate most effectively and about the widest range of topics, given the limited word set. (Vanderheiden & Kelso, 1987, p. 196)

Coverage vocabulary is highly dependent on the communication needs of an individual AAC user. As noted previously, these needs are likely to change, depending on the user's age and the communicative context. For example, the coverage vocabulary needed at a birthday party would be very different from that required during a physical therapy session. Coverage vocabularies for preliterate individuals are selected through careful analyses of their environmental and communication needs. (The details of these processes are discussed later in this chapter.)

Coverage vocabularies for preliterate individuals are commonly organized by context (environment or activity) so that the words are available when needed. Thus, AAC teams may design separate communication activity displays (also known as miniboards) to contain the vocabulary items that an individual needs while eating, dressing, bathing, playing a specific game, participating in specific school activities, and so forth. Team members or facilitators may situate these activity boards strategically in the environment where a particular activity takes place, such as in the kitchen, bathroom, or specific classroom area, so that they are available when needed. At other times, the individual may store activity displays in a carrying case or notebook so that the appropriate board is available for a specific communication context. (Additional activity board strategies are discussed in detail in Chapters 9, 11, and 12.) Alternatively, the AAC team may program vocabulary items into a voice-output electronic communication device, using "themes" or "levels" that are contextually relevant to the individual. Examples of this type of application with iconic encoding (e.g., Minspeak) have been provided by Bruno (1989).

Developmental Vocabulary

The vocabulary set for an AAC system may also include words that the individual does not yet know and that are selected not so much for "functional" purposes but to encourage language and vocabulary growth. At least some developmental vocabulary words should be provided to people across the age range because language growth is an ongoing process (Romski & Sevcik, 1996). For example, if a preliterate child is about to experience something for the first time, such as a circus, then his or her AAC team may include vocabulary items associated with the new context on the communication display even though the child has never before used them. During the circus, the child's parent or friend may point to various vocabulary items on the display that are associated with the circus events such as CLOWN, LION, FUNNY, and SCARY. This gives the child opportunities to develop language and learn new vocabulary items through exposure, just as children who speak learn new words by hearing people say them over and over again.

For beginning communicators of any age, developmental vocabulary items should include words or messages that encourage them to use various language structures and combinations. For example, beginning communicators should have access to words such as *more* to indicate continuation, *no* to indicate negation, and *there* to indicate location. AAC teams might include a variety of nouns, verbs, and adjectives to support the individual's use of word combinations (e.g., *more car, no eat*). As the person's language abilities expand, team members should select vocabulary to encourage the use of combinations of two, three, and four words or more. Lahey and Bloom (1977) suggested that developmental vocabulary should include words from at least the following semantic categories:

- Substantive words (i.e., people, places, things)
- Relational words (e.g., *big, little*)
- Generic verbs (e.g., *give, get, make*)
- Specific verbs (e.g., *eat, drink, sleep*)
- Emotional state words (e.g., *happy, scared*)
- Affirmation/negation words (e.g., *yes, no, not*)
- Recurrence/discontinuation words (e.g., *more, all gone*)
- Proper names for people first and personal pronouns later; initially, proper names can be used instead of pronouns for possessives (e.g., *Mike car* instead of *his car*) as well as object–agent relations (e.g., *Pat want* instead of *I want*)
- Single adjectives first (e.g., *hot, dirty*) and their polar opposites later (e.g., *cold, clean*); initially, *not* + adjective can be used for a polar opposite (e.g., *not* + *hot* = *cold*)
- Relevant colors
- Relevant prepositions

Vocabulary Selection for Nonliterate Individuals

Nonliterate individuals are unable to spell well enough to formulate their messages on a letter-by-letter basis and are not expected to develop or regain these spontaneous spelling skills. Most of these individuals are also unable to read, except perhaps for functional sight words that they have memorized. The vocabulary selection process for nonliterate individuals primarily aims to meet their daily, ongoing communication needs in a variety of environments. Nevertheless, the messages selected for these individuals may differ in a number of ways from those selected for preliterate individuals.

First, messages selected for nonliterate AAC users are nearly always chosen from a functional rather than a developmental perspective. Single words or, more often, whole messages are selected to meet individual communication needs. These messages are represented by one or more types of symbols, as discussed in Chapter 3. Second, it is very important that the coverage vocabulary selected for nonliterate individuals is age and gender appropriate. Many of these individuals, especially those with mental retardation or other developmental disabilities, may be adolescents or adults; special care must be taken not to select words and messages for them that are appropriate only for infants or young children. For example, a symbol of a happy face may be used for a young child to represent the word *happy,* whereas for an adolescent this same symbol might be translated to mean *awesome.* Even better, a THUMBS UP symbol might be used to represent *awesome* or *way to go* on an adolescent's display.

It is also appropriate to include at least some developmental vocabulary in the AAC systems of nonliterate individuals. For example, new messages should be added whenever new environments or participation opportunities are included in the individual's life. However, the goal is to expand the words and concepts about which the individual can communicate rather than to increase his or her use of complex syntactic forms. Again, efficient, functional communication in a variety of age-appropriate contexts is of paramount importance for these individuals.

Vocabulary Selection for Literate Individuals

AAC users who are able to read and spell have access to a greater variety of message preparation options. Literate individuals are able to formulate messages on a letter-by-letter and word-by-word basis and to retrieve complete messages, with appropriate AAC equipment, once they have been stored. Depending on the communication needs of an individual, AAC teams may prepare three different types of messages for quick retrieval: those related to timing enhancement, those related to message acceleration, and those related to fatigue reduction.

Timing Enhancement

Some messages require careful timing in order to be appropriate. Although a literate AAC user may have the ability to spell timely messages, their meanings may be lost if they are not communicated quickly. For example, if the message PLEASE PICK UP MY FEET BEFORE YOU ROLL MY WHEELCHAIR FORWARD is not delivered in a timely manner, then it loses its relevance when the wheelchair is moved while the person is formulating the message. Thus, messages that have important timing requirements are usually stored and retrieved in their entirety. Additional examples of such messages include WAIT JUST

A MINUTE, I'M NOT FINISHED YET; BEFORE YOU GO, WOULD YOU HELP ME WITH THIS?; and WHEN WILL WE MEET AGAIN? AAC users and their facilitators are the best sources for identifying unique messages related to timing enhancement.

Message Acceleration

In addition to timing enhancement, AAC teams often select vocabulary items to accelerate a user's overall communication rate. Vanderheiden and Kelso (1987) introduced the term *acceleration vocabulary* to refer to words or messages that occur so frequently and are so lengthy that the use of an encoding strategy to retrieve them results in substantial keystroke savings for the AAC user (see Chapter 3 for a more complete discussion of message encoding and communication rate enhancement). Thus, the AAC team chooses words for a message acceleration vocabulary set not to allow an AAC user to communicate particular ideas but rather to speed up the rate at which he or she can communicate them.

Typically, the first 50 (most frequently occurring) words will account for 40%–50% of the total words communicated, even though they account for only ½% of a 10,000-word vocabulary. One hundred words would account for approximately 60%, 200 words 70%, and 400 words 80%. (Vanderheiden & Kelso, 1987, p. 196)

Fatigue Reduction

The third type of vocabulary set that AAC teams typically select for people who are literate is one that will result in reduced fatigue. In many cases, words and phrases that compose the acceleration vocabulary set are the same as those that are encoded to reduce fatigue. In certain situations, however, selecting vocabulary to reduce fatigue requires a slightly different approach than when selecting other kinds of vocabulary. For example, fatigue is a cumulative problem for some AAC users. Early in the morning, they may be able to use their AAC systems with more physical efficiency than later in the day or the evening. In such cases, AAC teams should select fatigue reduction vocabulary items to cover these individuals' communication needs during the portion of the day when their fatigue levels are highest (e.g., the evening). In this way, they can avoid having to spell out words when they are tired. Analyses of communication patterns during periods of high fatigue can guide the selection of words and messages that will be most helpful to reduce fatigue.

VOCABULARY RESOURCES

Rarely does one individual have enough knowledge and experience to select all the vocabulary items needed by an AAC user in a specific environment. Rather, it is necessary to obtain this vocabulary information from a variety of sources. This section summarizes the sources that AAC teams commonly use during vocabulary selection and includes indications of the situations in which particular sources are most useful.

Core Vocabulary

Core vocabulary refers to words and messages that are commonly used by a variety of individuals and occur very frequently. Empirical research or clinical reports that assess vocabulary-use patterns of a number of individuals generally identify core vocabulary items. AAC teams have used three sources to identify core vocabularies for specific individuals: 1) word lists based on the vocabulary-use patterns of other successful AAC system users, 2) word lists based on the use patterns of the specific individual, and 3) word lists based on the performance of natural speakers or writers in similar contexts.

Vocabulary-Use Patterns of AAC Users

Of particular interest in developing core vocabulary lists is the performance of individuals who are operationally and socially competent with their AAC systems. Researchers have collected communication samples from these individuals over extended periods of time and analyzed their word-use patterns. The first of these studies involved the entire body of words produced on a letter-by-letter basis over 14 days by five young adults with disabilities who used Canon Communicators (Beukelman, Yorkston, Poblete, & Naranjo, 1984). From a composite list that consisted of all words produced by all five individuals, experimenters identified the 500 most frequently occurring words (see Table 2.5). Approximately 80% of the words communicated by the five individuals were represented by these 500 most frequently occurring words.

In subsequent research, Yorkston, Smith, and Beukelman (1990) compared the vocabulary lists produced by 10 AAC users during communicative interactions with six different composite word lists selected from published vocabulary sources. The 10 individuals all used spelling to express their messages. The results indicated that the individuals actually used between 27% and 60% of the words included in the various published lists.

A manual entitled *See What We Say: Vocabulary and Tips for Adults Who Use Augmentative and Alternative Communication* (Collier, 1997) is available through Harmony Place Support Services in Ontario, Canada. Written with input from 15 adult AAC users, the manual contains suggested vocabulary items for numerous situations, including communication about seating, participating in a case conference, self-advocacy, sexuality, and banking and finances.

Vocabulary-Use Patterns of a Specific AAC User

Individualized word lists, which are word lists compiled from the past performance of the specific individual for whom an AAC system is being developed, are even more efficient vocabulary sources than composite lists (Yorkston et al., 1990). This is not unexpected, as it could be assumed that the past performance of an individual AAC user would be the best predictor of his or her future performance. Unfortunately, in many cases, it is difficult to obtain and analyze communication samples from an individual AAC user in order to develop an individualized word list. Nonetheless, efforts to obtain this information appear to be important. The most common way of doing so is to record all of the words that a user produces over a period of time.

Table 2.5.   500 most frequently occurring words produced by five adult AAC users (listed from most to least frequently occurring)

I	had	something	hope	away	years	yourself	late
to	dad	buy	keep	TV	big	morning	part
you	need	night	eye	enough	radio	listen	normal
the	where	say	went	walking	looking	wonder	wrap
a	room	talk	cold	school	happened	miss	type
it	here	his	hot	move	told	pay	sleep
my	he	should	water	heard	rather	cars	notes
and	back	after	always	hour	oh	able	insure
in	some	ask	board	bad	bring	these	real
is	she	try	which	using	care	clothes	asked
me	they	little	hospital	working	breakfast	called	horn
on	about	than	love	once	he'll	stop	guy
have	no	better	money	shoes	life	show	might
do	could	does	getting	plug	six	hand	days
of	down	computer	pee	glad	hit	haven't	tired
that	tell	before	hate	many	face	save	slow
get	home	thing	leave	whole	suppose	broke	sitting
for	her	same	arm	man	huh	sun	nose
what	good	tonight	pack	yet	most	easy	lift
but	too	again	old	took	looks	second	comes
if	why	only	garage	red	forgot	thanks	card
can	ok	feel	hard	because	bit	pass	coming
don't	because	bag	pop	ago	half	moved	thinking
be	from	eat	doctor	blue	saw	tapes	month
I'm	much	has	guess	walker	mine	makes	sounds
with	car	find	week	block	made	gone	study
are	very	then	let	line	beautiful	full	pins
like	use	four	thought	name	three	gift	read
was	can't	maybe	under	hold	therapy	hair	feet
mom	work	left	pretty	ever	program	tomorrow	trying
how	now	last	mean	fell	own	leaving	such
this	more	those	kind	towel	building	stay	seeing
so	didn't	dinner	way	isn't	open	year	kept
will	help	doing	crib	floor	every	place	he's
go	him	first	might	doesn't	two	sit	stereo
not	who	stand	great	table	live	plus	walked
or	right	pleased	push	noise	yesterday	important	laundry
want	that's	battery	even	side	pick	mind	instead
would	day	said	head	check	anyway	months	job
when	tomorrow	people	both	pot	number	handle	door
up	foot	won't	wouldn't	believe	box	juice	wondering
all	long	a lot	far	since	their	track	low
out	were	give	set	boy	minutes	food	hello
it's	an	I'd	things	damn	she's	afraid	toilet
your	today	clean	game	words	fine	dumb	lap
at	by	turn	hurt	knee	understand	word	surgery
going	over	watch	stuff	gets	twenty	between	sound
put	them	well	music	talking	girl	run	probably
take	I've	remember	wait	hurts	close	carry	clear
we	really	other	next	problem	lot	supper	purse
did	walk	yes	done	mouth	shirt	lay	Friday
please	two	anything	also	what's	myself	doctors	cream
time	any	new	anyone	nurse	tube	ice	brain
know	let's	nice	our	while	started	cost	fall
one	chair	pants	sorry	came	least	feels	tight
see	still	never	until	write	there's	everything	diamond
just	I'll	fix	wear	cookies	best	apple	awful
am	look	lunch	making	weight	almost	nothing	shop
off	bed	tape	book	into	thank	speed	free
as	play	call	cave	bath	through	must	
think	wish	used	eyes	wrong	minute	dead	
there	may	been	skin	being	later	piece	
make	sure	light	paper	you'd	cut	already	

From Beukelman, D., Yorkston, K., Poblete, M., and Naranjo, C. (1984). Frequency of word occurrence in communication samples produced by adult communication aid users. *Journal of Speech and Hearing Disorders, 49,* 367; reprinted by permission.

Vocabulary-Use Patterns of Typically Developing Speakers or Writers

A considerable number of studies have examined vocabulary use patterns of typical natural speakers and writers. These composite lists provide a rich source of core vocabulary information and can be useful when developing vocabulary lists for specific AAC users. As noted previously, Yorkston et al. (1990) indicated that vocabulary selection for individual AAC users is quite complex because a composite vocabulary list contains only a fraction of the total words that will be needed. These authors summarized their views about the role of core vocabularies in AAC applications in the following statement:

> Our data . . . suggest that [standard word lists] are an excellent source of potential words to be included in an AAC application. The inclusion of standard word lists in the memory of an AAC device is a great time savings for augmented communicators and their facilitators. However, these standard lists must not be taught without careful consideration. Systematic strategies are required to eliminate unnecessary or "costly" words from the standard vocabulary lists as an AAC device is individualized for a given client. (1990, p. 223)

Fringe Vocabulary

Fringe vocabulary refers to vocabulary words and messages that are specific or unique to the individual AAC user. For example, these might include names of specific people, locations, and activities, as well as preferred expressions. Such words serve to personalize the vocabulary included in an AAC system and to allow expression of ideas and messages that do not appear in core vocabulary lists. By their very nature, fringe vocabulary items must be recommended by AAC users themselves or by informants who know them or their communicative situations quite well. The most important potential informant is the individual who will be using the AAC system. AAC users' abilities to act as informants about their own vocabulary and message needs depend on numerous factors including age, cognitive and language abilities, and the level of facilitator support provided.

Informants

In clinical work, there is a tendency for one or two AAC team members, often professionals, to select fringe vocabulary items without consulting a sufficient number of informants. A study by Yorkston, Fried-Oken, and Beukelman (1988) indicated that only about half of the top 100 fringe vocabulary words selected for AAC users by two types of informants were the same. Thus, it is clear that AAC teams should consult multiple informants to obtain the best possible list of fringe words. The most obvious informants are spouses, parents, siblings, teachers, and other caregivers. Informants such as employers, co-workers, peers, and friends often offer valuable vocabulary suggestions as well. Of course, whenever possible, AAC users themselves should identify potential informants as well as suggest words and messages to be included or retained in the vocabulary.

Very little research has examined the performance or role of informants in vocabulary selection. One exception is a study of three types of informants—parents, speech-language pathologists, and teachers—who often select vocabulary for AAC users (Morrow, Beukelman, Mirenda, & Yorkston, 1993). Results indicated that each of the informants contributed an important number of fringe words to the composite vocabularies for the child participants and that none of the informants could be eliminated from the vocabulary selection process. Specifically, for three of the six children involved in the study, their mothers contributed the most fringe words. For the other three children, their speech-language pathologists offered the most fringe words. Fringe words contributed by teachers, although fewer in number, were particularly crucial to classroom participation.

Vocabulary Selection Processes

Although there has been very little research regarding how to select fringe vocabularies, important suggestions to guide this process have been made. Musselwhite and St. Louis (1988) suggested that initial vocabulary items should be of high interest to the individual, have potential for frequent use, denote a range of semantic notions and pragmatic functions, reflect the "here and now" for ease of learning, have potential for later multiword use, and provide ease of production or interpretation. Several processes have been widely used in the AAC field to facilitate achievement of these criteria, including environmental or ecological inventories and communication diaries and checklists.

Environmental or Ecological Inventories

In an effort to personalize the vocabulary of AAC users, several authors have presented environmental or ecological inventory processes that AAC teams can use to document how the individual participates in and observes various activities (Carlson, 1981; Mirenda, 1985; Reichle, York, & Sigafoos, 1991). Carlson stated, "By discriminating between observation and participation events, it is possible to gain a better picture of the [individual's] actual experiences within the area rather than the [facilitator's] perception of the experience" (1981, p. 142). During an environmental inventory, the AAC team observes and documents the vocabulary words used by peers both with and without disabilities during frequently occurring activities. The team then reduces this pool of vocabulary items to a list of the most critical words that the AAC user can manage.

Parental vocabulary diaries . . . are invaluable supplements to professional observations. I find it is not possible to rely on such diaries for information about pronunciation or grammar, but most parents have little trouble learning how to keep a list of words used by the child during the day. (Crystal, 1987, p. 41)

Communication Diaries and Checklists

Vocabulary diaries are records of the words or phrases needed by an AAC user in a variety of contexts. Usually, communication diaries are kept by informants who simply record the needed vocabulary on a blank piece of paper throughout the day. Carefully constructed vocabulary checklists such as the MacArthur Communicative Development Inventory: Words and Sentences (Fenson et al., 1993b) can also be useful as a short-cut to vocabulary selection, as they provide informants with ideas about potential vocabulary words from which to choose. Morrow et al. (1993) studied informants' reactions to the communication diary, environmental inventory (after Carlson, 1981), and vocabulary checklist processes (Bristow & Fristoe, 1984). Parents, teachers, and speech-language pathologists all rated the communication diary and environmental inventory methods as being moderately easy to use and rated the vocabulary checklist as slightly more satisfactory.

CONCLUSIONS

Various aspects of the initial vocabulary selection process have been discussed in this chapter. It is important to emphasize that vocabulary selection also involves the ongoing process of vocabulary *maintenance.* AAC users employ some words and phrases so commonly that it is easy for them and their facilitators to decide to retain them in the system. Other words and phrases may be used much less often, either because they were poorly chosen in the first place or because they have outlived their usefulness. The latter applies particularly to vocabulary items that AAC teams selected for specific contexts, such as a particular unit of study in the classroom, or for special events, such as Thanksgiving or other holidays. Items for use in special contexts should be eliminated from the available lexicon once they are not needed, to make space for other, more important words and to reduce the cognitive load for users, who must scan many items prior to selection. Although there is no research about systematic vocabulary maintenance processes and the decision making involved in these processes, such research is sorely needed.

3

Symbols and Rate Enhancement

It's summertime, and you're in the car on the way home. The light turns red, so you stop; then it turns green, and you begin driving again. While you drive, you think about the chapter you just read on messaging and find yourself wondering, "What is the relationship between messages and symbols?" As you ponder this, you notice a detour sign pointing to a side street because of construction, and you follow the detour. You pass by an ice cream store and decide to stop for a treat. When you walk into the store, the clerk asks for your order, and you say, "I want that," and point to a full-color picture of a hot fudge sundae. The clerk gives you your sundae and your change, and you smile and wave as you leave. As you begin driving again, you continue to wonder, "Messages? Symbols? How are they related?" Little do you realize that you've just experienced five examples of this relationship. *Can you find all five in the story?*

The relationship between symbols and messages is actually quite simple. All of us—not just augmentative and alternative communication (AAC) users—communicate messages and represent those messages with symbols. Symbols can be used both with and without communication aids such as electronic devices. As illustrated in the previous example, symbols can convey whole messages such as *Stop, Go, Turn here, Thanks,* and *Good-bye,* as well as partial messages such as *(I want a) hot fudge sundae.* Even those of us who can speak use symbols every single day to both receive and send messages. Without symbols, we would not be able to communicate in writing or send nonverbal messages conveying empathy, warmth, and approval. There would be no golden arches! No mouse ears! No logos (imagine no golden arches!), no labels, no warning signs, no newspapers, and no textbooks! Without the ability to send messages via gestures, body language, written words, and other symbols, communication as we now know it would be a vastly different—and much less rich—experience.

For someone who is unable to speak, to "talk," and for someone who is unable to write, to place words on paper . . . is improbable, it is magical. (Beukelman, 1991, p. 2)

Much of the magic of AAC lies in the vast array of symbols and signals, other than those used in speech, that people can employ to send messages. Especially for individuals who cannot read or write, the ability to represent messages and concepts in alternative ways is central to communication. Acknowledgment of the importance of symbols has prompted much of the research and clinical effort devoted to studying and developing comprehensive symbol systems that are easy to use and learn. In this chapter, we review many of the most commonly used types of symbols and discuss their usefulness for various individuals.

OVERVIEW OF SYMBOLS

A number of definitions and taxonomies have been used to describe symbols and their various forms (see Fuller, Lloyd, & Schlosser, 1992, for the most recent taxonomy). Basically, a *symbol* is "something that stands for or represents something else" (Vanderheiden & Yoder, 1986, p. 15). This "something else" is termed its *referent.*

Symbols can be described in terms of many characteristics, including iconicity, ambiguity, complexity, figure–ground differential, perceptual distinctness, acceptability, efficiency, and size (see Fuller, Lloyd, & Stratton, 1997, for a review of these issues). Of these, iconicity has received the most attention from both researchers and clinicians. The term *iconicity* refers to the "visual relationship of a symbol to its referent" (Lloyd & Blischak, 1992, p. 106). At one end of the iconicity continuum are *transparent* symbols, in which "the shape, motion, or function of the referent is depicted to such an extent that meaning of the symbol can be readily guessed in the absence of the referent" (Fuller & Lloyd, 1991, p. 217). At the other end are *opaque* symbols, "in which no [symbol–referent] relationship is perceived even when the meaning of the symbol is known" (Fuller & Lloyd, 1991, p. 217). For example, a color photograph of a shoe is transparent, whereas the written word *shoe* is opaque. Between the two extremes are *translucent* symbols, "in which the meaning of the referent may or may not be obvious but a relationship can be perceived between the symbol and the referent once the meaning is provided" (Fuller & Lloyd, 1991, p. 217). For example, the gesture commonly used in North America for *peace* in which the index and middle fingers are raised to form a *V* is translucent in that one needs to be aware of the *V for victory* slogan used during World War II in order to understand the gesture's meaning. Translucent symbols are often defined by numerical ratings of the amount of relationship to a referent perceived to be present in the symbol (Lloyd & Blischak, 1992).

Symbols can be divided into those that are *aided,* which require some type of external assistance such as a device for production, and those that are *unaided,* which require no external device for production (Lloyd & Fuller, 1986). Aided symbols include real objects and black-and-white line drawings, and unaided symbols include facial expressions, manual signs, and natural speech and vocalizations. In addition, some symbol sets incorporate the use of aided and unaided elements; we refer to these as *combined symbol sets* (e.g., the Makaton Vocabulary [Grove & Walker, 1990]).

Numerous variables beyond those related to the characteristics of symbols themselves interact during the symbol learning process. For example, iconicity and symbol learning appear to be, at least to some extent, "culture-bound, time-bound, and, in general, experience-bound" (Brown, 1977, p. 29). Thus, Dunham (1989) found that adults with and without mental retardation differed in their abilities to guess the meanings of manual signs that adults without disabilities rated low in transparency (i.e., guessability). The different cultural and experiential backgrounds of these two groups are among the factors likely to have influenced the results. In addition, the longitudinal work of Romski and Sevcik (1996) suggested that spoken language comprehension plays a critical role in the symbol learning process. In their work with youth with severe cognitive disabilities, these researchers found that those who understood the meanings of specific referents learned to recognize the referents' abstract lexigrams more readily than did individuals without such comprehension skills. Several researchers have suggested that the reinforcement value of a referent is also likely to affect its learnability (Schlosser, Lloyd, & McNaughton, 1996). For example, Reichle, York, and Sigafoos argued that "the reinforcing value of an item might have a greater effect on the rate at which the corresponding gesture is acquired. That is, a candy bar represented by an opaque gesture might be more easily acquired than a highly guessable gesture for water" (1991, p. 54). Instructional factors, such as the availability of voice output (Schlosser, Belfiore, Nigam, Blischak, & Hetzroni, 1995) and the teaching strategies used during instruction (Schlosser & Lloyd, 1993), also appear to influence both initial and generalized symbol learning. Finally, numerous developmental factors appear to influence the ability to learn to recognize, use, and understand various types of relationships between symbols (specifically, pictures) and their referents (Stephenson & Linfoot, 1996). In short, numerous factors in addition to symbol iconicity clearly affect how, where, when, and by whom symbols are acquired and used.

In European countries, the term *sign* is used instead of *symbol* as a generic term for "linguistic forms that are not speech, (including) all kinds of manual and graphic forms." (von Tetzchner & Jensen, 1996, p. 10)

UNAIDED SYMBOLS: GESTURES AND VOCALIZATIONS

There's language in her eye, her cheek, her lip,
Nay her foot speaks; her wanton spirits look out
At every joint and motive of her body.
(Shakespeare, *Troilus and Cressida*, Act 4, Scene 5)

Nonverbal behavior can repeat, contradict, substitute for, complement, accent, or regulate verbal behavior (Knapp, 1980). Nonverbal behavior includes gestures, vocalizations, and other paralinguistic elements; physical characteristics (e.g., physique, body and breath odor); proxemics (e.g., seating arrangements, personal space requirements); artifacts (e.g., clothes, perfume, makeup); and environmental factors that may influence impressions and interactions (e.g., the neatness or disorder of a room may affect how one interacts with the person who lives there). Although all of these are important elements of communication, gestures and vocalizations are perhaps the most extensive forms of nonverbal behavior and are therefore discussed in more detail in the following sections.

At 20 months, Amy conveyed the message "You (one of several adults present in the room) give me that (a glass of water)," by orienting toward her potential partner, staring intently at her and then, once the communicative channel was open, pointing with one hand to the agent, the other to the object. (L. Adamson and B. Dunbar, describing the communication of a young child with a tracheostomy, in Adamson & Dunbar, 1991, p. 279)

Gestures

Gestural behavior includes fine and gross motor body movements, facial expressions, eye behaviors, and postures. Ekman and Friesen (1969) developed a classification system for describing these behaviors in terms of the communicative and adaptive purposes they generally serve. According to this system, *emblems* are gestural behaviors that can be translated, or defined, by a few words or a phrase and that can be used without speech to convey messages. There is usually high agreement about the meaning of emblems among members of the same culture. For example, in North America, head shaking is generally understood as an emblem for *no*, whereas head nodding is an emblem meaning *yes*. People usually produce emblems with their hands, although they may use their entire bodies, as in pantomime.

As is the case for verbal speech, people interpret emblems differently depending on circumstances; for example, a nose wrinkle may mean *I'm disgusted* or *Phew! That smells bad!* depending on the context. Some emblems, such as those used for *eating* (bringing the hand to the mouth) and *sleeping* (tilting the head to the side and closing the eyes or placing the hands beneath the head like a pillow), have been observed in several cultures (Ekman, 1976). Other emblems are quite culture specific. For example, Figure 3.1 displays suicide emblems that reflect the methods usually used for this act (hanging, shooting, stabbing) in three different cultures.

Some emblems are age specific, and their comprehension may depend on a person's cognitive and language abilities. For example, Hamre-Nietupski and her colleagues (1977) devised a list of 147 such emblems, which they called *generally understood gestures*, which were found to have a 77% recognition rate by people serving individuals with severe disabilities (Fiocca, 1981). Doherty, Karlan, and Lloyd (1982), however, found that adults with mental retardation in sheltered workshops understood fewer than 40% of these gestures. Similarly, some adults with aphasia secondary to stroke have been noted to have difficulty in using and understanding even common gestural emblems (Rosenbek, LaPointe, & Wertz, 1989). For such individuals, the apparent simplicity of even common gestures may be misleading.

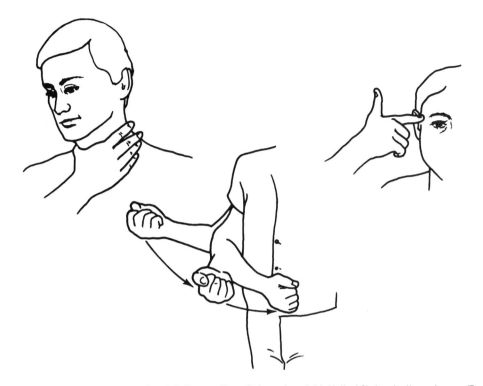

Figure 3.1. Emblems for suicide. Top left, Papua, New Guinea; top right, United States; bottom, Japan. (From Ekman, P. (1976). Movements with precise meanings. *Journal of Communication, 26,* 23; reprinted by permission of Oxford University Press.)

Ruth talks through her eyes, facial expressions, grunts and sighs and other sounds, and selects two- or three-word messages/fragments/clues from her word boards to germinate the conversation. . . . Ruth's communication is, in the most fundamental sense, pure poetry. (Steve Kaplan, describing the communication skills of his coauthor for the book *I Raise My Eyes to Say Yes,* in Sienkiewicz-Mercer & Kaplan, 1989, pp. xii–xiii)

Illustrators are nonverbal behaviors that accompany speech and illustrate what is being said (Knapp, 1980). Among other functions, illustrators 1) emphasize a word or a phrase (e.g., pointing emphatically to a chair while saying "Sit down"), 2) depict a referent or a spatial relationship (e.g., spreading the hands far apart while saying "You should have seen the size of the one that got away"), 3) depict the pacing of an event (e.g., snapping the fingers rapidly while saying "It was over with before I knew it"), or 4) illustrate a verbal statement through repetition or substitution of a word or a phrase (e.g., miming the action of writing while saying "Where's my pencil?"). Knapp (1980) suggested that people use illustrators less consciously and less deliberately than emblems and that speakers use them most frequently in face-to-face interactions when they are excited, when the receiver is not paying attention or is not comprehending the message, or when the interaction is generally difficult.

Affect displays are facial expressions or body movements that display emotional states. Affect displays differ from emblems in that they are more subtle, less stylized, and less intentional (Knapp, 1980); in fact, in many cases, an affect display may contradict a concurrent verbal statement. The person using these subtle gestures may be largely unaware of them, although the gestures may be obvious to the receiver of the message. Affect displays that convey happiness, surprise, fear, sadness, anger, and disgust or contempt may occur cross-culturally, although their contextual appropriateness is governed by specific social rules regarding age, sex, and role position (Ekman & Friesen, 1969).

Saying "I agree completely" while shaking the head *no* and crossing the arms in front of the body is one example of an affect display that contradicts a concurrent verbal statement.

Regulators are nonverbal behaviors that maintain and regulate conversational speaking and listening between two or more people. Regulators may function to initiate or terminate interactions or to tell the speaker to continue, repeat, elaborate, hurry up, talk about something more interesting, or give the listener a chance to talk, among other functions (Ekman & Friesen, 1969). Similar to emblems, regulators tend to be quite culturally bound (Hetzroni & Harris, 1996). In North America, head nods and eye behaviors are the most common regulators of turn-taking interactions for most people. For example, when one wishes to terminate an interaction, the amount of eye contact often decreases markedly, whereas nodding accompanied by wide-eyed gazing can urge a speaker to continue. Like illustrators, regulators are thought to be learned from watching others interact, but, unlike illustrators, they are emitted almost involuntarily. However, we are usually aware of these behaviors when they are sent by those with whom we interact.

The final category of gestures, *adaptors,* are learned behaviors that a person generally uses more often when he or she is alone; adaptors are not intentionally used in communication. Nevertheless, their use may be triggered by verbal interactions that produce emotional responses, particularly those associated with anxiety of some sort (Knapp, 1980).

Adaptors can be divided into three types: self, object, and alter adaptors. *Self-adaptors* refer to manipulations of one's own body and include holding, rubbing, scratching, or pinching oneself. People often use self-adaptors with little conscious effort and with no intention to communicate, and these behaviors receive little external feedback from others; in fact, other people rarely wish to be caught looking at them. Rubbing one's nose when feeling stress and wiping around the corners of the eyes when feeling sad are two examples of this type of self-adaptor. *Object adaptors* involve the manipulation of objects, are often learned later in life, and have less social stigma associated with them. Often, the person producing these gestures is aware of them and may intend to communicate a message with them. Chewing on a pencil instead of smoking a cigarette when anxious is an example of an object adaptor. *Alter adaptors* are thought to be learned early in life in conjunction with interpersonal experiences such as giving and taking or protecting oneself against impending harm. Ekman (1976) distinguished these learned behaviors by their adaptability. For example, a child who has been physically abused may react to an adult's sudden advance by crouching and moving his or her hands toward his or her face in a protective motion. Later in life, this alter adaptor may be manifest as a step backward with a slight hand movement toward the body when a stranger approaches; this is an alteration of the initial, self-protective behavior.

When conducting an AAC assessment, keep the following questions in mind in order to incorporate and acknowledge the differences in nonverbal communication across cultures.

- Is eye contact expected when listening? When talking? For children? For adults? Does eye contact (or a lack thereof) have social significance? Is it a sign of respect? Disrespect? Insincerity?
- Is touching or hand holding a social norm? Do gender differences govern touching? What are the social norms related to personal space? Displaying particular body parts?
- Is silence expected of listeners? Of learners? As a respect signal? Does it indicate lack of interest?
- Is laughter a communication device?
- Are gestures acceptable? What do they mean?
- What types of nonverbal cues are used to assist communication? To commence and terminate communication? Is turn taking consecutive or concurrent? (Adapted from Harris, in Blackstone, 1994a; Hetzroni & Harris, 1996)

Vocalizations and Speech

People who have difficulty with speech often produce vocalizations that are communicative in nature. These may range from involuntary sounds, such as sneezing, coughing, hiccuping, and snoring, to voluntary vocalizations, such as yawning, laughing, crying, moaning, yelling, and belching, that often signify physical or emotional states. Some individuals are also able to produce vocalizations that substitute for speech, such as "uh-huh" for "yes" or "uh-uh" for "no." Such vocalizations may be idiosyncratic and may require interpretation by people who are familiar with these individuals' repertoires of vocal signals.

Communication partners may also use vocalizations and speech as all or part of the communication or message display. For example, auditory scanning, either unaided or aided, can be particularly appropriate for AAC users with severe visual impairments who understand spoken language (Blackstone, 1988a). Beukelman, Yorkston, and Dowden (1985) described the use of auditory scanning by a young man who sustained a traumatic brain injury in an automobile accident. Because of the resulting impairments, he was unable to speak and was cortically blind. He communicated by having his partner verbally recite numbers corresponding to "chunks" of the alphabet, for example, 1 = *abcdef* and 2 = *ghijkl.* When his partner gave the number of the chunk he desired, he indicated his choice by making a predetermined motor movement. His partner then began to recite individual letters in the chunk until he signaled that the letter he desired had been announced. This laborious process continued until he spelled out the entire message. Similarly, Shane and Cohen (1981) described a commonly used process they called "20 questions," in which the communication partner asks questions and the person who uses AAC responds with "yes" or "no" answers. Many available electronic AAC devices and software programs provide an aided form of this technique, in which the options are announced via digitized or synthesized speech (see Blackstone, 1994a, for a review).

Toni can say one word. She can raise her hand to say "yes." Kerry will say, "Some juice please, Mom." As soon as she says that, Toni will make loud noises. So I'll ask her if she wants some juice, and she'll raise her hand. A couple of months ago, we had supper and we got done eating and Kerry said, "More spaghetti please." As soon as Kerry said that, Toni, who was sitting between Dad and me, made loud noises. I said, "You want more spaghetti?" Then she shot up her hand. Now, when Toni gets off the school bus (or is taken off in her wheelchair), and the minute I pick up my teacup, she'll start with the noises. That's your cue to ask if she wants a drink. So she's figuring out ways to get her point across. (A mother describing the communication of her foster daughter, Toni, in Biklen, 1992, p. 56)

UNAIDED SYMBOLS: GESTURAL CODES

In addition to common nonverbal signals, formalized gestural codes have been developed for use by people who have communication impairments. These codes differ from sign languages because they do not have a linguistic base. Formalized gestural codes have been developed as idiosyncratic systems for individuals in nursing homes, hospitals, and residential centers (Musselwhite & St. Louis, 1988). Few gestural codes are widely used and disseminated in North America, with the exception of Amer-Ind and the Tadoma Method.

Cathy White, who has a severe hearing loss as well as cerebral palsy with severe upper extremity involvement, developed White's Gestural System for the Lower Extremities with assistance from her mother, Harriet. The system consists of 125 leg signs, which use leg, foot, toe, heel, knee, ankle, calf, and thigh touch points to convey messages in a variety of linguistic categories (e.g., people, actions, objects) (Huer, 1987).

Amer-Ind

Amer-Ind is based on American Indian Hand Talk, a system used by a variety of Native American tribes to communicate across intertribal language barriers. Developed by a communication specialist who was taught Hand Talk by her Iroquois relatives (Skelly,

1979), the current system consists of 250 concept labels that are equivalent to approximately 2,500 English words because each signal has multiple meanings (Musselwhite & St. Louis, 1988). Additional meanings can be achieved through a process called agglutination, in which words can be combined to create new concepts (e.g., garage = *place* + *drive* + *shelter*). Skelly and her colleagues (Skelly, 1979; Skelly, Schinsky, Smith, Donaldson, & Griffin, 1975) reported that untrained observers accurately recognized between 80% and 88% of the hand signals. Later studies have suggested that adults who do not have disabilities can guess between 50% and 60% of the signals when the signals are presented without reference to their conceptual categories (Daniloff, Lloyd, & Fristoe, 1983; Doherty, Daniloff, & Lloyd, 1985). Nonetheless, these signals are still considerably more guessable than American Sign Language (ASL), which has reported guessability levels between 10% and 30% (Daniloff et al., 1983).

Amer-Ind has been used with some success by children who have severe to profound cognitive disabilities (e.g., Daniloff & Shafer, 1981) as well as by adults who have aphasia, apraxia, dysarthria, dysphonia, laryngectomies, and glossectomies (Bonvillian & Friedman, 1978; Daniloff, Noll, Fristoe, & Lloyd, 1982; Rosenbek et al., 1989; Skelly, 1979; Skelly et al., 1975; Skelly, Schinsky, Smith, & Fust, 1974). It appears that the average Amer-Ind signal can be produced at an earlier stage in motor development and requires less complex motor coordination than does the average ASL sign (Daniloff & Vergara, 1984). Therefore, this system might have advantages for people with upper-extremity impairments.

Tadoma Method

Individuals with dual sensory impairments (i.e., both deafness and blindness) who have minimal or no functional use of either visual or auditory modalities may use the Tadoma Method to tactually read the speech of others. With this technique, the person with dual sensory impairments places his or her hand on the speaker's face and neck. The thumb covers the speaker's mouth to feel movements of the lips, jaw, and tongue. The other four fingers are spread over the cheek, jaw, and throat to detect vibrations (Jensema, 1982; Mathy-Laikko, Ratcliff, Villarruel, & Yoder, 1987). Research has shown that experienced Tadoma users can track connected speech at rates of 30–40 words per minute with 50%–85% accuracy for key words (Reed et al., 1992). Vanderheiden and Lloyd (1986) noted that this and other vibrotactile techniques are relatively easy to learn by people who do not have any additional physical impairments.

UNAIDED SYMBOLS: MANUAL SIGN SYSTEMS

A number of manual sign systems, the majority of which were originally designed for and used by people who have hearing impairments, also have been employed by people with severe communication disorders who are able to hear. Manual signs, used alone or combined with speech, appear to be the form of augmentative communication used most often with people labeled as having autism or cognitive disabilities in the United States (Matas, Mathy-Laikko, Beukelman, & Legresley, 1985), the United Kingdom (Kiernan, 1983; Kiernan, Reid, & Jones, 1982), and Australia (Iacono & Parsons, 1986). This approach has also been used to some extent in the remediation of developmental apraxia (Culp, 1989).

In 1985, Bryen and Joyce published an analysis of 43 language intervention studies published in the United States and the United Kingdom between 1969 and
1979, of which 81% involved some type of manual sign system with people with
cognitive disabilities.

Despite the popularity of manual signing, controlled research studies with people
with cognitive disabilities have reported mixed success, with many reports indicating
that self-initiated spontaneous use of learned signs or structures often does not occur
(see Bryen & Joyce, 1985, and Kiernan, 1983, for reviews). Failure to implement recommended practice strategies in manual sign assessment and intervention appears to be
the primary reason for such poor clinical results (Bryen & Joyce, 1985).

Regardless of concerns related to efficacy with certain populations, manual signs
continue to be useful with a wide variety of people with severe communication disorders. Lloyd and Karlan (1984) suggested six reasons why manual sign approaches
might be appropriate alternatives to speech-only approaches. First, input is simplified
through the use of manual signs (i.e., verbiage is reduced and the rate of presentation is
slowed). Second, expressive responding is facilitated by reduction in the physical demands and psychological pressure for speech and by the enhancement of the interven-
tionist's ability to shape gradual approximations and provide physical guidance. Third,
vocabulary that is limited yet functional can be taught while maintaining the individual's attention. Fourth, manual signs allow simplified language input while minimizing auditory short-term memory and processing requirements. Fifth, stimulus processing is facilitated with the use of the visual mode, which has temporal and referential
advantages over the speech mode. Sixth, manual signs have the advantage over speech
or symbolic representation because signs are closer visually to their referents than are
spoken words.

Considerations for Use

As noted previously, manual sign languages permit the coding of an essentially infinite
number of messages; they also allow nuances of meaning to be added through accompanying body language. Some of the considerations relevant to the effective use of
manual signs include intelligibility, motoric complexity and other considerations, and
combining signs and speech or other AAC techniques, as discussed briefly in the sections that follow.

Intelligibility

The majority of ASL and Signed English signs cannot be guessed by unfamiliar individuals such as those who might be encountered on buses, in stores, recreational
facilities, and other community environments (Lloyd & Karlan, 1984). This concern was illustrated in a study of two students with autism who were taught to
use both manual signs and the Picture Communication Symbols (PCS) system (Johnson, 1994) to order food in a restaurant (Rotholz, Berkowitz, & Burberry, 1989). On average, between 0% and 25% of the manual sign requests by one student and none of
the signed requests by the other student were successfully understood by the restaurant counterperson without assistance from the students' teacher. Average successful

request rates of 80%–88% and 95%–100%, respectively, were reported when PCS symbols were used in the students' communication books. This study illustrates clearly the intelligibility limitations of manual signing when it is used with untrained community members and suggests that multimodal systems (e.g., manual signing plus a pictorial communication book) may be necessary. In addition, research has shown that signs that are high in iconicity are both easier to learn and easier to recognize (Karlan, 1990). Thus, facilitators who are teaching single, functional signs to beginning communicators may find it advantageous to select individual vocabulary items from several different manual sign systems (e.g., ASL, Signed English) to maximize both learnability and intelligibility. Of course, if manual signing is being taught as a language system, such selective use of signs across systems is inadvisable.

Motoric Complexity and Other Considerations

Reviews of the literature on manual sign learnability (Doherty, 1985; Karlan, 1990) have indicated that the easiest signs to learn are those that 1) require contact between the hands; 2) are symmetrical (i.e., both hands make the same shape or movement); 3) are produced within the user's visual field; 4) require a single, simple hand shape; and 5) require that the same hand movement be repeated. In addition, signs taught in the same environment or time frame should be dissimilar from other signs being taught; for example, teaching the signs for both EAT and DRINK during lunch in the school cafeteria is probably not a good idea because these signs are both motorically and conceptually similar. Finally, and most important, manual signs selected for instruction should be motivating and functional for the user. Selecting signs for initial instruction that meet all of these requirements is a formidable task because it appears that functionality and learnability may be at least somewhat incompatible (Luftig, 1984). Nonetheless, Musselwhite and St. Louis (1988) provided a useful matrix to make decisions about signs to be included in an initial lexicon. A modified form of the matrix is presented in Table 3.1.

Combining Signs and Speech or Other AAC Techniques

Simultaneous or total communication requires that manual signs be presented at the same time as words are spoken, usually in the context of a telegraphic or key-word signing approach (see Bonvillian & Nelson, 1978; Casey, 1978; Konstantareas, 1984; and Schaeffer, 1980). Multiple research studies have found a combined manual sign plus speech intervention to be more effective in establishing production and/or comprehension skills than either mode taught singly (e.g., Barrera, Lobato-Barrera, & Sulzer-Azaroff, 1980; Brady & Smouse, 1978). However, some individuals may be more apt to attend to the manual sign component than the speech component when the two modes are combined (Carr, Binkoff, Kologinsky, & Eddy, 1978). Furthermore, some research has suggested that the usefulness of simultaneous instruction may depend on whether the individual has mastered generalized imitation at the point of intervention (Carr & Dores, 1981; Carr, Pridal, & Dores, 1984).

Interventions combining manual signs, speech, and other AAC techniques may also be useful for some individuals for reasons other than enhanced intelligibility to unfamiliar partners. For example, a series of studies by Iacono and her colleagues demonstrated that instruction with manual signs plus line-drawing symbols on a voice-output communication device appeared to have advantages over sign-alone instruction in teaching the use of more complex language forms (e.g., two-word utterances) (Iacono &

Table 3.1. Decision-making matrix for selecting manual signs for initial instruction

Directions:
Using input from family and other team members plus suggested core vocabulary lists, select a vocabulary pool of at least 15–20 items for initial instruction. Rate each sign relative to the relevant features, using the following code.

Code:
Numbers in parentheses in each category indicate weightings that reflect the relative importance of the factor. For example, "user preference" has a weight of 3, compared with "contact," which has a weight of 1. This indicates that user preference is considered to be 3 times more important than contact. A plus sign (+) indicates that the sign meets this requirement (1 point × weighting), a slash (/) indicates that the sign partially meets this requirement (.5 points × weighting), and a minus sign (−) indicates that the sign does not meet this requirement (0 points).

Example:
Tim is a 10-year-old boy with autism who loves to eat and engage in self-stimulation by dangling strings in front of his eyes. He also enjoys music, although not as much as food and strings. He does not particularly like physical contact. Note that the signs for MORE, EAT, and STRING appear to be good initial instructional targets and that TOILET is least applicable, despite its high functionality. MUSIC might be introduced at a later time after introducing other, more motivating signs, and HUG should be eliminated from consideration because of its low "user preference" rating.

| | Learner and conceptual factors | | | | | Motoric factors | | | | |
Sign	(3) User preference	(2) Used frequently	(1) Ionic	(1) Contact	(1) Symmetric	(1) Visible	(1) Simple hand shape	(1) Simple movement	(1) Repetitive	Total score
MORE	+++	++	/	+	+	+	+	+	+	11.5
TOILET	−	+	−	−	−	+	−	+	+	4.0
EAT	+++	++	+	+	−	/	+	+	+	10.5
MUSIC	++	+	−	−	−	+	+	+	+	7.0
HUG	−	−	+	+	+	+	+	+	−	6.0
STRING	+++	++	+	/	+	+	−	+	−	9.5

Source: Musselwhite and St. Louis (1988).

Duncum, 1995; Iacono, Mirenda, & Beukelman, 1993; Iacono & Waring, 1996). In addition, the use of a multimodal system has the advantage of "covering all the bases" in instances in which it is not clear which symbol system might be best (Reichle et al., 1991). Finally, for some individuals, such as children with developmental apraxia of speech (DAS), a multimodal AAC system might well be the system of choice (Blackstone, 1989e; Cumley, 1997).

A videotape, *Early Use of Total Communication: Parents' Perspectives on Using Sign Language with Young Children with Down Syndrome,* and an accompanying booklet by Gibbs and Springer are available from Paul H. Brookes Publishing Co. The videotape illustrates how total communication, an approach in which speech and sign language are used simultaneously, creates an avenue for children with Down syndrome to communicate successfully.

There simply are no clear, empirically validated guidelines to use when making decisions about when and with whom to use manual signs in combination with other techniques. Thus, facilitators must make such decisions based largely on experience and logic. The available evidence suggests that multimodal instruction does not appear to reduce an individual's motivation to speak and may in fact enhance it (e.g., Cregan, 1993; Silverman, 1995).

Types of Manual Sign Systems

The term *manual sign system* actually refers to three main types of systems: 1) those that are alternatives to the spoken language of a particular country (e.g., ASL, Swedish Sign Language), 2) those that parallel the spoken language (manually coded English [MCE]), and 3) those that interact with or supplement another means of transmitting a spoken language (e.g., fingerspelling). We review the primary manual sign systems used in North America in the sections that follow, with particular reference to their applicability to AAC interventions.

National Sign Languages

In most countries, national sign languages have been developed through use by the Deaf community for many years. In the United States and most of Canada, ASL or Ameslan is used within the Deaf community for face-to-face interactions. In the province of Quebec, Canada, a distinctly different system, La Langue des Signes Québecoises (LSQ), is used by people who are deaf.

LSQ, the sign language of Quebec, is heavily influenced by brothers (monks) from the United States who taught deaf boys using ASL signs in French word order and by nuns from France who taught French deaf girls using French Sign Language. (J. Jamieson, personal communication, May 12, 1997)

ASL is related neither to English nor to the sign languages of other countries, so Deaf communities in China, France, Great Britain, Japan, Norway, Sweden, and many other countries have their own distinct languages. Only a few teachers of people with hearing impairments in the United States appear to use ASL with their students; thus, it is not a pedagogical language, although it is the predominant language of the Deaf community (Hoffmeister, 1990). Because ASL does not follow or approximate English word order, it is not used concurrently with speech.

Sign It is a game that teaches more than 800 ASL signs as players move their markers to complete a treacherous journey on the board. An accompanying book, *Signing Illustrated,* illustrates more than 1,350 ASL signs and expressions. The game is available from Permanent Reflections in Toronto, Ontario, Canada.

Pure-form ASL is rarely used with people who have communication difficulties not primarily due to a hearing impairment. Instead, an invented manual signing approach, in which ASL signs are combined with speech and produced in English word order, is often used. This technique is termed *key-word signing* (KWS) and is discussed in a following section in this chapter.

A historical note: The Paget-Gorman Sign System (Paget, Gorman, & Paget, 1976), developed in England, was the first MCE sign system and is composed largely of pantomimes and hand signs. Seeing Essential English (SEE-1; Anthony, 1971) was the first MCE developed in North America, and it was originally intended for use with individuals who were both deaf and had cognitive disabilities. Duffysigns (Duffy, 1977) was developed for use by individuals with both cognitive and physical disabilities (e.g., cerebral palsy) and requires less motor control than do other MCE systems.

Manual Sign Parallel Systems (Manually Coded English)

In North America, a number of manual sign systems that code English word order, syntax, and grammar have been developed for educational use with individuals with hearing and other communicative impairments. These systems have been referred to as educational sign systems (Musselwhite & St. Louis, 1988), pedagogical signs (Vanderheiden & Lloyd, 1986), and MCE (Karlan, 1990; Vanderheiden & Lloyd, 1986). We use the term *MCE* in acknowledgment of its common use in the Deaf community (Stedt & Moores, 1990).

Outside North America, many MCE systems have been developed for use by people with severe communication disorders. For example, in Ireland, Language Augmentation for Mentally Handicapped signs are used widely by children with cognitive disabilities (Kearns, 1990). Similarly, simplified sign lexica based on Finnish Sign Language (Pulli & Jaroma, 1990) and Swedish Sign Language (Granlund, Ström, & Olsson, 1989) have been employed in Scandinavia.

The three most commonly used MCE systems in North America are Sign English (Woodward, 1990), Signed English (Bornstein, Saulnier, & Hamilton, 1983), and Signing Exact English (SEE-2) (Gustason, Pfetzing, & Zawolkow, 1980). In addition, KWS, a type of MCE, has been developed primarily for use with people who have communication disorders and cognitive disabilities but can hear. We discuss these four MCE systems in the sections that follow.

Sign language videotapes for both ASL and MCE, sign language coloring books, and See 'n Sign cards that depict illustrated signs combined with Touch 'n Talk symbols are available from Imaginart Communication Products.

Sign English

Sign English, also known as Pidgin Sign English (PSE), is perhaps best described as ASL-like English when used by people who can hear and English-like ASL when used by people who have hearing impairments (Woodward, 1990). Many versions of Sign English have evolved from interactions between skilled deaf and hearing signers. Thus, Sign English is not considered to be a language separate from ASL and English; rather, it incorporates elements of each (Woodward, 1990). Because of this intermediate status and the fact that there is considerable geographical variability in Sign English dialects, few studies have described the grammatical characteristics of this manual system. Sign English appears to be used extensively in the education of students who have hearing impairments in a total communication context, in conjunction with speech or extensive mouthing of English words (Woodward, 1990).

Signed English and SEE-2, which were developed by teachers and hearing parents of deaf children, borrow liberally from the vocabulary of ASL but also include many non-ASL signs for word endings, verb tenses, and other elements that would ordinarily be fingerspelled or omitted. (Karlan, 1990)

Signed English

Signed English was designed in the early 1970s as a simple and flexible alternative to existing manual English systems. Although originally designed for preschoolers with hearing impairments, it has been expanded and adapted so that it can be used by older students as well (Bornstein, 1990). Signed English consists of more than 3,100 signs and uses 14 sign markers (e.g., *-ed, -ing*).

Signed English has been used for many years in conjunction with speech with students with cognitive disabilities, and it was the first manual sign system reported to be successfully implemented with children with autism (Creedon, 1973). Bryen and Joyce (1985) reported that Signed English was identified in the majority of studies of students with cognitive disabilities that named a specific manual sign system.

There are a wide variety of support materials for classroom and community use of Signed English, including illustrated dictionaries, texts, storybooks, flash cards, videotapes, coloring books, songbooks and records, poems, and posters. These are available through Gallaudet University Press.

Signing Exact English

SEE-2 was developed as an alternative to its predecessor, SEE-1, after the members of a SEE-1 work group became dissatisfied with its direction (Gustason, 1990). SEE-2 consists of approximately 4,000 signs and more than 70 word ending, tense, and affix signs (e.g., *-est, -ed, -ing, -ment, un-*). The system was developed around 10 basic grammatical principles that ensure internal consistency and provide guidelines for adding new signs (see Gustason, 1990).

SEE-2 is motorically and linguistically more complex than Signed English and may, therefore, be less useful for people with severe communication disorders not due primarily to hearing impairments (Musselwhite & St. Louis, 1988). For example, only two of the studies reviewed by Bryen and Joyce (1985) reported use of SEE-2 with students who had severe disabilities. It is also likely that references to the use of SEE-2 with people with cognitive disabilities actually refer to selective use of the signs from this system rather than to use of the complete system.

Numerous SEE-2 support materials, including articles, storybooks, videotapes, illustrated dictionaries, flash cards, songs, and posters are available for parents, teachers, and others through the Modern Signs Press (United States) and Wuerz Publishing (Canada).

Key-Word Signing

With KWS (Grove & Walker, 1990; Windsor & Fristoe, 1989), spoken English is used simultaneously with manual signs for the critical words in a sentence, such as base nouns, base verbs, prepositions, adjectives, and adverbs. Thus, the sentence *Go get the cup and put it on the table* might involve the use of the signs GET, CUP, PUT, ON, and TABLE while the entire sentence is spoken.

The term *key-word signing* probably most accurately describes the majority of interventions that use manual signs in English word order and that have been used with people with disabilities other than hearing impairments. Because these interventions almost always include the use of speech in addition to manual signs, they have been referred to as total communication or simultaneous communication approaches. Bryen and Joyce (1985) reported that of 25 studies they reviewed in which some type of manual sign system was used with students with severe cognitive disabilities, 4 purported to have used ASL, 6 used Signed English, 2 used SEE-2, and 13 used other or unspecified systems. It is quite likely that KWS, using signs from the other named systems, was the approach actually used in the majority of these studies.

It is important to make a distinction between ASL, Signed English, KWS, and other manual sign systems in order to respect the legitimacy of ASL as the language of the Deaf community as well as to be precise in sharing empirical and clinical results of interventions.

Tactual Reception of Signing

Tactual reception of signing is commonly used by individuals with dual sensory impairments who acquire their knowledge of sign language before becoming blind (Reed, Delhorne, Durlach, & Fischer, 1995). In this method, the deaf-blind person places one or two hands on the dominant hand of the signer and passively traces the motion of the signing hand. Thus, the various formational properties of signs are received tactually by the deaf-blind person, who then communicates expressively using conventional sign language. Tactual signing can be used in conjunction with ASL, Sign English (i.e., PSE), or Signed English. Research suggests that individuals with experience in the tactual reception of signing can receive approximately 1.5 signs per second; this compares favorably with typical signing rates of 2.5 signs per second for visual reception of signs by individuals who can see (Bellugi & Fischer, 1972; Reed, Delhorne, Durlach, & Fischer, 1995).

Manual Supplements to Spoken Language

Manual systems that interact with or supplement spoken English have been used with children who have hearing impairments and, to a limited extent, with individuals with communicative disorders to support the development of speech and literacy skills. Nevertheless, most of these techniques (including gestural or eye-blink codes) have not achieved widespread use in the field of AAC. One exception is cued speech (Kipila & Williams-Scott, 1990), a system of eight hand shapes that represent groups of consonant sounds plus six positions around the face that represent groups of vowel sounds and diphthongs. Combinations of these hand configurations show the exact pronunciation of words in concurrent speech (Jensema, 1982; Musselwhite & St. Louis, 1988). People with dual sensory impairments have used cued speech, often in combination with the

Tadoma Method (Reed et al., 1992). Cued speech is also used to encourage natural speech development in individuals with developmental apraxia of speech and autism. (See Musselwhite & St. Louis, 1988, and Silverman, 1995, for overviews of other manual supplements to English.)

Information and materials on cued speech are available from the National Cued Speech Association.

AIDED SYMBOLS: TANGIBLE SYMBOLS

Rowland and Schweigert (1989) coined the term *tangible symbol* to refer to two- or three-dimensional aided symbols that are permanent, manipulable with a simple motor behavior, tactually discriminable, and highly iconic. The term is used here in a more restricted sense to refer to symbols that can be discriminated on the basis of tangible properties (e.g., shape, texture, consistency); thus, most two-dimensional (i.e., pictorial) symbols are not included. Tangible symbols are typically used with individuals with visual or dual sensory impairments and severe cognitive disabilities, but they may also be appropriate for other populations (e.g., beginning communication symbols for children with visual impairments). Tangible symbols discussed in the following sections are real objects, miniature objects, partial objects, artificially associated and textured symbols, and other tangible symbols.

Instructional materials and videotapes developed by Rowland and Schweigert related to the use of tangible symbols are available through The Psychological Corporation and Communication Skill Builders (United States and Canada). A manual for using tangible symbols with individuals with autism (Vicker, 1996) is available from the Indiana Resource Center for Autism.

Real Objects

Real object symbols may be identical to, similar to, or associated with their referents. For example, an identical symbol for *brush your teeth* might be a toothbrush that is the same color and type as the individual's actual toothbrush. A similar symbol might be a toothbrush of a different color and type, whereas an associated symbol might be a tube of toothpaste or container of dental floss. Other examples of associated symbols include a sponge that represents *cleaning the kitchen counter* or an audiocassette that represents *music time* in the preschool classroom. Associated symbols may also include remnants of activities—items such as a ticket stub from the movies or a hamburger wrapper from a fast-food restaurant.

Many people with cognitive disabilities are able to match identical and nonidentical (i.e., similar) object symbols with similar accuracy (Mirenda & Locke, 1989). This suggests that both types of object symbols may be equal in enabling recognition of their referent; however, it is important to be cautious in this assumption, especially with beginning communicators. It is also important to consider the individual sensory input needs of individuals with visual impairments when selecting real objects for them to use. Rowland and Schweigert (1989, 1990) reported numerous examples of successful use of real object symbols with individuals who have visual and dual sensory impairments.

Miniature Objects

Miniature objects may be more practical than real objects in some situations but need to be selected carefully to maximize effectiveness (Vanderheiden & Lloyd, 1986). For example, miniatures that are much smaller than their referents may be more difficult for students with cognitive disabilities to recognize than some types of two-dimensional symbols (Mirenda & Locke, 1989). Nevertheless, miniature objects that are reasonably smaller than their referents have been used successfully with individuals with cerebral palsy (Landman & Schaeffler, 1986), dual sensory impairments (Rowland & Schweigert, 1989), and developmental disabilities (Rowland & Schweigert, 1996).

In addition to size, tactile similarity is also critical when using miniature objects with people who cannot see. It is unlikely that an individual with visual impairments will readily recognize the relationship between a miniature plastic toilet and a real toilet because they feel different with respect to size, shape, and texture. In this case, a real object associated with the toilet (e.g., a small roll of toilet paper) might be more appropriate as a bathroom symbol.

People with visual impairments "see" with their fingers and hands, so the tangible symbols they use should be tactually similar to or associated with their referents. For example, Catherine, a woman with dual sensory impairments, wears a pair of leather half-gloves (i.e., gloves with the fingers cut off) whenever she goes horseback riding. She uses the same gloves as tangible symbols for horseback riding in her schedule system at home because they remind her of (and smell like!) this activity.

Partial Objects

In some situations, particularly those that involve referents that are large, partial objects may be useful symbols. For example, the top of a spray bottle of window cleaner may be used to represent *washing the windows* at a vocational site. Also included in this category are "symbols with one or two shared features" (Rowland & Schweigert, 1989, p. 229), such as thermoform symbols that are the same size and shape as their referents. The use of partial objects may be a good alternative when tactile similarity cannot be met with miniature objects.

Artificially Associated and Textured Symbols

Tangible symbols may also be constructed by selecting shapes and textures that can be artificially associated with a referent. For example, if a wooden apple is attached to a cafeteria door, then a similar apple could be used to signify *lunchtime* (Rowland & Schweigert, 1989). Textured symbols, a subtype of artificial symbols, may be either logically or arbitrarily associated with their referents. For example, a piece of spandex material would be a logically associated textured symbol to represent a bathing suit because many suits are made of this material. Alternatively, a square of velvet could be arbitrarily selected to represent a favorite snack. Several case studies have documented the successful use of textured symbols with individuals with one or more sensory impairments in addition to severe cognitive disabilities (Locke & Mirenda, 1988; Mathy-Laikko et al., 1989; Murray-Branch, Udvari-Solner, & Bailey, 1991).

Other Tangible Symbols

Case study reports have documented the usefulness of adapting line-drawing symbols, such as Blissymbols, for use with people with visual impairments (Edman, 1991; Garrett, 1986). This approach creates a tactually discriminable relief symbol using a thermoform process, photoengraving, or other method. The user then learns to associate the raised outline of the symbol with its referent.

Instructional materials and videotapes related to the use of tangible symbols are available through The Psychological Corporation and Communication Skill Builders (United States and Canada).

AIDED SYMBOLS: REPRESENTATIONAL SYMBOLS

Many types of two-dimensional symbols can be used to represent various concepts. These representational symbols include photographs, line drawings, and abstract symbols. We review here the major representational symbol types used in North America in terms of their relative iconicity, as well as in terms of the populations of AAC users with whom they have been successfully used.

In Canada, numerous representational symbol sets, including many of those mentioned in this chapter, are available from Betacom-Bridges.

Photographs

High-quality color or black-and-white photographs may be used to represent objects, verbs, people, places, and activities. Photographs may be produced with a camera or obtained from catalogs, magazines, coupons, product labels, or advertisements (Mirenda, 1985). A research study found that people with cognitive disabilities matched color photographs to their referents somewhat more accurately than black-and-white photographs (Mirenda & Locke, 1989). Another study found that people with intellectual disabilities matched black-and-white photographs to their referents more accurately than line drawings (Sevcik & Romski, 1986). Dixon (1981) found that students with severe disabilities were more able to associate objects with their color photographs when the photographic objects were cut out than when they were not. Reichle et al. (1991) suggested that the context in which a photograph appears may affect an individual's ability to recognize it; for example, a photograph of a watering can may become more recognizable when it appears next to a photograph of a plant.

Sets of high-quality color or black-and-white photographs are available from companies such as the Mayer-Johnson Co., Attainment Co., Imaginart Communication Products (United States); and The Psychological Corporation and Communication Skill Builders (United States and Canada).

Line-Drawing Symbols

Picture Communication Symbols (PCS)

The first column in Figure 3.2 illustrates PCS, a widely used system of more than 3,000 clear, simple line drawings that are available with either written English labels or no labels (Johnson, 1994). PCS symbols can be purchased in a variety of formats, including stamps and photocopiable symbol books. A Macintosh software program, Boardmaker (Mayer-Johnson Co., 1995), can generate communication boards made of either black-and-white or colored PCS symbols in 10 languages (Danish, Dutch, English, French, German, Italian, Norwegian, Portuguese, Spanish, and Swedish). In addition, a wide variety of PCS teaching materials are also available.

Three research studies (Mirenda & Locke, 1989; Mizuko, 1987; Mizuko & Reichle, 1989) indicated that both PCS symbols and Picsyms are more transparent than Blissymbols for preschoolers without disabilities and for school-age and adult individuals with cognitive disabilities. In a comparative study of Blissymbols, PCS symbols, Pictogram Ideogram Communication (PIC) symbols (now called Pictogram Symbols), Picsyms, and rebus symbols, PCS symbols and rebuses were learned more easily across nouns, verbs, and modifiers (Bloomberg, Karlan, & Lloyd, 1990). In general, research studies on the learnability of PCS symbols indicated that preschoolers without disabilities learned more PCS symbols over three trials than either Picsyms or Blissymbols (Mizuko, 1987), whereas adults with cognitive disabilities appeared to find PCS symbols and Picsyms equally learnable (Mizuko & Reichle, 1989). AAC teams have used PCS symbols successfully in AAC interventions with people with cognitive disabilities (Heller, Allgood, Ware, Arnold, & Castelle, 1996; Mirenda & Santogrossi, 1985), cerebral palsy (Goossens', 1989), deaf-blindness (Heller, Allgood, Ware, et al., 1996), and autism (Hamilton & Snell, 1993; Rotholz et al., 1989), among other impairments.

Rebus Symbols

A *rebus* is a picture that visually or nominally represents a word or a syllable. For example, a rebus of a knot could be used to symbolize either *knot* or *not* (see Figure 3.2).

Figure 3.2.   Examples of Picture Communication Symbols, rebuses, Picsyms, and Blissymbols. (From Brandenburg, S., & Vanderheiden, G. (1988). Communication board design and vocabulary selection. In L. Bernstein (Ed.), *The vocally impaired: Clinical practice and research* (3rd ed., p. 94). Needham Heights, MA: Allyn & Bacon. Copyright © 1988; reprinted/adapted by permission.)

There are many types of rebuses (Vanderheiden & Lloyd, 1986), but the most common collection of these in North America was developed as a mechanism for teaching young children without disabilities to read (Woodcock, Clark, & Davies, 1968). This work has been adapted and expanded as a system of communication symbols for people with communication impairments, both in the United States (Clark, Davies, & Woodcock, 1974) and in the United Kingdom (Van Oosterum & Devereux, 1985; Walker, Parsons, Cousins, Henderson, & Carpenter, 1985). As of 1998, there are more than 3,500 rebuses in the British Rebus collection.

A study of children and young adults without disabilities in four age groups found rebus symbols to be equivalent to Picsyms in transparency, and both were more transparent than Blissymbols (Musselwhite & Ruscello, 1984). Another study found rebus symbols and PCS symbols easier to learn than Picsyms, PIC symbols, and Blissymbols (Bloomberg et al., 1990). Rebus symbols were found to be superior to Blissymbols in learning and short-term recall tasks with both typical preschoolers (Ecklund & Reichle,

1987) and preschoolers who had language delays (Burroughs, Albritton, Eaton, & Montague, 1990). Rebus symbols have been used in communication applications with a variety of individuals, including children with Down syndrome (Pecyna, 1988) and adults with autism (Reichle & Brown, 1986).

Rebus dictionaries and software products are available in North America from Don Johnston, Inc., and in the United Kingdom from Widgit Software, Ltd. Rebus products are also distributed in Australia, Finland, New Zealand, Singapore, South Africa, and Sweden (contact Widgit Software, Ltd., for information).

Picsyms

Picsyms is a logical system of visual-graphic symbols that were developed according to an internally consistent set of principles. The core system, which was developed through work with young children who were unable to speak (Carlson, 1985), consists of 880 line drawings accompanied by written labels (see Figure 3.2). New Picsyms can be created by following the generative rules that are included with the dictionary of symbols. As noted previously, Picsyms appear to be similar to or slightly more difficult to learn than PCS symbols and rebus symbols but easier to learn than Blissymbols, in both transparency and learnability (Bloomberg et al., 1990; Mirenda & Locke, 1989; Mizuko, 1987; Mizuko & Reichle, 1989; Musselwhite & Ruscello, 1984). They have been used in AAC interventions with individuals of all ages and ability levels.

The Picsyms dictionary can be obtained from Poppin and Company (United States). A children's songbook (Musselwhite, 1985) with a dictionary containing more than 100 manual signs, Picsyms, PCS symbols, and Blissymbols is available from Special Communications (United States).

DynaSyms

Faith Carlson, the author and inventor of Picsyms, also developed DynaSyms (see Figure 3.3). Originally designed to be used on a dedicated communication device called the DynaVox, they are also available in printed form. DynaSyms are based on Picsyms but were adapted for a computer format, with additional changes based on Picsyms consumer feedback over the years (F. Carlson, personal communication, February 4, 1997). The current disk-based system for the DynaVox-2 family of computers consists of approximately 2,000 symbols, whereas the printed version consists of more than 1,700 symbols that come in both black and white and color. Each symbol comes with the printed word above it. Generally, DynaSyms appear to be more transparent than Picsyms, although no research comparing them with other types of symbols has been conducted.

Figure 3.3.   DynaSyms. (From Glennen, S., & DeCoste, D. (1997). *The handbook of augmentative and alternative communication* (p. 122). San Diego: Singular Publishing Group; reprinted with permission by Singular Publishing Group, Inc., 401 West A Street, Suite 325, San Diego, CA 92101-7904 (800-521-8545).)

DynaSyms are available in both printed and computerized formats from Sentient Systems Technology, Inc. In addition, printed DynaSyms are available in cut-and-paste or self-adhesive sticker formats from Poppin and Company. (They also carry DynaSyms Christmas cards!)

Pictogram Symbols

Often confused in name with Picsyms and PCS, the unique Pictogram Symbols (formerly called PIC symbols) set consists of almost 1,000 white-on-black symbols designed to reduce figure–ground discrimination difficulties (Maharaj, 1998). Figure 3.4 illustrates four of these symbols.

Reichle et al. (1991) and Vanderheiden and Lloyd (1986) summarized a number of studies that indicate that white-on-black pictures are not necessarily more visually salient than standard black-on-white drawings. In a study with adults who did not have disabilities, PIC symbols were found to be less translucent than PCS symbols and rebus symbols but more translucent than Blissymbols (Bloomberg et al., 1990). Leonhart and Maharaj (1979) reported that adults with severe to profound cognitive disabilities learned PIC symbols faster than Blissymbols. PIC symbols have also been used with people with other severe or profound disabilities (Leonhart & Maharaj, 1979; Reichle & Yoder, 1985) and with people with autism (Reichle & Brown, 1986), typically in conjunction with communication books or boards.

Figure 3.4. Examples of Pictogram Ideogram Communication symbols. (From Maharaj. S.C. (1980). *Pictogram ideogram communication.* Portland, OR: ZYGO Industries; reprinted by permission.)

Pictogram Symbols (formerly called PIC symbols) are very popular in Scandinavian countries and Portugal. According to von Tetzchner and Jensen (1996), there are 563 Norwegian, 705 Danish, and 400 Portuguese Pictogram Symbols. In addition, a Dutch system called Vijfhoek Pictogrammen Systeem is based on Pictogram Symbols (Welle-Donker Gimbrère & van Balkom, 1995). Pictogram Symbols are available in North America from ZYGO Industries, Inc.

Blissymbolics

The history of Blissymbolics is complex and fascinating (see the original work by Charles Bliss, 1965, as well as historical records of Blissymbolics development in Canada in the early 1970s [Kates & McNaughton, 1975] for an in-depth explanation of the history of Blissymbolics). Generally, the system was developed to function as an auxiliary language for international written communication. It consists of approximately 100 basic symbols that can be used singly or in combination to encode virtually any message (Silverman, 1995). The current system is composed of more than 2,200 symbols (Wood, Storr, & Reich, 1992), more than 900 of which have been added since the original Blissymbolics dictionary was published in 1980. New Blissymbols are added periodically by an international panel affiliated with Blissymbolics Communication International (BCI) (see Figure 3.2 for examples of several Blissymbols).

In addition, a collection of Blissymbols is available that has been enhanced by pink line-drawing cues (BCI, 1984). These enhanced Blissymbols are designed to remind both the beginning user and the novice instructor of the concepts that the symbols represent, and they appear to have positive effects on both acquisition and retention of Blissymbols (Raghavendra & Fristoe, 1990, 1995). Figure 3.5 offers examples of enhanced Blissymbols paired with their traditional counterparts.

Blissymbolics is used in more than 33 countries and has been translated into 17 languages. Blissymbolics dictionaries, software, research reports, videotapes, teaching materials, and training workshops can be obtained through Betacom-Bridges and BCI (Canada). Enhanced Blissymbols books, a teaching manual, stamps, and flash cards are also available through BCI.

Numerous studies have indicated that of all the representational symbols in common use, Blissymbols are the least transparent, the most difficult to learn, and the hardest to retain (Bloomberg et al., 1990; Hurlbut, Iwata, & Green, 1982; Mirenda & Locke, 1989; Mizuko, 1987). Why, then, is this system so widely used in the AAC field? Vanderheiden and Lloyd (1986) noted some major strengths of Blissymbolics:

1. The principles and strategies for combining symbols enable expression of thoughts not on the communication board. The symbols are conceptually based and constructed using consistent, systematic rules.
2. The symbols can be introduced simply and later expanded.

Figure 3.5.   Examples of enhanced Blissymbols. (From Musselwhite, C., & St. Louis, K. (1988). *Communication programming for persons with severe handicaps* (2nd ed., p. 193). Austin, TX: PRO-ED; reprinted by permission.)

3. The use of Blissymbolics is compatible with other techniques including reading and writing.
4. Originally intended for use with children with cerebral palsy, Blissymbolics has been used with varying degrees of success in the remediation of virtually every known communication impairment (see Musselwhite & St. Louis, 1988; Silverman, 1995; and Vanderheiden & Lloyd, 1986, for applications).

I see the value of Bliss more and more as a transition "language" between pictures and print, for all who can achieve literacy, and a long-term language for those who cannot become fluent at spelling. . . . Pictures, Bliss, orthography, each offer different strengths to the developing child when introduced at the appropriate stage of development. All of them are important. Pictures offer immediate recognition and reduced cognitive demands, freeing attention for communication—important when the child is just learning what communication is all about. Blissymbols offer an explicit language scaffolding, preparing the way for independent mastery of what will always be a challenge—trying to replicate the accomplishments of speech. Orthography offers the ability to generate any utterance and to access all of the opportunities afforded by literacy. (Shirley McNaughton, in response to the question "What is your latest thinking on Bliss?" in McNaughton, 1995, pp. 22–23)

Other Pictorial Systems

Additional representational symbol systems have become available, although they have not been studied in terms of relative guessability and learnability. Some of these merit brief mention.

Numerous symbol systems have been developed to meet individual communication needs around the world. For example, the computerized COMPIC system from Australia contains 1,670 pictographic symbols based on international symbol conventions (Bloomberg, 1990). COMPIC symbols, software, videotapes, and instructional materials are available from COMPIC in Victoria, Australia. In Quebec, a line-drawing symbol system, Communimage, with French labels, is available through the Association de Paralysie Cérébral du Québec. Germany, Belgium, and the Netherlands also have national symbol systems (von Tetzchner & Jensen, 1996).

Self Talk

Self Talk symbols are among the commercial symbol sets available in color as well as in black and white. Originally available only on communication boards (Johnson, 1986), these simple symbols are printed with orthographic labels and may be purchased as separate stickers as well (Johnson, 1988). Students with cognitive disabilities were found to match colored Self Talk and various black-and-white line-drawing symbols with their object referents equally well, suggesting that Self Talk symbols are equivalent to these other types of symbols in guessability (Miranda & Locke, 1989).

Self Talk symbols and communication boards are available from The Psychological Corporation (United States and Canada).

Pick 'n Stick and Touch 'n Talk

Pick 'n Stick symbols are colored pictographs arranged categorically and available on peel-back pages. The 1,400 symbols available are not accompanied by written labels, so each symbol can be used flexibly to represent one of many related concepts (e.g., a symbol of a person sunbathing may be used to mean *sunbathe, relax, weekend,* or *suntan*). A black-and-white version of these symbols, Touch 'n Talk symbols, is also available. There is no available research concerning the relative iconicity of these symbol sets.

Pick 'n Stick symbols, Touch 'n Talk symbols, and related communication products are available from Imaginart Communication Products (United States). Both Pick 'n Stick and Touch 'n Talk symbols are also available from Imaginart as clip art libraries for Macintosh and IBM-compatible computers.

Talking Pictures I, II, and III

Talking Pictures I, II, and III are kits of black-and-white line drawings on cards, with printed labels in ASL, English, French, German, Italian, or Spanish on the reverse side of each card. They depict a range of functional, community living, and daily living vocabulary words. They are available in a variety of formats with support materials.

Talking Pictures I, II, and III can be ordered from the Crestwood Company (United States).

Oakland Schools Picture Dictionary

The Oakland Schools Picture Dictionary, a representational symbol system, consists of approximately 600 black-and-white line drawings, more than 75% of which are nouns (Kirstein, 1981). Included are symbols for vocational concepts and adult vocabulary items not found in other similar sets of symbols. Oakland symbols compared favorably with PCS symbols and rebus symbols on both transparency and translucency tasks with adults who had cognitive disabilities and those who did not in a study of symbols representing emotions (Francis, Nail, & Lloyd, 1990).

The Oakland Schools Picture Dictionary is available in limited quantities from Don Johnston, Inc. (United States and Canada). CD-ROM galleries of full-color PCS symbols, DynaSyms, Blissymbols, COMPIC symbols, and Pick 'n Stick symbols are also available from this company. They also carry CD-ROM galleries of *Kids in Action*, symbols that depict boys and girls engaging in everyday activities (400 symbols), and the *Core Picture Vocabulary* symbols of nouns, verbs, and adjectives relevant to young children (300 symbols). All of the symbol galleries are designed for use with Don Johnston, Inc.'s, Ke:nx or other Discover products.

AIDED SYMBOLS: ABSTRACT SYMBOL SYSTEMS

Abstract symbol systems include symbols for which form does not suggest meaning. The most widely known and used abstract symbol set is Yerkish Lexigrams. Blissymbolics is not considered abstract because at least some symbols are pictographic.

Yerkish Lexigrams

The abstract Yerkish Lexigram symbols resulted from a primate research project designed to develop a computer-based system for studying language acquisition in chimpanzees (Rumbaugh, 1977). The lexigrams are composed of nine geometric forms used singly or in combinations of two, three, or four to form symbols. As depicted in Figure 3.6, they may appear as white element combinations on black backgrounds (Romski, Sevcik, & Pate, 1988). They may also be reproduced on one of seven color-coded backgrounds (Silverman, 1995). Generally, the lexigrams are used on an illuminated computer-assisted AAC device (Romski et al., 1988) that produces synthetic speech when the lexigram is touched (Romski & Sevcik, 1988b).

Lexigrams were originally used in studies investigating the symbol-learning abilities of institutionalized adolescents and young adults with mental retardation requiring extensive support (Romski et al., 1988; Romski, White, Millen, & Rumbaugh, 1984). Lexigrams have been used successfully as symbols on voice-output communication devices with children with mental retardation requiring limited and extensive supports (Romski & Sevcik, 1996). Lexigrams probably will not gain widespread popularity as an AAC system because they are so opaque, and they should probably not be used except with AAC systems that translate them into some type of intelligible speech.

AIDED SYMBOLS: ORTHOGRAPHY AND ORTHOGRAPHIC SYMBOLS

Traditional orthography refers to the written characters used to transcribe a particular linguistic system (e.g., English letters, Chinese characters). Orthography has been used in AAC systems in the form of single letters, words, syllables (e.g., prefixes, suffixes),

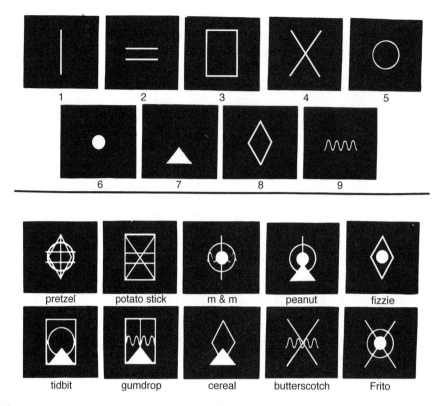

Figure 3.6.   Examples of lexigrams. (From Romski, M.A., Sevcik, R., & Pate, J. (1988). Establishment of symbolic communication in persons with severe retardation. *Journal of Speech and Hearing Disorders, 53,* 98; reprinted by permission.)

sequences of commonly combined letters (e.g., *ty, ck, th*), and phrases or sentences (Beukelman et al., 1985; Goodenough-Trepagnier, Tarry, & Prather, 1982) (see Mussel-white & St. Louis, 1988, for a comprehensive overview of traditional orthography and AAC applications).

The term *orthographic symbol* is used to refer to aided techniques that represent traditional orthography, such as braille and fingerspelling. These are differentiated from *orthographic codes*, which use letters as message abbreviations and are discussed later in this chapter.

Braille

Braille is a tactile symbol system for reading and writing that is used by people with visual or dual sensory impairments. Braille characters are formed by combinations of six embossed dots arranged within a cell of two vertical columns of three dots each (see Figure 3.7). The dots are numbered 1–3 on the left column and 4–6 on the right. The characters represent letters, parts of words, or entire words. Each character is formed according to a standard pattern within the six-dot cell and can be arranged into a total of 63 configurations.

Braille is organized and taught in three levels or grades. Grade 2 is the most widely used form of braille and in 1932 was accepted for standard use in the United States

(Scholl, 1986). It allows certain contractions that enhance reading and writing speed. Grade 1 braille is uncontracted and uses the alphabet symbols to spell out all words. Grade 3 braille is a shorthand form of the symbol set, used mainly for personal note taking. Braille is used internationally, and different countries change the code to suit their language patterns and needs. English Braille, American Edition, 1994, is the official system adopted in the United States and Canada (F. Poon, personal communication, May 2, 1997).

In addition to being the standard literacy code for reading and writing, braille symbols are also used with different meanings for other purposes, including Braille Music Code, the Nemeth Braille Code for Mathematics and Science, and Computer Braille Code. The Braille Music Code assigns braille symbols to standard music notations. The Nemeth Braille Code is used to write arithmetic and mathematical computations, chemical formulas, and scientific notations. In the Nemeth Braille Code, braille dots are positioned one level lower in the individual cells to denote numbers. The Computer Braille Code is part of an effort to standardize all operational commands for different types of computer equipment (Rossi, 1986). In general, although there are hundreds of symbols in the various codes, all codes use the standard six-dot cell design but assign different meanings to the same symbol (Huebner, 1986).

The International Council on English Braille, which has representatives from Australia, Canada, New Zealand, Nigeria, South Africa, the United Kingdom, and the United States, is conducting the Unified Braille Code Research Project. The goal of this project is to develop a single braille code providing notation for mathematics, computer science, and other scientific and engineering disciplines as well as general English literature.

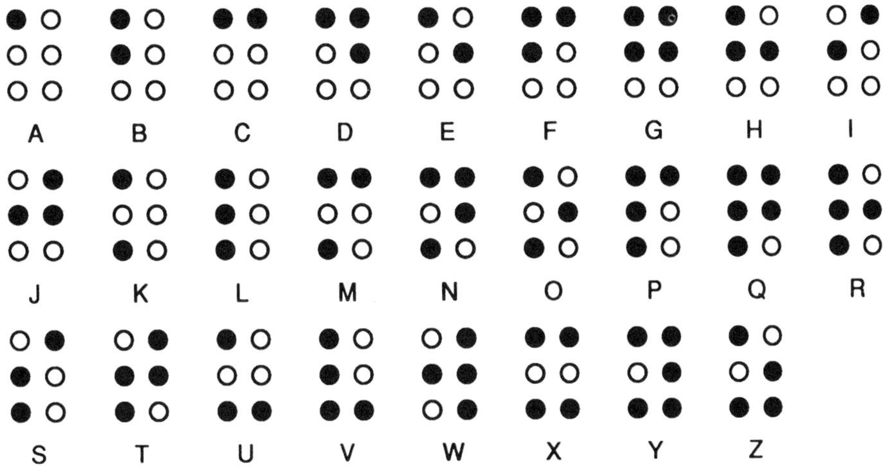

Figure 3.7.   English braille alphabet. Darkened circles represent embossed dots.

Fingerspelling (Visual and Tactual)

Sign language systems such as ASL use fingerspelling to represent single letters of the alphabet that can be combined to spell words for which there are no conventional signs (i.e., proper names). Interest in literacy instruction for AAC users has drawn attention to this feature of sign language because of its potential to assist beginning readers to learn the phonological code needed for reading and writing. Because many fingerspelled letters appear to be visually similar to their graphic counterparts, the learning of letter–sound relationships might be enhanced by pairing the two, at least during initial instruction (Koehler, Lloyd, & Swanson, 1994). There is some evidence of the efficacy of such an instructional strategy with individuals who can speak but have difficulty learning to read (Blackburn, Bonvillian, & Ashby, 1984; Wilson, Teague, & Teague, 1984).

In addition, the tactual reception of fingerspelling is a mode of communication that is commonly used by people with dual sensory impairments who are literate. Information is transmitted in fingerspelling by placing the hand of the information receiver over the hand of the individual formulating the letters (Jensema, 1982; Mathy-Laikko et al., 1987; Musselwhite & St. Louis, 1988). Research has shown that, at communication rates of approximately two syllables per second (roughly half that of typical speaking rate), experienced deaf-blind users can receive key words in conversational sentences at roughly 80% accuracy using tactual reception of fingerspelling (Reed et al., 1990).

COMBINED SYMBOL SYSTEMS (AIDED AND UNAIDED)

Formal symbol systems that incorporate the use of at least manual signs with graphic symbols became popular in North America in the 1980s and have been used with people who do not speak. In general, use of such systems is based on the assumption that if a single augmentative communication technique works, then using more than one technique should work even better. These combined systems differ from individualized communication systems that incorporate multiple modes (e.g., Hooper, Connell, & Flett, 1987) in that symbols are combined in a standard intervention package. Two combined symbol systems that have been used in augmentative communication are Sigsymbols (Cregan & Lloyd, 1990) and the Makaton Vocabulary.

Sigsymbols

Sigsymbols were originally designed in Great Britain for adolescents with severe disabilities who are learning or have learned manual signs. Some of the symbols (called "sigs") are simple black-and-white line drawings (pictographs), some are rule-based abstract symbols (ideographs), and some are drawings of manual signs (sign-linked symbols). Examples of these symbols are shown in Figure 3.8.

Different sets of Sigsymbols are linked to different manual sign systems, including British Sign Language (Cregan, 1989a), Finnish Sign Language (Cregan, 1989b), and Signed English (Cregan & Lloyd, 1990). No information concerning the relative transparency or translucency of the Sigsymbol system is available. There is one published report of the successful use of this system by an adolescent with severe cognitive disabilities (Cregan, 1993).

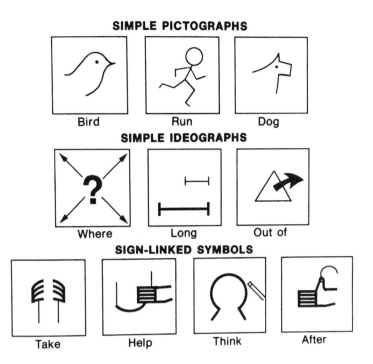

Figure 3.8. Examples of Sigsymbols. (From Musselwhite, C., & St. Louis, K. (1988). *Communication programming for persons with severe handicaps* (2nd ed., p. 215). Austin, TX: PRO-ED; reprinted by permission.)

Sigsymbol information is available in North America from Don Johnston, Inc.

Makaton Vocabulary

The Makaton Vocabulary is "not an [AAC] system itself, but rather an organizational approach to the teaching of language and communication, which can be combined with any modality" (Grove & Walker, 1990, p. 25). The approach combines speech, manual signs, and graphic symbols, and the National Curriculum Council in the United Kingdom has adopted it as the "official" AAC system that is used in schools with students with cognitive disabilities (M. Walker, personal communication, February 26, 1997). The core vocabulary consists of approximately 470 concepts organized in a series of nine stages, plus an additional section, that correspond to the order in which the words are introduced. For example, Stage 1 consists of 39 concepts that meet immediate needs and can establish basic interactions, whereas Stage 5 consists of 38 words that can be used in the general community. In addition, there is a large resource vocabulary of approximately 7,000 concepts, about two thirds of which are illustrated with symbols devised by the Makaton Vocabulary Development Project (MVDP). Makaton symbols are illustrated in Figure 3.9.

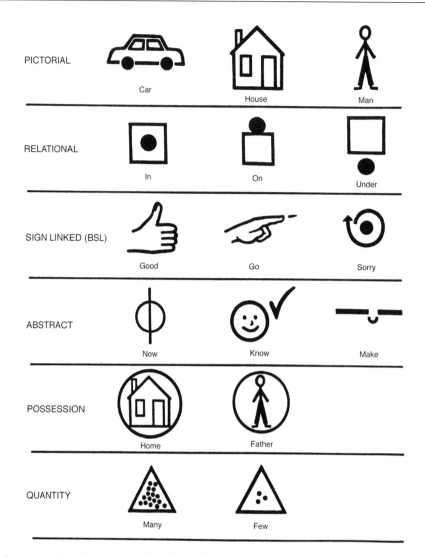

PICTORIAL — Car, House, Man

RELATIONAL — In, On, Under

SIGN LINKED (BSL) — Good, Go, Sorry

ABSTRACT — Now, Know, Make

POSSESSION — Home, Father

QUANTITY — Many, Few

Figure 3.9.   Examples of Makaton symbols. (From Grove, N., & Walker, M. (1990). The Makaton Vocabulary: Using manual signs and graphic symbols to develop interpersonal communication. *Augmentative and Alternative Communication, 6,* 23; reprinted by permission.)

The Makaton Vocabulary program has been adapted for use in more than 40 countries, including Australia, Bahrain, Bangladesh, Canada, China, Egypt, France, Germany, Greece, India, Japan, Kuwait, Malta, Namibia, Nepal, New Zealand, Norway, Pakistan, Portugal, Saudi Arabia, Spain, Sri Lanka, Switzerland, Turkey, Uganda, and the United States.

No invented or modified manual signs are used with the Makaton Vocabulary. The MVDP recommends that users from different countries adopt the sign language used locally by members of the Deaf community or in educational settings with deaf students. Thus, in the United Kingdom, a combination of British Sign Language (BSL) and British Signed English signs are used, whereas in the United States, the signs are largely taken from the SEE-2 lexicon (Gustason et al., 1980). The MVDP has produced a specific collection of Makaton signs and symbols that are related to the main core subject areas of the British National Curriculum, including information on developing literacy skills through Makaton.

With regard to instruction, Makaton can be used and taught either with a *key-word approach*, in which only the main information-carrying words are spoken, signed, and represented graphically, or with a grammatical translation approach, in which the complete word order of the language is used (much like SEE-2 is used with students who are deaf in North America). Makaton is taught through structured behavioral interventions and in natural contexts (Grove & Walker, 1990). The developers of Makaton emphasized that although the program is organized in stages and within a structure, practitioners are free to modify the system to meet individual student needs regarding the symbols used; the vocabulary introduced; and the procedures for assessment, instruction, goal setting, and data collection (Grove & Walker, 1990). The Makaton approach has been used successfully with children and adults with mental retardation, autism, specific language disorders, multiple sensory impairments, and acquired neurological problems affecting communication (Walker, 1987).

The Makaton Vocabulary Development Project distributes a variety of Makaton resource and training materials and organizes training courses in Great Britain and other countries. Their World Wide Web site is at http://www.makaton.mta.ca.

RATE ENHANCEMENT TECHNIQUES

The conversational speaking rates of natural speakers who do not have disabilities vary from 150 words per minute to 250 words per minute (Goldman-Eisler, 1986). These speaking rates allow for efficient communication of extensive messages, which are formulated and spoken virtually simultaneously. One has only to view the interaction patterns among a talkative, animated group of friends to realize the importance of efficiency in communication in order for all speakers to take their conversational turns and communicate their messages before someone else claims the floor.

In addition to communicating efficiently, natural speakers formulate spoken messages to meet the needs of the particular communicative situation. During spoken interaction, much of the meaning of a message can be derived from the context and the timing of the message. For example, we frequently mumble greetings to friends or colleagues as we pass them in the hallway at work. It is only because of the context that such poorly articulated messages can be understood. As we watch sporting events with our friends, someone may exclaim, "What an idiot!"—a message with no referent, which can be understood and appreciated only if it is produced in a timely fashion, not 3 minutes after someone has fumbled the ball.

Unfortunately, communication inefficiencies and message-timing limitations interfere with the communication interactions of many AAC users who use symbols to communicate. For example, the AAC rates of aided symbol users were reported to be usually less than 15 words per minute under most circumstances (Foulds, 1980, 1987). In many cases, the rates are much less—often two to eight words per minute. These rates are only a fraction of those achieved by natural speakers. Clearly, such drastic reductions in communication rate are likely to interfere significantly with communication interactions, especially in communicative situations with natural speakers who are accustomed to exchanging information at a much more rapid pace. Because of this problem, the AAC field has developed a number of strategies to accelerate communication rate and improve the timing of messages that are constructed with aided symbols. These strategies are described in the next section.

Message Encoding

One factor contributing to the slowed communication rates of AAC users is that users must often compose messages by selecting component parts (e.g., pictures, words, symbols, letters of the alphabet) one item at a time. A strategy to increase communication rates for frequently used messages or messages that must be timed precisely is to compose complete sentences or phrases and store them in AAC systems. Rather than communicate these messages word by word, the user is able to convey an entire message by using one appropriate code.

AAC teams have developed and implemented a number of coding and retrieval strategies over the years. The term *encoding* identifies any technique in which the user gives multiple signals that together specify a desired message (Vanderheiden & Lloyd, 1986). This means that the user encodes a message with a sequence of items from the selection set. How codes are represented—that is, the type of symbols used—is an individual decision that should be matched to the AAC user's capabilities. Some strategies for encoding messages include the use of numbers, letters, or icons (see Table 3.2).

Alpha (Letter) Encoding

Letters of the alphabet are used to encode messages in a wide range of AAC systems. Generally, AAC teams select a code for a message through one of the strategies discussed in the following sections.

Salient Letter Encoding

In salient letter encoding, the initial letters of salient content words in the message are used to construct the code. For example, the message *Please open the door for me* might be coded OD, because these are the initial letters of the primary words in the message *open door*. This technique attempts to establish a logical link between the code and how the message is spelled. Although user capability requirements for salient letter encoding have not been studied in detail, it seems that some familiarity with traditional orthography and the ability to spell at least the first letter of a word are necessary. In addition, this technique would probably be most effective for users who are able to recall messages in their correct syntactic forms, as the codes are often determined by the usual word order of the most salient items.

Table 3.2. Sample message encoding strategies

Strategy	Code	Message
Salient letter encoding	HH	*Hello,* how are you?
Letter-category encoding	GH	*(Greeting) Hello,* how are you?
Alpha-numeric encoding	G-1	Hello, how are you? *(Greeting #1)*
Numeric encoding	5-1	Hello, how are you? *(Arbitrary numbers)*
Iconic encoding	Lei you	Hello, how are you? *(LEI icon associated with greeting; YOU icon designates addressee)*

Letter-Category Encoding

When letter-category encoding is used, the initial letter of a code is determined by an organizational scheme that categorizes messages. For example, the messages *Hello, how are you? It's nice to see you, See you later,* and *Good-bye for now* could be grouped in the category of greetings. The first letter of the code for each of these messages would then be the letter *G,* which represents the category. The second letter of the code would be the specifier within the category, which is based on the specific content of the message. Thus, the message *Hello, how are you?* might be coded GH, and the message *It's nice to see you today* might be coded GN (for *nice*).

Abbreviation expansion is a term that has also been applied to alpha encoding techniques. Vanderheiden and Lloyd defined abbreviation expansion as "a technique that can be used in conjunction with all techniques that include an alphabet in their selection vocabulary. . . . Words, phrases, or entire sentences can be coded and recalled by the user using a short abbreviation." (1986, p.135)

Alpha-Numeric Encoding

Alpha-numeric encoding involves the selection of codes that include both letters and numbers. Generally, the alphabetic part of the code refers to the category of messages, such as G for greetings, T for transportation, and F for food. The number is used arbitrarily to specify an individual message within the category. Thus, G1 might refer to *Hello, how are you?* and G2 might refer to *I haven't seen you in a long time!*

Numeric Encoding

Occasionally, numeric codes only are used to represent messages. For example, numeric codes may be used when a communication display must be quite small in order to accommodate the user's limited motor capabilities. In this case, it is to the user's advantage if items in the selection set can be combined in many ways to code messages.

Usually the relationship between the code and its corresponding message is completely arbitrary; thus, 13 might be the code for *Can we leave now?* and 24 might be the code for *I like this a lot.* Most systems that use numeric encoding display the codes and the associated messages on a chart or a menu as part of the selection display so that neither the AAC user nor the communication partner must rely on their memory for recall or translation. Extensive learning and instruction is necessary to memorize the codes if this option is not available.

Morse Code

Morse code is an international system that uses series of dots and dashes to represent letters, punctuation, and numbers (see Figure 3.10). When used in AAC applications, the dots and dashes are transmitted via microswitches through a device called an emulator that translates them into orthographic letters and numbers.

Morse code emulators are available in a number of communication devices and communication software products, including Aurora for DOS and Windows (Aurora Systems, Inc.), CarryCom2 (Great Talking Box Co.), EZ Keys (EZK) (Words+, Inc.), HandiCODE (Microsystems Software, Inc.), Ke:nx (Don Johnston, Inc.), Liberator II (Prentke Romich Co.), Macaw (ZYGO Industries, Inc.), and Scan Com-PS (Med Labs, Inc.).

A	. _	V	... _
B	_ ...	W	. _ _
C	_ . _ .	X	_ .. _
D	_ ..	Y	_ . _ _
E	.	Z	_ _ ..
F	.. _ .	1	. _ _ _ _
G	_ _ .	2	.. _ _ _
H	....	3	... _ _
I	..	4	.... _
J	. _ _ _	5	.....
K	_ . _	6	_ ....
L	. _ ..	7	_ _ ...
M	_ _	8	_ _ _ ..
N	_ .	9	_ _ _ _ .
O	_ _ _	0	_ _ _ _ _
P	. _ _ .	period	. _ . _ . _
Q	_ _ . _	comma	_ _ .. _ _
R	. _ .	?	.. _ _ ..
S	...	error	....
T	_	wait	. _ ...
U	.. _	end	. _ . _ .

Figure 3.10. Morse code.

Studies investigating the learnability of Morse code by AAC users are limited. One exception is a case study of a man with a spinal cord injury who wrote using Morse code at a rate of 25–30 words per minute. He learned to produce basic Morse code using a sip-and-puff switch within 2 weeks and became proficient in use of the system within approximately 2 months (Beukelman, Yorkston, & Dowden, 1985). Marriner, Beukelman, Wilson, and Ross (1989) also described the learning of Morse code by 10 individuals, ranging in age from 8 to 26 years, who activated their communication systems with bilateral head switches. Eight people learned to send Morse code with 95% accuracy within 4 weeks, and two required 5 months to reach this level. Based on these data, the authors suggested that the threshold for learning Morse code is a second- or third-grade reading level. (See McDonald, Schwejda, Marriner, Wilson, & Ross, 1982, for a discussion of some of the advantages of Morse code.)

Many software applications for the iconic encoding technique called semantic compaction are available for users across the age and ability ranges from the Prentke Romich Co. These include the integrated Unity software packages (all ages); Power in Play+ (preschoolers); Interaction, Education, and Play+ (school age); Learning and Living (adolescents); and Words Strategy (WS) (school age to adult). A Blissymbol component application using Minspeak is also available, and versions of WS have been developed in German (Braun & Stuckenschneider-Braun, 1990) and in Swedish (Hunnicutt, Rosengren, & Baker, 1990).

Iconic Encoding

Baker (1982, 1986) proposed an iconic encoding technique referred to as *semantic compaction*, or Minspeak. In this system, sequences of icons (i.e., pictorial symbols) are combined to store word, phrase, or sentence messages in one of the voice-output devices constructed to incorporate this technique. The icons used for this encoding are deliberately selected for their rich semantic associations.

Iconic encoding is available in a number of aided communication products, including the AlphaTalker, DeltaTalker, Liberator II, and Vanguard (Prentke Romich Co.); DigiVox (Sentient Systems Technology, Inc.); Macaw (ZYGO Industries, Inc.); Ke:nx (Don Johnston, Inc.); and Talking Screen (Words+, Inc.).

Using iconic encoding, an apple icon might be associated with *food, fruit, snack, red,* and *round;* a sun icon might be used to refer to concepts such as *weather, yellow, hot, summer,* and *noon;* or a clock icon might represent *time, numbers,* and a *daily schedule.* Some of the codes that an AAC user might construct from these three icons are depicted in Figure 3.11. As illustrated in this figure, the message *Let's have a barbecue* might be encoded with an apple icon (food) and a sun icon (summer). Or, an apple icon might be combined with a clock icon to encode the message *It's time to have a snack.* Or a sun icon might be combined with a clock icon to signify *It's time to catch some rays!* These sequences and their corresponding messages are stored in the electronic voice-output de-

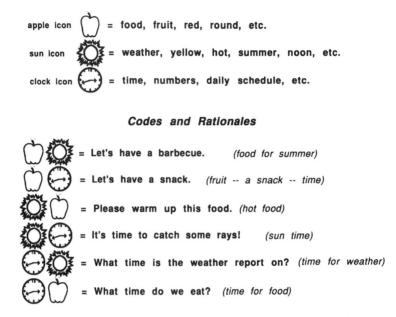

Figure 3.11.   Examples of iconic codes. (Picture Communication Symbols copyright © 1994 by Mayer-Johnson Co.; reprinted by permission. Some symbols have been adapted.)

vice that the user may activate to produce synthetic speech for the message. Using iconic encoding, messages can be semantically organized by activities, topics, locations, or other categories to enhance retrieval.

Color Encoding

Color has also been utilized to encode messages, usually in conjunction with specifiers such as numbers or symbols. In particular, color encoding has been used to formulate messages for eye-pointing communication systems (Goossens' & Crain, 1986a, 1986b, 1987). Imagine an eye-gaze display with colored squares in the eight common locations with letters of the alphabet assigned to each square. Such a display is depicted in Figure 3.12, using the standard ETRAN letter and number arrangement. A user might have a series of colored and alpha codes to represent various messages that are cataloged in a decoding book for partners. For example, the message *Turn on the music* might be symbolized as BLUE M and the message *Can you scratch my foot?* might be PURPLE F. In order to select the first message, the AAC user would first gaze at the blue square on the display and then shift his or her gaze to the letter *M*. The communication partner would then find the message that corresponds with BLUE M in the decoding book and follow with the requested action. Color coding can be used with other types of access techniques, such as low-tech communication books, to help the AAC user to locate a symbol more easily. For example, all of the people symbols might be colored with yellow backgrounds, all of the food symbols colored green, and all of the things-to-do symbols colored blue.

MESSAGE RETRIEVAL AND LEARNABILITY

Encoding strategies refer to the ways in which codes are associated with specific messages. In this section, we outline the strategies used to retrieve the encoded messages.

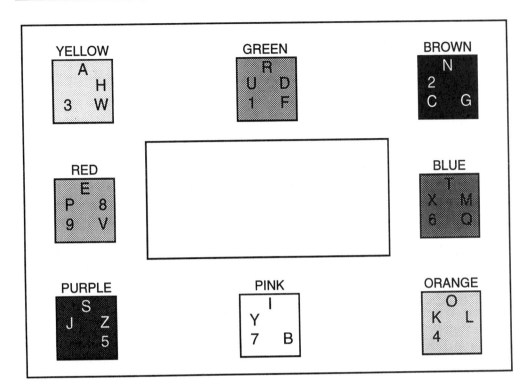

Figure 3.12. Color eye-gaze display.

There are three main retrieval strategies: memory based, chart based, and display (or menu) based (Vanderheiden & Lloyd, 1986).

Memory-Based Retrieval Strategies

Memory-based retrieval strategies require the AAC user to memorize the codes associated with specific messages. This can be accomplished either through rote memorization (e.g., for numeric encoding) or through the use of a mnemonic strategy that assists recall, such as salient letter encoding or letter-category encoding. In iconic encoding strategies, the semantic associations with icons assist with retrieval, as do the icon prediction lights available on some electronic communication systems (e.g., the Liberator II, Prentke Romich Co.).

Memory-based techniques are efficient and relatively easy to implement from a technical perspective. If users are able to retrieve codes from memory, they do not have to consult charts or menus in order to send a message. Users simply activate the appropriate codes in the selection set. Thus, static (unchanging) selection displays can be used instead of dynamic displays.

Word Codes

The learning curves of typical adults for five encoding strategies used to represent single words were investigated (Beukelman & Yorkston, 1984). These five strategies were 1) arbitrary numeric codes, 2) alphabetically organized numeric codes in which consecutive numbers were assigned to words based on their alphabetic order, 3) alpha-numeric codes, 4) letter-category codes, and 5) menu-prompted codes in which words were organized by their initial letters into computer menus and assigned number codes on the menus. Menu-prompted codes require the AAC user to call up a menu by typing the first letter of a target word and then to enter the number of the target word by consulting the menu. Thus, this technique is a combined memory- and display-based encoding strategy, whereas the others are entirely memory based.

Ten literate adults who did not have disabilities served as participants, with two participants serving in each of the five conditions. In each condition, individuals were introduced to 200 codes and the associated words during 10 sessions. Individuals performed most accurately and retrieved the codes most quickly when using encoding approaches that grouped words by meaning—that is, the alpha-numeric, alphabetically organized numeric, letter-category, and menu-prompted codes. The participants were least effective using arbitrary numeric codes. The learning curves for the random numeric codes and the alpha-numeric codes did not show as much improvement over time as did learning curves for the other three encoding strategies.

Three single-word encoding techniques were also investigated (Angelo, 1987), including 1) truncation codes in which the ends of words were eliminated (e.g., HAMB = hamburger), 2) contraction codes in which the most salient letters in words formed codes (e.g., COMUNCTN = communication), and 3) arbitrary letter codes. The 66 individuals without disabilities in this study attempted to learn 20 words during a series of 10 trials. The results indicated that the individuals recalled truncation codes most accurately, followed by contraction and arbitrary letter codes, respectively.

It is clear that some types of memory-based codes are easier to learn than others. Individual assessment is needed in order to identify the type(s) of encoding most appropriate for individual AAC users in terms of their memory, cognitive, and motor capacities.

Message Codes

Three studies have investigated learning and instructional issues associated with message encoding techniques (Egof, 1988; Light & Lindsay, 1992; Light, Lindsay, Siegel, & Parnes, 1990). One study used undergraduate university students as participants (Egof, 1988), whereas the others (Light & Lindsay, 1992; Light et al., 1990) involved individuals with disabilities. In the Light et al. (1990) study, 30 salient letter, 30 letter-category, and 30 iconic codes were taught in three 15-minute sessions. In the Light and Lindsay (1992) study, 80 codes of each type were taught over an extended training period with multiple sessions. Overall, the results of both studies indicated that the letter-based codes were recalled most accurately, whereas the iconic codes were associated with the least accurate performances. The question of whether personalized codes—those selected by the AAC user rather than by a researcher or a clinician—improve performance was also explored in these studies. For AAC system users, Light and Lindsay (1992) did not find an overall differential effect for self-selected codes compared with nonpersonalized codes.

Clearly, the learning issues associated with memory-based encoding techniques are extensive; however, little research has been done in this area. Additional investigation to clarify the relative advantages and disadvantages of various encoding strategies for both literate and nonliterate AAC users is urgently needed.

Chart-Based Retrieval Strategies

Chart-based retrieval strategies may be used in a variety of encoding applications. With this strategy, codes and their corresponding messages are listed on a chart, usually in alphabetic, numeric, or categorical order. The charts are fixed and do not change to accommodate varying communication requirements. For low-tech AAC techniques, such as eye-gaze displays, static charts may be used by both the communication partner and the AAC user. The AAC user indicates a code, and the partner then reads the code and consults the chart to determine the associated message. The encoding chart may be separate from the communication display, or the chart may be located on the display itself.

A chart-based display that might be used for eye pointing is illustrated in Figure 3.13. In this figure, the AAC user looks at the numbers 5 and 2 sequentially. The partner decodes this message, which represents the letter *d*, using her chart. The user might then continue to spell a message or send an alphabetic code by indicating additional letters.

The primary advantage of a chart-based display is that neither the AAC user nor his or her communication partner is required to memorize the codes because both people can use the chart to identify the appropriate codes and to retrieve messages. Obviously, the rate of communication depends on how efficiently the user and the partner can visually locate the desired code or message on the chart.

Message Prediction

In addition to message encoding, message prediction, a dynamic retrieval process in which options offered to the AAC user change based on the portion of the message that

Figure 3.13. Chart-based display used for eye pointing.

has already been formulated, can also be used to enhance communication rates. Message prediction algorithms generally occur at one of three levels: single letter, word, or phrase/sentence.

Single-Letter Prediction

In virtually all languages that can be represented orthographically (i.e., with letter symbols), individual letters of the alphabet do not occur with equal probability. Some letters occur more frequently than others; for example, in English, the letters *e, t, a, o, i, n, s, r,* and *h* occur most frequently, and *z, q, u, x, k,* and *c* occur least frequently (as any frequent watcher of the television show *Wheel of Fortune* is well aware!).

Orthographic languages are also organized so that the probability of the occurrence of a letter in a word is influenced by the previous letter. In English, the most obvious example of this is that the letter *q* is always followed by the letter *u*. Some letter combinations occur with more frequency than others. For example, *ch-, -ed, tr-, str-,* and *-tion* are frequent letter combinations in English, whereas combinations such as *sz, jq,* and *wv* occur rarely if at all.

Electronic AAC letter prediction systems rely on the probability of these letters and letter combination relationships so that when a letter is activated, a menu of the letters that are most likely to follow will be offered on a dynamic display. When this technology was first introduced, often the entire display of a scanning system was electronically reorganized each time a new letter was selected. Users complained, however, that this required extensive scanning to find the letter they wanted to enter. In response to this problem, letter prediction systems were redesigned to keep the overall letter display intact and to include an additional, dynamic line of letter prediction at the top or the bottom of the device.

Word-Level Prediction

There are three basic types of prediction strategies that can occur at the word level: word prediction, word-pattern prediction, and linguistic prediction. These are discussed in the following sections.

Word Prediction

Electronic word prediction, in its simplest form, involves a computer program that provides a set of likely words (e.g., words weighted for frequency of use) in response to a user's keystrokes. As an example, a typical word prediction system with a dynamic menu display is illustrated in Figure 3.14. Words are displayed in a menu or "window" at the upper right of the screen. The letters that the AAC user selects determine the specific words that the computer program presents in the menu. For example, if the user types the letter L, the six most frequently used words that begin with L will appear on the menu. If the word of choice is not included in the listing, then the user types the next letter (e.g., E), and six frequent words that begin with LE will be presented in the menu. This process continues until the desired word is displayed in the menu. Once the AAC user sees the desired word, he or she can simply type its associated number code to insert the word in the text being formulated on the screen. Thus, this form of word prediction can also be thought of as a numeric encoding technique with dynamic displays.

Predictive Adaptive Lexicon (PAL) software, developed at the University of Dundee, Scotland, provides word prediction similar to that displayed in Figure 3.14. The words displayed in the menus are selected by the program algorithm on the basis of frequency of occurrence and recency of use (Swiffin, Arnott, Pickering, & Newell, 1987). Children and adults who experience physical, language, or learning disabilities or mental retardation have used PAL successfully (Beattie, Booth, Newell, & Arnott, 1990; Newell et al., 1992). It is available from Scotlander, Ltd. (Scotland).

The symbols or messages included in word prediction software can be selected in several ways. Some software contains preselected messages determined by the manufacturer. Other products allow users to enter specific words in the menus. Other programs monitor the communication performance of the AAC user and update menu content based on frequency of word use. More than one of these options may be available in the same product.

Word-Pattern Prediction

Some AAC systems predict words based on the patterns of word combinations likely to occur in conversational interactions. For example, the probability is high that an article such as *a, an,* or *the* will follow a preposition in a prepositional phrase (e.g., *on the bed,*

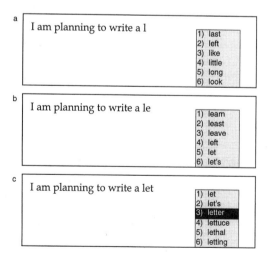

Figure 3.14.   Dynamic menu display with word prediction (selecting the word *letter*). a) Screen displays the six most likely words that begin with *l* when the letter is typed; b) screen changes to the six most likely words that begin with *le* when the letter *e* is added; c) screen changes to six words beginning with *let* when user hits *t*. User can now type 3 to select the word *letter*.

under a *tree*). Designers of AAC systems have translated this word pattern information into prediction algorithms. These systems offer the user a menu of words that are likely to follow each word that the user selects. Thus, the words offered depend not on the letters typed (as with word prediction) but rather on the word *patterns* in the text.

Linguistic Prediction

In an effort to refine prediction strategies, some system designers have included algorithms that contain extensive information about the syntactic organization of the language. The predictions offered to the user in these systems are based on grammatical rules of the language. For example, if an AAC user selects a first-person singular noun as the subject of a sentence (e.g., Chris, mom), only verbs that agree in subject and number will be presented as options (e.g., is, likes, is going). If the user selects an article (e.g., *a, an,* or *the*), the system will predict nouns rather than verbs as the next word because it is unlikely that a verb will follow an article. Obviously, the algorithms that support linguistic-based prediction are complex. This type of message enhancement is becoming increasingly available, however, with decreasing costs of computer processing. Not only does this type of prediction enhance communication rate, but it may also enhance the grammatical performance of some people who have language or learning disabilities.

Phrase/Sentence-Level Prediction

A team of researchers in Scotland has developed several communication computer programs that incorporate sophisticated algorithms for predicting language units longer than single words. For example, Conversation Helped by Automatic Talk (CHAT) stores individualized conversational phrases (i.e., speech acts) that can be retrieved easily and combined (Brophy-Arnott & Campbell-Sutherland, 1992; Newell, 1992). TALK stores utterances of three types: topic content contributions, fillers, and content-sensitive comments (Todman, Elder, & Alm, 1995). Information about these prototype projects, which seek to apply artificial intelligence techniques to communication rate enhancement, is available from the Department of Applied Computing at the University of Dundee, Scotland.

Talk:About is software for Macintosh computers that enables users to converse. It provides the part of conversation that is social, such as greetings, responses, small talk, continuers, wrap-ups, and farewells. Then it allows users to follow through on conversations by telling "stories" that can be related to the subject or the conversation partner. Talk:About is based on the CHAT program developed at the University of Dundee and is available from Don Johnston, Inc. (United States). Talk Boards, a set of social conversation boards for Speaking Dynamically Pro software, are also based on the conversational modeling research based at the University of Dundee. They are available from the Mayer-Johnson Co. (United States).

RATE ENHANCEMENT RESEARCH

Both encoding and message prediction strategies are generally employed for three purposes: to enhance message timing, to assist grammatical formulation of messages, and
to enhance communication rates. A wide variety of encoding and prediction strategies
are continually being developed and implemented for AAC systems. A growing number of researchers are also investigating the efficacy of these approaches from a variety
of perspectives.

The study of rate enhancement in the AAC field can be illustrated by the fable
about the elephant and the four wise men who could not see. The men were
trying to describe an elephant and were forced, by the nature of their shared
impairment, to use their sense of touch to do so. The first man ran his hands up,
down, and around the beast's round, rough leg and declared, "An elephant is
like a tree!" The second man felt the elephant's long, wavy trunk and announced, "No, no, an elephant is like a snake!" The third man laughed at his
friends as he felt the animal's bristly tail and challenged, "You two are both
wrong! An elephant is like a broom!" And the fourth man, feeling the elephant's
high, broad side, exclaimed, "What are you talking about? An elephant is like a
wall." In fact, all four were right—and all four were wrong, for it is only through examination of the interaction among the separate factors that the true picture
can be understood.

Because a number of human factors affect various rate enhancement strategies, the
extent to which these strategies actually enhance communication rates may not be as
great as implied by studies that have examined only one factor. For example, measuring the average number of motor acts—also referred to as keystrokes—avoided
through the use of an encoding technique does not take into account the visual, timing,
linguistic, and cognitive factors that also influence communication rates. The human
factors associated with encoding or predicting also vary depending on the interactions
between visual monitoring and motor control. In acknowledgment of the complexity of
this issue, researchers have proposed several factors that should be considered when
evaluating the efficacy of various rate enhancement strategies:

- Linguistic cost (i.e., the average number of selections needed to communicate a
  word) (Rosen & Goodenough-Trepagnier, 1981)
- Motor act index (i.e., the number of keystrokes necessary to produce a message)
  (Rosen & Goodenough-Trepagnier, 1981; Venkatagiri, 1993)
- Time or duration of message production (i.e., how long it takes to produce a mes-
  sage) (Rosen & Goodenough-Trepagnier, 1981; Venkatagiri, 1993)
- Cognitive processing time needed to decide which selections or acts are necessary
  (Light & Lindsay, 1992)
- Productivity and clarity indices (i.e., measures of *which* meanings may be encoded
  and *how well* they are encoded) (Venkatagiri, 1993)

Several studies, summarized in the sections that follow, have examined the effects of
one or more of these factors on message production.

Theoretical Studies of Rate Enhancement

Theoretical studies of rate enhancement typically have investigated the number of keystrokes required to communicate messages in various encoding strategies. Other human-influenced variables such as motor control, visual scanning, cognitive load, learning, and fatigue are not considered. For example, one study investigated the keystroke savings that might be achieved by retrieving frequently occurring words either through encoding or linguistic prediction strategies (Vanderheiden & Kelso, 1987). The authors reported that a relatively small number of words account for the majority of word usage and suggested that

> Providing quick access to the first 100 words will have a much greater impact on the person's speed of communication than quick access to the next 1,000 words. As a result, most of the acceleration techniques tend to focus on the most-frequently used words to optimize their effectiveness. (p. 197)

Obviously, this approach assumes that there is considerable commonality of word usage across individuals. A summary of research in this area noted that "the most-frequently used words do differ among studies. However, there is a fair degree of commonality, and a set of 50–200 'frequently used words' can be constructed which will apply across most word samples" (Vanderheiden & Kelso, 1987, p. 198).

Vanderheiden and Kelso (1987) also considered word length. Obviously, a longer word requires more letters than a short word. Thus, encoding or prediction strategies applied to longer words will yield greater keystroke savings than those used with shorter words. The authors conducted a theoretical analysis of the percentage of keystrokes that would be saved through the use of various encoding techniques and suggested that, depending on the type of encoding, keystroke savings might range from 20%–50% compared with typing letter by letter. Furthermore, this research suggested that the keystroke savings for message prediction systems would not be likely to exceed those achieved through encoding.

In another study (Higginbotham, 1992), keystroke efficiency was compared for a number of encoding and prediction strategies, including EZK (Words+, Inc.); Words Strategy (WS; Prentke Romich Co.), the Predictive Linguistic Program (PLP, a forerunner of Predict It by Don Johnston, Inc.), Write 100 (W100; Goodenough-Trepagnier et al., 1982), and Generic Encoding Technology software (GET; Vanderheiden, 1988). Experimenters typed twenty 500-word text passages using each of the techniques and analyzed the number of keystrokes in several ways. The results indicated that, when all words in the text were considered, EZK and W100 both reduced the total keystrokes per word by 45%, compared with PLP (41%), WS (36%), and GET (31%). When only the words contained in the lexicons of each system were considered (i.e., when words that had to be spelled letter by letter were removed), however, WS saved 60% of keystrokes, compared with PLP (48%), EZK (46%), and GET (40%). The 24% difference between the two results for WS was due in part to the fact that two additional keystrokes were needed to enter and exit the letter-by-letter spelling mode of this system; this need has been circumvented in subsequent versions of WS software (Higginbotham, 1994). A second report informally evaluated the potential keystroke savings of several additional programs that can be used on MS-DOS computers (Higginbotham, Bak, Drazek, Kelly, & White, 1992). The results indicated that KeyWiz software saved 47% of keystrokes, compared with the PAL software (44%), Access 1-90 (40%), Write-Away (37%), and Handiword (31%). Overall, these studies suggest that, theoretically, keystroke savings of between 35% and 50% are possible with most rate enhancement software available for both MS-DOS and dedicated AAC systems.

> The software for the Liberator II (Prentke Romich Co.) combines both iconic encoding and word prediction, based on the recommendations of Higginbotham (1992, 1994). As of 1998, studies of keystroke savings using this combined approach were still in progress. (D.J. Higginbotham, personal communication, May 7, 1998)

Other theoretical research has attempted to delineate specific system design factors that might influence rate enhancement. For example, Venkatagiri (1994) examined the effect of the size of the menus offered in word prediction programs. He examined menus with 5, 10, and 15 words in a writing task using participants who did not have disabilities and found that message preparation time in the 15-word menu was equal to that in the 5-word menu, although the rate of prediction was highest and the number of keystrokes required was lowest in the 15-word condition. Thus, if fatigue is a problem for a particular AAC user, larger menus have some clear advantages, but if reducing cognitive load is desired, smaller menus might be preferable. Studies such as this one that examine specific human factors and how they interact with various aspects of rate enhancement can provide useful theoretical information for the development and application of these technologies.

Rate Enhancement Studies with AAC Users

Studies of AAC users have generated very little information about the efficacy of various rate enhancement techniques. One exception is the work of Koester and Levine (1996), which compared spelling with a letter-plus-word prediction technique in six men with cervical spinal cord injuries (SCI) and eight men who were able bodied (AB). All of the participants were given comparable sentences to transcribe with a standard keyboard and a mouthstick using either letter-only or letter-plus-word prediction, in which six numerically coded words at a time appeared on the screen based on the letters typed (see Figure 3.14). The authors analyzed the data along several dimensions and found that the benefits of any keystroke savings for the word prediction system were generally offset or even exceeded by the keystroke cost of making each selection. Thus, improvements in text generation rate with the prediction system relative to letters only were "much less than would be expected based on keystroke savings alone" (Koester & Levine, 1996, p. 164). The participants without disabilities selected items between 25% and 40% more slowly with the prediction system than with letters only, and the participants with SCI made selections from 50% to 70% more slowly. Much of the extra time was spent searching the menus; even by the end of the study (i.e., after several sessions of practice), the average search time was 0.47 seconds for the AB participants and almost twice as long for those with SCI. Both groups of participants also rated the letter-plus-word prediction strategy as more difficult to use than the letter-only strategy, implying that the former placed higher cognitive demands on the participants than the latter. Additional studies with actual AAC users are needed to delineate the costs and benefits of various rate enhancement techniques in a variety of contexts.

For example, studies examining the impact of various strategies during conversational exchanges or during independent text-generation (as opposed to transcription) tasks are necessary.

Human and theoretical issues related to AAC rate enhancement are complex and have only begun to receive research attention in the 1990s (e.g., Venkatagiri, 1995). Communication rate and timing gains made possible by encoding and prediction strategies are potentially very important and can result in substantive interaction gains. Nevertheless, each strategy is also associated with human factors that involve learning, memory, cognitive load, and visual scanning. AAC users and their facilitators must weigh the relative benefits and costs of available strategies without much assistance from a research base. Research in message encoding and prediction should continue to clarify the interactions among various human factors, whereas development efforts should focus on innovative strategies that minimize costs to AAC users.

4

Alternative Access

In a junior high school in Edmonds, Washington, I received my first extensive lesson in alternative access. Kris, a junior high student with severe athetoid cerebral palsy, was "talking" with her mother at the end of a school day. As I observed from across the room, they faced each other. Her mother stared intently at Kris's face and talked quietly throughout the interaction. Kris did not speak at all; however, after watching for a while, it was clear to me that she was communicating a great deal. At the time, I was impressed with the magic of the interaction. Her mother was "reading" Kris's face, and they were discussing the schoolwork to be completed at home over the weekend. I was "listening" to a sincere interaction in which both individuals were contributing, adding their opinions, and arguing a bit.

My curiosity led me to move behind Kris's mother, where I observed a series of very rapid eye movements that were somehow being translated into letters, words, and eventually messages. As I came to know Kris and her mother better, they let me know the nature of their code. When Kris directed her eyes at her mother's feet, she was communicating the letter *F.* When she directed her eyes toward her mother's elbow, she signaled an *L.* When she looked at her mother's nose, she signaled the letter *N.* After they explained these codes to me, they seemed rather logical. Then, they told me that when Kris raised her eyes and looked slightly to the left, she was signaling the letter *Y,* referring to the "yellow curtains in the living room," the location where this eye code had been developed!

At one point, I attempted to communicate with Kris using her system and quickly found that, although the system was technically inexpensive, it required extensive learning and ability on the part of a listener. I didn't have the training and practice to be an effective communication partner for Kris, so her mother and her speech-language pathologist patiently interpreted for me. Eventually, Kris developed other forms of alternative access in order to control an electronic communication system, as well as computer equipment, so that she could talk with people like me, complete high school and university, and eventually enroll in a doctoral program. (D. Beukelman, personal communication, February 1991)

Those of us who speak learned our verbal communication skills at an early age. These skills and processes are now so automatic that we have little awareness or understanding of them. Only when we begin to translate our spoken language into written form do we begin to realize that we code messages by combining and recombining a relatively small set of elements. In the English language, those who are literate are able to write nearly anything they wish by combining and recombining a set of 26 letters. The child's task in learning to write is to select the appropriate letters from the set of 26 and to formulate them so that they meet certain standards of accuracy, intelligibility, and aesthetics. Similarly, people who speak are able to say every word in spoken English by combining approximately 45 sounds. Only those who have difficulty learning to speak need to know that words are made up of sounds and that certain sounds require special attention in order to be spoken correctly.

Communication is based on the selection of one or more types of symbols used alone or in combination to express messages. In natural speech, a person produces messages by combining specific sounds. In writing, a person forms orthographic symbols (i.e., letters) and places them in a systematic order. People who are unable to speak or write through traditional means need alternative strategies in order to communicate. The task of learning alternative access methods is easier to understand when the organization of natural language is first considered. For a person with a severe communication disorder, learning alternative access methods involves the selection of messages or codes from a relatively small set of possibilities. The person then uses these elements alone or combines them in ways that allow for the communication of a variety of messages. Obviously, the person must present the message to the listener in a way that the listener can understand.

In the past, many people with disabilities operated standard communication devices such as typewriters by using headsticks and keyguards. If individuals were unable to use these devices, interventionists considered them to be inappropriate candidates for electronic communication options. During the 1970s and 1980s, however, alternative access options for people with severe disabilities expanded dramatically. Since then, dozens of new communication products and devices have entered the commercial market, and older products and devices have been discontinued. In order to adequately cover the influx of new technology without making this book outdated before it went to press, we decided to offer readers only limited examples of communication devices that represent specific access techniques or features. This is in no way meant to imply that the products mentioned in this chapter are the only examples or even the "best" examples of the concepts they illustrate. It was not our intention to attempt to offer a comprehensive overview of the latest technology. The Resource List at the conclusion of this book contains the names and addresses of many of the major communication device manufacturers and distributors (see Appendix). In addition, the Barkley AAC Center's World Wide Web site (http://aac.unl.edu) contains links to most of the manufacturers associated with the augmentative and alternative communication (AAC) field.

The *Trace Resourcebook (1996–1997)* and a CD-ROM called *Co-Net* are available through the Trace Center at the University of Wisconsin–Madison. The book lists more than 1,500 assistive device products and more than 400 manufacturers. The CD-ROM database contains more than 21,000 assistive technology products, from wheelchairs, to devices, to computer keyboards. Pictures are also included for about 650 communication and computer access products. The Trace Center's World Wide Web site is located at http://trace.wisc.edu/.

THE SELECTION SET

Typewriters and computers are perhaps the most familiar AAC communication options used by people who have difficulty writing by hand. A keyboard contains a finite set of symbols, which compose the selection set. These symbols include individual letters of the alphabet; punctuation symbols; numbers; and control commands for the device, such as enter, control, tab, and return. Although not all AAC systems involve computer technology, the example of a computer keyboard is useful because many AAC systems use similar components, even if they are not electronically based.

Many AAC techniques utilize visual displays of items in the selection set. When visual displays are inappropriate because of an individual's visual impairments, however, the selection set may be displayed auditorily or tactually. Auditory displays usually involve presentation of the selection set through spoken words or messages. Tactile displays are composed of tactile representations of items in the selection set using real or partial objects, textures, shapes, or raised dots (e.g., braille).

Components of the Selection Set

The *selection set* of an AAC system includes the visual, auditory, and tactile presentation of all available symbols (Lee & Thomas, 1990). The symbols in a selection set are determined in a number of ways. In the case of standard computers, the manufacturer assigns the symbols (numbers, letters, punctuation symbols, and commands). It is the task of the user to learn what the various symbols mean and how to use them. For individuals who use AAC systems, however, symbols are typically selected on an individual basis so that relevant messages can be represented in a way that the user can understand and use efficiently. The components of the selection set can generally be divided into three groups: messages, symbols and codes, and operational or interactional commands.

Messages

A communication board with a variety of selection items is illustrated in Figure 4.1. An AAC team developed this particular board to facilitate communication for a Chicago Bulls fan as he watched professional basketball with his friends and family. Because this individual reads and spells, the team decided to display items of the selection set orthographically rather than pictorially or in some other way. They included complete messages as well as individual alphabet items for two reasons. First, the individual must communicate some messages immediately if they are to have meaning. For example, the message WHAT A GREAT PLAY! is only meaningful if the individual produces it at exactly the right moment during a fast-moving basketball game. If the individual has to spell the message letter by letter, he or she would not meet this timing requirement, and the message—completed long after the play that elicited the comment—would lose its meaning. Facilitators chose to include other phrases because the AAC user communicates them frequently, and the ability to retrieve them intact saves time and reduces fatigue. HI, HOW ARE YOU? and SEE YOU LATER are examples of such messages. Obviously, choosing messages to be included in a selection set requires cooperative effort by the user and his or her facilitators. The symbolization and coding of the messages depends on the individual's linguistic and learning abilities, as well as on personal preference.

Symbols and Codes

Not all items included in the selection set in Figure 4.1 are complete messages. A number of the items are symbols, including individual letters of the alphabet, numbers, and

	Coaches	**Players**	Points
How are you?	Jackson	Booth	Fouls
See you later.		Brown	Personal
Just a minute.	What a great play!		Technical
Thanks for coming.	Greatest!!	Buechler	Assists
Next time.	Fantastic!	Burrell	Turnovers
This team	Incredible!	Caffey	Free throws
Past teams	Awful!	Calabria	Rebounds
United Center	Idiot!	Gingold	Yes
Draft pick	Never!	Gorenc	No
Championship	What's the score?	Harper	Maybe
Bulls Opponents	Legal	Jordan	I don't know.
Atlanta	Illegal	Kerr	Forget it.
Charlotte	A B C D E F	Kleine	I have something to say.
Miami	G H I J K L	Kornel	
New York	M N O P Q R		This is important!
Orlando	S T U V W X	Kukoc	Start over.
Utah	Y Z 1 2 3 4	Larue	
	5 6 7 8 9 0	Longley	Please repeat each word I say, so I know you understand.
Former Players	I will spell the word.	Pippen	
Armstrong	I will point to the letter as I say the word.	Rodman	
Boozer		Wennington	
Grant			
Paxson	Wait a minute!	Whitfield	You misunderstood!
Thesus			

Figure 4.1.   A communication board designed to facilitate communication for a Chicago Bulls fan.

punctuation marks. The AAC user must combine these symbols in certain ways in order to communicate messages. One way to accomplish this is to combine the symbols, one at a time, to spell out words for a communication partner to read. Alternatively, the individual could form codes with the symbols—in this case, letter or number abbreviations—that represent longer messages. For example, the AAC user might tell someone to LMA, which means *Leave me alone now.* When the individual employs codes, the communication partner must understand the code, or the AAC device must interpret it via an output mechanism (see Chapter 3 for an extensive discussion of the types of codes commonly used in AAC applications).

Operational or Interactional Commands

On many communication displays, a small number of items are assigned as operational or interactional commands. In electronic communication systems, as well as in computers, some of these commands direct the operations of the technical equipment (e.g., enter, backspace, delete, print, speak). In other cases, the AAC user may direct communication partners with commands. In Figure 4.1 several of these interactional commands are included on the communication board, including START OVER, FORGET IT, and WAIT A MINUTE. Some of these commands allow the communication partner to interpret messages formulated by the user, whereas others allow the user to exert some control over turn taking in the conversation.

Physical Characteristics of Selection Set Displays

After the vocabulary items to be included in a selection set have been chosen (see Chapter 2) and the symbolization or encoding strategies for the various items have been identified (see Chapter 3), several physical characteristics of the selection set display must be considered. Intervention decisions should be based on a match among the cognitive, language, sensory, and motor capabilities of the user and the characteristics of the AAC technique.

Number of Items

Whether a display is visually, auditorily, or tactually based, the actual number of items in a selection set is a compromise of many factors. The most important factor is the number of messages, symbols, codes, and commands that are required by the user. When symbols other than those representing letters or codes (e.g., traditional orthography, braille, Morse code) are used exclusively, the size of the selection set increases with the number of messages because there is a one-to-one correspondence between messages and symbols. Thus, 500 symbols are required for 500 messages. When encoding strategies are used, the number of items in the selection set may be greatly reduced, depending on the number of codes used. Thus, if a large number of codes are used, the display may contain fewer items than if a small number of codes are used. This is because each item can be used in multiple ways to make up numerous codes; for example, literally thousands of two-letter codes can be constructed by combining each of the 26 letters in the alphabet with each of the other 25. Once symbol and encoding decisions have been made and the potential items the AAC user needs in the display have been established, the actual number of items on a visual display will be determined by size and spacing considerations.

Size

Intervention teams should consider two issues related to size when making selection set decisions: individual item size and overall display size. For visual displays, the actual size of the symbols or messages on the display is determined by the user's visual capabilities, the motor access technique employed, the type of symbol, and the number of items to be displayed. For many individuals, visual capabilities determine individual item size; this factor is discussed in more detail in Chapter 6. For other AAC users, motor control is the critical variable because items need to be sufficiently large to allow accurate and efficient selection.

The overall size of the visual display also involves compromises among the number of items that must be displayed, the size of individual items, the spacing of items, mounting and portability factors, and the AAC user's physical capabilities. For example, if the system is to be carried around by the AAC user, the shape and weight of the display must be manageable and nonfatiguing, and its exact dimensions will depend on the user's physical capabilities. If the individual uses a wheelchair, the AAC display must not be so large that it obscures vision. If the AAC user selects items using finger pointing or a headstick, the overall size of the display must accommodate the user's range of movement or some items will be inaccessible.

The Portacom is a lightweight, modular symbol display unit designed for ambulatory AAC users. In Figure 4.2a–b, the Portacom base unit is shown in the closed and fully open positions, with a pocket page for carrying extra symbols. Symbols attach to the display with Velcro. The Portacom was designed by the mother of twin girls who use AAC techniques and is available from Made by Mom Creations (Canada).

With auditory displays, the size of the display is determined by the user's memory and ability to retain the organizational scheme of the display. When large auditory displays are employed, users need to remember that a particular item will eventually be displayed (i.e., announced) if they wait long enough. When multilevel displays are available in electronic auditory scanners, the user must be able to remember the categorical scheme used for organization. For example, if messages are organized by main topic (e.g., food, drinks, places, people), the user must remember that COKE is a message under DRINK, whereas SHOPPING MALL is stored under PLACES. If the display contains more than two levels, this categorical scheme becomes even more complex, and COKE might be a message under SODA POP, which is a subcategory of DRINKS.

For tactile displays, the size of the selection set depends on the tactile recognition capabilities of the AAC user. Some users, such as those who use braille, require very little information to recognize options presented tactually, whereas others with less cognitive or tactile ability may require larger tactile symbols or actual objects.

Spacing and Arrangement of Items

Spacing and arrangement of items on a visual or tactile selection display is determined largely by the visual and motor control capabilities of the individual user. For example, some users are more able to discriminate among items on the display if the items are widely separated and surrounded by a large empty area. For others, performance may be improved if the space surrounding the items is colored to contrast with the rest of the communication board. Other AAC users may have field cuts or blind spots that require irregular spacing arrangements to match their visual capabilities. Assessors make determinations such as these on an individual basis (see Chapter 6).

The motor control profile of each user also influences the spacing arrangement. Many people with physical disabilities who use AAC systems have better control of one hand than the other. The items on the display should be positioned accordingly to enhance access. For example, Figure 4.3 illustrates a communication board in which frequently used items are displayed to be most accessible to the user's right hand, which has better motor control. In addition, the size of the items in the area where the user has his or her best motor control (i.e., the right side of the board) is smaller than in areas of reduced motor control (i.e., the left side of the board).

a

b

Figure 4.2.   Portacom base unit in the a) closed and b) fully open positions.

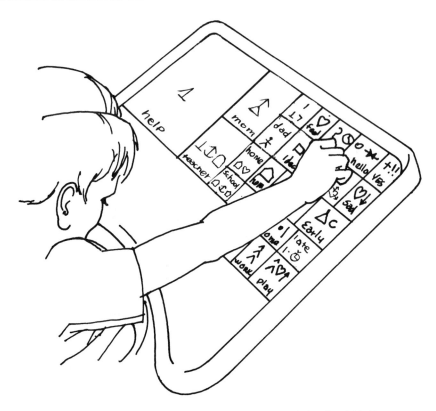

Figure 4.3.   A communication board for an individual with better motor control on the right side.

Another example of a communication board display, a curved array, is provided in Figure 4.4. This arrangement is designed to accommodate the motor control capabilities of a person using a headstick. By positioning the items in an arch, the forward and backward movements of the head and neck are minimized, compared with movements needed to reach items in a square or rectangular display.

Orientation of Display

Orientation refers to the position of the display relative to the floor. The orientation of a visual or tactile display is dependent on the postural, visual, and motor control capabilities of the AAC user. Visual and motor capabilities are the most critical in a direct selection display, where the user points in some way to items on the display. If a scanning approach is used, visual and postural factors will probably determine the orientation decisions because these are critical skills for the switch activation required by this technique. These issues are detailed later in this chapter.

A visual/tactile display mounted on a table or wheelchair tray that is horizontal to the floor provides considerable arm and hand support, as well as stabilization, if weakness, tremor, or extraneous movements are present. This display orientation requires that the user maintain upright posture (either independently or with adaptive equipment) while viewing and using the display. Alternatively, a display positioned at a 30°–45° angle to the floor provides a compromise position for many people with physical disabilities. This orientation allows the user to see the display clearly but avoids the neck flexion required by the horizontal display, while still providing some degree of hand and arm support and stability. Many people with very limited motor control due

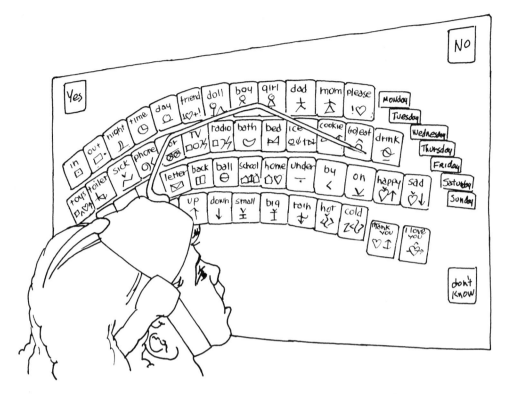

Figure 4.4   A communication board with a curved array for an individual using a headstick.

to weakness or extraneous movements may experience difficulty using a display that is oriented in this way. For these individuals, mobile arm supports may be used to elevate their arms and hands so that they can access a slanted display. Finally, displays that are used in combination with light or optical pointers are usually oriented at a 45°–90° angle to the floor, again depending on the vision, motor control, and posture of the user. When a display is positioned at a 45°–90° angle, care must be taken not to obstruct the user's vision for other activities, especially operating a wheelchair or viewing instructional materials.

Types of Displays

The display of a selection set depends on the technique and device employed in the AAC application. Displays are generally one of two main types: fixed or dynamic.

Fixed Displays

The communication board illustrated in Figure 4.1 is a fixed display because the symbols and items on the board are fixed in a particular location. Most displays used in the AAC field are of this type. The number of symbols that a fixed display can include is limited, depending on the AAC user's visual, tactile, cognitive, and motor capabilities. This means that AAC users typically must use a number of fixed displays in order to accommodate all needed vocabulary items. For example, if the user wishes to change the topic of discussion from professional basketball to plans for an upcoming holiday, he or she might need to change from the display with sports symbols to one with travel and family vocabulary items.

Because of the obvious limitations imposed by the use of multiple fixed displays (e.g., lack of portability, inefficiency), interventionists have made extensive efforts to compensate for the limited symbols that a fixed display can contain. One compensatory technique is to organize a number of displays into levels. For example, a communication book in which symbols are arranged topically on pages is an example of a fixed display with several levels (in this case, each page is a different level). Many electronic communication aids that contain visual or auditory selection sets also incorporate levels in their design and operation. Another compensatory technique involves various encoding strategies by which an individual can construct multiple messages by combining one, two, three, or more items on a fixed display. Obviously, by coding messages this way, the number of messages a person can communicate can exceed the number of items on the display (see Chapter 3).

Dynamic Displays

Two types of dynamic displays are commercially available in the AAC field. The first utilizes a computer screen with electronically produced visual symbols representing messages. Certain areas of the screen, when activated, automatically change the selection set on the screen to a new set of programmed symbols. For example, if the individual using the communication board in Figure 4.1 had access to a dynamic display, he might first see a screen displaying symbols related to a number of different conversational topics, such as professional basketball, plans for the day, personal care, work, or family members. By touching the BASKETBALL symbol, he would activate the screen so that the items contained in Figure 4.1 would be displayed. When the basketball game ends, he could return to the initial screen by touching the appropriate symbol. Then he could select a new topic symbol (e.g., a calendar representing "plans for the day") that would cause the screen to change to a new set of related vocabulary items.

Several commercial AAC products in North America offer this type of dynamic display. Users can access one dynamic display program, Speaking Dynamically for Macintosh computers, via a mouse, trackball, joystick, head pointer, keyboard, touch screen, or switches for scanning (see Figure 4.5). Other options, such as the Talking Screen and Logical Language programs, are designed for IBM-compatible computers, and individuals can access them with either a touch screen or a scanning technique. Finally, DynaVox is a dedicated AAC device with a dynamic screen controlled either through a touch screen or scanning.

The Mayer-Johnson Co. distributes Speaking Dynamically; Words+, Inc., publishes Talking Screen; Innocomp produces Logical Language; and Sentient Systems Technology, Inc., produces DynaVox.

The second type of dynamic display informs the user which items in the selection set are available for activation. In this display, the symbols are static, but the indicator changes with each selection. This technique is used in the Liberator II (Prentke Romich Co.), an AAC device that uses sequences of iconic codes to represent messages (see Chapter 3). When a user activates the first icon in a sequence, indicators on the display screen light up next to each icon that could be chosen next. After the user selects from one of these options, the lights change to indicate the icons that could come next in the sequence. AAC specialists designed this technique as a memory aid, particularly for individuals who use numerous icon sequences to communicate. Because dynamic screen technology is new to the AAC field, practitioners have accumulated little information regarding the user capabilities required for operation.

Product designers included early versions of dynamic displays based on virtual reality strategies in Freestyle (Assistive Technology, Inc., United States) and Scaena (for Dutch, German, and English speakers) (Kompagne VOF, the Netherlands). Typically, messages (or message scripts) are stored as a virtual space. For example, the display might depict an environment, such as a restaurant, with message scripts that might typically be associated with making a reservation, ordering food, and paying the bill stored in the virtual locations associated with these activities.

SELECTION TECHNIQUES

The term *selection technique* refers to the way the user of an AAC system selects or identifies items from the selection set. People who use AAC systems may choose from two principal approaches to item selection: direct selection and scanning.

Direct Selection

The AAC user indicates the desired item directly from the selection set with direct selection techniques. Most of us have experienced several types of direct selection. When typing, we are able to directly choose or activate any item on the typewriter or computer keyboard by depressing a key. Even those of us who are single-finger typists have the option to select any key that we wish. In addition, most of us have used natural speech and gestures, and many have either observed or used manual signing. These modes are direct selection techniques because we can directly select gestures or signs to communicate specific messages from a large set of options.

Direct selection via finger pointing or touching is a common selection method for many AAC system users. Other AAC users employ optical pointers, light pointers, or headsticks to select items or point their gaze in order to indicate choices (see Kris's story at the beginning of this chapter). Options for direct selection are reviewed briefly in the following sections.

Physical Pressure or Depression

Individuals may activate many AAC devices by depressing a key or a touch-sensitive pad. A standard keyboard requires this activation mode, as does the touch pad (i.e., membrane switch) on many microwave ovens and AAC devices. If a device requires pressure for activation, an individual usually generates it with a body part, such as a finger or a toe, or with some device that is attached to the body, such as a headstick or a splint mounted on the hand or arm. The movement of the body part or body-part extension (e.g., a headstick) must be sufficiently controllable so that only a single item is activated with each depression. Facilitators can usually help individuals set pressure-sensitive keys and touch pads to a variety of pressure thresholds that enhance accurate activation.

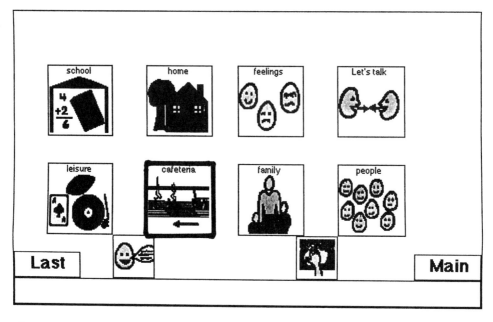

a

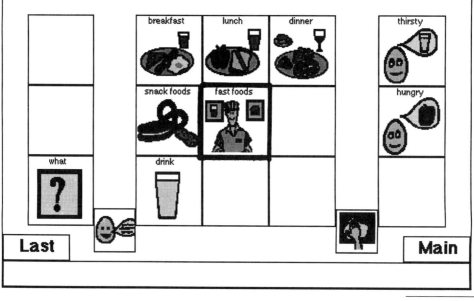

b

(continued)

Figure 4.5.   Example of a series of dynamic display screens using Speaking Dynamically. a) The main screen contains symbols depicting activity options; b) when the CAFETERIA symbol is selected, the screen changes to symbols for various food and drink categories; c) when FAST FOODS is activated, the screen changes to display food and drink items available in that type of environment; d) finally, when HOW MUCH? is activated, the screen changes again to display money, coin, and amount symbols. Note that the user can return to the previous screen at any time by activating LAST and can return to the main screen by selecting MAIN.

Figure 4.5. (*continued*)

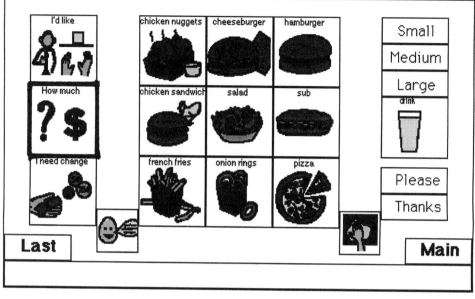

c

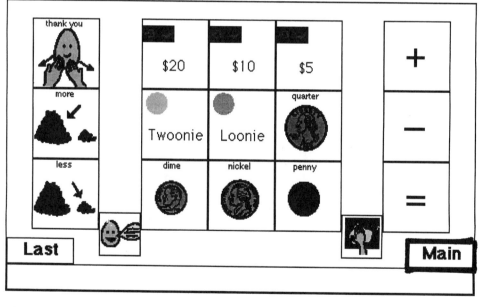

d

Physical Contact

With many nonelectronic AAC options, individuals select items with physical contact rather than pressure or depression. For example, the man who uses the communication board shown in Figure 4.1 identified items from the selection set by touching them with his finger. Because electronic activation was not involved, pressure was not required.

Manual signs and gestures fall into this category because they are formed by hand and body movements rather than by pressure or pointing.

Pointing (No Contact)

The user does not always need to make actual physical contact when selecting an AAC option. For example, in eye pointing (eye gazing), the AAC user looks at an item from the selection set long enough for the communication partner to identify the direction of the gaze and confirm the selected item. Many individuals who are unable to speak as a result of physical impairments employ eye pointing because these people often retain relatively accurate eye movements. In addition, eye pointing is often employed by young AAC users who have not yet learned other communication techniques as well as by those with poor positioning, chronic fatigue, or ongoing medical conditions that prevent them from utilizing more physically demanding options. Some nonelectronic eye-gaze communication techniques are quite advanced and incorporate complex encoding strategies (Goossens' & Crain, 1987). Figures 4.6 and 4.7 illustrate an eye-pointing display and an eye-gaze communication vest, respectively.

AAC users can also use pointing without contact with an optical or light-generating device that is mounted on the head in some way (e.g., on a headband, attached to glasses) (see Figure 4.8) or held in the hand. This technique can be used with both high- and low-tech AAC options. For example, the individual who used the communication board in Figure 4.1 could indicate his choice by directing a light beam toward the desired item. Individuals may also activate electronic AAC systems with optical or light pointing. Systems that incorporate this selection technique electronically monitor the position of the light beam or optical sensor and select an item if the beam or sensor remains in a specific location for a period of time. The two primary motor requirements

Figure 4.6.   Eye pointing display. (From Goossens', C. (1989). Aided communication intervention before assessment: A case study of a child with cerebral palsy. *Augmentative and Alternative Communication, 5,* 20; reprinted by permission.)

Figure 4.7.   An eye-gaze vest. (From Goossens', C., Crain, S., & Elder, P. (1992). *Engineering the preschool environment for interactive, symbolic communication* (p. 68). Birmingham, AL: Southeast Augmentative Communication Conference Publications; reprinted by permission.)

for use of this technique are the ability to direct the light beam to a desired item and the ability to maintain the direction for a prescribed period of time. Because light pointers and optical sensors are usually mounted on the head, individuals must have head control without excessive tremor or extraneous movements for accurate and efficient use of these options.

The AAC user can also make selections with sonar or infrared technology instead of direct physical contact. A receiving unit positioned near a computer screen display generates sound or infrared signals that are imperceptible to human senses. By moving his or her head, the AAC user controls the cursor on the computer screen to indicate items from the selection set. Motor control requirements of sonar or infrared systems are similar to those for light pointing and optical systems.

Voice Recognition

In the past, individuals who could speak but were unable to write or control a computer keyboard opted primarily for voice-recognition strategies. However, in the 1990s, AAC researchers and developers have made considerable progress in the area of voice recognition as an alternative access selection mode for people who can produce consistent speech patterns. Depending on the technology, the facilitator can develop the selection set for voice recognition in a variety of ways. In some cases, the system is trained to recognize certain words, phrases, codes, or commands as well as the voice of a specific individual. Thus, the selection set is limited to those items the system has been trained to recognize; usually these are limited to letters, numbers, and basic computer commands. The newer commercial voice-recognition systems include an extensive vocabulary of frequently occurring words. The user selects these words by speaking the words or by speaking the alphabetic or numeric codes displayed on the screen. This practice increases the rate of message composition considerably. In addition, as the user works

Figure 4.8.   Headlight pointing (yes/no communication). (Reprinted by permission of Singular Publishing Group, Inc. From Glennen, S.L. Augmentative and alternative communication systems. In S.L, Glennen & D. DeCoste (Eds.), *The handbook of augmentative and alternative communication* (p. 61). San Diego: Singular Publishing Group.)

with the system, recognition accuracy improves as the system continuously learns and relearns the user's voice patterns.

Gradually, people with increasingly severe disabilities have opted for speech-recognition systems. Noyes and Frankish (1992) provided an overview of the use of speech recognition technology for communication, environmental control, and medical applications. Ferrier, Shane, Ballard, Carpenter, and Benoit (1995) investigated the DragonDictate speech recognition system as a writing aid for 10 individuals with spastic dysarthria due to cerebral palsy. They reported that most speakers with low intelligibility experienced considerable variation across dictations in their percentage of word recognition, with fatigue apparently an important factor. However, speakers with high intelligibility showed less variability, and their final recognition scores resembled those of speakers without disabilities. Two speakers from the low-intelligibility group also achieved accuracy scores in the typical range.

Activation Strategies

When a user selects an item from an electronic display, he or she must then activate the item so that the AAC system recognizes and translates it into usable output. Because many AAC users have limited motor control capabilities, they must employ alternative activation strategies. For example, some individuals may be unable to isolate a pressure key on a selection display without occasionally dragging their fingers across the display, inadvertently activating other items. Several electronic options can compensate for these difficulties.

Timed Activation

Most electronic AAC devices that allow for direct selection offer the option of timed activation. This strategy requires the AAC user to identify an item on the display in some way (e.g., through physical contact, by shining a light beam) and then sustain the contact for a predetermined period of time in order for the selection to be recognized by the device. Timed activation allows AAC users to move their fingers, headsticks, or light beams across the display surface without activating each item that they encounter. The clear advantage of this strategy is that it reduces both inadvertent activations and the motor control demands placed on the user.

Release Activation

Release activation is another activation strategy available in electronic AAC devices. The individual can use release activation only with displays controlled by direct physical contact, either with a body part or with an extension of some type. The strategy requires the AAC user to contact the display, for example, with a finger and keep contact until the desired item is located. The individual can move his or her finger anywhere on the display without making a selection as long as direct contact is maintained. To select an item, the AAC user releases contact from the display. The advantage of this strategy is that it allows an individual to use the display for stability and that it minimizes errors for users who move too slowly or inefficiently to benefit from timed activation.

Filtered or Averaged Activation

Some AAC users are able to select a general area on the display but have difficulty maintaining adequately steady contact with a specific item for selection. In other words, their selection ability is so limited that it is impossible to set a sufficiently low activation time to accommodate them. Often, there are AAC users who are able to use head-mounted light or optical pointers but who do not have the precise and controlled head movements needed for accurate selection. Devices with filtered or averaged activation "forgive" (i.e., ignore) brief movements away from a specific item and sense the amount of time the pointer spends on each item in the general area. The device averages this accumulated information over a short period of time and activates the item to which the light or optical device was pointed the longest. Facilitators can set the amount of time that elapses prior to activation to personalize the system for an individual.

Scanning

Some individuals who require AAC systems are unable to choose items directly from the selection set. Although a variety of reasons may explain this inability, the most common reason is lack of motor control. In such situations, the items in the selection set are displayed either by a facilitator (i.e., a trained communication partner) or by an electronic device in a predetermined configuration. The AAC user must wait while the facilitator or electronic device scans through undesired items before reaching the item of choice. At this point, the user indicates in some way that the desired item has been presented. This type of item selection is called *scanning*. We discuss various aspects of scanning selection in the following sections.

Scanning Patterns

The configuration in which items in the selection set are presented to the AAC user is one important feature of scanning. It is important that items in the selection set be identified systematically and predictably so that the intention of the AAC user and the actions of the facilitator or device are coordinated. Three primary selection set patterns are circular, linear, and group–item scanning techniques.

Circular Scanning

Circular scanning is the least complicated pattern that electronic devices use to present items in the selection set (see Figure 4.9). The device displays individual items in a circle and scans them electronically, one at a time, until the AAC user stops the scanner and selects an item. The scanner is usually a sweep hand like the big hand on a clock or takes the form of individual lights near each item in the selection set. Although circular scanning is visually demanding, it is relatively easy to master cognitively and for this reason is often introduced first to new AAC users.

Horn and Jones (1996) provided a case report of a 4-year-old child involving circular scanning. They found that scanning was more difficult than direct selection via headlight pointing, even though assessment information suggested that scanning would be the more appropriate option.

Linear Scanning

In visual linear scanning, a cursor light or an arrow moves across each item in the first row, each item in the second row, and each item in the subsequent row, until the AAC user selects an item. Figure 4.10 illustrates a visual display in which items in the selec-

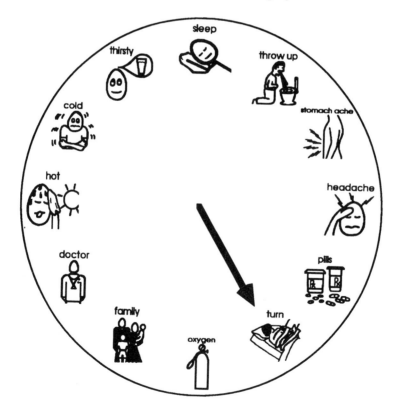

Figure 4.9.   A circular scanning display for an individual in an intensive care unit. (Picture Communication Symbols copyright © 1994 by Mayer-Johnson Co.; reprinted by permission.)

tion set are arranged in three lines or rows. In auditory linear scanning, a synthetic voice or a human facilitator announces items one at a time until the AAC user makes a selection. For example, the facilitator might ask, "Which shirt do you want to wear today? The red one? The blue one? The striped one? The purple and green one?" until the user answers YES. Linear scanning, although more demanding than circular scanning, is straightforward and easy to learn. Nevertheless, because items are presented one at a time in a particular order, it may be inefficient if the selection set contains many items.

Light (1993) reported a case study documenting a developmentally based instructional protocol to teach automatic linear scanning to a 5-year-old child with severe physical and communication disabilities. Previously, the child had failed to learn scanning from instruction focused primarily on the motor control process. Analyses of the performances of successful scanners suggested that the task of automatic linear scanning involves coordination of the relation of the cursor to the target symbol in the array and the relation of the switch to the selection process. Instruction was effective in providing the conceptual bridge that this child required to progress from her partial representation of the task (relation of the switch to the selection process) to the representation that allowed her to scan successfully.

Group–Item Scanning

AAC device developers have come up with group–item scanning approaches in an effort to enhance scanning efficiency. Group–item scanning involves identifying a group of items and then eliminating options gradually until a final selection is made. For example, in auditory group–item scanning, the device or facilitator might ask, "Do you want food items? Drink items? Personal care items?" and continue until the AAC user identifies the group or topic. Then, the device or facilitator recites a predetermined list of options within that group. For example, if the AAC user selects DRINK, the facilitator might question, "Water? Pop? Tea? Beer?" until the user makes a choice. Clearly, this

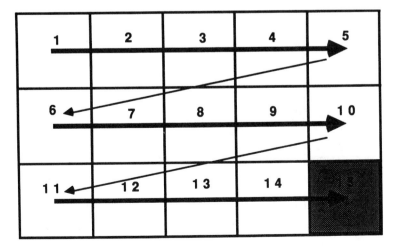

Figure 4.10. A linear scanning display with three rows of symbols.

would be more efficient than if the facilitator first went through a list of food items and then repeated the process for drink items before the user could make a selection.

One of the most common visual group–item strategies is row–column scanning (Figure 4.11). Each row on the visual display is a group. The rows are each electronically highlighted in presentation until the user selects the row containing the target item. Then, individual items in that row are highlighted one at a time until the user stops scanning at the specific item desired.

There are also a number of row–column scanning variations. To increase efficiency, sophisticated AAC systems that contain many items in the selection set often employ group row–column scanning, a common variation of row–column scanning. Group row–column scanning requires the user to make three selections. First, the entire display is highlighted in two or three groups. When the AAC user identifies a group—for example, the group at the top of the screen—each row in that group is scanned. When the user selects a specific row, the scanning pattern changes to highlight each item in that row. Finally, the user identifies the desired item within a row.

Another variation is horizontal group–item scanning. Figure 4.12 illustrates a horizontal group–item scanning array of the type employed in Ke:nx (Don Johnston, Inc.), which allows users to control Macintosh computers through alternative access options. The horizontal display occupies minimal space on the computer screen, thus allowing the AAC user to see nearly all of the application display for word processing, game, or educational programs. Horizontal group–item scanning operates identically to row–column scanning except that the rows are replaced by groups of symbols (in most cases, letters) that are highlighted one at a time before individual within-group items are presented.

Scanning Timing and Speed

In addition to customizing the scanning pattern, the speed and timing of scanning must be personalized according to the AAC user's physical, visual, and cognitive capabilities. When nonelectronic scanning is used, the facilitator can announce the items audibly or on a communication display (e.g., an alphabet or communication board) as quickly or as slowly as the user requires. The facilitator can usually observe the indi-

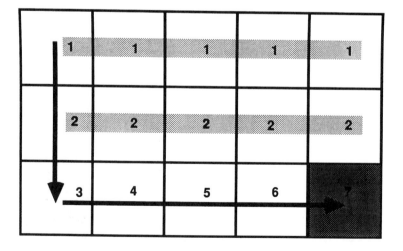

Figure 4.11.   A row–column scanning display.

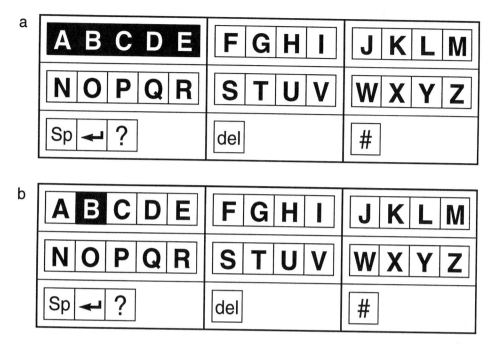

Figure 4.12. A horizontal group–item scanning display at the bottom of a computer screen. a) The user selects a group on the display, b) then selects an item from the selected group.

vidual's response patterns and adjust the speed of scanning accordingly. When electronic equipment is used, however, scanning speed must be individualized for or by the AAC user because a facilitator is not involved in the scanning presentation. Most electronic AAC devices have sufficient scanning speed options to meet the needs of individual users.

Selection Control Techniques

The user must be able to select an item while a facilitator or device systematically scans items in a display. Generally, three selection control techniques are used: directed (inverse), automatic (regular or interrupted), and step scanning.

Directed (Inverse) Scanning

In directed scanning, the indicator or cursor begins to move when the AAC user activates (i.e., holds down) a microswitch of some type. As long as the switch is activated, the indicator moves through the preset scanning pattern (e.g., circular, linear, row–column). The selection is made when the user *releases* the switch. Directed scanning is particularly useful for people who have difficulty activating switches but who can sustain activation once it occurs and can release the switch accurately.

Automatic (Regular or Interrupted) Scanning

The movement of the indicator or cursor in this type of scanning is automatic and continuous according to a preset pattern (e.g., circular, linear, row–column). The user activates the switch to interrupt the indicator at the group or item of choice in order to make a selection. This type of scanning is particularly useful for people who are able to activate a switch accurately but who have difficulty sustaining activation or releasing the switch. This is also the type of scanning that is employed when the display presentation is auditory. The facilitator might recite names of movies, for example, until the AAC user stops (or interrupts) the recitation at the one he or she wishes to see.

Step Scanning

In step scanning, the indicator or cursor moves through a preset selection pattern, one step (i.e., one group or item) at a time for each activation of the switch. In other words, there is a one-to-one correspondence between cursor movement and switch activation. In order to select a specific item, the AAC user simply stops activating the switch for an extended period of time or activates a second switch that indicates selection of the item displayed. Step scanning is often used by individuals who have severe motor control or cognitive restrictions or who are just beginning to learn to operate electronic scanners. Because step scanning requires repeated, frequent switch activations, it is often fatiguing for complex AAC applications.

FEEDBACK

The two primary purposes of feedback from a communication system are 1) to let AAC users know that an item has been selected from the selection display (activation feedback) and 2) to provide AAC users with information about the message they have formulated or selected (message feedback). Some communication systems provide neither type of feedback, some provide one but not the other, and some provide both. Feedback can be visual, auditory, tactile, or proprioceptive.

Activation Feedback

Lee and Thomas defined activation feedback as "the information sent back to the user upon activation of the input device" (1990, p. 255). Activation feedback differs from message feedback in that it informs the user that activation has occurred but does not provide information about which symbol or message has been selected. It differs from output in that it provides information that is useful to the AAC user but not, generally, to the communication partner.

Activation feedback must occur in a sensory modality that is within the user's capabilities. Auditory activation feedback may be a beep, click, or other generic sound produced by an electronic communication device. Nonelectronic displays do not provide auditory activation feedback. Visual activation feedback on an electronic communication device may be provided via a light flash after a switch has been activated or via an area or symbol flash on a backlit display. Visual activation feedback on a nonelectronic display may consist of seeing one's body part contact the device (Lee & Thomas, 1990). Contact with the textured surface of symbols on either electronic or nonelectronic devices provides tactile activation feedback. Finally, proprioceptive activation feedback is obtained when the user applies pressure against a resistant surface (a switch or key) that moves when the pressure threshold is exceeded. AAC users who produce manual signs and gestures also get proprioceptive and kinesthetic feedback from the position and movement of their hands in space.

Message Feedback

Message feedback provides the AAC user with information about the symbol or message itself after it has been formulated. Unlike activation feedback, message feedback may be useful to the communication partner as well, although this is of secondary importance. For example, when an AAC user interacts with a keyboard that echoes each letter as it is typed via synthetic speech, the echo provides the user with message feedback. The echo may also serve as output for the communication partner, if he or she can hear the echo and chooses to listen, but this is not its primary purpose. Similarly, a device may provide the AAC user with message feedback in the form of a screen display of symbols as they are activated in a sequence (e.g., DynaVox).

Message feedback, like activation feedback, is available through auditory, visual, tactile, or proprioceptive modalities. Auditory message feedback may be provided on an electronic device as either a key echo (e.g., a speech synthesizer announces each alphabet letter as it is activated by an AAC user using orthographic symbols) or a word/phrase echo (e.g., a speech synthesizer says individual words or phrases in a message as they are produced). With nonelectronic displays (both aided and unaided), the communication partner often provides auditory message feedback by echoing each letter, word, or phrase as it is produced or selected by the user. Visual message feedback may be provided on electronic devices as computer screen displays of letters, words, or phrases as they are selected. Several communication devices (e.g., DynaVox) and software products (e.g., Writing with Symbols [Don Johnston, Inc.]) are available that provide message feedback in screen displays of symbol sequences as each symbol is selected.

Visual message feedback from aided and unaided nonelectronic devices is generally identical to activation feedback—the AAC user sees the symbol he or she produces. AAC applications do not provide tactile and proprioceptive message feedback, with the exception of writing aids used by people with visual impairments.

RESEARCH ON ALTERNATIVE ACCESS

The usefulness of a variety of alternative access options has been discussed in this chapter and is illustrated more comprehensively in Chapters 10–18. There has been considerable speculation but little systematic research regarding the effectiveness of various alternative access options.

> It has been speculated that scanning is more difficult than direct selection for several reasons. First, scanning is a slower selection technique than direct selection. . . . Using direct selection, the rate of production ranges from 6 to 25 words per minute (Yoder & Kraat, 1983); using scanning, it ranges from 5 to 10 words per minute (Foulds, 1985).The slow rate of scanning may place extra demands on . . . memory and attention. Others have speculated that scanning is cognitively more difficult than direct selection and have hypothesized that different forms of direct selection and scanning vary in their cognitive complexity. . . . However, there is limited empirical evidence to support any of these speculations about the cognitive differences between direct selection and scanning. (Mizuko & Esser, 1991, p. 44)

Research studies have addressed only some of these issues. Ratcliff compared direct selection and row–column scanning performance among typically developing children. The study reported that the children "made significantly more errors, and took longer to respond" (1994, p. xi) using scanning as opposed to direct selection. Ratcliff suggested that scanning requires more user attention and short-term memory than direct selection. Nevertheless, the results of another study regarding the cognitive demands of direct selection and row–column scanning techniques appear to contradict those of Ratcliff. Mizuko and Esser (1991) found no significant differences among typically developing 4-year-old children on a visual sequential recall task performed with direct selection and circular scanning. The task in this study, however, was considerably less demanding than that used in the Ratcliff study. In a related report, Fried-Oken (1989) presented evidence suggesting that electronic auditory scanning places higher information-processing demands on adults without disabilities than does electronic visual scanning. Researchers have not confirmed these results either with children or adults who have disabilities. As is apparent from this brief discussion, research examining the requirements (sensory, motor, cognitive, and language) and the effects (rate, accuracy, and fatigue) of various access options is still limited.

Despite extensive research, AAC users of all ages and abilities have used and are using alternative access successfully because AAC teams can match the abilities and needs of individuals with the characteristics and capabilities of techniques. Although one might think that there is a "best" or "ideal" alternative access method for each user, in reality most individuals utilize several different access options depending on the communication task, the time of day, and their fatigue level. The story of Kris, presented at the beginning of this chapter, illustrates this. Although Kris initially communicated using eye pointing, she eventually learned to control a Morse code–based AAC device with bilateral head switches in order to participate in school classes. Ten years later, she was communicating with eye pointing as well as with her Morse code device, depending on the situation. She uses eye pointing when she "talks" with her family, when she is tired or ill, and when she is not in her wheelchair. She sends Morse code when she is at the university to operate her computer, write papers, and talk with people who cannot comprehend her eye-pointing system. In addition to her electronic communication device, Kris controls other assistive devices such as a powered wheelchair and a page turner.

MESSAGE OUTPUT AND INPUT

The auditorium was nearly full as Michael Williams lectured, from his own experience, about AAC use in society. He illustrated his comments about how AAC users interact with the public by recounting his most recent shopping trip to purchase a new suit. The story was funny and poignant. Looking around the room at the audience who were laughing, many with tears in their eyes, I realized how effectively Michael was communicating with more than 500 people. His message was not interpreted by a natural speaker or illustrated by text projection. He spoke independently using a Liberator AAC device with DECtalk (Perfect Paul) voice. When the "suit story" was finished, I imagined how completely proud Dennis Klatt would have been that day. Dennis was a noted speech acoustics researcher who had developed the DECtalk algorithms to simulate his own voice. That is, the voice that he had before the onset of throat cancer. Dennis died in 1987, so he had little opportunity to realize his impact on the AAC field; however, I suspect that he probably foresaw it. I also reflected on the fact that, while Michael Williams spoke that day in North America, AAC users in many countries were speaking with synthetic voices (American English, British English, French, German, Italian, Norwegian, Spanish, and Swedish) that had been developed by Karoly Galyas and his colleagues at the Royal Institute of Technology in Stockholm, Sweden. Although Karoly also died of cancer, he had the opportunity to observe the impact of these voices on AAC users before he died. (D. Beukelman, personal communication, August 1997)

AAC users, like all of us, are both the senders and the receivers of messages during communicative interactions. In this section, the term *message output* refers to the information that AAC users send to their communication partners. Examples of message output modes include synthetic speech, print, gestures, manual signs, and nonelectronic aided symbols. Conversely, the term *message input* refers to the information that AAC users receive from others. Message input usually takes the form of natural speech, gestures, and vocalizations (assuming that most partners do not have disabilities), although input may also take the form of written or printed materials (e.g., letters, notes) or manual signs.

It is important to distinguish message input and output from *feedback,* which is primarily provided during rather than at the end of message construction. Feedback lets the AAC user know that an item has been selected and, in some cases, also provides the user with information about the selected item.

For some AAC users, the input mode through which they receive messages may be as much of an intervention concern as the output mode by which they send messages. For example, Beukelman and Garrett noted that "the incidence of auditory reception problems among the adult population with aphasia is large" (1988, p. 119), and these individuals may need augmented input in the form of gestures, pictures, or writing in addition to natural speech. People with impairments that affect cognitive, sensory, and linguistic processing (e.g., mental retardation, traumatic brain injury [TBI]) may also require and benefit from augmented input techniques. The following sections review the major types of message output and input used in AAC applications in terms of general characteristics and the learning and performance abilities that they require of AAC users and their communication partners.

Synthesized Speech

The advances in synthetic speech technology in the AAC field since the mid-1980s have been nothing short of remarkable! AAC users who once had no choice but to use devices that produced robotic, barely intelligible English are now able to choose from an array of natural-sounding male, female, and childlike voices in dozens of languages! The main types of synthesized speech are described in the following sections.

Types of Synthesized Speech

Synthesized speech is produced from stored digital data. Discussions of the methods used to develop the digital data stores and to retrieve these data to produce synthesized speech follow.

Text-to-Speech

A common method employed to generate synthetic speech in AAC devices is text-to-speech synthesis. According to Venkatagiri and Ramabadran (1995), this is a three-step process. First, text (words or sentences) that a user has typed into an AAC device or retrieved from its memory as codes are transformed into phonemes and allophones. Second, the device uses the stored speech data to generate digital speech signals that correspond to phonetic representations of the text. Finally, the device converts the digital signals to analog speech waveforms that listeners can interpret and understand.

Rule-generated speech involves a flexible mathematical algorithm representing the rules for pronunciation, pronunciation exceptions, voice inflections, and accents. In standard text-to-speech synthesis applications, the algorithms generate speech sounds that reflect the phonetic representation of the text. The device does not store speech itself in digitized form; rather, the device generates speech for each utterance by the rule-based algorithm. A complete discussion of the algorithms used for these applications is beyond the scope of this text (see Venkatagiri and Ramabadran, 1995, for additional information).

A second type of text-to-speech synthesis uses concatenated diphones to produce speech. This method employs approximately 1,300 diphones, which are sound units that begin at the steady-state frequency midpoint of one phoneme, include the natural transition to the next phoneme, and end at the steady-state midpoint of the succeeding phoneme (Boubekker, Foulds, & Norman, 1986). Because the diphones are extracted from carrier words recorded by natural speakers, the resulting speech is intended to be more natural sounding than conventional text-to-speech synthesis. Diphone-based synthesizers, however, require considerably more memory and faster microprocessing speeds for operation than do text-to-speech synthesizers.

A third type of text-to-speech synthesis employs a phoneme-to-speech method, in which the device produces synthetic speech output from words entered into the algorithm on a phoneme-by-phoneme basis. The resulting speech of any of the three text-to-speech methods sounds less natural than that produced by other methods of speech synthesis (e.g., digitization), but the text-to-speech method is flexible and requires relatively little computer memory.

Digitized Speech

Digitized speech, also called waveform coding, is another type of electronic speech used in AAC systems. This method consists primarily of natural speech that has been recorded, stored, and reproduced. In digitized speech, natural speech is recorded with a microphone and passed through a series of filters and a digital-to-analog converter (Cohen & Palin, 1986). When reproduced, the speech is a close replica of the original speech entry. The primary disadvantage of this process is that it requires considerable computer memory. In addition, because messages can be entered only through a microphone and cannot be typed as in text-to-speech methods, it can be inconvenient to enter messages. Despite these drawbacks, a number of AAC devices with digitized speech are available in response to consumer demand for high-quality speech output.

Some AAC devices that use digitized speech include MessageMate (Words+, Inc.), AlphaTalker (Prentke Romich Co.), and Macaw and Parrot devices (ZYGO Industries, Inc.).

Combination

Some individuals use a combination of text-to-speech and digitized speech techniques. The AAC device converts text entered via a keyboard to a pronunciation code using a dictionary and a set of rules in an algorithm. The device converts this code again to produce intonation, duration, and proper stress. Finally, the device creates speech from the code with a digital-to-analog converter (Cohen & Palin, 1986). The process requires a moderate amount of computer memory, involves no more time for the user than the standard text-to-speech method requires, and results in very natural-sounding speech.

Digital Equipment Corporation's DECtalk system combines text-to-speech and digitization to produce a variety of voices, including Huge Harry, Perfect Paul, Doctor Dennis, and Frail Frank (male); Beautiful Betty, Rough Rita, Uppity Ursula, and Variable Val (female); and Whispering Wendy and Kit the Kid (child). The DECtalk is also available in a portable, battery-operated unit, the MultiVoice, that weighs 3 pounds and can produce 2–3 hours of continuous speech following an overnight battery charge. It is available through Assistive Technology, Inc., and its distributors.

Intelligibility and Comprehensibility of Synthesized Speech

Beukelman and Yorkston (1979) found that the ability of unfamiliar listeners to comprehend messages read by dysarthric speakers deteriorated markedly once the speakers' sentence intelligibility fell below 81%. If this figure is used as the benchmark or cutoff point for acceptable intelligibility, very few speech synthesizers in early generations of AAC devices produced output that was adequately intelligible to children or adults without disabilities. However, several of the voices used in modern AAC devices achieve relatively high sentence intelligibility scores. Mirenda and Beukelman (1987) found three DECtalk voices (Perfect Paul, Beautiful Betty, and Kit the Kid) to be 81%–97% intelligible. Rupprecht, Beukelman, and Vrtiska (1995) reported that the male and female MacinTalk Pro voices were similar in sentence intelligibility to the DECtalk voices.

A variety of factors other than the quality of the synthetic voice itself have been reported to affect speech intelligibility:

- **Rate of speech:** One study provided evidence that listeners summarized complex passages more accurately when produced by DECtalk at slow rates (approximately 5.5 words per minute) instead of normal rates (approximately 140 words per minute). Less complex passages were summarized with similar accuracy at either slow or normal rates (Higginbotham, Drazek, Kowarsky, Scally, & Segal, 1994). In a related study, both younger and older adults indicated that the most comfortable listening rate for the DECtalk voice was 150–200 words per minute (Sutton, King, Hux, & Beukelman, 1995).
- **Output methods:** Higginbotham and his colleagues studied the relative effects of three different synthetic speech message output methods (Higginbotham, Scally, Lundy, & Kowarsky, 1995). In the *word method*, the words in a sentence were interspersed with periods of silence (e.g., The++ dog++ is++ ferocious). In the *sentence method*, consecutive sentences were interspersed with periods of silence (e.g., ++ The dog is ferocious.++ The cat is cute). Finally, in the *mixed method*, both intra- and inter-word pauses were utilized (e.g., The++ dog++ is++ f+e+r+o+c+i+o+u+s). Word-method listeners produced more accurate summarizations of the text spoken

with DECtalk than sentence-method listeners, who, in turn, did better than the mixed-method listeners.

- **Noise:** DECtalk voices Perfect Paul and Beautiful Betty were found to be significantly less intelligible in noisy conditions (signal-to-noise ratio of 10+ decibels) than in ideal listening conditions (Fucci, Reynolds, Bettagere, & Gonzales, 1995; Reynolds, Bond, & Fucci, 1996). Similarly, noise was found to have more deleterious effects on the intelligibility of DECtalk than on that of natural speech (Koul & Allen, 1993).
- **Nonnative speakers of English:** In noisy conditions, nonnative speakers of English were found to make significantly more errors transcribing sentences produced with DECtalk than native speakers (Reynolds et al., 1996).
- **Older adults with hearing loss:** For older adults, speech-recognition performance has been correlated negatively with hearing sensitivity. In one study, listeners with the greatest hearing loss had the most difficulty understanding both natural and synthetic speech (DECtalk) (Humes, Nelson, & Pisoni, 1991).
- **Practice:** Repeated listening opportunities clearly improve listeners' ability to understand synthetic speech. For example, McNaughton, Fallon, Tod, Weiner, and Neisworth (1994) demonstrated significant improvement between the first and the last of five listening sessions with the DECtalk Kit the Kid voice. Similarly, a group of listeners exposed to synthetic speech at least 1 hour per working day for at least 6 months achieved higher intelligibility scores for DECtalk and MacinTalk Pro voices than did inexperienced listeners or speech-language pathologists (Hustad, Kent, & Beukelman, in press). The positive effects of practice have also been demonstrated in nonlaboratory settings, such as secondary school classrooms (Rounsefell, Zucker, & Roberts, 1993).
- **Synthetic speech via telephone:** Japanese female listeners had more positive impressions than did male listeners to telephone calls made via synthetic speech (with the Fujitsu voice synthesis unit) (Nakamura, Arima, Sakamoto, & Toyota, 1993).

Most studies that have examined the intelligibility of synthetic speech have been conducted with individuals who do not have disabilities serving as listeners. In order to assess whether the results of these studies are generalizable, however, it is important to know whether people with disabilities (especially potential users of AAC systems) experience synthetic speech in the same way as their peers without disabilities. One study attempted to provide this information as it relates to people with aphasia and found that high-quality synthetic speech combined with sufficient exposure and practice appear to positively affect intelligibility for adults with aphasia. These individuals often rejected low-quality synthetic voices (Carlson, Hux, & Beukelman, 1994).

One of the few studies (Massey, 1988) in which children with disabilities served as listeners investigated comprehension of the DECtalk Perfect Paul voice by elementary school–age students. The results after a single experimental session indicated that not only did children with language impairments have significantly more difficulty understanding synthetic speech than did children without disabilities, but they also scored significantly lower on a test presented by synthetic speech than on the same test presented by natural speech. Another intelligibility study compared DECtalk and Votrax synthesizers with natural speech, using elementary school–age children who did not have disabilities and those who had learning disabilities or mental retardation requiring intermittent supports (Dahle & Goldman, 1990). The results indicated that 1) for all three listener groups, significant differences existed across intelligibility scores for the three voices, with natural speech better than DECtalk, which was better than the Votrax voice; 2) the response times of all children were faster for natural speech than DECtalk; and 3) listeners with mental retardation exhibited significantly slower response times for synthetic speech than did children with learning or other disabilities. Koul and Hanners (1997) compared the performance of a group of individuals who had mental retardation with a control group on word-recognition and sentence-verification tasks using the DECtalk Perfect Paul and Beautiful Betty voices and Realvoice synthesized voices. The DECtalk voices were superior to Realvoice for both groups. No significant differences in word identification and response latencies were observed between the two groups. However, the listeners with mental retardation performed more poorly than the listeners without disabilities on the sentence verification task.

No studies have been conducted regarding the intelligibility of digitized speech, probably because researchers presume it to be close to or identical to that of natural speech. There may be differences, however, in the quality of the digital-to-analog converters, playback mechanisms, or other components that produce better speech in some systems than in others. This evaluation awaits future comparative research.

Acceptability of Synthesized Speech

If the intelligibility of synthesized speech is poor, listeners are likely to rate it poorly along other dimensions as well, such as gender and age appropriateness and overall social acceptability. Indeed, two studies that examined this issue found that for hypothetical contexts involving people, low-intelligibility voices that are no longer in common use in the AAC field were consistently rated no higher than 2 on a 5-point scale on which 1 signifies "I wouldn't like the voice at all" and 5 signifies "I would like the voice a lot" (Crabtree, Mirenda, & Beukelman, 1990; Mirenda, Eicher, & Beukelman, 1989).

But what of synthesizers whose intelligibility seems reasonably good? How do communication partners rate these voices for overall acceptability? No research data are available in this area for digitized speech, although, presumably it would be highly rated because it is essentially natural speech that has been stored and played back. Crabtree et al. (1990) and Mirenda et al. (1989) found that listener attitudes varied considerably depending on the age and gender of the potential user, even for voices such as DECtalk that are rated relatively high in intelligibility. For example, of the three DECtalk voices included in the study (Perfect Paul, Beautiful Betty, and Kit the Kid), none were considered comparable in acceptability to age- and gender-appropriate natural speech. In a related study, 9-year-old children without disabilities also rated a natural female child's voice as preferable to three synthetic alternatives (Bridges Freeman, 1990). When asked about their attitudes toward the hypothetical children's voices using the four options, the children in this study rated no significant differences across the voices on a standard attitude scale. Thus, although they appeared to prefer the natural voice, this preference did not seem to affect the children's attitudes toward potential synthetic speech users. Gorenflo, Gorenflo, and Santer (1994) reported similar attitudes and found that the easy-to-listen-to synthetic voices positively influenced the attitudes of listeners without disabilities, but their gender appropriateness did not. In the end, it appears that high-quality speech is more important than gender- or age-appropriate speech, although these factors appear to be desirable "add-ons" to sufficient intelligibility.

Advantages and Disadvantages of Synthesized Speech

From the perspective of a communication partner, the major advantages of reasonably intelligible synthesized speech are that it 1) may significantly reduce the partner's burden in the interaction because interpretation of the output requires only the ability to understand spoken language, 2) provides information in a mode that is relatively familiar and nonthreatening, 3) allows communication if an individual is nonliterate but understands spoken language or if an individual has visual impairments, 4) allows the AAC user to send messages without first obtaining the partner's attention through some other mode, and 5) allows communication to occur at a distance.

Consider a boy with severe disabilities who is included in a general kindergarten classroom of 25 children, has limited receptive language skills, and does not speak. If he uses an unaided AAC technique such as manual signing or a low-tech aided system such as a communication board, his teacher and classmates must also learn to use and understand the symbols in that system. In fact, if the boy uses a communication board, they must be near him when he communicates so that they can see the symbols on the display. Now, imagine that same child using an AAC device that produces high-quality synthetic speech output when a symbol is touched on the display. The teacher and the other students now face fewer learning demands regarding reception and comprehension of the output, and the child can communicate from anywhere in the classroom assuming that he can adjust the volume on the device sufficiently. Older people who want to communicate with their young, nonliterate grandchildren; adults who work in vocational environments who need to communicate with co-workers at a distance; and any other potential AAC users may also find substantive advantages in the use of speech output.

Researchers at the Artificial Language Laboratory (ALL) at Michigan State University developed a Hebrew-speaking voice-output device that is used primarily in Israel (Eulenberg, 1987). The ALL is also involved in the India Voice Project, which seeks to develop a synthesizer that can speak many of the languages in India, such as Bengali and Hindi (Kaul, 1990).

Speech output has disadvantages for communication partners as well. Even when synthetic or digitized speech is fairly intelligible, it may be difficult to hear and understand in noisy environments by people with hearing impairments, nonnative language speakers, or those with reduced receptive language ability (e.g., aphasia, congenital learning disabilities, cognitive disabilities). AAC teams must consider such limitations individually before deciding whether speech output is appropriate for a particular user.

Visual Output

As the quality of synthetic speech has improved through the years, visual output has changed from being a primary output method in AAC to being a supportive one. Generally speaking, visual output serves to clarify messages when the listener does not understand synthetic or natural speech. When an AAC device has a computer output screen, the listener may request clarification or message reformulation less frequently

(Higginbotham, 1989). Visual output is particularly important for communication partners who have hearing impairments, who are unfamiliar with the AAC user and his or
her system, or who communicate in noisy environments where synthetic speech may
not be intelligible. In addition to employing visual output to supplement synthetic
speech output, many AAC users utilize printed output in many of the same ways as do
the rest of us—to write letters, complete assignments, leave notes, make lists, and keep
personal journals.

AAC teams have often considered the type of visual display that electronic devices
provide to be secondary to selection of the symbol set, access mode, and encoding technique. Nevertheless, as an increasing number of options have become available and as
stationary AAC computer displays have become increasingly common in schools and
vocational settings, information concerning visual display options has become more
relevant to device selection. A detailed discussion of the visual technology used in AAC
devices, however, is well beyond the scope of this book (see Cook & Hussey, 1995, for a
discussion of visual screens).

Hard Copy Print

A printer that may be part of the communication device or an adjunct to it produces
permanent, "hard copy" output on paper. Many communication devices can be connected to standard peripheral printers or interfaced with small, portable printers. The
printer may produce full-page, wide-column, or strip output in many paper and font
sizes. With some software/hardware combinations, the user may also print messages with
nonorthographic symbols. For example, Macintosh computers can display and print
PCS symbols using software programs such as Boardmaker (Mayer-Johnson Co., 1995)
and Speaking Dynamically (Mayer-Johnson Co., 1990), and Blissymbols can be printed
using programs such as StoryBliss and AccessBliss (McNaughton, 1990a, 1990b).

Computer Screen Messages

Computer-generated messages are widely used in AAC devices as feedback and output. This technology can manage both orthographic and specialized symbols. A variety
of technologies help display computer generated symbols on screens (see Cook &
Hussey, 1995, for detailed information).

Unaided Symbols

Nonelectronic forms of output such as gestures or manual signs impose memory requirements on both of the participants in the communicative exchange. Because no permanent display is available, all of the gestures or manual signs must be produced from
memory by the sender and processed in memory by the receiver. These may be very
difficult tasks for people who have memory impairments (e.g., people with TBI) or who
have difficulty processing transitory information (e.g., people with autism). Mirenda
and Schuler (1989) and Reichle and Karlan (1985) have encouraged the use of aided
systems with permanent displays as a solution for people with memory impairments.

Another major concern regarding unaided symbol output is that relatively few
people without disabilities are likely to understand it. For instance, in Chapter 3 we
mentioned that researchers found that only 10%–30% of American Sign Language
(ASL) signs and 50%–60% of Amer-Ind gestures were guessable by typical adults

(Daniloff et al., 1983; Doherty et al., 1985). Thus, when the user produces unaided symbols as the sole output to unfamiliar partners, he or she will almost always require a translator. Again, multimodal systems that incorporate both aided and unaided symbols often serve to resolve this dilemma.

Aided Symbol Displays

In nonelectronic applications that use aided symbols, communication partners interact directly with the symbol set itself. As the user identifies the symbols of choice, the partner formulates the message, often speaking it aloud as feedback to the user. Whenever unfamiliar (i.e., translucent or opaque) symbols are used to form messages in communication systems, constraints may be placed on the range of communication partners who will comprehend the message. Potentially problematic aided symbols include textured symbols with arbitrarily assigned meanings, selected symbols from all the pictorial line-drawing sets discussed in Chapter 2, many Sigsymbols and Blissymbols, orthographic symbols, lexigrams, and other symbols such as braille and Morse code. To maximize aided output intelligibility in such situations, AAC teams often choose systems that provide simultaneous written translations of aided messages for literate communication partners. To facilitate interactions with nonliterate partners, AAC teams may opt for a multimodal AAC system with at least one component that provides synthetic speech output for the communication partner(s).

Another difficulty with the output provided by nonelectronic AAC options has to do with partner attention to the display. When AAC users communicate with books, boards, or other low-tech displays, these individuals must first get their partners' attention. Then, the partners must be able to turn or move toward the AAC users in order to see the boards, books, or devices that display their message symbols. Finally, communication partners must possess sufficient sensory acuity to see the output. There are many situations in which one or more of these requirements is difficult or impossible to fulfill. Such situations include communicative interactions in which a partner has a visual impairment and interactions in busy, crowded, or dimly lit environments, or places that allow limited mobility (e.g., classrooms, factories, movie theaters, football games). The best solution in these situations may be for AAC teams to introduce one or more forms of speech or print output as part of a multimodal, individualized communication system.

The role and potential impact of communicative (input). . . has been underutilized in intervention approaches to date. . . . Research focus should be directed to the influence of the partner's communication (input) in (AAC) system exchanges. (Romski & Sevcik, 1988b, p. 89)

Visual Input

The availability of visual input appears to facilitate receptive language comprehension for some individuals. People with autism, for instance, have been found to process concrete visuospatial information more readily than temporal or visual-temporal information such as speech or manual signs (Biklen, 1990; Mirenda & Schuler, 1989). Providing visual input models to AAC users also appears to enhance their communication and language abilities or literacy skills, as exemplified by the work of Romski and Sevcik (1996; see Chapter 12 for additional information). Some individuals with aphasia may also benefit from augmented input, as discussed in Chapter 16.

Unaided Symbols

Gestures and signs are convenient types of input because they require no additional paraphernalia (e.g., books, boards, computers) and are always available for use because they do not have to be switched on as do electronic devices. Teachers and family members of AAC users with developmental disabilities often use manually signed input within a total (or simultaneous) communication paradigm, in which the communication partner accompanies spoken words with their corresponding signs (Carr, 1982). Some evidence suggests that communication partners who use total communication slow their rates of both speaking and signing and insert more pauses than when they use speech alone (Windsor & Fristoe, 1989, 1991). This may account, at least in part, for the expressive and receptive language gains that some people with autism and other developmental delays display when using this approach (Kiernan, 1983). The type and amount of input that partners should provide to the AAC user are, however, major considerations. Should manually signed input accompany all or most spoken words, or should communication partners opt for a telegraphic or key-word approach instead? Should the individual employ a total communication approach throughout the day or only during designated instructional periods? Unfortunately, existing research does not supply the answers to these important questions.

Aided Symbols

Communication partners can also provide AAC users with input consisting of symbols of many types. For example, a facilitator may draw simple pictures or write letters and words while speaking to a person with receptive aphasia to help him or her to comprehend messages (see Chapter 16). The two most prevalent input methods that utilize aided symbols are aided language stimulation (Elder & Goossens', 1994; Goossens' et al., 1992) and the System for Augmented Language (Romski & Sevcik, 1996). In both methods, a facilitator points to key symbols while speaking in a manner parallel to that used in total communication. In order to accomplish this, facilitators must have the necessary symbols available for transmission and must organize the environment in order to apply the symbols appropriately. For aided language stimulation, facilitators must prepare activity boards with the necessary symbols in advance and have them available when needed (Goossens', 1989). The logistical demands of aided symbol input often prevent facilitators from using the technique extensively, despite research evidence that it can have positive effects on both speech and language development over time (Romski & Sevcik, 1996; see Chapter 12 for additional information about these techniques).

5

Team Building for
AAC Assessment and Intervention

AAC IN TRANSITION

Knowledge about augmentative and alternative communication (AAC) has increased dramatically since the 1970s. Specifically, AAC technology has evolved at a remarkable pace, and intervention strategies have been developed for people with a wide array of severe communication disorders. Concurrently, models for delivering AAC services have also undergone changes in order to accommodate the growth in the knowledge and resource base of the field. Such changes in the patterns of service delivery can perhaps best be characterized as a "transition from the pioneering to the public policy phase" of the AAC field (Beukelman, 1990, p. 110).

The Pioneering Phase

During the pioneering phase of AAC development, successful interventions were viewed as the exception rather than the rule. When children or adults with severe communication disorders were successfully provided with AAC systems and when they learned to use the systems to communicate effectively, their achievements were often celebrated by the local media, presented at professional meetings, and perhaps written up as a case study in a professional journal. The successful intervention demonstrated what was possible at that point in the AAC field, and it was viewed as a pioneering effort.

As is common during the pioneering phase of any field, AAC professionals celebrated successes and often minimized or ignored failures. For example, it was the responsibility of potential AAC users, their families, or professionals to make the unusual efforts necessary to obtain services. When there was no one to make such efforts for a child or adult with a severe communication impairment, he or she received minimal or no services. Thus, there was a far greater incidence of failures and inequities with service delivery than successes, although the inequities were not publicized or acknowledged.

The Public Policy Phase

The public policy phase of the AAC field has progressed differently in every country in which AAC is used. Zangari, Lloyd, and Vicker (1994) provided an excellent chronology of AAC public policy development around the world. In the following sections, we describe this development briefly as it has occurred in the United States and internationally.

United States

The impetus to move the AAC field beyond the pioneering phase to a public policy phase has differed from country to country. In the United States, several legislative efforts have moved the AAC field solidly into the public policy arena and have guaranteed access to AAC devices to those who need them. Perhaps the most important of these is the Technology-Related Assistance for Individuals with Disabilities Act of 1988, PL 100-407, which stipulates that efforts should be made to provide assistive technology services to all citizens in a state, regardless of age, disability, or location. The law provides financial incentives in the form of grants to enable states to make assistive technology services equitably available. In addition, the Americans with Disabilities Act (ADA) of 1990, PL 101-336, extends federal civil rights to protect people with disabilities from discrimination in the workplace and to provide them with equal access in many other areas. This act promotes the integration of assistive technology as a civil right for all people with disabilities. Similarly, the Individuals with Disabilities Education Act (IDEA) of 1990, PL 101-476, provides for the following:

> If a child with a disability requires assistive technology devices or services, or both, in order to receive a free appropriate public education, the public agency shall ensure that the assistive technology devices or services are made available to that child, either as special education, related services, or as supplementary aids and services that enable a child with a disability to be educated in general education classes.

These service requirements were updated in the IDEA Amendments of 1997, PL 105-17. IDEA '97 also stipulates an individualized assessment process to determine the need for assistive technology, as well as funding for research and training on assistive technology. Finally, the Rehabilitation Act Amendments of 1992, PL 102-569, require state rehabilitation agencies to provide similarly equitable access to technology devices and services as part of the rehabilitation process for individuals with acquired disabilities.

International

The emergence of the public policy phase was also seen in numerous other countries around the world starting in the 1980s. Of course, specific legislation, policies, funding mechanisms, and resources vary greatly from country to country. In 1980 and 1982, the first International Conferences on Nonspeech Communication were held in Toronto, Ontario, Canada. In 1983, the International Society for Augmentative and Alternative Communication (ISAAC) was formed, which, as of 1998, had a membership of more than 2,300 individuals from more than 50 different countries (for more information about ISAAC, visit their World Wide Web side at http://isaac-online.org). ISAAC supports a biennial AAC conference; the *ISAAC Bulletin*, a quarterly newsletter; and *Augmentative and Alternative Communication*, the first refereed journal in the field of AAC, published since 1985. As of 1998, 10 countries have national chapters of ISAAC: Canada, Denmark, Finland, Germany, Israel, Netherlands–Flanders (a joint chapter), Norway, Sweden, the United Kingdom, and the United States. Other countries also have active organizations focusing on AAC that are not formally affiliated with ISAAC, such as Interface in South Africa and the Australian Group on Severe Communication Impairment.

The ISAAC head office, located in Toronto, Ontario, Canada, is an excellent source of information about AAC activities, policies, and services around the world. Information about *Augmentative and Alternative Communication, ISAAC Bulletin,* and other AAC publications such as *Communication Outlook, Communicating Together, Augmentative Communication News,* and *Alternatively Speaking* can be obtained from the ISAAC office.

As shown in this brief overview, the AAC field has developed and continues to develop in the context of a broad-based international community of consumers, family members, professionals, researchers, developers, and manufacturers. (See Zangari et al., 1994, for a detailed chronology of the development of the AAC field and for additional information about ISAAC and related activities around the world.) Although the models used to deliver AAC services vary widely from country to country, one common goal unites these efforts: to enable people to communicate to the best of their abilities. And, although the policies, legislation, and organizations that affect AAC continue to change, the efforts of a team of people, including the AAC user and his or her family, are essential during the assessment and intervention process. Because a team approach is so important to the success of any AAC intervention, the remainder of this chapter focuses on the skills needed for effective collaboration within a team.

Some kind of help
Is the kind of help
That helping's all about.
And some kind of help
Is the kind of help
We can all do without.
(Silverstein, 1974, p. 101)

TEAM DEVELOPMENT

Why work within a team structure anyway? Wouldn't it be easier for professionals to "do their own thing" in each specialty area and have occasional meetings to share information? The answer is yes, it would be easier for professionals, but it would *not* be better for the AAC user and his or her family! It is essential to involve AAC users as well as family members and other significant individuals as members of the team from the outset of intervention. Furthermore, AAC teams should base intervention decisions on a broad range of information. For example, teams need information regarding the cognitive, language, sensory, and motor capabilities of the individual, as well as information regarding the operational, linguistic, social, and strategic competence of the individual's current communication. Teams also need to know about current and future communicative contexts and about the support system available to the potential AAC user. Intervention teams must also identify and respect the preferences of AAC users, their families or guardians, and their personal advisers. Few individual AAC specialists are capable of assessing and intervening in all these areas; therefore, it is nearly always necessary to involve a team of individuals to provide appropriate AAC services. When it comes to AAC, the old adage that "two heads are better than one" holds true—collaborative efforts are integral to the success of most interventions!

Early efforts to build inclusionary, cooperative teams may prevent problems and discord later on. "Consensus today keeps dissension away."

Two kinds of issues affect the ability of a team to function harmoniously and efficiently: structural issues and relational issues. *Structural issues* include concerns such as

- The model of service delivery that guides the functioning of the team
- The goals and purposes of the team
- Membership on the team
- Who can be referred to the team and how the referral process is organized
- How services are organized and delivered
- How resources are managed
- How and by whom team meetings are run

Blackstone (1990) identified several structural factors deemed critical by AAC clinicians. These include conducting interventions in natural contexts, involving families throughout the assessment and intervention, and using a team approach (Blackstone, 1990). She also noted several structural factors that clinicians believe impede service delivery, such as insufficient funding, center-based evaluations, lack of a team approach, lack of follow-up, and pull-out therapy services. Structural problems often appear in the form of confusion about the purposes of the team or how it operates; a perception that services are delivered inequitably; long lag times between referral and service delivery because of inefficient team operation; team meetings that are disorganized and consume inordinate amounts of time; and, ultimately, less-than-adequate outcomes for the consumer.

Similar problems can also be the result of *relational problems* on the team, including

- Frequent violation of the implicit and/or explicit social norms established by the group for interaction
- A feeling that it is not safe for team members to express their feelings and opinions
- Inequitable or dysfunctional interactions among team members
- An inability to give and receive criticism, resolve conflicts, and take others' perspectives
- Decision-making processes that leave some members feeling devalued or marginalized
- Team members who regularly dominate meetings and interactions

- A lack of creative problem-solving skills among team members
- Freeloading, perpetual lateness, or work avoidance by some team members
- A lack of positive interdependence ("all for one, one for all")

Initially, relational problems affect how team members interact and cooperate, but over time they also affect team functioning and productiveness. Team members often ignore relational issues until the problem is like a "whale in the living room"—so big that it can't be ignored any longer! Unfortunately, by this time team members are often so angry and demoralized that it is difficult for them to deal openly and honestly with the concerns. The trick, of course, is to avoid such problems by setting up the team in ways that are likely to prevent it from becoming dysfunctional. The sections that follow focus on strategies for building functional, effective teams.

STRUCTURAL ISSUES

Teams can be organized in a variety of ways. On a *multidisciplinary team*, each specialist independently completes his or her portion of an AAC assessment and makes discipline-specific intervention decisions. The team members then share the assessment results and intervention plans at a team meeting, after which each team member provides direct services to the individual. Within an *interdisciplinary team* model, specialists also assess students individually but then meet to discuss their individual findings and make collaborative recommendations regarding an intervention plan. Team members may meet regularly to discuss progress and make revisions in the intervention, which is usually overseen by one team member (often called the "case manager"). Alternatively, all of the interdisciplinary team members may meet regularly to discuss progress and make revisions in the intervention. Finally, on a *transdisciplinary team*, information is shared among professionals so that direct services providers become proficient in areas other than their primary specialties (Locke & Mirenda, 1992). Assessment is often completed through the collaborative efforts of all team members and is followed by a team meeting to establish the goals and objectives for intervention. According to Hart (1977), once decisions are made, each team member is responsible for the care of the whole individual, rather than only one facet of his or her life.

What is the "best" structure for an AAC team? This question cannot be answered without first considering the goals and purposes of each team and who it is meant to serve. Thus, successful AAC teams may work within any of these models, although Yorkston and Karlan (1986) suggested that the interdisciplinary model is perhaps the most common. There is certainly a growing trend toward and a need for service-delivery structures in which center-based and community-based programs work together in one system. Alm and Parnes recommended models that combine community-based rehabilitation with "Centers for Excellence" (1995, p. 183) that focus on specialty areas of AAC, research and development, and high-tech assistive technology approaches. The trend toward such models is becoming increasingly prevalent around the world in such places as Sweden, South Africa (Alant, 1993; Alant & Emmett, 1995), the United Kingdom (Leese et al., 1993), and the United States. Alm and Parnes noted that systems that operate as a "dynamic continuum" (1995, p. 183) are more likely to encourage accessible and flexible programs that are effective and cost-efficient while also providing for a concentration of expertise as needed for technological and training supports. Alant suggested that, especially in less developed countries, community-based service delivery requires a "dialogical strategy" (1996, p. 3), which accommodates both an intellectualized level of knowledge (from professionals) and an experiential level of attitudes and social structures (from the community at large).

One factor that hampers intervention in less developed countries can be identified as the separation of the technical AAC strategy skill of professionals and their ability to understand the contextual demands for implementation. . . . This . . . often contributes to a superficial understanding of the reality within which service provision occurs within these contexts, leading to inappropriate recommendations of "what is needed." . . . It is clear that, when dealing with different communities, one of the most important issues remains the redefinition of AAC strategies within the infrastructure of that community. (Alant, 1996, p. 2)

Team membership often needs to be quite broad and must include the AAC user and family members as integral—not just "token"—members. Several negative outcomes can result if the user and his or her family are not incorporated into the team before the assessment and intervention-planning processes. First, the team will lack information that pertains to subsequent intervention efforts. Second, an AAC user and his or her family may not be able to assume "ownership" of interventions that are formulated by others on the team without the family's input and agreement. Third, distrust of the agency delivering AAC services may develop if the family is not permitted to participate, regardless of the quality of the evaluation or interventions. Fourth, the AAC user and family members may not learn to participate as team members if they have been excluded when team dynamics and interaction styles are established.

These consequences are also likely to result if key professionals, especially those who manage the natural environments in which the AAC user participates, are excluded or ignored as team members. For example, general and special education teachers usually manage a child's educational environment, speech-language pathologists often manage the communication-conversation environment, employers manage the work environment, and family members or residential staff may manage the living environment. One or more of these individuals is likely to be affected by any of the team's decisions. Therefore, their involvement is absolutely critical in order to avoid later problems that are related to a lack of collaboration or a failure to follow through with team decisions.

Another important structural issue involves the creation of systems for managing resources. In particular, it is important to have ready access to rental or loan equipment that can used for trial periods during an AAC evaluation. Rental equipment can be housed in centralized loan banks or can be located in community settings such as health units or school districts (Blackstone, 1990, 1994b). In fact, loan banks or similar systems may help to reduce the prevalence of technology abandonment, which occurs worldwide. The phenomenon of technology abandonment, which is all-too-familiar to most AAC professionals, occurs when communication technology is discarded by the AAC users whom it was meant to benefit! As Turner et al. noted, "At first glance, technology abandonment seems somewhat understandable because people with disabilities are the ones sticking technology in their closets, attics, and basements. Yet the responsibility for this phenomenon does not rest solely with the disability community"

(1995, p. 288). Technology abandonment appears to be the result of a number of interrelated factors, including the following:

- Recommendations for high-tech AAC devices that produce inadequate synthetic speech or that make message programming or retrieval demands that are too complex for the user (Jinks & Sinteff, 1994)
- The use of professional- rather than consumer- and family-centered decision-making processes (Turner et al., 1995)
- Inadequate availability of AAC systems in relevant environments, a lack of responsive communication partners, inadequate training of communication partners, insufficient time for consumer training and support (i.e., follow-up), inadequate selection of vocabulary for systems, and lack of acknowledgment of the multimodal nature of communication (Murphy, Marková, Collins, & Moodie, 1996)
- Poor or inadequate services related to the mounting and portability of AAC systems (Jinks & Sinteff, 1994; Murphy, Marková, Collins, et al., 1996)

Clearly, these are all issues related to the adequacy of assessment and implementation (i.e., issues related to the quality and quantity of available services), not simply issues that stem from simple consumer or family "noncompliance." Service delivery systems that are structurally sound and that have efficient systems for managing resources are more likely to experience fewer problems in this area. Table 5.1 lists symptoms of structural difficulties that may be found in agencies that deliver AAC services.

RELATIONAL ISSUES

How do a "collection of people" come together to form a team? If you're lucky enough to be a member of a team that functions like a well-oiled machine, you may not have had the need to stop and ask yourself how it came to be that way. But if you (like most of us) are now or have ever been on a team whose gears are sometimes out of align-

Table 5.1.   Symptoms of structural difficulties in AAC service delivery programs

1. Because the AAC program includes people from many professional disciplines, there is no administrator who assumes overall responsibility for the program.
2. The agency has no policies regarding the use of AAC equipment or materials.
3. There is no staff development plan for the AAC team members.
4. An AAC user is placed at the beginning of the school year in a classroom in which the "new" teacher has had no preparation regarding AAC.
5. The AAC efforts of the agency are inefficient or haphazard because there is no designated team leader.
6. AAC interventions are often "stalled" because it is not clear who is responsible for obtaining funds to purchase AAC systems for potential users.
7. Funds for purchasing the AAC equipment and materials that are needed for assessment must be "squeezed out" of the budgets of the speech-language pathology and occupational therapy departments because the AAC program has no independent budget.
8. People with AAC systems receive as much (or less) intervention time from the speech-language pathologist as people with mild communication impairments (e.g., mild articulation disorders).
9. Although one or two schools in a school district have well-developed AAC programs, there is no systematic plan for establishing such programs in other schools that serve students who are potential AAC users.
10. Although a potential AAC user and family desire AAC services, they cannot figure out how to obtain them or who is responsible for delivering services.

> Having a collection of people is not the same as having a team. (Giangreco, 1996a, p. 21)

ment, this is more than an academic question. When conflicts occur, the roots frequently can be traced to early failure to develop productive consensus patterns among team members. Table 5.2 lists 10 symptoms commonly seen among AAC teams that do not practice consensus-building strategies during assessment and decision making.

Fortunately, we know a lot about what helps and what hinders the ability of a collection of people to collaborate efficiently and effectively as a team. According to Thousand and Villa (1992), all members of truly collaborative teams employ a process that involves 1) regular face-to-face interactions in which each member's input is equally valued; 2) positive interdependence; 3) practicing, monitoring, and processing interpersonal skills; and 4) individual accountability. We examine each of these in detail.

Regular Face-to-Face Interactions

It might seem obvious that team members need to meet regularly in order to function as a team, but there are many ways in which teams can compromise this most basic requirement. Groups can be so large that there is little opportunity for each member to express his or her ideas or feelings. Scheduling a common meeting time for people who are very busy can be very difficult. Then there are the latecomers, the early leavers, and the sporadic attenders; teams thus have the challenge of efficiently communicating decisions and assignments to members who are absent. There may also be power imbalances or learning style differences among team members that create challenging interpersonal dynamics. Even physical arrangements can make it difficult to interact and plan effectively. It's no wonder that the simple requirement for face-to-face interaction is often problematic!

Table 5.2.   Ten symptoms of AAC teams that do not practice consensus building

1. Parents or guardians who have not been included in the assessment or decision-making processes are asked to sign individualized education programs (IEPs) that delineate AAC interventions.
2. AAC users are not asked for input during assessment or intervention planning.
3. A person's new AAC system is a surprise to his or her classroom teacher, parents, or employer.
4. Although many team members attend a meeting, only a few give reports. These few team members also control the discussion so that other members are neither required nor expected to contribute their opinions or preferences.
5. A parent or guardian refers to an AAC intervention as something "they" said to do.
6. Paraprofessionals, educational aides, or direct care staff are not invited to attend team meetings.
7. A school administrator rejects an intervention plan without having attended the team meeting at which it was formulated.
8. Parents or guardians are not provided with opportunities early in the assessment process to express their opinions and preferences.
9. When parents speak at a team meeting, team members do not take notes as they do when other team members speak.
10. The members of the AAC team have never met the staff who manage the AAC user's residence or employment site.

Haaf, Millin, and Verberg described the ideal relationship between a consumer and a team of AAC professionals in a story about Sheila, a fictitious 16-year-old girl with cerebral palsy:

When decisions are being made regarding assistive technology, Sheila's opinions and ideas are listened to, and *her* needs (not the preferences of the professional team or convenience of family member(s) or school staff) are paramount. . . . Recently, Sheila expressed a desire to try a standard keyboard with a keyguard on her computer at school. Although clinicians on her team expressed their opinion that this was not as functional for her as using her Touch Talker, the clinicians recognized that Sheila needed to try it for herself and make her own decision. The consequence of this level of responsibility is that although the decision is ultimately Sheila's, she needs to assume responsibility for the decisions that are made, even if they turn out to be wrong. (1994, pp. 4–6)

Team Membership and Size

It is important to make thoughtful decisions about who should be on a team. The following three questions should be asked when formulating any team:

1. **Who has the expertise needed by the team to make the best decisions?** The days when "the more, the merrier" was the predominant approach to team membership are long past. Funding, time, and other constraints often make it necessary to economize for the sake of efficiency, but smaller teams can also be more effective. The literature on this issue suggests that a team of four to six members is ideal to ensure diversity of viewpoints while supporting effective communication (Johnson & Johnson, 1987b). However, at any given point in time, team membership might change as the consumer's needs dictate. For example, during the initial assessment for an AAC system or device, the involvement of one or two team members might be sufficient if the issues are quite clear. Later on, teams might invite additional members to consult about specific motor, sensory, or other concerns that arise. This concept of utilizing a small "core team" of people who are most immediately and directly involved with a specific AAC user plus an "expanded team" of people with additional expertise as needed is likely to enhance both team effectiveness and team efficiency (Swengel & Marquette, 1997; Thousand & Villa, 1992).

2. **Who is affected by the decisions?** In almost all cases, the answer to this question is simple: the AAC user and his or her family. Ironically, these are often the individuals who are least involved and least consulted in the AAC assessment and intervention process! As a result, the outcomes desired by the consumer may take a "backseat" to the goals identified as important by the professionals on the team. For example, one of us was told about the experience of an older man with cerebral palsy who lives in a group home and whose speech is insufficient for talking on the telephone (but is sufficient for most day-to-day interactions). During the initial meeting with the AAC team, he made it quite clear that all he wanted was to be able to use the telephone to talk to his family and order pizza or do other tasks. Six months later, after many hours of assessment and experimentation, he ended up with a very sophisticated voice-output communication device that can do just about everything, including help him talk on the telephone—and that's exactly what he uses it for! The rest of the time,

this $10,000 piece of equipment sits by the telephone waiting for the next time he has a taste for pizza! When members of the AAC team that provided the device were told about this outcome, they shook their heads and bemoaned his lack of vision for himself and his reluctance to use the technology provided to him. This example illustrates the kind of problem that can arise when the consumer and family members are "token" but not "real" members of the team and when goals and outcomes are professionally defined rather than consumer defined. As Michael Williams asked, "Whose outcome is it anyway?" (1995b, p. 1).

3. **Who has an interest in participating?** This question is meant to encourage the team to think beyond the obvious. In every community, there are people who might be interested in helping to solve particular problems or in loaning their expertise. For example, we know a high school computer science teacher, Mr. Reilley, who acts as an informal "technology consultant" to his daughter's elementary school. In this capacity, he has made numerous suggestions for simple adaptations that have resulted in better computer access for students with physical disabilities. Although unusual, Mr. Reilley's membership on the team has been a critical factor in those students' successful use of technology. Thinking broadly about team membership will often reveal such opportunities to "build bridges" into the larger community.

The speech teacher did ask me if I liked it (a Canon Communicator) and I said "no" but she said, "Hang in there; it's not going to be overnight." Most of the time nobody asked. And, if they did, it didn't seem to make them change anything. I felt like they were the experts; listen to them. . . . My doctor told my speech teacher what to put on my board so I could tell him what my problem is. . . . Nobody asked me if the pictures were okay. The doctor said it and the speech teacher did it. . . . They made me feel like I'm not the one who has to carry it and use it; but I am. Does it matter if they are wrong? No. Just do what they say and don't make waves! (Dawn, a young woman with cerebral palsy, describing the "flip side" of the consumer–professional relationship, in Smith-Lewis & Ford, 1987, p. 16)

Team Member Participation

More challenging than decisions about who should be on a team are decisions about how to create an environment in which team members can function most efficiently and effectively. This goes beyond arranging the physical environment and encompasses such nitty-gritty issues as organizing meetings for maximal effectiveness, establishing guidelines for communication and attendance, and dealing with time constraints. Some of the most important considerations in this regard are summarized in the first section of the survey entitled "How Are We Doing as a Team?" that is presented in Figure 5.1. You might find it interesting to have the members of your team complete the survey independently and then share and discuss the results together. It is critical that the team address from the outset structural issues such as those examined under "Meeting Structure Skills" on this survey.

Circle the points to the right of each item only if *all* team members answer "yes" to the item. Total the number of points circled per section.

I. Meeting Structure Skills

1. We meet regularly as a team.   2

2. We meet in a comfortable physical environment.   2

3. We start our meetings on time.   2

4. We arrange ourselves in a circle when we meet.   2

5. The size of our team does not exceed six members at a time.   2

6. Needed members
    - Are invited (*Note:* Needed members may change from week to week based on the agenda items.)   2
    - Attend   2
    - Arrive on time   2
    - Stay until the end of the meeting   2

7. We have regularly scheduled meetings that are held at times and locations agreed on in advance by the team.   2

8. We do not stop the meeting to update tardy members. Updates occur at a break in the meeting.   2

9. We have a communication system for
    - Absent members   2
    - "Need to know" people who are not part of the core team   2

10. We use a structured agenda format that prescribes that we
    - Identify agenda items for the next meeting at the prior meeting   2
    - Set time limits for each agenda item   2
    - Have public minutes   2
    - Process group effectiveness regarding both task accomplishment and social skill performance   2
    - Review and modify the agenda, whenever necessary   2

11. We have identified ways for "creating" time for meetings.   2

12. We summarize the discussion of each topic before moving on to the next agenda item.   2

13. We end meetings on time.   2

Total   _____ / 42

II. Team-Building Skills (Positive Interdependence)

14. Our meetings are structured so that there is ample "air time" for all participants.   2

15. We have publicly agreed to the group's overall goals.   2

16. We have publicly shared our individual "agenda"; that is, we have each stated what we need from the group to be able to work toward the group goals.   2

17. We distribute leadership functions by rotating roles (e.g., recorder, timekeeper, observer).   2

18. We coordinate our work to achieve our objectives (as represented by agenda items).   2

19. We discuss situations from the perspective of absent members.   2

20. We generate and explore multiple solutions before selecting a particular solution.   3

(continued)

Figure 5.1.   The How Are We Doing as a Team? checklist. (From Thousand, J.S., & Villa, R.A. (1992). Collaborative teams: A powerful tool in school restructuring. In R.A. Villa, J.S. Thousand, W. Stainback, & S. Stainback (Eds.), *Restructuring for caring and effective education: An administrative guide to creating heterogeneous schools* (pp. 91–94). Baltimore: Paul H. Brookes Publishing Co.; adapted by permission.)

Figure 5.1. *(continued)*

21. We consciously identify the decision-making process we will use for making a particular decision (e.g., majority vote, consensus, unanimous decision).	2
22. We devote time at each meeting for positive comments.	2
23. We structure other group awards and "celebrations."	2
24. We distribute among ourselves homework/action items.	2
25. We generally accomplish the tasks on our agenda.	3
26. We have fun at our meetings.	3
Total	____ / 29

III. Interaction Skills

27. We have established group social norms (e.g., "no put downs," all members participate) and confront one another on norm violations.	3
28. We have a "no scapegoating" norm. When things go wrong, it is not one person's fault but everyone's job to make a new plan.	3
29. We explain the norms to new members.	2
30. We feel free to express our feelings and opinions (positive and negative).	3
31. We call attention to discussions that are off task or that stray from the agenda topics.	2
32. We openly discuss problems in social interaction among team members.	3
33. We set aside time to process social interactions and feelings.	2
34. We spend time developing a plan to improve social interactions.	2
35. We have arranged for training to increase our small-group skills (e.g., giving and receiving criticism, perspective taking, creative problem solving, conflict resolution).	3
36. We view situations and solutions from various perspectives.	2
37. We treat each other with respect, even if we don't always agree.	3
Total	____ / 28

IV. Summary

Meeting Structure Skills	____ / 42
Team-Building Skills	____ / 29
Interaction Skills	____ / 28
Total	____ / 100

> Positive interdependence is the perception that one is linked with others in a way so that one cannot succeed unless they do (and vice versa), and that their work benefits you and your work benefits them. It is the belief that "you sink or swim together." (Johnson & Johnson, 1987a, p. 399)

Positive Interdependence

Perhaps the most important aspects of team functioning are the relationships and interactions among team members. Often, the mutual respect and ability to work in an "all for one and one for all" atmosphere will determine the success of a team effort. Four processes are particularly relevant to interdependence, especially when new teams are being formed or when new members join an existing team.

Discussing Individual Philosophies, Goals, Roles, and Needs

Having team members discuss individual philosophies, goals, roles, and needs is an important yet often-overlooked step in forming a collaborative team. It is natural for each member of the team to have his or her own experiences, goals, perception of his or her roles, and needs. However, it is generally assumed that individuals will put all of these preconceptions aside "for the greater good," even during team conflict. When teams first come together, it is important for members to discuss individual goals and needs publicly. This is particularly important in order to involve consumer and family members productively because their perceptions of their needs and the perceptions of the rest of the team may differ. In addition, the needs and priorities of parents may change over time, as reflected in two related studies that examined this issue in families with young children (Angelo, Jones, & Kokoska, 1995) and with adolescents or young adults who use AAC (Angelo, Kokoska, & Jones, 1996). Table 5.3 summarizes the top needs and priorities identified by both mothers and fathers across these two studies, which may differ quite dramatically over the years as mothers and fathers assume different roles on the AAC team.

Similarly, professional members of the team, especially those who join the team on a case-by-case basis (e.g., a vision specialist who participates on behalf of particular

Table 5.3. Needs of mothers and fathers of AAC users in two age groups

Priority	Families with young children		Families with adolescents and young adults	
	% Mothers (n = 56)	% Fathers (n = 35)	% Mothers (n = 85)	% Fathers (n = 47)
Increasing knowledge of assistive devices	44.4	48.5	46.4	44.7
Planning for future communication needs	42.8	45.7	44.6	50.0
Integrating assistive devices in community settings	49.0		48.8	
Integrating assistive devices at home		41.1		44.7
Getting computer access	44.4			43.2
Developing community awareness and support for assistive device users	47.2			
Finding advocacy groups for parents of children using assistive devices	41.0			
Finding trained professionals to work with my child	41.0			
Finding volunteers to work with my child		44.1		
Getting funding for an assistive device		42.8		
Knowing how to teach my child using an assistive device		41.1		
Having social opportunities with peers without disabilities			54.1	
Having social opportunities with other assistive device users			47.6	
Knowing how to maintain or repair an assistive device				48.9
Integrating assistive devices in educational settings				43.5
Knowing how to program an assistive device				43.5

Sources: Angelo, Jones, and Kokoska (1995) and Angelo, Kokoska, and Jones (1996).

consumers but is not a consistent member), should be included in a discussion related to their needs and roles from the beginning of their involvement. For example, Locke and Mirenda (1992) reported that teachers on AAC teams often assume a wide variety of responsibilities, ranging from traditional "teacher roles," such as writing goals and objectives for AAC users (82%) and assessing cognitive abilities (81%), to those that might be within the traditional domain of other team members, such as designing and constructing adaptive devices (35%) or assessing symbolic representation (34%). Thus, these individuals join each new team with expectations colored by their past experiences (positive and negative) that may not represent the expectations of the rest of the team. It is important to achieve clarity and negotiate agreement on such issues early in the collaborative process.

A major reason for having team members clearly articulate their needs, role perceptions, and priorities is to avoid some of the negative effects of not doing so! Such effects may include the sabotage of team efforts by individual members, passive-aggressive behaviors such as "forgetting" to come to meetings or "not having time" to complete essential tasks, or even expressions of outright hostility in some cases. If everyone declares their personal agendas "up front," these agendas are more likely to be met or accommodated. Most important, declaring one's own goals and needs publicly is the first step in establishing a standard of honest, trusting, and trustworthy behavior among all team members (Locke & Mirenda, 1992).

Ms. Huston is a speech-language pathologist who worked for the past 6 years in a school district where she had a caseload of 52 students, 6 of whom were AAC users (see Blackstone, 1997, for information about "typical" speech-language pathologist caseloads in schools and other settings). She is most familiar with a two-tiered AAC service delivery model in which school district personnel assess and serve students with less complex communication needs and specialists help those with more complex needs at a regional assessment center. Recently, she moved to a new city and is now part of a team that supports children and adults with acquired disabilities. When she meets the other members of her team for the first time and they each talk about their personal goals, she says that she wants to learn more about AAC technology for children and adults. She also says that her long-term goal, maybe 5 years down the road, is to start a private practice specializing in communication supports for children and adults with traumatic brain injury.

Identifying Learning and Work-Style Needs

One area in which goal and need identification is particularly important for AAC professionals has to do with learning and work-style issues, especially as they relate to technology learning. From both our clinical and our classroom experiences, we have come to think about professionals in three groups: mastery learners, performance learners, and social learners. *Mastery learners* are individuals who prefer to work alone and will strive to master completely new pieces of software or equipment. They tend to be very systematic in their learning; they will often read instruction manuals thoroughly, explore all of the options and features of each new product, and so forth. These individuals are usually solitary learners who prefer to be self-directed rather than work in groups. In contrast are *performance learners,* who work well in a team structure and usually learn new technologies primarily for the sake of a particular AAC user. Their goal is to learn what they need to enhance client performance rather than to completely master the technology; they learn best when they are faced with actual clinical problems that they can resolve as part of the learning process. Because performance learners are more "practically oriented" than "thoroughness oriented," they may appear (at least to mastery learners) to be rather haphazard in their approach, when, in fact, they are simply more focused on technology as a means to an end rather than as an end in itself. Finally, *social learners* enjoy the social aspects of team participation. They dislike self-instruction and usually prefer to work in interactive groups so that their social needs can be met while they are learning. Social learners tend to provide the relational "glue" for an AAC team.

Clearly, it is important for each team member to think about and articulate his or her technology learning style needs early in the formation of the team. In that way, accommodations can be made for the different (and sometimes conflicting!) styles. For example, performance and social learners are often intimidated by mastery learners who, in turn, may be quite impatient and frustrated with their extremely people-oriented colleagues! Putting these three types of learners together to learn a new product is often a recipe for stress and conflict! Yet, mastery learners are invaluable on a team because they are the ones to whom everyone turns when there is a technological problem or unusual challenge. By the same token, social learners have the "people skills" that make them good group instructors for other social learners (once they have learned the technology themselves). Similarly, performance learners often make good technology instructors because they can appreciate and explain both the clinical implications and the technical aspects of a product. We find that effective teams often have a good "mix" of each type of learner and assign responsibilities within the team to take advantage of each person's learning and work-style strengths.

Ms. Huston and her colleagues talk at their first meeting about learning and work styles. She admits (somewhat sheepishly) that she has not had a lot of experience with high-tech AAC devices and computer software and that she is a bit worried about her ability to contribute to the team efforts in this area. She says that she is used to being socially active throughout her day and, although she is quite able to be independent, she prefers collaborating with others to learn and to solve problems. Her colleagues laugh and tell her to "stay away from Jake," the physical therapist on the team who they fondly call a "tech-head" because his style is exactly the opposite! Two team members suggest that she participate in a series of hands-on workshops they are running for parents and teachers over a 6-week period to learn the basic operations of several pieces of equipment, and she quickly agrees. They also reassure her that they all learn differently and that she'll do just fine (as long as she steers clear of Jake!).

Agreeing on Mutual Team Goals

Once individual goals have been identified, the team can move on to identifying mutual goals that are needed for effective functioning. Some of these may be congruent with individual goals, and some may conflict. When conflicts occur, it is important for members to examine the conflict within a "win-win" framework (Fisher, Ury, & Patton,

1991) and attempt to discover together how the goals of all conflicting parties can be accommodated. This may take some time but is surely worth the effort in the long run because the process of arriving at solutions together can help the team to develop some of the negotiation and listening skills that are critical for long-term success. The process of identifying mutual goals is really a process of "vision planning" and should be repeated periodically in teams that are long standing.

At the rehab team's first meeting, members also did some "vision planning" for 1-year and 3-year markers. They decided that their 1-year goal was to explore ways to improve the efficiency of their service delivery model in light of the funding restrictions imposed by managed care. Specifically, they decided to modify the transdisciplinary, or "arena assessment," model they've used in the past. Within this model, all team members meet to complete the assessment and then establish collaborative goals and objectives for intervention. They decided to try a modified approach in which the team will first meet to decide who should be involved in the assessment for each client (Glennen, 1997). The selected members will then work collaboratively as a "mini-team." They also decided that, over the next 3 years, they want to improve their ability to do field-based research to document the outcomes of their interventions. A subgroup volunteered to discuss some strategies for accomplishing this and report back with suggestions in 1 month's time.

Creating Positive Resource, Role, Task, and Reward Interdependence

Positive interdependence means that team members share resources and take different roles as needed, create an equitable division of labor, and create common rewards for group members' work. It also means that the team shares the knowledge, skills, and material resources of each member to complete the job at hand and that team roles may be explicitly distributed and shared among members during team meetings on a rotating basis. Some of the most common of these roles are summarized in Table 5.4. Finally, interdependence requires that all members participate equally in completing the necessary tasks, even if this means crossing "disciplinary boundaries" at times. For example, the motor specialist on a team might offer to assist her "temporarily swamped" speech-language pathologist colleague to create communication displays. Her colleague might then reciprocate later by helping to create a specialized switch mount for a wheelchair. When task interdependence is held as the norm, work assignments should be reviewed periodically by the team to ensure that no one is either "freeloading" by taking on fewer tasks or having trouble "letting go" of tasks that could be shared with others. Finally, when successes are celebrated collectively so that no one person gets special recognition, all team members can share in the gratification of having contributed to the achievement. By the same token, teams that swim together may sometimes sink together—so when things don't go the way they were planned, the collective "we" rather than a single person takes responsibility for setbacks.

Practicing, Monitoring, and Processing Interpersonal Skills

People are born into the world one at a time, not in groups—perhaps that's why most of us don't automatically have the skills needed to collaborate in group situations! Al-

Table 5.4.   Areas of expertise for an AAC team

Speech-Language Pathology
  Communication sciences
  Normal and disordered communication
  Receptive and expressive language
  Development and disorders
  Alternative and augmentative aids, symbols, techniques, and strategies
  Management of communication interventions

Medicine
  Management of therapeutic program
  Natural course of the disorder
  Medical intervention
  Management of medication regimes

Physical Therapy
  Mobility aids
  Motor control and motor learning
  Positioning to maximize functional communication in all environments
  Maintenance of strength and range of motion
  Physical conditioning to increase flexibility, balance, and coordination

Occupational Therapy
  Activities of daily living
  Positioning to maximize functional communication in all contexts
  Adaptive equipment
  Mobility aids
  Access to aids, computers, and splints

Engineering
  Application and modification of existing electronic or mechanical aids and devices

Education
  Planning for appropriate social and academic experiences
  Development of cognitive/conceptual objectives
  Assessment of socio-communicative components in the classroom
  Integration of augmentative components in the classroom
  Development of an appropriate vocational curriculum

Psychology
  Documentation of level of cognitive functioning
  Selection of appropriate learning styles
  Estimation of learning potential

Social Services
  Evaluation of total living situation
  Identification of family and community resources
  Provision of information about funding options

Vocational Counseling
  Assessment of vocational potential
  Identification of vocational goals
  Education of co-workers
  Identification of augmentative components in vocational settings

Computer Technology
  Evaluation of software programs for potential use by clients
  Modification of existing software programs
  Developing programs to meet existing communication needs

Adapted from Yorkston and Karlan (1986).

It is now 4 months after the team's first meeting, and Ms. Huston has been busy! She's had to get used to working in a setting where resources and job responsibilities are shared. At first, she felt a bit threatened and was concerned that her skills were not respected or utilized, because everyone on the team seemed to know a lot about everything! Over time, though, she has realized that her expertise is valued and that she can be an active contributor to the AAC assessment and intervention process. Plus, she's learned a lot of things that she never imagined she would learn—from the operation of several new devices to how to recognize primitive reflex patterns that might interfere with their use. She's also learned about how *not* to conduct team meetings—it seems to her that her colleagues waste a lot of time each week complaining about their workloads! Ms. Huston, however, does enjoy the 10 minutes at the end of each meeting when the outreach team reports about the status of individuals who have been discharged because most of them are doing well in the community. Overall, she's a bit overwhelmed but proud to be part of a team that works and celebrates their successes together!

though such skills go far beyond those required in one-to-one interactions or most other social situations, it is not unusual for teams to assume that all members will just "have" the interpersonal skills that are needed to work together effectively. Of course, that's not always the case—and problems with interpersonal communication among the members of a team are both common and stressful for all involved. In this section, we examine some of the strategies that might be useful to teams who are dissatisfied with the ways in which members interact with one another.

Establishing Group Norms

All groups have norms (i.e., expectations about standard practices and operations), but they are usually informal (i.e., unstated) rather than explicit. Norms are important because they help to equalize the influence between powerful and more timid group members and because they establish a set of expectations that are understood by all. For some teams, it is important to discuss and determine group norms quite explicitly, especially if there is frequent staff turnover or if some team members tend to function more autonomously than others. It might even be useful to post the agreed-on norms or include them as part of a new staff orientation handbook. Some of the social norms that might be stated explicitly include, for example, not using foul language or sarcasm, treating each other with respect and dignity at all times, understanding that the process is just as important as the product, and so forth. The team may also decide to be explicit about one or more task-related norms, such as, "We will get all reports done by the third Thursday of the month" or, "We will start and end all meetings on time."

Over time, Ms. Huston learned that a social norm on her new team is that everyone uses first names when addressing each other, so she had to get used to being called Lavinia by her colleagues. She also learned that there is a very strong ethic that everyone participate actively at team meetings, which she knows will be a challenge for her because she is quite shy by nature. But it's all part of the growth process!

Practicing Interpersonal Skills for Collaboration

Johnson, Johnson, Holubec, and Roy (1984) identified four sets of skills needed for effective collaboration:

1. **Forming skills:** Forming skills are the initial trust-building skills needed to establish a team. They include basic elements such as arriving at meetings on time, looking at people when they speak, using appropriate voice tone and volume, refraining from using "put-downs," and so forth. Forming skills are necessary to establish trust as well as to ensure that everyone is focused on the task at hand.

2. **Functioning skills:** Functioning skills are the communication and leadership skills needed for management and organizational purposes. They are also needed to ensure that tasks are completed and relationships are maintained. They include such skills as sharing ideas, resources, and materials; sharing feelings when appropriate; volunteering for roles that are shared; asking for help, clarification, or assistance; praising other team members' contributions (both verbally and nonverbally); using humor as appropriate (e.g., to relieve tension or motivate the group); explaining or clarifying when asked to do so; and so forth. When functioning skills are present on a team, they are often taken for granted, but when they are not present, they are sorely missed! It is important that all team members value the same functioning skills; otherwise, mixed messages are likely to abound, with the associated stresses that accompany them. For example, if some team members are "solo players" and others are "team players," there is likely to be a conflict each time one of the latter members asks one of the former for assistance, unless it is clear that such coteaching is expected and valued as part of the job.

3. **Formulating skills:** Formulating skills are those skills needed for learning, creative problem solving, and decision making, such as asking why or how a particular solution was chosen or asking for feedback, rationales, or elaboration. Formulating skills also include diagnosing and talking about group difficulties regarding both tasks and interpersonal problems and generating multiple solutions through creative problem-solving strategies. Many teams exert insufficient effort in this area in terms of both in-service education and actual practice. One formulating process that can be particularly useful is called the Creative Problem-Solving Process (Osborn, 1963; Parnes, 1985, 1988). This process consists of five basic steps for problem solving: 1) fact finding (gathering information), 2) problem finding (clarifying the problem), 3) idea finding (brainstorming and generating many ideas without judging them), 4) solution finding (selecting the best ideas based on criteria), and 5) acceptance finding (making a plan of what to do next and taking action). Whether this particular approach is used, each team needs to either develop or adapt its own process for equitable and efficient problem solving.

4. **Fermenting skills:** Fermenting skills are needed to manage controversy and conflicting opinions, search for more information, and stimulate revision and refinement of solutions. The better the fermenting skills of a team, the more likely it is that members will see diversity as an asset rather than as a problem. Fermenting skills include being able to explain how or why decisions were made, extend or build on other members' ideas or conclusions, generate additional solutions or strategies, see ideas from others' perspectives, criticize ideas without criticizing people, and resolve differences of opinions using respectful negotiation skills. This list shows that, without fermenting skills, a team is likely to be discordant and dysfunctional. It is important to note that although fermenting skills often do not come naturally, they can be learned. Some useful resources include game theory (Zagare, 1984) and the "win-win" techniques developed by Fisher et al. (1991).

No wonder so many teams have a hard time functioning harmoniously and productively! The interpersonal skills needed for collaborative teaming are multiple and complex! Maybe that's why, on so many teams, many important decisions are made autocratically (i.e., by one person) rather than after consultation with all members. The problem is that autocratic decision making is likely to perpetuate disjointed and fragmented service delivery as well as create conflicts among team members. An often-used alternative is to take a democratic approach to decision making in which the "majority rules"—but this, too, may be problematic in that it tends to polarize factions within teams and discount the potential value of dissenting opinions. A democratic approach is particularly problematic when the dissenting opinion is held by the AAC user and/or family members who, after all, will ultimately be the most affected by decisions. Arriving at decisions through consensus may take more time in the short run but can save time by avoiding the aftermath of more "efficient" processes over the long run. Regardless, as each team decides on its own decision-making process and style, the skills needed for cooperation and collaboration must be part of the members' learning agenda.

Ms. Huston and her team have decided to "tackle" the complaints about workload that seem to be growing in both frequency and magnitude. At a team meeting, they each take 5 minutes to share their experiences and their perceptions of the causes of the problem. They identify several issues: a perception that some members are overworked whereas others are not very busy, differences in individual work styles that make some appear to be more efficient than others, and the belief that there are just too few professionals for the number of individuals referred to the team. They spend some time brainstorming potential solutions without making any judgments about their potential efficacy and then talk about each idea in turn. By the end of the meeting, they have made two decisions: 1) to institute an absolute moratorium on complaining about the workload for 2 weeks and 2) to devise a system for collecting data that will allow them to identify how much time the various tasks assigned to each member currently take. They figure that, with such data, they will be able to determine whether they are actually short-staffed or whether they need to work on improving efficiency. They all agree that they are "sick and tired" of listening to each other complain and that they feel better now that they have an action plan that might help to institute change. They decide to meet again in 2 weeks to review the workload study proposal (see Blackstone, 1997, for three examples of how this might be done).

Monitoring and Processing Group Functioning

There's not much point to having norms and identifying interpersonal skills that need refinement without having some way to monitor and process the outcomes. Are team members honoring the agreed-on norms? Are certain interpersonal problems occurring regularly among team members? Are problems solved collaboratively and efficiently? If there are difficulties, what solutions can be created and implemented? Finally, how well do the solutions work? Teams can employ many strategies to monitor and process the answers to such questions. For example, Thousand and Villa (1992) suggested that a different team member be assigned the role of observer from week to week or meeting to meeting to observe and record the frequency of use of specific interpersonal skills of concern (e.g., the fermenting skill of "criticizing ideas without criticizing people"). Alternatively, the team could ask an outside observer to provide such input; or both types of individuals could assist. Another strategy is to take time regularly (e.g., during the last 10 minutes of each team meeting, once a month) to discuss team dynamics openly, using a comfortable format. This might include a "group sharing" process, in which team members discuss what they think is going well and not so well with regard to collaboration, or periodic use of the How Are We Doing as a Team? checklist presented in Figure 5.1. The point is to have some way of monitoring the use (or lack of use) of interpersonal skills that team members themselves have identified as needing work and then to share and process this information with the group as a whole. This helps to foster the "all for one and one for all" attitude that is central to the collaborative team process.

Individual Accountability

The final element necessary for effective teamwork is individual accountability. This exists when team members believe that their work is both identifiable and valued and that they must fulfill their responsibilities in order for the group (and themselves) to be successful. There are two sides to this issue, both of which are important. One side is the question of how the team can provide incentives and rewards for performance that meets or exceeds expectations; the other side is the question of what to do when a team member is not fulfilling his or her responsibilities. With regard to the first issue, the principles of teaming suggest that any extrinsic rewards be distributed to the team as a whole rather than to individuals because public recognition of one individual over another is likely to promote competition rather than collaboration (Villa, Thousand, Stainback, & Stainback, 1992). Even more desirable is the fostering of intrinsic rewards such as feelings of personal satisfaction and pride in one's accomplishments. Traditional management theory is based on the principle "what gets rewarded gets done" (Sergiovanni, 1990, p. 22). A better strategy on which to base our efforts is "what is rewarding gets done. When something is rewarding, it gets done even when no one is looking."

This is not to say that teams should avoid giving extrinsic rewards, particularly those that are ongoing and social in nature. No one likes to go to work day after day when the atmosphere is one in which productivity and excellence are taken for granted or ignored altogether! In fact, productive teams are characterized by the offering of frequent and mutual praise (by team members, not just by administrators), complimenting, and other forms of positive acknowledgment for efficient, high-quality work. These are the elements that make team efforts seem both reward*ed* and reward*ing*.

And what about the other side of the issue—the team member who is *not* doing his or her part? If dysfunctional behaviors occur infrequently or in isolated situations, the best strategy is to ignore them—after all, no one is a perfect team player all of the time. But if behaviors such as freeloading, rudeness, sloppy or late work, or other problems persist, direct confrontation is the best strategy. Of course, this should always be done on an individual basis and in private so that the person doesn't feel that the team is "ganging up" on him or her. Any team member can initiate the process if it is likely that the person will respond positively; otherwise, either a supervisor or one of the team members with whom the person has a positive relationship should offer the feedback. Although this kind of interaction is always uncomfortable for both the giver and the receiver, it is important to deal with such situations as soon as they are identified. Otherwise, team unity and morale is likely to be negatively affected as team members begin to complain to each other behind closed doors about the problem member.

After Ms. Huston has been on the job for about 6 months, one of her colleagues asks to meet with her for coffee. At that time, he tells Ms. Huston that he has some concerns about the fact that she was late the last few times they were scheduled to do an AAC evaluation together and asks if they could talk about it. Ms. Huston is initially quite defensive, saying that he should "cut her some slack" and implying that he is making a big deal about nothing. But her colleague persists, reminding her that last week he and a client had to wait 15 minutes before she appeared. She acknowledges that he is correct and that punctuality has never been her strong point. Together, they discuss some strategies for improving her time management skills, and she decides to invest in a digital watch with an alarm that can be set for 10 minutes before each appointment of the day. Although Ms. Huston feels embarrassed about being confronted, she is also grateful that her colleague brought it to her attention rather than just grumbling to himself about her lateness. She resolves to conquer her "time gremlins," and they part on a positive note.

The process of team development requires commitment, energy, patience, and practice from all concerned. Effective teams are not built in a day, and ineffective teams are often the result of inattentiveness to the "little things" that eventually grow to be "big things." Effective teams are structured in ways that allow team members to deal with internal business regularly and openly in order to both solve and prevent problems.

6

Principles of Assessment

In the broadest sense, the goal of augmentative and alternative communication (AAC) interventions is to assist individuals with severe communication disorders in becoming communicatively competent in order to meet their current communication needs and to prepare them to meet their future communication needs. AAC assessment involves the gathering and analysis of information so that users of AAC systems and those who assist them can make informed decisions about the adequacy of current communication, the individual's communication needs, AAC systems and equipment, instruction, and outcomes evaluation. This chapter presents some of the general principles and procedures of AAC assessment. (See Chapter 7 for information about assessment of specific capabilities related to selection of an AAC system.)

AAC ASSESSMENT MODELS

Many models have been developed over the years to guide the AAC assessment process. These include candidacy models (which are, for the most part, no longer used but are of historical significance), communication needs models, and the Participation Model on which this book is based. We describe each of these briefly in the following sections.

Candidacy Models

A primary goal of an AAC assessment is to determine whether an individual requires or continues to require AAC assistance. Initially, this might appear to be a trivial task, as it seems obvious that people who are unable to meet their daily communication needs through natural speech require AAC interventions. Nevertheless, since the 1970s, considerable controversy has been generated about candidacy for AAC services.

A review of the history of the field reveals that interventionists have held a variety of candidacy requirements. Formerly, AAC teams provided assistance primarily to those individuals who demonstrated chronic expressive communication disorders along with relatively strong cognitive and linguistic capabilities. For example, teams often provided AAC services to people with degenerative diseases such as amyotrophic lateral sclerosis (ALS), in which individuals lose the ability to speak but experience no impairments in cognitive and linguistic functioning. Similarly, interventionists considered individuals with spinal cord injuries to be good candidates for AAC services directed toward improving writing abilities because these individuals' primary impairments were motoric rather than cognitive or linguistic in nature. AAC teams also considered people with severe speech disorders due to cerebral palsy to be appropriate candidates for AAC services, if they demonstrated relatively intact cognitive and language skills.

In addition, teams tended not to provide AAC systems to people who might eventually develop natural speech. Thus, they often excluded children with developmental apraxia of speech in the hope that their phonologic abilities might improve. They often assumed (or feared) that if these children received AAC systems, they might not exert the effort required to become natural speakers. Similarly, AAC professionals often considered adults with aphasia and individuals with traumatic brain injury to be inappropriate candidates for AAC interventions until it became clear—sometimes months or even years after their injuries—that speech recovery had failed to occur. Consequently, these individuals were deprived of the ability to communicate their wants, needs, preferences, and feelings, often during the very period of time when they were attempting to restructure their lives in order to live with their severe communication disorders and other disabilities.

In these early years, interventionists also exercised a strong bias against providing AAC services to people with developmental cognitive limitations. Many of these individuals had severe expressive communication problems secondary to mental retardation, autism, congenital dual sensory impairments, or multiple disabilities, and their cognitive and linguistic limitations were taken as evidence that they were not appropriate candidates for AAC services. This thinking predominated so much that the service delivery guidelines of local educational agencies often imposed specific requirements of cognitive or linguistic performance before interventionists would consider an individual to be an appropriate AAC candidate. This effectively excluded most individuals with mental retardation from receiving AAC services.

Communication Needs Model

"Candidacy" guidelines for AAC intervention have been gradually replaced by guidelines based on communication needs, as a result of several influential factors. First, the definition of AAC services expanded to include communication strategies and technologies that could be used by individuals who were not literate (i.e., those who could not type messages letter by letter). Initially, this expanded view of AAC allowed teams to provide communication options to individuals who were preliterate, such as preschoolers. In time, AAC teams also extended these options to people who were nonliterate.

Marvin and his teacher sat facing each other on low chairs. The teacher would say, "Look at me," and Marvin would occasionally comply. The teacher would then give him a raisin to eat. After a while, the teacher began to touch some of her body parts—head, nose, and eyes—and would prompt Marvin to imitate her actions. When he did, he received a sip of juice. I asked, "Why are you doing these activities?" and the teacher replied, "To teach him the prerequisites for communication." (D. Beukelman, personal communication, July, 1997)

Second, it became increasingly clear that when people were excluded from AAC services because of their "inadequate" capabilities, they were also usually excluded from the experiences, instruction, and practice necessary to improve their capabilities (Kangas & Lloyd, 1988; Reichle & Karlan, 1985; Romski & Sevcik, 1988a). People who were excluded in this way worked on "perpetual readiness" activities that were hypothetically designed to teach them the "prerequisite" skills that they lacked. Most of these activities, such as learning about object permanence by finding toys hidden under towels or learning about visual tracking by following stuffed animals moved across the line of visual regard, were nonfunctional and often age inappropriate.

In time, the concept of prerequisite skills was abandoned, and interventions were organized to match the individual's needs and capabilities for today while building future capabilities for tomorrow (see Chapter 7 for more complete discussion). As a result of these changes, AAC teams now determine candidacy for communication intervention based on an individual's unmet communication needs rather than on some profile of his or her impairments. Beukelman et al. (1985) described the Communication Needs Model and its goals:

- Document the communication needs of an individual
- Determine how many of these needs are met through current communication techniques
- Reduce the number of unmet communication needs through systematic AAC interventions (See also Dowden, Beukelman, & Lossing, 1986.)

The Communication Needs Model works well for assessment and intervention when the communication needs of an individual are easy to define. For example, some adults with severe communication disorders have well-established lifestyles with consistent support systems. They are often successful in reaching consensus with their families and attendants about their communication needs; as a result, intervention plans can be quite straightforward. Determining the communication needs of individuals with less clearly defined or changing lifestyles is, however, more difficult. For these individuals, the Communication Needs Model has limitations because it is not sufficiently comprehensive and does not facilitate planning for the future.

Participation Model

In an effort to broaden the Communication Needs Model, Beukelman and Mirenda (1988) expanded on concepts that were initially described by Rosenberg and Beukelman (1987) to guide AAC decision making and intervention. The Participation Model, shown in Figure 6.1, provides a systematic process for conducting AAC assessments and designing interventions based on the functional participation requirements of peers without disabilities of the same chronological age as the potential AAC user. This is similar to the Human Activity Assistive Technology (HAAT) model proposed by Cook and Hussey (1995), in which interventionists consider the interactions among the human user, the activity to be completed, and the context in which the activity is performed when making decisions about appropriate assistive technology (see Cook, 1994, for a synopsis of the HAAT model).

Throughout this text, we use the Participation Model to discuss assessment and intervention strategies in AAC. First, however, we define and examine basic principles that underlie the Participation Model. These include the need for multiphase assessment and the importance of consensus building.

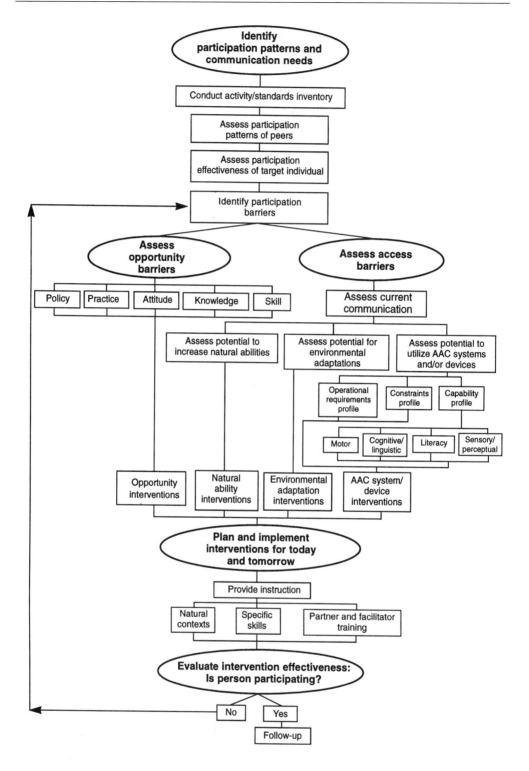

Figure 6.1.   The Participation Model.

Principle 1: Assessment is not a one-time process. Assess to meet today's needs, then tomorrow's, and tomorrow's, and tomorrow's. . . .

PHASES OF AAC ASSESSMENT

AAC interventions are usually ongoing, long-term processes, because the individuals who require them usually are unable to speak or write due to chronic rather than temporary disabilities. The communication problems of these individuals usually persist because of severe physical, cognitive, language, and sensory impairments. Nevertheless, as AAC users mature and age, their communication needs and capabilities often change. Some people experience an expanding world with increased opportunities, whereas others become less able to participate as they age or as their impairments become more severe. Thus, AAC assessment and intervention is a dynamic process and usually consists of three general phases.

Phase I: Initial Assessment for Today

During this phase, the AAC team assesses the individual's current communication interaction needs and physical, cognitive, language, and sensory capabilities so that efforts to support immediate communication interaction and communication can begin. Thus, the goal of initial assessment is to gather information to design an initial intervention to match today's needs and capabilities. These initial AAC interventions usually undergo continuous, subtle refinements as users learn about the operational requirements of their AAC techniques. Gradually, the AAC team develops a basic communication system to facilitate interactions with family members, friends, and other individuals familiar with the AAC user. Beukelman et al. (1985); Blackstone, Cassatt-James, and Bruskin (1988); Culp and Carlisle (1988); Glennen and DeCoste (1997); Goossens' and Crain (1986b); and Musselwhite and St. Louis (1988) reported detailed discussions of useful assessment processes in the initial phase.

Phase II: Detailed Assessment for Tomorrow

The goal of assessing for tomorrow is to develop a communication system that will support the AAC user in a variety of specialized environments, beyond the familiar ones. These environments reflect the individual's lifestyle and may include school, employment, independent living, and recreational and leisure environments. Such settings require basic conversational communication as well as specialized communication that matches the participation requirements of each setting. For example, a child in a classroom must have access to a system that allows academic and educational participation as well as social participation. Similarly, an adult at work might need to write and talk on the telephone as well as to converse with co-workers during breaktimes. Thus, this phase requires careful assessment of the individual's expected participation patterns, as well as assessments to refine the basic communication system to accommodate future participation.

Phase III: Follow-Up Assessment

Follow-up, in general, involves maintaining a comprehensive AAC system that meets the changing capabilities and lifestyle of the individual. Assessment in this phase may involve periodically examining communication equipment to detect replacement and repair needs, assessing the needs and abilities of communication partners and facilitators, and reassessing the capabilities of the AAC user if his or her capabilities change. For individuals whose lifestyles and capabilities are relatively stable, follow-up assessment may occur irregularly and infrequently; for others, such as those with degenerative illnesses, follow-up assessments may be a major part of intervention planning.

IDENTIFY PARTICIPATION PATTERNS AND COMMUNICATION NEEDS

The remainder of this chapter follows the Participation Model flowchart depicted in Figure 6.1. The top part of the model depicts the process for describing the participation patterns and communication needs of the individual, referenced against the participation requirements made of same-age peers without disabilities. The sections that follow describe this process.

> Principle 2: The purpose of an AAC intervention is to facilitate meaningful communication and participation in daily life activities.

Conduct an Activity/Standards Inventory

The assessment of a potential AAC user's participation patterns begins with an Activity/Standards Inventory (see Figure 6.2). All specific daily activities in which the individual must participate, at home, school, work, or other settings, are outlined by the AAC team. Obviously, an individual's specific activities will depend on social, vocational, and educational factors. In any case, it is important at this stage of assessment for team members to reach a consensus regarding the activities included on the Activity/Standards Inventory, because this list will influence the subsequent assessment process and intervention program. Furthermore, if the team cannot reach a consensus about the activities important to a person, it will be very difficult to determine later if the AAC intervention has been effective. (We use the term *standards* throughout this book to refer to standards of performance, and we do not mean to imply that participation standards are based on arbitrary or norm-referenced criteria.)

Assess the Participation Patterns of Peers

The next step of assessment is to determine the participation patterns of peers. The importance of this step varies depending on the individual of concern. For example, if the potential AAC user is a young child or an older adult who participates in few general activities outside of the home, documentation of peer participation may be inappropriate. In most cases, such as with a potential AAC user who participates in educational, vocational training, employment, or residential environments, this step of the assessment is quite important.

Directions:

1. List the *primary and secondary activities* in which peers without disabilities are expected to participate.
2. Select one or more peers without disabilities who are typical in terms of their ability to achieve the expected standards. After observing one of the peers in each activity listed, indicate the *level of peer participation* achieved by entering a *P* in the appropriate category for each activity.
3. After observing the target individual in each activity, indicate the *level of participation* achieved by entering a *T* in the appropriate category for each activity.
4. In the Discrepancy column, indicate *yes* if a participation gap exists for the target individual compared to peers and *no* if a participation gap does not exist.
5. Based on your observations and impressions, indicate if the barrier to participation appears to be related to *opportunity barriers*, *access barriers*, or *both*.

| Activity | Level of peer participation | | | | | Discrepancy | | Type(s) of barrier(s) | |
	Independent	Independent with set-up	Verbal assistance	Physical assistance	Unable to participate	Yes	No	Opportunity	Access
1.									
2.									
3.									
4.									
5.									
6.									

Figure 6.2.   Activity/standards inventory.

151

Again, assessors can use the form in Figure 6.2 to gather and record information. The team should select as a model a peer of the same gender and approximately the same age as the individual, whose participation is representative of the desired performance in a given situation. This may necessitate selecting several peers, depending on the environments involved in the analysis. As team members observe and document participation patterns in each delineated activity, they base performance standards on the following criteria:

- **Independent:** The peer is able to participate in the activity without human assistance.
- **Independent with setup:** The peer is able to participate independently once human assistance has been provided to set up the activity (e.g., art materials are laid out for an individual student, the raw data for an engineering report are compiled for an employee).
- **Verbal assistance:** The peer is able to complete an activity if provided with verbal prompts or instruction (e.g., in an educational setting, it is very common for a teacher or educational aide to prompt students verbally as they work through a new assignment or process).
- **Physical assistance:** The peer is able to participate in an activity if provided with physical assistance (e.g., a parent or a teacher provides hand-over-hand guidance or holds certain materials while the peer completes the activity).
- **Unable to participate:** The peer cannot or does not participate in the activity.

Accurately determining participation patterns of peers is an important step in the AAC assessment process. AAC users, their teachers, co-workers, or family members may at times set unrealistic standards for an activity. For example, a junior high school social studies teacher once indicated to us that a student in her class who had severe cerebral palsy should be prepared to attend class and to discuss the assigned readings during every class. An assessment of the peer participation patterns in the classrooms revealed that few, if any, of the peer students were prepared to discuss the readings daily, and, in fact, some of them were almost never prepared to do so. If the AAC team had accepted the teacher's standard as its goal, they would have placed excessively high expectations on the student with the AAC system. Instead, the teacher, who was a member of the team, agreed to alter her expectations of the target student once she received the results of the peer participation analysis.

Assess the Participation Effectiveness of the Target Individual

When team members have identified participation standards for peer individuals, they can assess and document actual participation patterns of the target individual with the same criteria they used to establish participation standards. The individual may be able to participate in some activities at a level similar to the peer, and in such situations, no participation gap exists. For other activities, however, discrepancies will be evident between the participation level of the peer and that of the individual. Figure 6.2 contains a space to designate whether such a discrepancy exists. In addition, the form encourages a preliminary assessment of the types of barriers to participation in each activity.

Identify Participation Barriers

According to the Participation Model, two types of barriers may result in a failure to participate—those related to opportunity and those related to access. *Opportunity barri-*

ers refer to barriers that are imposed by people other than the individual with the severe communication disorder and that cannot be eliminated simply by providing an AAC system or intervention. For example, an individual may be unable to participate at the desired level because of the attitudes of those around him or her, even though an appropriate AAC system has been provided. Access barriers are present primarily because of limitations in the current capabilities of the individual or his or her immediate support system. For example, an access barrier might occur because there is no AAC system in place or because the vocabulary in the AAC system is outdated. Assessments aimed at identifying the source of barriers to participation are needed in order to formulate effective assessment and intervention strategies for each barrier.

Principle 3: The mere provision of an AAC system is often not enough. Thus, identification of actual or potential opportunity barriers is a critical component of the assessment process.

ASSESS OPPORTUNITY BARRIERS

The AAC team can complete an Opportunity Assessment using the form in Figure 6.3. First, the team can list a summary of the activity inventory in the left column. After making observations in various environments, the assessment team meets to discuss and identify opportunity barriers that might apply to each activity. Team members should consider five types of opportunity barriers (see Figure 6.3) during this assessment process.

Severe-profound students in our school district don't qualify for AAC services until they've reached sensorimotor stage 5. It's the school district policy. (A speech-language pathologist, personal communication, 1989)

Policy Barriers

Policy barriers are the result of legislative or regulatory decisions that govern the situations in which AAC users find themselves. In schools, vocational environments, residential centers, hospitals, rehabilitation centers, and nursing homes, policies are usually outlined in the written documents that govern the agency. In less formal situations, such as the AAC user's family's home, policies may not be written but are nonetheless set by the decision makers (e.g., parents, guardians) in the environment. A wide variety of policies can act as barriers to participation; the following sections describe two of the most prevalent.

Segregation Policies

Many educational agencies and school districts still have policies that segregate students with disabilities into classrooms or facilities that separate them from their peers

154

Directions:
1. List the activities for which potential opportunity barriers have been identified for the target individual.
2. Indicate the nature of the opportunity barrier (e.g., policy, practice, attitude, knowledge, skill).
3. Briefly describe the intervention plan and individual(s) responsible for implementation.

Activity	Opportunity barrier					Intervention plan and individual(s) responsible
	Policy	Practice	Attitude	Knowledge	Skill	
1.						
2.						
3.						
4.						
5.						
6.						

Figure 6.3. Opportunity assessment.

without disabilities. In such situations, by policy, students with disabilities cannot be included in general education classrooms, participate in the school district's general education curriculum, or communicate regularly with peers who do not have disabilities. Furthermore, because many school districts with segregation policies offer such educational programs only in "cluster sites" or special schools, students may be bused to facilities far away from their neighborhoods. This not only limits these students' access to peers without disabilities during the school day, but it also greatly reduces these students' opportunities to make friends in their neighborhoods. The combination of these restrictions severely limits the communication opportunities afforded to students with disabilities. Similar situations can occur in sheltered workshops, segregated group homes or institutions, and in other "disabled-only" settings.

Limited-Use Policies

It is still fairly common for educational agencies to limit the use of AAC systems that are purchased with school district funds. Usually, *limited-use policies* mean that students who use AAC devices in school are not permitted to take them home after school or, in some cases, are not permitted to take them out of the school building for community-based instruction (e.g., vocational training). Thus, by policy, some students cannot use their communication systems during evenings, weekends, holidays, and summer vacations, unless the systems are purchased with nonschool funds. The opportunity barriers to participation imposed by such policies are obvious.

Similarly, limited-use policies may exist in intensive care units (ICUs) that contain complicated and expensive equipment. In order to prevent mechanical or electronic interference with this equipment, some hospitals have stringent policies regarding other types of equipment that patients can bring into ICUs. People with electronic AAC devices may face opportunity barriers in some medical settings due to such policies. This situation may also exist in agencies or nursing homes that serve adult AAC users.

If parents ask that their handicapped child be placed in a general education classroom, we see what we can do. We cross that bridge when we come to it. It's certainly not something that we encourage, but I guess we don't really have a policy against it. (A school administrator, personal communication, 1990)

Practice Barriers

Whereas policy barriers are legislated or regulated procedures, *practice barriers* refer to procedures or conventions that have become common in a family, school, or workplace but are not actual policies. The staff of an agency may think that long-standing practices are legislated policies, but a review of actual agency policies usually reveals that this is not the case. For example, it is a matter of practice in many school districts to restrict the use of district-funded AAC equipment outside the school, although this is not part of "official" district policy. We know of several cases in which school district representatives have told families and staff that such practices are state education department policies, although no such policies existed. The same may be true of the segregation practices of many schools or businesses. In fact, it is illegal in many countries, including the United States, to institute *policies* that prevent students with disabilities from attending general education classes or that prevent workers with disabilities from obtaining competitive employment. Nevertheless, there are often very strong *practices* in place that do not encourage or permit such participation.

Professional practices may also limit participation opportunities for individuals with AAC needs. Early in AAC history, for example, some speech-language pathologists made it their practice not to work with individuals who were unable to speak, believing that this would be inappropriate because they were trained to assist people with speech problems. Since then speech-language pathologists have largely abandoned this practice, although it may still exist within some agencies.

I had just described the summer school program of a young girl who is unable to speak and has cerebral palsy. She has an AAC system, and for 8 weeks during the previous summer she had worked for 3 hours each morning on an intensive literacy program. I explained that the program was designed to assist the student to compete at the third-grade level during the following school year. An experienced special education teacher in the audience raised her hand and indicated that she would never recommend such a summer school program for her students. "Summer is a time for socialization and fun," she said. Then she added, "We don't expect these children to be competitive students, anyway." (D. Beukelman, personal communication, April, 1991)

Attitude Barriers

An attitude barrier occurs when the beliefs held by an individual, rather than an agency or establishment, present a barrier to participation. For example, we were involved in a situation in which a university professor did not want to permit a student with a disability to enroll in his class. The *policy* of the university was clear: People with disabilities who had been admitted to the university were entitled to attend all classes. It was also the *practice* of the university to comply with this policy, even if this meant moving classes to more accessible locations. Nevertheless, an individual professor, because of his *attitude* toward students with disabilities, attempted to set up a barrier. Of course, he was not permitted to maintain this barrier in the face of the actual policies and practices of the institution.

The negative or restrictive attitudes that can form barriers to participation are extensive. Parents, relatives, co-workers, supervisors, professionals, peers, and the general public may hold negative or restrictive attitudes. At times, attitude barriers are quite blatant, but, more often, they are subtle and insidious because most people realize the social unacceptability of such views. The result of most attitude barriers is that family members, professional personnel, and employers have reduced expectations of individuals with disabilities, which in turn results in limited participation opportunities. It is outside the scope of this book to discuss the wide range of attitude barriers that exist. However, assessors should be sensitive to attitudes that may prevent an individual with a severe communication disorder from participating in daily activities.

While we were writing this book, a junior high teacher called us and said that her school district would be enrolling a student with a severe visual impairment at the beginning of the next school year. During a team meeting in preparation for the student's arrival, it became clear that no one in the school knew very much about the technology available for individuals with visual impairments. The teacher was calling because she had volunteered to learn about this technology and identify services that might be of assistance to the team.

Knowledge Barriers

A knowledge barrier refers to a lack of information on the part of someone other than the AAC user that results in limited opportunities for participation. Knowledge barriers may initially seem like attitude barriers because many professionals often have difficulty admitting a lack of knowledge. It is often "easier" to say "I won't" than to say "I can't" or "I don't know how." Regardless, lack of knowledge about AAC intervention options, technology, and instructional strategies often presents tremendous barriers to effective participation by individuals with disabilities. Knowledge barriers on the part of some members of the intervention team are likely to exist at some point during nearly every AAC intervention. One purpose of assessment is to identify these barriers in advance, so that information can be provided in order to eliminate or minimize them.

"Where is Steven's communication device?" I asked. "In the closet," his group home supervisor replied sheepishly. "No one knows how to turn it on since Marge left last year. I guess we should have called sooner, but we were so embarrassed. . . ."

Skill Barriers

Skill barriers occur when, despite even extensive knowledge, supporters have difficulty with the actual implementation of an AAC technique or strategy. For example, we have all had the experience of attending a class, conference, or workshop that was full of good ideas and information and then encountering difficulty putting our newly acquired knowledge into practice at work on Monday morning! Numerous technical and interaction skills are often necessary to assist someone to become a competent communicator. It is important to assess the skill level of individuals who will be responsible for various aspects of the AAC user's intervention plan in order to identify skill impairments and to design interventions to reduce these barriers to communicative competence.

ASSESS BARRIERS TO ACCESS

In the Participation Model (Figure 6.1), *barriers to access* pertain to the capabilities, attitudes, and resource limitations of potential AAC users themselves, rather than to limitations of their societies or support systems. Many types of access barriers can interfere with an individual's participation. Although access barriers related to communication are of primary importance in this book, it is important to remember that access barriers might also be related to lack of mobility, difficulty with manipulation and management of objects, problems with cognitive functions and decision making, and sensory-perceptual impairments (i.e., vision, hearing, or touch impairments). The purpose of assessing AAC access is to identify the nature and extent of the potential AAC user's capabilities as they relate to communication.

Principle 4: Everyone can communicate. Everyone does communicate.

Assess Current Communication

It is important to remember that everyone communicates in some fashion. Thus, the initial step in assessing communication access is to determine the effectiveness and the nature of the individual's current communication system.

Figures 6.4 and 6.5 provide profiles for assessing and documenting the individual's communication techniques. Figure 6.4 helps the AAC team gather information about different communication techniques, because most individuals use a variety of techniques as part of an overall communication package. The assessment of current communication focuses on two aspects of communicative competence: operational and social. Some individuals have a very difficult time using a particular communication technique. For example, a child may be unable to use eye gaze consistently, or an adult with aphasia may be unable to write legibly with a standard pen or pencil. Some individuals, however, may be operationally competent but not socially competent with a specific technique. For example, an individual might be able to operate an electronic communication device but might never use it to initiate interactions. Therefore, when assessing the current communication system, it is necessary to rate both the individual's operational and social competence for each technique currently used.

Figure 6.5 helps the team gather information about what types of messages the individual currently communicates. This form is deliberately open ended, so that the team can supply the communicative functions of interest to the individual. Nevertheless, efforts should be made to compile information in all four of the areas outlined, through observation, interview, or both. A number of excellent assessment instruments that provide more detail are also available in this regard. One such tool is the Communication Matrix (Rowland, 1996), which was designed for use with children or adults who are in the earliest stages of communicative development and can be completed through observations, interviews, and direct elicitation of communicative behaviors. This tool can be used both to gather information about current communication and to assist with intervention planning.

The Communication Matrix (Rowland, 1996) and two copies of the one-page summary profile are available at a low cost from the Oregon Health Sciences University, Center for Self-Determination.

The AAC team can assess the potential of various solutions to the existing communication barriers only after it has described the current communication system and how it is used. One solution might be to help increase the person's natural communication abilities, as the following section discusses briefly.

Directions:
1. List all of the various *techniques* the target individual currently uses to communicate. Examples: natural speech, vocalizations, gestures, body language, manual signs, pointing to a communication board with pictures, eye gaze to photographs, scanning with _____ device, typing on a type-writer, headlight pointing to _____ device.
2. Describe the *body part* used for each technique listed (e.g., both eyes, right hand, left thumb, right side of head).
3. Describe any unique *adaptations* needed for each technique (e.g., must sit on Mom's lap, uses keyguard, needs to have eye-gaze chart held 6 inches from face).
4. After observing use of the technique, rate the person's *operational competence* (1 = poor, 5 = excellent). (Operational competence is the person's ability to use the technique *accurately and efficiently* over time without becoming fatigued.)
5. After observing and interacting with the person, rate his or her *social competence* (1 = poor, 5 = excellent). (Social competence is the person's ability to use the technique in an interactive, socially appropriate manner.)

Technique	Body part	Adaptations	Operational competence					Social competence				
			Poor 1	2	3	4	Excellent 5	Poor 1	2	3	4	Excellent 5
1.												
2.												
3.												
4.												
5.												
6.												

Figure 6.4. Current communication techniques.

	Not at all				Very much		Context-specific comments
Expression of needs and wants							
Overall	1	2	3	4	5	N/A	
Home	1	2	3	4	5	N/A	
School	1	2	3	4	5	N/A	
Work	1	2	3	4	5	N/A	
Other _____	1	2	3	4	5	N/A	
Other _____	1	2	3	4	5	N/A	
Sharing information							
Overall	1	2	3	4	5	N/A	
Home	1	2	3	4	5	N/A	
School	1	2	3	4	5	N/A	
Work	1	2	3	4	5	N/A	
Other _____	1	2	3	4	5	N/A	
Other _____	1	2	3	4	5	N/A	
Social closeness							
Overall	1	2	3	4	5	N/A	
Home	1	2	3	4	5	N/A	
School	1	2	3	4	5	N/A	
Work	1	2	3	4	5	N/A	
Other _____	1	2	3	4	5	N/A	
Other _____	1	2	3	4	5	N/A	
Social etiquette routines							
Overall	1	2	3	4	5	N/A	
Home	1	2	3	4	5	N/A	
School	1	2	3	4	5	N/A	
Work	1	2	3	4	5	N/A	
Other _____	1	2	3	4	5	N/A	
Other _____	1	2	3	4	5	N/A	

Figure 6.5.   Communication interaction effectiveness.

Assess Potential to Use and/or Increase Natural Speech

Many individuals with severe communication disorders demonstrate some ability to communicate using natural speech. Functionally, the effectiveness of natural speech for communicative interaction can be divided into 10 levels, according to the Meaningful Use of Speech Scale (MUSS; Osberger, 1992):

1. Vocalizes during communicative interactions
2. Uses speech to attract others' attention
3. Vocalizations vary with content and intent of messages
4. Is willing to use speech primarily to communicate with familiar people on known topics
5. Is willing to use speech to communicate with unfamiliar people on known topics
6. Is willing to use speech primarily to communicate with familiar people on novel topics or with reduced contextual information
7. Is willing to use speech primarily to communicate with unfamiliar people on novel topics or with reduced contextual information
8. Produces messages understood by people familiar with his or her speech
9. Produces messages understood by people unfamiliar with his or her speech
10. Uses appropriate repair and clarification strategies

The AAC team can assess natural speech by interviewing family members using the MUSS to get an estimate of typical speech usage. Each item is scored on a scale of 0–4, with 0 indicating that the behavior never occurs and 4 indicating that it always occurs. Although the MUSS was designed for use with children with severe hearing impairments, Kent (1993) suggested that it can also be used appropriately with any children who produce speech with reduced intelligibility of any kind. More specific information related to speech intelligibility in children can be obtained through the use of standardized measures such as the Assessment of Phonological Processes–Revised (Hodson, 1986), the Children's Speech Intelligibility Test (Kent, Miolo, & Bloedel, 1992), and the Preschool Speech Intelligibility Measure (Morris, 1995). Adult intelligibility can be assessed with measures such as the Quantitative Rating of Performance (Bross, 1992) and the Sentence Intelligibility Test (Yorkston, Beukelman, & Tice, 1996).

It is important to note that intelligibility, which refers to the adequacy of the acoustic signal to convey information, is affected by many intrinsic factors such as articulation, respiration, phonation, rate of speech, positioning, utterance length, and so forth (Kent, Miolo, & Bloedel, 1994; Yorkston, Strand, & Kennedy, 1996). Typically, intelligibility scores for an AAC user will be either extremely low or widely fluctuating because of the combined influence of these factors. Thus, Yorkston, Strand, et al. (1996) proposed a second, more useful measure, which they refer to as speech *comprehensibility*. This refers to the extent to which a listener can understand an individual's speech in a natural communicative context. It is a measure of the *functionality* of speech that, as many readers already know, can be much better than suggested by the low intelligibility scores of many AAC users.

In response to the need to assess comprehensibility, specialists have developed two assessment tools for clinical use. The first, the Index of Contextual Intelligibility (ICI), was developed for use with adults with severe dysarthria (Hammen, Yorkston, & Dowden, 1991). The second, the Index of Augmented Speech Comprehensibility in Children (I-ASCC), is based on the ICI but was developed for use with children as young as 30 months of age (Dowden, 1997). The structure of these two tools is similar.

Target words from common categories such as "something children eat at snacktime," "things children play with in the bathtub," and "a number less than 11" are identified. The target words are then elicited via speech in the following order: 1) picture cue only (e.g., "What is this?"); 2) picture plus context cue (e.g., "It's a place you might go with your family. What is it?"); and 3) picture plus an embedded model ("It's a shirt. Now you say it."). Assessors tape-record the speech productions of the individual being assessed and then familiar and unfamiliar listeners review the recordings with and without supporting contexts. In the no-context listening task, assessors ask listeners to play the recording of each word twice and then write down what they hear. In the context condition, listeners receive a context cue phrase (e.g., "Something a person might eat for dinner") related to each word and are asked to listen and then write down the word they hear that best fits the context. This assessment is designed specifically to evaluate the extent to which speech is comprehensible under different conditions rather than the degree to which speech is simply intelligible without context. Dowden (1997) provided several illustrative clinical examples of the applicability of such assessment and suggested that it be used primarily to help to determine the effects of speech supplementation strategies on an individual's functional speech, help to resolve disagreement about the need for alternative communication strategies, assist in guiding a team that sees a voice-output device as a quick solution when it might not be, and help clarify the role of speech and alternative strategies with unfamiliar partners in particular.

We observed a young girl who used an electric wheelchair and a communication board that did not have voice output. Educators made an attempt to include this child in a busy preschool classroom in which most of the children did not have disabilities. The teacher was experiencing difficulty during "circle time" as the children gathered around her to discuss the calendar, weather, and the schedule for the day. Because the children without disabilities could move quickly, they would cluster around the teacher, who was seated with her back to a wall. By the time the student with disabilities approached the group with her wheelchair, there was no way for her to make her way through the crowd. Thus, she was always positioned at the back of the class and off to the side, with relatively poor access to instructional materials and few opportunities to communicate. After assessing the communication barrier in this situation, the staff decided to institute a number of environmental adaptations. The teacher began to position herself in the center of the room and had the children sit on a rug in front of her. In this configuration, the student with disabilities was able to drive her wheelchair around the cluster of students and position herself alongside the teacher, close to her peers. This allowed her to use her communication board successfully and to be near the instructional center of the class.

Assess Potential for Environmental Adaptations

Environmental adaptations may be successful and relatively simple solutions to communication access barriers. As previously illustrated, such adaptations may include altering physical spaces or locations or altering physical structures themselves. For example, in the classroom, teachers can lower a blackboard or create a storage area that a student in a wheelchair can reach. School staff can raise or lower desks and tables, create a vertical work surface with a slanted board, or cut out countertops to accommodate wheelchairs or standing frames. Assessment of the need for such adaptations is a common-sense process and teams can almost always conduct such assessments by observation of problematic situations.

Assess Potential to Utilize AAC Systems or Devices

In the Participation Model (Figure 6.1), three assessments determine an individual's ability to use AAC systems or devices in order to reduce access barriers. These include an operational requirements profile, a constraints profile, and a capability profile. We discuss the first two of these profiles in the following section, and the capability profile is discussed in Chapter 7.

Operational Requirements Profile

Often, AAC teams will need to institute either low-tech (nonelectronic) or high-tech (electronic) techniques to reduce existing access barriers to communication. Thus, it is necessary to identify which of the many AAC device options may be appropriate. The first step is for the assessment team to become familiar with the operational requirements of the various AAC techniques. For example, there may be display requirements regarding the size, array, and number of items in the selection set. There are always alternative access system requirements regarding the motor and sensory interface between the individual and the device, so that the individual can operate the device accurately and efficiently. In addition, the output provided by the device may require the individual to have certain skills or abilities. (See Chapters 3 and 4 for descriptions of the operational and learning requirements of many AAC options.)

Principle 5: Technology alone does not make a competent communicator any more than a piano makes a musician or a basketball and a hoop make an athlete.

Constraints Profile

Practical issues, aside from those directly related to potential AAC users and techniques, may influence the selection of an AAC system and the strategies for instruction. The AAC team should identify such constraints early in the assessment process so that subsequent decisions do not conflict with the constraints and so that team members can make efforts to reduce them whenever possible. The most common constraints are those related to user and family preferences, the preferences and attitudes of other communication partners, the abilities of communication partners and facilitators, and funding.

User and Family Preferences

Undoubtedly, the most important constraints that AAC teams must assess are those related to user and family preferences (Blackstone, 1989b; Norris & Belair, 1988). These may include concerns about 1) system portability, durability, and appearance (i.e., cosmesis); 2) time and skills required to learn the system (this may be particularly relevant for manual sign and technology-based approaches); 3) quality and intelligibility of synthetic speech output; and 4) the "naturalness" of the communication exchange achieved through the system. For example, some users and families may prefer to use low-tech AAC approaches (e.g., gestures, alphabet boards) because they believe that these techniques allow greater social closeness and are less cumbersome than electronic devices (Harris, 1982). Others may have strong negative reactions to technological solutions for other reasons, such as the amount of learning time or physical effort that may be required (see Chapter 1). Family members may express hesitation at assuming the extra maintenance of a high-tech system or may be averse to the speech produced by some devices, though increased availability of high-quality speech output has greatly reduced this problem. Although some AAC users may be unable to express their preferences as straightforwardly as others, assessors can often determine preferences by carefully observing the individual's affective, motor, and other behaviors (Campbell, 1989).

It is not at all uncommon to find that family members and potential users do not share the same concerns or preferences. For example, one parent of a child with a communication disorder may be very interested in an electronic AAC option, whereas the other parent may strongly prefer a low-tech approach. The basis for such disagreements may come from a variety of sources. One individual may be more experienced with technology than the other, or one of the parties involved may be lured by the magic of technology, regardless of its appropriateness in a given situation.

Another issue is that potential users and their families may have completely negative attitudes toward using AAC techniques of any kind. This most often occurs in one of three situations. First, the parents of young children may be biased against AAC because they are worried that natural speech will not develop if an alternative option is available. Second, the families of older adults may resist implementing AAC options. For example, it is often very difficult for the spouse and children of an older individual to accept the sudden onset of communication impairments secondary to stroke. In this situation, family members may reject AAC options because they have a strong desire that their spouse or parent regain the use of natural speech. At other times, concerned individuals reject certain electronic options because they just cannot imagine their older relative operating a system that produces artificial speech. Third, individuals may reject AAC options when they are overwhelmed with a medical situation. For example, some individuals do not wish to attempt alternative forms of communication in an ICU, even if they cannot communicate important information because of a temporary absence of speech. It often seems that such individuals simply do not have the cognitive or emotional resources that are needed to acquire basic operational skills in the midst of high levels of existing stress.

In an assessment of constraints, it is important to help potential users and their families identify their preferences and attitudes concerning various AAC options so that AAC teams can consider these during subsequent decision making. Sensitivity and attention through consensus building are critical in an assessment of constraints, even if this means that the final assistive device decision is less than perfect from the perspective of the AAC professionals on the team. After all, it is the AAC user and his or her family who will have to live with whatever decision is made. Failure to consider user and family preferences will almost certainly result in a widespread lament: The individual has this great system/device but hardly ever uses it (Creech, Kissick, Koski, & Musselwhite, 1988)!

Preferences and Attitudes of Other Communication Partners

Less important than user and family preferences, but still of concern, are the technology-related preferences and attitudes of other individuals with whom an AAC user either regularly or occasionally interacts. Several studies have sought to empirically measure the influence of various communication techniques on the perceptions of unfamiliar communication partners. Individuals without disabilities in these studies typically have watched videotapes of interactions between an AAC user and a natural speaker and have rated their perceptions or attitudes along a number of dimensions. For example, one study indicated that college-age young adults had less favorable attitudes about an individual who used a nonelectronic AAC system (i.e., an alphabet board) than one who used an electronic system (i.e., voice-output device), regardless of whether the study participants received written information about the AAC users (Gorenflo & Gorenflo, 1991). People with previous personal exposure to AAC users have displayed the opposite preference pattern, however, preferring low-tech devices because they allowed more active involvement in the communication process (Mathy-Laikko & Coxson, 1984). In another study, children who attended inclusive elementary schools (i.e., schools attended by students both with and without disabilities) rated videotaped scenes of a peer using aided electronic, aided nonelectronic, and unaided (i.e., manual sign) systems (Blockberger, Armstrong, O'Connor, & Freeman, 1990). The results indicated that, regardless of the type of system used by the target peer, fourth-grade children gave similar estimates of her chronological age and school grade and responded similarly (and, in general, positively) to an attitude measure of social acceptability. In a related study, fifth graders from four different schools—two that were inclusive and two that were not—viewed videotapes of a child using an alphabet board or an electronic device in conversational interactions with an adult (Beck & Dennis, 1996). Students from the inclusive schools had more positive attitudes about the child with disabilities than those from the noninclusive schools, but there were no differences related to the AAC system used. From these studies, it appears that children are less influenced by the type of AAC system than are adults, although additional research is needed to clarify this issue. In addition, information about attitudes of communication partners from various cultural, ethnic, and socioeconomic backgrounds is needed in order to consider these preferences realistically and sensitively.

Abilities of Communication Partners and Facilitators

It is essential for the AAC team to assess the general abilities of potential communication partners because it is imperative that they are able to understand the messages conveyed through a communication system. For example, if unfamiliar listeners cannot readily understand the system output, as may be the case with manual signs or low-quality synthetic speech, frequent communication breakdowns will occur (see Chapter 4). Other constraints that may guide the selection of one system over another are the ages and literacy skills of potential partners and other display-related issues. At present, common-sense considerations such as these guide the assessment of partner abilities, because the field has accumulated little empirical research investigating the impact of such issues on AAC system use.

Partners affect communication in other ways as well. Literature in the AAC field abounds with empirical studies of interactions among users and partners. These studies clearly indicate that the skills of partners are at least as critical as those of users in creating successful communicative exchanges (e.g., Higginbotham, Mathy-Laikko, & Yoder, 1988; Kraat, 1985). Facilitators who provide extensive support to AAC users by virtue of either their familial or professional connections play a unique role during initial and long-term intervention. The knowledge and skills of these individuals frequently must exceed those needed to interact with natural speakers. For example, it is not uncommon to find that facilitators are operationally competent in the programming, use, and maintenance of the user's electronic AAC device. Facilitators must also demonstrate social and strategic competence with AAC techniques in order to provide good models and instruction to the users they support. For these reasons, lack of adequate facilitator skills may place constraints on the intervention selected, simply because the necessary, ongoing expertise is unavailable. Failure to specifically consider adequate facilitator skills in the assessment process will almost always result in implementation failure later on; this is especially true for more demanding high-tech devices.

Unfortunately, few assessment tools for evaluating the capabilities of potential facilitators are in widespread use. One exception is a Partner Rating Scale designed by Culp and Carlisle (1988) that assessors can use to evaluate facilitator attitudes and knowledge concerning AAC techniques. Figure 6.6 contains selected items from the Partner Rating Scale. In the absence of a wide variety of assessment instruments, the AAC team must evaluate facilitator expertise more informally.

Funding

The funding of AAC technology and intervention services is a complex process within and across countries. As the AAC field has moved into the public policy phase of devel-

---

Directions:
The partner is asked to use the following scale to respond to all questions:
   Strongly disagree, disagree, neutral, agree, strongly agree

1. I like _____ (AAC user's name) to use his or her _____ (augmentative technique).

2. Other people like _____ (AAC user's name) to use _____ (augmentative technique).

3. I feel good about the way _____ (AAC user's name) uses _____ (augmentative technique).

4. I think it is important for _____ (AAC user's name) to use _____ (augmentative technique).

5. I understand how to use _____ (AAC user's name)'s _____ (augmentative technique).

6. When using _____ (augmentative technique), _____ (AAC user's name) can say most things he or she wants to say.

7. When _____ (AAC user's name) uses _____ (augmentative technique), he or she can make most people understand.

8. Using the _____ (augmentative technique) may improve _____ (AAC user's name)'s speech.

9. The rewards for using _____ (augmentative technique) justify my efforts to do so.

10. _____ (AAC user's name)'s present augmentative technique(s) suits his or her current needs and abilities.

Figure 6.6.   Selected items from the Partner Rating Scale (based on Culp & Carlisle, 1988).

opment, the funding base to cover AAC services and equipment has shifted and expanded. In some countries with nationalized (i.e., centralized) health and social service systems such as Australia, Canada, Sweden, and the United Kingdom, the shift to a public policy phase has resulted in the inclusion of new groups of people eligible to receive support for AAC services and the development of service delivery capacities to meet the needs of these individuals. In such instances, increased funding support has generally accompanied the authorization of new service delivery programs, although this is not always the case.

In contrast, in countries with decentralized or individualized health and social programs, funding patterns are more difficult to summarize because they are so diverse. Thus, it is impossible to cover this topic adequately in this book. For detailed information related to funding in the United States, see *Assistive Technologies: A Funding Workbook* by Morris and Golinker (1991) as well as additional discussions by Cook and Hussey (1995), Ourand and Gray (1997), and Wallace (1995). In addition, readers in the United States can find out how to contact the Assistive Technology Center in their state by accessing the World Wide Web site at http://www.asel.udel.edu/at-online/pro grams/tech_act.

It may be helpful to develop a funding profile for an individual AAC user by using the Personal Funding Worksheet contained in Figure 6.7 when attempting to locate AAC funding in a decentralized system. The Personal Funding Worksheet contains intervention activities and potential funding sources for each activity. AAC teams can use this tool to develop a funding strategy that accommodates individual AAC users' ages and available support services. Two examples follow.

First, consider a kindergarten-age child in a school district with an AAC program. In this case, the school district will probably manage AAC referral. The district will also fund assessment and evaluation, which school district personnel will conduct, perhaps with the assistance of a consultant. In difficult cases, the school district might refer a child to a regional specialty center and assume the costs of referral. The district will probably fund any resulting AAC prescription and report as part of the evaluation process. The district, however, may or may not support the actual procurement of necessary equipment. If it does not, AAC teams will need to approach health insurance, social service, or other agencies for funding support in this area. Finally, school district personnel will probably deliver intervention training for the student, although it would not be uncommon for the school district to enlist a consultant to prepare school staff to provide this training.

Now consider a 45-year-old individual with ALS. In this case, the individual, a family member, or the primary physician will probably make the referral for services. A regional specialty center or a professional in private practice will probably conduct the assessment, evaluation, and prescription of an AAC program. The individual's health insurance company or a social agency will probably pay for these services, at least in part. Individuals who do not have such support may need to use personal finances or obtain community support. These adults may have difficulty purchasing needed technical equipment, because there may be no social agency responsible paying for their equipment. The person's health insurance company may or may not support the purchase of equipment, depending on a variety of factors. If an insurance agency rejects a funding request, it may be necessary to prepare an appeal or to enlist the assistance of a social agency. As a last resort, the family may need to seek community funding of some type for the AAC equipment. Similarly, funding for intervention training may or may not be covered by insurance or social agencies. Thus, such support may simply be lacking, or it may have to be paid for with private funds.

Funding source	AAC intervention activities			
	Assessment prescription	Equipment purchase	System personalization	Instruction and follow-up
Adoption/foster care agency				
Adult services agency				
Community organizations				
Disability organizations				
Employer				
Legal settlement				
Long-term disability insurance				
Medicaid				
Medicare				
Parent/family/self				
Private health insurance				
School				
State agency				
Vocational rehabilitation				
Other (specify)				

Figure 6.7.   Personal Funding Worksheet.

As is obvious from this discussion, patterns of funding vary tremendously from individual to individual. We recommend the following general steps to develop a funding strategy for an individual within a decentralized funding system:

1. Survey the funding resources that are potentially available to the individual.
2. Identify potential funding sources for the various activities in an AAC intervention (see Figure 6.7).
3. Prepare a funding plan with the AAC user and family members.
4. Assign responsibility to specific individual(s) for pursuing funding for each aspect of the AAC intervention.
5. Prepare necessary documentation for the funding request. Be sure to make all requests in writing so a written record is available if an appeal is necessary.
6. If the initial request is denied, appeal (with the AAC user's permission) for reconsideration, or identify new funding sources.
7. Proceed to a hearing (with the AAC user's permission) if appeals are denied, or identify new funding sources.

Despite careful planning, families and potential users may have to wait to receive services while funding is sought (Beukelman, Yorkston, & Smith, 1985). Similarly, after the AAC team has completed assessment and made assistive device decisions, an AAC user may face a lengthy wait while additional third-party payment for the device is secured. Unless private funds are readily accessible, the "least dangerous assumption" (Donnellan, 1984, p. 141) with regard to funding is that such time lags will occur. Therefore, the AAC team must plan during assessment to 1) institute an interim system or device; 2) seek minor funding for equipment rental, which itself may take considerable time to obtain; 3) use an equipment loan service if one is available; and/or 4) arrive at some other creative solution to circumvent this constraint. In the United States, federal funds available in response to the Americans with Disabilities Act (ADA) of 1990, PL 101-336, and the Technology-Related Assistance for Individuals with Disabilities Act of 1988, PL 100-407, should allow states to develop cohesive and coordinated interagency plans for funding AAC devices and systems.

7

Assessment of Specific Capabilities

OVERVIEW OF APPROACHES TO CAPABILITY ASSESSMENT

Capability assessment is the process of gathering information about an individual's capabilities in a variety of areas in order to determine appropriate augmentative and alternative communication (AAC) options. In this chapter, we present some general principles and procedures for constructing a capability profile. In Chapters 9–18, we review additional capability assessment considerations for people with various disabilities.

According to Yorkston and Karlan (1986), capability assessment involves identifying an individual's level of performance in critical areas that pertain to AAC intervention, such as cognition, language, literacy, and fine motor control. An assessment should result in a profile of the individual's capabilities that can be matched to the operational requirements of particular AAC options. One of the characteristics of a capability profile is that it emphasizes an individual's strengths and unique skills rather than his or her impairments. A "strengths" approach is critical to the endeavor because the assessor will match these strengths to one or more AAC techniques. In general, the AAC team might consider two or three approaches to capability profiling.

Principle 1: A primary purpose of AAC capability assessment is to identify strengths and abilities, not weaknesses and impairments.

Maximal Assessment

Most AAC specialists have been trained in a maximal, or comprehensive, assessment approach. The goal of this approach is to construct a comprehensive profile of, for example, an individual's receptive language level, reading level, and motoric capabilities. Examples of broad-based comprehensive assessment tools include the Comprehensive Screening Tool for Determining Optimal Communication Mode (House & Rogerson, 1984) and the Non-Speech Test (Huer, 1983).

Maximal assessment is a time-consuming process for both the individual with AAC and his or her professional staff. Such an assessment often yields a great deal of information about the person's capabilities, but the professional uses only a small portion of this information to make AAC intervention decisions. For these reasons, maximal assessment strategies are often unnecessary and impractical for AAC applications and have been replaced by criteria-based assessment.

Criteria-Based Assessment

AAC specialists use criteria-based assessment to determine whether an individual meets the performance thresholds necessary for successful implementation of specific communication techniques or devices. The Non-Oral Communication Assessment (Fell, Lynn, & Morrison, 1984) and the Assessment for Non-Oral Communication (Mills & Higgins, 1983) are representative of criteria-based assessment packages. Yorkston and Karlan described this approach in detail:

> The team frequently has at its disposal some basic information regarding the individual. This information is usually obtained through a screening procedure that may involve a survey of the broad areas of cognitive and language function, hearing, and speech as well as environmental factors. Based on this screening, a decision is generally made not to conduct a comprehensive assessment. For example, when the goal of assessment is to select a portable writing/text editing system for an individual who has successfully attended a community college, in-depth assessment to identify the specific grade level in spelling or grammatical composition may not be necessary.
>
> The criteria-based assessment approach is used to expedite assessment because it is based on a series of branching decisions that allow the team to exclude a large number of possible questions and proceed to critical decisions. For example, when selecting the most appropriate interface by which an individual can access an AAC device, one of the first questions asked is, "Can this individual access the aid in a direct selection mode?" If the answer is no, then a number of scanning options are explored in more detail. However, if the answer is yes, then a large number of scanning options are eliminated from consideration, and attention is focused on selecting the most appropriate direct selection option. (1986, pp. 175–176)

From this description, it should be clear that criteria-based assessment requires the professionals involved in the process to work together when gathering information and making decisions.

Predictive Assessment or Feature Matching

Several authors have suggested predictive profiling or "feature matching" as an extension of the criteria-based approach (Costello & Shane, 1994; Glennen, 1997; Yorkston & Karlan, 1986). In the predictive assessment approach, the team first assesses the capabilities of the individual using a number of carefully selected tasks. Based on this initial assessment, the AAC team predicts the efficiency with which the individual might utilize one or more devices or techniques. The team then uses its predictions to set up a "trial" of the selected AAC system for a designated period of time (e.g., from a few weeks to several months, depending on the technique involved). Feature matching requires that AAC team members be knowledgeable about the operational and learning requirements of a wide variety of AAC options. If the team does not use predictive profiling, it is often necessary to have many AAC options available at the time of the assessment or later so that members can complete successive trials with each device. In many settings, such equipment availability is simply impossible. When the team has decided which capability assessment approach it will use, its specific assessment strategies will then depend on the individual's age, disability, and other factors, as described in the remainder of this chapter.

LIMITATIONS OF NORM-REFERENCED STANDARDIZED TESTS

Many professionals in fields such as psychology, education, and speech-language pathology have been trained to use norm-referenced tests designed to compare an individual's abilities with those of same-age peers. These professionals may be frustrated when they attempt to evaluate people who require AAC systems because they cannot administer the norm-referenced tests in a standardized manner. For example, the assessor cannot use tests that require verbal responses if the individual is unable to speak. Tests that require object manipulation may be useless for assessing people who have upper-extremity impairments. Even instruments that incorporate multiple-choice formats, which are useful in assessing people with limited speech and motor abilities, can present difficulties because individuals may not be able to complete the tests within standard time limitations.

Fortunately, AAC assessment rarely requires that professionals administer norm-referenced tests in a standardized manner because the purpose of the assessment is not to compare the individual with peers of the same age. Thus, many professionals perform AAC assessments with norm-referenced tests that contain appropriate content; they simply modify the tests to obtain capability or predictive profiling information. For example, some individuals may require response options to be presented in a yes/no format instead of an open-ended format or multiple-choice array. Many formal language assessment instruments can be adapted for use with people who have upper-extremity impairments and need to use eye gaze or alternative techniques to respond (for adaptations see Bigge, 1991; Goossens' & Crain, 1986b; Johnson-Martin, Wolters, & Sowers, 1987; and Wasson, Tynan, & Gardiner, 1982).

Although standardized tests usually are not necessary for AAC assessment, there are certainly situations in which educational or similar agencies require the administration of standardized tests to verify an individual's eligibility for services. Verification testing is one of the most frustrating aspects of agency policy and practice for those who serve people with severe communication disorders. Frequently, agencies simply cannot administer tests in a standardized fashion to AAC users, and, as a result, people with AAC systems may not receive services. The AAC team may need to address the problem of verification testing, which is an excellent example of a policy and practice issue that can become a barrier to communication opportunities. Professionals, AAC users, their families, and involved individuals may need to advocate to change such policies or practices so that service availability is not limited by such a barrier.

Principle 2: Address seating and positioning concerns before finalizing motor access assessment.

ASSESS POSITIONING AND SEATING

Assessment of positioning and seating is critical for individuals with a range of motor impairments. People with disabilities that severely restrict movement (e.g., cerebral palsy, spinal cord injury, amyotrophic lateral sclerosis [ALS]) may spend the majority of the day in a seated position; therefore, they need to be able to do so safely and without sacrificing functional communicative effectiveness. Other individuals may have more subtle motor impairments that affect their concentration, range of movement, and ability to use AAC functionally in a variety of positions. Consequently, it is important to consult with clinicians such as physical and occupational therapists, who specialize in motor control and can aid in assessing seating and positioning, as an initial step toward capability assessment in general. In that spirit, we welcome the contributions of Donna Drynan, an occupational therapist from the Sunny Hill Health Centre for Children in Vancouver, British Columbia, Canada, who assisted us with developing this section on seating and positioning.

Neuromotor Impairments

Several types of neurological and motor impairments can affect positioning and movement. Some individuals have increased or decreased *muscle tone,* which refers to the "degree of vigor or tension in skeletal muscles" (Fraser, Hensinger, & Phelps, 1990, p. 279). Too much tone makes voluntary movement difficult, whereas too little tone creates problems with maintaining posture, balance, and strength. Many individuals have high tone in their extremities and low tone in their trunk area and, therefore, may experience all of the above problems, depending on the task at hand. Efficient use of AAC devices necessitates adapting to compensate for these difficulties.

Other problems can result from the presence of *primitive reflexes,* involuntary muscle responses that are present in typically developing infants but disappear as they grow and mature. For example, you may have noticed that, if you stroke an infant's cheek, the child will turn his or her head and open his or her mouth to that side. This response is the *rooting reflex,* which usually disappears within the first few months of life. If the reflex persists it can interfere with voluntary head control, especially during meals (Orelove & Sobsey, 1996).

Other reflex patterns, such as the asymmetrical tonic neck reflex (ATNR), can affect the motor control needed for the use of switches or other adaptive devices. ATNR usually disappears by the time the infant is 6 months of age. It is activated when the infant's head is turned to the side, causing the child to extend the arm and leg on the same side to which his or her face is turned and also prompting the flexion of the infant's arm and leg on the opposite side (see Figure 7.1a). Once the reflex has been activated, many individuals become "stuck" in the abnormal motor pattern and are unable to resume a mid-line position without assistance. Therefore, AAC systems for individuals who exhibit ATNR should be designed to prevent the need for head rotation to scan a display because once the person's head is turned, he or she will be unable to use the arm on that side for direct selection (see Figure 7.1b, c). Similarly, the AAC team should place switches that are manually activated toward the mid-line of the body, rather than off to the side, and should also move them away from the head altogether, if possible (see Figure 7.1d, e).

Another common reflex pattern is the symmetrical tonic neck reflex (STNR), which occurs in response to either extension or flexion of the neck. When the individual's neck

Figure 7.1.   a) Asymmetrical tonic neck reflex (ATNR); b) facilitator and/or augmentative and alternative commu-nication (AAC) display should not be placed to the side; c) mid-line placement of the facilitator and/or AAC dis-play is preferred; d) switches should not be placed to the side; e) mid-line placement of switches is preferred. (From Goossens', C., & Crain, S. (1992). *Utilizing switch interfaces with children who are severely physically chal-lenged* (pp. 40, 43, 44). Austin, TX: PRO-ED; reprinted by permission.)

flexes (i.e., bends forward), STNR prompts flexion of the arms at the elbows and extension of the hips (see Figure 7.2a). The opposite occurs when his or her neck extends (i.e., moves backward): The individual's arms extend outward and his or her hips flex (see Figure 7.2b). Again, the individual often becomes "stuck" in the reflex position and requires assistance to resume a functional position. Because STNR interferes with the individual's functional use of his or her arms, its presence affects AAC motor access. To avoid triggering the reflex, individuals with strong STNR responses should not use displays or switches that are oriented horizontally (e.g., on a desk); instead, they should use displays that are oriented vertically (see Figure 7.2c, d). Similarly, people interacting with the individuals should not approach them from above (see Figure 7.2e) but should approach them at eye level (see Figure 7.2f).

Some individuals also have *skeletal deformities* that affect various aspects of positioning. Two common examples include scoliosis (lateral curvature of the spine), which can affect upright posture as well as comfort, and the windswept position of the hip (i.e., hip dislocation, pelvic rotation, and scoliosis), which affects sitting balance and posture. Prevention of such conditions is of primary importance, but if they have already developed in the individual and are fixed, the professional AAC staff will need to compensate for the resulting difficulties.

Finally, *movement disorders* such as athetosis, which is characterized by involuntary movements of the face and limbs during muscle activation, are common in people with certain types of brain lesions. These individuals may not have sufficient control of their upper extremities to be able to write or point to symbols on a display, and as a result they may need to use switches to activate AAC devices.

Principles and Techniques

Most individuals with neuromotor impairments are likely to use their AAC devices while in a seated position—in a wheelchair, at a school or work desk, or at home. It is possible to grossly underestimate an individual's capabilities if he or she is not properly positioned and supported in a seated position. Improper positioning and inadequate physical support can affect a person's fatigue and comfort levels, emotional state, and ability to move and attend to a task. Therefore, the first step in an assessment should involve optimizing the individual's positioning so that the AAC team can assess cognitive, language, and motor capabilities. This does not mean that the team should delay all AAC assessments until the optimum wheelchair or seating insert has been developed to improve an individual's posture. Rather, it means that the team members who are experts at evaluating physical posture and control should be prepared to at least temporarily position the individual so that they can complete an appropriate physical functional assessment. Over time, a comprehensive assessment of the individual's seating and positioning needs should be completed so that solutions for the individual's postural and movement difficulties can be implemented as part of the AAC intervention.

Ideally, a symmetrical seated position should be the goal; however, this will not be possible for many individuals with severe neuromotor impairments, especially those with fixed deformities. A number of principles should guide the assessment of (and the later design of supports for) positioning and seating. These principles, adapted from Radell (1997) and York and Weimann (1991), include the following.

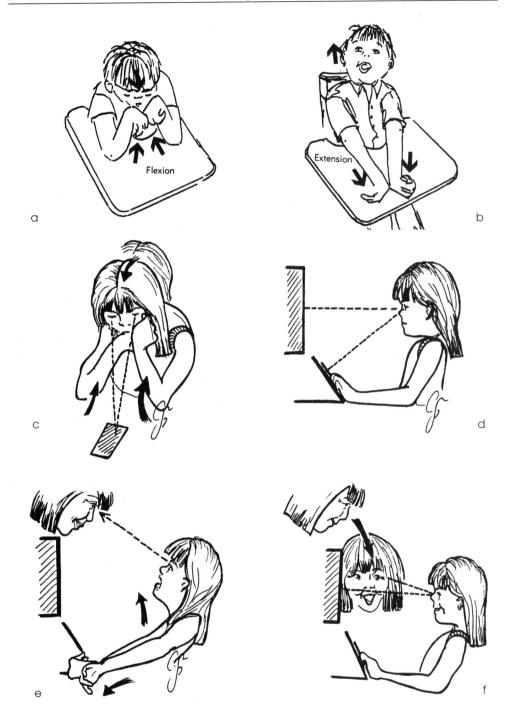

Figure 7.2. a) Symmetrical tonic neck reflex (STNR) in response to neck flexion; b) STNR in response to neck extension; c) horizontal placement of AAC display and/or switches may activate STNR; d) augmentative and alternative communication (AAC) display should be placed at eye level and switches should be aligned vertically; e) approaching from above may activate STNR; f) facilitator should approach the user at eye level. (From Goossens', C., & Crain, S. (1992). *Utilizing switch interfaces with children who are severely physically challenged* (pp. 40, 43, 44). Austin, TX: PRO-ED; reprinted by permission.)

1. **Use yourself as a reference.** Almost automatically, people without disabilities position themselves for comfort, stability, and functional movement during tasks. Therefore, in evaluating the position of a person with motor impairments, using yourself as a reference is usually a good idea. The process of using yourself as a reference involves engaging in a task (e.g., activating a switch, using a keyboard) and asking yourself questions such as "How would I position myself for this task?" "How would I align my trunk?" and "How would I position my head, arms, and legs?" The answers can then be used as guidelines to optimize positioning for the individual who is being assessed.

2. **Obtain a stable base of support.** It is impossible for a person to move in functional ways if his or her trunk and extremities are not sufficiently stable. For instance, if you place a piece of paper on a table and try writing without resting your forearms on the table surface, you will probably find the task fairly difficult. This is because the forearms stabilize the arms, shoulders, upper trunk, and wrists; so, in order to use any of these, the forearms must be supported. Similarly, the feet stabilize the lower part of the body and the trunk, which is why it is difficult to sit for long periods of time without resting your feet on the floor. For the individual undergoing AAC assessment, this stability can be achieved through the use of seat belts, bars, harnesses, lap trays, and other adaptive devices designed for static positioning (see Figures 7.3–7.5).

3. **Decrease the influence of atypical muscle tone.** An individual with low muscle tone often requires external supports to achieve a proper seated position for AAC assessment. For example, a person who cannot keep his or her head in an upright position may need a headrest or neckrest, either temporarily or permanently. Individuals with high muscle tone (i.e., spasticity) require the careful positioning of AAC displays, switches, and other assistive devices to avoid triggering reflex patterns and to maximize their ease of movement. Often, professionals use a trial-and-error approach to identify the position(s) that allows the individual to have the most functional movement.

4. **Accommodate fixed deformities and correct flexible deformities.** As noted previously, the ideal seated position is one that is symmetrical and stable. By applying the first principle ("use yourself as a reference"), AAC team members can correct most flexible deformities through the appropriate use of positioning devices. In many cases, fixed deformities may prevent the attainment of symmetry, and the individual may require accommodations to maintain residual movement, maximize comfort, decrease fatigue, and minimize the effort required for movement. For example, an individual with severe scoliosis or other deformities may be unable to sit in an upright position and the team will need to utilize either temporary or permanent supports to achieve alignment in as functional a position as possible (McEwen & Lloyd, 1990).

5. **Provide the least amount of intervention needed to achieve the greatest level of function.** It is important that the individual not be so rigidly supported in a seated position that he or she is unable to move. As the person's center of gravity changes with upper-body shifting (e.g., leaning forward, reaching, leaning back), his or her feet and arms must be free to move and compensate. In addition, most people both enjoy and need to assume a variety of positions throughout the day.

Several general procedures are usually involved in the assessment of positioning and seating that is related to AAC use (Cook & Hussey, 1995; McEwen & Lloyd, 1990; Radell, 1997; York & Weimann, 1991). First, the AAC team should observe the individual in his or her wheelchair or while he or she is seated in a standard chair. If the per-

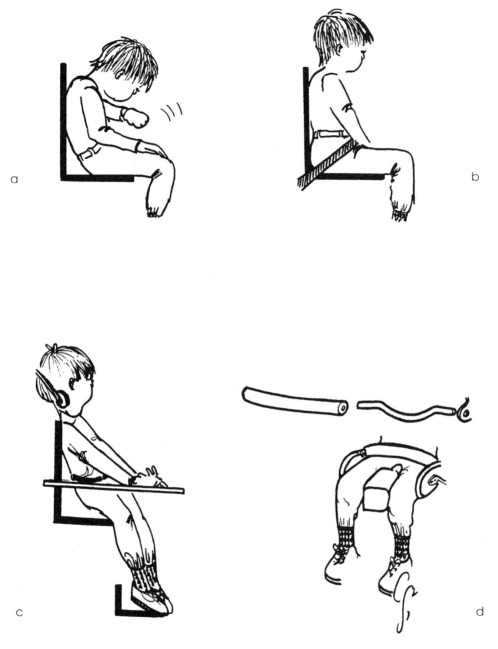

Figure 7.3. a) Poor positioning in a chair; b) good positioning with pelvis back in the chair and stabilized with a seat belt at a 45° angle across the hips; c) extensor thrust with hips extended and buttocks raised off the seat; d) subasis bar in place (rigid pelvic restraint used to stabilize the pelvis and prevent extensor thrust), with two variations shown. (From Goossens', C., & Crain, S. (1992). *Utilizing switch interfaces with children who are severely physically challenged* (p. 26). Austin, TX: PRO-ED; reprinted by permission.)

son's hips have slid down in the chair, the team should lift the individual so that his or her pelvis is centered on the back edge of the seat or on a custom insert. The person's feet and arms should be supported as needed for proper alignment and movement, and so forth. If the person is likely to use an AAC device frequently in other positions,

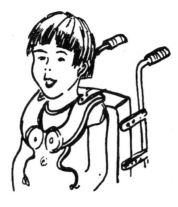

a

b

c

Figure 7.4.   Devices used for trunk and shoulder stability. a) Butterfly harness; b) Danmar harness; c) shoulder retractors. (From Goossens', C., & Crain, S. (1992). *Utilizing switch interfaces with children who are severely physically challenged* (p. 32). Austin, TX: PRO-ED; reprinted by permission.)

the team should observe the individual in these other situations as well. Second, if the person cannot assume or maintain a proper seated position independently, the AAC team should provide assistance in this regard while allowing as much participation by the individual as possible. The assessor(s) should provide firm support to allow the person to achieve a stable and well-aligned position on his or her chair, beginning with his or her pelvis, which provides the base of support and therefore must be stable. Next, the AAC team should position the individual's lower extremities, followed by his or her trunk, upper extremities, head, and neck. In effect, the support provided by the hands of the team members simulates the type of support that might be sought through the use of assistive equipment. Third, the team should help the person under observation move out of the chair (if possible) so that team members can take note of the seat, back angles, and any adaptations already in place (e.g., a contoured seat back). Fourth, the staff should assess the individual while he or she is out of the chair, looking for any deformities, pressure sores, contractures (i.e., shortening of certain muscle groups), and other physical problems.

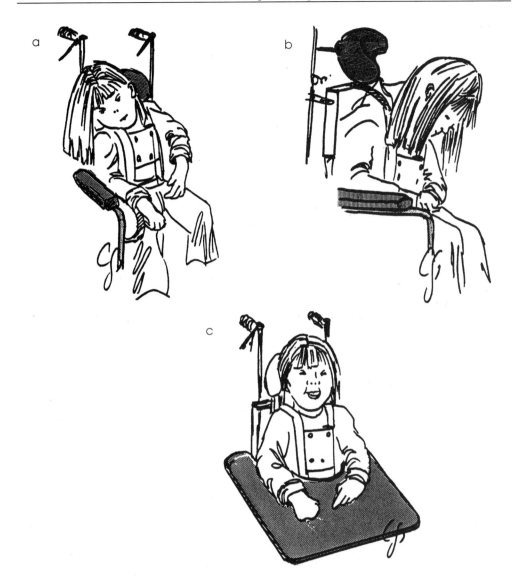

Figure 7.5.   a, b) Without a lap tray, the head and arms are unstable; c) the lap tray provides trunk, shoulder, neck, and head stability. (From Goossens', C., & Crain, S. (1992). *Utilizing switch interfaces with children who are severely physically challenged* (p. 36). Austin, TX: PRO-ED; reprinted by permission.)

Once the AAC team has completed its observations, temporary changes can be implemented to improve the individual's positioning. Table 7.1 summarizes the elements of an optimal seated position, although not all of these elements may be attainable for every individual. After the team has properly positioned the person's pelvis, hips, and thighs and secured them to create a stable base, his or her trunk, upper extremities, lower extremities, head, and neck can also be supported. Rolled towels, foam inserts, heavy cardboard supports, temporary splints, Velcro straps, blocks, and other nonpermanent materials can serve as "mock-ups" for any supports that will eventually need to be custom made. The goal at this stage is simply to optimize positioning so that assessment of the motor skills necessary for AAC use can proceed. Over time, a variety of permanent supports may be needed to ensure that the individual has the efficiency and

Table 7.1.   Elements of an optimal seated position

Ideally, the **pelvis, hips, and thighs** should be positioned so that
- The sitting bones (i.e., ischial tuberosities) bear equal weight
- The pelvis is tilted slightly forward or in a neutral position
- The pelvis is centered in the back edge of seat
- The pelvis is not rotated forward on one side
- The hips are flexed to 90°
- The pelvis is secured to the chair with a belt at a 45° angle across the hips (not across the abdomen)
- The thighs are equal in length
- The thighs are slightly abducted (apart)

Ideally, the **trunk** should be positioned so that it is
- Symmetrical, not curved to the side
- Curved slightly at the low back
- Upright or leaning forward slightly

Ideally, the **shoulders, arms, and hands** should be positioned so that
- The shoulders are in a relaxed, neutral position (not hunched up or hanging low)
- The upper arms are flexed slightly forward
- The elbows are flexed in mid-range (about 90°)
- The forearms rest on a tray for support, if necessary to maintain alignment
- The forearms are neutral or rotated downward slightly
- The wrists are neutral or slightly extended
- The hands are relaxed, with fingers and thumbs opened

Ideally, the **legs, feet, and ankles** should be positioned so that
- The knees are flexed to 90°
- The feet are aligned directly below or posterior to the knees
- The ankles are flexed to 90°
- The feet are supported on a footrest
- The heels and balls of the feet bear weight
- The feet and toes face forward
- The feet can be moved backward behind the knees when the upper body moves forward (i.e., no straps or other restrictive devices unless needed)

Ideally, the **head and neck** should be positioned so that
- They are oriented toward the mid-line of the body
- The chin is slightly tucked (i.e., the back of the neck is elongated)

From York, J., & Weimann, G. (1991). Accommodating severe physical disabilities. In J. Reichle, J. York, & J. Sigafoos (Eds.), *Implementing augmentative and alternative communication: Strategies for learners with severe disabilities* (p. 247). Baltimore: Paul H. Brookes Publishing Co.; adapted by permission.

accuracy of movement needed for communication in a seated position. These permanent supports may be relatively simple in nature, such as floor sitters or seating orthoses that support children while they are seated on the floor, in the bathtub, or on other horizontal surfaces (see Figure 7.6). The supports can also be quite sophisticated, including those used to stabilize and align the pelvis, trunk, hips, thighs, legs, shoulders, and/or head. Figures 7.7–7.9 depict some of the most common permanent components used to support seating.

Principle 3: The goal of motor assessment in AAC is to discover motor capabilities, not to describe motor problems.

Figure 7.6.   Floor sitter. (From Sunny Hill Health Centre for Children, Ministry of Health, and Ministry Responsible for Seniors. (1992). *A conceptual model of practice for school system therapists* (p. 56). Vancouver, British Columbia, Canada: Author; reprinted by permission.)

ASSESS MOTOR CAPABILITIES

As was the case with assessment of seating and positioning, the involvement of physical and/or occupational therapists in the assessment of motor access is critical for individuals with severe motor impairments. There are two related motor assessment concerns: identifying a motor technique that the individual can use during the assessment process and identifying a technique that the individual can use for alternative access in the long term. (At this point, readers might wish to review the alternative access options presented in Chapter 4.) These two concerns might result in the selection of the same motor technique for both the assessment and for long-term access, or the team might choose two techniques that are quite different, depending on the AAC user.

Identification of Motor Skills for Assessment

The AAC assessment process requires identification of a number of cognitive, symbolic, language, literacy, and other skills related to communication. Therefore, whoever is involved in the assessment must ensure that the individual has a reliable and reasonably efficient way to answer questions and provide other information. The means of communication will need to be a direct selection technique because scanning appears to add cognitive difficulty to tasks (Ratcliff, 1994; Szeto, Allen, & Littrell, 1993), at least when the array has more than 40 items (Mizuko, Reichle, Ratcliff, & Esser, 1994). In addition, Glennen (1997) noted that when the team uses scanning for initial assessment it is difficult to determine the source of errors—the individual may not understand how scanning works, may not be able to access the switch in time to select a correct response, may have forgotten the question while waiting for the scanning cursor to move

Posterior Shoulder Support

Lateral Thoracic Support

Lumbar Support

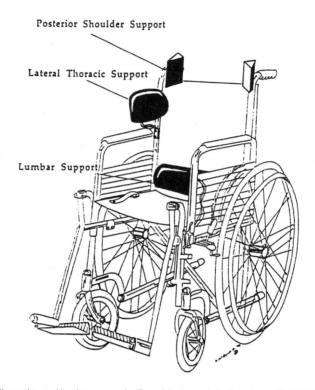

Figure 7.7.   Shoulder, thoracic, and lumbar supports. (From Medhat, M.A., & Hobson, D. (1992). *Standardization of terminology and descriptive methods for specialized seating: A reference manual* (p. 26). Washington, DC: RESNA Press; reprinted by permission.)

to the correct answer, or simply may not know the answer! For these reasons, choosing one of the direct selection options is important, at least during assessment.

Temporary assessment of a direct selection technique can be quite straightforward and usually begins with assessment of the person's ability to answer yes/no questions because such a format can be used for adaptations most easily. It is important to ask questions that are developmentally appropriate, such as asking a child "Is your name Santa Claus?" or "Is this a car?" (while holding up a car or another item), asking an adult "Did you get here today in an airplane?" and so forth. Many individuals will be able to respond to such questions quite accurately with vocalizations; eye blinks; facial expressions; head shakes, turns, or nods; and other gestures. If the team plans to use a yes / no format during the remainder of the assessment, it is critical that the individual's responses be highly accurate and unambiguous. If the person's responses are vague, the team usually proceeds to examine finger/hand use as a second option. To do this, the assessor may place a variety of food items, toys, or other motivating items on a table or lap tray. He or she can then encourage or ask the person under observation to reach for, pick up, or point to the objects while the assessor notes accuracy, range, and movement patterns (e.g., ability to cross the mid-line of the body). If the individual's hand and arm use are limited, the assessor can hold up items in front of the person at various distances and locations in the visual field in order to assess his or her eye gaze in a similar manner. Finally, if absolutely necessary, the team can provide the individual with a headstick or headlight pointer; however, this is usually the least desirable option because it requires the person to have some training and practice in order to use the headstick or pointer with sufficient accuracy.

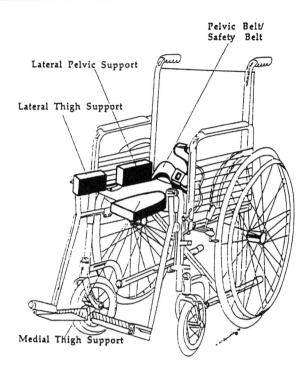

Figure 7.8.   Pelvic and thigh supports. (From Medhat, M.A., & Hobson, D. (1992). *Standardization of terminology and descriptive methods for specialized seating: A reference manual* (p. 26). Washington, DC: RESNA Press; reprinted by permission.)

It is important to allow adequate time for response during a preliminary direct se-lection assessment because individuals who do not regularly use these techniques may require considerable processing time before they can execute the necessary motor ac-tions. For example, one woman we know had been deemed unassessable by two con-secutive AAC teams because she could not demonstrate a reliable motor behavior dur-ing the initial screening. In reality, she could point to pictures and objects with her hand quite accurately—as long as assessors were willing to wait for up to 2 minutes so that she could drag her hand across the lap tray to select an answer! Although this method was too slow to be useful as a permanent access technique, it was used successfully during assessment to identify this woman's language, symbol, and literacy skills, which were considerable.

Identification of Long-Term Motor Skills

Once the team has identified a temporary response technique, the assessment may pro-ceed to determining the best long-term technique. As we have seen, there are two ap-proaches to indicating items in the selection display: direct selection and scanning. During this portion of the process, the philosophy of the AAC team influences the depth and detail of the assessment. Some teams prefer a maximal assessment strategy, in which the members assess the voluntary control of all sites of the body that might be involved in alternative access (e.g., Lee & Thomas, 1990). More often, however, the team uses a predictive- or criteria-based assessment to determine whether the individ-ual can access an AAC system through a direct selection technique.

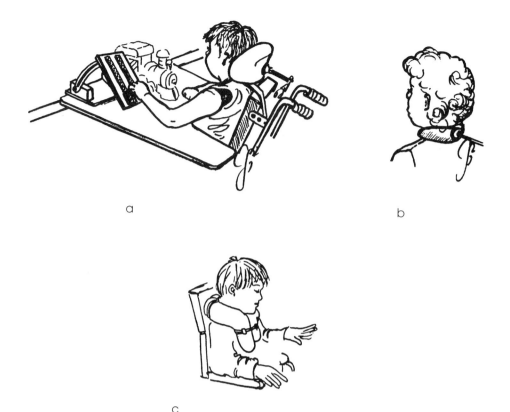

Figure 7.9.   Head and neck supports. a) Curved headrest; b) neck ring; c) Hensinger head collar. (From Goossens',
C., & Crain, S. (1992). *Utilizing switch interfaces with children who are severely physically challenged* (p. 34). Austin,
TX: PRO-ED; reprinted by permission.)

Direct Selection

"Direct selection techniques can be more efficient for individuals with sufficient motor control, and are generally preferred to scanning selection techniques" (Lee & Thomas, 1990, p. 98). Therefore, motor assessment usually focuses first on direct selection, and the team initiates scanning assessment only if the AAC user's control of direct selection options is inaccurate, very slow, or fatiguing. Although the philosophy stated above is quite prevalent in the AAC field, a word of caution is in order. As more and more AAC devices are manufactured with both scanning and direct selection options, many users can incorporate both into their systems. For example, some AAC users communicate using direct selection in the morning but change to scanning in the afternoon or evening when they are tired. Others are able to use a direct selection technique when they are properly positioned in wheelchairs, but they control their communication systems or computers through scanning when they are in other types of chairs or in bed.

An assessment of direct selection capabilities generally occurs in the following stages (Lee & Thomas, 1990): 1) assessment of hand and arm control, 2) assessment of head and orofacial control, and 3) assessment of foot and leg control. The individual's upper limbs are assessed first because the hand potentially provides the most discrete control and has the greatest social acceptance as an alternative access site. Second, head, neck, and orofacial movements (e.g., eye pointing, head pointing) may be used but often interfere with the AAC user's natural movements and actions. Third, the team usually assesses the individual's foot and leg control last because few people with physical impairments have the necessary fine motor control of their lower extremities needed for direct selection techniques.

The form in Figure 7.10 has been developed to collect and summarize the information from a direct selection survey. Some of the techniques that teams may use to gather this information are summarized in the sections that follow.

Observation and Interview

First, a team usually begins an assessment of direct selection capabilities by observing the individual for a period of time to determine the types of movements he or she makes during communication or other routine activities. Interviews with the individual, family members, caregivers, and others also provide information about current movement patterns and activities. For example, some individuals may already point with their hands or their eyes to indicate items of choice. Such information is useful in guiding the assessment.

Assess Range and Accuracy of Movement

Next, the assessment generally involves testing the individual's range and accuracy of movements without using adaptations. The AAC team usually assesses hand or head-stick control by using a horizontal grid surface, and eye pointing or headlight pointing is assessed using a vertical grid surface (see Figure 7.11). Of course, the individual must understand the task requirements in order for the results to be valid; therefore, the team should try to minimize the cognitive, linguistic, and technical aspects of the assessment so that motor control can be isolated and studied. For this reason, the team usually does not use AAC symbols or technology during this initial screening process. Rather, the members begin by placing various types of targets on the display surface and indicating that the individual is to touch, look at, or shine the light on each target. We have found that coins make excellent targets for children, especially when the children are told they can keep each coin that they touch with their hands or feet, "hit" with a head-stick or light pointer, or look at using eye gaze. We have found that even children with severe cognitive impairments often understand this task almost immediately. Alternatively, the team can use small edible items, toys, or other motivating items as targets. In some cases, individuals may be able to reach for items with their hands, but they lack the ability to point accurately and efficiently. If this is the case, the AAC assessors can provide a variety of manual supports or devices to facilitate pointing during assessment. These aids include, for example, temporary finger or wrist splints, hand-held pointers (e.g., a pencil, a small flashlight), or mobile arm supports such as slings or hinged arm positioners.

The AAC team may need to enlarge targets to assess headlight (optical) pointing, at least initially, so that the individual experiences success. For adults who understand the task, colored circles of construction paper positioned on a large display surface, such as a light-colored wall, may be sufficient. For children, the assessment may include asking them to shine the headlight on large animal pictures or some other motivating targets. Some children are also willing to try to play tag with the light pointer in an assessment. By "chasing" targets (the assessor's hand, toy animals, or large pictures) as they move slowly across a solid background, children may be able to demonstrate the range and accuracy of their head control. Many of these same techniques are useful for screening for eye-pointing capabilities as well.

Movement pattern	Direct selection device	Adaptations used (e.g., splint, textured surface, keyguard)	Target (size, number, distance/ orientation to body)	Times hit/missed target	Negative impact (e.g., muscle tone, reflexes, postures, fatigue)	Comments
Right upper limb						
Left upper limb						
Head/neck	Headlight pointer					
Head/neck	Headstick/ mouthstick					
Eyes						
Other (e.g. lower limbs, sign of voice recognition)						

Figure 7.10. Direct selection survey.

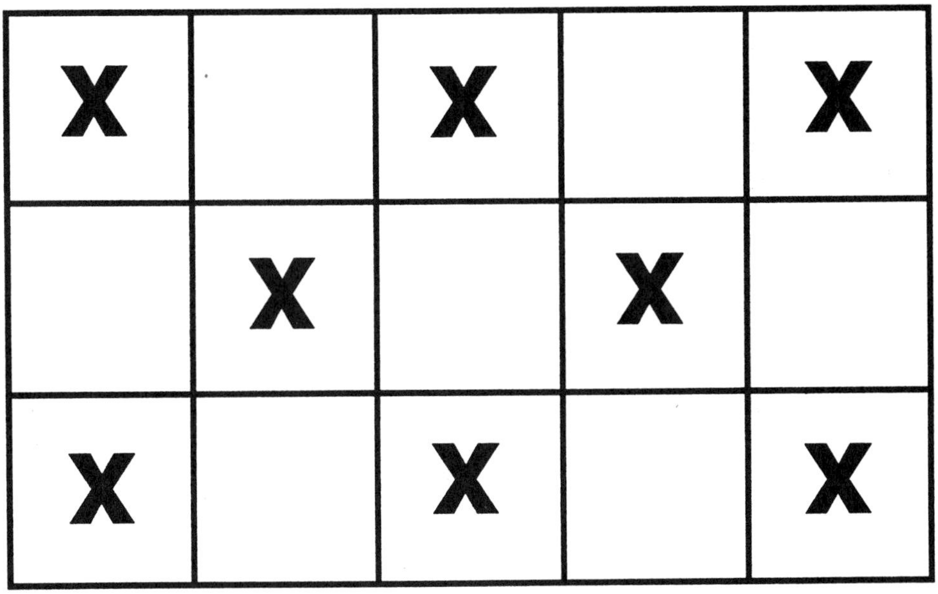

Figure 7.11.   A targeting grid for motor assessment.

Optimizing Control

For motor techniques with which the individual was somewhat successful during screening, additional assessment can help to further define capabilities in areas such as 1) the degree of accuracy with which the person can use the technique to access targets of various sizes; 2) the maximum range and number of targets that he or she can access; and 3) the extent to which adaptations such as keyguards, various display surface angles, various textured surfaces (e.g., slick versus rough), head supports, and trunk supports can optimize his or her accuracy, efficiency, and range of motion. Because people with severe disabilities may have had little experience with the access options used in the assessment, the AAC team members should be quite conservative in their judgments about motor control. During an initial evaluation, an individual may demonstrate little of the ability that instruction and practice might produce. This is particularly true for techniques such as headlight pointing because few individuals are likely to have had any experience with this method of alternative access prior to an evaluation. Therefore, the team should reassess options that appear even marginally viable—if possible, after the individual has practiced for a few weeks.

Assess Negative Impact

Throughout the motor control assessment, the AAC team should also focus on the overall impact each access technique has on the individual. For example, some direct selection control techniques can lead to unwanted consequences such as persistent abnormal reflexes, excessive muscle tone, abnormal postures, or excessive fatigue. In the assessment, the AAC team members must determine the extent to which they can minimize the negative impact of various alternative access options while preserving the potential benefits. Often, a compromise may be reached; however, the negative consequences associated with a particular alternative access option occasionally can be so detrimental that the team must abandon the option for the moment. Such techniques often can be considered later with additional instruction, practice, or adaptations.

Manual Signing

If manual signing is being considered for an individual, the AAC team may undertake assessment of the fine motor skills used for manual signs or formalized gestures, such as Amer-Ind. Dennis, Reichle, Williams, and Vogelsberg (1982) and Doherty (1985) reviewed a number of studies that examined the motoric dimensions that appear to be related to manual sign acquisition and retention. In addition, formal protocols for fine motor assessment related to the use of signs were developed by Dunn (1982) and described by Dennis et al. (1982). Although available assessment protocols in this area lack formal reliability measures, some are based on the research literature and therefore appear to be reasonably valid. We summarize these protocols in Table 7.2.

Switch Assessment for Scanning

The AAC team will need to complete a switch assessment for scanning if an individual is unable to directly select items from a display. Switch assessment involves identification of body sites that the individual can use to activate one or more switches, as well as assessment of the individual's ability to use various scanning strategies and arrangements (see Chapter 4).

Screening for a switch activation site on the body is the first step of a scanning assessment. A note of caution: AAC teams have a tendency to utilize tasks that are too complex when identifying an individual's switch activation sites. The team should attempt to reduce the cognitive, visual, and communicative demands in a switch control assessment; for this reason, we rarely use AAC equipment to gather this information. We have found that asking an individual to activate a tape recorder and play music (or to turn on a battery-operated toy) is an effective way to provide a consequence during the scanning assessment. To perform the assessment, we attach a switch to the remote-control port of a tape recorder and insert an audiocassette tape appropriate for the age and interests of the potential AAC user. A team can then try different switches as it assesses various motor control sites, such as fingers, hands, head, and feet.

Generally, we use a criteria-based assessment approach to identify a switch activation site. To this end, we begin a switch assessment with the most socially appropriate body site for switch control: the hands. If hand or finger control of a switch sufficiently allows accurate, efficient, and nonfatiguing alternative access, we do not continue the assessment with other body parts. If hand control seems insufficient, we usually assess the head next, followed by the feet, legs, and knees.

Table 7.2.   Selected instruments for assessment of manual signing capabilities

Instrument	Source
Pre–Sign Language Motor Skills (Klein, 1988)	Communication Skill Builders c/o The Psychological Corporation, 555 Academic Court, San Antonio, TX 78204-2498
Purdue Perceptual-Motor Survey (Roach & Kephart, 1966)	Charles E. Merrill Publishers, Columbus, OH 43216-0508
Illinois Test of Psycholinguistic Abilities, Manual Expression Subtest (Kirk, McCarthy, & Kirk, 1968)	University of Illinois Press, Urbana, IL 61801
Early Manual Communication Skills Assessment (Sweeney & Finkley, 1989)	D. Blackstone, E. Cassatt-James, & D. Bruskin (Eds), *Augmentative communication: Intervention resource* (pp. 3-159–3-168). Rockville, MD: American Speech-Language-Hearing Association

Components of Switch Control

There are essentially six components of switch control. In order to operate an electronic scanner, the individual must first be able to wait for the right moment, in order to avoid inadvertently activating the switch. Some individuals have difficulty waiting because of cognitive or motor control problems. The second step in controlling a switch is activation, or closing the switch. During assessment, the team should determine whether the individual can activate a variety of switches, note the approximate length of time it takes for each activation to occur, and observe the efficiency with which the person completes the activation movements. The third step in controlling a switch is to hold it in an activated position for the required time. Some individuals who are able to activate the switch accurately and promptly are not able to hold or maintain switch closure. The fourth step in switch control is the ability to release the switch accurately and efficiently, a step that may be problematic for some people. Finally, the fifth and sixth steps involve the individual waiting and then reactivating the switch at the appropriate times.

The team can assess each of these components by using the tape recorder or toy strategy described previously. Members may ask the individual to turn the tape recorder on and off according to directions designed to assess each component, such as "Wait, don't play it yet," "Okay, play it now," "Stop," and "Play it again." The AAC team may need to observe individuals who are unable to follow verbal directions because of cognitive or other limitations while the individuals use switches to control appliances in natural environments. Regardless of the environment, this assessment should give the team an overall indication of the individual's ability to activate switches at various motor control sites. We provide a form to record the results of this assessment in Figure 7.12. Again, we remind readers that, although many body parts are listed on this form, it is often unnecessary to evaluate all of them.

Detailed instructions for switch assessment and mounting, as well as techniques for teaching scanning skills to young children, can be found in Goossens' and Crain (1992).

Cursor Control Techniques and Switch Control Capabilities

The choice of cursor control technique for scanning (e.g., automatic, directed, step scanning) is influenced by an individual's motor control capabilities. This match between techniques and capabilities is illustrated in Tables 7.3 and 7.4. The types of scanning are found across the top of Table 7.3, and the six components of switch control described previously are listed along the left side. The table includes the motor component skill-accuracy requirements for each type of scanning. Therefore, in the case of automatic scanning, in which the cursor moves automatically across the selection set and the AAC user is required to stop it at a desired item, there is a high skill-accuracy requirement for the user to wait until the cursor is in the correct location. There is also a high skill-accuracy requirement for the user to activate the switch to stop the cursor. Because the item is selected at the moment of switch activation, it does not matter how long the user holds the switch closed, and the accuracy requirements for holding are low. The release phase also has a low skill-accuracy requirement because nothing is required during this

Voluntary motor control (single switch)

	Is able to wait		Is able to activate		Is able to hold		Is able to release		Is able to wait		Is able to reactivate		Accuracy*
	Yes	No	Yes	No	Yes	No	Yes	No	Yes	No	Yes	No	
Fingers on left hand													
Fingers on right hand													
Left hand (palm? back?)													
Right hand (palm? back?)													
Left shoulder													
Right shoulder													
Head rotation (R? L?)													
Head flexion													
Head-side flexion (R? L?)													
Head extension													
Vertical eye motions													
Horizontal eye motions													
Tongue or chin													
Left outer leg/knee													
Right outer leg/knee													
Left inner leg/knee													
Right inner leg/knee													
Left foot (up? down?)													
Right foot (up? down?)													

*Accuracy = rate of overall accuracy on a 0–4 scale in which 0 = never and 4 = always.

Figure 7.12. Assessment of motor (switch) control for scanning.

Table 7.3.   Skill accuracy requirements of cursor control techniques for scanning

Motor component	Cursor control technique		
	Automatic scanning	Directed scanning	Step scanning
Wait	High	Medium	Low
Activate	High	Low	Medium
Hold	Low	High	Low
Release	Low	High	Low
Wait	High	Medium	Medium
Reactivate	High	Medium	Medium
Fatigue value	Low	Medium	High

phase of automatic scanning. Finally, the user requires high skill accuracy for waiting and reactivating the switch. Automatic scanning relies on timing rather than on repeated movements or endurance, so it produces a low level of fatigue.

In directed scanning, the cursor moves to the desired item only when the switch is activated, and the user must release the switch to make a selection. A review of Table 7.3 for this type of scanning indicates that waiting prior to activation has a medium skill-accuracy requirement. Although waiting does not affect accurate item selection directly, inadvertent activation at this point will initiate cursor movement before the individual is ready to begin. Switch activation has a low skill-accuracy requirement in directed scanning because activation does not involve precise timing. Holding in directed scanning has a high skill-accuracy requirement because the individual must hold the switch closed until the cursor is positioned at the desired item; therefore, a person's inability to adequately hold the switch closed will result in a selection error. During directed scanning the individual makes a selection in the switch release phase, requiring high skill-accuracy, whereas waiting and reactivation have medium skill-accuracy requirements. The fatigue value in directed scanning is medium because the individual must have some motor endurance to hold the switch closed for a period of time.

In step scanning, the cursor moves one step with each activation of the switch. Therefore, the individual's ability to wait has a low skill-accuracy requirement because it is not involved in item selection. Switch activation has a medium skill requirement because, although the activation does not have to be rapid, accurate, or well timed, it may be quite fatiguing. Holding in step scanning requires only low skill-accuracy because the cursor moves one step with each activation and therefore holding is not part of the selection process. For the same reason, releasing is also a low skill-accuracy requirement. Waiting and reactivation require medium motor control abilities because inadvertent switch activation at these phases will result in erroneous selections. Fatigue is high in step scanning because of the multiple, repeated switch activations.

The preceding discussion is based on clinical experience, not research—in fact, we are unaware of any research that exists to support this model. Nonetheless, professionals with whom we have worked tell us that generally applying these guidelines helps them achieve effective matching between an individual's motor control capabilities and a cursor control pattern for scanning. We illustrate clinical applications of these guidelines in the following sections by discussing three AAC users who use scanning for alternative access.

Table 7.4.   Clinical illustrations of ease of motor control and capabilities for scanning

Motor component	Ease of motor control		
	Francesca (athetosis)	Isaac (spasticity)	Jin (weakness)
Wait	Difficult	Medium	Easy
Activate	Difficult	Medium	Medium
Hold	Medium	Easy	Difficult
Release	Easy	Difficult	Easy
Wait	Difficult	Medium	Easy
Reactivate	Difficult	Medium	Medium
Fatigue value	Medium	Medium	Difficult

Clinical Illustration: Francesca (Athetosis)

The results of a switch assessment for Francesca, a child with athetoid cerebral palsy, are illustrated in Table 7.4, in which we describe the ease or difficulty with which Francesca was able to accomplish the various components of switch activation. As is the case for many individuals with athetosis, accurate waiting was difficult for her. Because of involuntary motor movements ("overflow") associated with her athetosis, Francesca inadvertently activated the switch during the waiting phase. Similarly, accurate and efficient switch activation was also difficult because Francesca's overflow movements are accentuated in times of stress or anticipation. Therefore, she was unable to activate the switch quickly on command. We see that the holding phase was of medium ease for Francesca because she was able to maintain contact with the switch once she managed to activate it. In contrast to the difficulties associated with switch activation, the release phase was easy for this child, for she was able to release the switch efficiently and accurately. Finally, Francesca found that waiting and reactivation were again difficult because of her extraneous motor movements.

A comparison of Francesca's switch control profile with the requirements of cursor control in Table 7.3 suggests that directed scanning might be an alternative access mode for her. Directed scanning has high skill-accuracy requirements for holding and releasing, which match her capabilities. Conversely, automatic scanning has high skill requirements for waiting and activating, the two phases of switch activation that Francesca found most difficult. Step scanning would probably exacerbate her involuntary motor movements because it requires the greatest amount of actual motor activity and is quite fatiguing.

Clinical Illustration: Isaac (Spasticity)

Isaac is a young man with severe spasticity resulting from a traumatic brain injury; as in the case of Francesca, we provide a summary of his switch activation profile in Table 7.4. The assessment showed that Isaac had medium ease with waiting and switch activation, and that his activations were rather deliberate and slow. He found it easy to hold the switch closed briefly but difficult to release it in a timely and accurate manner. Release was difficult for Isaac because the spasticity prevented him from relaxing his contact with the switch when he wanted. He experienced medium ease with waiting and reactivation.

A review of the requirements of cursor control patterns suggests that Isaac's difficulty with switch release will probably make it difficult for him to use directed scanning successfully. Instead, automatic scanning might be a more appropriate choice for him because it has high waiting and activation requirements, activities that Isaac found moderately easy. Automatic scanning also has low skill requirements for switch releasing, the phase with which this young man has the most difficulty.

Clinical Illustration: Jin (Weakness)

Jin, a woman with ALS that causes severe weakness throughout her body, could operate a very sensitive switch affixed just above her eyebrow by raising her forehead slightly. Jin found waiting quite easy and was able to activate the switch with moderate ease when asked. She experienced difficulty holding the switch closed because of her weakness, but she could easily release it. She then had no difficulty waiting and could reactivate the switch with medium ease. As can be seen by consulting Table 7.3, the optimal cursor control pattern for Jin appeared to be automatic scanning because this option requires the greatest amount of waiting and causes the least fatigue, a major concern for someone like Jin who has little motor stamina.

We remind the reader that the clinical interpretations made in these case studies are illustrations only. In no sense do we mean to suggest that all individuals who experience athetosis, spasticity, or weakness will have switch activation profiles similar to those in this section. We simply present these examples to illustrate the process of matching an individual's capabilities with the motor control requirements for scanning. Readers should also note that the goal of the type of motor assessment described here is to screen an individual's motor capabilities so that intervention can begin. In addition to this initial process, the AAC team should continually assess an individual's motor control after an intervention is in place in order to further refine the alternative access technique and ensure that the AAC user's performance becomes increasingly more accurate and efficient and less fatiguing.

Principle 4: Assessment of cognitive and linguistic capabilities should enhance the process of matching an AAC user to an appropriate AAC technique or device. Thus, the goals of such assessment are inclusionary, not exclusionary.

ASSESS COGNITIVE/LINGUISTIC CAPABILITIES

In the Participation Model, assessment of an individual's current communication skills occurs at an earlier phase of assessment (see Chapter 6). At this point in the assessment process, we can use additional assessments to gather relevant information about specific cognitive, language, and related skills.

Cognitive Assessment

The purpose of cognitive assessment in AAC is to determine how the individual understands the world and how the AAC team can best facilitate communication within this understanding. Ultimately, the team should use this information to achieve a good match between the person and one or more AAC techniques. Unfortunately, however, the cognitive requirements of most AAC options have been described only minimally in the clinical and research literature, even though it is quite obvious that the operation of AAC techniques requires various types of cognitive abilities, ranging from basic to quite sophisticated. For example, in order to use even a basic communication board with pictorial symbols, the AAC user must understand that when he or she indicates an item on the board, the communication partner will respond accordingly. Some beginning AAC users may not fully understand this basic concept of communicative cause and effect.

As of 1998, no formal tests are available that predict the user's ability to meet the cognitive requirements of various AAC techniques. Rather, the AAC team must analyze the cognitive requirements of a particular approach and then estimate the extent to which the individual will be able to meet these requirements. The team may need to conduct intervention trials with one or more AAC techniques or devices in order to determine an individual's capabilities. Thousands of successful AAC interventions have been instituted without formal documentation of the cognitive abilities required to use various techniques.

Aside from the goal of achieving a good match between user and AAC technique, there are often other situations in which assessment of an individual's cognitive abilities may be necessary or useful. For example, we are frequently asked to suggest instruments that can be used in educational settings for cognitive assessment related to individual education planning, especially for individuals with severe and/or multiple disabilities. The assessment measures listed in Table 7.5 may yield useful information concerning the sensorimotor skills of beginning communicators, such as alertness, attentiveness, vigilance (i.e., ability to visually or auditorily process information over time), understanding cause and effect, and understanding object or pictorial permanence. In addition, the "Communication Matrix" (Rowland, 1996) can be used in the assessment of early cognitive skills related to communication, as can the "Communication and Symbolic Behavior Scales" (Wetherby & Prizant, 1993). Several reasonably reliable and valid standardized intelligence tests also can be used with children as young as 2½ years of age who are unable to speak. These tests include the Columbia Mental Maturity Scale (Burgemeister, 1973), the Bracken Basic Concept Scale (Bracken, 1984), the Test of Nonverbal Intelligence, Second Edition (Brown, Sherbenou, & Johnsen, 1990), and the Leiter International Performance Scale (Leiter, 1969). In addition, the Psychological S–R Evaluation (PSR), although lacking in reliability and valid-

Table 7.5.   Selected instruments for sensorimotor assessment related to curriculum

Instrument	Source
Callier-Azusa Scales for the Assessment of Communicative Abilities (Stillman & Battle, 1985)	University of Texas at Dallas, Callier Center on Communication Disorders, Dallas, TX 75235
Nonverbal Prelinguistic Communication (Otos, 1983)	Oregon Department of Education, 700 Pringle Parkway SE, Salem OR 97310
Sequenced Inventory of Communication Development (Hedrick, Prather, & Tobin, 1984)	University of Washington Press, Seattle, WA 98195
Sensorimotor Assessment Form (Robinson, Bataillon, Fieber, Jackson, & Rasmussen, 1985)	Meyer Rehabilitation Institute, 44th & Dewey, Omaha, NE 68198-5450

ity data, was designed as a tool to assess verbal and visual-motor intelligence in developmentally young children with severe, multiple disabilities (Mullen, 1985).

Johnson-Martin et al. (1987) presented an excellent review of several nonverbal cognitive tests along with suggestions for empirically validated adaptations, and they also discussed the pros and cons of using such tests for AAC assessment. In addition, clinicians working with individuals with physical and sensory impairments have developed informal modifications of Piagetian assessment tasks (e.g., Goossens', Heine, Crain, & Burke, 1987). Such adaptations include, for example, cutting up test pages with pictures into separate items that can then be arranged on an eye-gaze display or individualized array for pointing, limiting the number of choices from which they ask the individual to choose, enlarging test stimuli (i.e., pictures) for individuals with visual impairments, and using a yes/no or multiple-choice format instead of asking open-ended questions (Glennen, 1997). For example, if the original test question is "How are an orange and an apple the same?" the assessor might ask the question and then present a series of yes/no options in random order: "Are they both red?" "Are they both round?" "Are they both fruit?" "Are they both toys?" and so forth. Although such adaptations technically invalidate many cognitive assessments so that the scores obtained cannot be reported as "mental age" or IQ scores, the modifications may have practical value in that they do allow the team to assess the individual's cognitive skills that are measured by the test items.

Symbol Assessment

Symbols or codes represent a majority of the messages included in AAC systems. People who are unable to read or write may use one or more of the symbol options described in Chapter 3. It is not uncommon to see AAC users successfully employ not just one set but rather a variety of symbol types. Thus, the goal of symbol assessment is not to identify a single symbol set to represent all messages. Instead, the goal of assessment is to select the types of symbols that will meet the individual's current communication needs and match his or her current abilities as well as to identify symbol options that might be used in the future.

Assessment of an individual's ability to use symbols usually involves several steps. Before starting, the team members responsible for the symbol assessment should identify 10 or so functional items with which the individual is familiar, basing their selections on the recommendations of the individual's family members, teachers, or frequent communication partners. These functional items might include a cup, brush, washcloth, spoon, and so forth. Next, the assessment team members should reach a consensus about the individual's familiarity with the selected items because one of the most common errors is to attempt a symbol assessment using items that the individual does not understand or know. When the team reaches a consensus on an item, it can indicate this in the appropriate column on the symbol assessment form; otherwise, members may replace items if they are found to be unfamiliar. Then, from a variety of sources, the team should compile symbols that represent the selected items. These symbols might include color and black-and-white photographs, miniature objects, various types of line-drawing symbols (see Chapter 3), and written words. Figures 7.13–7.15, 7.18, and 7.19 contain spaces for recording the items and symbols selected for assessment.

Functional Use Format

At the most basic level of symbol use is the ability to understand the functional use of objects (Glennen, 1997). An AAC team can assess a child's level of functional understanding in a play context by giving him or her the items selected for the assessment and observing whether the child uses them functionally (e.g., trying to drink when presented with a cup). With older individuals, the team can make direct requests related to functional objects' uses, such as "Show me what you do with this." Often, interviewing family members, teachers, or others reveals useful information in this regard—for example, a child's mother might report that he gets excited whenever she gets out his "going to the park" jacket, indicating that he recognizes its function. Finally, individuals with severe motor impairments that prevent them from manipulating objects can be assessed for functional understanding of object use if the assessor is willing to act as a "demonstrator." In this case, the demonstrator mimes both correct and incorrect uses of each object and observes the individual's reactions. For example, the assessor might brush her hair with a spoon or put a cup on her head as a hat, and then wait for the person under observation to give gestural or other indications that the demonstrated action is "wrong." The individual's responses should be quite different from those elicited by a "correct" mime (e.g., eating from a spoon, drinking from a cup). Success in one or more of these formats would suggest that the person recognizes that the test objects have specific uses. Figure 7.13 provides a format for assessing functional object use.

Receptive Labeling and Yes/No Formats

Observing an individual's receptive labeling ability is often the next step in symbol assessment because this is the most straightforward way to establish whether an individual can recognize a symbol as representing its referent. The person conducting the assessment presents the individual with two or more symbols of a particular type and asks him or her to point out the presented item. Of course, obtaining the requested motor response depends on the person's motor abilities. Alternatively, the assessor can use a yes/no format, in which he or she holds up one symbol at a time and asks, "Is this a _____?" The assessor should arrange the trials so that yes/no questions are presented randomly for all target items. This testing format is only appropriate if the individual understands the concept of yes/no and has a clear and accurate way of answering yes/no questions. The team can assess several types of symbols, one type at a time, using any of these formats. The assessor records on a form (see Figure 7.14) whether the individual can identify target items from the various symbol sets.

Alternative Visual-Matching Format

In the cases of some individuals, AAC team members cannot use receptive labeling or yes/no formats because the people undergoing symbol assessment do not understand either the task expectations or the verbal labels presented or because they lack motivation. However, there is evidence that a visual-matching format produces similar results to those elicited from the receptive labeling format, when used with 2- and 3-year-olds without disabilities and individuals of similar developmental ages with severe cognitive disabilities (Franklin, Mirenda, & Phillips, 1994). Thus, a visual-matching format similar to the one provided in Figure 7.15 may serve as a useful alternative to the receptive labeling option. In a standard matching assessment, the team provides the individ-

Format used: Direct request ("Show me what you do with this") _____   Caregiver interview _____

Assessor demonstration of correct usage _____

Instructions used _____

Response accepted as correct _____

List objects used	Confirmation of item knowledge by informant?

Indicate whether trial is correct or incorrect in appropriate column and describe responses

Trial no.	Object	Function correct? (describe)	Function incorrect? (describe)
1			
2			
3			
4			
5			
6			
7			
8			
9			
10			
11			
12			

Figure 7.13.   Functional object use assessment.

Format used: Receptive labeling _____   Yes/no ____

Number of items in array _____

Instructions used _____

Response accepted as correct _____

List items used	Confirmation of item knowledge by team?

Indicate whether trial is correct (+) or incorrect (−) in appropriate column

Trial no.	Target item	Real objects	Color photographs	Line drawings	Other (specify)
1					
2					
3					
4					
5					
6					
7					
8					
9					
10					
11					
12					

Figure 7.14.   Symbol assessment: Receptive labeling and yes/no formats.

Format used: Standard matching _____   Sorting _____

Number of items in array _____

Instructions used _____

Response accepted as correct _____

List items used	Confirmation of item knowledge by team?

Indicate whether trial is correct (+) or incorrect (−) in appropriate column

Trial no.	Target item	Real objects	Color photographs	Line drawings	Other (specify)
1					
2					
3					
4					
5					
6					
7					
8					
9					
10					
11					
12					

Figure 7.15.   Symbol assessment: Visual-matching format.

ual with a single object and places two or more symbols, one of which matches the object, on the table (see Figure 7.16a). The assessor then asks the individual to match the object to the corresponding symbol, using eye gazing, pointing, or direct selection. Alternatively, the team may give a single symbol to the individual, who then attempts to match the symbol to the correct object in an array (see Figure 7.16b). A study examining alternative symbol assessment strategies found these formats to be equivalent in difficulty (Franklin et al., 1994). The AAC team can also adjust the configuration, spacing, and number of items in the array in order to meet the needs of specific individuals. The goal is to make systematic adjustments that facilitate the acquisition of accurate and useful information about the person's ability to associate objects with their referents on the basis of perceptual characteristics.

Several cautions are in order with regard to the matching format. First, it is not essential for an individual to be able to match objects and symbols in order to learn to use symbols successfully (Romski & Sevcik, 1996). If a person can do this, he or she understands (at least at a visual level) the relationship between symbols and their referents, but if an individual lacks this understanding, it does not mean that he or she cannot learn to use symbols. Second, the matching assessment is not a standardized testing protocol; rather, it is a flexible format that the team can alter to suit the individual's abilities and interests. For example, many people with limited cognitive abilities may need to learn to match items and symbols before actual assessment. The team can usually accomplish this instruction in a short time using a "teach–test" approach. During the "teach" phase, team members can introduce and gradually fade out physical or other prompts in order to teach the person to match identical real objects. Once he or she can do this independently and fairly accurately, the team can present various object–symbol matching tasks as described previously (see Mirenda & Locke, 1989, for a more complete description of this approach).

Pulling It All Together

By this point in the assessment, two things should be clear: whether the individual understands the functional use of selected, familiar objects and whether the person can either recognize the verbal labels for a variety of symbols or match them to their referents. If one or both of these skills is not evident, this may indicate that, at this particular

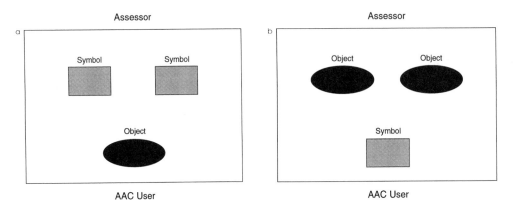

Figure 7.16.   a) Single-object-to-multiple-symbol matching format, b) single-symbol-to-multiple-object matching format.

time, the person will be best served by several "beginning communicator" strategies designed to build communicative skills while teaching symbol–referent associations. These strategies include schedule systems and "talking switch" techniques, as described in Chapter 11. The individual's ability to perform the assessment tasks successfully can be used to predict the type(s) of symbols with which he or she is most likely to be successful, at least initially. The initial symbol set(s) selected should enable accurate, efficient, and nonfatiguing communication with very little instruction required. Over time, the AAC user can learn and use more sophisticated types of symbols. Symbol sets such as manual signs, Blissymbols, and others that require extensive learning and practice may be excellent choices for the future but may not be appropriate for initial use.

Because real communication rarely involves either receptive language labeling or symbol matching, we have found it useful to extend the assessment beyond these basic tasks to determine whether an individual can use symbols in a more communicative manner. The AAC team should include this portion of the assessment process regardless of whether the individual is successful during the initial symbol tasks because some individuals may find it easier to demonstrate symbolic understanding during natural interactions. However, Blockberger noted that typically developing children can talk for up to a year before they are able to use pictures symbolically, around 24–30 months of age. She commented that

> It may not be realistic for us to assume that the child with severe speech impairment will be able to use graphic symbols symbolically and communicatively at the same developmental age that a typical child begins to speak. When children are able to point to graphic symbols on request but do not spontaneously use that symbol communicatively, [it may be because] the child [has not] grasped the symbol's referential function. (1995, p. 225)

AAC team members can use one or both of the following formats to assess a person's symbol use in context.

Question-and-Answer Format

Figure 7.18 contains a form with which a team can assess whether an individual can use symbols to answer verbal questions. As in the basic assessment, the assessor should first identify items or concepts that are known to the individual by interviewing familiar communication partners and listing items on the form. The assessor should select two or more symbols of a specific type—such as objects, photographs, or line drawings—and present them to the individual, asking a question that the individual can answer correctly by indicating one of the symbols. Receptive labeling questions such as "Can you show me the car?" or "Where is the picture of your dog?" should not be used in this situation. Instead, the assessor may ask simple knowledge-based questions such as "What did you eat for breakfast?" while presenting symbol choices such as the person's favorite breakfast food, a car, and a dog or ask "Who likes to ride in the car?" with symbol options such as a boy and a horse.

In order to successfully complete this task, the individual must understand the task expectations, the questions, and the symbol options presented, and he or she must be motivated and cooperative during the evaluation. If the individual performs poorly in the assessment, it is important for the team to try to determine which of these aspects of the question-and-answer task is responsible for the individual's difficulties. Alternative formats, such as question-and-answer assessments in natural contexts, may be useful to counteract some factors contributing to poor performance, especially with people who have severe cognitive impairments. For example, many individuals may be able to

Number of items in array _____

Instructions used _____

Context: Out of context _____   In context (specify) _____

Response accepted as correct _____

List items used   Confirmation of item knowledge by informant?

Indicate whether trial is correct (+) or incorrect (−) in appropriate column

Trial no.	Question asked	Real objects	Color photographs	Line drawings	Other (specify)
1					
2					
3					
4					
5					
6					
7					
8					
9					
10					
11					
12					

Figure 7.18.   Symbol assessment: Question-and-answer format.

answer the "breakfast" question if they are seated in the kitchen where they usually eat rather than in a classroom where meals never take place. The form in Figure 7.18 allows the assessor to provide relevant information related to context.

Requesting Format

Individuals with severe communication and cognitive limitations may be able to match symbols to objects and even answer simple questions using symbols, yet they may still be unable to use symbols to make requests. In Figure 7.19, we provide a form to guide the team's assessment of symbol use in this requesting format. An AAC team usually conducts this assessment in an appropriate natural context, such as during snacktime, a play activity, the performance of some domestic task (e.g., washing the dishes), or in any other context that is of interest to the person being assessed. As before, the team lists and confirms items that the person knows and that are available in the context. Then the assessors provide symbols representing two or more of the available options, trying one type of symbol at a time. The structure of the interaction provides opportunities for the person to request objects or actions by selecting one of the available symbols without the assessor instructing him or her to do so. Indirect cues such as "I don't know what you want. Can you help me out?" may be used to elicit requests, but direct instructions such as "Touch the picture to tell me what you want" should be avoided because the purpose of this assessment is to determine whether the individual can make spontaneous, unprompted requests.

Pulling It All Together

The question-and-answer and requesting formats provide basic information about how the person can communicate with symbols; they do not indicate which symbols he or she recognizes linguistically or perceptually. Individuals who can do only one or neither task will need instruction to be able to use, in functional contexts, the symbols that were identified during the basic assessment. The strategies described in Chapter 11 for teaching requesting, rejecting, and so forth may be useful in this regard. Individuals who are able to answer questions or make requests using symbols may have the skills needed for more advanced symbol use, as assessed through the next two formats.

Advanced Symbol Use

Individuals who are adept at single-symbol use in communicative contexts may be able to use symbols for words other than nouns and/or chain two or more symbols together to construct messages. The team can assess both of these abilities through the use of an activity display with symbols that represent various syntactic elements—nouns, verbs, adjectives, and so forth. For example, we often use dual Go Fish displays with symbols representing the various elements of this simple card game because it is appropriate for individuals across the age range (see Figure 7.20). While playing the game, the assessor produces multiple one- and two-symbol messages using his or her display, thus providing models for advanced symbol use. The AAC user will often learn how to use the display quite quickly, and then the assessor can observe whether the individual uses any non-noun symbols or makes a sequence of two symbols when provided with opportunities to do so. For example, at appropriate times, the assessor can create opportunities for the individual to communicate two-symbol messages such as GO + FISH, YOUR + TURN, YOU + LOSE, I + WIN, and so forth. The absence of one or both types of advanced symbol use suggests that the team should construct the initial system with single-symbol messages, keeping the goal of moving toward multiple-symbol messages. Of

Number of items in array _____

Instructions used _____

Were options: Visible? _____   Out of sight?_____

Context: Out of context _____   In context (specify) _____

Response accepted as correct _____

List items used	Confirmation of item knowledge by informant?

Indicate whether trial is correct (+) or incorrect (−) in appropriate column

Trial no.	Items available	Real objects	Color photographs	Line drawings	Other (specify)
1					
2					
3					
4					
5					
6					
7					
8					
9					
10					
11					
12					

Figure 7.19.   Symbol assessment: Requesting format.

Figure 7.20. Go Fish display for assessment of advanced symbol use.

course, an individual with motor impairments that limit hand use will need to play the game with a partner who manages the cards, and he or she may need to use an eye-gaze display with the appropriate messages as well. Alternative activities, such as playing Space Invaders with young children, can also be used during such assessments.

Symbol Categorization and Association Assessments

Some individuals might be able to use systems that depend on various categorization strategies, or they might be candidates for iconic encoding. Teams can assess simple categorization skills with symbols of various items placed in two or more semantic categories, such as vehicles, foods, clothing, and animals. The individual is asked to sort the symbols into categories ("Put all of the animals in this box and all of the vehicles in that box") or is helped to do so using eye gazing ("Which box should I put this one in?"). Alternatively, a team can assess categorization abilities by asking the person to sort symbols for two very different activities, such as going to the beach and going to a birthday party ("Put the ones you'd use at the beach in this box and the ones you'd need at a birthday party in that box"). The results of this type of assessment can be useful to determine whether to incorporate categorization into AAC system design and in what manner to do so. For example, symbols in communication books or boards may be organized in semantic or activity category sections. Similarly, dynamic display devices require the ability to recognize and use categorization techniques. Individuals who cannot categorize will require additional instruction in this regard to use such AAC systems effectively.

The use of iconic encoding techniques such as Minspeak requires a related skill, that of association. Individuals need to be able to use various aspects of a symbol to "remind" them of associated concepts or words in a flexible manner. Several basic techniques for informal assessment of an individual's associative abilities with symbols have been developed for clinical use. Generally, the team provides an individual with a small set of colored symbols that he or she can already recognize by name (e.g., *sun, apple, car, clock*). The assessor then asks the person to use those symbols to answer questions requiring different types of associations. Assessment protocols designed by Elder, Goossens', and Bray (1989) and Glennen (1997) suggested that these questions should include associations such as the following:

- Object function (e.g., "What do you use to tell time?" CLOCK)
- Part/whole concepts (e.g., "Where is the wheel?" CAR)
- Similar item associations (e.g., "What goes together with rain?" SUN)
- Associations related to physical properties such as color, size, shape, texture or temperature, and substance (e.g., "Find something red" APPLE, "Find something hot" SUN, "Find something metal" CAR)
- Category associations (e.g., "What makes you think of food?" APPLE)
- Rhyming or "look-alike" associations (e.g., "What sounds like 'knock'?" CLOCK; "What looks like 'truck'?" CAR)

Assessors can ask individuals who make several types of associations correctly to select two- or three-symbol sequences to represent phrases such as "Let's walk the dog" (e.g., CAR + DOG) or "It's time to go eat" (CLOCK + CAR + APPLE). At issue is whether the person uses some kind of internal logic to select the sequences, not whether the assessor agrees with the selections made. Whether the individual uses internal logic will often be revealed by the team asking the person to recall the same sequences 10–15 minutes later—recall is more likely if the sequences were made logically than if they were selected arbitrarily. Thus, someone might choose the symbols APPLE + DOG for "What's for breakfast?" because he or she likes to eat fruit and protein every morning—not a choice likely to be obvious to most assessors but one that may enhance recall for the user! Success at one or more levels of an association assessment would suggest that an AAC strategy that incorporates iconic encoding might be appropriate for the individual.

The assessment questions and materials needed for the Semantic Compaction Proficiency Profile–Experimental Edition (Elder et al., 1989) can be purchased from Southeast Augmentative Communication Publications in Birmingham, Alabama.

Language Assessment

Language assessment should include an evaluation of the AAC user's single-word vocabulary capabilities as well as his or her use of common language structures (i.e., morphemes, syntax) (Roth & Cassatt-James, 1989). Basic strategies for assessment in these areas are discussed in the sections that follow.

Single-Word Vocabulary

Two types of language assessment typically are completed for AAC purposes. In the first assessment, the AAC team makes an attempt to measure vocabulary (i.e., single-word receptive language) comprehension in relation to the individual's overall level of functioning. Assessment instruments such as the Peabody Picture Vocabulary Test–Revised (PPVT–R), Form M (Dunn & Dunn, 1981) may be used to assess nonrelational words, which researchers have defined as "words that have referents in the real world such as chair, dog, shirt, etc." (Roth & Cassatt-James, 1989, p. 169). Teams often prefer this test for AAC evaluations because they can modify it easily without sacrificing validity to meet the needs of individuals with motor limitations. For example, Bristow and Fristoe (1987) compared PPVT–R scores obtained using the standard protocol with those obtained using six alternative response modes, including eye gaze, scanning, and headlight pointing. The participants were children without disabilities in four age groups. The results indicated that, with few exceptions, scores obtained under the modified conditions correlated highly with those obtained using standard test protocols. In addition to assessing nonrelational words, it is important for the team to assess the individual's comprehension of relational words (i.e., those that do not have real-world referents), such as *in* and *out* or *hot* and *cold* (Roth & Cassatt-James, 1989). The Boehm Test of Basic Concepts (Boehm, 1986) is one instrument that assessors might use to assess this kind of comprehension. For individuals who are unable to complete formal tests, a team can often obtain an estimate of vocabulary comprehension by having family members, caregivers, and school personnel develop a diary of the words and concepts that the individual appears to understand.

Standardized Spanish and British English versions of the Peabody Picture Vocabulary Test are also available from the American Guidance Service in Circle Pines, Minnesota.

Language Abilities

In many cases, it is important for assessors to attempt to determine the individual's syntactic or grammatical knowledge, depending on the nature and extent of the communication disorder. For people who can participate in formal testing, a number of tests that are based on simple multiple-choice or pointing formats are available. These tests include selected subtests from one of the Clinical Evaluation of Language Fundamentals instruments (Semel, Wiig, & Secord, 1995; Wiig, Secord, & Semel, 1992); the Preschool Language Scale–Third Edition, Auditory Comprehension Scale (Zimmerman, Steiner, & Evatt-Pond, 1992); and the Test for Auditory Comprehension of Language–Revised (Carrow-Woolfolk, 1985). We refer readers to Roth and Cassatt-

James (1989) and to the March 1990 and September 1997 issues of the *Augmentative and Alternative Communication* journal for additional information about language assessment.

Traditional language sampling usually cannot be completed because most individuals participating in AAC assessments have no formal communication systems. Informal language sampling, however, often yields useful information and should be attempted when appropriate. Alternatively, family members, caregivers, and school personnel may be asked to keep a diary of the word combinations that the individual understands and produces through either natural speech or augmented modes.

Pulling It All Together

Once again, it must be emphasized that the purpose of language assessment, both formal and informal, is not to assign a score or developmental age to the individual but rather to gather information that is needed for intervention planning. The goal is to develop a functional profile of the person's current language capabilities so that appropriate symbols, vocabulary items, and instructional procedures can be selected. There is no recipe for matching specific AAC strategies and techniques with the characteristics of the individual's language profile because this information must be considered in its totality along with information about the individual's motor, sensory, and other capabilities. For example, imagine a language profile for an individual with no motor or vision impairments indicating that she has a one-word vocabulary of 300 line-drawn symbols, produces no two- or three-word combinations, and initiates simple requests and answers questions with symbols. It is likely that the initial AAC intervention would involve either a low- or high-tech system with a large vocabulary capability that can be expanded easily and would include techniques aimed at encouraging multi-word combinations and increasing communicative competence in conversational and other interactive contexts. Contrast this with the profile of an individual with severe motor and vision impairments who has a vocabulary of 10 manual signs, cannot make choices, and initiates no interactions. Clearly, the recommended intervention would be much different for the second individual than for the first one—not just because of differences in language ability but because of a combination of *many* factors. These two examples illustrate the importance of considering language assessment information as part of the "big picture" of all intervention information.

Literacy Assessment

Literacy encompasses a multitude of skills that, cumulatively, result in a person's ability to read, spell, and write. Literacy assessment is particularly important for AAC users, who may have received very irregular instruction in this area and may present with scattered profiles of ability as a result. The primary areas in which literacy assessment should be conducted are discussed in the sections that follow.

Print and Phoneme Recognition Assessment

Screening for recognition of letter names and sounds is useful as a beginning step in an overall literacy assessment. AAC teams can conduct such screening quite easily using simple letter boards, eye-gaze displays, or keyboards. Assessors can ask the individual to point to or look at specific letters by name ("Show me *A, H,* and *M*") and/or identify them by sound ("Show me the one that sounds like /ah/"). Team members can ask individuals who can write to produce letters or their corresponding sounds by printing.

It is important to note that some individuals who can read are unable to recognize letters in either manner in isolation, so additional literacy assessment should proceed even in the absence of these basic skills.

Word Recognition and Reading Comprehension Assessment

People who are even partially literate may be able to use their reading skills in AAC contexts. Assessment of reading skills for AAC usually involves checking both word recognition and reading comprehension. A variety of assessment instruments incorporate these components, including the Metropolitan Reading Readiness Test, Level II (Nurss & McGauvran, 1986); the Gates-MacGinitie Reading Tests (MacGinitie & MacGinitie, 1980); reading subtests of the Peabody Individual Achievement Test–Revised (Markwardt, 1989), and the Woodcock Reading Mastery Tests–Revised (Woodcock, 1987). All of these require a simple pointing response or can be adapted for use with alternative response modes.

Canadian versions of all levels of the Gates-MacGinitie Reading Tests (MacGinitie, 1980) are available from Nelson Canada in Toronto, Ontario, Canada.

It is often advisable to conduct an informal, interactive word recognition reading assessment as well, especially with individuals who demonstrate limited skills on standardized tests. For example, some people may recognize words visually either on flash cards or in natural contexts, perhaps because the words have been paired with symbols on their AAC displays. AAC teams can conduct informal assessments using words to which the individual has been exposed either formally or informally (e.g., *enter* or *exit*, *women* or *men, stop*, names of favorite foods or restaurants). Or assessors may use multiple-choice questions of increasing difficulty to determine contextual reading abilities. For example, teams can construct sentences such as "I like to eat (pizza, chair, dog, shoe)" using information from family members or teachers. If the person succeeds at this level, assessors may gradually increase the similarity among options over subsequent trials so that the answer sets for the above sentence might change to (doors, horses, donuts, arms [all plural]) and then to (come, cook, cane, cake [all with same initial letter]).

Spelling Assessment

Spelling abilities are also important targets during AAC assessment. Because various AAC techniques require different types of spelling skills, a nontraditional language or spelling evaluation may be necessary. Overall, three components of spelling ability should be assessed: spontaneous spelling; first-letter-of-word spelling; and, if necessary, recognition spelling.

Spontaneous Spelling

In spontaneous spelling, the individual is required to spell words letter by letter. The spelling subtest of the Wide Range Achievement Test (Wilkinson, 1993) provides good estimates of spontaneous spelling abilities. Individuals who can spell, at least phonetically (e.g., *fon* for *phone*), can use these skills when operating dedicated or computer-based AAC devices that rely on orthography.

First-Letter-of-Word Spelling

In our experience, individuals with minimal performance on spontaneous spelling tests often perform quite well on first-letter-of-word tasks. Several AAC techniques require first-letter-of-word spelling so that the individual can use word menus for each of the letters of the alphabet. Thus, it is also important to evaluate the extent to which people can spontaneously indicate the first letters of words, even if their other spelling skills are minimal or nonexistent. Tests such as the BRIGANCE® Comprehensive Inventory of Basic Skills (Brigance, 1981)[1] allow assessment of this skill. Otherwise, this can be done informally in two ways. The first (and more difficult) procedure involves showing the person pictures of common items and asking "What's the first letter of this word?" without saying the word out loud. The second procedure is to say the word while asking the question, such as "What's the first letter in *cat?*" In order to use first-letter-of-word spelling for AAC, individuals without speech need to be able to do the first of these tasks; however, it is also important to identify skills in the easier assessment task so they can be built on and expanded, if necessary.

Recognition Spelling

Many individuals who acquired literacy skills without appropriate writing systems learned to spell on a recognition basis—that is, they can recognize words that are spelled correctly but cannot spontaneously produce those words or their first letters. They have, in effect, a "sight word vocabulary" in that they have memorized the configurations of certain words. Assessment of recognition spelling is only necessary if the individual can produce neither the first letters of words nor their correct spellings spontaneously. To assess recognition spelling, the individual is asked to recognize either the correct or the incorrect word from a series of options. For example, assessors might present the words *esarar, eraser,* and *erisir* with a picture of an eraser, and the individual's task is to identify the word that is spelled correctly. The Peabody Individual Achievement Test measures recognition spelling ability (Markwardt, 1989).

Pulling It All Together

AAC teams should incorporate any reading skills that are identified during assessment into the overall design of the AAC system at an appropriate level of difficulty. At the most basic level, printed words can be used as symbols instead of or in addition to pictorial symbols. Otherwise, displays using single-word options in a multiple-choice format can be provided, as reported for adults with aphasia in Chapter 16. In addition, reading assessment information can be used to design an appropriate literacy program of instruction. We discuss the importance of literacy instruction for AAC users in detail in Chapter 13.

It is not at all unusual for AAC users to have very uneven spelling and reading profiles; often, individuals with fairly good reading skills are not able to spell at the same level. Assessors should not overestimate the spelling skills of these individuals because the implications for each type of spelling skill with regard to AAC intervention differ considerably. For example, in order to learn Morse code, it appears that people need spontaneous spelling skills to at least the second-grade level (Marriner et al., 1989). Nevertheless, individuals who are not this proficient but who have first-letter-of-word spelling abilities and adequate reading abilities may be able to use a word predic-

---

[1]BRIGANCE® is a registered trademark of Curriculum Associates, Inc.

tion or word menu selection technique (e.g., Co:Writer or EZ Keys software). As with other types of assessments, it is important that the AAC team be aware of the available intervention options and the operational requirements to ensure a good client–system match.

Sensory/Perceptual Assessment

Because vision impairments accompany many of the developmental and acquired disabilities that are common in AAC users, an accurate vision assessment is quite important. Decisions about the type, size, placement, spacing, and colors of symbols will often be guided by the results of such an assessment. Assessment of hearing capabilities, although less critical, will also allow the AAC team to make decisions about output options (e.g., types of synthetic or digitized speech the AAC user can hear) as well as options related to language input (e.g., whether to supplement speech with manual signs or symbols). Assessment in both of these areas is discussed in the sections that follow.

Vision Assessment

Vision is a three-stage system that involves *sight*, the reception of sensory stimulation through the eye; *transmission* of an image along the optic nerve; and *interpretation* of the image in the visual cortex of the brain. During interpretation images are transformed into meaningful information. The interpretation of the image is a result of all that an individual brings to the task, including motivation, experience, and self-image, which are the tools of functional vision. How an individual actually uses and enhances his or her existing vision through various means is at least as important from a functional perspective as is the nature or severity of the visual impairment itself. This certainly applies to AAC system considerations; thus, it is important for intervention teams to consider not only the individual's impairment but also the AAC user's perceptions of his or her visual abilities and disabilities.

Assessment of an individual's visual status involves evaluation of a number of components, including *visual acuity, visual field magnitude, oculomotor functioning, light and color sensitivity,* and *visual stability.* Each element contributes to an individual's functional vision skills. Most of these components will require assessment by ophthalmologists, optometrists, or vision specialists either before or during the AAC evaluation process.

Visual acuity, or clarity of vision, allows an individual to discriminate details. Visual acuity is expressed by notations that describe the size of a visual target and the distance at which the target is identified. Fractional notation is most commonly used, with the numerator indicating the testing distance and the denominator indicating the size of the test item that can be identified on an eye chart (see Figure 7.21). The designation for *normal vision* is 20/20 (Cline, Hofstetter, & Griffin, 1980). People with acuities of 20/70–20/200 are considered to be *partially sighted,* and those with less than 20/200 vision are labeled *legally blind.* When vision decreases to awareness of light only, visual level is referred to as *light perception,* and a person is considered to be *totally blind* in the absence of light perception.

Visual acuities should be measured close up and at a distance because visual performance may differ depending on the task, as well as on the person's overall abilities and the visual condition causing the impairment. Some of the most common visual acuity assessment formats that can serve as an alternative to traditional eye charts are presented in Table 7.6 (Cress, 1987; Cress et al., 1981). In addition, Sobsey and Wolf-

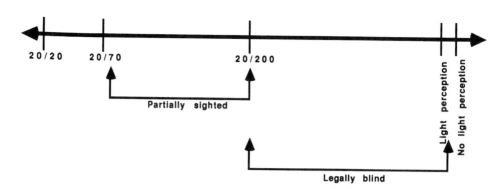

Figure 7.21.   Continuum depicting the range of visual impairments.

Schein (1996) described a forced-choice preferential looking (FPL) procedure that is easy to administer and can provide basic information about functional visual acuity. In the FPL procedure, two computer screens with the same illumination or one large split screen is used. Two images, one of which contains no pattern and the other of which is boldly striped, checkered, or has wavy lines, are displayed on the screen(s) over several trials in alternating order (see Figure 7.22). Because most individuals will consistently look at the patterned screen, vision assessors can determine the person's ability to see at all. If the person orients toward the bold pattern, repeated pairings can then be presented with increasingly finer patterns until reaching the stage at which the person is unable to make a discrimination. Assessors can also vary the size of the squares systematically to approximate the size of potential communication symbols (e.g., 4″ × 4″, 2″ × 2″). In addition, the distance from the screen can be varied to determine the minimum and maximum distances within which the person demonstrates pattern preferences. Although the FPL procedure provides only an informal estimate of visual acuity, it can be useful in the absence of alternative tests.

Table 7.6.   Selected instruments for vision assessment

Instrument	Source
Lippman HOTV (Lippman, 1971)	Good-Lite Company, 7426 W. Madison Street, Forest Park, IL 60130
Lighthouse Flashcard Test	New York Association for the Blind, 111 E. 59th Street, New York, NY 10022
Parsons Visual Acuity Test (Spellman, DeBriere, & Cress, 1979)	Bernell Corporation, 750 Lincolnway, East, Post Office Box 4637, South Bend, IN 46634
Teller Acuity Cards (Teller, McDonald, Preston, Sebris, & Dobson, 1986)	Vistech Corporation, 4162 Little York Road, Dayton, OH 45414
Vision Assessment and Program Manual for Severely Handicapped and/or Deaf-Blind Students (Sailor, Utley, Goetz, Gee, & Baldwin, 1982)	San Francisco State University, Bay Area Severely Handicapped/ Deaf-Blind Project, 612 Font Boulevard, San Francisco, CA 94132

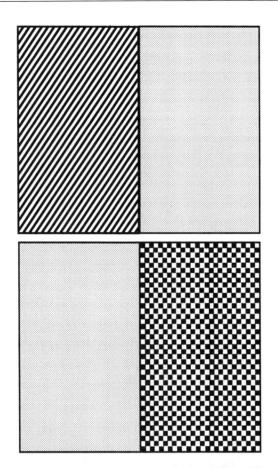

Figure 7.22.   Examples of screens used for the forced-choice preferential looking (FPL) procedure for functional visual acuity.

AAC teams need information about visual acuity in order to decide whether to use aided symbols or unaided symbols (e.g., manual signs for someone with vision), and, if aided symbols are chosen, the type(s) of symbols to use, their size, their distance from the AAC user's eyes, and so forth. Even individuals who are considered legally blind often have some residual vision that they can use for communication.

Visual field refers to the area in which objects are visible to the eye without a shift in gaze, normally extending in arcs of 150° horizontally and 120° vertically (Jose, 1983). The central visual field corresponds to the foveal and macular areas of the retina, which contain the cells most adapted to yield high visual acuity. Stimulation of these areas by visual impulses produces vision of the greatest clarity. Normal acuity decreases in proportion to the distance of the target from the fovea and macula. Thus, vision in the peripheral visual field is less clear than in the central visual field. The peripheral visual field detects movement and assists with vision in conditions of decreased illumination (Cline et al., 1980).

There are many impairments associated with the visual field, including 1) decreased vision in either the central or the peripheral field; 2) depressed visual sensitivity in specific areas; 3) blind spots (also referred to as opacities or scotomas) of varying shapes and sizes; 4) hemispheric losses; and 5) field losses that may occur subsequent to acquired brain injury, stroke, or other causes, in which entire segments of the visual field are missing. These losses can occur in one or both eyes and are depicted in Figure 7.23. An individual with a *central visual field loss* has difficulty seeing a visual target presented at the mid-line of the body. This person must shift his or her focus off center to bring a target into view, generally by moving the head or eye horizontally or vertically. Individuals with *peripheral visual field losses* tend to experience difficulties when moving because they may be unable to detect movement or locate objects to their sides or beneath them. *Depressed sensitivity* results in areas of decreased acuity, which affect functional vision depending on the location of the affected areas and their shape and size (Harrington, 1976). Similarly, *blind spots* or *hemispheric losses* in the visual field can create a variety of problems that require adjustment of the point of visual fixation, head position, and the placement of materials. Such adjustments are often difficult to achieve for individuals with visual impairments who use AAC because they may experience additional physical impairments that interfere with their ability to move, maintain head control, or precisely direct their eye gaze. A qualified professional should make a careful assessment of visual field impairments in order to ensure proper placement and arrangement of communication symbols and devices for such individuals.

Oculomotor functioning refers to the operation of the eye muscles that enable the eyes to move together smoothly in all directions. These muscles allow the eyes to move into position and to place and maintain the image of an object on the optimal area of the retina. Oculomotor functioning includes movements that allow the eyes to establish and maintain visual fixation, locate and scan for objects, and follow moving objects. Problems with oculomotor functioning impair an individual's ability to direct precisely his or her gaze and may result in *double vision* or other problems. For example, a person

Central visual field loss

Peripheral visual field loss
with decreased central
sensitivity

Multiple "blind spots"
in the visual field

Loss of the left visual field

Figure 7.23.   Examples of visual field impairments and their effects. (Picture Communication Symbols copyright © 1994 by Mayer-Johnson Co.; reprinted by permission.)

with *strabismus* is unable to maintain the eyes in a position of binocular fixation because of weak eye muscles, and, thus, the eyes either converge (i.e., cross) or diverge. *Nystagmus,* another oculomotor disorder, is characterized by various involuntary movements of the eye and results in significantly reduced visual acuity. Individuals with this oculomotor disorder often attempt to compensate for it by repositioning their eyes, their head, and/or the materials they are examining. Thus, the detection of oculomotor disorders is of particular importance when an intervention team designs AAC systems for an individual with physical disabilities because the individual may lack the ability to freely adjust his or her body positions in order to compensate for the oculomotor disorder. Decisions regarding the positioning of an AAC device, the configuration of a symbol array, and the spacing of items on the display are all affected by the user's ocular motility and coordination. In addition, an individual with oculomotor problems may have great difficulty using scanning devices that require him or her to track moving lights on a display.

Light sensitivity must also be considered when evaluating an individual's visual status. Some disorders necessitate reduction or intensification of ambient light in order to achieve optimal visual functioning. For example, individuals with retinal problems may demonstrate abnormal sensitivity to light and require low light conditions for maximum performance. Individuals with conditions such as *degenerative myopia* (nearsightedness) require significantly increased levels of illumination in order to see. In addition to various disorders affecting light sensitivity, *glare* is a consideration for all but those individuals with the most severe visual impairments. Glare is the dazzling sensation that is caused by bright light or the reflection of bright light, and it produces discomfort and interferes with optimal vision (Cline et al., 1980). Glare is a concern for all AAC users whose displays are laminated or otherwise covered by plastic because such coverings heighten the reflection of light off the surface of the page. In addition, glare may be a problem for users of AAC devices with computer screen displays, especially those that are highly reflective. Attention to ambient light sources used for illumination, as well as to the positioning of displays with reflective surfaces, are important in order to minimize glare.

Color perception occurs when certain eye structures are stimulated by specific wavelengths of light and may be impaired in ways that affect accurate visual discrimination of contrast and detail. Generally, problems occur in the ability of the eyes to interpret particular (but not all) wavelength frequencies, so total color blindness is quite rare. People can learn to accommodate color vision problems, but the problems may be difficult to identify in very young children or in those who have difficulty labeling or matching. Nonetheless, AAC teams need to identify color impairments accurately to ensure that functional implications are minimized. For example, color codes using color wavelengths involved in an individual's particular impairment may serve only to reduce communication accuracy and frustrate the AAC user. Colors used on AAC displays for organizational or coding purposes must be discriminable and helpful to the user and must be used in ways that enhance communication accuracy rather than detract from it (see Bailey & Downing, 1994).

Another visual component affecting AAC use is *visual stability.* Some individuals have eye conditions that are stable and relatively unchanging over time. Others have conditions that fluctuate, sometimes daily, depending on the individuals' physical status or on environmental factors. In addition, some conditions deteriorate over time, with variability in both the rate of deterioration and the final visual outcome. For example, individuals with *retinitis pigmentosa* (a progressive genetic visual impairment) experience a gradual reduction in the size of their visual field, along with night blindness, abnormal sensitivity to light, and color impairments. They may retain some vision throughout life, or they may eventually lose most or all vision. Because the condition is progressive and unpredictable and because it cannot be treated, these individuals must consider their current and potential visual status when making long-term decisions. Teams should consider AAC techniques for both current and future use even at the point of initial assessment.

In addition to the measures mentioned previously, informal vision assessment procedures such as Langley's (1980) Functional Vision Inventory may provide AAC team members with useful strategies for gathering information relevant to *visual competency.* This term refers to how an individual actually uses and enhances his or her existing vision through various means and is at least as important from a functional perspective as is the nature or severity of any visual impairments that may exist. For example, consider two individuals with the same eye condition that results in identical visual acuities of 20/200 (the limit for legal blindness). One person lives a typical life: She uses adaptations to perform certain tasks but continues to work, raises a family, and generally functions independently in society. Her counterpart functions much less independently and is unable to perform basic tasks, including those necessary for employment. The major difference between these two individuals is in the functional use of the vision they have, not in their impairments. This variation in functional use of vision certainly affects AAC system considerations because it is important to consider not only the individual's impairments but also the AAC user's perceptions and ability to compensate for them.

Pulling It All Together

Throughout this section, we suggest how information in each area might be useful in the overall design of an AAC system. In our experience, it is not at all uncommon for inadequate vision assessment or inadequate application of assessment information to cause individuals to abandon using their systems. Information about a person's visual *abilities* is far more important for AAC application than information about his or her visual *impairments.* Questions to ask include the following: What *can* the person see accurately? How close to the person and how large do stimuli need to be? How far apart should they be arranged? Would colored or dark backgrounds help accommodate for problems of contrast? Are there blind spots or areas of reduced vision, and, if so, where in the visual field is vision most accurate? How should displays be positioned to allow maximal visual efficiency? If oculomotor problems are present, how are they best minimized or accommodated? Which colors can be seen? What lighting is required for optimal vision? If additional visual losses will occur over time, what is the time line and predicted progression? The answers to such questions are often implicit in formal vision assessments but may not be addressed explicitly by an examiner without prompting from other team members. It is up to the AAC team to ensure that information needed for system design is made explicit to the person conducting a vision assessment, and we have found that most vision specialists are able and willing to provide such information if it is requested.

Hearing Assessment

Assessment of hearing capabilities is important, especially if the selection set is displayed auditorily, as with auditory scanning. AAC teams usually select auditory display systems for people with severe visual impairments, and these systems require that

users be able to hear and understand the items in the selection set as they are announced. If interventionists consider auditory scanning via synthetic or digitized
speech as an option, the hearing assessment should also serve to determine the individual's ability to comprehend the particular type of synthesized speech used in the system. In many electronic devices, feedback is also auditory and may be in the form of a
beep to indicate that an item has been selected or a spoken echo produced via synthetic
or digitized speech. Finally, many AAC devices utilize speech synthesis or digitization
for output. Although such output is provided primarily for the benefit of the communication partner, not the AAC user, auditory comprehension of the output signal by the
user is generally desirable.

Assessment of hearing capabilities is usually straightforward and can be conducted by a qualified audiologist who does not necessarily have experience with AAC.
If needed, evaluation of a potential user's ability to understand synthetic or digitized
speech may be requested as an additional service. Of course, for some individuals, examiners may need to employ alternative response modes. For example, Bristow and
Fristoe (1988) reported data supporting the use of a speech audiometry procedure in-
corporating eye gaze as the response mode for people with physical disabilities. Additional alternative formats were described by Sobsey and Wolf-Schein (1996). People
with severe cognitive impairments may require considerable instruction prior to formal
testing in order to establish a reliable operant response to sound. The empirically validated procedures developed by Goetz, Gee, and Sailor (1983) may be useful during
such instruction. Examiners may test individuals who cannot participate actively in audiological assessment using an auditory brain stem response procedure (Berlin &
Hood, 1987).

Assessment is a process during which information is gathered in order to make
clinical, educational, or vocational management decisions. (Yorkston & Karlan,
1986, p. 164)

CONCLUSIONS

The goal of assessment is to gather a sufficient amount of information for the AAC
team—the user, family members, professionals, and other facilitators—to make intervention decisions that meet both the individual's current and future communication
needs. Because of the many complex issues that must be considered in such assessments, there is a widespread tendency to overassess capabilities. Too much testing of
an individual's motor, cognitive, linguistic, and sensory performance can actually interfere with AAC intervention because it takes so much time and places so many demands
on the family and the potential user. In this chapter, we have provided a framework for
completing assessments that are broad-based in scope but not necessarily exhaustive.
Additional details regarding the assessment of people with acquired communication
impairments appear in Chapters 15–18.

8

Principles of
Decision Making and Intervention

Once the assessment process has been completed, the augmentative and alternative communication (AAC) team can finalize decisions about intervention. Some guidelines for decision making are presented in Chapters 6 and 7. In this chapter, we discuss additional principles that can be used in the intervention process. However, the issues discussed in this chapter are general. (See Chapters 9–18 for specific intervention guidelines and techniques for AAC users with various types of disabilities.)

Principle 1: Build on the consensus already achieved during the assessment process.

CONSENSUS BUILDING DURING INTERVENTION

In Chapter 5, we discuss the importance of using a team approach to AAC assessment and intervention planning. During decision making and intervention, the AAC user, his or her family, and the professionals involved must continue to work together to share information about preferences and strategies. Two strategies in particular are important during this phase of the process:

- Continue to make decisions as a team after the assessment has been completed, rather than asking team members to "sign off" on an idea or decision in which they have not been involved. If even one member of the team disagrees with a decision, negotiation and compromise should be clearly established as the appropriate team responses.
- Create an atmosphere in which team members feel free to raise issues or problems. Team members may not be comfortable expressing concerns for fear of "hurting someone's feelings" or "making someone angry." It is important to establish an at-

mosphere of trust and interdependence from the outset so that each person on the team can offer his or her opinions and ideas to the intervention process. The extra time this may take in the beginning will be well worth it in the end!

A consensus-building approach to team management may be ineffective if the basic principles of consensus building are violated. During ineffective consensus building, an agreement to compromise typically means that one or more of the team members (almost always those in the minority) have been manipulated, intimidated, coerced, or otherwise persuaded to agree with the rest of the team. This may resolve the immediate conflict but will come back later to haunt the overall team efforts through subtle (or not so subtle) sabotage of the plan. Instead, the goal should be a compromise that emerges when all team members engage in an open dialogue about the issue and arrive at truly "reciprocal concessions" (Chadsey & Wentworth, 1974, p. 121).

To accomplish this compromise, all members of the team must be willing to state their opinions openly, engage in dialogue to share rationales and information, and state their revised opinions. Team members must be willing to repeat the dialogue as many times as necessary to resolve the conflict. In order to negotiate, the consensus facilitator (i.e., team leader) must be prepared to confront the behavior of individual team members who refuse to engage in discussions or reveal their biases and opinions or who otherwise remain uninvolved in the decision-making process. The team must work to achieve consensus without anyone "losing face" or agreeing to tasks that are clearly "above and beyond the call of duty." Finally, all team members, including administrators and support personnel, should be prepared to state their understanding of the compromise and their willingness to participate. Again, we emphasize that the long-term detrimental effects of a failure to build consensus cause far more delays and problems with service delivery than do the efforts that may be needed to achieve consensus.

In this chapter, we continue discussing the steps in the Participation Model and focus on steps that take place after the assessment of participation needs, opportunity barriers, current capabilities, and constraints. General interventions related to opportunity barriers are discussed briefly and then expanded in the chapters pertaining to specific impairments.

OPPORTUNITY BARRIER INTERVENTIONS

The reason for assessing the nature of opportunity barriers in the first place is to facilitate appropriate interventions at this stage of the process. *Policy barriers*, which are the official written laws, standards, or regulations that govern the contexts in which AAC users find themselves, will need to be resolved through advocacy efforts aimed at changing the restrictive legislation or regulations. Such efforts will usually require the efforts of large groups of parents and professionals working together to institute change. For example, in the United States, the passage of the Technology-Related Assistance for Individuals with Disabilities Act of 1989, PL 100-407, and the Americans with Disabilities Act (ADA) of 1990, PL 101-336, has resulted in the dissolution of many barriers that formerly made AAC services inaccessible to many people who needed them. In addition, the National Joint Committee for the Communicative Needs of Persons with Severe Disabilities has made a series of policy-level recommendations that have been influential in the AAC area. The committee consists of individuals from professional organizations representing the fields of AAC, speech-language pathology, occupational therapy, physical therapy, and education, as well as those concerned specifically with services for individuals with mental retardation and other severe disabilities. In 1992, the committee produced a document entitled *Guidelines for Meeting the Communication Needs of Persons with Severe Disabilities,* which contains a list of numerous "recommended practices" for assessment, goal setting, intervention, service delivery, and the knowledge needed by members of an interdisciplinary team. It also contains a *Communication Bill of Rights,* which is presented in Table 8.1. These guidelines and rights are rapidly becoming the standards for established practice in the United States and are used to challenge policy and practice barriers that contradict them. Clearly, changing barriers at the policy level often requires organized and widespread efforts.

Practice barriers refer to procedures or conventions that have become common in a family, school, or workplace but that contradict official policies that allow for service provision. For example, parents in a school district that has a policy to support inclusion might still need to advocate within their specific school to counteract existing barriers against inclusion and ensure that the policy is carried out. Advocacy efforts are often needed to address practice barriers, but they should almost always be combined with educational and sensitization efforts as well. For instance, if parents simply advo-

Table 8.1.   A communication bill of rights

All persons, regardless of the extent or severity of their disabilities, have a basic right to affect, through communication, the conditions of their own existence. Beyond this general right, a number of specific communication rights should be ensured in all daily interactions and interventions involving persons who have severe disabilities. These basic communication rights are as follows:

1. The right to request desired objects, actions, events, and persons, and to express personal preferences, or feelings.
2. The right to be offered choices and alternatives.
3. The right to reject or refuse undesired objects, events, or actions, including the right to decline or reject all proffered choices.
4. The right to request, and be given, attention from and interaction with another person.
5. The right to request feedback or information about a state, an object, a person, or an event of interest.
6. The right to active treatment and intervention efforts to enable people with severe disabilities to communicate messages in whatever modes and as effectively and efficiently as their specific abilities allow.
7. The right to have communicative acts acknowledged and responded to, even when the intent of these acts cannot be fulfilled by the responder.
8. The right to have access at all times to any needed augmentative and alternative communication devices and other assistive devices, and to have those devices in good working order.
9. The right to environmental contexts, interactions, and opportunities that expect and encourage persons with disabilities to participate as full communicative partners with other people, including peers.
10. The right to be informed about people, things, and events in one's immediate environment.
11. The right to be communicated with in a manner that recognizes and acknowledges the inherent dignity of the person being addressed, including the right to be part of communication exchanges about individuals that are conducted in his or her presence.
12. The right to be communicated with in ways that are meaningful, understandable, and culturally and linguistically appropriate.

From the National Joint Committee for the Communication Needs of Persons with Severe Disabilities. (1992). Guidelines for meeting the communication needs of persons with severe disabilities. *Asha, 34*(Suppl. 7), 2–3; reprinted by permission.

cate a change in practice without acknowledging that school staff will need education and support in order to make this happen, the practice barrier is likely to remain. Practice barriers may be easier to eliminate than policy barriers, especially if policies are already in place to support the need for change.

A third type of barrier is related to *attitude*. Here, the beliefs held by an individual, rather than by an agency or by an establishment, present a barrier to participation. Often, attitude barriers will persist even when policy and practice barriers do not. For example, a group home run by a very progressive agency has clear policies related to the importance of providing supports to enable the men who live there to make choices and control their own lives as much as possible. In fact, in this group home, the general practice is in compliance with this policy; the men are encouraged to participate in designing meal menus, decorating their home, determining their own activity schedules, and so forth. However, one particular staff member's attitude presents an opportunity barrier in that he does not believe that the men should be "allowed to have" as much control and choice as they do. The result is that he limits their communication opportunities by failing to both provide them with choices and honor the choices they make. Clearly, this is not an issue for which advocacy efforts are appropriate. Instead, attitude barriers are best approached with such strategies as providing information about the issue of concern, arranging to have the person talk with or visit colleagues with more appropriate attitudes, providing time for open discussion of ideas about the issue, and modeling appropriate practices. In other words, it is easier to reduce attitude barriers with personalized educational efforts directed at change rather than with administrative or legislative solutions. In the preceding example, the "problem" staff member at the group home was provided with readings about choice and empowerment of people with disabilities, instruction related to how to facilitate choice making, and ample opportunities to discuss his feelings and concerns with other staff. Over time, his attitude barriers fell away as he was able to incorporate a new way of thinking into his existing repertoire.

Knowledge barriers are the result of a lack of information on the part of someone other than the AAC user that results in limited opportunities for participation. Knowledge barriers can be one of several barriers or can occur even when policies, practices, and attitudes in support of communication are in place. These barriers are best remediated through educational efforts such as in-service training, courses, workshops, directed readings, and so forth. Related to these are *skill barriers*, which occur when team members have difficulty with the actual implementation of an AAC technique or strategy despite even extensive knowledge. Education efforts need to be directed toward additional practice, the provision of technical assistance, and other individualized and "hands-on" efforts. Skill barriers are what all of us have experienced after coming back from an exciting course or workshop only to realize that actually *implementing* all of the new information is a formidable task! Working with other colleagues who have more experience in the area or asking someone to brainstorm about strategies for translating theory into practice are two good examples of appropriate skill-building strategies.

Once a plan is in place to deal with the identified opportunity barriers over time, team members can compile assessment information and compare it with the requirements of various communication options. Two sets of communication options are generally available: 1) those designed to increase natural abilities and 2) those designed to utilize environmental or communication adaptations. We cannot overemphasize that these options are not mutually exclusive. Indeed, many individuals may be best served by a combination of natural ability interventions and environmental adaptations.

NATURAL ABILITY INTERVENTIONS

The first decision that the team must make often involves the relative emphasis to be placed on natural ability interventions and adaptive approaches. Of course, this consideration depends on the origin, stage, and course of the AAC user's communication disability. For example, an individual with end-stage amyotrophic lateral sclerosis (ALS) will not benefit from interventions designed to increase natural speech, whereas a preschool child with cerebral palsy is likely to require extensive attention in this area (see the chapters discussing specific disabilities in Parts II and III). Regardless, the team may need to resolve misconceptions and disagreements concerning this decision.

Resolving Misconceptions

Family members may perceive discussions about the relative emphasis of AAC (i.e., adaptive) versus natural ability interventions as leading to dichotomous, either/or outcomes. Perhaps the most common scenario is that family members resist AAC interventions because they are afraid that these will inhibit the individual's natural speech development. For example, the family of a young adult with traumatic brain injury (TBI) who has some speech but who cannot be understood by unfamiliar people may perceive a team's recommendation to provide an AAC system as an indicator that the team will exert no further therapeutic efforts to improve the young adult's speech, even if this is not the team's intended message. Or the motor specialists working with a young child with severe cerebral palsy may recommend a single-switch scanning device with a head switch because this best matches the child's current capabilities. The other members of the team and the family may view this decision negatively if they interpret it to mean that the team will discontinue current therapeutic interventions to improve the child's upper-extremity motor function.

The team must identify and articulate such misconceptions early in the decision-making process so that they can be discussed and corrected. If the team does not deal with these misconceptions, the issue is almost certain to surface again, during either intervention planning or implementation. Sometimes, providing concerned individuals and families with information from research regarding the effects of AAC on natural speech development is sufficient to alleviate their concerns (Dowden, 1997).

Simple assurances that AAC interventions are unlikely to be detrimental to natural speech development, however, are usually insufficient to dispel such misconceptions. The AAC team should include a plan describing 1) the amount of speech therapy services that will be provided, 2) the intervention goals, and 3) information about the approaches to be used in the individual's educational or rehabilitation plan, if applicable. In addition, it is important to share information about any progress in natural abilities with the entire team (including the individual and his or her family) on a regular basis to avoid the perception that agreement to work on these skills was a token gesture rather than a serious commitment.

Resolving Disagreements

More than simple misconceptions about the intended emphasis of natural ability interventions in the overall communication plan may exist. In fact, some team members may even suggest that work on natural abilities not be initiated, be terminated after a

trial period, or be increased or decreased markedly. Typically, disagreements about recommendations to terminate or decrease instruction arise from perceptions or evidence
that efforts to increase natural ability have not proved effective for the individual of
concern. For example, an older adult with aphasia secondary to stroke who has had
years of speech therapy may indicate that he or she no longer wishes to receive such
services, against the wishes of his or her spouse. Disagreements about whether to initiate natural ability interventions almost always stem from differing opinions about the
prognosis of such efforts. For example, the family of a child with autism and little
speech may be unwilling to place the child in a modified curriculum because they believe that he or she may be able to communicate through reading and writing if given
the necessary instruction. Finally, disagreements about whether to increase or maintain
the emphasis on natural ability often arise when team members are more familiar with
natural ability options than with AAC options. Consider the example of a child with severe motor and speech apraxia who has been using both AAC and natural speech approaches for several years. Her family moved to a new town where she attends a school
in which there has never been a child who uses AAC. None of the professionals involved in her educational program are familiar with either the AAC field or her particular communication system. Hence, a recommendation was made at the initial team
meeting to place major emphasis on developing the child's natural speech and to minimize or discontinue the use of the AAC system at school. Her parents protested that intensive speech therapy was tried for several years with minimal results and insisted
that her AAC system be fully incorporated into the overall plan.

Whatever the source of the disagreement, certain outcomes can be predicted if a
consensus is not achieved prior to intervention planning. First, members of the team
representing the minority position are at risk for being labeled by the others as uncoop-
erative, unrealistic, or "in denial" about the abilities in dispute. The parents of the child
with apraxia in the previous example were labeled overly pessimistic because they did
not wish to expend undue time and energy on natural speech instruction, and they
were considered to be "parents who think technology will solve everything" because of
their support of the child's AAC system. Second, the intervention plan as a whole is at
risk for failure because it is almost certain that the team members who disagree will
pursue implementation of the plan with less than full commitment and enthusiasm.
Third, and most important, the AAC user is at risk for continued and future communication problems as a result of the interpersonal conflicts and intervention failures that
are likely to occur as a result of the lack of consensus.

Clearly, none of these outcomes is acceptable. Concerted and ongoing efforts to resolve the disagreement through consensus building are critical if an impasse occurs.
The first step in resolution is to identify the source of the disagreement through a discussion with all team members—including the AAC user's parents; the individual,
when appropriate; and professional, support, and administrative staff. In many cases,
the real source of the disagreement may stem from policies or practices of the agency
providing services. Failure to involve agency administrators can result in ineffective
and inefficient consensus building. For example, consider a disagreement between the
family of a 17-year-old boy with learning disabilities and the student's speech-language
pathologist and teachers. The family wanted their son to be allowed to use a portable
computer in the classroom with a spelling checker, grammar checker, and linguistic
predictor to produce written work such as tests and reports. The professionals on the
team refused, ostensibly because they believed that he should work to remediate his
natural reading and writing skills exclusively. In fact, however, they were acutely

aware that none of them possessed sufficient computer skills to provide the student with the necessary support, and they were worried about the implications for their workloads if this adaptation were to be instituted. Of course, none of the team members admitted these real issues to the family, and it was only when one of the teachers made a reference to being wary of computers and other gadgets at the consensus meeting that the true nature of the problem began to emerge. The disagreement was eventually resolved, with the help of the principal, who had the authority to initiate districtwide interventions to increase computer skills among the staff. Although this particular situation may be unique, there are similar situations in which the apparent source of the disagreement differs from the real source. Regardless of the issue, resolution of a disagreement is impossible until its source and dynamics are clear to all team members.

In disagreements in which neither clear evidence nor history supports one position over another, outcomes that reflect compromise are preferable to those in which some team members win while others lose. Compromise is a likely solution in most cases, considering the advances in both natural and augmented communication approaches. For example, who is to say that the family of the aforementioned child with autism was wrong in their assessment of his potential literacy abilities? Indeed, splinter skills in literacy are fairly well documented in this population, and some believe that they may be more common than previously thought (Biklen, 1990).

Principle 2: Communication is multimodal in nature. AAC interventions should also be multimodal in nature.

In reality, for decisions about natural ability interventions, the evidence for one position and the accuracy of predictions concerning outcomes are often weak at best. Therefore, in order to reach consensus, professionals, family members, support personnel, and AAC users all must be willing to grant the possibility that a novel approach or combination of approaches merits consideration (see Dowden, 1997, for examples). Often, we approach compromise with the analogy of an investment portfolio, in which negotiable percentages of professional time are allocated to natural speech and AAC investments, respectively. Thus, the team might decide to invest 50% of available intervention time in therapies to increase natural speech and motor skills and 50% of its time to AAC system development and use, or 10% to natural ability areas and 90% to the area of AAC, or whatever reasonable compromise can be reached by the team. When a compromise is reached, it is critical that the team follow through with the negotiated plan and meet regularly to share progress or lack thereof so that adjustments can be made in the "investment portfolio" accordingly.

ENVIRONMENTAL ADAPTATION INTERVENTIONS

The second intervention option in the access strand of the Participation Model (Figure 6.1) involves resolving communication difficulties through environmental adaptations. The need for environmental adaptations may have been identified in the assessment of participation patterns or in the capability assessment, or both. Environmental adaptations, when indicated, are as critical to the overall success of the communication intervention as are other options. These adaptations can be divided into two main categories: space/location adaptations and physical structure adaptations.

Space/Location Adaptations

It is important to distinguish space/location adaptations from those made to eliminate identified opportunity barriers. Major lifestyle concerns regarding physical segregation and isolation from people because of lack of opportunity require policy- and practice-level interventions such as legislation, regulation, or education and are not solved by simple space/location adaptations. Space/location issues are specific to each intervention and should be solvable by the AAC team without major policy-level changes—assuming that consensus building has been effective, as discussed previously.

Space adaptations may be necessary for removing physical barriers to the AAC system itself. For example, a woman with a brain-stem stroke who lives in a residential care home may be unable to bring her communication device into the cafeteria because the tables and chairs are too close together for the device to pass when mounted on her power wheelchair. Or, a college student with cerebral palsy may not be able to install his adapted word processing equipment in his dormitory room because there is not enough space. In the first case, the necessary adaptations are simple: move the chairs and tables farther apart; in the second case, more complex accommodations will be necessary.

Location adaptations are more related to the location of the AAC user him- or herself than to the equipment. For example, a young girl with an AAC system in a classroom may be seated in the back of the room, making it difficult for her to regularly interact with the teacher. In addition, if she uses an AAC device with synthetic speech output, her teacher may have difficulty hearing the device without being near the student for every interaction. One teacher's initial solution in such an instance was to turn off the individual's speech-output device because "No one could hear it anyway!" In such cases a location adaptation to move the child's seat near the front of the room would be more appropriate (this was eventually done for the girl mentioned previously).

Physical Structure Adaptations

Physical structure adaptations go beyond space and location adjustments and are necessary for accommodating the communication system or for facilitating its use. Obvious examples include adjusting tables or classroom desks to accommodate a student and his or her AAC system, adapting beds with adjustable swing arms in order to mount AAC systems for users who are partially bedridden, and widening doorways to allow passage of wheelchair-mounted equipment. Physical structure adaptations related to making public places accessible are required in the United States by the ADA.

AAC INTERVENTION PLANNING AND IMPLEMENTATION

In Chapters 6 and 7, we discuss strategies for constructing a technology requirement profile and a capability profile to achieve an appropriate match between the AAC user's current abilities and the requirements of the available options. We also discuss which information is needed to compile a profile of constraints that might affect the AAC system or device plan. The process of achieving an effective match between a user and an AAC intervention involves a number of important considerations related to both long- and short-term communication goals. These considerations are explored in the sections that follow.

Principle 3: Plan for today and tomorrow.

Planning and Implementing Interventions for Today and Tomorrow

With initial assessments completed, the team should be prepared to make a decision about AAC devices or systems for the individual. Actually, two sets of decisions should be made from the outset: those aimed at "today" and those aimed at "tomorrow" (Beukelman, Yorkston, & Dowden, 1985). The relationship between decisions for today and decisions for tomorrow is depicted in Figure 8.1. The "today" decisions should meet the user's immediate communication needs and match the current capabilities and constraints identified during the assessment process. The "tomorrow" decisions are based on projections of future opportunities, needs, and constraints, as well as capabilities that result from instruction. Both decisions are critical to the long-term success of an intervention plan.

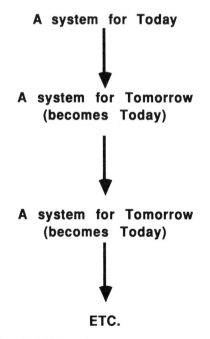

A system for Today

A system for Tomorrow (becomes Today)

A system for Tomorrow (becomes Today)

ETC.

Figure 8.1.   The longitudinal nature of AAC interventions.

Interventions for Today

When planning for today's needs, it is important to first consider the AAC technique(s) that meet the user's immediate needs within the available opportunities and are accurate, efficient, and nonfatiguing. An accurate system is one that the AAC user can use to produce intended messages with a minimum number of communication breakdowns and errors. This means that the system for today should match the user's current linguistic, cognitive, sensory, and motor abilities as closely as possible. An efficient system enables the AAC user to produce messages in an acceptable amount of time, again without extensive practice or training. This requirement can be met by achieving a good match between the system and the user's motor and sensory abilities, in particular, and those motor and sensory abilities required by the system. A nonfatiguing system enables the AAC user to communicate for as long as necessary without becoming excessively tired or experiencing significantly reduced accuracy or efficiency. This requirement, like accuracy, is met only by considering various linguistic, cognitive, motor, and sensory factors. In short, today's system should require a minimum of training and practice in order for the individual to use it effectively to communicate messages about his or her most important and immediate needs. Of course, the AAC team should select a system for today with a consideration of the existing constraints and unresolved opportunity barriers.

When we first got the light talker (sic), Ana had very poor head control. Getting the light to hit the right squares became a daily battle. But she carried on with a determination I found extraordinary. She must have known that this device was eventually going to liberate her, at least from the confines of speechlessness. I have never been so proud of my daughter as I was during those times. (Cy Berlowitz, describing his daughter who has severe cerebral palsy, in Berlowitz, 1991, p. 16)

In order to avoid situations in which an AAC user must wait for months or years before he or she can communicate effectively, it is of utmost importance that the individual have the ability almost immediately to use a system. Unfortunately, this sense of urgency is not always a major consideration of the AAC team. One study of 118 school-age students with mental retardation requiring extensive to pervasive support who were provided with manual sign instruction indicated that the average student was able to imitate nine signs and spontaneously produce four signs after 2.9 years of instruction (Bryen, Goldman, & Quinlisk-Gill, 1988). Obviously, this is an unacceptable outcome. Two primary failures account for these disappointing figures: 1) a failure to gather sufficient assessment information for decision making and 2) a failure to consider the need for instituting systems for today that match students' current abilities (Bryen et al., 1988). Although the problems in this case were twofold, it is just as likely that this result might have occurred even if the assessment had been complete. For example, most readers can probably think of at least one AAC user who has struggled for months or even years to learn to operate a manual AAC system despite severe upper-extremity athetosis or to communicate with a headlight pointer despite insufficient head control, meanwhile having no way to achieve accurate, efficient, and nonfatiguing communication. What a disappointment it must be for people who have never been able to communicate to discover that communication involves a great deal of hard work with very little payoff! Of course, some initial instruction or training must occur in most situations, but both the length and complexity of training should be minimized.

Interventions for Tomorrow

Decision making for tomorrow should be concurrent with decision making for today under most circumstances. That is, as the AAC team institutes a communication system that matches the individual's current abilities and immediate needs, it should also develop plans for broadening the user's skill base in preparation for a system for tomorrow. These plans might involve providing instruction to improve specific motor, symbol recognition, pragmatic, or literacy skills. The plans might involve remediating identified barriers that limit the quantity or quality of communication opportunities. Whatever the focus of planning for tomorrow, the goal should be to institute an intervention that will enable more of the user's communication needs to be met and/or to increase the accuracy, efficiency, and ease of use of the current system.

The system for tomorrow may be an expansion or extension of the system for today, or it may involve a different device or technique. For example, a component of the system for today for a young man with TBI early in recovery may be a series of eye-gaze communication boards with color photographs that represent the major choices available in his day. An expansion of this system for tomorrow might introduce Picture Communication Symbols (PCS symbols) for the same messages by placing them next to the photographs and then fading the photos as he becomes able to accurately eye point to the PCS symbols. As another example, perhaps the photographic eye-gaze system for today was intended as a temporary measure to allow the motor therapists to develop the adaptations and skills needed for more effective hand and arm use. If this is the case, the eye-gaze system might be discontinued when motor control is sufficient and can be replaced with a lap-tray communication board containing the same photographs. In either case, once the system for tomorrow has been instituted, it becomes the new system for today, and planning can begin immediately for yet another tomorrow. Thus, a longitudinal AAC plan should always be two-pronged by including plans for both today and tomorrow—although the time between successive tomorrows is likely to lengthen as the AAC system comes closer and closer to meeting all of the user's communication needs.

Another example illustrating the ongoing nature of interventions for today and tomorrow might prove useful. Mirenda, Iacono, and Williams (1990) described one possible series of such interventions appropriate for a student with multiple disabilities who has some volitional movement of the head. A system for today for such a student might consist of a head-activated microswitch that turns on single, prerecorded audiocassette tapes for eliciting attention and requesting food, objects, or activities (Wacker, Wiggins, Fowler, & Berg, 1988). Other components might include the use of nonsymbolic gestures, vocalizations, and other natural modes in the context of predictable routines to signal rejection, emotions, and preferences (Siegel-Causey & Guess, 1989). At the same time, an intervention for tomorrow consisting of the use of a "calendar box" with symbols of real objects for daily activities (Rowland & Schweigert, 1989) could be introduced, although it may be beyond the student's current level of ability during the initial planning stages. The purpose of introducing the calendar box at this point would be to begin teaching symbol–activity associations in natural contexts. Once the student begins to show the ability to make such associations, the object symbols could be used for making simple choices with eye gaze (if the student has sufficient vision) or with direct selection of the object symbols through a tactile mode (if the student's vision is limited). As the student's eye gaze or tactile symbol skills develop, one of these options could become the new system for today and replace the initial, limited microswitch and tape device. At this point, planning and instruction would begin for the next system for tomorrow that would continue to meet communication needs and to build skills in natural contexts. Additional examples of the today and tomorrow principle can be found in a number of case studies (Beukelman, Yorkston, & Dowden, 1985; DeRuyter & Donoghue, 1989; Dowden, 1997; Goossens', 1989; Light, Beesley, & Collier, 1988; Yorkston, 1989).

In some cases, it might be fairly obvious what the system for today should be but not at all clear how to plan for tomorrow logically. This is often the case if the individual's motor impairments are very severe and not easily remediable. In such cases, it is often advisable to institute multiple and simultaneous training programs for tomorrow, each designed to improve the AAC user's ability to control and use a different motor site. For example, consider a young man with severe athetoid cerebral palsy and good literacy skills. It was apparent from assessment that a simple orthographic eye-gaze system (Goossens' & Crain, 1987) combined with dependent auditory scanning (a 20-questions approach) was the best match for his current abilities. It was also apparent that in order for him to gain access to a more efficient and comprehensive system, he would need to achieve increased control of at least one motor movement sequence. It was not at all clear, however, which motor movement sequence could be taught best. Therefore, training programs designed to increase his ability to operate a single switch using his head, right hand, and left foot, respectively, were instituted at the same time. It became apparent that his head control was improving at the fastest rate, and after 6 months of work, he was able to use a head switch to control a single-switch scanner accurately, efficiently, and without unreasonable fatigue. When the logical direction for tomorrow is not clear, such a multiple target approach is vastly preferable (and certainly less frustrating!) to one in which single training targets are tested in succession until the best one is selected.

Providing Instruction to AAC Users and Facilitators

After drawing up a comprehensive plan for natural skill development, environmental adaptations, and assistive device adaptations, the AAC team needs to select vocabulary items that will be represented on the system (see Chapter 2). Instruction of the AAC user, communication partners, and the facilitators who manage the ongoing intervention must be initiated. Although many instructional techniques are specific to the AAC user and his or her impairment (see Chapters 9–18), there are several general principles that guide instruction. These are discussed briefly in the following section.

Principle 4: Provide both contextual and specific skill instruction, as needed.

Natural Contexts

Instruction in AAC techniques has come a long way from the days when one or two professionals did the majority of such work in isolated therapy rooms (Musselwhite & St. Louis, 1988). It is now well established in the AAC literature that much, if not most, of the focus of intervention should take place in natural contexts such as classrooms, homes, community environments, and workplaces (Calculator, 1988a; Montgomery, 1987). Instructional plans that emphasize natural context interventions appear to result in better response generalization (to novel targets within the same response class) and better stimulus generalization (to novel people, environments, materials, and situations) than do instructional plans that emphasize isolated skill training (Musselwhite & St. Louis, 1988; Reichle, York, & Sigafoos, 1991). Natural context instructional strategies specific to AAC users with various backgrounds and abilities are discussed in Part II of this book.

Specific Skills

Regardless of the importance of natural context instruction, it is also important to provide specific skill instruction, which may occur in separate training sessions, as part of the intervention plan when necessary. Specific skill training, unfortunately, may be labeled "nonfunctional" and discounted or ignored by proponents of natural context instruction, even if training is the most functional response to remedy a skill impairment (e.g., Arwood, 1983). Specific skill training is particularly useful if the individual needs instruction in new skill areas and needs to compensate quickly for past instructional deficiencies.

Initiating New Skill Learning

Basic instruction of most new skills is best conducted in natural contexts from the very beginning of intervention. However, if sensory or motor skills are to be taught, at least some specific skill instruction in separate training settings may be necessary as well as desirable. It is important to remember that the motor skills necessary for natural speech or AAC device use typically involve fine discrete movements and that most AAC users have motor impairments that are sometimes quite severe. In addition, many AAC users are easily startled and distracted by noise, movement, activity, or other extraneous environmental stimuli. For all of these reasons, it is often difficult for them to maintain concentration and to achieve control of the target motor site. An individual with such multiple obstacles in busy, distracting, everchanging natural contexts may not make steady improvement in the skill being taught, and to expect him or her to do so is unrealistic. Rather, a judicious blend of natural and specific skill training is often necessary to achieve the desired result in a reasonable period of time.

Principle 5: Minimize the cognitive, linguistic, sensory, and motor demands of specific skill training.

Specific skill training is appropriate only when the target skill is particularly challenging for the AAC user, so it stands to reason that the other skills required during training sessions should be minimally demanding. For example, if an adult with spinal cord injury (SCI) is learning to use a sip-and-puff switch so that he or she can send Morse code, it does not make sense to teach him or her to control the switch at the same time that he or she is learning and memorizing Morse code. Rather, the AAC team should introduce nonlinguistic practice tasks (e.g., pattern imitations) designed to teach him or her to sip and puff accurately and efficiently first. Then, using a visual display chart, he or she could learn to produce Morse code sequences for single letters or numbers during some practice sessions, while learning and memorizing the codes without using the switch during others. Finally, the team could have the individual integrate motor and symbol skills gradually toward the goal of mastery (Matas & Beukelman, 1989). Similarly, the cognitive, linguistic, and sensory requirements for training the motor skills for tasks such as headlight pointing (Blackstone, 1988b), manual signing (Carr & Kologinsky, 1983), and visual scanning (Blackstone, 1989e) should be reduced as much as possible during initial instruction.

This principle also applies to teaching cognitive/linguistic and sensory skills. For example, Keogh and Reichle (1985) recommended providing difficult-to-teach students with mental retardation opportunities for specific "match-to-sample" training when introducing new pictorial symbols. Similarly, specific skill instruction for the linguistic and pragmatic components of a low-tech communication system for an older AAC user with Broca's aphasia has been described (Garrett, Beukelman, & Low-Morrow, 1989). Other examples of this principle can also be found in Beukelman, Yorkston, and Dowden (1985) and Glennen and DeCoste (1997).

Compensating for Past Instructional Deficiencies

In some cases, the institution of an optimal system for tomorrow is entirely dependent on the AAC user acquiring rather complex, specific skills. Perhaps the clearest examples of this situation are young adult AAC users, many of whom have severe cerebral palsy, who have the ability and the motivation to learn to read and write but who have not been provided with sufficient instruction (Berninger & Gans, 1986a; Smith, Thurston, Light, Parnes, & O'Keefe, 1989). These individuals need to acquire literacy skills in order to use AAC systems with flexible, orthographic displays. In addition, many who use and are satisfied with nonorthographic AAC systems may want to be able to read and write for personal or educational reasons. Intensive specific skill instruction in literacy will be necessary to compensate for past instructional deficiencies in this area, as we describe in Chapter 13.

Principle 6: Provide information, training, and support to AAC users, their communication partners, and their facilitators to build communicative competence.

Building Communicative Competence

Light (1989b) identified four types of competencies that are necessary for successful augmented communication: 1) operational competence, 2) linguistic competence, 3) social competence, and 4) strategic competence. Light and Binger (1997) published the results of an extensive project that sought to identify and then teach specific skills as they are related to communicative competence in each of these domains. We discuss the specific skills they taught and describe the instructional procedures they used in Chapter 11 but provide a brief overview of the four domains in this section.

Operational Competence

The most immediate need for AAC users and those who support them is to acquire operational competence as quickly as possible when an AAC system is introduced. This requires instruction in all operational and maintenance aspects of the device or system (see Lee & Thomas, 1990, for details). Often, the AAC user is not the primary recipient of much of this instruction, and facilitators may take on much of the responsibility for operational competence. These facilitators may be parents, spouses, or other family members; educational, residential, or vocational staff; friends; and other people who are involved in and committed to the AAC user's communicative well-being. In school settings, new facilitators may have to be trained in AAC operation each school year to keep pace with staff turnover and teacher and staff rotations. For example, one fourth-grade student who has worked with the same speech-language pathologist and paraprofessional since kindergarten has nonetheless had 16 people trained in operational aspects of her system over a 5-year period (Beukelman, 1991). AAC users, facilitators, or both, need to 1) keep the vocabulary in the device up to date; 2) construct overlays or other displays as needed; 3) protect the device against breakage, damage, or other problems; 4) secure necessary repairs; 5) modify the system for tomorrow's needs; and 6) generally ensure day-to-day availability and operation of the device. Generally, unaided or low-tech devices require less operational competence, which is one reason why they may be preferable when facilitator availability is identified as a constraint (see Chapter 6).

Linguistic Competence

Linguistic competence involves a functional mastery of the symbol system or linguistic code used for the display. Equally important, the AAC user must learn the language spoken by communication partners in order to receive messages. For the bilingual user, this may mean learning his or her family's native language as well as that of the community at large (Light, 1989b). For AAC users with acquired disabilities, much of this learning may be in place at the time of intervention, leaving only AAC-specific tasks to be mastered. For people with congenital disabilities, however, all of these skills must be learned within the accompanying physical, sensory, or cognitive constraints.

Parents, communication specialists, friends, and other facilitators can play a major role in assisting AAC users to master this formidable set of tasks. First, facilitators can offer ongoing opportunities for practicing expressive language (both native and augmentative) in natural contexts (Romski & Sevcik, 1996). In some cases, this may be simply helping the AAC user learn the augmentative symbol system or code. In other cases, especially if the user has a history of poor generalization, facilitators may themselves have to learn the symbol system in order to provide sufficient opportunities for practice (e.g., manual signing [Loeding, Zangari, & Lloyd, 1990; Spragale & Micucci, 1990]). It is also important for facilitators to provide augmented input models in the language of the community and family as well as in the symbols or codes used in the AAC display. Receptive language input strategies may include aided language stimulation vests or boards (Goossens', 1989), symbol song strips used with music (Musselwhite & St. Louis, 1988), joint use of the AAC user's display by the facilitator (Romski & Sevcik, 1996), or key word input provided through manual signing (see Blackstone, Cassatt-James, & Bruskin, 1988, for additional strategies). Specific strategies for encouraging linguistic competence in relation to the AAC system are discussed in greater detail in Chapter 12.

Principle 7: Meaningful communication is a shared responsibility.

Social Competence

Of the four areas identified by Light (1989b), social competence has been the focus of most of the research in the AAC field (e.g., Kraat, 1985; Light, 1988). Social competence requires the AAC user to have knowledge, judgment, and skills in both the sociolinguistic and sociorelational aspects of communication or "competence as to when to speak, when not [to], and as to what to talk about, with whom, when, where, in what manner" (Hymes, 1972, p. 277). For example, sociolinguistic skills include abilities to 1) initiate, maintain, and terminate conversations; 2) give and take turns; 3) communicate a variety of functions (e.g., requesting, rejecting); and 4) engage in a variety of coherent and cohesive interactions. Light (1988) suggested that some sociorelational skills that are important for AAC users include 1) a positive self-image, 2) an interest in others and a desire to communicate, 3) active participation in conversation, 4) responsiveness to partners, and 5) the ability to put partners at ease.

Opportunities to practice social competence skills in natural contexts are critical for AAC users and facilitators. A number of facilitator training manuals and approaches have been developed for AAC users who have a variety of backgrounds and AAC system needs (e.g., Blackstone et al., 1988; Culp & Carlisle, 1988; Light & Binger, 1997; Light, Dattilo, English, Gutierrez, & Hartz, 1992; Light, McNaughton, & Parnes, 1986; MacDonald & Gillette, 1986; Manolson, 1985; McNaughton & Light, 1989; Reichle et al., 1991; Siegel-Causey & Guess, 1989). Both the number and the quality of such efforts are indicative of the importance of providing extensive training in social competence skills to both AAC users and their facilitators.

Information, training, and support efforts related to social competence must often go beyond specific training for AAC users and facilitators. In many cases, it is also important for AAC teams to work directly with communication partners who encounter the AAC user only on social occasions. For example, the AAC user's friends and peers may need information about how to adjust their interactions to accommodate the requirements of the AAC system (e.g., allowing sufficient pauses for message composition). The AAC team may need to explain how to interact with the user of a low-tech display (e.g., echoing messages as the user indicates them in order to provide feedback). Brief in-service training to an AAC user's entire school class may help to demystify the AAC system, and in many cases users can participate in or conduct these sessions. Whatever the content and however brief, communication partner interventions such as these are often just as critical as more extensive facilitator training endeavors.

Strategic Competence

Because even the most flexible AAC systems impose some interactive limitations on their users, people who use AAC need the knowledge, judgment, and skills that allow them to "communicate effectively within restrictions" (Light, 1989b, p. 141). Instruction in strategic competence involves teaching various adaptive or coping strategies to use when communication breakdowns occur. For example, an AAC user may learn to transmit the message "Please slow down and wait for me to finish," or learn to use a gesture that means "No, you misunderstood." This is another area of training from which both facilitators and AAC users can benefit. For example, many AAC users appreciate the increased efficiency that results if the communication partner helps to co-construct messages by guessing. In order for this to occur, however, a facilitator or the AAC user him- or herself must teach the partner how to guess accurately. Unfortunately, few guidelines for facilitator or partner training exist in this domain.

Assign Responsibilities

In addition to providing instruction in operational, linguistic, social, and strategic competence, facilitators assume other responsibilities. For example, someone must be responsible for planning and executing the AAC user's educational and vocational programs, securing funding for AAC interventions, providing ongoing technical supports, and ensuring that efforts are coordinated and properly sequenced. Usually, the facilitators for these tasks are members of the AAC user's assessment and intervention team. One team member/facilitator is usually responsible for each area, and others are assigned to assist. For example, the speech-language pathologist is usually responsible for managing interventions to increase the AAC user's linguistic competence, and teachers, parents, and paraprofessionals may serve as assistants. An adult AAC user and his or her spouse may agree to manage funding for the intervention with assistance from a social worker or vocational rehabilitation specialist. As part of decision making and planning, the team (including the family and AAC user) must determine how various facilitators' instructional and support responsibilities will be delegated. Specifically, the team decides who will serve as the manager and who will assist in each major area. One of the greatest mistakes a team can make is to fail to make these roles and responsibilities explicit, thereby assuming that everyone understands what needs to be done and who will do it. The result is that efforts are poorly coordinated and that important tasks do not get done. In addition, unless facilitator roles are explicitly assigned to specific team members, accountability is difficult to achieve. A planning form (Cumley, 1991) is provided in Figure 8.2 that the team can use to decide who will perform which facilitator roles and responsibilities.

Social Network Interventions

In addition to facilitators who assume instructional and managerial roles, other members of an AAC user's social network may also need specific support and guidance. The availability and skills of communication partners affect the overall quality of AAC users' social environments and are thus critically important. Initiation of an AAC system may require more social adjustment than anything else, particularly for adults with acquired and degenerative impairments. Facilitators and AAC team members may need to encourage friends and relatives to visit as the individual becomes less able to use natural speech and as communication becomes more difficult. An older individual may require glasses or hearing aids in order to hear or see the AAC system of his or her companion. Grandchildren may need to be reassured that even though their grandfather's speech sounds different after his stroke, he is still able to "read" stories to them

Directions: In the appropriate space, indicate who is responsible for each role:
Manager (M): Assumes primary responsibility (usually one person for each area of responsibility)
Assistant (A): Provides instructional assistance or other supports (one or more people per area of responsibility)

Team member/facilitator responsible

Area of responsibility	AAC user	Parent/guardian/spouse	Speech-language pathologist	General/special educator	Personal assistant/paraprofessional	Motor therapist (OT, PT)	Other (specify)
AAC operational competence							
AAC linguistic competence							
AAC social competence							
AAC strategic competence							
Educational program							
Vocational program							
Home program							
Overall coordination							
Funding							
Technical support							
Other (specify)							

Figure 8.2. Team member/facilitator responsibilities and roles. (*Source:* Cumley, 1991)

by pointing to pictures or by using another technique. If concerted efforts are not made to maintain a broad social network, AAC users with acquired disorders may find themselves "all dressed up with no one to talk to" as their social lives become limited to immediate family members and caregivers.

Social network interventions may also be necessary for people with congenital impairments, particularly during times of transition. The first years spent in a preschool, elementary school, junior high, senior high, college or university, new job, or new neighborhood are all periods when social network interventions may be particularly necessary to help the AAC user adjust interaction habits and priorities. To assume that an AAC user will be able to initiate and establish social networks without assistance during transitional periods is often unrealistic and is likely to result in disappointment. Clearly, the overall AAC intervention plan must anticipate such transitions and attempt to minimize their impact through social network interventions.

Outcomes measurement should be consumer driven, flexible, and enduring. The result of AAC interventions should be an improved quality of life for people who use AAC. The results of outcomes measurement also should be used to improve cost-effectiveness and to improve the quality of equipment and services. (Consensus statement developed by participants in Alliance '95, an international conference on AAC outcome evaluation, in Blackstone & Pressman, 1995)

MEASURING AND EVALUATING INTERVENTION OUTCOMES

The final steps of the Participation Model (Figure 6.1) refer to strategies for measuring and evaluating the outcomes of AAC interventions. As reflected in the consensus statement made by Alliance '95 conference attendees, AAC outcome evaluation should measure parameters that are important to the user and to his or her family (e.g., "Does the person have a better life as a result of this AAC intervention?") and that can lead to improved services. Unfortunately, this rarely occurs, for numerous reasons: 1) payer resistance to or lack of acceptance of measures that reflect quality-of-life issues, 2) possible increased costs of intervention, 3) time limits set by payers on interventions, 4) high demands on professionals to achieve and maintain skills, 5) family and user response to the increase in their responsibilities when they assume a leadership role, 6) difficulties experienced by families when they are asked to envision the future for their relative with disabilities, and 7) cultural differences inherent in many professional–family relationships (Blackstone & Pressman, 1995). Despite the enormity of the task, it is critical for professionals in the field to grapple with these issues and persist in developing useful tools to measure meaningful outcomes. Outcome evaluation can be conceptualized as occurring at three levels: 1) evaluation that relates to impairment, 2) evaluation that relates to functional limitations, and 3) evaluation that relates to disability (Nagi, 1991).

Providers must not only do the right thing, they must do the right thing right. (Parnes, 1995)

Impairment refers to "anatomical, physiological, mental, or emotional abnormalities or loss" (Nagi, 1991, p. 322). Evaluation of the degree to which communication interventions compensate for impairments involves measuring specific cognitive, language, motor, and sensory skills that have changed as a result of intervention. Culp (1987) referred to two types of measures in this area: operational parameters and representational parameters. *Operational parameters* reflect the AAC user's ability to interact with the system itself. For example, evaluation at this level of an effort to teach headlight pointing might entail trial-by-trial assessment of correct and incorrect responses to various targets. *Representational parameters* evaluate the AAC user's symbol and grammatical abilities. For example, measurement of the effectiveness of a pictorial symbol intervention might entail daily or weekly data collection of an individual's ability to identify and match the symbols with their referents.

Data collection in educational and rehabilitation settings has traditionally focused on evaluating the impact of an intervention on the impairment. Although outcomes measurement at the level of impairment may be useful for gauging operational and representational skill acquisition, this kind of measurement may not be sensitive to larger issues related to functional social or strategic competence (Calculator, 1988a). Evaluation that is focused on impairment can demonstrate positive outcomes in the absence of real change in the quality of life or on consumer and family priorities.

What do you think?

Granlund suggested that, in the measurement of AAC outcomes, "norm-referenced criteria do not have any real relevance, because it's not normal to be normal, if you're not normal" (1995, p. 32).   *What do you think?*

Functional limitations refer to "limitations in performance at the level of the whole organism or person" (Nagi, 1991, p. 322). This aspect of a disorder is related to the individual's reduced ability to walk, reach, reason, see, hear, talk, and so forth because of his or her impairment. Thus, an individual who has multiple sclerosis (MS) has a neurological condition (impairment) that may affect his ability to walk, see, eat, or talk (functional limitations). An individual with Down syndrome has a chromosomal abnormality (impairment) that may affect her ability to reason, walk, talk, and so forth (functional limitations). Measurements of the impact of AAC interventions at this level seek to judge improvements in functional communication skills. Culp referred to a number of "interaction parameters" (1987, p. 174) that might be measured with regard to functional communication, such as how much and which modes of communication an individual uses, how many times a user initiates or responds to a partner's message, and how the user repairs communication breakdowns. A number of specific evaluation tools, both criterion and norm referenced, have been used to measure the impact of intervention on the AAC user's functional limitations (e.g., Bolton & Dashiell, 1984). Examples of protocols in this area can be found in Culp (1987, 1989), Culp and Carlisle (1988), Garrett et al. (1989), and Romski and Sevcik (1988a).

What is the price of a dream not dreamed?
What is the price of a word not spoken?
What is the price of a voice not heard?
What is the price of a vision not imagined?
What is the price of a life not lived?
(Williams, 1995a, p. 30)

Finally, *disability* refers to "limitation in performance of socially defined roles and tasks within a sociocultural and physical environment" (Nagi, 1991, p. 322). Outcome evaluation related to disability focuses on the impact of the AAC intervention on improved quality of life in school, community, home, recreational, and vocational environments. The importance of outcome evaluation at this level has become increasingly recognized in the mid-1990s (Blackstone & Pressman, 1995; DeRuyter, 1992; Heaton, Beliveau, & Blois, 1995). This is exemplified by the international conference entitled Alliance '95, which focused on outcome issues in AAC. There is no doubt that, as governments and other systems increasingly shift from a "social/ethical agenda to an economic policy agenda, . . . [and as] payers [scramble] to find ways to maximize limited funds and insure that no funds are wasted" (De Ruyter, 1995, p. 13), the need for data to answer "big picture" outcome questions is critical. These questions include, for example, questions about whether the AAC system or device has resulted in increased

- Self-determination and control for the AAC user
- Inclusion of the user in social groups
- Independence, to the degree the AAC user desires it
- Participation in the community
- Gainful employment
- Academic achievement
- Social connectedness
- Educational inclusion or decreased special class placement (Blackstone & Pressman, 1995)

The Participation Model emphasizes outcomes at this level by determining the AAC user's participation in the activities identified during the initial needs assessment. Measurement of intervention effectiveness then seeks to quantify or describe the observed or reported level of participation after the AAC intervention is in place. If the desired level of participation is not achieved, the Participation Model requires reexamination and remediation of the opportunity and access factors that may be barriers.

Evaluations related to disability may also seek to measure the degree to which an AAC intervention is positively perceived by others (i.e., consumer satisfaction measures) and affects the attitudes of communication partners. Culp referred to these as "psychosocial parameters" (1987, p. 174), such as the attitudes of AAC users and their partners about the communication system or the adjustment patterns of users and significant others. Protocols adapted from empirical studies may be useful to AAC teams as they gather some of this information. For example, Mathy-Laikko and Coxson (1984) used a 7-point scale for communication partners to rate their reactions to various types of AAC output devices in terms of pairs of opposites (e.g., intelligible/unintelligible, fast/slow, clear/unclear). A tool that measures certain aspects of consumer satisfaction was developed at the University of North Carolina to measure professional and family perceptions of family participation in decision making, assessment, team meetings, and provision of family goals and services (Bailey, Buysse, Edmondson, & Smith, 1992). Other consumer satisfaction measures can be found in the manual for Partners in Augmentative Communication Training (Culp & Carlisle, 1988). Unfortunately, few validated and reliable instruments exist in this area.

(My daughter) says she wants to be a veterinarian. Can someone with severe cerebral palsy come close to that goal? In 10 or 15 years, will medicine and technology have caught up with Ana's aspirations? (Cy Berlowitz, describing his daughter who has severe cerebral palsy, in Berlowitz, 1991, p.16)

FOLLOW-UP

According to the principle of interventions for today and tomorrow discussed previously, most AAC interventions never end! That is, once an AAC user has mastered a device or system for today, parallel training and practice can begin to prepare for one that is even more accurate, efficient, and nonfatiguing for tomorrow. Once these new skills are acquired, today becomes yesterday, tomorrow becomes today, and planning can begin for a new tomorrow!

If the AAC user is a child, this cycle is likely to require repetition at each transition—from preschool to kindergarten, from elementary school to junior high, from junior high to senior high, and from senior high to either employment or post-secondary schooling. Adults with either congenital impairments (e.g., cerebral palsy) or acquired, nondegenerative impairments (e.g., SCI) are likely to need system alterations less frequently, unless their employment, residence, or family status changes markedly. Adults with degenerative illnesses (e.g., ALS, MS), however, may require frequent system changes as their abilities deteriorate and living situations change. Finally, long-term AAC users will require additional modifications to their systems as they approach retirement age, begin to shift priorities, and experience changes in ability that occur as a result of aging (see Light, 1988).

Augmentative and Alternative Communication Interventions for Individuals with Developmental Disabilities

9

AAC Issues for People
with Developmental Disabilities

This chapter provides a context for the information presented in Part II, which addresses the communication needs of individuals who are acquiring communication and language skills for the first time. These individuals have disabilities that were either present since birth or before the age of 18 and that affect one or more aspects of development (e.g., physical, sensory, cognitive). Augmentative and alternative communication (AAC) techniques are used quite routinely with people who experience developmental disabilities, including cerebral palsy, cognitive disability (i.e., mental retardation), autism and the associated spectrum disorders, and developmental apraxia of speech. Blackstone and Painter (1985) estimated that 900,000 individuals in the United States are unable to speak as a result of one or more such impairments. In this chapter, each of these impairments is defined and explained briefly in terms of its description, prevalence, and major characteristics. An overview of the AAC issues most pertinent to each impairment follows.

CEREBRAL PALSY

It is difficult when you are a child to relate to strangers. It is also difficult when you have no voice. I was nonverbal and all these . . . adults had complete power over my life. I cried. I had pain in my body. I had pain in my heart. . . . I cried because I was lonely and afraid. I cried because people couldn't understand me—my words or my feelings. I was often sent to a special room because I was too noisy. I guess I can thank God for giving me a fighting spirit, because the harder it got, the harder I struggled. (Justin Clark, describing his experiences as a child with cerebral palsy living in an institution, in Clark & Pellerin, 1996, p. 7)

Definition, Prevalence, and Causes

The term *cerebral palsy* is typically used to refer to a developmental neuromotor disorder that is the result of a nonprogressive abnormality of the developing brain (Hardy, 1983). It is estimated that the incidence of cerebral palsy is between 0.6 and 2.4 cases per 1,000, depending on the study, and varies little across industrialized countries (Paneth & Kiely, 1984). The overall prevalence of cerebral palsy has not increased significantly despite improved neonatal intensive care (Hagberg, Hagberg, & Zetterstrom, 1989). Despite the multiplicity of problems associated with cerebral palsy, most children with the disorder will live to adulthood. These individuals, however, do have a significantly lower life expectancy compared with the population in general (Blackman, 1983).

There are a number of etiologies that result in early lesions or malformations of developing brain tissue. Data compiled by Batshaw (1997) indicated that, in approximately 24% of all people with cerebral palsy, there is no identifiable cause. Problems during intrauterine development account for the majority of known causes (44%), including exposure to radiation, intrauterine infection, exposure to teratogens, chromosomal abnormalities, and brain malformations. Problems during labor and delivery account for another 19%, and complications in the perinatal period or during childhood result in the final 13% of all cases.

Characteristics

Motor Problems

Individuals with cerebral palsy primarily experience motor problems, which vary depending on the location of the brain lesion. The most common type, pyramidal (spastic) cerebral palsy, results in hypertonia (increased muscle tone) and occurs in about 50% of all cases (McDonald, 1987). It may manifest as diplegia, in which the legs are affected more than the arms; hemiplegia, in which one side of the body is primarily affected; or quadriplegia, in which there is diffuse and severe damage, and all four limbs are affected (Batshaw, 1997). A second type is called extrapyramidal (athetoid) cerebral palsy, which is marked by the presence of abrupt, involuntary movements of the extremities. Unlike pyramidal cerebral palsy, in which the problem is initiating movement, individuals with athetoid cerebral palsy have difficulty regulating movement and maintaining posture. Finally, some individuals experience either rigid or atonic cerebral palsy. Rigid cerebral palsy is characterized by "lead pipe rigidity," in which the limbs appear rigid but can be bent with persistent pressure, whereas atonic cerebral palsy involves "floppy" muscle tone (hypotonia). In addition, mixed-type cerebral palsy, which includes both pyramidal and extrapyramidal elements, may occur in approximately 12% of these individuals (McDonald, 1987). The wide diversity of motor problems associated with cerebral palsy presents significant challenges to AAC teams serving this population.

Associated Disorders

A number of associated disorders are also common in people with cerebral palsy. Batshaw (1997) stated that 60%–70% of all children with cerebral palsy also have some degree of mental retardation; individuals with hemiplegia are the least likely to be affected, whereas those with extrapyramidal symptoms are most likely to have mental retardation. In addition, approximately 46% of individuals with cerebral palsy have visual problems that may include eye muscle imbalances (e.g., strabismus), visual field cuts, visual-perceptual problems, and/or loss of visual acuity, any of which can significantly affect educational and communication programming. The incidence of hearing loss in this population has been estimated at 30%, and the brain injury that results in cerebral palsy precipitates seizure activity in roughly 50% of these individuals (Batshaw, 1997).

Speech and Communication Disorders

Speech disorders are also common sequelae to this neurological disorder, with the incidence of dysarthria estimated to occur in a significant portion (estimates range from 31% to 88%) of all people with cerebral palsy (Yorkston, Beukelman, & Bell, 1988). The speech problems are associated with poor respiratory control as a result of muscular weakness and other factors, laryngeal and velopharyngeal dysfunction, and oral articulation disorders that result from restricted movement in the oral-facial muscles. The incidence of dysarthria varies in relation to the type and degree of motor impairment. Other communication characteristics (e.g., overall language delay) may be associated with the problems of mental retardation, hearing impairment, and learned helplessness that often co-occur with the disorder.

> Whenever I entered a new area of experience, my mother would always pave the way for me. I always let her. After all, it was so much easier than doing it myself. I couldn't talk, she was very articulate. . . . This had a subtle but profound effect on my personality. When you have someone representing you at the bargaining table of life, all you have to do is sit back and reap the benefits. (Michael B. Williams, recalling his experiences as a child with cerebral palsy, in Williams, 1992, p. 19)

Unique AAC Issues

Learned Helplessness

Many individuals with cerebral palsy do not have a history of being able to successfully control their environments, placing them at high risk for developing the behaviors and attitudes associated with learned helplessness. In this regard, Seligman (1975) found that people who were frequently exposed to situations where they could control their fate were more resistant to the development of helpless behavior. Thus, strategies designed to prevent the development of learned helplessness should be a high priority for AAC teams planning for children with severe motor impairment. Early intervention should be aimed at constructing situations to teach them that they can control people and objects in their environment through the use of augmentative communication aids and techniques as well as adapted toys and environmental control devices. They need to be provided with opportunities to make choices, decisions, and even mistakes on occasion, just like their typically developing peers! In addition, it is imperative that interventionists provide children who have upper-extremity involvement with adapted techniques for literacy instruction (i.e., reading, writing, and spelling) prior to entering kindergarten so that they are empowered to learn literacy skills alongside their typically developing peers.

Empowering a child with a disability creates much more work for the parents; it is much easier to do everything for them and be done with it, especially if there is a communication problem. But this creates a set of psychological and social problems that the disabled adult will have great difficulty dealing with later in life. (Williams, 1992, p. 19)

Team Approach to Intervention

Communication interventions with individuals who experience cerebral palsy require the expertise of a team of professionals from a number of disciplines, perhaps more so than with any other developmental disability. The wide variety of motor impairments in this population necessitates the involvement of professionals such as occupational and physical therapists, orthotics specialists, and rehabilitation engineers in the assessment process for determining the appropriate communication system for each individual. Professionals should be familiar with positioning and seating adaptations that must be developed on an individual basis in order to ensure optimum stability and the movement efficiency necessary to access a communication system. The team should also be familiar with the wide range of communication options available as well as with the special considerations necessary to achieve the optimal client–system match. The importance of such individualization was emphasized in a study by Lafontaine and DeRuyter (1987), in which they reported that, across 64 individuals with cerebral palsy who were assessed and fitted with AAC devices, a total of 17 different types of communication devices were prescribed. These included several different types of non-electronic devices such as picture or word boards and 13 different types of electronic devices. Although 47% of the individuals in Lafontaine and DeRuyter's study were able to access their devices through the use of a finger, the remainder used a number of alternative access techniques, including optical indicators, chin pointers, joysticks, and a variety of switches for scanning. Similarly diverse patterns of AAC system use were reported by Murphy, Marková, Moodie, Scott, and Boa (1996).

In addition, visual acuity and visual-perceptual problems will affect decisions regarding the size and figure-ground contrast of the symbol system chosen for communication, and comprehensive assessment by a pediatric ophthalmologist or other team member trained to assess these issues is often required (DeCoste, 1997a). Perceptual impairments or other disorders (e.g., hearing loss) can impede the process of learning to read or spell in those individuals who have this capability, requiring input from professionals such as speech-language pathologists or educators who specialize in remediation of these problems. Finally, but certainly of no less importance, the input of speech-language pathologists and both general and special educators will be necessary during the assessment process to train the user and facilitators and to manage the intervention process.

For an AAC user, the development of one's voice poses (a) . . . challenge because AAC devices can be limiting. A symbol or word might not appear on a board. A voice synthesizer might not have the right intonation. All of this can limit or change what is trying to be said. . . . Because I rely on AAC, it has taken me many years to learn how to communicate effectively. I now use a combination of "agencies," including speech, written words, telecommunications, a word board, and a voice output device. All of these devices allow my "voice" to be heard. But the other, and most important component of being heard, is having people who want to listen to you. (Nola Millin, a young woman with cerebral palsy, in Millin, 1995, p. 3)

Balanced Approach to Intervention

Beukelman (1987) emphasized the need for a "balanced approach" to communication programming for people with severe expressive communication disorders. In the case of people with cerebral palsy, emphasis on augmentative communication treatment needs to be balanced with motor development training, speech therapy, and academic instruction, as necessary. For example, some individuals will require extensive motor training in order to use adaptive access techniques such as headlight pointing or scanning. However, in the search for a technique that an individual can use immediately, a frequent mistake is to abandon such motorically demanding options. The result is that long-term efficiency is often sacrificed for short-term gains. Instead, a longitudinal program designed to meet the person's immediate communication needs with a number of readily accessible approaches, which also "invests in the future" through a systematic motor or speech therapy program to train more complex skills, may be more fruitful and, ultimately, more balanced.

This principle also applies to the selection of multimodal communication systems for individuals with cerebral palsy. A number of augmentative techniques may be used in different contexts and with different people to communicate a variety of messages (see Light, Collier, & Parnes, 1985a, 1985b, 1985c). In addition, although speech, gestures, and facial expressions may be severely affected as a result of motor impairment, this does not mean that people with cerebral palsy should be discouraged from using these natural modes for communication. Rather, a balanced approach calls for efforts to encourage and support the use of such multimodal systems, including training of both individuals and their communication partners concerning the most effective techniques to use in various situations. For example, the individual may be able to communicate with family members very effectively using natural modes, whereas he or she may need to rely on AAC techniques with unfamiliar partners.

MENTAL RETARDATION

The day and hour had finally arrived. This was to be the day when the consulting speech pathologist was going to let us know when Vi was finally going to get her augmentative communication system. Anticipation loomed like the hot sticky July air, which pervaded her unit cubicle (in the institution where she lived), where we all had gathered to hear the news. Five minutes into his polite but rambling recitation, though, it became apparent that the only news he had for

us that day was no news at all: a glitch had developed here or there, a microswitch had failed, a proverbial monkey wrench had been thrown into the
works again. . . . I asked how much longer it'd take to get back on track this time.
"Why," he quizzically replied, "Is there any special reason for all the rush???" "No,
no special reason," I said. . . . "No, no special reason at all. . . except that she has
had 50 years of no special reasons." (Bob Williams, talking about Vi, a friend with
mental retardation, in Williams, 1989, pp. 16–17)

People like Vi, who are labeled as having mental retardation, have only been recognized as appropriate candidates for AAC interventions since the mid-1980s. Indeed,
many school districts, adult services agencies, and residential facilities still maintain
candidacy criteria to ascertain whether such individuals are likely to qualify for AAC
services. Nonetheless, the 1980s and 1990s have seen important positive changes in societal and professional attitudes toward these individuals. People with intellectual disabilities increasingly are being provided with the opportunities and technology needed
to assist them to communicate in inclusive, dynamic environments (see also Mirenda,
Iacono, & Williams, 1990).

Definition and Causes

Mental retardation (also called intellectual disability) is characterized by

> significantly subaverage intellectual functioning, existing concurrently with related lim-
> itations in two or more of the following applicable adaptive skill areas: communication,
> self-care, home living, social skills, community use, self-direction, health and safety,
> functional academics, leisure, and work. Mental retardation manifests before age 18.
> (Luckasson et al., 1992, p. 5)

The American Association on Mental Retardation (AAMR) definition de-emphasizes
ability-level (or IQ-based) classifications (mild, moderate, severe, profound) in favor of
a focus on the level(s) of support a person needs (Luckasson et al., 1992). Thus, an individual with mental retardation may be described as requiring intermittent, limited, extensive, and/or pervasive supports in one or more areas. This new descriptive system
acknowledges that appropriate supports can have a significant impact on the ability of
individuals with mental retardation to live, work, recreate, and learn successfully in
community environments typical of their same-age peers.

The majority of incidences of mental retardation are the result of either congenital
anomalies of the developing brain (20%) or genetic factors (45%). Other influences,
such as peri- or postnatal trauma (6%–10%), environmental toxins (e.g., lead poisoning), and infections account for the remaining 35% (Batshaw, 1997). Most prevalent
among the genetic disorders are Down syndrome and fragile X syndrome, although literally hundreds of other disorders and syndromes are also associated with cognitive
impairments. As is the case with cerebral palsy, mental retardation can co-occur with
hearing, vision, motor, seizure, and communication disorders.

What is retardation? It's hard to say. I guess it's having problems thinking. Some people think that you can tell if a person is retarded by looking at them. If you think that way you don't give people the benefit of the doubt. You judge a person by how they look or how they talk or what the tests show, but you can never really tell what is inside the person. (A man labeled as having mental retardation, in Bogdan & Taylor, 1994, pp. 90–91)

Prevalence

Although figures for the school-age population are difficult to obtain, it is estimated that 0.5% of the preschool-age population is identified as having disabilities (Blackman, 1983). Because learning difficulties are often not recognized until the child enters school, this figure jumps to about 10% in the 6- to 16-year-old age group (Blackman, 1983), approximately 2% of whom have severe disabilities (Evans, 1991). Overall, researchers estimate that 0.8%–1.2% of all people in the United States have mental retardation (Batshaw, 1997).

A demographic study conducted in the state of Washington indicated that people with mental retardation comprise the largest percentage of the school-age population of individuals who are unable to speak (Matas et al., 1985). This study estimated that 4%–12% of school-age children with mental retardation requiring intermittent to limited support and 92%–100% of children with mental retardation requiring extensive to pervasive support were nonspeaking. It is becoming increasingly accepted that AAC teams can and should deliver communication services of some type to these individuals regardless of the degree of impairment (e.g., Calculator & Jorgensen, 1994; Johnson, Baumgart, Helmstetter, & Curry, 1996; Linfoot, 1994; Mirenda, 1993; Reichle et al., 1991).

Unique AAC Issues

Opportunity Factors

When designing communication interventions for people with mental retardation, it is vital to address their lack of naturally occurring communication opportunities. Such opportunities can exist only when responsive communication partners interact in real (not artificial) home, school, and community environments (Mirenda, 1993). Unfortunately, many people with mental retardation continue to live, work, and recreate in segregated environments where the only people available as communication partners are other individuals with communication impairments or paid staff members. In addition, the notion persists that AAC instruction with this population should be conducted in highly structured, artificial settings until some arbitrary criterion is reached; only then is the individual exposed to natural situations in which communication skills are actually required. Unfortunately, given the generalization difficulties common in people with mental retardation, this approach is usually futile. In an extensive discussion of this issue, Calculator and Bedrosian noted that "there is little justification for conducting communication intervention as an isolated activity because communication is neither any more nor less than a tool that facilitates individuals' abilities to function in the various activities of daily living" (1988, p. 104). The presence of integrated, natural communication opportunities will directly affect the vocabulary selected as well as the instructional techniques used and must be considered an integral part of any AAC intervention.

Challenging Behavior

Most people with mental retardation do not engage in socially inappropriate behaviors. Behavior problems, however, do occur in these individuals more often than in people without disabilities (Batshaw, 1997), for reasons that should be quite obvious—a lack of preferred and functional places to go, people to be with, things to do, and ways to communicate. For decades, the primary strategies that have been used to "manage" the behavior of people with cognitive disabilities include incarceration (i.e., institutionalization), medication, and the use of aversive (i.e., punishment based) behavior modification techniques. Since the mid-1980s, the emphasis has shifted to the use of proactive, ecological strategies to prevent behavior problems, as well as numerous strategies for teaching functional communication skills as alternatives for challenging behavior (Carr et al., 1994; Durand, 1990; Koegel, Koegel, & Dunlap, 1996; Reichle & Wacker, 1993). This shift has great relevance to AAC because many individuals with cognitive disabilities do not use speech as their primary mode of communication. It is critically important that AAC facilitators working with individuals who engage in challenging behavior familiarize themselves with the literature on communication approaches for behavior support so that they can act as both facilitators and advocates in this regard (see Mirenda, 1997, for a review).

AUTISM AND PERVASIVE DEVELOPMENTAL DISORDERS

Autism is something I cannot see. It stops me from finding and using my own words when I want to. Or makes me use all the words and silly things I do not want to say. Autism makes me feel everything at once without knowing what I am feeling. Or it cuts me off from feeling anything at all. Autism makes me hear other people's words but be unable to know what the words mean. . . . Autism makes me feel sometimes that I have no self at all, and I feel so overwhelmed by the presence of other people that I cannot find myself. (Donna Williams, an Australian woman with autism, in Williams, 1994, pp. 237–238)

Definition, Prevalence, and Causes

All of the diagnostic systems commonly used to describe autism agree that there are three main diagnostic features of the disorder: 1) impairments in social interaction; 2) impairments in communication; and 3) restricted, repetitive, and stereotypical patterns of behaviors, interests, and activities (American Psychiatric Association, 1994; World Health Organization, 1992). Although the syndrome is defined in terms of a number of behaviors, it is not a "behavior disorder" but rather a profound social, communicative, and cognitive impairment that is lifelong in nature (Freeman & Ritvo, 1984).

It is increasingly accepted that autism and a number of related pervasive developmental disorders (PDDs) occur as a spectrum of impairments of different etiologies (Wing, 1996). On the one end of the spectrum are individuals with autism who also have mental retardation requiring extensive to pervasive support. On the other end are socially eccentric or "odd" individuals who may get married, hold down jobs, and are never diagnosed as having a disability. For example, individuals with Asperger's syndrome (high-functioning autism) may have no cognitive or language impairments but exhibit a number of unusual social and behavioral characteristics. Between the extremes are individuals with one of the disorders related to autism (e.g., Rett syndrome) or with PDD not otherwise specified.

Although the cause of autism is not known, a large body of research is available to demonstrate that it is not caused by family, emotional, or environmental factors (Wing, 1996). In the 1990s, researchers have focused on a number of genetic and neurological factors that may cause the syndrome. Prevalence estimates vary widely across studies, depending on the criteria used and the breadth of the spectrum examined. Wing (1996) estimated that autism spectrum disorders occur in at least 58 per 10,000 people. Freeman (1993b) stated that autism (not including the associated spectrum disorders) occurs in approximately 2–4 people per 10,000. It is generally accepted that there is no cure for autism, although educational and related interventions can make a real difference in functional abilities.

Characteristics

Cognitive Impairments

The question of whether people with autism have mental retardation is impossible to answer because the disorder is so pervasive that it affects virtually every aspect of functioning as measured by standardized intelligence tests. Approximately 50% of all individuals with autism, however, do function in the same IQ range as individuals with mental retardation throughout life (Freeman, 1993b); whether this is a reflection of how we educate and intervene or is inherent in the disorder is less clear. Another 25%, who usually have relatively normal motor development and develop communicative language before the age of 5 years, will require support as adults but have less severe disabilities. The final 25% have typical intelligence, can work independently, and may even marry and have children, although the last is rare (Ritvo, Freeman, Mason-Brothers, & Ritvo, 1993).

As she grew, the problem of her speech took precedence over all the others. It was through speech that she must join the human race. (C.C. Park referring to her daughter with autism, in Park, 1982, p. 198)

Social/Communication Impairments

Because autism is, by definition, primarily a social/communicative disorder, a comprehensive description of the communication characteristics is beyond the scope of this book (see Cohen & Donnellan, 1987, and Wing, 1996, for more complete descriptions and intervention implications). Nevertheless, individuals with autism present with a wide range of complex issues related to both the means and the forms of language and communication. Approximately 50% of people with autism never develop sufficient speech as a means for communication (Wing & Atwood, 1987). If speech and language do develop, certain abnormalities are common, including echolalia, repetitiveness, literalness of meaning, monotonous intonation, and idiosyncratic use of words or phrases.

Most striking in individuals with autism are a number of verbal and nonverbal impairments of social interaction. In fact, autism has several core symptoms that, if noted before 18 months of age, are usually good predictors for a later diagnosis of autism. These include lack of pretend play, lack of protodeclarative pointing (i.e., use of an index finger to indicate to another person an object of interest, as an end in itself), lack of social interest, lack of social play, and lack of joint attention (i.e., showing objects to others and gaze monitoring) (Baron-Cohen, Allen, & Gillberg, 1992; Osterling & Dawson, 1994). Impairments in nonverbal communication, including an inability to "read" the facial expressions or take the perspective of others, are also central features of the syndrome (Frith, 1989; Happé, 1994).

Emotional hypersensitivity made contact with gentle affectionate people give me the effect of being force fed with a box of lemons. (Donna Williams, an Australian woman with autism, in D. Williams, 1996, p. 5)

Language Impairment

People with autism often have language impairments as well, and substantial delays in receptive language ability are not uncommon. These problems may be masked, however, by unusual skills in other areas that make it seem that people with autism understand everything that is said to them. Indeed, many people with autism have visual-spatial and visual-memory skills that far surpass their apparent abilities in the language area, which may account for reports of unusual reading and spelling abilities (hyperlexia) (Tirosh & Canby, 1993). In fact, it appears that at least some individuals with autism may have relatively intact language systems despite appearances to the contrary, as evidenced by reports of some who have progressed from typing with assistance to typing independently through use of *facilitated communication* (Biklen, 1993; see Chapter 11). Other individuals with autism may use such visual-spatial splinter skills to compensate for a lack of linguistic understanding by memorizing routines and attending to the subtle situational cues that accompany spoken language (Schuler & Prizant, 1987).

As a child, the "people world" was often too stimulating to my senses. Ordinary days with a change in schedule or unexpected events threw me into a frenzy, but Thanksgiving or Christmas was even worse. At those times our home bulged with relatives. The clamor of many voices, the different smells—perfume, cigars, damp wool caps or gloves—people moving around at different speeds, going in

---

different directions, the constant noise and confusion, the constant touching, were overwhelming. . . . This is not unusual for autistic children because they are over-responsive to some stimuli and under-sensitive to other stimuli. . . . (They) have to make a choice of either self-stimulating like spinning, mutilating themselves, or escape into their inner world to screen out outside stimuli. Otherwise, they become overwhelmed with many simultaneous stimuli and react with temper tantrums, screaming, or other unacceptable behavior. (Temple Grandin describing her experience as a child with autism, in Grandin & Scariano, 1986, pp. 24–25)

Processing Impairments

Underlying the speech/language/communication impairments of autism are a number of developmental and cognitive processing issues that directly affect social and communication interventions. For example, researchers in the United Kingdom have provided evidence that people with autism lack a "theory of mind"—the ability to "attribute independent mental states to oneself and others, in order to explain behavior" (Happé, 1994, p. 41). This could account for the inability of even the most capable individuals with Asperger's syndrome to take the perspective of others into account in social situations. In addition, Prizant (1983) described people with autism as "gestalt processors," referring to their tendency to process the gestalt, or "whole," of a situation or utterance rather than its component parts; this could account for much of the echolalic language frequently observed in these individuals, at least during the early stages of language development (Prizant, 1983). Overall, it is clear that autism spectrum disorders are extremely complex and varied both within and across individuals and present numerous challenges with regard to both speech-based and AAC interventions.

Unique AAC Issues

Early Intervention

There are several elements that research has shown to be critical in intervention programs for individuals with autism. The most important of these are

1. Start early
2. Start early
3. Start early
4. Start early
5. Start early!!

There is no doubt that early intervention with emphases on speech, language, and communication as well as on social and play skills development is perhaps more important for individuals with autism than for children with any other developmental disability (Dawson & Osterling, 1997). Advances in the field have made it possible to recognize the disorder at a very early age, so that accurate assessment and diagnosis may be possible before the age of 18 months (Baron-Cohen et al., 1992; Osterling & Dawson, 1994). Although it is not clear exactly *how* such intervention is best conducted, the fact is that "the earlier the better" is more than just an option here; it is a necessity. Although early intervention is appropriately aimed at encouraging the development of speech, AAC interventions are often critical as well, either temporarily (i.e., until speech develops) or permanently.

Professionals from each of these different camps (approaches to dealing with autism) didn't become extinct as new camps arose. They are still out there beating their drums and beating down each other's doors. Like dinosaurs, some professionals have believed their ideas are the only ones which are right. Others have been a bit more open minded, holistic, imaginative and less resistant to change. Some professionals are the dinosaurs of today and some are the dinosaurs of tomorrow and some try hard not to be dinosaurs at all. (Donna Williams, an Australian woman with autism, in D. Williams, 1996, p. 7)

A Range of Intervention Approaches and Need for Collaboration

Perhaps more so than with any other disorder, the field of autism is a "field of fads." Throughout the years, treatments have included (and still do include) holding therapy, megavitamin therapy, various diets, and many others. As of 1998, two approaches relevant to AAC are receiving considerable "popular press" in North America (and elsewhere)—facilitated communication (Biklen, 1993) and intensive behavior therapy based on the work of Lovaas and his colleagues at UCLA (Lovaas, 1987; McEachin, Smith, & Lovaas, 1993). Although it is beyond the scope of this chapter to either summarize or critique these approaches, the point is that families are continuously faced with the task of deciding what to do for their child with autism and how best to do it from an unusually wide range of options. Some of these decisions may drastically affect the extent to which AAC techniques of various types will be accepted and used by the family (e.g., in an intensive behavior therapy approach, manual signing may be accepted but graphic symbols often are not; see Sundberg, 1993). Thus, AAC interventionists may need to work with other professionals whose views are quite divergent from (and perhaps even incompatible with) their own; this may require considerable skill at negotiation and collaboration.

We offer two sets of guidelines in this regard. The first (see Table 9.1) is a set of guidelines for evaluating treatments for autism, adapted from a set of principles developed by Freeman (1997). The second (see Table 9.2) is a compilation across two synopses conducted 10 years apart of the key factors that appear to be critical for successful outcomes, based on existing research (i.e., outcomes in which the child develops speech or at least good language skills and is able to function in general classrooms with same-age peers without substantial supports). Both synopses are in general agreement about the critical factors in this regard (Dawson & Osterling, 1997; Simeonsson, Olley, & Rosenthal, 1987).

If everybody else in the room is also banging their head on the table and pulling their hair, then that must be the accepted norm. I think no matter how severely retarded our kids with disabilities are, they are not dumb. I think they really can perceive themselves in relation to other people around them. Peers exert a lot of pressure on each other. Some of that is positive and some of it is negative. I have heard kids in Ben's class say to him when he is doing something that looks dumb, "That looks dumb." . . . If kids stay away from him because he is doing something that looks stupid or hurtful, he is aware of that; and he doesn't like to be alone. So he will make the effort to try to stop because he wants to be with the kids. (Sue Lehr, talking about her son who has autism, in Biklen, 1992, p. 78)

Communication in a Social and Developmental Context

Because autism profoundly affects the very nature of communication as a social mediator, it is critically important that interventions emphasize the pragmatic aspects of communication rather than merely aspects related to form (Duchan, 1987). To quote Rees, "morphology plus syntax plus semantics does not equal communication" (1982, p. 310) for most individuals with autism. Especially for beginning communicators with autism, the development of spontaneous communication as a dynamic, interpersonal process is critical. Related to this is the need to teach the individual to use communication skills in the context of naturally occurring routines related to functional activities in daily life.

It is also important that interventions start at the individual's level of social/communicative/cognitive development and build skills in a natural developmental progression. A number of researchers have demonstrated that the developmental profiles of children with autism, unlike those typically found in children with mental retardation, are characterized by an uneven distribution of skills; this is often referred to as "developmental discontinuity" (Fay & Schuler, 1980). On a sensorimotor assessment battery, for example, children with autism tend to perform markedly better in the areas of object permanence and tool use (causality) than in areas requiring interpersonal in-

Table 9.1. Guidelines for evaluating treatments for autism

---

1. *Approach* any new treatment with hopeful skepticism. *Ask yourself,* to what extent is this treatment aimed at helping the person with autism become a fully functioning member of society?

2. *Beware* of any program or technique that
   - Claims to be appropriate (or desirable) for every person with autism
   - Prevents or interferes with individualization
   - Potentially results in harmful program decisions

3. *Be aware* that treatment should always be based on individual assessment information that points to a particular choice of one or more treatments for an individual. If assessment procedures to determine whether a particular treatment might be appropriate for an individual are not available—*BEWARE.*

4. *Beware* of new treatments that have not been scientifically validated. *Ask* for research evidence that provides support for a treatment, and examine it critically.

5. *Ask yourself*
   - Will this treatment result in potential harm to the child?
   - How will failure of the treatment affect the child and his or her family?
   - Has the treatment been validated scientifically?

From Freeman, B.J. (1997). Guidelines for evaluating intervention programs for children with autism. *Journal of Autism and Developmental Disorders, 27*(6), 647; adapted by permission.

Table 9.2.   Factors related to favorable outcomes of intervention for young children with autism

Factor	Simeonsson, Olley, and Rosenthal, 1987	Dawson and Osterling, 1997
Treatment at an early age: as young as possible (i.e., most programs begin with children at 30–36 months, if possible)	C	C
Family participation: parents and other family members actively involved in treatment	C	C
Intensity: a large number of hours are needed for intervention, particularly during the first 6 months; positive outcomes reported from 20 to 40 hours per week	C	C
Structured, behavioral emphasis in highly supportive teaching environments	C	C
Predictability and routine: use of visual cues, schedules, and other techniques to assist with transitions between environments and activities		C
Emphasis on generalization of skills across people and environments; instruction in home, integrated preschool, and community environments	C	C
Functional approach to problem behaviors: emphasis on a proactive rather than a reactive approach to behavior problems		C
Integration with children without disabilities in preschools, with instruction on how to interact with their peers	M	M
Transition planning from preschool to kindergarten, with emphasis on teaching kindergarten "survival" skills as part of the preschool curriculum	M	C
Comprehensive curriculum across all domains (attending, imitation, language comprehension and use, social skills, and toy play most important)		C

C = factor identified as critical, M = factor mentioned but not highlighted.

teraction, such as gestural or vocal imitation, use of adult-as-agent (means–ends), symbolic understanding, or language comprehension (Curcio, 1978; Wetherby & Prutting, 1984). This information has direct implications for AAC interventions, as it is important to gear such interventions to the child's social and linguistic abilities rather than object ability. For example, it is not unusual to see manual sign language or other formalized communication systems (e.g., pictorial systems) recommended for children with autism who do not speak. This presumes that the problem is simply lack of an output mode and that communicative intent or language is intact. In fact, many such children have neither the language nor the social base on which communication must be built, even though they demonstrate substantial abilities in nonlanguage areas such as fine and gross motor skills or areas that involve object manipulation (e.g., puzzle assembly). Formal language or communication approaches with children who show evidence of significant developmental discontinuity should be preceded by interventions designed to build imitation, social, and natural gestural communication skills. Premature initiation of formal language-based AAC (or speech) approaches will often result in nonfunctional, stereotypical behavior, with resulting frustration on the part of both the child and his or her facilitators.

DEVELOPMENTAL APRAXIA OF SPEECH

Katie was a girl with developmental apraxia of speech who was adopted at age 2 after spending her infancy in a number of different foster homes. Her mom recalled that at first, "Katie was easily distracted, particularly in groups or where there was a lot going on in the environment. She was constantly on the move (and) did not stick with any task for more than a few minutes (or less). She had very poor fine motor skills (i.e., difficulty stringing beads, buttoning, doing puzzles). She screamed frequently, not in rage or anger, but I interpreted this as the only way she could "communicate." (Katie's mother, personal communication, July 17, 1991)

Katie was an active child who showed evidence of upper limb apraxia, in addition to an extremely limited vocal repertoire. At age 8, her speech consisted primarily of single sounds, with imitative attempts at two-syllable words or sound patterns. Her primary communicative behaviors included pointing, nodding "yes," waving, various facial expressions, and pantomimes. She achieved age-equivalent scores of 4 years, 11 months on both the Peabody Picture Vocabulary Test–Revised (Dunn & Dunn, 1981) and the Test for Auditory Comprehension of Language–Revised (TACL-R; Carrow-Woolfolk, 1985). Her hearing and vision were within normal limits.

Description and Characteristics

The term *developmental apraxia of speech* (DAS; also known as childhood verbal apraxia and childhood dyspraxia, among other terms) has been used since the 1970s in the United States to refer to children with articulation errors who also have difficulty with volitional or imitative production of speech sounds and sequences (Bernthal & Bankson, 1988). Aram and Nation (1982) listed a number of behavioral symptoms commonly attributed to children with DAS. These include a difference between voluntary and involuntary use of speech articulators, difficulty in selection and sequencing of phonological articulatory movements, slow improvement with traditional articulation treatment, fine and gross motor incoordination and nonfocal neurological findings, and frequent oral apraxia. It is assumed that the speech problems of DAS stem from a motor control impairment that affects the ability to execute and plan motor routines and activities (Guyette & Diedrich, 1981; Robin, 1992), although research suggests that it may be a disorder of inappropriate stress (Shriberg, Aram, & Kwiatowski, 1997a, 1997b, 1997c). Marquardt, Dunn, and Davis (1985) noted that positive neurological signs, including difficulty with gait and coordination; electroencephalogram abnormalities; and delayed development of or clumsiness in dressing, feeding, writing, and walking, are characteristic of children with DAS. Research related to the physiology of speech production has indicated that DAS is the result of faulty timing, coordination, and transitioning among dynamic motor subgroups (Blackstone, 1989c). The assumption is made that these problems are due to a neurological impairment that affects motor programming, the nature of which has not been documented empirically (Guyette & Diedrich, 1981).

DAS is often associated with other impairments, including mental retardation and neuromuscular disorders (Hall, Jordan, & Robin, 1992). Although individuals with DAS often have language problems as well, it appears that these co-occur with the speech impairment but are not directly related (Hall, 1992). In addition, the difficulties with motor planning during volitional nonspeech activities may account for the disorders found in approximately 40% of these children in such areas as reading, spelling, and writing (Aram & Nation, 1982). Shriberg (1994) estimated the incidence of speech delay plus DAS as 1–2 cases per 1,000, with 80%–90% of these being males. They often come from families with a history of speech and/or language problems. The speech of children with severe DAS may not be intelligible enough to meet their daily communication needs at home or in school; such children may be candidates for communication augmentation.

At one point, Katie's family contacted two speech-language pathologists to inquire about possible speech therapy for her. Katie's mother reported that they were told, "We cannot work on speech until we have speech" (Katie's mother, personal communication, July 26, 1991).

Unique AAC Issues

AAC as a Secondary Strategy

One of the major concerns voiced by parents and others is whether the provision of AAC techniques to individuals with DAS will inhibit their speech. A 1997 study provided evidence that should alleviate this concern. Cumley (1997) provided activity-based AAC displays to young children with DAS during play activities with an adult and analyzed the level and type of comprehensible communicative behaviors across different modalities, among other variables. He found that the children who used their AAC displays most frequently were those who had the most severe speech disorders, relative to the entire group. The availability of the activity displays did not inhibit their speech production but replaced their use of gestures with a more symbolic form of communication, thus raising their likelihood of being more comprehensible. Yet, when AAC displays were provided to the children with "less severe DAS," they continued to use either spoken words and/or gestures as their primary modes of communication and used the AAC displays only as secondary strategies. This study is the first to demonstrate empirically that the provision of AAC does not appear to inhibit speech in individuals with DAS. The goal of AAC is to support the child's attempts to communicate successfully, until such time as (hopefully) speech is adequate to meet ongoing communication needs. If speech does not develop to this extent, the AAC system will need to be revised so that it can function as a long-term, multipurpose system.

Of course, it goes without saying that intensive work to improve natural speech production should be part of every intervention for children with DAS. As Blackstone noted, "Every intelligible word/phrase is worth it" (1989c, p. 4). Several natural-speech treatment approaches for DAS incorporate AAC techniques such as gestures in conjunction with speech. These include movement techniques such as arm swinging (Yoss & Darley, 1974) and conventional gestures (Klick, 1985). Klick (1994) described the successful use of what she termed an *adapted cuing technique*, in which manual cues that reflect the shape of the oral cavity, the articulatory placement and movement pattern, and the manner in which a sound is produced are presented with the speech sounds. Similarly, a touch cue method (Bashir, Grahamjones, & Bostwick, 1984) and the Prompts for Restructuring Oral Muscular Phonetic Targets (PROMPT) system (Hayden & Square, 1994) incorporate systematic manual-tactile cues to the face concurrent with speech to elicit specific sounds in therapy sessions.

Manual signing has also been used to promote speech development. For example, the efficacy of "melodic intonation therapy" was reported for two children with DAS (Helfrich-Miller, 1994). This multiphasic technique involves the use of manual signs (in this case, Signed English) with intoned phonemic sequences, and the technique was reported to result in a gradual decrease in articulation and sequencing errors over the course of training. Similarly positive results were reported as a result of "signed target phoneme" therapy, in which fingerspelled letters from American Sign Language are paired with difficult sounds during therapy (Shelton & Garves, 1985).

At age 3, Katie received early childhood home-based services for 1 year before entering a preschool classroom for children with hearing impairments. The preschool placement was chosen because it was believed that she should be taught to use manual signs to communicate. Signing Exact English (SEE-2) was used in the classroom, and her parents used it at home as well. Her mom recalls that due to Katie's fine motor problems and hyperactivity, it was very difficult for her to focus when someone signed to her. One day, out of frustration, she said to Katie, "Don't you want to learn sign language so we can talk?" and Katie shook her head "No." Finally, the family's continued frustration with Katie's lack of progress in signing prompted them to withdraw her from school in order to provide her with home schooling.

Multimodal Communication

Children whose speech is largely unintelligible may benefit, at least in a practical sense, from an intervention package that includes AAC techniques. Children with DAS may show evidence of significant language delays that can be traced (at least hypothetically) to their inability to "practice" language in their early years (Stromswold, 1994). Delayed language development is a high price to pay while either waiting for speech to develop naturally or devoting 99% of the available therapy time to speech intervention. Rather, it is critically important to provide children with DAS with one or more appropriate AAC modalities from an early age so that they have ample opportunities to use and "play" with language. For example, Cumley and Swanson (1997) provided a case study example of a preschool child with DAS whose mean length of utterance increased from 2.6 words per utterance without AAC to 4.6 words per utterance with AAC supports. These included a voice-output communication device with Picture Communication Symbols on activity displays.

From the outset, AAC systems should almost always include at least gestures and visual-spatial (i.e., pictorial) symbols in addition to manual signs, if these are appropriate. Children whose fine motor abilities are not compromised (i.e., children without accompanying limb apraxia) may benefit from a total communication approach (speech plus manual sign) or one that incorporates the use of highly iconic gestures, such as Amer-Ind (Crary, 1987). Motivation for communicating may also be increased through the use of pictures or other symbols (e.g., rebus symbols, Blissymbols) that are visual and concrete in nature (Haynes, 1985). Nonelectronic communication/conversation books, miniboards, wallets, and other formats are often useful, as are aids that supply voice output (Blackstone, 1989c). The advantage of these methods, particularly if they incorporate line drawings or orthographic symbol output, is that they are often more intelligible to unfamiliar communication partners than are manual signs. The main disadvantages are the vocabulary and portability constraints that they can impose on the AAC user. Kravitz and Littman (1990) emphasized the importance of providing an adequate number of vocabulary items, noting that for many DAS individuals with whom they have worked, communication books are often nonfunctional unless they have 400–500 items. In terms of motor ability, individuals with DAS can almost always manage multiple overlays and pages, so extensive vocabulary displays can be carried, worn, or strategically placed in the environment.

Katie was home schooled (a legal educational option in her state) for approximately 2 years, along with several other children. When Katie was 8 years old, her family contacted a speech and hearing clinic at the state university to inquire about possible services. After assessment was completed, a multimodal intervention was introduced with the goals of improving Katie's natural speech and augmenting her communication while building her language skills through the use of communication miniboards. A modified phonological processing approach (Hodson & Paden, 1991), with hand gestures used to cue specific sounds, was initiated. Functional, motivating games and activities—not only drill and practice sessions—formed the context for systematic speech intervention.

Careful, flexible combinations of aided and unaided approaches can be effective in enhancing the advantages and minimizing the disadvantages of each approach. For example, Blockberger and Kamp (1990) reported the use of multimodal systems consisting of natural speech, gestures, manual signs, and voice-output communication aids with school-age children with DAS. The children and their families generally preferred to use unaided approaches and only resorted to aided techniques when communication breakdowns occurred. Kravitz and Littman (1990) provided another example in their discussion of an adult with DAS, among other impairments. This woman used sign language to exchange basic information rapidly, whereas she used her communication book primarily to achieve social closeness and to engage in more elaborate conversational interactions. She also used a simple AAC device with voice output for specific situations such as introductions, asking for assistance at the bank, or ordering at fast-food restaurants.

It is also important to remember to plan ahead to make aided AAC techniques portable and easy to manage because most individuals with DAS are ambulatory. One child with DAS who used a multimodal system consisting of natural speech, gestures, manual signs, and voice-output communication aids (Culp, 1989) relied primarily on speech, gestures, and manual signs, largely because of the lack of portability of her communication book. Some alternative techniques that may help to circumvent the lack of portability include communication miniboards mounted on walls, mealtime place mats, car dashboards, refrigerators, bathtub tiles—in short, in any and all of the places the child may go, so that opportunities and vocabulary for communication are abundantly available (Blackstone, 1989c). Many of the available direct selection electronic devices are also appropriate for literate and preliterate children and can be transported with shoulder straps, carrying cases, or briefcases.

In addition, individuals with DAS need to learn the following three sets of skills for conversational interactions: strategies for topic setting, strategies for clarification and repair, and strategies for decision making about when to use which communication modality. Strategies for topic setting are usually related to the use of natural speech, which is almost always the child's mode of choice even when intelligibility is poor. The difficulty is that when the child attempts to introduce a new topic of conversation with one or more poorly articulated words, the communication partner is required to guess what the word is from a virtual universe of possibilities. If the child can narrow the range of possibilities by referring to a topic card, remnant book, or other option (see Chapter 11), his or her communication partner may find it easier to guess the spoken words that are difficult to understand.

Clarification and repair strategies include repetition, rephrasing, adding or changing communication modes, using a cuing display (e.g., first sounds, rhyming words), gesturing, using body language/pantomime, and pointing to environmental cues (Blackstone, 1989c). Instructions for communication partners concerning useful ways to resolve breakdowns are often necessary and beneficial as well (e.g., "Try asking me the question another way"). The child may need to learn a decision-making strategy regarding when to use manual signs, a communication book, or an electronic aid. For example, Reichle and Ward (1985) taught an adolescent to point to the orthographic message "Do you use sign language?" when asked a question by an unfamiliar person and then to use either manual signs or his electronic aid depending on the partner's response.

Concurrent with intensive work on natural speech, miniboards with black-and-white line-drawing symbols were introduced to Katie in the context of motivating activities. The boards were designed to encourage multiword combinations, teach Katie to use specific language structures (e.g., prepositions, descriptors), and enhance her overall communication. Katie also began to use the miniboards at home during activities with her family (e.g., making cookies or popcorn, playing with dolls). A remnant book was also introduced at home and in the clinic to help Katie to introduce and establish topics.

Parent Support

Because children with DAS do speak, parents (and many clinicians) are often reluctant to augment verbal communication "too soon," for fear that speech will fail to progress if other communication modes are available. Furthermore, parents may assume that a decision to augment communication is tantamount to "giving up on speech" or may be unable to understand why AAC interventions are recommended for an otherwise healthy, intact child. Sensitive but systematic parent counseling is often necessary to adequately discuss these issues and to assure family members that the intention is to augment communication in the truest sense of the word rather than to replace speech. It may be useful to have parents visit classrooms where other children are using augmentative communication systems so that they can see for themselves how the system can be integrated into efforts to enhance natural speech. In addition, parents and other primary communication partners will usually require input related to strategies that facilitate communication interactions once the decision to augment speech has been made. Such efforts may require considerable time and energy on the part of the clinician and should be geared to increasing the parents' understanding of the nature of communication and the importance of supporting the child's efforts in this regard. Blackstone (1989c) provided additional suggestions about parent support strategies.

Closely related to the issue of parent counseling is that of when intervention should begin. If the family or clinician views the decision to augment communication for a child with DAS as a last resort, there will almost always be great reluctance to initiate such an intervention with very young, preschool-age children. Unfortunately, the child may enter kindergarten or first grade unequipped to deal with the extensive written and spoken communication demands of an academic setting. For example, because many of these children also exhibit fine motor planning problems that affect handwriting abilities, they may be at risk for problems with learning to read and spell because these areas appear to be closely intertwined (Gloeckler & Simpson, 1988). Obviously, if the child with DAS is mildly affected, augmentative writing or verbal expression techniques may not be necessary. However, AAC teams should consider providing children who have more severe conditions with augmentation in these areas even prior to entering school to ensure that their verbal and fine motor planning problems do not stand in the way of academic proficiency.

After 7 months of multimodal communication work, Katie's mom reported that "within a few days (maybe 2 weeks), I saw some changes as we continued working intensely at home. . . . After a few weeks—a month or so . . . I began to hear others, outside the family, remark at the improvement in Katie's speech. I have seen gradual but fairly steady improvement—the changes may seem quite slight to anyone else. . . . Katie is making a greater effort to take time to get more information across. Often, with a simple reminder, she will attempt a word again with greater clarity. She is beginning to attempt combinations of words (occasionally). . . . She has enjoyed making use of her book to communicate information to others. We as her family have learned a lot that will help her, too. (For) example, I will no longer hesitate to use the book, signs, pictures, or whatever else seems appropriate to help Katie get started with some dialogue or provide a beginning point for others." (Katie's mother, personal communication, July 17, 1991)

10

AAC Strategies
for Beginning Communicators

Building Opportunities and Nonsymbolic Communication

We use the term *beginning communicators* to refer to individuals *across the age range* who have one or more of the following characteristics:

- They rely primarily on nonsymbolic modes of communication such as gestures, vocalizations, eye gaze, and body language.
- They do not demonstrate communicative intentionality.
- They are learning to use aided or unaided symbols to represent basic messages for communicative functions such as requesting, rejecting, sharing information, and engaging in conversations.
- They use nonelectronic communication displays or simple technology (e.g., switches and electronic devices with limited message capabilities) for participation and communication.

Beginning communicators may be young children with various types of disabilities whose communication is developing in accordance with their chronological ages. They may be children, adolescents, or adults with one or more developmental disabilities such as cerebral palsy, autism, dual sensory impairments, mental retardation, or developmental apraxia of speech. They may be individuals who are in the early stages of recovery following traumatic brain injury or some other neurological trauma. Regardless of their ages or the etiologies of their communication impairments, they require support to learn that through communication they can have a positive impact on their environments and the people around them. In this chapter, we discuss interventions for beginning communicators that are related to opportunity barriers and nonsymbolic communication.

COMMUNICATION OPPORTUNITY INTERVENTIONS

Planning and implementation within the context of the Participation Model (Figure 6.1) requires assessment of the individual's participation needs, including those related to communication, in natural contexts such as community, home, and school environments. As we discuss in Chapter 6, the Participation Model requires that the participation patterns of typically developing peers in relevant environments be assessed for comparison. The participation patterns of the target individual are assessed in the same contexts and compared with those of the peer. Interventions are then designed to increase the participation levels of the target individual to match peer levels more closely. For infants and toddlers, this requires analyzing the interaction patterns of peers in home and community settings. When dealing with preschoolers and school-age children, teams also need to conduct this kind of examination in the classroom. When dealing with adults who are beginning communicators, teams should perform participation analyses in home, community, and work environments.

Young Children

> We purchased (our son) Dustin's computer system in February of 1984. He was 3½ years old. . . . We did not pay attention to psychologists' reports. They said that Dustin functions at an 8-month level. Considering that the evaluations have been based on motoric indicators, an 8-month level might be generous. It tells us nothing, however, about Dustin's strengths: his personality, his ability to learn, his appreciation of music, his ability to make friends. (Webb, 1984, p. 4)

Early Intervention Philosophy

Webb (1984) highlighted a number of important points that are appropriate for guiding augmentative and alternative communication (AAC) interventions for young children. First, she alluded to the dearth of norm-referenced assessment tools that accurately and meaningfully measure the abilities of children with complex sensory, motor, and speech problems. Second, she cautioned against putting much credence in the results of such assessments, especially if observation provides information and impressions that are contradictory to the test results. Third, she emphasized the importance of building on the child's strengths rather than focusing on the child's impairments. Finally, she reminded us that AAC interventions with young children should operate under the assumption that all children have the potential to make significant skill gains.

In addition to following these basic principles, AAC teams should conduct communication interventions with the view that outcome predictions are almost always inappropriate when addressing the needs of young children. Thus, without exception, strategies for supporting the development of natural speech should always be included in communication interventions for this age group. Similarly, teams should include strategies for supporting the development of literacy skills (e.g., reading, writing) in all intervention plans, even in those for children who may seem unlikely to acquire such skills. In addition, AAC professionals should base their intervention strategies on the assumption that general kindergarten placement is the goal for *all* young children. This aggressive approach can result only in positive outcomes for the child and will guard against the all-too-frequent later realization that a child with many skill deficits might have been able to develop a number of skills if he or she had received communication opportunities in earlier years. Interventions designed to increase communication opportunities as well as those designed to teach specific communication and social interaction skills are usually necessary for positive outcomes.

Participation in mainstreamed (preschool) programs is an essential component for improving the peer social competence of young children with disabilities. (Guralnick, 1990, p. 11)

Early Intervention Services

During the first few years of a child's life, his or her primary caregivers usually deliver early intervention services in the home. These people generally learn to provide appropriate inputs and supports, including those related to communication, from teachers and therapists who visit the home regularly. Starting at approximately 2 or 3 years of age, the child usually attends a preschool program for at least part of the day, where he or she receives direct services from professional staff. The type of preschool program may vary greatly; for example, it may accommodate only children with disabilities or may serve primarily typically developing children.

There is no doubt that preschool environments that include at least some typically developing children are vastly preferable to segregated classrooms for social interaction and communication (Hanson & Hanline, 1989; Peck & Cooke, 1983). Guralnick noted, "A mainstreamed preschool appears to provide a challenging and developmentally appropriate social/communicative environment for the child with disabilities, one that cannot be replicated in specialized programs due to the linguistic and other limitations of the handicapped children themselves" (1990, p. 10). In this chapter and subsequent chapters, we assume that some amount of regular, systematic integration with peers without disabilities exists in the preschool setting, and, if it does not, this should be recognized as an opportunity barrier and targeted for remediation. We also use the generic term *children* to refer to the people targeted for early intervention, although this may include infants, toddlers, and preschoolers, depending on the intervention discussed.

The Augmentative Communication Online User's Group is an Internet discussion group open to all AAC users and their supporters. To subscribe, e-mail acolug request@vm.temple.edu.

Communication Opportunities

Table 10.1 displays an example of a participation analysis and intervention plan for a preschool-age child's daytime activities. In this example, the AAC team identified discrepancies between the participation patterns and teachers' expectations of the target

Table 10.1.   Sample participation analysis and intervention plan for a preschool-age child

Activity	How do peers participate? (What is expected?)	How does child participate?	Intervention plan
Music (group)	Choose songs, sing repetitive parts of songs, put record on player, do hand or body movements to songs	Does not choose or sing, does not put on record, does hand and body movements with aide's assistance, mostly sits and watches/listens	Provide taped songs that she can turn on with a switch to sing along, provide picture symbols representing songs so she can choose, continue to imitate hand/body movements with aide
Snacktime (group)	Wash hands with help, sit down, ask for snack item, ask for drink, ask for help as needed, eat/drink appropriately, take dirty plate/cup to sink and rinse, wash hands/face with help	Washes hands and sits with help; does not ask for snack, drink, or help; needs help to eat and drink; does not take or rinse plate/cup at sink; hands and face washed by aide	Provide real object choices of two snacks and drink options, look for eye gaze or reach to indicate choice; talk to physical therapist about facilitating standing at sink so she can participate in cleanup routine
Pretend-play time (solo or small group)	Doll play in kitchen or grooming area, block and car play, dress up play: children expected to play appropriately with peers while teacher encourages verbal language according to IEP goals	Tues. & Thurs.: sits in wheelchair and watches peers play in an area; Mon., Wed., & Fri.: practices switch use with battery-operated toys (solo)	Encourage peers to use her lap tray as a play surface, adapt toys with Velcro so she can pick up with adapted Velcro glove, use Fisher-Price stove and sink on lap tray instead of large play kitchen furniture, adapt battery-operated blender and mixer for switch activation, use activity frame to display small items within reach

student and other children. The team then designed assistive device and environmental adaptations to reduce discrepancies at certain times in the child's day, such as during music and pretend-play time. The team identified the need for both adaptations and instructional modifications (e.g., adapting toys with Velcro) during other activities, such as pretend-play time. In all cases, the basic principle of the Participation Model is reflected: The first step to increasing communication is to increase meaningful participation in natural contexts. Some of the basic strategies for accomplishing this in preschool settings are summarized in the sections that follow.

Creating Predictable Routines at Home and in the Preschool Classroom

Daily living routines can provide many opportunities for communication, if caregivers help structure them with this purpose in mind. In most homes and classrooms, routines such as dressing, bathing, eating, and changing the child's position occur at regular times and intervals throughout the day. If this is not the case, these routines should be regularized as much as possible so that the child can begin to anticipate their occurrence. In addition, caregivers should perform routines in roughly the same sequence each time so that the child can begin to anticipate what happens next. Whenever possible, caregivers should allow sufficient time to carry out the routine so that contextual communication instruction can occur concurrently with the activity. Specific strategies for using regular, predictable routines to teach communication skills are discussed later in this chapter.

Participation is the only prerequisite to communication. Without participation, there is no one to talk to, nothing to talk about, and no reason to communicate. For young children, the primary participation context is *play.*

Adaptive Play

Because the primary "business" of young children is play, their primary communicative opportunities occur in play contexts. By increasing participation in play activities, we automatically increase the quality and quantity of communication opportunities (Brodin, 1991).

In *Adaptive Play for Special Needs Children,* Musselwhite noted that play is an intrinsic activity that is "done for its own sake, rather than as a means to achieving any specific end. . . . [It is also] spontaneous and voluntary, undertaken by choice rather than by compulsion. . . . Play includes an element of enjoyment, something that is done for fun" (1986a, pp. 3–4). Unfortunately, when play skills are taught in classrooms, these characterizations of play are often ignored, and play becomes, quite literally, the child's "work." This is not to imply that educators cannot use play as a vehicle to promote the development of gross motor, fine motor, social, cognitive, self-help, and (of course) communication skills. In fact, whenever possible, it is desirable to "telescope" goals and activities by working on one primary and one or more secondary goals simultaneously in a play context (Musselwhite, 1986b). For example, a "dress the doll" activity might require a preschool child to work primarily on fine motor skills related to dressing and to work secondarily on social and communication skills. Nevertheless, it is important that the activity remain *playful* and not become one in which toys are used as vehicles for work. This requires careful selection of play materials and the ways they are used.

For play activities to foster the development of communication skills, parents and educators must select toys and play materials with interaction goals in mind. For example, some types of toys (e.g., blocks, balls, toy vehicles, puppets) have been found to be more facilitative of peer interactions than other, more solitary play materials (e.g., books, paper and crayons, playdough, puzzles) (Beckman & Kohl, 1984). Other important considerations in selecting a toy include safety, durability, motivational value for children with various types of disabilities, attractiveness, and reactivity (Musselwhite, 1986a). Reactivity refers to the extent to which the toy "does something" (e.g., produces sound, sustains movement, creates a visual display). Research has demonstrated that young children with severe disabilities engage in longer periods of manipulative play with reactive toys than with nonreactive toys (Bambara, Spiegel-McGill,

Shores, & Fox, 1984). Finally, parents and teachers should select toys for realistic and imaginative play so that children have opportunities to engage in both concrete and pretend (i.e., symbolic) play.

Another way to increase the probability that children will play with toys is to make them easy to hold, carry, and manipulate. This is particularly important for children with motor impairments because the quality of early communication and the motor ability to manipulate objects appear to be related (Granlund & Olsson, 1987). Numerous authors have described assistive device play adaptations that can be made at home or at school (Burkhart, 1993; Goossens' & Crain, 1986a; Musselwhite, 1986b). These include activity frames, adjustable easels, learning boxes, play boxes, and other means of stabilizing and presenting manipulable toys so that they are accessible to children with limited hand and arm control. Toys can also be attached to lap trays with Velcro or elastic cords so they are within reach. Books can be adapted with small foam or carpet tape squares pasted on the corners to separate pages for easier turning (these are often called "page fluffers"). Small magnets or squares of Velcro can be attached to toys so that the child can then pick them up with a headstick or mitten affixed with the same material. Toys with movable parts (e.g., levers, knobs) can be adapted with plastic or Velcro extenders for children with sensory or motor impairments. Figure 10.1 illustrates some of the many possible toy adaptations.

If a child with motor impairments has battery-operated toys and appliances (e.g., blenders, slide projectors), these also will require adaptation so that he or she can operate them successfully. Parents and school staff can either purchase the switches through commercial distributors or manufacturers or construct them inexpensively at home or at school using readily available components (Burkhart, 1980, 1982, 1988; Goossens' & Crain, 1986a, 1986b; Levin & Scherfenberg, 1988; Wright & Nomura, 1987). Playing with battery-operated toys should serve as the means to an end (i.e., participation), not as an end in itself. All too often, children with motor or other impairments can be found sitting in the corner of a classroom with a paraprofessional, playing with a battery-operated toy and a microswitch while the other preschoolers are having fun playing house, garage, or dress-up! Unfortunately, this is often made worse when teachers provide a child with only one or two battery-operated toys for switch activation, apparently under the assumption that a monkey (or a bear, or a dog) hitting a drum (or crashing a pair of cymbals, or riding a car) is so fascinating that it will sustain the child's attention for an extended period of time, day after day! None of these practices reflect an understanding of the principles of the Participation Model or the appropriate use of microswitch technology in general, and they are almost certain to result in the widespread lament, "We spent all that money to buy a switch and a toy and the child gets bored with it after 2 minutes!" York, Nietupski, and Hamre-Nietupski (1985) described a step-by-step process for determining the appropriateness of microswitch usage. Table 10.2 summarizes some suggestions for using microswitches to enhance participation in home and preschool activities for children.

Detailed information about assessment and intervention planning for children who use switches for communication and participation can be found in *Utilizing Switch Interfaces with Children Who Are Severely Physically Challenged* by Goossens' and Crain (1992).

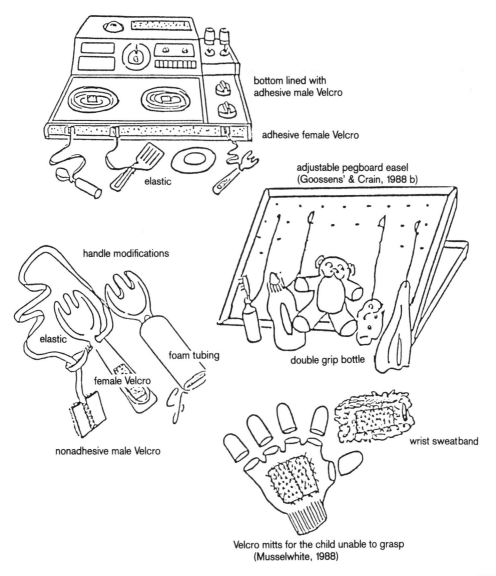

bottom lined with
adhesive male Velcro

adhesive female Velcro

adjustable pegboard easel
(Goossens' & Crain, 1988 b)

elastic

handle modifications

elastic

foam tubing

female Velcro

double grip bottle

wrist sweatband

nonadhesive male Velcro

Velcro mitts for the child unable to grasp
(Musselwhite, 1988)

Figure 10.1.   Examples of play adaptations that can be made at home or at school. (From Goossens', C. (1989). Aided communication intervention before assessment: A case study of a child with cerebral palsy. *Augmentative and Alternative Communication, 5,* 17; reprinted by permission.)

Communication opportunities can also arise or be created in the context of music, movement, puppetry, acting, and other fine arts activities for young children. Like other play activities, these may require adaptations in order to be accessible to children with disabilities. Musselwhite (1985, 1986b) described strategies and resources for using music (alone or in conjunction with adaptive play) to create opportunities for interaction and communication. For example, she described strategies for writing simple songs that can be easily represented through manual signs or pictorial symbols and for adapting songs to enhance their usefulness as contexts for encouraging speech and manual sign skills.

Movement activities (e.g., fingerplay songs such as "Where Is Thumbkin?"; gross motor games such as Red Light, Green Light) are excellent vehicles for teaching basic

Table 10.2.   Suggestions for using microswitch technology to enhance participation of preschoolers

Environment	Activity	Participation via microswitch technology
School	Transition from one activity to another	Child activates switch attached to a cassette tape recorder with a recorded tape of the teacher singing the cleanup song or saying, "Time to get ready for x," or whatever the verbal transition routine usually is.
	Snacktime	Child uses a switch to operate a toy car or truck that "delivers" the snack of the day to each of his or her friends at the table.
	Free playtime	Child uses a switch to operate simple computer game with a peer (e.g., Interaction Games, Don Johnston, Inc.). Child controls a battery-operated toy in play interaction with a peer.
Home/school	Playtime	Child in a crib accidentally activates a switch placed near a mobile body part to turn on a toy that provides stimulating and enjoyable feedback (e.g., a light display, a music tape, a mobile).
	Music time	Child activates a switch to turn on a sing-along tape or a prerecorded tape of a same-gender child singing his or her part in a song.
	Pretend-play time	Child uses a switch to activate a battery-operated car, truck, robot, toy blender, or toy mixer, depending on the theme of the pretend play.
	Art time	Child uses switch to operate a broken record player (no arm or needle) with paper affixed to the turntable and a blob of paint placed on the paper to make a swirly design pattern. Child provides power for electric scissors used by a peer or adult to cut paper.
	Storytime	Child uses a switch to operate a recorded tape of an adult reading the "story of the day," as he or she looks at the book to read along.
	Cooking	Child operates a blender with a switch to make a milkshake, uses a mixer to make cake batter, or uses a food processor to make salad.

cognitive/communication skills such as following directions, imitation, sequencing, and concept development. However, many standard movement activities and songs require one or more of the following modifications to be used for communication purposes: 1) simplifying target movements so that the child can participate meaningfully (this is also a good place to incorporate movement goals identified by therapists); 2) slowing the speed of the song/activity; 3) making directions shorter, simpler, and more repetitive; 4) simplifying the vocabulary; 5) pairing words with manual signs; 6) accompanying movements with sounds or words to encourage speech; and 7) including visual aids or concrete materials for children who do not yet engage in pretend play (Musselwhite, 1985). Arts activities such as acting (Stuart, 1988) and puppetry (Musselwhite, 1985) can also serve to create communication opportunities. For example, the teacher can attach a puppet to the child's foot or wrist rather than to his or her hand, or the child's wheelchair can be decorated so that it can be used as a prop or stage in a play or puppet show.

Sherazad is a 4-year-old girl who lives in a Canadian city with her mother, father, and brother. She is ventilator-dependent as a result of a high spinal cord injury from a fall when she was 2 years old. She cannot speak and depends on others for all of her personal care needs. She is learning to use a sip-and-puff switch in the context of daily activities at home and in her preschool. For example, with her switch she can turn the lights on and off in the classroom; turn music on and off during music time; help to make blender drinks daily during snacktime; and play adapted versions of Candyland, Chutes and Ladders, and other children's games using a battery-operated "spinner" attached to her switch. Paper templates with colored or numbered sections are fitted under the spinner dial. When she sips on her switch, the spinner spins around and when she puffs, it stops. Her game partner then moves her token to the color or the number of spaces selected (Canfield & Locke, 1997). She can also play computer games with her friends; operate a battery-operated toy mixer, blender, and microwave during "house play" time; tell the teacher to turn the pages of a book during storytime by activating a small communication device with a single recorded message; and operate electric scissors and a hot glue gun to make art projects with a helper during art time. Once Sherazad enters kindergarten, she will use the switch to type letters and words in Morse code into a computer emulator at the same time that her classmates learn to write letters with pencil and paper.

SCHOOL-AGE INDIVIDUALS

Communication Opportunities

Where do typically developing children and adolescents find communication opportunities, meet communication partners, and learn to communicate in a variety of ways? As most parents know, these opportunities all occur primarily at school, when children interact with classmates and other peers. Since the mid-1980s, the school reform movement has emphasized the importance of including students with disabilities in general education classrooms along with their typically developing peers (Stainback & Stainback, 1996). This greatly increases the likelihood that students with disabilities will have numerous, daily opportunities for natural communication with a variety of partners. At the same time, inclusion presents greater challenges to those who provide classroom support, in that students in general education classrooms usually have a broader range of communication needs than do students in segregated situations. In general education classrooms, students need to be able to ask and answer questions on a number of topics, give reports, participate in instructional groups, and participate in a wide variety of social exchanges (Nelson, 1992). In social environments, students encounter communication opportunities that go beyond simple requesting, rejecting, and identifying wants and needs as they interact with classmates and friends. For example, if an adolescent is sitting in the cafeteria with his high school friends and one of them is helping him eat lunch, he probably does not have to communicate many wants and needs messages because his needs are already being met. Instead, he may be asked by his friends to share information about what he did last weekend or be expected to contribute to the conversation by sharing the latest teenage joke. In order for students to be fully included in social as well as educational activities, it is critically important that they have strategies for communication in areas such as information sharing, social closeness, and social etiquette (Light, 1988).

Of course, there is no guarantee that just because students are enrolled in general education classrooms, they will be included in the educational and social milieu of the school in ways that promote communication. Across North America, a number of models for inclusion have been developed to assist administrators (Villa et al., 1992), educators (Falvey, 1995; Stainback & Stainback, 1996), and related services personnel (Calculator & Jorgensen, 1994; Rainforth, York-Barr, & Macdonald, 1997) to accomplish these goals. The following sections summarize the primary approaches to inclusion.

MAPs, Circles of Friends, and PATH

Making Action Plans (MAPs; Pearpoint, Forest, & O'Brien, 1996), Circles of Friends (Snow & Forest, 1987), and Planning Alternative Tomorrows with Hope (PATH; Pearpoint, O'Brien, & Forest, 1993) are three related models that have been used primarily to facilitate the inclusion of school-age individuals with severe disabilities into general classroom settings, although they certainly can be used to create inclusive neighborhoods, workplaces, and other settings as well. When applied to school inclusion, these dynamic processes involve family members, school principals, both general and special education teachers, paraprofessionals, support personnel, and general class peers. The processes involve strategies for building school communities in which an individual with disabilities can be supported and develop friendships (Pearpoint et al., 1996; Vandercook, York, & Forest, 1989).

MAPs is a "collaborative planning process for action that brings together the key actors in a child's life" (Pearpoint et al., 1996, p. 68). These people can use MAPs to carefully consider a student's strengths, lifestyle, and dreams and develop a concrete plan of action for helping the student reach his or her dreams. MAPs is not a case conference or planning meeting for developing an individualized education program (IEP), although the results may be useful in this regard. Interventionists often use the Circles of Friends process in conjunction with MAPs to support the development of friendships among classmates and peers. Finally, PATH is an in-depth, eight-step process for helping people assist a student by solving complex individual, family, or system problems through focused planning. These three approaches have been used widely in both the United States and Canada to facilitate social inclusion in general classrooms and in the community for children and adults.

A variety of written materials and training videotapes on Circles of Friends, MAPs, and PATH are available from Inclusion Press International in Toronto, Ontario, Canada.

COACH and VISTA

COACH (Choosing Outcomes and Accommodations for Children; Giangreco, Cloninger, & Iverson, 1998) and VISTA (Vermont Interdependent Services Team Approach; Giangreco, 1996b) are two related approaches used to develop a student's IEP and to assist the educational team in developing collaborative support teams for implementing IEPs in inclusive classrooms. COACH is a process in which family members and others are interviewed by a member of the educational team to identify a long-term vision for the student as well as annual educational goals. Interventionists then identify members of the educational team who will implement the plan, and program content is defined in a format that facilitates implementation in general classrooms and other settings. VISTA picks up where COACH leaves off and provides alternative ways for the student's educational support team to integrate related services (e.g., speech-language pathology, occupational and/or physical therapy) in general classrooms. Research on COACH has indicated that it is highly rated by parents, teachers, and educational "experts" along a number of dimensions when it is used as intended. In particular, use of COACH appears to facilitate the provision of natural supports by peers (see Giangreco, 1996a, for a summary of COACH research). When used together, these tools can be very useful in assisting professionals in creating meaningful communication opportunities for AAC users in general classrooms.

If she needs something, if she needs help opening the paint, she'll tap one of the other kids and hand them the jar like, "You know, I can't get this cover off." And they have gotten so they've been as excited as I have. "Hey, Holly wants me to open it! Holly asked me to do it! She's communicating!" (A mother whose daughter was supported in an general classroom using COACH, in Giangreco, 1996a, p. 252)

Program Development Process

The step-by-step program development process combines elements of the Participation Model (see Mirenda & Calculator, 1993) as well as elements of Circles of Friends, MAPs, and COACH to support students who use AAC in general classrooms (Calculator, 1997; Calculator & Jorgensen, 1991, 1994). The process begins with identification of the student's abilities and needs and then utilizes additional strategies to 1) identify barriers to inclusion and time lines to address those barriers; 2) develop a process for facilitating friendships and natural supports (e.g., through Circles of Friends); 3) choose priority learning goals, participation goals, and short-term objectives for the school year (e.g., through COACH); 4) develop instructional and curriculum modifications as needed; and 5) evaluate the quality of inclusion and the effectiveness of instruction periodically.

The Ability OnLine Support Network is an electronic mail system that connects young people with disabilities or chronic illness to peers and mentors with and without disabilities. It is offered free of charge, other than long distance tariffs that apply outside the Toronto area. Access to the network is available through the use of a computer, modem, and telephone, either by dialing directly into the system (416-650-5411) or by telnet via the Internet (bbs.ablelink.org). First-time users can register on-line.

ACE

Interventionists can use the ACE (Analyzing the Communication Environment) inventory (Rowland & Schweigert, 1991, 1993) to identify ways to encourage communication in activities within the classroom. The ACE is unique in that it targets the properties of specific daily activities rather than the student's skills; thus, it identifies barriers to communication opportunities rather than what or how to teach the student. The ACE consists of 52 statements grouped in six categories: 1) the activity, 2) the student's communication system, 3) adult interaction, 4) group dynamics, 5) materials, and 6) specific opportunities for communication. When intervention teams administer the ACE inventory, they observe an activity at least twice, check off statements that describe strategies used in the activity, and calculate a score for the activity. The intent is to assist educational personnel to identify barriers to communication, which can then be remediated. Research investigating ACE suggests that both its reliability and its validity are excellent and that the relationship between the ACE score and fluency of a student's communicative behavior appears to be strong (Rowland & Schweigert, 1993).

In the next decade, with advancements in knowledge and availability of AAC technology, a generation of children who successfully communicate using AAC will grow into adults with developmental disabilities. . . . There will be an obligation from AAC professionals and program administrators to (ensure) that the communication gains made in childhood transfer into successful integration of AAC into the adult community. (Delsandro, 1997, p. 672)

Adults

Communication Opportunities

Since the mid-1970s, a number of authors have argued that adults who are beginning communicators, like other citizens, should be fully included in the community and should participate in the same types of vocational, recreational and leisure, and other activities as typical adults (Meyer, Peck, & Brown, 1991). In order to accomplish this, these adults must have access to a community-referenced support model, within which they can learn the skills needed to participate in activities that are age appropriate, functional (i.e., directly useful in their daily activities), taught in the actual community or vocational environments where they are needed, and taught with reference to the cues and corrections that are naturally available (Falvey, 1986; Ford & Mirenda, 1984). Such activities may occur in home, recreational and leisure, community, vocational, or school environments.

Adoption of a community-referenced approach to instruction has a direct, positive impact on the quantity and quality of the participation and communication opportunities that are available. Because of increased involvement in the community, the individual may, for example, need to order food in a restaurant, cheer for the local basketball team, ask for help at the library, or chat with co-workers at breaktime—the list of natural opportunities for things to say and people to say them to becomes endless! Careful analysis of the settings in which the individual participates helps to identify the opportunities available for communication and to ensure that necessary adaptive and AAC techniques are included in an intervention. The "ecological inventory" process has been used successfully for this purpose for many years, and Reichle et al. (1991) described it as it applies to communication interventions. In brief, the ecological inventory process involves the following:

- Observing a peer without disabilities engage in the activity of interest
- Writing a step-by-step list of the skills required
- Assessing the target individual against the skill inventory to identify discrepancies
- Designing communication adaptations and instructional programs to teach compensatory skills

Figure 10.2 provides excerpts from an ecological inventory completed for an adult in a community environment, along with suggested participation and communication adaptations in discrepancy areas. AAC teams can apply this basic format to activities at home, in the workplace, or in the community. If the individual is not supported to participate in functional, age-appropriate activities in a wide variety of settings, this restriction clearly should be considered an opportunity barrier and targeted for remediation.

Self Advocates Becoming Empowered (SABE) is a new self-advocacy organization for people with developmental disabilities in North America. Their goal is to support people so that they have the same "choices, rights, responsibilities, and chances to speak up to empower themselves, as well as to make new friendships and renew old friendships, just like everyone else" (Kennedy & Shoultz, 1997, p. 7). For additional information about the self-advocacy movement around the world, see *New Voices: Self-Advocacy by People with Disabilities* (Dybwad & Bersani, 1996).

Communication Partners

Who is there to talk to? For most adults with severe disabilities; the answer is family members; adults who are paid to be communication partners; and, perhaps, other people with severe disabilities. These are all perfectly *acceptable* communication partners—but they should not be the *only* communication partners. Imagine what it would be like, day after day, to communicate only with your parents, teachers, and other people who have at least as much difficulty as you do in getting messages across! A planning and support model designed to increase the number and types of other adult communication partners—also known as acquaintances and friends—is described in the following section.

Support Helps Others Use Technology (SHOUT) is a group of AAC users and professionals whose mission is "to study and advocate for the employment of people who could benefit from augmentative communication to overcome significant speech, language, and multiple impairments" (Creech, 1993, p. 4). SHOUT sponsors the annual Pittsburgh Employment Conference for Augmented Communicators (PEC@) and supports ongoing self-advocacy projects for AAC users.

Environment: Prendle's Drug Store
Target Individual: Sarah, age 20
Activity: Purchasing personal care items
Set-up: In the store with a friend who also needs to do some shopping, friend is wheeling Sarah in
         wheelchair

Skill (as performed by a peer without a disability)	Participation (person with a disability)	Possible participation or communication adaptations
1. Enter store.	–	Pause before entering, wait for signal indicating anticipation/ acceptance.
2. Greet salesperson at jewelry counter, if present.	+ (vocalized)	In addition, consider single message loop tape with greeting that can be activated with microswitch by left hand.

	Items to Purchase			
Repeat for each item:	**1**	**2**	**3**	
3a. Walk/wheel along front of store, looking down each aisle until desired aisle is identified.	–	–	–	Encourage Sarah to look down aisle, pause and look for accept signal, proceed down aisle after signal.
3b. Walk/wheel down aisle.	–	–	–	Friend can wheel her slowly down aisle.
3c. Locate correct section.	–	–	–	As she wheels past the sections, look for an accept signal and stop.
3d. Examine options.	P	P	P	Friend can hold up two options at a time to make this easier.
3e. Choose desired item.	P	P	P	Look for eye gaze or arm movement toward one of the two options presented. If none, try another two options.
3f. Converse with friend as desired/needed.	P	–	P	Consider a multiple message loop tape with topic-setter statements that can be activated with microswitch by left hand: "Have you seen any good movies lately?"
3g. Check to see if next item is in the aisle. If yes, go to step 3a. If no, go to step 2.	–	–	–	Friend can push her down aisle again slowly, looking for signal to stop.

Skill	Participation	Possible participation
4. Locate checkout stand.	–	Wheel to front of store and pause within view of stand, pause and wait for a signal to proceed.
5. Greet cashier.	P (smiled slightly)	Consider single message loop tape as in Step 2.

(continued)

Figure 10.2. Excerpts from an ecological inventory with suggestions for participation and communication adaptations.
(Key: + = performed independently by target individual; – = not attempted by target individual; P = attempted.)

Figure 10.2.   (*continued*)

Skill (as performed by a peer without a disability)	Participation (person with a disability)	Possible participation or communication adaptations
6. Put items on counter.	–	Friend can do this.
7. Get out money.	–	Friend can do this.
8. Give cashier money when requested to do so.	–	Place a Velcro strap around her left hand and tuck bills under it. Have her extend her left hand toward the cashier, who can then remove the money.
9. Receive change.	–	Friend can do this.
10. Put change away.	–	Friend can do this.
11. Take bag with purchases.	–	Take bag from counter and hold in front of Sarah, and pause. Look for an accept signal and place bag on lap.
12. Exit store.	–	Pause before door, look for an accept signal, and leave store.

Personal Futures Planning

The Personal Futures Planning process emphasizes assisting supporters to "focus on opportunities for people with severe disabilities to develop personal relationships, have positive roles in community life, increase their control of their own lives, and develop the skills and abilities to achieve these goals" (Mount & Zwernik, 1988, p. 1). It can be used to facilitate community integration of individuals of all ages, but it has been particularly successful in assisting adults with disabilities to make successful transitions from institutional to community settings and from segregated community settings to more integrated ones. Personal Futures Planning is as much a process for organizational change as for individual planning (Mount, 1994).

Personal Futures Planning consists of several basic steps. First, a "vision plan" is developed from a group interview of the "focus person" and all of the people involved in his or her life ("supporters") to gather information about past events, relationships, places, preferences, choices, ideas about the future, obstacles, and opportunities. The goal of this first step is to develop a collective vision of the future that emphasizes the person's capacities and gifts, rather than his or her impairments and problems. Next, the group develops both short- and long-term goals based on the vision plan. Finally, supporters make commitments of various types and levels to help the individual carry out the plan over time. Additional activities may include interactive problem solving; strategic redesign of the support system or agency to facilitate the vision plan; and other activities that facilitate harmony among the person's vision, the community opportunities available, and the system resources (Mount, 1994). A complimentary process for organizational change, *Framework for Accomplishment* (O'Brien & Lyle, 1987), presents additional tools to help people bridge the gap between person-centered planning and organizational change.

Written materials, videotapes, and other information about Personal Futures Planning are available from Inclusion Press International in Toronto, Ontario, Canada.

THE BOTTOM LINE

Over and over again, friends, parents, professionals, and community members have documented the incredible impact of integrated communication opportunities—or the lack thereof—on the communication abilities of people who are beginning communicators (e.g., Perske & Perske, 1988). There is simply no doubt about it: The availability of genuine and motivating communication opportunities in integrated and inclusive settings is *at least* as important to the success of a communication intervention as the availability of an appropriate access system. This is perhaps more true for people who are just learning the basics of communication than for anyone else because these individuals are among those with the fewest personal resources and the most need for assistance from others. If the communication partners of these individuals do not include a substantial number of people who are not paid to interact with them, who are not likely to leave for a new job next year, and who do not believe that their primary task is to make the individual more like everyone else, the communication interventions are almost certainly going to have a limited impact!

Once the AAC team has created communication opportunities and identified communication partners, it can begin to plan a multimodal and multi-element approach for building communication skills. For many beginning communicators, initial interventions may be aimed at strengthening their repertoires of nonsymbolic communication behaviors.

Augmentative Communication Empowerment Supports (ACES) is an international support and training program established in 1988 at Temple University in Philadelphia. The purpose of ACES is

> To assist individuals with significant speech and physical disabilities to develop a literal, social, and political voice in order to remove the perceived "cloak of incompetence." An additional purpose is to enhance opportunities to live independently and to gain access to further education and employment. (Bryen, Slesaransky, & Baker, 1995, p. 80)

For information about ACES, contact the Institute on Disabilities at Temple University (http://www.temple.edu/inst_disabilities).

NONSYMBOLIC COMMUNICATION INTERVENTIONS

Often, facilitators who support beginning communicators fail to build a strong communicative foundation before instituting AAC interventions to teach the use of symbols. Initial interventions often involve introducing a formal symbolic communication system that uses manual signing or pictures, even though the individual may not understand many basic elements of communication, such as turn taking, joint attending, and the role of other people as communication partners. In typical development, early forms of communication such as gestures and vocalizations are gradually augmented by new forms and eventually result in an integrated multimodal system, which includes speech. With a developmental model as the basis, facilitators should promote the use of natural gestures and vocalizations in a variety of natural contexts with individuals of any age who show little evidence of intentional communication. The goal of such nonsymbolic communication interventions is to build a strong foundation for the development of speech and/or symbolic AAC techniques.

Relationship Between Communication and Challenging Behavior

It is not unusual for individuals who are beginning communicators to engage in nonsymbolic behaviors that create unique challenges for those with whom they live, learn, play, and/or work. These might include behaviors such as tantrums, hitting, screaming, pushing, various forms of self-injurious behavior, and many others. Numerous authors have suggested that most challenging behavior can be interpreted as communicative in nature and treated as such (Carr et al., 1994; Donnellan, Mirenda, Mesaros, & Fassbender, 1984; Durand, 1990; Reichle et al., 1991). Throughout this chapter, communication interventions related to individuals who exhibit challenging behavior are discussed in the context of other communication interventions.

Three important principles are common to both nonsymbolic and symbolic communication interventions for challenging behavior. First is the *principle of functional equivalence:* Sometimes, the most appropriate intervention involves teaching the individual an alternative behavior that serves the same function as the problem behavior. This means that interventionists must undertake a holistic and often extensive analysis of the behavior of concern to identify its current function(s) so that they can design an appropriate alternative (see Carr et al., 1994; Durand, 1990; and O'Neill et al., 1997, for examples of procedures). For example, if the function of the behavior is to get attention, the new behavior must result in attention; or if the current behavior allows the individual to avoid nonpreferred events, the new behavior must also allow the individual to accomplish this. The second principle, called the *principle of efficiency and response effectiveness*, states that people communicate in the most efficient and effective manner available to them at any given point in time. This means that the alternative behavior must be at least as easy for the individual to produce as is the problem behavior and must also be as effective in obtaining the desired outcome. If the new behavior is more difficult or less effective, the old behavior will persist.

"Circle time. You need to sit down. You need to look out the window. Is it a sunny day or is it a rainy day? Jimmy, you need to look out the window." All expressed, of course, with exaggerated facial movements and sign language and pictures of yellow balls with spikes and smiling faces and gray clouds with little Velcro bits on the back. "You need to keep your hands to yourself. Turn the cloud over, Jimmy, you're not supposed to feel the Velcro, you need to put it in the calendar." Finally, Jimmy and his little cohorts have had enough of little red blocks and pegs, throw them at the teacher when she dumps the box on the little table in front of them for the 100th time, and the teacher finally says, "Do you want time out?" Behavior problems? The only thing the kids are allowed to want or choose is their own punishment. (H. Rader, personal communication, March 7, 1997)

The third principle is the *principle of appropriate listening*, which says that sometimes the most appropriate response is to identify the function of the problem behavior and alter the environment accordingly, rather than to teach an alternative behavior.

Consider, for example, a woman who is hanging out the window of a burning building, screaming and hitting herself. Most people would agree about the function of her behavior and the message therein: "Get me out of here! I'm really scared, and it's getting hotter all the time!" probably comes pretty close. Everyone would also agree that the appropriate response would be to listen to her message and rescue her, not to try to teach her to produce an alternative behavior for screaming and hitting, such as showing a manual sign for "help" or showing a photograph of fire! Unfortunately for many people with severe disabilities, their "burning buildings" are not usually so obvious—they appear in the form of isolated, noninteractive environments; boring, nonpreferred tasks; and rigidly structured schedules over which they have no control or choice (see Brown, 1991, for examples). Carr, Robinson, and Palumbo (1990) noted in their eloquent discussion of this issue that the appropriate response in such situations is to focus on changing the environment or the sequence of events, not the person. As we learn more and more about the relationship between behavior and communication, it becomes increasingly important to remember that it is critical to provide opportunities for communication and control in the context of meaningful, interactive activities and environments.

Sensitizing Facilitators

As mentioned in Chapter 2, the term *facilitator* refers to an individual who assumes or is assigned responsibility for supporting a person's communicative attempts. Several studies have highlighted the importance of teaching facilitators to identify and respond to children's emerging signals. For example, Houghton, Bronicki, and Guess (1987) observed 37 students with severe multiple disabilities across 12 classrooms. They coded the frequency of student initiations related to expression of preferences, as well as facilitator responses to these initiations. The results indicated that body movements and facial expressions were the most frequently observed communicative behaviors produced by the students. The students initiated such behaviors approximately once per minute in both structured and unstructured situations, but facilitators responded to these communications only 7%–15% of the time! Unfortunately, a study of preschoolers with dual sensory impairments reported similarly dismal data (Rowland, 1990). In general, the data from these two studies suggest that 1) the facilitators were largely unaware of or insensitive to students' attempts to communicate and/or 2) the constraints imposed by the demands of the classrooms precluded the level of facilitator attentiveness that was desirable. Regardless, the critical need for training and environmental adjustments in this area is obvious.

In their excellent text on nonsymbolic communication interactions, Siegel-Causey and Guess (1989) suggested that the first step in teaching facilitators to "tune in" to early preference behaviors is to foster an atmosphere of security and warmth through nurturing relationships. This includes encouraging facilitators to provide comfort, support, and affection; create positive environments for interactions; and focus on the individual's interests at the moment. For example, AAC teams should encourage facilitators working with young beginning communicators to use animated facial expressions such as smiles and wide eyes to display enjoyment, and simple verbalizations with rhythmic intonation patterns to convey affection and emotional warmth. Facilitators who support older individuals need to use age-appropriate interaction styles that communicate acceptance, respect, and positive regard.

Responding to Spontaneous Signals

Individuals who communicate primarily through gestures and vocalizations initially do so when the need arises, rather than in response to queries or directives from their communication partners. Initially, an individual's spontaneous signaling behavior is not intended to be communicative but simply occurs at random. When facilitators consistently interpret and respond to such behaviors as if they were intentional, the individual gradually learns to initiate them intentionally. Interpretation and responsiveness continue to be important facilitator techniques to expand communication repertoires, even after individuals begin to attach meaning to their gestures and vocalizations. Although most adults are attuned to gestures and vocalizations of typical children and adults, they often either ignore or misinterpret many of the more subtle and idiosyncratic behaviors exhibited by children and especially adults with disabilities (Houghton et al., 1987; Rowland, 1990).

Parents rely heavily on their own intuition and ability to interpret their child. . . . (This) involves a great degree of guesswork. . . . Parents are often regarded with suspicion about the validity of their interpretations. They often hear from other people that they over-interpret the child and that their comprehension is only an expression of wishful thinking. . . . Parents have a unique competence in knowing their children and understanding their children's communication. (Brodin, 1991, p. 237)

Building a Communication Foundation

Three essential building blocks of communication are signals for attention-seeking, acceptance, and rejection. Even individuals who have a limited repertoire of gestural or vocal behaviors may be able to communicate these signals. Attention-seeking signals are those the individual uses primarily to initiate social interactions with others, such as laughing, crying, or making eye contact. Acceptance signals are those used to communicate that whatever is currently happening is tolerable, okay, or enjoyable. Familiar communication partners are usually able to describe these behaviors if asked questions such as "How do you know when Joey doesn't mind or likes something?" or "How do you know when Quinta is happy?" Rejection signals are used to communicate that the individual finds his or her current status unacceptable, not enjoyable, or intolerable for some reason. Partners will often describe these behaviors when asked questions such as "How do you know when Leon doesn't like something?" or "How do you know when Jackie is unhappy or in pain?" Thus, the ability to signal "acceptance" and "rejection" is not the same as the ability to respond to yes or no questions—the latter involves a much more sophisticated set of skills. Accept and reject signals may be overt and obvious, such as smiling, laughing, frowning, or crying, or may be very subtle, such as averted eye gaze, increased body tension, increased rate of respiration, or sudden passivity. Most individuals are able to signal acceptance and rejection in some way, although this may be quite idiosyncratic. If clear and socially appropriate attention-seeking, acceptance, and rejection signals are not part of an individual's communication repertoire, initial interventions should include strategies for developing these behaviors.

Attention-Getting Signals

It is particularly important that facilitators be attuned to attention-seeking behaviors initiated by the individual. Initially, facilitators should respond to any such behavior that is socially and culturally acceptable so that the person can repeatedly experience the communicative results of his or her efforts (Smebye, 1990). For example, a facilitator might respond to a behavior such as pounding on a lap tray or vocalizing loudly as an indicator of a desire for attention (Baumgart, Johnson, & Helmstetter, 1990). After a repertoire of acceptable attention-seeking behaviors has been established and is used intentionally, facilitators can limit their responses to the most desirable and frequent behaviors only.

Simple technology can also serve to enhance the salience of attention-getting behaviors, especially for learners whose behaviors are quite subtle and easily missed. For example, one study investigated the use of switch-activated attention-getting devices such as call buzzers and a single-message tape recording that said COME HERE, PLEASE (Gee, Graham, Goetz, Oshima, & Yoshioka, 1991). The study used an "interrupted behavior chain" intervention to teach use of the devices to three children with mental retardation requiring extensive or pervasive support and sensory, physical, and medical disabilities who were extremely limited in their ability to participate in daily school routines (a more extensive discussion of this teaching technique appears later in this chapter). Teachers identified three or four routines that could be interrupted to provide opportunities during the school day for the students to use their attention-getting devices. For example, one such opportunity occurred during a transfer activity when a student, Erik, was told it was time to get out of his wheelchair, had his straps loosened and tray removed, but was not then moved. Erik's teacher waited for him to initiate a gestural or vocal behavior to call attention (e.g., extending his arms, making agitated noises, whimpering) and then prompted him to activate a switch mounted in an appropriate location and connected to one of the attention-getting devices described previously. When the device was activated after teacher prompting, the routine continued as planned (i.e., Erik was moved from the wheelchair). Over time, instructional prompts for switch activation were gradually faded using a time-delay procedure (see discussion later in this chapter). All three students learned to activate their attention-getting switches independently across several such routines within a maximum of 63 instructional opportunities. This study demonstrated clearly that well-planned instruction using appropriate contexts and technology can result in the acquisition of at least simple communicative behaviors even by individuals with very severe disabilities.

Rowland and Schweigert (1991, 1992) have developed a systematic intervention process for introducing microswitch technology to beginning communicators to teach attention-getting and other early communicative behaviors. A manual and related videotape of this process are available from The Psychological Corporation (United States and Canada).

Relationship to Challenging Behavior

It is important to note that, for many individuals, attention-getting signals take the form of socially unacceptable behaviors, such as screaming, grabbing, hitting, throwing tantrums, performing self-injurious behaviors, and others. In the 1990s, a technique known as functional communication training (FCT) has been used widely in response to such challenging behaviors. FCT involves a set of procedures designed to reduce challenging behavior by teaching functionally equivalent communication skills. FCT requires a thorough assessment to identify the function (i.e., message) of the behavior of concern and systematic instruction related to the new communicative behaviors. In a review of research in which AAC techniques were incorporated into FCT interventions, Mirenda (1997) reported that 31% of the 52 interventions included in the review involved teaching alternative attention-getting behaviors. This was accomplished by teaching use of nonsymbolic gestures such as a hand tap or arm wave (Lalli, Browder, Mace, & Brown, 1993; Sigafoos & Meikle, 1996), conversation books (Hunt, Alwell, & Goetz, 1988, 1990), a microswitch and taped message that said PLEASE COME HERE (Northup et al., 1994; Peck et al., 1996), and an electronic communication device with the message I WANT TO BE WITH THE GROUP (Durand, 1993). The AAC techniques and the specific messages that were taught varied to match the context of the challenging behaviors. Systematic teaching strategies such as prompting and fading were used to teach the new attention-getting behaviors in natural contexts, and brief attention was provided in all cases as a response.

Accept/Reject Signals

The basic principles of contingent interpretation and responsiveness are the cornerstones for building other communicative behaviors, including those signaling acceptance or rejection. These signals may be subtle; for example, an individual might not display behavior changes when he or she is content but might whimper slightly when distressed or uncomfortable. In other cases, a person might give more overt indicators such as limb movements, smiling, or crying. Initially, it is necessary for facilitators to respond to and comply with any communicative behaviors that can be socially and culturally tolerated in order to strengthen the behaviors over time and teach the power of communication. Occasionally, facilitators express concern about the implications of this strategy, worrying that people will become "spoiled" if they always "give them what they want." This need not be a concern if facilitators are attuned to the amount and level of responsiveness the individual needs so that they can decide when to begin to respond intermittently to these signals.

Relationship to Challenging Behavior

Some individuals may use unconventional gestural behaviors to signal acceptance or rejection. For example, self-stimulatory behaviors (e.g., spinning objects, gazing at a light) and aggressive behaviors (e.g., throwing tantrums, causing self-injury) both can be interpreted as rejection messages for many individuals (Siegel-Causey & Downing, 1987). Other people may flap their hands, squeal repetitively, or become aggressive when they are happy or excited, which are two clear occasions for sending acceptance messages. As is the case with inappropriate forms of attention getting, FCT can be used to teach alternatives to inappropriate acceptance and rejection signals. For example, Monica used to bang loudly on her wheelchair lap tray when she did not want to eat an offered food while she was being fed. Her mother began to watch to see whether Monica produced more subtle rejection cues before she started banging. She noticed that occasionally Monica would purse her lips and turn her head away first, so Monica's mother started to respond to this behavior whenever it occurred by removing the rejected food. At the same time, when Monica banged on the lap tray, her mother would prompt her to turn her head instead. Over a 2-month period, Monica's lip pursing behavior increased and she stopped banging on the tray almost completely because she now had another way to tell her mother "No, thanks!"

Researchers in Sweden and other Scandinavian countries use a two-pronged approach to assessment and intervention of beginning communicators. *Disability-related interventions* seek to reduce the impact of the disability by teaching new communication skills to beginning communicators. *Handicap-related interventions* focus on potential communication partners and physical environments in order to remediate opportunity barriers and enhance generalization of communication skills (Granlund, Björck-Åkesson, Brodin, & Olsson, 1995; Granlund, Terneby, & Olsson, 1992a, 1992b).

Parent Training Programs

AAC teams have developed several Interactive Model programs (Tannock & Girolametto, 1992) to train parents of young beginning communicators to facilitate their child's communication development using the principles reviewed in the previous sections. These programs include the Ecological Communication Organization Program (MacDonald, 1989; MacDonald & Carroll, 1992), the Transactional Intervention Program (Mahoney & Powell, 1986), and the Hanen Early Language Parent Program (Girolametto, 1988; Girolametto, Greenberg, & Manolson, 1986; Manolson, 1985; Manolson, Ward, & Dodington, 1995). Although almost no researchers have investigated the efficacy of these programs for young AAC users, we include them here because the principles on which they are based are prevalent in many agencies that support young beginning communicators.

Interactive Model programs share a number of intervention techniques, which can be summarized as follows:

- **Be child oriented:** Respond to the child's focus of attention, follow the child's lead, match the child's style and abilities, organize the environment to promote communication, and maintain face-to-face interaction with a positive affect.
- **Promote interaction:** Take one turn at a time, wait with anticipation, signal for turns, and decrease directiveness.
- **Model language:** Comment on the ongoing activity; use contingent labeling; use repetition and short, simple utterances; and expand or extend the child's turn (Tannock & Girolametto, 1992).

In the Interactive Model, the child is not expected to produce specific communication behaviors during interaction and is not explicitly prompted to do so (Tannock & Girolametto, 1992). Instead, facilitators train parents to facilitate and encourage their child to use his or her communication skills during natural routines and activities such as preparing food, making music, sharing books, playing games, and creating art together (e.g., Manolson et al., 1995). The principles of the Interactive Model have been incorporated into at least one program aimed at beginning communicators who use AAC techniques: Partners in Augmentative Communication Training (Culp & Carlisle, 1988). Such systematic training approaches can be quite successful in teaching facilitators to be aware of and responsive to children's efforts to communicate non-symbolically.

Scripted Routines

In addition to responding to spontaneous attention-getting, acceptance, and rejection signals, facilitators can provide structured opportunities for beginning communicators to practice these behaviors in the context of naturally occurring routines (e.g., Baumgart et al., 1990; Carlson, Hough, Lippert, & Young, 1988; Oregon Research Institute, 1989). Routines can be established informally or formally through the use of planned dialogues (Siegel-Causey & Guess, 1989) or scripted routines. Table 10.3 displays part of a scripted routine created for Adam, a young man with dual sensory impairments (i.e., deafness and blindness) and severe physical disabilities, to use while preparing for swimming. As can be seen from this example, scripted routines may consist of five elements, depending on the type of routine and the person's disability. These five elements—touch cue, verbal cue, pause, verbal feedback, and action—are described with reference to Table 10.3.

1. **Touch cue:** Touch cues are information provided in addition to spoken words and should be provided before each step in the routine. The touch cue for a step should be the same each time, and all facilitators should use the same cues. Touch cues are critical for individuals with one or more sensory impairments (e.g., vision, hearing, or both) and are often useful with other individuals as well. For example, in Step 2 of Table 10.3, the touch cue associated with putting on Adam's swimsuit is the suit brushing against his wrist.

2. **Verbal cue:** The verbal cue is a general description of what the facilitator should say while providing the touch cue. For example, while rubbing Adam's swimsuit against his wrist before putting it on, the facilitator might say, "It's time to put on your swimsuit" (Step 2, Table 10.3). Facilitators should not be rigid about the precise structure of verbal cues and should provide necessary information as naturally as possible. Facilitators should always use verbal cues, even with individuals who have hearing impairments because most of these individuals have at least some residual hearing.

3. **Pause:** After each touch cue and verbal cue pair, the facilitator should pause for 10–30 seconds and observe the person for a response. A response means any motor movement or vocalization that appears to be deliberate or can be interpreted as deliberate. If the person responds with a signal that can be interpreted as an acceptance signal after the pause, the facilitator should continue the routine. If the individual gives a rejection signal, the facilitator may stop the routine briefly and then try again, explore an alternative way of proceeding, or terminate the routine altogether. If neither type of signal is produced, the facilitator should repeat the paired touch and verbal cues and wait 10–30 seconds again for a signal. If the individual still gives no signal, the facilitator should continue the routine. The length of the pause depends largely on the individual's level of responsiveness and the extent of motor involvement. Individuals with severe disabilities require much longer pauses in order to have time to formulate and produce signals.

4. **Verbal feedback:** After the individual's acceptance signal, verbal feedback in the form of a comment about what the person did and what action the facilitator will do in response should be provided in conjunction with the appropriate action. For example, after pausing (Step 2, Table 10.3), Adam's facilitator might say, "Oh, you

Table 10.3. Example of a scripted routine

	Touch cue (how you give nonverbal information)	Verbal cue (what you say)	Pause (wait for at least 10 sec., and look for a response)	Verbal feedback (what you say while performing the action)	Action (what you do after the person accepts or the second pause is over)
1.	Rub seat belt under Adam's elbow. Release buckle so that a sound is made.	"Time to get ready for a swim."	Pause, observe	"Okay, I hear you *making a noise*; let's put on your swimsuit."	Continue to Step 2.
2.	Rub the waist band of swimsuit against his wrist.	"It's time to put on your swimsuit."	Pause, observe	"Oh, *you moved your foot*; okay, let's get undressed."	Continue to Step 3.
3.	Unzip coat/sweater.	"It's time to take off your coat/sweater."	Pause, observe	"I see *you moved your arm*; here, I'll help you take off your coat."	Continue to Step 4.
4.	Rub Adam's back.	"Let's lean forward now."	Pause, observe	"I hear *you make a noise*; good, you can lean forward now."	Lean him forward.
5.	Tug coat collar behind Adam's head and rub your hand on the back of his head.	"Going to pull this over your head now, Adam."	Pause, observe	"*You moved your head*, so I'll help you take off the sweater."	Pull up back of coat all the way and over Adam's head.
6.	Pat his first arm where the sleeve ends.	"Time to take off your sleeve."	Pause, observe	"I see you *trying to move your hand*; I'll help you get your hand out."	Remove hand from sleeve.
7.	Pat his second arm where the sleeve ends.	"Let's take off the other sleeve now."	Pause, observe	"Good for you, you're *trying to get the other hand out*. Let's take it out."	Remove hand from sleeve.
8.	Tap his first shoe, hard.	"Time to take off your shoes."	Pause, observe	"I hear *you making a noise* to tell me to take off your shoe."	Untie shoe, and remove.
9.	Tap second shoe, hard.	"Time to take off your other shoe."	Pause, observe	"*You moved this foot*, I guess you want the other shoe off."	Untie shoe, and remove.

moved your foot; okay, I'll unzip your coat first" or "I see you moved your arm; here, I'll help you take your coat off."

5. **Action:** For each step in the scripted routine, the facilitator performs an action at the same time as the verbal feedback. An action is the actual step in the routine that is identified through a task analysis. The facilitator may have to assist individuals who are unable to perform the action independently. The facilitator should adjust the amount of assistance provided to the individual's needs. It is important to remember that the point of a scripted routine is *not* to teach the person to perform the action; rather, it is to facilitate the development of communicative signaling within the context of a familiar activity.

To teach scripted routines for play to young children, the facilitator can utilize a simplified format similar to the one used for the dressing/undressing routine, but without the touch and verbal cues. For example, the facilitator can create an interactive routine for singing "Row, Row, Row Your Boat" by sitting on the floor facing the child while holding his or her hands. As the facilitator sings the song, he or she rocks to and fro in a boat-like motion with the child. Once the routine has been established and the child is seen to enjoy it, the facilitator pauses after every two lines in the song and watches for any indication that the child wants to continue the game. The facilitator can apply this basic format—action, pause, action—to other interactive games and songs as well. Individuals older than 5 years of age may swim, play video or pinball games, run relay races, go to dances, listen to music, or engage in a wide variety of other recreational activities. Table 10.4 illustrates how some of these activities can be adapted for scripted routines. (See McLean, McLean, Brady, & Etter, 1991, and Snyder-McLean, Solomonson, McLean, & Sack, 1984, for informative suggestions for making such adaptations.)

Over a 6-month period, Adam gradually began to participate in the dressing and undressing routine for swimming by moving his left arm or leg or by vocalizing during the pauses in the routine. At first, these movements occurred infrequently, but they gradually became more common as his support staff responded to them. Additional scripted routines were introduced during mealtimes, position changes, and bath time in the evening. Now, 5 years later, Adam has changed from a 27-year-old man who spent 99% of his day either sleeping or passively allowing people to care for him to a 32-year-old man who spends most of his day awake and actively involved in activities through gestures or by operating a large switch positioned by his head. He is developing clear signals for acceptance and rejection and appears to have preferences among support staff, activities, and musical selections. Adam is becoming a beginning communicator!

Movement-Based Approach

A more systematic method for facilitating the development of communicative signals and natural gestures is based on the work of Van Dijk (1966) and his colleagues at the Institute for the Deaf in Sint Michielsgestel, the Netherlands. They first described this approach for enhancing the social and communicative abilities of young children with

Table 10.4.   Examples of scripted routine segments for older individuals

Touch cue (how you give nonverbal information)	Verbal cue (what you say)	Pause (wait for at least 10 sec., and look for a response)	Action (what you do after the person accepts)
Swimming			
1. Move an inner tube up and down when the person is safely seated in it.	"Get ready to float. 1, 2, 3. . . . "	Pause, observe	Verbally acknowledge, and push the inner tube gently across to a partner, 2–3 feet. Repeat.
2. Float the person in a life jacket under the spray fountain in the middle of the pool. Let the water spray on his or her body.	"Getting wet, going under the water. . . . "	Pause, observe	Verbally acknowledge, and keep the person in the spray for 2–3 minutes. Repeat.
Video or pinball game			
1. Place hand on video joystick or pinball lever.	"Okay, it's time to fire/shoot. Here we go."	Pause, observe	Verbally acknowledge, and use hand-on-hand assistance to fire/shoot. Repeat.
Going to a school dance			
1. Wheel the person onto the dance floor and spin around once or twice.	"What great music for dancing!! Let's go for it!"	Pause, observe	Verbally acknowledge, and dance around with chair for 2–3 minutes. Repeat.
2. Go to the refreshment table and get some punch. Brush the cup along the person's lower lip.	"Here's some punch. I bet you're thirsty from all that dancing."	Pause, observe	Verbally acknowledge, and give a sip of punch. Repeat.
Relay race			
1. As each team member runs and the line moves forward, the person's team partner shakes the wheelchair slightly before moving up in line.	"Okay, here we go, we need to move closer to the front to take our turn."	Pause, observe	Verbally acknowledge, and move the chair forward. Repeat.
2. Before taking a turn in the race, place the baton in the person's hands.	"Ready, on your mark, get set. . . . "	Pause, observe	Push wheelchair, and run as required, then go to the back of the line when finished.

dual sensory impairments (i.e., deafness and blindness). The Van Dijk technique and its adaptations are based on the principle that "learning through doing" enables people to acquire concepts, form social relationships, and influence the environment as communicators. Thus, these approaches emphasize movement as a way for the individual to be actively involved in the ongoing activities of daily life.

It is perhaps not surprising that movement-based techniques were first developed for use with individuals who can neither see nor hear and for whom movement in its many forms, such as touch, motion, or object manipulation, represents the most viable way of learning about the environment. This approach has been successfully adapted and used since the 1960s with individuals with mental retardation requiring extensive to pervasive support, multiple disabilities, autism, and other disabilities in addition to sensory impairments (e.g., Rowland & Schweigert, 1989, 1990; Siegel-Causey & Guess, 1989; Sternberg, 1982; Stillman & Battle, 1984; Writer, 1987). The six levels of the approach described by Van Dijk are summarized in the sections that follow, with particular emphasis on adaptations described by Writer (1987).

Nurturance

The aim of nurturance is to develop a warm, positive relationship between the individual with disabilities and the facilitator. Siegel-Causey and Guess described this as a relationship "that promotes interest in communicative interactions and enhances a willingness to participate in social exchanges" (1989, p. 23). According to Writer (1987), Van Dijk's suggestions for establishing this social bond include 1) limiting the number of people working with the individual so the facilitator and the person can get to know each other through continual contact, 2) building a routine of daily activities for the individual, and 3) distributing external stimuli to avoid over- or understimulation. Siegel-Causey and Guess (1989) suggested that nurturance is provided when the facilitator gives support, comfort, and affection; creates a positive setting for interaction; expands on behaviors initiated by the individual; and focuses on the individual's interests. They offered the following example:

> When it is time to go out to recess, the paraprofessionals need to make sure everyone is dressed properly in coats, gloves, and hats. Sarah, one paraprofessional, using an affectionate tone of voice, directs Ken, a student, toward the coat rack. She holds his hand and as they walk, they swing their arms back and forth slightly. While smiling at Ken, Sarah's voice is warm as she says to him, "It's almost time for recess now, what do you need to do?" Ken returns the smile and looks delighted as he reaches for his coat. He obviously enjoys the attention Sarah pays him and uses his nonsymbolic behaviors (e.g., reaching, smiling) to communicate with her. (Siegel-Causey & Guess, 1989, p. 28)

Resonance

Activities related to resonance are designed to shift the individual's attention from him- or herself to the external world of people and objects. Similar to scripted routines, resonance activities consist of rhythmic movements that the individual and the facilitator perform while in direct physical contact. For example, the facilitator might use a full hand-on-hand prompt to assist the individual to wipe a tabletop with a sponge. After several back-and-forth wiping movements, the facilitator pauses and waits for a signal that the movement should start again. Or, the facilitator may sit on the floor with a young child on his or her lap and rock back and forth to music, pausing regularly to provide opportunities for the child to signal a desire to continue. The facilitator may also use tactile and object cues associated with specific activities, people, or items to communicate with the individual (Oregon Research Institute, 1989).

Coactive Movement

Coactive movement is an extension of resonance with the basic difference being the amount of physical distance between the facilitator and the individual with disabilities (Siegel-Causey & Guess, 1988). The goal of coactive movement is to develop sequence and anticipation by gradually building activities that the individual and the facilitator do together (Sternberg, 1982). The establishment of such predictable sequences facilitates communicative development by allowing the individual to anticipate and become actively involved in daily routines.

Coactive movements are executed when the individual is parallel to or next to a peer or adult model (Writer, 1987). The facilitator may use full-body movements, limb or hand gestures (e.g., kicking a ball, waving good-bye, making the manual sign for *eat*), and tactile cues to help the individual initiate the coactive movement, with the goal of fading these cues. Coactive movement activities, like resonance activities, follow a "start-stop" format, in which the facilitator is sensitive and responsive to signals from the individual.

Nonrepresentational Reference

Nonrepresentational reference involves teaching the individual to identify body parts on models that are initially three-dimensional (e.g., a doll, another person) and later, two-dimensional (e.g., a stick figure, a line drawing) (Writer, 1987). These activities develop body image, teach pointing, and encourage the individual to be somewhat independent of the facilitator (Sternberg, 1982). The facilitator should conduct these activities as much as possible during routine activities (e.g., during a dressing routine at home, during make-believe time in a preschool classroom).

Deferred Imitation

Deferred imitation teaches the individual to imitate movements after the facilitator has completed them, starting with full-body movements (e.g., standing up, sitting down) and eventually proceeding to functional limb and hand movements (e.g., putting on a hat, kicking a ball). Van Dijk (1966) recommended that such imitative movements be taught with familiar objects and through natural daily routines, using the types of cues described in the section on coactive movement. In fact, deferred imitation is the direct result of further fading of the cues used during coactive movement.

Natural Gestures

The final component of the movement-based approach involves encouraging the individual to produce communicative gestures that are "self-developed" (Sternberg, 1982, p. 214) and that motorically represent how the target individual typically uses an object or participates in an event. Writer (1987) noted that many manual signs that are highly iconic—for example, a sign for *car* that involves the motion of holding and moving an invisible steering wheel—represent how an adult facilitator typically experiences objects or activities. Thus, according to the principles set forth by Van Dijk, it would not be appropriate to introduce this particular gesture as a sign for car because a child typically experiences a car as a passenger. Other iconic gestures or manual signs typical of the individual may be encouraged during this stage, such as waving good-bye, patting the mouth to ask for food or drink, or pointing at a desired item to request it.

Gesture Dictionaries

By the time facilitators have instituted interventions successfully to teach signals for attention, acceptance, and rejection, the individual has probably developed a fairly large repertoire of vocalizations and gestures for communication. Many of these signals may be idiosyncratic, so that a few close facilitators (e.g., parents, support workers) are able to understand and respond to them consistently, whereas people less familiar with the person may have difficulty understanding and interpreting the messages. This may result in unnecessary, problematic communication breakdowns. For example, the babysitter may not know that the child's way of asking someone to change the channel on the television is to walk over to the television and bang on it repeatedly with moderate force. If the sitter tries to dissuade the child from engaging in this seemingly destructive act, the child's efforts will intensify until both individuals are frustrated and dissatisfied! Such communication breakdowns may be avoided by using a "gesture dictionary" in which descriptions of the person's gestures, along with their meanings and suggestions for appropriate responses, are compiled. The dictionary may take the form of a wall poster in the classroom or home or may be an alphabetized notebook with cross-referenced entries. For example, in the previous situation, the babysitter might look in the child's gesture dictionary under *B* for banging or *T* for television. Under either (or both), he or she might find a description of the behavior, its meaning, and how to respond (e.g., "Banging means he wants you to change the channel on the television. Get him to try to say 'Help me,' and then change the channel for him"). Table 10.5 displays a portion of a gesture dictionary created for Shawn, an adolescent with visual and cognitive impairments. The gesture dictionary can also be used for individuals well beyond preschool age. In fact, this technique has been used effectively as a method of orienting new staff to the communication patterns of residents with severe disabilities in group homes and other adult residential environments that have a high staff turnover.

A variety of strategies are available to build communication opportunities and to establish a nonsymbolic communication foundation. In Chapter 11, we continue this discussion and introduce additional strategies to teach the use of symbols in functional contexts.

Table 10.5. Example of a gesture dictionary

What Shawn does	What it means	What you should do
Manual sign for *T* to chin	Wants to go to the bathroom	Give him permission, and help him to door.
"Sshh" sound	"Yes"	Respond according to situation.
Shakes head back and forth	"No"	Respond according to situation.
Reaches out his hand to other person	"I want to shake your hand." (Greeting)	Shake his hand.
Clapping other's hand when offered	"I'm feeling sociable/affectionate."	Respond according to situation.
Puts both arms around his stomach	Wants a hug	Encourage him to shake your hand by prompting, or give him a hug, if appropriate.
Hands crossed at chest and tapping both shoulders		
Pulls your hand to bring you close to him		
Tapping his opposite shoulder with one hand		
Hand flat across mouth	Wants food	If mealtime or near mealtime, help him to table or ask him to wait a few minutes.
Hand sideways to mouth	Wants a drink	If between meals, provide small amount of milk or bland food (ulcer).
Hand to mouth with grinding teeth	"I'm *really* hungry!"	
Jumping up and down	In a good mood	Respond in kind.
	Needs to go to the bathroom	Give permission, and take to the door.

Kevin is a 3-year-old boy with autism who attends a preschool for young children both with and without disabilities. At the beginning of the school year, he was extremely withdrawn and antisocial. His teachers and family worked very hard to implement the principles of a movement-based approach to intervention. They paid attention to when he seemed receptive to having people near him and engaged in parallel play during those times, talking their way through each activity. If Kevin showed interest, they included him in the activity by showing him materials and offering to help him use them. Gradually, as their relationships with him developed, he began to allow them to use hand-over-hand instruction (resonance activities) to help him with self-care skills such as putting on his coat and with play skills such as assembling simple puzzles. As Kevin learned the skills for these activities, his teachers began to fade the prompts (coactive movement) and encourage him to do more on his own. At the same time, they began to work on imitation skills in both structured and natural contexts and came up with scripted routines to encourage the development of socially appropriate natural gestures for acceptance and rejection. By the end of the year, Kevin had developed a large repertoire of nonsymbolic behaviors for communication, which were documented in a portable gesture dictionary that could be used both at home and at school.

11

AAC Strategies for Beginning Communicators

Symbolic Approaches to Communication

In Chapter 10, we introduce strategies for establishing communication opportunities and encouraging the development of nonsymbolic communication. The strategies in that chapter are meant to include the individual in communicative interactions and build a foundation for symbolic communication. In this chapter, we describe some of the most common techniques for teaching functional communication skills using symbols. We begin by discussing some of the issues for consideration when choosing aided and unaided symbols and then describe a range of instructional approaches that have been reported in the augmentative and alternative communication (AAC) literature.

INTRODUCING SYMBOLIC COMMUNICATION

A number of strategies for communication participation are particularly applicable to individuals who have developed the basic skills of attention getting, accepting, and rejecting and are being introduced to symbolic communication. It is important to expand the repertoires of these individuals to include basic skills such as following a symbol schedule and engaging in simple social routines. We summarize briefly a few of the most prevalent or innovative introductory symbol techniques.

Calendar/Schedule Systems

A calendar or schedule system represents each activity in the person's day with symbols and may serve several purposes: 1) to introduce the individual to the concept of symbolization, which is the idea that one thing can stand for another; 2) to provide an overview of the sequence of activities; 3) to provide specific information about what will happen next; 4) to ease transitions from one activity to the next; and 5) to serve as one component of a behavioral support plan for individuals who have a high need for predictability (Flannery & Horner, 1994). This schedule strategy came from the work of

Stillman and Battle (1984) and other practitioners who helped individuals with dual sensory impairments. It has also been described for use with people who have visual, cognitive, or multiple disabilities (e.g., Hodgdon, 1996; Rowland & Schweigert, 1989, 1990, 1996; Vicker, 1996). Schedule systems can be effective in home, school, and community settings for beginning communicators across the range of age and ability. Table 11.1 outlines how to create and use a schedule system.

Table 11.1.   Creating/using a calendar/schedule system

Organizing the Calendar/Schedule System

The *first step* in putting together a schedule system is to identify the individual's daily schedule across relevant home, school, and community environments. This schedule should include all of the activities he or she does every day or during a relevant portion of the day. Make a list of the activities in order as they occur.

Second, symbols that can be used to represent each of these activities should be identified. For most beginning communicators, these symbols will probably be real object or partial object symbols, although they may be photographs, line drawings, or any other type of symbol the individual can recognize. Once you have identified the appropriate types of symbols, you should gather symbols representing each of the activities in the schedule. For example, if you use real objects, a brush might represent morning grooming activities, a milk container might represent eating breakfast, and socks might represent getting dressed. Collect the symbols in one place (such as a cardboard box) so that they are readily available. The same objects should represent the activities every time.

Third, a container for the schedule system should be constructed. You can place real objects in a series of shallow containers arranged in a left-to-right order. These can be a series of empty shoe boxes or cardboard magazine holders taped together, a series of transparent plastic bags hung on cup hooks, or maybe just a long cardboard box with cardboard dividers taped into it at intervals. If you chose photographs or other graphic symbols, you can place them in the slots of a slide projector page, on the pages of a photo album, or in some other portable carrier. Figure 11.1 depicts a schedule box system with real objects laid out in order to represent the first six activities of the day.

Fourth, you should devise a system for identifying finished activities. If you use real objects, this system can be a "discard box" into which the individual can deposit each object after finishing the activity. If you selected photographs or other graphic symbols, the individual can simply turn them over at the end of each activity.

Using the Calendar/Schedule System

Before each activity, you should prompt the individual to go to the schedule box or to open the schedule book. The symbol for the first activity should be selected or identified. If real objects are used, the object should be taken to the related activity and used during the activity. For example, the symbol for BREAKFAST (a milk container) might have been selected because the first thing that happens at breakfast is that someone pours the milk. Perhaps the individual could be assigned this task as his or her way of participating in breakfast preparation. This will help him or her make the connection between the symbol and the activity.

When the activity is completed, the person should discard the symbol in the manner determined. The discarded symbols should be readily accessible to the individual at all times. He or she thus has the option of going to the box and taking out a symbol of an activity that has been completed if he or she wants to ask to do that activity again. If this ever happens, facilitators should make *every attempt* to respond to the request—let the individual do the activity the symbol represents, if at all possible!

Positive signs that might indicate that the person is making the connection between a symbol and the activity it represents include 1) taking a symbol and then wheeling or walking to the room or area where the activity typically occurs (e.g., to the bathroom for grooming, to the table for eating) and 2) smiling or laughing when the individual picks up a symbol for something he or she likes to do.

Schedules can incorporate real objects or tangible symbols as well as photographs or line-drawing symbols in age-appropriate daily appointment books, wall displays, or other formats (see Glennen & DeCoste, 1997; Hodgdon, 1996; and Johnson et al., 1996, for examples). Instruction in the use of a schedule system is generally conducted in loosely structured naturalistic formats, with a hierarchy of prompts that are gradually faded. Figure 11.1 provides an example of a schedule used at home and in the community by a man with autism.

Talking Switch Techniques

Burkhart (1993) referred to a number of talking switch devices with which facilitators can introduce symbolic communication and provide limited context communication using voice output. One device is the BIGmack, a small, single-message, battery-powered communication aid that has 20 seconds of memory. The BIGmack has a built-in microswitch that, when activated, plays a recorded message. A more cumbersome alternative involves multiple, single-message cassette tapes and a tape recorder operated with a microswitch (Fried-Oken, Howard, & Prillwitz, 1988). In either case, the facilitator can record human voice messages, music, or other sounds (e.g., a dog barking), and the AAC user can play the recording with a simple switch activation. Ideally, the person who records the message should be the same age and gender as the AAC user. Activation may be direct (i.e., the individual with sufficient fine motor skills activates the BIGmack or turns on the tape recorder) or remote. In the latter case, some type of switch (e.g., one that is operated by the head) is connected to the device in some way (e.g., through a latch timer or other adapter). Such simple voice-output techniques

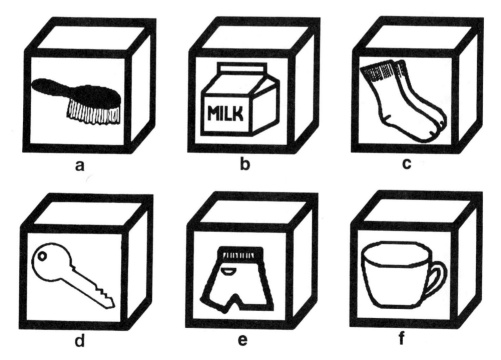

Figure 11.1.   A calendar/schedule system using real object symbols for six activities. a) Morning grooming activities, b) eating breakfast, c) getting dressed, d) going in the van, e) swimming, f) stopping for a snack.

might be particularly appropriate for beginning communicators who use wheelchairs and who are learning to employ microswitches to participate in communication (see Rowland & Schweigert, 1991). Because the BIGmack is lightweight and transported easily (a carrying strap is available from the manufacturer), it can also be used by ambulatory individuals in a variety of settings.

The BIGmack and other technologies for communication participation are available through AbleNet, Inc.

The most obvious context for using a talking switch technique is one in which the individual can participate in a preferred activity. In this case, a single symbol representing the message should be fastened with Velcro to the switch prior to use. The type of symbol (e.g., real object, tangible symbol) can vary, depending on the needs and abilities of the individual (see Chapter 7 for assessment information). For example, a talking switch technique might be used in a preschool or elementary school classroom

- During opening "circle time" (e.g., the child activates a message to sing his or her part in the greeting song)
- At transition times (e.g., the child activates a recording of someone singing the cleanup song or of a voice saying "Time to clean up!")
- Whenever a request for continuation or turn taking is appropriate (e.g., the child plays a recording that says "More, please" or "My turn")
- Any time the schedule dictates that a specific activity take place (e.g., in the morning the child plays a recording that says "Take my coat off, please")
- During any activity that requires a leader to announce movements to be performed by the other children (e.g., "Put your right foot in, put your right foot out," "Simon says clap your hands")
- Any time an interjection during an activity is appropriate (e.g., "Wowee!" "Cool!")

Older AAC users can employ talking switch techniques for similar purposes in age-appropriate contexts, during activities such as the following:

- Participating in specific events that require contextual messages (e.g., singing "For He's a Jolly Good Fellow" to a co-worker, singing "Happy Birthday" at a party)
- Cheering (or booing) a favorite sports team on television or in person
- Conversing on the telephone by activating a single message—a nice way for beginning communicators to keep in touch with friends and relatives
- Greeting (e.g., "Hi, how are you today?") or saying farewell (e.g., "Good-bye," "Good to see you," "Let's get together soon")
- Making single requests in predictable situations (e.g., "I'd like a cheeseburger and small fries, please")
- Initiating conversations or introducing topics (e.g., "So, how was your weekend?")
- Making introductions (e.g., "Hi, my name is George; what's yours?")

In some cases, beginning communicators might be able to understand all of the words in such messages, although in other cases, they may participate beyond their level of receptive language understanding. For example, Jeremiah is a young man with multiple disabilities who communicates primarily with facial expressions and body language. When he uses a talking switch technique to say the blessing before dinner with his family, he does not understand all of the words, nor does he recognize the *pray* symbol on his switch. Jeremiah, however, smiles broadly when it is time for him to hit his switch and lead this ritual and appears to enjoy participating in it. As he leads his family in the blessing, he also learns about basic concepts such as cause and effect (hit the switch and your whole family talks!) and using symbols to participate in a meaningful communication context. The application of talking switch techniques by individuals like Jeremiah is limited only by the budget available for equipment and by the facilitator's imagination.

Some devices that accommodate one or more switches for single or multiple messages include the AlphaTalker (Prentke Romich Co.), Parrot and Macaw with an interface box (Zygo Industries, Inc.), SpeakEasy (AbleNet), Switchmate (Tash International, Inc.), VoicePal (AdapTech), Talk Back (Crestwood), and Lynx (Adamlab). Readers may also refer to Burkhart (1993) for information about using switches for computers with speech synthesizers.

TEACHING BASIC CHOICE MAKING AND REQUESTING

Do you remember our discussion about teaching people to accept and reject in Chapter 10? Those actions relate directly to choice making. The development of nonsymbolic behaviors to signal acceptance and rejection shows an implicit awareness of *preference.* Preference is evident when an individual indicates acceptance and rejection after he or she is offered options *one at a time.* For example, when Maxwell's mom tries to help him put on his red shirt, he squirms around and begins to whine. When she gets the message and offers his Power Rangers shirt, he smiles and cooperates with dressing.

In the above example, Maxwell showed that he preferred the Power Rangers shirt and could communicate his preference with gestures. The development of preferences and a way to communicate them through nonsymbolic means is a necessary first step to choice making. *Choice making* occurs when an individual indicates his or her preference from *two or more options,* either spontaneously or when someone else offers them. People who don't have preferences find it difficult to make choices—think of the last time you went shopping and couldn't find anything you really liked! You might have bought something anyway, but it was more difficult to make the choice because nothing really caught your eye! The same thing applies to people who are learning to make choices, at least in the beginning of instruction—if they don't have preferences, they will find it hard to make choices. In particular, this applies to older individuals who have spent years in institutional settings in which they were provided with few opportunities to express their preferences or make choices. As these individuals begin to move into communities, they may need to be exposed to many, many new activities, environments, foods, drinks, and people before they begin to develop preferences and communicate them through "accept" and "reject" behaviors. (See Chapter 10 for a discussion of AAC strategies related to this concern.) Once they have developed such preferences, they can learn to make choices among them.

There are several different types of choice-making and requesting actions, which differ in terms of whether they are initiated by the facilitator (elicited) or by the AAC user (self-initiated) and whether they incorporate generic or explicit communication forms. It is not clear from research exactly how these skills are ordered in terms of ease of acquisition (Reichle et al., 1991). Thus, the order in which we present them here is derived from our clinical experience, not research. In any case, there is probably some degree of variability across beginning communicators who are learning these skills.

The first skill on the continuum, an elicited or "offered" choice, is initiated by a facilitator rather than by the AAC user and involves a restricted array of items from which the AAC user can choose. For example, Jordan's teacher offers him a red crayon and a blue crayon (or symbols thereof) and asks which one he wants for drawing. The second skill adds a step to offered choices by requiring the AAC user to initiate the interaction through a generic request such as "want" or "please." The facilitator then offers a restricted array of items from which the user can choose. For example, Jordan now approaches his teacher with a WANT symbol, and in response she offers him the red and the blue crayon (or corresponding symbols) and asks which one he wants. The only difference between the first two skills on the continuum is the person who initiates the offered choice. Finally, the third choice-making option requires the AAC user to both initiate the request and discriminate among symbols to make a choice, as occurs when Jordan spontaneously scans his array of crayon color symbols, chooses the picture of the red crayon, and hands the picture to his teacher.

Again, we base this continuum on clinical experience rather than empirical data, and it should not be applied in a rigid fashion. We do know, however, from research that many beginning communicators have significant problems learning to engage in spontaneous communication (Carter, Hotchkis, & Cassar, 1996; Halle, 1987). Thus, we usually begin choice-making interventions by teaching offered choices that a facilitator initiates because this seems to be the easiest of all the choice-making skills for many beginning communicators to learn.

Teaching Offered Choice Making

The following sections examine some of the major issues involved in teaching offered choice making.

Choice-Making Opportunities

People who are learning to make offered choices need frequent, meaningful opportunities to control their environments in this way. Thus, the AAC team's first step in teaching choices is to identify when, where, and by whom choices can be offered to an individual throughout the day. Some occasions for choice making are obvious: deciding which food to eat or drink, which music to listen to, which television shows to watch, and which clothes to wear. Other instances may be less obvious, such as choosing whom to sit next to (or avoid!) during an activity, how to complete an activity, and the order in which to complete a multicomponent task (e.g., a personal care routine in the morning). Still other choice-making opportunities depend on the extent to which the individual is included in school and community life. These instances include, for example, choices about what brand of beer to order in the pub, which team to cheer for, which store to shop in, whom to call on the telephone, or whom to invite to a slumber party. Without exception, the number of choices available in the course of a day directly reflects the quality and quantity of integrated opportunities in an individual's life. Sigafoos and his colleagues, who successfully developed strategies to increase choice-making opportunities in both classroom and group home settings, demonstrated this in a series of Australian studies (Sigafoos, Kerr, Roberts, & Couzens, 1994; Sigafoos, Roberts, Couzens, & Kerr, 1993; Sigafoos, Roberts, Kerr, Couzens, & Baglioni, 1994). Thus, facilitators should focus initial choice-making interventions toward expanding opportunities rather than toward new and more sophisticated ways to teach AAC users the essential skills.

Choice-Making Items or Symbols

During choice-making interventions for individuals who are just learning the concept of "choice," facilitators should employ real, meaningful items (e.g., drinks, foods, toys) rather than symbols of those items. For example, a facilitator might offer a girl or woman who is learning to make choices both a toothbrush and a washcloth and ask, "What should we do first?" during a personal care routine. The facilitator could then help her to use whichever object she chooses. There is no correct or incorrect answer during such early choice-making interactions because the person is learning that "what you point to/reach for/look at, you get." Even this basic concept may be quite novel for many individuals, especially those who have lived in segregated or institutional settings, because they have not been provided with opportunities to make choices in the past. Facilitators may need to offer such individuals simple, motivating choices many times each day before they begin to understand what choice making is all about.

People who can make choices using real items can begin to learn the use of symbols for offered choice making. As with all AAC interventions, those that pertain to choice making should incorporate symbols with which the individual is likely to have the most success. This may require the facilitator to provide real object symbols (e.g., an empty cola can to represent *soda* or *pop*) or tangible symbols for people with vision impairments. Or, the facilitator may furnish more abstract aided symbols such as color photographs, commercially available line drawings, or written words, depending on the person's symbol abilities. Individuals who use manual signs as their primary symbol system may find it easier to learn about initial choice making with aided symbols because they can offer and manipulate these symbols more easily. Some evidence also indicates that augmented choice making—that is, choice making using aided symbols—can result in greater accuracy for individuals who can speak but have difficulty with behavioral regulation (Vaughn & Horner, 1995). (See Chapter 7 for a discussion of symbol assessment strategies related to this issue.) When in doubt, it is probably better for facilitators to err on the side of caution by selecting a more concrete rather than a more abstract type of symbol during the introductory stages of teaching symbol use for choice making.

Choice-Making Formats

Facilitators must offer motivating choices in natural contexts, and they must present them in a manner that the individual understands. Making the choices simple enough so that the person can choose successfully requires the facilitator to carefully consider the individual's symbolic, yes/no, and receptive object labeling abilities because many choice-making formats typically used in natural settings require one or more of these skills. Table 11.2 displays clinically derived formats that facilitators can use to offer

Table 11.2.   Two-item offered choice-making formats in approximate order of difficulty (Levels 1–3)

Level	Strategy	Examples
Level 1 Simple active/ passive choice system with two options	Person gets choice A when passive (i.e., for doing nothing) and choice B when active (i.e., for doing something) (Wacker, Wiggins, Fowler, & Berg, 1988).	Monika is at home, watching TV (choice A). A caregiver enters the room and says "Do you want to go for a walk?" and holds up Monika's coat (choice B). She must do something active to choose the walk: for example, point at the coat, reach for it, put it on, stand up, or vocalize. If she wants to watch TV, she can be passive and do nothing. Monika vocalizes and reaches for the coat, so they go for a walk.
Level 2 Two-item active choices using real objects or object symbols in natural contexts	Show two objects or symbols, label the choices, and say "What do you want?" Look for an indicator (e.g., eye gaze, reaching) that one is preferred over the other, and comply.	Harold is in the store buying clothes with his support worker. The worker says, "You can buy a red shirt (holds it up) or a blue shirt (holds it up). Which one do you like?" Harold looks at the red shirt and smiles.
Does not require either yes/no or object labeling concepts	Show one object or symbol and ask "Do you want the _____," show second item as well, and finish, " . . . or the _____?" Provide the item indicated (Baumgart, Johnson, & Helmstetter, 1990).	Sam's dad is helping him with self-care activities in the morning. These consist of toothbrushing, hair combing, and face washing. Dad holds up a toothbrush and says "Should we brush your teeth first . . . "; then he holds up the comb as well and finishes, ". . . or comb your hair?" Sam looks at the toothbrush and Dad complies. After this activity is done, Dad repeats the routine with the washcloth and the comb.
Level 3 Two-item choices using real objects or object symbols in natural contexts; requires yes/no concept but not object labeling	Show one option and ask "Do you want the _____?" Pause and look for an accept response; comply if given. If the person gives a reject or no response, hold up a second option and ask "Do you want the _____?" Continue until the person accepts an option (Musselwhite, 1986b).	Franklin is swimming with his friend Alec. Alec points to an inner tube, asks "Do you want to swim in the tube?" and pauses. Franklin does not respond, so Alec points to a rubber raft, asks, "How about the raft?" and pauses again. Franklin grins and reaches for the raft. At a fast-food restaurant, Susan shows Minae an empty french fry container and an empty apple pie container and says, "You can have french fries or apple pie today." She then holds out *only* the french fry container and asks "Do you want french fries?" Minae extends her arms, an indicator of acceptance, so Susan complies.

choice-making opportunities, arranged from simple to complex. People should offer choices to the AAC user in the format that most closely corresponds to his or her abilities. Facilitators can teach the skills needed for more sophisticated levels concurrently.

Choice-Making Arrays

In addition to choosing the choice-making format, the facilitator must select the choices that will be available in the array. When doing so, the facilitator has several options: He or she 1) may select two preferred options (Writer, 1987), 2) may opt for one preferred and one nonpreferred option (Burkhart, 1988), or 3) may use one preferred option and a "blank" or "distractor" option for teaching initial choice making (Reichle et al., 1991; Rowland & Schweigert, 1990, 1996). (Note that a fourth option promoted by some in the past, which involves using one preferred and one aversive item, does not appear in our list of acceptable strategies.) No empirical data guide decisions in this area, and reasonable arguments can be made in support of each option. Our preference, particularly when teaching individuals to choose between two real items, is to start out with two preferred options (i.e., items known to be acceptable to the individual) because this is the most natural choice format (see also Rowland & Schweigert, 1991). If there are indications that the person is having difficulty making choices—for example, if he or she frequently chooses an option and then rejects it or if he or she always chooses the item on one side of the array—one of the other array formats might help to clarify the task. Other strategies to consider for individuals who seem to find initial choice making difficult include spacing options closer together or farther apart, aligning them vertically rather than horizontally, and holding them out of reach from individuals who are impulsive (Burkhart, 1988).

Size of Array

Size of array refers to how many options are available at one time. Usually, initial choice arrays utilize two options, progressing gradually to three, four, and so forth as the individual learns to scan and select from more options. Large choice arrays for individuals with physical impairments may require aids such as an eye-gaze board, scanning device, or other system for displaying the options so that they are motorically accessible.

Instructional Techniques

As is the case for choice arrays, AAC specialists have a variety of opinions about how to best teach choice making once symbols are introduced. One approach is to offer choices using appropriate symbols and then provide the item selected as feedback (e.g., Locke & Mirenda, 1988; Sigafoos & Dempsey, 1992; Sigafoos, Laurie, & Pennell, 1995). With this approach, the facilitator evaluates whether the choice is "correct" or "incorrect" in light of the person's behavior once he or she receives the selected item. If the individual takes the item, uses it appropriately, and appears to enjoy it, the facilitator can assume that the choice was "correct" for that individual at that time and in that place. Conversely, if the person rejects the item selected, refuses to use it appropriately, or expresses distress when it is offered (e.g., crying, screaming), the facilitator can assume that the choice was "incorrect" for that occasion. Facilitators can utilize this feedback approach with any of the array options presented previously, as the approach is based on the notion that people learn to make "correct" choices by experiencing both the pleasant and the unpleasant consequences of their actions. How many of us, for example, have bought a shirt or a pair of shoes that we disliked after a single wearing or, even worse, have experienced the pain of making a relationship choice that later proved to be problematic? This "natural consequences" approach to choice making relies on the tendency of people to gradually learn to make more and more accurate choices if facilitators provide them with adequate exposure and practice.

A second common approach to teaching choice making with symbols employs a basic procedure for assessing and teaching symbol comprehension (Rowland & Schweigert, 1996). First, the facilitator offers the person a choice of two preferred items. After the person chooses an item, the facilitator offers two corresponding symbols. A "correct" response occurs if the person selects the symbol that represents the chosen item, whereas an "incorrect" response occurs if the person selects the opposite symbol. In the latter case, the facilitator may provide a second trial with an appropriate type of prompt to elicit a correct response.

Alternatively, facilitators may implement the reverse of this symbol assessment and teaching procedure. In this case, the person first selects the symbol, and the facilitator then provides him or her with an array of items. If the person selects the item corresponding to the chosen symbol, he or she has offered a situationally correct response (Frost & Bondy, 1994; Stephenson & Linfoot, 1995). Ultimately, of course, the person should always receive the chosen item once he or she selects the correct symbol. Both versions of this procedure are designed to provide the person with more specific feedback related to the symbol–referent connection than the "naturalistic" approach provides. Both versions of the procedure also assess the individual's comprehension of the symbol in a meaningful context.

A third approach to teaching choice making is to use a distractor symbol along with one for a preferred item (Reichle et al., 1991). Physical or gestural prompts are provided within an errorless learning paradigm to teach the person to select the symbol for the preferred item, which is then provided. In errorless learning, facilitators provide the prompt *before* the individual has a chance to make a "mistake," and this process thus ensures a correct response. The facilitator fades prompts as quickly as possible and then consequates any incorrect responses (i.e., choices of the distractor symbol) accordingly (i.e., the person receives nothing when this is selected). Over time, the facilitator introduces the symbol for a second, less preferred item instead of the distractor.

As of 1998, there are no empirically validated guidelines regarding the selection of one instructional approach over another, either in general or for individual AAC users. Thus, facilitators can only employ whichever approach seems to "best fit" the person involved and switch to another approach if this is not fruitful over time. Regardless of the instructional technique selected to teach offered choices, it will always be critical for the facilitator to provide natural consequences following a selection.

Natural Consequences

As stated previously, beginning communicators need to experience natural consequences in order to learn, even if this means that sometimes they do not get what they want because they were not paying sufficient attention or failed to weigh the options adequately. A common mistake that facilitators make is to offer the individual two options and then to provide corrective input if the individual selects the option that the facilitator presumes or knows to be less preferred. The following scene in a kitchen illustrates this mistake (T = Tom, N = Nancy):

T: Do you want milk [shows empty milk carton] or juice [shows juice container]?
N: [looks at and points to milk]
T: [suspects that Nancy doesn't really want milk]: Do you want *milk*?
N: [looks at and points to juice]
T: Yes, okay, you want the juice.

Providing corrective feedback in this way almost certainly ensures that problems will occur later in instruction. Nancy will learn that it is not necessary to pay attention or think about her response because Tom will always "make it better" in the end. Instead, it would be preferable for Tom to let the natural consequence of a bad choice occur and then offer an opportunity for Nancy to try again, as illustrated in the following scene in a fast-food restaurant (T = Tom, N = Nancy):

[Nancy has just chosen a hamburger. Tom suspects that Nancy really wants french fries.]

T: [gives Nancy the hamburger that she selected]

N: [pushes the hamburger away and begins to whine, cry, and scream]

T: Oh, you don't want the hamburger? Okay, we'll try again in a minute. [removes the hamburger, pauses at least 30–60 seconds, and presents a new opportunity to choose between the hamburger and the french fries]

Facilitators commonly make another feedback error when they check an individual's response for correctness by providing a second or even a third opportunity to make the same choice. The following scene in a video arcade illustrates this kind of mistake (M = Martin, Z = Zach):

M: Do you want to play Pac-Man [points] or Space Invaders [points]?

Z: [gestures toward Pac-Man]

M: Okay, let's try it again. Do you want to play Space Invaders [points] or Pac-Man [points]?

Z: [assumes he must have misunderstood the first time and gestures toward Space Invaders]

M: You need to start paying attention. Do you want to play Pac-Man [points] or Space Invaders [points]?

Z: [does not respond because there seems to be no way to win this game!]

The "massed trial" approach to choice making shown in this example is inappropriate and almost certainly will confuse the individual because the consequence of the choice is unclear. Instead, a natural consequence should follow *each* choice-making opportunity so that the individual can gradually learn the effects of his or her actions.

Age Appropriateness

Options available in choice-making instruction for beginning communicators should be appropriate for people of the same age who do not have disabilities. With sufficient exposure and encouragement from friends and others, most adolescents and adults with disabilities will acquire sensitivity to age-appropriate cultural norms. Unfortunately, many of these individuals may have had limited exposure to age-appropriate experiences, and when presented with such unfamiliar options, they may express no interest or may continue to choose options that are age inappropriate. This presents communication facilitators with a dilemma: Do we offer *age-inappropriate* options when teaching choice making because these are more motivating for the individual, or do we offer only *age-appropriate* options, although the person shows little interest in them?

The principle of *today and tomorrow* discussed in Chapter 8 offers a solution to this dilemma. According to this principle, decisions for today should meet the user's immediate communication needs and match his or her current capabilities and constraints identified during assessment. Decisions for tomorrow should be based on projections of future opportunities, needs, constraints, and capabilities as a result of instruction. In terms of the choice-making dilemma, the principle of today and tomorrow suggests that for today, choice-making options presented should be those that are valued by the individual, regardless of their age appropriateness. Nevertheless, the principle also *demands* that the facilitator take concurrent steps to expose the individual to a variety of age-appropriate options so that the facilitator can incorporate them into the individual's choice-making repertoire for tomorrow. Although the today decision may be necessary to provide motivation, it is certainly not an acceptable long-term solution.

Alternative Access

Individuals with severe motor impairments may have difficulty making choices or engaging in other basic communicative interactions because they are unable to point to, reach for, or otherwise indicate a choice. Of course, many of these individuals can use eye gazing as a motor access technique, and AAC teams can adapt any of the aforementioned techniques for teaching offered choice making in this response modality. In addition, many dedicated communication devices allow multiple-switch input and can be used to make offered choices (Burkhart, 1993). Alternatively, individuals can use two or more cassette tapes, each in a separate tape recorder with its own switch, to make multiple choices. In either case, facilitators should label each switch with a symbol representing the associated choice with appropriate object, tactile, or pictorial symbols. For example, a support worker offers Sophie a choice of two activities after dinner: listening to taped music or making popcorn for the movie later on that night. Switches with symbols for each activity are attached to the tape recorder and popcorn popper through a relay box. After showing her what each switch activates, her support worker in the group home asks, "Which one do you want to do?" Sophie activates the popcorn popper switch and makes her choice. She also experiences the direct effects of her choice as the popcorn begins to shoot out of the popper chute! This is one example of the use of talking switch technology to enable choice making for individuals with severe motor impairments. (See Burkhart, 1993, and Rowland & Schweigert, 1991, for additional suggestions.)

Darcy is a 23-year-old with cerebral palsy who lived in a hospital setting where she attended school for 15 years. She now lives in a group home with four other women. When she moved into the community 5 years ago, she had no formal communication system at all, although she could communicate her preferences quite well through facial expressions, vocalizations, and body language. Darcy's family wanted her to make choices and communicate her wants and needs more spontaneously and with greater clarity. To accomplish this, Darcy's support staff first made decisions about her daily schedule and provided her with real objects in a schedule system to represent each of the activities in her day. Through repeated exposure and practice over a 6-month period, she learned to recognize the objects as representing specific activities. Then her support staff offered Darcy choices among activities using the object symbols and constructed her daily schedule based on those choices. Once she made a choice between two object symbols, they showed a large Picture Communication Symbol (PCS) corresponding to her choice, as feedback. They did this to expose Darcy to the PCS symbol for *tomorrow*. She learned to make offered choices with objects within about 3 months and also began to recognize PCS symbols. Over the next 3 months, her support staff faded out the object symbols, and Darcy began making offered choices using only PCS symbols, which facilitators offer to her in pairs in appropriate contexts.

TEACHING REQUESTING

Requesting is clearly one of the most basic and essential communication skills, and facilitators need a systematic approach of some sort to teach this skill in many cases. The sections that follow summarize some of the most common techniques that facilitators have used to teach either elicited or self-initiated requesting. Facilitators may use some methods, such as the Picture Exchange Communication System (PECS) (Bondy & Frost, 1995) and the generalized requesting approach (Reichle et al., 1991), to teach specific forms of requesting, whereas others may be used to teach more than one form.

Relationship to Challenging Behavior

The ability to make self-initiated requests is a behavior skill as well as a communication skill. It is not uncommon for beginning communicators to use socially unacceptable behaviors to initiate requests for desired foods, drinks, toys, activities, or other tangible items (Durand, 1990). Mirenda (1997) found that approximately one third of published interventions that implemented AAC techniques to treat challenging behavior were related to inappropriate requesting behaviors. Interventionists offered alternative behaviors by teaching some participants in these interventions to produce generic communicative messages such as manual signs for *please* or *want* (Campbell & Lutzker, 1993; Day, Horner, & O'Neill, 1994), to show a tangible symbol for "want" (Durand & Kishi, 1987), to operate a voice output communication device programmed to say "I want more" (Durand, 1993), and to activate a microswitch and taped message that said "I'm bored; somebody give me something to do" (Steege et al., 1990; Wacker et al., 1990). Researchers provided other participants with AAC techniques that allowed them to request specific items using manual signs (Bird, Dores, Moniz, & Robinson, 1989; Horner & Budd, 1985), line drawings (Sigafoos & Meikle, 1996), photographs (Lalli, Browder, Mace, & Brown, 1993), or tangible symbols (Gerra, Dorfman, Plaue, Schlackman, & Workman, 1995). Clearly, learning some form of self-initiated requesting was important to these beginning communicators.

Teaching Generalized and Explicit
Requesting and Use of an Attention-Getting Signal

One of the most well-researched approaches in teaching attention-getting signals involves teaching both generalized and explicit requesting within natural contexts using a behavioral framework (Reichle et al., 1991; Sigafoos & Reichle, 1992). Generalized requesting is accomplished when the individual uses a single, uniform symbol (e.g., WANT) in different situations to initiate requesting, which is then completed by offering real-object choices. Generalized requesting requires fewer symbol discrimination skills than does explicit requesting, which necessitates using more than one symbol to make requests. Using the generalized requesting strategy, facilitators can also teach individuals to make requests composed of a single, specific symbol in order to obtain an item (e.g., a picture of ice cream to get ice cream), by simply substituting the specific symbol for the *want* symbol.

In order to make self-initiated generalized requests, the individual must be able to gain the attention of his or her communication partner. Facilitators should teach attention getting as part of the generalized requesting technique, although they can teach it separately. Keogh and Reichle (1985) noted that learners initially may use the attention-getting signal frequently until the novelty has worn off. They emphasized the importance of the facilitator's response to these initiations, even if the individual does complete the request sequence. Table 11.3 summarizes the instructional steps for teaching generalized requesting and the use of an attention-getting signal. This approach has been demonstrated to be effective with many individuals with developmental disabilities, including those with whom AAC interventions have often not been successful (e.g., Rett syndrome; Sigafoos, Laurie, & Pennell, 1995, 1996).

Milieu Teaching Interventions

Milieu teaching is a "naturalistic strategy for teaching functional language skills" (Kaiser, Yoder, & Keetz, 1992, p. 9). Interventionists have applied this method primar-

---

Table 11.3.   Teaching generalized requesting and use of an attention-getting signal

Teaching Self-Selection
1. *Provide* an assortment of potentially reinforcing items (e.g., toys, food, drinks) on a cafeteria tray.
2. *Hold tray* within the target individual's reach for 10–20 seconds, and encourage him or her to select an object.
3. *Accept* the individual's reach or point as an indicator.
4. When an item has been selected, *remove* the tray, *provide* the item, and *record* the selected item as data.
5. If no response occurs within 10–20 seconds, remove the tray, wait, and try again.
6. Repeat Steps 1–6 until Step 4 occurs three times in a row.
7. Repeat over 3–4 days to determine what the individual's preferences are and how long each practice session should last.

Teaching Use of a Generic *Want* Symbol with Arranged Cues
1. *Place* a *want* symbol (e.g., a Picture Communication Symbol for *want*) on a large cardboard in front of the individual within reach.
2. *Offer* the cafeteria tray with various items on it and ask, "What do you want?"
3. When the individual attempts to reach for a desired item:
    a. *Note* the item for which he or she was reaching.
    b. *Slide* the tray well out of reach.
    c. Physically (not verbally) *prompt* the individual to touch the "want" symbol.
4. After the "want" symbol has been touched, *provide* the desired item.
5. Over subsequent trials, gradually *fade* the physical prompt until the individual is consistently and independently touching the "want" symbol in response to "What do you want?"
6. Practice Steps 1–5 in a variety of natural contexts with a variety of items (e.g., at breakfast with food items, at the library with books, during a grooming session with self-care items). *Do not* practice in one context only, or the individual will fail to learn that *want* can be used anytime, anyplace.

Teaching Use of an Attention-Getting Signal to Initiate Requests
1. Be sure the *want* symbol is readily available to the individual.
2. Identify a manual or aided attention-getting signal that will be taught. Some possibilities include tapping a listener's arm or shoulder (manual), raising a hand until attended to (manual), ringing a bell (aided), and activating a call buzzer (aided).
3. If an aided call signal is selected, be sure it is accessible to the individual.
4. Use a physical prompt to teach the individual to use the signal to get a partner's attention.
5. When the partner's attention has been gained, the partner approaches the individual and repeats Steps 2–6 of Teaching Use of a Generic *Want* Symbol.
6. Be sure to fade the prompt used to teach the attention-getting signal.
7. Make the attention-getting signal available to the individual during as much of the day as possible to encourage spontaneous requests.

Adapted from Keogh and Reichle, 1985; Reichle et al., 1991.

ily with children who have language delays and are at a cultural disadvantage. AAC teams have used milieu teaching successfully in both aided and unaided AAC interventions to teach simple forms of communication (e.g., Glennen & Calculator, 1985; Hamilton & Snell, 1993; Heller, Allgood, Ware, Arnold, & Castelle, 1996; Kaiser, Ostrosky, & Alpert, 1993; Letto, Bedrosian, & Skarakis-Doyle, 1994; McGregor, Young, Gerak, Thomas, & Vogelsberg, 1992; Oliver & Halle, 1982; Peck, 1985; Turnell & Carter, 1994). Three milieu teaching strategies in particular have been used to teach basic requesting: incidental teaching (Warren & Kaiser, 1986); the mand-model technique (Halle, 1982); and the time-delay procedure (Halle, Baer, & Spradlin, 1981; Halle, Marshall, & Spradlin, 1979), singly or in combination. Milieu teaching differs from more traditional behavioral approaches in that the child rather than the adult initiates the teaching episodes, and the consequences are functionally related to the child's response, instead of being artificial in nature (Goodman & Remington, 1993).

There are similarities as well as distinct differences among the three primary milieu teaching strategies. All three are characterized by the use of dispersed (as opposed to massed) teaching trials in natural contexts and by attempts to base teaching on the individual's interests. In addition, all three methods require that facilitators learn to identify potential communicative contexts throughout the user's typical day and employ a variety of setup strategies to create communication opportunities. Setup strategies may include 1) placing a needed or desired item out of the individual's reach, 2) passively blocking access to a desired item, 3) intentionally giving the individual materials that are inappropriate to the context (e.g., providing a cup when it is time to put on a coat), or 4) presenting two or more options so the individual can make a choice (Haring, Neetz, Lovinger, Peck, & Semmel, 1987). All of these strategies are meant to elicit requesting behavior of some type.

Incidental teaching, the mand-model, and the time-delay procedure are meant to be used in similar but distinctly different situations. AAC teams employ the mand-model technique to teach elicited requesting skills to individuals who have no such behaviors in their repertoires. Incidental teaching encourages initiation and builds more sophisticated communication skills in individuals who already communicate using at least simple gestures in response to verbal cues. AAC teams use the time-delay procedure to teach self-initiated requesting when the individual already has the desired behavior in his or her repertoire but does not use it unless verbally prompted. Table 11.4 summarizes the basic elements of the three milieu teaching strategies. Another example of milieu teaching as it applies to teaching conversational commenting appears later in this chapter.

Interrupted Behavior Chains

Using the interrupted behavior chain, AAC teams teach either elicited or self-initiated requesting in natural settings. The method is based on milieu teaching and utilizes natural routines, or *behavior chains*, as contexts for communication (Alwell, Hunt, Goetz, & Sailor, 1989; Gee et al., 1991; Goetz, Gee, & Sailor, 1985; Hunt & Goetz, 1988a; Hunt, Goetz, Alwell, & Sailor, 1986). Behavior chains might include putting on a coat and then going outside, washing dishes after having eaten dinner, or any other multiple-step task that a person performs in the same way each time.

An example of the use of an interrupted behavior chain appears previously in this chapter as it relates to attention-getting devices (Gee et al., 1991). In general, interrupted behavior chains are particularly useful for teaching requesting to individuals

Table 11.4.   A summary of milieu teaching strategies

Mand-Model Technique (Halle, 1982)

1. *Provide* communication opportunities in natural contexts. For example, have favorite foods or recreational/leisure items readily available.

2. When the target individual approaches the target item(s), the facilitator *initiates* communication by asking for a request signal, for example, "What do you want?"

3. If the individual does not respond, *expand* the request and *model* desired behavior. For example, "Show me (models gesture)" or "Show me the sign" (models) or "Show me the picture" (models).

4. *Pause* and observe for response.

5. If the individual still does not respond, *provide* a second model and a physical prompt if necessary to assist imitation. For example, "Show me what you want" + *model* + *pause* + physical *prompt* if no response during pause.

6. As soon as the individual makes the desired response, provide the target item along with verbal feedback.

Incidental Teaching (Haring, Neetz, Lovinger, Peck, & Semmel, 1987; Peck, 1985; Warren & Kaiser, 1986)

1. *Arrange* a variety of communication opportunities in natural contexts. For example, place desired or needed items out of reach, "forget" to put silverware on the dinner table, or "lose" one of the individual's shoes prior to physical education class.

2. After the target individual has approached desired items and has attempted to get them through simple gestures (e.g., pointing, reaching, vocalizing), the facilitator *approaches* and *provides* instruction to elicit a more sophisticated response. Four levels of prompts may be used (Hart & Risley, 1975):

   a. *Natural prompt*, such as a question ("What do you want?") or receptive *adult attention*, perhaps with a questioning look.

   b. *Minimum prompt*, a nonspecific verbal direction from the facilitator, such as "You need to tell me what you want."

   c. *Medium prompt*, a request for a partial imitation. For example, the facilitator might say "You need to tell me what you want. 'Want _____,'" while pointing to the individual's hands or communication board to signal that he or she should complete the sentence.

   d. *Maximum prompt*, in which the facilitator asks, "What do you want? You need to tell me. Say '(label),'" and simultaneously models the manual sign or points to the appropriate communication symbol.

3. When the individual responds correctly, *confirm* the response and *provide* the desired items.

Time-Delay Procedure (Halle, Baer, & Spradlin, 1981; Halle, Marshall, & Spradlin, 1979; Oliver & Halle, 1982; Peck, 1985)

Required:

1. *Identify* and *arrange* communication opportunities.

2. When the individual stands by, looks at, or approaches a desired item, the facilitator *approaches* the individual within 3 feet but does not vocalize.

3. *Ensure* that the individual is aware of the facilitator's presence (e.g., via body language, clearing the throat).

4. *Pause* for at least 15 seconds for the individual to initiate the desired response and provide desired item when this occurs.

Optional (if the target individual does not respond after the pause):

1. *Provide* a visual prompt (e.g., gesture broadly to the cassette on the shelf, hold up coffee cup).

2. *Exaggerate* facial expression/body language (e.g., pursed lips, raised eyebrows, shoulders shrugged as if to say "I don't know what you want").

3. *Kneel* down to be on the individual's level.

4. Last resort: *Model* desired behavior or *use* incidental teaching prompts.

5. *Provide* desired item when desired communication behavior occurs.

who are not motivated to initiate communication or who have very limited response repertoires. First, the AAC team conducts preintervention assessment probes to identify the intervention variables related to success. Using this information, the team begins instruction by having the individual or a facilitator carry out the initial steps in the chain. Then, the team interrupts the chain in some prearranged manner to elicit targeted communicative behavior. Table 11.5 summarizes basic assessment and intervention steps for using interrupted behavior chains. Ample evidence indicates that once an individual has learned to produce the targeted communication response in the context of several different behavior chains, generalization to noninstructional settings occurs with little difficulty (Alwell et al., 1989; Hunt & Goetz, 1988a). The incidental teaching and time-delay strategies discussed previously can help facilitate such spontaneous requesting.

Table 11.5.   Assessment and instructional procedures of interrupted behavior chains

Selected Routines or Behavior Chains as Contexts for Instruction (Assessment)

1. *Identify* several behavior chains (routines) throughout the day 1) in which the target individual can at least initiate each step (may need some help completing some steps) and 2) that are not pivotal routines in the schedule (i.e., if they are not completed, an alternate activity can be substituted).
2. *Conduct* task analyses of the chains/routines.
3. *Choose* points in each chain where interruption and subsequent communication can occur (e.g., getting ready for recess routine, before zipping coat, dishwashing routine, before getting detergent from shelf).
4. *Allow* the individual to begin the routine, then interrupt the routine before the predetermined steps by
   a. Passively blocking the individual from taking the next step
   b. Delaying presentation of the item needed for the next step
   c. Placing a needed item out of the individual's reach
   d. Removing an item needed for the activity from view
   e. Allowing a natural interruption to occur
5. *Rate* the level of the target individual's frustration at being interrupted (1 = low, 2 = moderate, 3 = high) and motivation to continue the chain (1 = low, 2 = moderate, 3 = high).
6. *Repeat* Steps 4 and 5 on at least three occasions and average the ratings obtained.
7. *Select* chains for instruction for which the individual has an average frustration score of 1–2 and motivation score of 2–3.

Basic Instructional Procedure

1. Have picture symbols available for the target requests or have manual signs selected.
2. *Begin* the routine.
3. *Interrupt* the routine at the predetermined points using strategies in Assessment Step 4. Do not use verbal cues.
4. Trial 1:
   a. *Wait* 5–15 seconds for the individual to initiate communication.
   b. If the individual initiates, *continue* the chain (go to Step 6).
   c. If the individual does not initiate, *model* or *physically prompt* the desired communication behavior (e.g., touching the picture, manually signing).
   d. *Wait* 5–15 seconds.
5. Trial 2:
   a. If the individual initiates, *continue* the chain (go to Step 6).
   b. If the individual does not initiate, *discontinue* the chain and initiate alternate activity.
6. *Record* correct (+), incorrect (−), and prompted (P) responses for Trials 1 and 2.
7. If Step 5b is necessary for five consecutive sessions, *discontinue* instruction for that chain.

Adapted from Alwell, Hunt, Goetz, and Sailor, 1989; Goetz, Gee, and Sailor, 1985; Hunt and Goetz, 1988a, 1988b; and Hunt, Goetz, Alwell, and Sailor, 1986.

Verbal Prompt-Free and Expectant-Delay Procedures

Self-initiated requesting through the use of aided symbols (e.g., real objects, photographs) may be taught by a verbal prompt–free strategy (Locke & Mirenda, 1988; Mirenda & Dattilo, 1987; Mirenda & Santogrossi, 1985; Mirenda & Schuler, 1988). Experimenters introduced a variation of this procedure, termed *expectant time delay*, to students with severe physical disabilities to teach choice making (Kozleski, 1991). These strategies are particularly appropriate for individuals who are so dependent on verbal prompts to communicate that they rarely initiate requests without cuing from their partners (e.g., "What do you want?" "You need to tell me what you want"). Verbal prompt–free and expectant-delay procedures require the facilitator to refrain from using any verbal prompts from the outset of instruction to avoid the need to fade them later. Facilitators may implement both strategies in natural contexts with both children and adults with severe disabilities. Table 11.6 summarizes the basic steps for use of the verbal prompt–free strategy in natural routines (e.g., meals, recreation, grooming times). (See Kozleski, 1991, for a detailed description of the expectant time-delay procedure.)

Picture Exchange Communication System (PECS)

PECS is a behavioral approach that facilitators may employ to teach self-initiated requesting with aided symbols. The method teaches requesting as the very first skill in the person's communicative repertoire, without requiring the individual to have skills such as eye contact, imitation, facial orientation, match-to-sample skills, or labeling as prereq-

Table 11.6. Verbal prompt–free strategy

Basic Procedure:
1. *Identify* natural contexts in which multiple requests for food or leisure items are appropriate (e.g., mealtime, breaktime at work, free-choice recreational/leisure activity).
2. *Identify* a number of items (at least two or three) that may be requested and that are motivating to the target individual in the selected contexts, and *place* them within the individual's view.
3. *Choose* aided symbols (e.g., real objects, tangible symbols, photos, line drawings) corresponding to the items identified in Step 2.
4. *Position* self next to or across from the individual at a table and *place* one of the symbols on the table within the individual's reach.
5. *Wait* for 3–5 minutes. *Do not say anything.*
6. If the individual touches the symbol *accidentally or on purpose*, immediately *acknowledge* the touch verbally and *provide* the associated item (e.g., "Oh, you touched the picture of the juice—yes, you can have some juice! Here it is!").
7. If the individual does *not* touch the symbol within 3–5 minutes, *physically prompt* him or her to do so and *provide* the item associated with the symbol. Over subsequent trials, *fade* the prompt as quickly as possible.
8. *Repeat* Steps 4–7 until the individual has independently touched the symbol (without any type of prompt) five to six times in succession.
9. If accidental touches are still occurring, begin to *ignore* them while *continuing to respond* to deliberate touches only until the individual is consistently touching the symbol deliberately.
10. *Add* a second symbol, and continue as in Step 8 while alternating the positions of the symbols.
11. Continue to *add* one symbol whenever the Step 8 criterion is met.
12. Once the requesting behavior is solidly in place across a number of symbols, *begin to deny* the request occasionally when appropriate (e.g., "No, sorry, it's not time for that now, you'll have to wait").
13. *Place* symbols in a book or wallet that is portable and make it available in appropriate natural contexts.

Adapted from Locke and Mirenda, 1988; Mirenda and Dattilo, 1987; and Mirenda and Santogrossi, 1985.

uisites (Bondy & Frost, 1995). Although PECS was originally designed for preschoolers with autism, facilitators have also applied it successfully with individuals who have other developmental disabilities across the age range (Marriner, 1993). Outcome data for 66 nonspeaking children with autism ages 5 and younger who were taught via PECS over a 5-year period are quite encouraging. In 1995, Bondy and Frost reported that 34 of the children acquired functional speech and no longer required any AAC supports, that 14 used a combination of words and pictures or written words, and that the remaining 18 children continued to use aided symbols for communication in functional contexts.

Instruction in PECS begins after an assessment of potential reinforcers for the individual of concern. In the first phase of PECS, the person learns to pick up a single symbol (e.g., photograph, line drawing) and place it in the open hand of a facilitator, who gives the person the associated item (e.g., food, drink, toy). At first, an assistant to the facilitator provides physical and gestural prompts but no verbal prompts (e.g., "What do you want?" "Give me the picture"), as in the verbal prompt–free strategy described previously. As the person begins to make the picture exchange, the assistant gradually fades the prompts until the exchange is made unassisted. The assistant then gradually moves away so that the person learns to take the picture to the facilitator to exchange it for the desired item. Gradually, the number of symbols available is increased to teach symbol discrimination (Frost & Bondy, 1994). The facilitator conducts comprehension checks by asking the individual to select the requested item from an array after offering the symbol and by providing natural consequences and/or corrective feedback, as appropriate. Once the individual has mastered basic requesting, the facilitator may extend the program to build sentence structures (e.g., to teach the person to chain an *I want* symbol and a specific referent symbol), to teach the person to answer yes/no questions in a request context, and to label items (e.g., "What is this?"). (See Frost & Bondy, 1994, for additional information.)

General Case Instruction

Facilitators have relied on general case instruction since the early 1980s to teach functional living skills to people with severe disabilities (Horner, McDonnell, & Bellamy, 1986). However, only since the early 1990s have facilitators applied the method to teach a communication skill such as requesting (Chadsey-Rusch, Drasgow, Reinoehl, Halle, & Collet-Klingenberg, 1993; Chadsey-Rusch & Halle, 1992). General case instruction involves analyzing the relevant stimulus and response classes associated with particular tasks or situations and teaching individuals both when to respond and when *not* to respond under a variety of stimulus conditions (Chadsey-Rusch et al., 1993). For example, in order to teach beginning communicators to request assistance by signing HELP, the facilitator should first identify a number of opportunities across relevant environments in which the individual might require help. Such opportunities might occur, for example, when the individual prepares food (e.g., and needs to open a container) or when he or she encounters mobility barriers and/or doors. Next, the facilitator conducts a task analysis to identify the steps involved in the task (e.g., recognizing the need for help, gaining a listener's attention, asking for help) and the task variations that the individual might encounter at each step. For example, recognizing the need for help might require the individual to recognize various types of containers that need to be opened (e.g., cola cans, wrapped sandwiches), mobility barriers (e.g., speed bumps, curbs), and door barriers (e.g., heavy doors, hinges with too much tension for the door to open easily).

Once the facilitator has completed the preparatory steps, instruction is conducted by a number of facilitators who represent both genders and (as much as possible) a range of ethnic backgrounds, ages, heights, and hair colors, in order to facilitate generalization across people. For example, facilitators might offer verbal and modeling prompts that they fade quickly to teach the participant to sign HELP in the school cafeteria when presented with a closed food package. Once the participant learns the basic skill, facilitators arrange opportunities to ask for help across the day to sample from a range of identified variations. Finally, probes are conducted in novel settings and with novel people to assess generalized use of the new skill. Although the general case technique requires more time and instructional effort than teaching in only one or two restricted contexts, previous research suggested that it is also more likely to result in spontaneous use and generalization of newly acquired communication skills (Chadsey-Rusch & Halle, 1992).

Casey is 17 years old and attends a local high school. Two years ago, his educational team met to brainstorm about how to encourage Casey to make decisions for himself because it seemed like he always waited to be told what, when, with whom, and how to do things. He could choose between two objects or color photographs when they were offered to him, but he never initiated decisions on his own. The team decided to first teach Casey to make requests from more than two options. They constructed five choice displays for Casey with photographs representing preferred foods, drinks, school activities, friends, and recreation activities. The displays were arranged by type of choice (e.g., food, drinks), and each display had five photographs on it. They identified contexts during the day when they could ask him to use the displays, and they began to ask questions such as "What do you want?" to elicit requests in those contexts. They also implemented the interrupted behavior chain strategy to teach him to make spontaneous requests in natural contexts such as going through the cafeteria line, checking out books from the library, and getting equipment in gym class. Casey gradually learned to use the displays to make choices when people asked him to do so and when opportunities occurred within structured activity chains. Later, the facilitators provided Casey with the displays in natural contexts but refrained from asking him what he wanted. Instead, they used a time-delay procedure to encourage him to initiate requests. At first, Casey made slow progress, but once he caught on that he could ask for things by himself, he began to use the displays spontaneously in numerous contexts. During the next school year, facilitators expanded his choice displays in type, quantity, and size. Casey now makes both elicited and spontaneous requests using PCS symbols representing more than 150 options.

TEACHING BASIC REJECTING

Relationship to Challenging Behavior

Many individuals are highly motivated to communicate rejections (e.g., rejecting or terminating an undesired item or activity), perhaps even more so than requests. It appears that rejection is the underlying communicative function of many so-called behavior problems such as aggression, tantrums, and self-injury. In a review of intervention research related to functional communication training (FCT), in which experimenters taught specific communication skills to 52 participants as alternatives to challenging behavior, Mirenda (1997) found that rejection (i.e., escape) was the "message" underlying behavior 56% of the time. Thus, teaching individuals to communicate rejection messages is likely to have positive communicative as well as behavioral consequences. FCT interventions that have incorporated AAC techniques include teaching gestures such as a head shake (Lalli, Casey, & Kates, 1995), a tangible symbol for "break" (Bird et al., 1989), manual signs such as GO, NO, and DONE (Fisher et al., 1993; Northup et al., 1994; Peck et al., 1996), a card with the word *break* or *done* printed on it (Day et al., 1994; Peck et al., 1996), a microswitch with a taped message such as STOP! (Steege et al., 1990), and a voice-output communication device with the message I WANT A BREAK (Durand, 1993).

Leave-Taking

Reichle and colleagues (1991) described a basic strategy for teaching communicative leave-taking to individuals who usually cooperate in a particular activity for a brief period of time and then try to escape or otherwise terminate the activity (e.g., by having a tantrum). Here, the message of the behavior can be thought of as "I want a break," "I don't want to do this anymore," or something similar. Prior to intervention, facilitators need to identify the consistent behavioral antecedents to escaping. For example, perhaps the person begins to whine, or acts distracted, or stops working just before he or she tries to escape. The individual needs to have an *escape* symbol available during the activity (e.g., the manual sign for *stop*, a card with a *break* sign on it attached to a cord on the person's belt loop). As soon as the individual begins to exhibit the antecedent behaviors, the facilitator should physically prompt him or her to produce the *escape* symbol. When the individual produces this symbol, an immediate cessation of the activity for a few minutes should follow. The facilitator should fade the physical prompt gradually over subsequent trials until the person produces the *escape* symbol independently. When this basic rejecting behavior has been firmly established, the facilitator begins to delay stopping the activity for just a few seconds (e.g., "Oh, you want to stop. Okay, let's just finish wiping this one table") and gradually for longer periods (e.g., Bird et al., 1989; Lalli et al., 1995). Reichle and colleagues (1991) also discussed variations of this procedure involving use of a "safety signal."

Refusal

Alternatively, an individual may wish to reject an offered object or activity completely. For example, Reichle, Rogers, and Barrett (1984) taught an adolescent girl this rejection behavior, using the manual sign for *no*. They offered her a variety of nonpreferred items and asked her, "Want one?" Initially, they physically prompted her to produce the sign for *no*, and they gradually faded the prompts. Whenever she produced the sign or an approximation, a facilitator removed the nonpreferred item. Once an individual learns a rejecting behavior, it is important for facilitators to honor it in situations that may not be as clear cut, such as when the individual rejects a preferred item because he or she does not wish to have more (e.g., rejecting a third cup of coffee although the first two were accepted). (See Reichle et al., 1991, for additional discussion.)

No longer can we select communicative target behaviors for both the AAC user and partner from a magician's hat without considering the effects of these behaviors on perceptions of the AAC user's communicative competence. (Bedrosian, Hoag, Calculator, & Molineux, 1992)

TEACHING BASIC CONVERSATIONAL SKILLS

At a minimum, conversational interaction requires skills that include the ability to initiate the interaction; maintain the conversation by asking questions, answering questions, and commenting on the ongoing topic; and terminate the conversation appropriately. The following sections review several common strategies for facilitating some or all of these components.

Initiation and Topic-Setting Strategies

Initiation and topic-setting strategies allow beginning communicators to begin and establish topics of conversation using various types of basic symbols. We discuss six initiation and topic-setting approaches: badges, collections, topic-setting or remnant books, topic-setting cards, joke cards, and conversation displays.

Badges

A study involving two boys, ages 10 and 12, with cerebral palsy and cognitive disabilities examined the use of badges to initiate play activities (Jolly, Test, & Spooner, 1993). During free-play time at school, experimenters attached with Velcro four badges with photographs of preferred activities to the boys' lap trays. They taught the boys to pull off a badge and hand it to a peer who did not have a disability when the boys wanted to initiate a play activity. Play initiation for both boys increased after intervention, although their ability to sustain the play interactions was still limited. Badges, however, may be a simple way to promote at least basic social initiation in loosely structured settings.

Collections

Many individuals of all ages enjoy collecting various objects. Even preschoolers may begin to accumulate collections of items such as play necklaces, bracelets, toy cars, squirt guns, or stuffed animals. Older individuals may collect stamps, hockey cards, political buttons, or baseball caps—the possibilities are endless! Such collections, if facilitators systematically encourage them and display them appropriately, can stimulate adult and peer interactions with AAC users across the ability range. For example, a teenager could wear a different message button from her collection to school every day or a teacher could display a child's toy robot collection on a bulletin board at school. Facilitators could remind both adults and children to comment on the newest addition to the collection and could encourage the child's peers to look at the collection items and talk with the child about them. Items in some collections may also be shared as play or personal materials (e.g., toy cars, jewelry).

Remnant Books

A book or album made up of "remnants" or scraps saved from activities provides a way for beginning symbol users with limited verbal skills to tell people about past events, such as those that occurred during the school day or over the weekend. The remnant book allows the individual to answer questions such as "What did you do at school/work/home today?" or "What did you do over the weekend?" and to settle on a topic of conversation about an interesting event. Determining the topic of conversation may be a particularly useful skill for individuals who can talk somewhat but who have poor articulation. Once such an individual has narrowed down the topic of conversation by referring to a remnant in the book, his or her communication partner may find it easier to guess the parts of the individual's speech that are difficult to understand. Table 11.7 displays a strategy sheet that facilitators can use at home or school to establish a remnant book.

Work by Marvin and Privratsky (1996) compared the effects of child-focused materials (e.g., stickers, art products, mementos) and parent-focused materials (e.g., newsletters, journals, teacher memos) on conversations between young children without disabilities and their parents immediately after leaving preschool settings. The results indicated that the preschoolers initiated considerably more conversations and talked about more school-related events when they brought child-focused materials home. This suggests that remnant books might similarly facilitate such interactions, because the types of materials that facilitators and users place in them are user focused.

Musselwhite (1990) included suggestions for teaching the use of remnant books, including a sequenced partner training approach, which consists of three steps. She suggested that after the individual and the facilitator select a remnant and place it in the book, they rehearse using the remnant to introduce a topic through role playing or through puppets (with young children). Next, a third person begins interacting with

Table 11.7. Starting and using a remnant book

Putting things in the book

1. When you go somewhere in the community with the individual, *save a remnant* of the place you went. *Remnant* is a fancy word for something that the person used or encountered during the activity. The remnant should be something that is meaningful *to the individual* and that he or she will be able to associate with the place from which it came. Let the person help to select the remnant, if possible.

Examples:

- If you go to a movie, you might save a ticket stub, or the popcorn container, or the candy box—whichever one the individual prefers and finds most meaningful.
- If you go out to eat, you might save a napkin, or the hamburger wrapper, or the styrofoam chicken box, or the empty paper cup from pop—whichever one the individual prefers and finds most meaningful.
- If you do something interesting or special at home, save a remnant of that as well—such as birthday parties, watching a video, having a friend come for tea.

2. Help the individual to put the remnant in his or her communication book on the page marked with the correct day of the week (Monday, Tuesday, etc.). You may have to flatten the remnant to put it on the page under a plastic page cover. It will be bulky, but there's not much to do about that.

General strategies for using the book

Don't

- Ask the person "accuracy questions" with the book—"Show me where you went first on Monday," "Show me what you did next," and so forth—in which there is a "right" and "wrong" answer. This is not much fun for the individual and will make him or her hate the book very quickly!

Do

- Make interactions fun and casual.
- Use the book when the person indicates that he or she is interested.
- Encourage the person to try to say the words for the place or activity the remnant represents
- Make the book readily available at all times so that the individual can initiate interactions by simply opening the book and pointing to one or more remnants. When he or she does this, have a conversation about the place or activity the remnant represents.
- Ask the person what happened today/last night/over the weekend, and encourage him or her to get out the book. Talk about the places and activities the remnants represent (e.g., "Oh, I see you went to the basketball game. Did you have a good time?").
- Get out the book and go through it with the person to talk about what he or she has been up to lately—sort of like reading a story together, but it's a personal story that's being read!

the individual, and the facilitator coaches the person to use the remnant with the third person. Finally, the third person is asked to facilitate an interaction with another person. Musselwhite also suggested that the facilitator provide written cues with the remnants to assist literate communication partners to engage in multiexchange conversations with the remnant book user. For example, a cue card might read "Ask me what I did this weekend," "Ask me who I went with?" or "Ask me what funny thing happened there."

Topic-Setter Cards

Topic-setter cards are simple drawings or symbols on self-adhesive notes or index cards that present topics of interest to the user (Musselwhite & St. Louis, 1988). Topic-setter cards may be used in conjunction with collections, remnant books, or other techniques. For example, a card fastened to a wheelchair lap tray might display a symbol of a television along with a written message that faces the communication partner (i.e., upside down to the user) stating "My favorite television show is *The Simpsons*. Do you have a favorite show? Do you like *Home Improvement?*" A facilitator can also place the cards in a communication book or program an electronic device to speak the message (Musselwhite, 1990). The user simply points to the card in order to initiate the interaction.

Joke Cards

Individuals who have a sense of humor may enjoy initiating interactions with joke cards. We like to use 5" × 7" file cards with a riddle on one side and the answer on the other. For example, one side might have a picture or symbol of a chicken with the caption, *Why did the chicken cross the road?* and the directions on the bottom *Please turn over for answer.* The other side would bear a picture of a chicken across the road and the punch line, *To get to the other side.* The facilitator can teach the person to approach an appropriate partner and hand him or her the card, riddle-side up (color coding the correct side might be helpful). Some individuals use joke cards without really understanding the language of the joke—but who understands the chicken joke anyway?! The person is learning how to initiate an interaction and (most important) how to make a friend laugh and share a positive exchange—both valuable communication skills for beginning communicators.

Facilitators can make a slightly more advanced form of the joke card by using "knock, knock" jokes. The format of this joke (with which most people in North America are familiar) lends itself readily to simple conversational turn taking. A series of pictures representing the parts of the joke facilitate the telling of the joke. For example, the AAC user might first touch a picture of someone knocking on a door accompanied by a written label such as *Wanna hear a cool joke? Knock, knock. . . .* After the partner responds "Who's there?" the AAC user touches the next picture (e.g., a picture of plates and bowls labeled *dishes*). The partner responds "Dishes who?" and the AAC user touches the final picture, which is a photo of himself or herself with the caption *Dishes me, who is you?* and everyone groans together!

Conversation Displays

If we want individuals to initiate conversations with their AAC systems, the systems must be constructed and designed with this goal in mind. Toward this end, conversation displays (e.g., books, boards, wallets, electronic overlays) should contain messages related to favorite people, pets, places, activities, and other items important in the person's life. Past and upcoming events should also be represented. For example, one individual we know had a plastic bag containing grass clippings in his conversation book, so that he could tell his friends about learning how to mow the lawn over the weekend. Hunt, Alwell, and Goetz (1990) described a teenager who had a few pieces of dry cat food taped in her communication book to help her initiate conversations about taking care of her cat at home. The point is to provide AAC users, through a combination of media, with symbols and messages that promote topics of conversation that are interesting and motivating both to them *and to their communication partners.* Facilitators should change and expand these regularly so that the communication display reflects current events in the person's life.

Of course, the format and the content of conversation display should also look age appropriate. The covers of conversation books should be attractive and, if applicable, decorated in a manner appropriate to the individual's age. The symbols and messages should also reflect age-appropriate interests. Polite though they may be, the co-workers of an adult with a developmental disability are not going to be interested for long in photos of dolls or in cut-out pictures from the movies *Bambi* and *Snow White.*

The Yooralla Society of Victoria, Australia, developed an excellent videotape entitled *prAACtically speaking.* The tape, designed for staff who support adults with developmental disabilities in community settings, features gesture dictionaries, conversation books, calendar/schedule systems, and community request cards, as well as basic techniques for interaction. An information booklet accompanies the video, which is available from the Functional Communication Outreach Service.

Conversational Instruction

For many beginning communicators, acquiring the ability to have conversations involves learning both linguistic and social skills (Light, 1989b). That is, they must first learn to access appropriate messages on their displays (requiring linguistic skills) and then to use those messages to initiate, maintain, and terminate conversations (requiring social skills). Facilitators can teach these skills sequentially or simultaneously, depending on the individual and the characteristics of his or her AAC system. The following sections describe three approaches to teaching conversational skills.

Structured Practice

Experimenters have used a structured practice approach to teach the linguistic and social aspects of conversation either sequentially (Dattilo & Camarata, 1991) or simultaneously (Spiegel, Benjamin, & Spiegel, 1993). These two studies involved three adults with cerebral palsy who used iconic encoding (Minspeak) on voice-output communication devices (TouchTalkers). In the Dattilo and Camarata (1991) study, experimenters first taught two adults to produce a variety of conversational messages using their devices. After they learned the icon sequences needed to access a number of messages, experimenters provided a variety of leisure materials and encouraged the adults to use their systems to ask for or talk about the materials. In the Spiegel et al.

(1993) study, experimenters offered instruction related to production of the icon sequences concurrent with separate practice sessions for structured conversational role
playing. In practice sessions, a facilitator provided narrative cues to set the stage for
the participant's selection of programmed sentences. In both cases, the facilitator provided expectant pauses and minimal verbal prompts to facilitate initiation and commenting on the conversational topic. All three individuals showed marked improvement of their conversational skills and evidence of generalization to nontraining
settings within four to six practice sessions. The studies suggested that for some individuals the acquisition of basic conversational skills may require structured opportunities to practice basic skills in natural contexts.

Conversational Coaching

Hunt, Alwell, and Goetz (1988, 1990, 1991) and Storey and Provost (1996) introduced
another strategy that holds real promise for teaching AAC users to use communication
aids in conversation. This strategy requires a facilitator to provide unobtrusive conversational coaching to the person and to communication partners (e.g., friends, parents,
co-workers) during instructional sessions.

Figure 11.2 (Hunt et al., 1991b) illustrates the basic structure of this conversational
strategy. The facilitator provides physical, gestural, indirect verbal, and direct verbal
prompts to teach the basic conversational structure and fades these cues gradually.
First, the AAC user is prompted to initiate the conversation by taking the conversation
aid from its carrying case and pointing to a picture, remnant, or other topic-setter device to ask a question or make a comment. The partner then responds to the question or
comment, makes additional comments about the topic, and ends his or her turn by asking the AAC user a question about something else represented in the communication
aid. Finally, the facilitator prompts the AAC user to answer the question, comment as

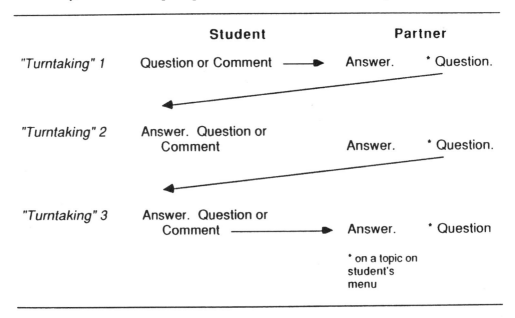

Figure 11.2. Basic conversational strategy. (From Hunt, P., Alwell, M., & Goetz, L. (1991b). Interacting with peers
through conversation turn taking with a communication book adaptation. *Augmentative and Alternative Communication, 7,* 120; reprinted by permission.)

desired, and ask another question. The facilitator repeats a loose form of this cycle until the conversation reaches its natural end point. Table 11.8 summarizes the conversational intervention strategy, which has been used successfully with aided communication only.

Several empirical studies regarding this strategy have indicated that even AAC users with severe disabilities and little or no speech can learn to initiate and maintain augmented conversations independently after several weeks of instruction. The results also indicated that this occurs only when interventionists also give communication partners a 5-minute briefing that includes the following basic information:

> You always do three things in the conversation: 1) talk about what [the individual] just pointed to in the book and anything else you want to talk about; 2) then ask him/her a new question; and 3) then be sure to wait until [the individual] has a chance to talk about other things as well. (Hunt et al., 1990, Appendix B)

This brief training also serves to emphasize the important role that facilitator training plays in AAC interventions, as we mention throughout this book.

Facilitators can implement a similar coaching strategy to introduce conversation boards during play interactions between young AAC users and their peers (Rao, 1994). First, using the communication display while speaking during activities, the facilitator acts as an active communicator, play partner, and model for the AAC user and at least one peer without a disability. The facilitator encourages peers without disabilities to use the display and assumes the role of translator of the AAC user's messages (e.g., "Grace

Table 11.8.   Summary of a conversational intervention strategy

I. Conversational Materials Needed
   1. Conversation book, board, or wallet (see related section in this chapter)
   2. Carrying case if the AAC user is ambulatory and requires portability (see Chapters 9, 15, and 16)
II. AAC User Instruction
   1. *Identify* naturally occurring conversational opportunities throughout the day in which interactions with peers without disabilities take place: during recess, breaktime at work, lunch at school, or transitions between classes. *Conduct* instruction in those settings.
   2. *Recruit* peers without disabilities as conversational partners.
   3. *Plan* for brief instructional sessions (preschoolers, 1–3 turns each; elementary students, 1–3 minutes; older students, 3–5 minutes, maximum).
   4. *Sit* by the AAC user and the partner and *coach* both through the steps involved. Use direct verbal and indirect verbal prompts (e.g., direct, "Point to the picture of your birthday party"; indirect, "What could you say about that?"). *Reinforce* AAC user with subtle verbal praise or a pat on the back as necessary.
   5. *Fade* the coaching as quickly as possible by providing subtle gestural cues or whispered verbal cues.
   6. *Remember:* The point is to facilitate conversations that are as normal as possible: Don't be rigid about the conversational structure or intrusive in the conversations.
   7. *Facilitate* generalization: *Teach* across multiple settings and partners, *ensure* that AAC users have their books available at all times, *provide* sufficient information to potential partners regarding their roles, *monitor and instruct* to repair breakdowns.
III. Partner Information
   1. *Tell* the partner to make comments related to the pictures in the book.
   2. *Tell* the partner to end his or her turn by asking a question about something in the book.
   3. *Cue* the partner as needed during conversational training sessions.
   4. *Stay out of the partner's way as much as possible.*

Adapted from Hunt, Alwell, and Goetz, 1988, 1990, 1991a, 1991b.

pointed to the picture of the horse. She's telling us that she wants to talk about horses"). Gradually, the facilitator transfers the role of translator to the peers, while continuing to prompt and model as needed (e.g., "Grace is showing us the picture for *hot*. What do you think she's telling us?"). The facilitator's goal is to fade out of the interaction altogether (or at least fade out but remain within earshot), as the peers become capable of both understanding the messages of and interacting with the AAC user.

Dual Communication Boards

Another technique for conversational instruction involves the use of dual communication boards (Heller, Allgood, Ware, et al., 1996; Heller, Ware, Allgood, & Castelle, 1994). The facilitator constructs two identical communication boards with symbols (e.g., PCS symbols) in four categories: 1) greetings, introductory phrases (e.g., HOW IS WORK GOING?), and responses to the greetings; 2) symbols for offering items of interest and responses to the symbols (e.g., WANT, THANK YOU); 3) questions and answers about activities of interest and whether the individual liked them (e.g., WHAT DID YOU DO LAST NIGHT?, FUN?, LIKE?); and 4); closing phrases and responses. Both the AAC user and the conversational partner receive a board, and each of them uses his or her own display to ask and answer questions. A facilitator gives prompts to the AAC user, such as signing, modeling, and physical guidance, to coach the conversations, in a manner similar to the conversation book technique described previously. AAC teams have implemented this technique successfully with individuals who have severe to profound hearing loss and reduced vision in community-based vocational sites. The dual display format has been shown to decrease communication errors by promoting natural turn taking and allowing both partners to interact at natural distances. Some evidence also suggests that communication partners who are not familiar with AAC prefer dual displays to the more typical single-display format (Heller et al., 1994).

My wife and I were driving to Colorado and stopped in North Platte, Nebraska, for breakfast. The town was holding its annual "Wild West Days" celebration, so the restaurant was very crowded. We went through the breakfast buffet and sat down at the last available table. We noticed a young man with Down syndrome who was standing near us looking for a seat, so we motioned to the empty chair at our table. He sat down, reached into his pocket, took out a small book with words and pictures in it, and opened it on the table in front of his plate. He looked at the book, looked up at me, and said, "Hi, how are you today?" I said I was fine and commented that it was really crowded in the restaurant. He nodded, turned the page of his book, looked at my wife, and said, "How do you like the weather?" She commented on the dreary rain and asked if he had come for the Wild West Days celebration. He nodded and smiled again, turned the page of his book, and asked me another question. The conversation continued like that all through breakfast. I found out later that he learned to use his conversation book from a graduate of our Nebraska Summer Institute on AAC. (D. Beukelman, personal communication, April 20, 1997)

TEACHING SKILLS RELATED TO COMMUNICATIVE COMPETENCE

Light (1989b) proposed a definition of communicative competence for people who use AAC. She argued that the development of communicative competence is a complex process that relies on knowledge, judgment, and skills in four domains: linguistic, operational, social, and strategic. Linguistically, AAC users need to learn the language(s) spoken in their homes and social communities as well as the linguistic code(s) of their AAC systems (e.g., Blissymbols, manual signs). Operationally, AAC users must learn the technical skills needed to operate their AAC systems, whether the systems are manual sign based, low tech, or electronic. Social domain skills include those related to discourse strategies such as initiating, maintaining, and terminating conversations as well as those needed for functional speech acts such as choice making, requesting, and rejecting. Social domain skills also include those that relate to interpersonal dynamics, such as knowing how to put partners at ease, actively participate in conversations, and so forth. Finally, strategic skills are those that allow AAC users to "make the best of what they do know and can do" (Light, 1996, p. 9).

Until the 1990s, researchers had conducted few studies to identify the precise skills that contribute to the attainment of communicative competence in AAC users. Logically, many of the basic skills discussed previously (e.g., initiating, requesting, rejecting) are probably related to communicative competence, but limited empirical evidence supports this. In the sections that follow, we offer intervention techniques that empirical studies have shown to be related to communicative competence. Many of the skills in the following sections are from the work of Light, Binger, and their colleagues and share the following instructional procedures (Light, 1996):

1. Define the specific goal (i.e., target skill) for the AAC user.
2. Explain the skill to the AAC user and why it is important.
3. Demonstrate how to use the skill or have the AAC user observe another person applying the skill while saying "think-aloud" statements that explain when to use the skill.
4. Ask the individual or significant others (as appropriate) to think of situations in which he or she might use the skill.
5. Set up situations for the AAC user to learn the skill, either during natural interactions or during a combination of role playing and actual interactions.
6. Use several different settings, partners, and sets of materials during instruction.
7. Start instruction in situations that are less demanding and, as the individual develops competencies, introduce more demanding situations.
8. Provide guided practice for the person to use the target skill in naturally occurring situations or role playing.
9. Always give the person an opportunity to use the skill spontaneously, and prompt only as required using a least-to-most cuing hierarchy (natural cue, expectant delay, general point and pause, and model).
10. Provide feedback on both appropriate use of the skill and problem areas after each instructional session.
11. Evaluate progress regularly to measure the effects of instruction.
12. Practice until the individual uses the skill spontaneously in 80% of opportunities during instructional sessions on at least two consecutive occasions.
13. Conduct probes in novel settings with novel partners to evaluate the generalized effects of instruction; offer "booster sessions" of role playing and practice, as needed, to facilitate generalization.

Researchers have demonstrated the effectiveness of this systematic approach to instruction in teaching a wide range of skills and strategies to students with learning disabilities (Deshler & Schumaker, 1988) as well as AAC users (Light & Binger, 1997). The strategies related to communicative competence that were taught through this approach are summarized in the sections that follow, along with related interventions taught with other instructional methodologies.

What do you think?

Partner reauditorization occurs when a speaking partner repeats and expands an AAC user's aided message without rising intonation. For example, an AAC user in a conversation with her friend says "TV." Reauditorization occurs when her partner then says, "Oh, you were watching TV last night, were you?" Three studies have provided evidence that reauditorization does *not* affect perceptions of an AAC user's communicative competence either positively or negatively (Bedrosian, Hoag, Calculator, & Molineux, 1992; Hoag & Bedrosian, 1992; Hoag, Bedrosian, Johnson, & Molineux, 1994). *What do you think?*

Introduction Strategy

An AAC user employs an introduction when he or she meets someone new. The message usually includes two components: information about the AAC user's means of communication and information about what the partner can do to facilitate the interaction. Light provided an example of an introduction strategy used by a 13-year-old with cerebral palsy:

> HI. I UNDERSTAND WHAT IS SAID TO ME, SO PLEASE SPEAK NORMALLY. I USE SIGN LANGUAGE TO COMMUNICATE SOMETIMES. IF YOU DON'T KNOW SIGN LANGUAGE, JUST LET ME KNOW, AND I WILL TYPE OUT THE THINGS I WANT TO SAY ON THIS COMPUTER. YOU WILL HEAR MY MESSAGE SPOKEN OUT ONCE I FINISH TYPING IT. PLEASE GIVE ME A FEW MINUTES TO ANSWER. I MAY BE SLOW, BUT IT'S WORTH WAITING FOR! (1996, p. 24)

Light, Binger, Dilg, and Livelsberger (1996) reported that use of an introduction strategy positively influenced perceptions of communicative competence, as rated by 30 adults and 30 adolescents without prior AAC experience and by 30 AAC professionals. In a related study, experimenters successfully taught the use of introductory strategies to five AAC users (ages 12–44 years) with cerebral palsy, autism, traumatic brain injury (TBI), or developmental delays (Light & Binger, 1997). The AAC users communicated via a variety of systems, including eye gazing, gestures, some speech, and various voice-output communication aids (VOCAs).

Regulatory Phrases

Regulatory phrases are similar to introduction messages, and they allow AAC users to manage and control aspects of interactions that are related to the operation of their AAC systems. Such phrases might provide directions to the communication partner with regard to positioning (e.g., CAN YOU COME OVER HERE WHERE I CAN SEE YOU?), effective use of the AAC system (e.g., SAY EACH LETTER AS I POINT TO IT), obtaining and securing conversational turns (e.g., I HAVE SOMETHING TO SAY), and repairing communication breakdowns (e.g., WAIT, LET ME SAY IT DIFFERENTLY). Buzolich and Lunger (1995) provided a case study in which a clinician taught an AAC user to interact with classmates who did not have disabilities by using a variety of regulatory phrases preprogrammed into a voice-output communication device. The clinician instructed the individual through both role-playing interactions and coached interactions with peers. Although the participant did not use more regulatory phrases during postintervention probes, she did initiate more topics, repair more conversational breakdowns, and use a wider variety of conversational strategies after instruction. For many AAC users, indirect strategies for conversational control and management may be more appropriate than the more blatant use of preprogrammed phrases (see the excellent discussion of mode devaluation by Calculator, 1988b).

What do you think?

Grammatically complete messages include all of the content words as well as the functional words required by the grammar of the language (e.g., "The boy and his dog went to the lake"). They differ from telegraphic messages, which contain the content words but not the functors (e.g., "Boy dog go lake"). Light et al. (1995) found that the use of grammatically complete messages was *not* consistently related to positive perceptions of communicative competence. They suggested that the grammatically complete message strategy interacts with communication rate such that the positive impact of the former might be "counterbalanced" by the added time required to produce the messages. *What do you think?*

Partner-Focused Questions

Partner-focused questions consist of questions about the conversational partner and his or her experiences. They might include, for example, "How was your weekend?" "What do you think?" "What's up?" and so forth. Light, Binger, Agate, et al. (1996) reported that this strategy was positively related to perceptions of communicative competence in observers with and without prior AAC experience. In a related study, they successfully taught the generalized use of partner-focused questions to six AAC users who ranged in age from 10 to 44 years (Light, Binger, Agate, & Ramsay, 1997). The study included individuals with cerebral palsy, mental retardation, or TBI who used various combinations of eye gazing, speech, gestures, a communication board with line drawings, and VOCAs.

Response-Recode

A simple form of a partner-focused question approach is the response-recode (R-R) strategy (Farrier, Yorkston, Marriner, & Beukelman, 1985). When an interactant responds to a question and then asks a related question in return (e.g., "My favorite coffee drink is cappuccino; what's yours?"), he or she has used the R-R form. O'Keefe and Dattilo (1992) taught the R-R strategy to three adult AAC users with developmental disabilities in the context of conversations about preferred leisure activities. Two participants used communication boards and one used a VOCA; in addition, the three participants used gestures, facial expressions, and a few spoken words. At the beginning of the conversation, the facilitator initiated a topic by asking a question and then provided the participant with graduated prompts to elicit the R-R form, consisting of 1) a verbal model (e.g., "After you answer me, I want *you* to ask *me* something. Like this: 'News. You?' Go ahead, you do it"); 2) a verbal model plus a model using the communication device or a communicative gesture; 3) a verbal model, communication device/gesture model, and manual assistance to produce an R-R with the device. All three individuals learned to produce the R-R form without prompting across both trained and novel interactants. Six weeks after they terminated intervention, experimenters interviewed family members and caregivers who reported lasting changes in the participants' conversational repertoires and who agreed that the R-R skill was "fundamental to true conversational involvement" (O'Keefe & Dattilo, p. 231).

Bedrosian, Hoag, and their colleagues examined the impact on communicative competence of using single words versus short phrases (two to four words). In the first study (Bedrosian, Hoag, Calculator, & Molineux, 1992), they found that only AAC professionals judged AAC users who used short phrases to be more communicatively competent than those who used single words; adults with no prior AAC experience were not similarly affected. However, in two subsequent studies with more subjects and slightly different methodologies, short phrases were found to positively affect perceptions of communicative competence by both groups of observers (Hoag & Bedrosian, 1992; Hoag et al., 1994).

Nonobligatory Turns

This type of conversational turn follows a partner's comment or statement (but not a question). Nonobligatory turns include interjections such as "Cool," "No way," and "Awesome!" as well as more substantive comments on the conversational topic. Light et al. (1995) found this nonobligatory turn taking to be related to positive perceptions of communicative competence. Light, Binger, Bailey, and Millar (1997) taught basic nonobligatory turn taking to five individuals (9–21 years of age) with developmental delays, mental retardation, cerebral palsy, or autism. The participants' communication systems consisted of speech, gestures, communication boards with line drawings and/or printed words, manual signs, and assorted VOCAs. All five individuals were able to take nonobligatory turns in conversations with new people in new settings after instruction.

Conversational Commenting

In a related study, Buzolich, King, and Baroody (1991) reported the successful use of a package of milieu teaching approaches for conversational commenting to three AAC users who used VOCAs. The intervention consisted of a time-delay procedure followed by graduated prompts similar to those used by Light and her colleagues. The comments consisted of phrases such as "This is fun," "Sounds good," "Yuck!" and "I didn't like it." Experimenters provided instruction in the context of a regular communication group that occurred daily in the students' classroom. All three students learned to produce the comments appropriately using a range of electronic communication aids, and two students generalized this ability to novel contexts.

What do you think?

Nonverbal feedback consists of eye gazes, facial expressions, head movements, and body postures that are used to provide listener feedback. Light et al. (1998) investigated the impact of nonverbal feedback on perceptions of the communicative competence of AAC users. They suggested that the use of videotaped interactions for scoring may have affected the results, in that it was difficult to capture the subtleties of nonverbal feedback on videotape. They found only weak evidence of the positive effects of nonverbal feedback on the perceptions of AAC professionals as well as adults and adolescents without AAC experience. *What do you think?*

FACILITATED COMMUNICATION

Sharisa Kochmeister is a person with autism who at one time had a measured IQ score somewhere between 10 and 15 (Biklen, 1996; Kliewer & Biklen, 1996). She does not speak. When she first began using facilitated communication (FC) several years ago to type on a keyboard, she required an FC facilitator to hold her hand or arm as she hunted for letters on a keyboard. No one thought she could read, write, or spell. She can now type independently (i.e., with no physical support) on a computer or typewriter. Sharisa addressed the 1994 conference of The Association for Persons with Severe Handicaps by typing, with a facilitator sitting nearby for emotional support. When asked what has made the biggest difference in her life now that she can type independently, Sharisa responded, OTHER PEOPLE KNOWING I'M SMART AND SELF-CONTROL AND ESTEEM (Kliewer & Biklen, 1996).

Sharisa joins a small group of people around the world who began communicating through FC and are now able to type either independently or with minimal, hand-on-shoulder support. There can be no doubt that, for them, FC "worked," in that it opened the door to communication for the first time. In addition, hundreds (or even thousands) of individuals use FC with physical support. To many observers, it does not seem clear whether or not these individuals are authoring their own messages. Thus, FC has become controversial and hotly contested as a valid and reliable technique (e.g., Green & Shane, 1994). We include FC here because of Sharisa Kochmeister, Lucy Blackman, Larry Bissonnette, and others who now communicate fluently and independently, thanks to FC. For them, the controversy has ended.

What Is Facilitated Communication?

Crossley (1988, 1990, 1991) first used FC in 1977 with Anne McDonald, a young woman with cerebral palsy, who was diagnosed as having profound disabilities and was institutionalized in Australia. The story of Anne's progress with FC and her eventual release from the institution was described in detail in *Annie's Coming Out*, which she and Crossley wrote (Crossley & McDonald, 1984). Crossley used the approach subsequently with individuals at the Dignity, Education, and Language (DEAL) Communication

Center in Melbourne, Australia, many of whom were diagnosed as having autism. The approach was introduced to a North American audience with the publication of a paper by Douglas Biklen, a professor of special education at Syracuse University, who spent several months in Australia observing Crossley's work and interacting with 27 facilitated communicators who had autism (Biklen, 1990). Biklen and his colleagues have implemented the approach in his community with children and adults with autism and has reported impressive results (Biklen, 1993; Biklen & Cardinal, 1997).

FC assumes communicative competence rather than impairment. FC facilitators are encouraged to expect that their communication partners with autism will produce meaningful, even complex, communicative messages with the proper supports. The technique involves the use of a keyboard communication device of some type (e.g., a Canon Communicator, a small portable typewriter). The FC facilitator physically supports the individual's forearm; wrist; and, if necessary, index finger. The individual is introduced to the keyboard device gradually and is initially physically prompted to touch the correct letter keys in response to simple questions (e.g., "Where is the letter *m*?" "Show me which letter 'dog' starts with"). The FC facilitator provides errorless teaching, including positive verbal feedback for correct responses, so that the person experiences successful interactions. Gradually, the FC facilitator asks the individual to type more complex responses, such as his or her name, simple questions, or fill-in-the-blank statements. Eventually, the individual is encouraged to initiate typing communicative messages and to carry on conversations with facilitation. Gradually, prompts and other supports are faded, although the FC facilitator may provide physical arm, wrist, and hand support as long as the individual indicates a need for it.

What Is the Controversy?

The central controversy has to do with the issue of authorship: Who is typing the messages, the FC user or the facilitator? Multiple experimental studies have been unable to confirm authorship by the FC user when experimenters controlled facilitator knowledge (e.g., when the FC user and facilitator were shown different pictures and the FC user was asked to type what he or she saw). In addition, multiple studies provide unequivocal documentation of instances in which facilitators have controlled the communicative content of messages, presumably without intending to do so. A few experimental studies, however, have provided preliminary evidence of communicative competence by FC users, although the degree of experimental control across these studies has varied widely (e.g., Cardinal, Hanson, & Wakeham, 1996; Sheehan & Matuozzi, 1996; Weiss, Wagner, & Bauman, 1996). In response to the predominant evidence against the validity of FC, numerous professional organizations in the United States have issued position statements urging members of their professions to consider FC an experimental intervention at best.

Where Does This Leave Us?

Overall, the "FC debate" leaves FC proponents in North America more cautious than they were after Biklen's 1990 article yet still determined to fight for the right of people with communication impairments to try FC and to continue to use it if their communication with the technique is validated. FC critics have been largely silent since the mid-1990s, perhaps because the preponderance of the evidence appears to support their position that FC is not a valid technique. Indeed, the use of FC in North America appears to have decreased markedly since the mid-1990s, and the intense media attention it once warranted has also faded.

Where all of this leaves AAC users is the more critical issue. Clearly, some individuals, such as Sharisa Kochmeister, eventually become independent typists through FC and find it to be a useful technique. However, we do not believe that FC works for everyone or even with *most* people. We believe that FC facilitators must obtain informed consent from the individual and his or her family, which includes making them aware of all of the potential problems associated with FC and the lack of empirical support available. We believe that FC facilitators and AAC experts who promote FC should obtain signed release forms from the individual and his or her legal representatives before instituting the intervention. FC facilitators must receive appropriate training about all aspects of the technique, including validation techniques and the importance of using them. FC facilitators must also address seating, positioning, and other support issues (e.g., assuming competence, providing emotional support, exerting backward resistance to the hand or arm during typing) on an ongoing basis, in order to give the technique a fair test. Critical decisions about legal, financial, and health matters, as well as those pertaining to residential, vocational, and educational placements, should not be made on the basis of FC messages unless multiple sources of evidence confirm that the individual constructed the messages without influence. Finally, interventionists should conduct regular, systematic attempts to verify messages produced through FC, starting from the beginning of intervention.

I HAVE A VOICE NOW—THEY WILL NOT RETURN ME TO PRISON. THEY WOULD NOT DO THIS TO HELEN KELLER AND SURVIVE UNSCATHED. THEY WILL NOT DO IT TO US, EITHER. IT'S OUR TURN NOW. (Typed independently by Sharisa Kochmeister, age 15, at a press conference in response to a television show criticizing FC, 1994)

12

Language Learning and Development

Test your knowledge of AAC history! When was this written?

"In general, there is a pervasive tendency to teach communication in stilted, stimulus-response paradigms (e.g., the practice of teaching comprehension of symbols in tasks that are low in communication saliency: 'Find pants,' 'Find shoes') as opposed to teaching augmentative and alternative communication (AAC) use in contexts that allow students to see symbols being used repeatedly, interactively, and generatively, during a meaningful ongoing activity."

Did you guess that this was written sometime in the 1980s? That would be a good guess because a number of authors have noted that during the 1980s researchers began to raise concerns about the highly structured, artificial nature of most "language training programs," including those that incorporated the use of symbols (Bricker, 1993; Glennen & DeCoste, 1997; Linfoot, 1994; Zangari, Lloyd, & Vicker, 1994). If you guessed the 1980s, however, you are wrong! The quote actually appeared in Goossens', Crain, and Elder's 1992 discussion of several issues related to augmentative and alternative communication (AAC) system training (p. 14). It is sad (as well as somewhat frustrating) to be reminded that, in many places, AAC techniques are still taught through the use of instructional strategies that are unlikely to result in spontaneous or generalized language use.

Although there is general consensus, at least within the AAC research community, about what *doesn't* work when it comes to language learning and development, it is still not very clear what *does* work, especially for children with developmental disabilities who use AAC. While we were writing the first edition of this book in the early 1990s, we talked about including a chapter on this topic and decided against it for one very simple reason: There wasn't enough to say! Since that time, numerous research studies and papers examining various aspects of AAC language learning and development have appeared in the journal *Augmentative and Alternative Communication*, as well as in other professional journals, books, and conference proceedings. Although there is still much for us to learn, in this chapter we describe and summarize the current knowledge of AAC language learning and development and implications for clinical practice, especially with regard to children and adolescents who use AAC.

WHAT WE KNOW ABOUT LANGUAGE DEVELOPMENT IN AAC USERS

Language is what allows us to talk, read, write, understand what others say, and learn about the world. When we have language, we can combine symbols in unique ways and describe our perceptions, thoughts, and experiences using spoken or written phrases and sentences. Regardless of the cultural, cognitive, social, and other factors that influence language development, all languages are composed of six domains: speech acts, pragmatics, phonology, semantics, morphology, and syntax. Summaries of current knowledge about AAC users' capabilities in each of these domains are provided in the sections that follow.

Speech Acts

Speech acts are communicative functions accomplished through language. Speech acts include structures that represent communicative functions such as *ritualizing* (e.g., greetings, introductions), *informing* (e.g., questions, answers, denials), *controlling* (e.g., requests for assistance, requests for permission to do something), and *feeling* (e.g., apologizing, bragging) (Sutton, 1989). The term *speech act* is actually quite misleading in that many of these functions appear in children without disabilities in the form of nonverbal communication long before speech is present. Numerous studies around the world have indicated that the range and general pattern of speech acts (i.e., communicative functions) produced by many AAC users tend to be restricted, regardless of the observational context (e.g., Basil, 1992; Calculator & Luchko, 1983; Kraat, 1985; Light et al., 1985b; Sutton, 1989; Udwin & Yule, 1991a; von Tetzchner & Martinsen, 1992). These studies have shown that, in general, AAC users tend to occupy a respondent role in their interactions with others; they seldom initiate conversations, respond primarily when obliged to do so, and produce utterances that are only as long as they need to be to get a message across.

Pragmatics

Related to speech acts is the domain of pragmatics, which describes the rules for using language contextually for social purposes such as conversation. For example, one of the pragmatic rules for conversations in North American culture is that when two strangers greet each other (a speech act), they do not typically kiss or hug. It is not unusual to find reports that AAC users have impaired pragmatic skills, especially in conversational interactions, which researchers have studied the most (e.g., Light et al., 1985a; O'Keefe & Dattilo, 1992).

Phonology

Phonology refers to the rules of the sounds of language. A person with phonological awareness can "manipulate the sounds of spoken language with or without alphabet knowledge" (Blischak, 1994, p. 246). So, for example, such a person could hear the difference between /pa/ and either /po/ or /ba/. Phonological awareness for individuals with little or no speech relates primarily to learning to read, spell, and write. Although much is known about the development of phonological awareness in speaking children (e.g., Bishop, Rankin, & Mirenda, 1994; Blischak, 1994), researchers have conducted few studies in this area for individuals with severe speech impairments. Exceptions include the work of Bishop and her colleagues in the United Kingdom, who investigated the abilities of youth with severe speech and physical impairments (e.g., cerebral palsy) on a variety of phonological awareness and phoneme discrimination tasks that did not require speech. They found that although the youth analyzed and manipulated phonologic information successfully (Bishop & Robson, 1989a, 1989b), they scored well below control participants on research tasks, regardless of whether other language problems were present (Bishop, Byers Brown, & Robson, 1990). This and other research (e.g., Dahlgren Sandberg & Hjelmquist, 1996) clearly reveal that at least some potential AAC users are at risk for delays in the area of phonology, in the absence of intervention.

Michael B. Williams talked to fellow AAC users about the importance of language learning in his Words+ lecture at the 1996 International Society for Augmentative and Alternative Communication conference:

> I fear some of you out there view your sessions with your speech language pathologist the way I used to view my sessions with speech therapists: They (the sessions) are just a bunch of hard work with little or no payoff. So let me ask you something: Have you got anything better to do? Listen to me: There is nothing more important for you to be doing right now than to learn how to express your thoughts and feelings to other people. I know how painful it is when people stare at you and think you are somebody other than who you really are because of how you look on the outside. Believe me, this won't change unless you have some way to tell people who you are on the inside. (M. Williams, 1996, p. 8)

Semantics

Semantics refers to understanding words and how they relate to one another. For example, a school-age child with intact semantic knowledge would know that the words *pin*, *pan*, and *pen* each refer to a different object and could discriminate among them. In Chapter 2, we discuss semantic development in terms of "messaging" or vocabulary development for AAC users. As summarized by Van Tatenhove (1996), a substantial body of research suggests that young AAC users often experience delays in this area because

- They cannot select their own lexicon (i.e., the corpus of words from which a word can be chosen) for their AAC displays but must depend instead on adults to do so for them (Beukelman, Jones, & Rowan, 1989; Nelson, 1992).
- Their external lexicon (i.e., the words on the communication display) may not reflect their internal lexicon (i.e., the words in their head) (Smith, 1996; van Balkom & Welle Donker-Gimbrère, 1996).
- As they select words from their communication displays, they do not receive symbol feedback from their partners, particularly if they overextend words (e.g., if they use the symbol COW to refer to a dog, they might be told the correct word verbally ["No, that's not a cow, that's a dog"] but they are unlikely to be shown the correct symbol on their display, even if it is there) (von Tetzchner & Martinsen, 1992).

An assumption underlying these concerns is that young AAC users learn new words through processes that are quite similar to those used by children without disabilities. If this is the case, the challenge for AAC teams in building semantic knowledge is primarily one of providing individuals with sufficient access to new vocabulary via some type of symbol system and then providing ongoing input to build semantic knowledge via this system. However, this is true only if AAC users are able to "fast map"—that is, learn new words with minimal exposure (Carey & Bartlett, 1978). Dollaghan (1987) has demonstrated that most children without disabilities as young as 12–15 months of age are able to learn new words after as little as one exposure. Most children with Down syndrome who can speak are also able to do this at a level commensurate with age-matched and language-matched children (Chapman, Kay-Raining Bird, & Schwartz, 1990). This accounts partially for the rapid growth in vocabulary size of young children; by one estimate, they learn an average of nine new words each day and know at least 14,000 words by the time they are 6 years old (Carey, 1978)! Clearly, the ability to fast map would greatly enhance the semantic learning process of young AAC users as well.

Can AAC users fast map? If so, how can AAC teams best facilitate this process? Two studies provide some answers. The first is from Romski, Sevcik, and colleagues on the System for Augmented Language (SAL) project at Georgia State University (Romski, Sevcik, Robinson, Mervis, & Bertrand, 1995). The study involved 12 young men with little or no functional speech and mental retardation requiring limited to extensive support. Each participant received four exposure trials in one sitting to each of four novel objects labeled with both nonsense words and lexigrams on a voice-output communication device. After four exposures, researchers tested the participants' ability to both comprehend and produce the lexigrams immediately as well as 1 day and 15 days later. Seven of the participants fast mapped the symbol meanings and retained their comprehension of some of the words for up to 15 days. Furthermore, they also generalized their knowledge from comprehension to production. Four of the five participants who did not fast map had historical symbol achievement patterns characterized by slower symbol acquisition and less generalization than those who did fast map. Thus, it appears in this case that at least some AAC users are able to fast map, despite moderate to severe cognitive impairments.

Fast mapping is one behavioral demonstration of the *novel name–nameless category principle* (N3C) that guides children's learning of words. The N3C principle states that "when a child hears a novel word in the presence of an unknown object, he or she will immediately map the novel name onto the novel entity" (Romski et al., 1995, p. 391). Interested readers can refer to Crais (1992) for a comprehensive discussion of N3C as it relates to fast mapping.

The second study provides some information about how AAC teams may best promote fast mapping. Hunt-Berg (1996) identified 22 AAC users between the ages of 3 and 10 years who were able to comprehend at least two different graphic symbols (all of the children in the study used either Picture Communication Symbols [PCS] or Oakland Schools Pictures). The experimenter presented the children with unfamiliar toys that were labeled with unfamiliar spoken words and graphic symbols. In Condition A, the children could see the toy but the experimenter pointed only to the symbol while providing the verbal label (e.g., saying "Look, it's a *toma*"), whereas in Condition B experimenters added an explicit pointing cue to visually link the toy to the graphic symbol (e.g., saying "Look, it's a *gazzer*" while pointing to the gazzer). The children received nine exposures in each condition, which is more than sufficient for fast mapping to occur (Crais, 1992; Romski et al., 1995). Results indicated that the AAC users in Hunt-Berg's study were able to fast map novel spoken words under both conditions but fast mapped only the graphic symbol meanings under Condition B (verbal labeling and pointing from the graphic symbol to the toy). None of the following were related to learning: the time the children spent looking at graphic symbols in response to pointing, the size of their receptive vocabularies, and their experience with graphic symbols. The results suggest that AAC teams can best facilitate fast mapping of new graphic symbols by AAC users with teaching strategies that make symbol–referent connections visually explicit through pointing or another technique that maintains joint attention. (It is interesting to note that this was part of the procedure in the Romski et al., 1995, study cited previously.) Fast mapping is discussed later in this chapter as it pertains to aided language stimulation and related techniques for language learning.

The problems experienced by AAC users in both comprehension and use of grammatical morphemes and syntactic structures challenge Pinker's suggestion that "as far as grammar learning goes, the child must be a naturalist, passively observing the speech of others, rather than an experimentalist, manipulating stimuli and recording the results." (1994, p. 281)

Morphology

The rules for building and changing words are referred to as *morphology*. For example, knowing that *pin* refers to one object and *pins* refers to more than one object or that *walk* describes a current action whereas *walked* describes a past action indicates an individual's morphological awareness. Researchers have conducted few studies to examine the ways in which AAC users either learn or develop morphological awareness, but most studies have demonstrated AAC users' marked difficulties with grammatical morphology (e.g., Berninger & Gans, 1986b; Kelford Smith, Thurston, Light, Parnes, & O'Keefe, 1989; Sutton & Gallagher, 1993). A 1996 study by Blockberger is particularly illustrative in this regard. She assessed the mastery of three grammatical morphemes (possessive -'s, third personal singular -s, and past tense -ed) in 20 AAC users from 5 to 17 years of age whose Peabody Picture Vocabulary Test–Revised (Dunn & Dunn, 1981) scores were matched with 40 typically developing 4- to 7-year-olds (10 children for each age). She found that participants without disabilities of all ages scored significantly higher on comprehension and grammar judgment tasks than the AAC users. The eight AAC users in the study who were literate were much less able to use the target morphemes in a structured output task than were the participants without disabilities. Subsequently, Blockberger (1997) reported that the AAC users in her study also performed significantly poorer on all three tasks than did a matched cohort of peers with language delays who could speak.

It is not clear why people who use AAC regularly experience problems with morphology, but at least five explanations are possible:

1. The symbols the AAC user needs to indicate (e.g., plural or past tense) are not available on his or her communication display (Blockberger & Johnston, 1997).
2. The AAC user chooses efficiency over accuracy as a strategy for enhancing the speed of communication (Light, 1989a).
3. The AAC user has not yet learned the morphological rules that apply to the situation (Sutton & Gallagher, 1993).
4. People who learn language late in life experience difficulty in this area because of a lack of practice and early feedback.
5. The AAC modality itself influences output and precludes the need for conventional English morphemes (Smith, 1996).

Smith (1996) provided an example of the latter possibility by referring to the PCS symbol for *sit*, which is a line drawing of a person sitting on a chair. When asked to symbolize the sentence "The girl is sitting on the chair," one of Smith's research participants pointed to SIT, rather than combining the PCS symbols GIRL, SIT, ON, and CHAIR. In fact, her participant was correct—the form of the PCS symbol for *sit* itself precluded the need for constructing the utterance word for word in this instance. It is likely that similar occurrences contribute to difficulties with grammatical morphology, but research to examine this issue is in its infancy.

An American movie titled *Field of Dreams* was about a man building a baseball field in his cornfield. A voice told him, "If you build it, they will come." The same voice is speaking for people using augmentative and alternative communication. It says, "If you build language, effective and independent communication will come." (Van Tatenhove, 1996)

Syntax

The term *syntax* refers to the rules for putting words into sentences; for example, if a person understands English syntax, then he or she would know that "I like this cake" is preferable to "Like I this cake," even though listeners might comprehend both. We actually know quite a bit about the syntactic difficulties of individuals who communicate with graphic symbols. Soto (1996) summarized the most commonly reported expressive syntactic characteristics identified in the literature:

• A predominance of one- or two-word messages, both in spontaneous and elicited conditions (e.g., Basil, 1992; Basil & Soro-Camats, 1996; Smith, 1996; Udwin & Yule, 1990; van Balkom & Welle Donker-Gimbrère, 1996; von Tetzchner & Martinsen, 1992)
• Difficulty with both receptive (Roth & Cassatt-James, 1989) and expressive word order tasks. For example, in message construction, AAC users often use unusual word orders, such as subject-object-verb order (e.g., GIRL + HOUSE + GO), verb-subject-object order (GO + GIRL + HOUSE), or even object-verb-subject order (HOUSE + GO + GIRL) in languages in which subject-verb-object order (GIRL + GO + HOUSE) is typical (e.g., Sutton & Morford, 1995; van Balkom & Welle Donker-Gimbrère, 1996). Even advanced AAC users often have word-order difficulty with compound sentences

(e.g., TWO + BED + SLEEP + BOY + ONE + GIRL + WHITE + BED + BROWN + BED for "The boy and the girl are sleeping in two beds, one in a white bed and the other in a brown bed") (van Balkom & Welle Donker-Gimbrère, 1996).

- The use of syntactic structures not commonly used in the individual's language (Soto & Toro-Zambrana, 1995)
- Omission of words that appear frequently in the individual's language, such as verbs and articles, even when these are available on the communication display (Soto & Toro-Zambrana, 1995; van Balkom & Welle Donker-Gimbrère, 1996)
- A prevalence of simple clauses, with limited use of complex structures such as questions, commands, negatives, and auxiliary verbs (Soto & Toro-Zambrana, 1995; van Balkom & Welle Donker-Gimbrère, 1996)
- Extensive use of multimodal combinations (e.g., gesture + symbol, vocalization + symbol), word overextensions (e.g., *dog* instead of *cow*), and other linguistic strategies that compensate for a lack of necessary symbols (Light et al., 1985c; Sutton, 1989)

In summary, we can make several statements about language learning and development in AAC users. First, many AAC users show evidence of both receptive and expressive language impairments. Second, although this may not be obvious from the above, some AAC users do not show evidence of both impairments. (See Sutton, 1996, for an excellent review of the opposing evidence.) Many individuals who have never been able to use natural speech have written and spoken eloquently about their experiences and their lives using AAC—clearly, such individuals have mastered the intricacies of language and are now able to pass their knowledge on to others (e.g., Joyce, 1993; Marshall, 1994; M. Williams, 1996)! Third, and perhaps most important, the language difficulties experienced by many AAC users are undoubtedly influenced by the fact that their language-learning experiences are so very different from those of individuals who can speak. Nelson so eloquently noted,

> How can [we] assess what words and structures a young child knows if the only words and structures available [to] the child . . . have been provided by someone else? How can [we] know whether a preliterate child might actually have a variety of words in mind to express a concept or communicate a feeling, but cannot because the words are inaccessible for expression? . . . How can [we] know if a child can generate multiword utterances if the child's computer is preprogrammed with frequently used phrases? (1992, p. 4)

How, indeed? Clearly, strategies specifically aimed at language development need to be an integral part of every communication intervention. In the section that follows, we describe some of the most commonly used and/or promising methods for language development.

Over the years, . . . (Adam) has added some of the structure, rules, and intricacies of language. He added these in the same way he adds to his vocabulary: when he wants and needs them to communicate, when he's given the words with which to do them, and when it isn't too much trouble to use them! Come to think of it, that's just about the way my daughter developed her language, and she doesn't use AAC. The only difference between the kids was that my daughter didn't have to wait for someone to give her a way to express those words. (The mother of Adam, a 9-year-old boy who uses a variety of AAC techniques, in Gregory & McNaughton, 1993, p. 22)

INTERVENTIONS TO SUPPORT
LANGUAGE LEARNING AND DEVELOPMENT

> The fact that we know very little about the development of language in young children with severe speech and physical impairments who require AAC is not surprising. At this point in time, we have many more questions than answers. . . . If we think of our knowledge in this area as a tootsie roll pop, we have barely taken the first lick. The chocolate goodie in the center is still a long way off. (Bedrosian, 1997, p. 179)

Graphic Symbols and Language

One of the most passionate debates in AAC revolves around the advantages and disadvantages of specific symbol systems or encoding techniques in terms of language development. In particular, this debate has focused over time on three approaches: Blissymbolics, semantic compaction (i.e., Minspeak), and manual signing. Despite the heat of the debate, researchers have done little to answer the central question, which can be summarized in the following way: "Do certain graphic symbol approaches facilitate language development (or certain aspects thereof) more than others?" We summarize the issues surrounding the debate in the sections that follow.

Blissymbolics

Proponents of Blissymbolics have stated for many years that the use of this pseudolinguistic system allows users to learn about the rules of morphology, syntax, and message construction (Soto, 1996). The "Why Bliss?" page on the World Wide Web site for Blissymbolics Communication International (http://home.istar.ca:80/~bci/index. htm/) describes this advantage as follows:

> Blissymbolics is a language with a wide vocabulary, a grammar that allows for sentences in past, future and present tenses, and markers for possession, plurality, questions and commands. There are many strategies within the system of Blissymbolics which enable the user to create new symbols. It is a totally generative system with each new symbol interpretable by the receiver through analyzing the component parts. In the same way that letters represent sounds that are used to create words in print, meaning-based Bliss units are sequenced to define the meaning of each compound symbol. Because there are a limited number of elements (called key symbols), the learner need only master the meaning of approximately 100 elements.

There is no question that many individuals who learned to use Blissymbols as children have developed into adults who are excellent users of their native language (for examples, see Soto & Toro-Zambrana, 1995, and any issue of *Communicating Together*). However, there is also ample evidence that this is not a universal outcome, and some researchers have challenged the rationales typically provided to support the use of Blissymbols (e.g., Besio & Chinato, 1996). In the absence of studies comparing, for example, the outcomes for long-term Bliss users with those of long-term users of other systems, it is impossible to know whether Blissymbolics does, indeed, facilitate language development better than other systems. In the interim, it seems that, at least theoretically, Blissymbolics offers some advantages over less linguistically oriented systems.

For those children who must rely primarily on graphic symbols for their vocabulary, the challenge is representing *all* the needed concepts in ways that are understood, memorable, and generative. Given these requirements, I believe the kind of system is important! (McNaughton, 1993b, p. 23)

Semantic Compaction (Minspeak)

Considerable debate has also focused on semantic compaction, or Minspeak, as a technique to support language. The debate has centered on two main questions: 1) Is Minspeak a language? and 2) Does Minspeak promote language development? In a series of articles from 1992 and 1993 on these two topics, both proponents and critics of Minspeak appeared to agree on the answer to the first question (Deegan, 1993; Jennische, 1993; McNaughton & Jennische, 1992; Nyberg, 1993):

- Minspeak *is not* a language. It does not have an established rule system, set of icons, or set of meanings associated with particular icons.
- Minspeak *is* an iconic encoding technique whereby "symbols are organized so that they can be joined together to access a vocabulary with a minimum of keystrokes" (Nyberg, 1993, p. 21). A variety of symbols, including Minsymbols, Blissymbols, PCS symbols, and written words (among others) have been and can be used within Minspeak. The rules for assigning meanings to the symbols and for organizing them in sequences are flexible and can be individualized.

The answer to the second question, "Does Minspeak promote language development?" is more complex. Some researchers have argued that Minspeak does promote language development because of the similarities among semantic compaction, language learning, and literacy learning and use. In this view, both literate adults and semantic compaction users learn a certain set of words and icon sequences and then apply knowledge of that set to decode and spell new words and select new icon sequences (Erickson & Baker, 1996). Thus, semantic compaction, language, and literacy all share the characteristic of being generative in nature. Others argue that the question is not a fair one because *no* symbol or encoding system itself promotes (or impedes) language development—it all depends on how it is taught and used! Nyberg noted that Minspeak (like all messaging approaches) should be provided within a "comprehensive . . . teaching paradigm that is not only accessible to the child, but also helps to enrich the development of his or her cognitive skills and interactive capabilities" (1993, p. 20). Finally, skeptics of semantic compaction have questioned its use entirely, especially for individuals who have not achieved a strong language base and for whom early language concepts are still developing (e.g., Jennische, 1993). Such critics question both the theoretical underpinnings of the technique and the practical implications of spending many hours teaching an individual to encode messages in a way that is quite different from the way spoken and written language is encoded. The bottom line, though, is that the jury is still out on the impact of Minspeak on language development of AAC users.

Case study evidence in support of semantic compaction as a technique that supports language development can be found in any of the eleven volumes of the *Proceedings of the Annual Minspeak Conference* in the United States, as well as in the proceedings of similar annual conferences held in France, Germany, Spain, and the United Kingdom. Contact Semantic Compaction Systems for ordering information.

Manual Signing

One of the clearest potential advantages of manual sign systems, whether in the form of a national sign language such as American Sign Language (ASL) or a manually coded language such as Signed English, is that they are linguistic in nature. In North America, most AAC users who are not deaf learn Signed English because it follows the word order and grammar of the spoken language. Language studies in AAC have focused to date on the use of signing more than any other symbol system, and two things seem clear: 1) Individuals with a range of disabilities are often able to acquire extensive manual sign vocabularies in the course of intervention (e.g., Kouri, 1989; Weller & Mahoney, 1983); and 2) manual sign learning often stalls at the one-word stage of development, especially when individuals with cognitive disabilities use it (Karlan et al., 1982; Romski & Ruder, 1984). The latter occurs even though manual sign systems seem particularly suited to teaching multiword utterances as well as the principles of syntax and morphology because of their linguistic base (Fay & Schuler, 1980; Kiernan, 1983). Some researchers have suggested that this is more a function of how manual sign systems are typically taught in school and residential settings than of the systems themselves, and considerable evidence supports this position (e.g., Bryen, Goldman, & Quinlisk-Gill, 1988; Bryen & McGinley, 1991; Udwin & Yule, 1991b). Nonetheless, despite some clear theoretical advantages in favor of manual signing as a technique for language learning, the research suggests that there may be no *real* advantage to using this symbol system rather than others for AAC users who can hear.

The problem here is not with the kind of AAC symbol system used. Any symbol system can have the missing words added to the vocabulary. The problem is with having to use AAC. (Gregory & McNaughton, 1993, p. 21)

In summary, the issues raised by proponents of each of these symbol systems are both thoughtful and cogent. Unfortunately, aside from numerous published case studies, little empirical evidence is available to either refute or support any of the positions mentioned. Thus, perhaps the best advice for now is to find ways to create links between *whichever* system the developing child uses for face-to-face communication and *whichever* system he or she uses for language and literacy instruction so that he or she is not faced with the daunting task of learning completely separate systems for each of these domains (Pierce, Steelman, Koppenhaver, & Yoder, 1993).

Instructional Strategies and Language Learning

Because it is not clear that one symbol system has clear advantages over others for language learning (wouldn't that have been easy?!), we turn now to instruction for solutions. By *instruction* we mean methods for organizing and teaching the use of symbols, in this case, to encourage language development. It is important to note that there is not one best way to do this, and little research exists in this area, overall. Thus, the strategies we summarize in this section are drawn from current state-of-the-art of practice, as well as (in some cases) the research base of the field.

Organizational Strategies

When an individual uses graphic symbols of any kind for AAC, the symbols must be organized in ways that promote maximally efficient and effective communication. This is particularly crucial when an individual has a large number of symbols in his or her system. Several organizational strategies are commonly used, some of which have the potential to encourage language learning.

Environment or Activity Displays

Many AAC users begin using pictorial or other graphic symbol displays that are organized for different environments or activities. These can function as overlays on electronic devices or as stand-alone, low-tech communication aids (see Musselwhite & St. Louis, 1988, for examples). Each display contains vocabulary items that are specific to an environment (e.g., a fast-food restaurant) or an activity (e.g., washing the dishes). Activity displays allow individuals to participate in both special events and regular activities by ensuring that a rich variety of needed vocabulary items are available. In so doing, the displays also provide vehicles for promoting language development and more complex expressive output (e.g., multiword combinations). Some evidence suggests that, from a purely developmental perspective, this strategy is most likely to encourage early language use (Blockberger, 1995).

Mirenda (1985) described a variety of strategies for designing and organizing low-tech activity displays in order to facilitate their usefulness. For example, AAC teams can place divider tabs in communication books to separate activity sections and facilitate easy access or can provide core displays with supplemental border overlays for people who use lap-tray aids (Goossens' & Crain, 1986a). Such strategies are important in order to provide a wide selection of vocabulary items while allowing the AAC user to find a desired display quickly. In addition, Burkhart (1994) provided principles for designing the pages of electronic devices with dynamic displays. She suggested that activity-based vocabulary organization is preferable to categorical organization because the latter adds to the cognitive demands of the task for the AAC user who might not think in categories.

Participation is enhanced when multiple activity displays are available, perhaps in addition to a generic communication board or overlay that is used routinely. Several authors have discussed the construction of activity displays for children who use eye gazing, rotary scanners, communication books, dynamic display devices, and other display formats (Burkhart, 1994; Goossens', 1989; Goossens' & Crain, 1986a; Goossens' et al., 1992; Musselwhite & St. Louis, 1988). Low-tech activity displays can be mounted in specific locations, such as on the wall (e.g., in each room of the home at the child's height), on aquatic flotation devices (e.g., kickboards, inner tubes), or on the dashboard of the car. Activity displays can also be designed for use by individuals across the age range in community, school, and vocational settings (Elder & Goossens', 1994). The advantage of using this organizational strategy is that facilitators can construct new displays relatively quickly using only the vocabulary items appropriate to the activity or event. Low-tech displays for special events can be constructed and stored until the next occasion for their use (e.g., next Christmas, the next time Grandma visits). This strategy enhances the probability that specialized vocabulary items for specific contexts will be available when they are needed.

In addition to enhancing participation, activity displays also can promote the use of multiword linguistic structures and build a strong receptive language base. Unfortunately, many AAC users do not have access to vocabulary items that they can combine flexibly; instead, they have boards that contain only symbols that represent their "wants and needs," such as basic objects, people, places, and food items, plus a few verbs such as *eat, drink,* and the inevitable *go bathroom.* Thus, it is not surprising that their language development and use patterns often lag behind those of their peers who do not use AAC. Facilitators can provide relevant vocabulary items from a variety of semantic categories for specific activities with multiple low-tech activity displays. Figure 12.1 shows an example of such a display for playing the game Space Explorer.

Also, the *natural branching* capabilities of dynamic display devices can be used to promote sentence construction within specific activities. Burkhart (1994) suggested that, at first, partial sentence starters (e.g., *see, can't see*) should appear on the first page with a natural branch to a second page after any selection (see Figure 12.2a). Page 2 should have vocabulary items that might naturally come next as options (e.g., *big, quiet, good*), as

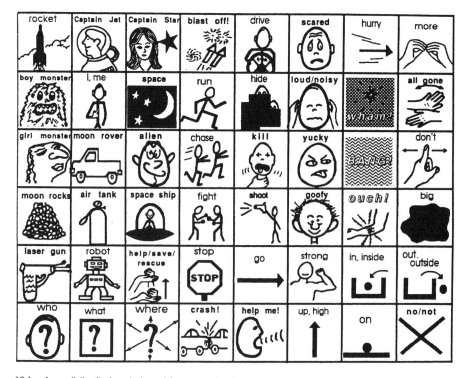

Figure 12.1. An activity display designed for a preschool-age child to encourage language development. (Picture Communication Symbols copyright © 1994 by Mayer-Johnson Co.; reprinted by permission. Some symbols have been adapted.)

depicted in Figure 12.2b. When an individual selects one of the second options, the display would naturally branch to a third page (see Figure 12.2c) with final-position words or phrases (e.g., animals, vehicles, people).

Grammatical Categories

Facilitators usually opt to use a grammatical category strategy for the explicit purpose of encouraging the AAC user to learn language by mapping the symbols according to spoken word order and/or usage. This strategy involves organizing vocabulary items by grammatical function (Brandenberg & Vanderheiden, 1988). A commonly used grammatical category strategy is the Fitzgerald key or some modification thereof (McDonald & Schultz, 1973). The original form of the Fitzgerald key organizes symbols from left to right into categories such as *who, doing, modifiers, what, where, when,* and so forth, with frequently used phrases and letters clustered along the top or bottom of the display. The order was intended to facilitate word-by-word sentence construction from left to right. Bruno (1989) described the design of a Minspeak display for a young child using a modified Fitzgerald key that involved a left-to-right clustering of symbols for people (nouns and pronouns), verbs, adjectives, prepositions, object nouns, time words, and place words. Goossens', Crain, and Elder (1994) standardized their published activity displays using a modified Fitzgerald key with the following categories: miscellaneous words (e.g., social words, *wh-* words, exclamations, negative words, pronouns), verbs, descriptors, prepositions, and nouns. Burkhart (1994) also recommended that activity displays with a consistent grammatical organization across displays be used to organize vocabulary for dynamic display devices. Regardless of the categorization strategy used, symbols in the grammatical categories are usually color-coded to allow easier visual access.

Semantic Categories

A third organizational strategy involves grouping symbols according to superordinate semantic categories such as *people, locations,* and *activities.* Garrett, Beukelman, and Low-Morrow (1989) used this scheme to develop an AAC system for an older man with aphasia because he had retained substantial semantic knowledge despite a severe expressive language impairment. Mirenda, Malette, and McGregor (1994) described a similarly organized system for an adolescent with cognitive disabilities in which symbols were placed on pages (i.e., categories) for snack foods, lunch foods, transportation, after-school activities, weekend activities, personal care activities, friends, and family members. Of course, facilitators can use this strategy in combination with the activity-board concept and even as a subcategorization scheme within a grammatically organized system. Although this might be a more practical strategy for individuals who can relate to semantic categories, it is less likely (at least theoretically) to facilitate language learning because of its nonlinguistic nature.

Other Categorical Arrangements

Some individuals may have skills that facilitate the use of unique categorical arrangements. For example, we know of a man who, after his stroke, retained his ability to map information according to its geographical and spatial location. His communication system consists of a series of pictorial maps with which he guides his listener to desired topics. He might start out by pointing to a map of Nebraska to locate his hometown of Hastings. He then uses a Hastings map to identify his street name and then a street map to locate his house. A house map guides the listener into the kitchen, and a kitchen

Figure 12.2.   Dynamic displays for sentence construction. a) Partial sentence starters on page 1 of display, b) descriptors on page 2, c) final-position words on page 3. (Boardmaker and Picture Communication Symbols copyright © 1994 by Mayer-Johnson Co.)

map takes the listener to the refrigerator where he locates the word *orange juice* to tell his wife what he wants for breakfast! Although communicating with this strategy takes time, it is the only categorical system that he can use easily and accurately. Similarly, another man, who could categorize alphabetically after his stroke, communicated with the Yellow Pages before a formal AAC intervention was instituted! For example, when he wanted to talk about his car, he flipped to the "Automobile Dealers" section, and when he wanted to eat a particular food, he opened the "Restaurant" section and found an establishment that served the type of food he desired! Although unusual, such unique organizational strategies may be the preferred way to support language learning and use for some individuals.

Teaching Strategies

In order to use symbols effectively, AAC users must learn both their meanings, alone and in combination (receptive language), and how to produce them in communicative contexts (expressive language). Some instructional approaches treat receptive and expressive language as separate instructional entities, whereas others take a more holistic perspective. In the sections that follow, we describe the primary approaches related to teaching one-word labeling skills (i.e., semantics) and more complex language skills (i.e., morphology and syntax), along with the empirical evidence that relates to their effectiveness. In Chapter 13, we deal with instructional approaches related to literacy (including phonological skills). Readers may refer to Chapter 11 for information about teaching functional speech acts such as requesting and rejecting, along with a range of conversational skills that are related to communicative competence.

Structured Approaches

In the beginning of this chapter, we introduced criticism of highly structured language training approaches that endeavor to teach language forms absent their function or that teach new vocabulary words solely as labels rather than in communicative contexts. Such techniques are characterized by repeated, discrete trials delivered within a facilitator-directed drill-and-practice format, usually conducted one to one or in a small group. For example, a facilitator might present a learner with a symbol of a shoe and a cookie and ask him or her to touch the cookie or to produce a particular manual sign in response to a verbal cue (e.g., "show me EAT"). When the individual produces the target response, the facilitator may or may not provide reinforcement related to the target language form (Goodman & Remington, 1993). Often, the facilitator delivers several such trials in quick succession. This approach is grounded in the traditions of both experimental (e.g., Remington & Clark, 1993a, 1993b) and applied behavior analysis (e.g., Reichle, York, & Sigafoos, 1991).

It is important to acknowledge that the field of AAC has benefited greatly from experimental work on language learning within a behaviorist framework. The early work of Premack with graphic symbols and chimps (1970); the more recent work of Rumbaugh (1977) and Savage-Rumbaugh (1984) with Yerkish lexigrams; and the contributions of researcher-practitioners such as Carr et al. (1994), Durand (1990), and others in the area of functional communication training for challenging behavior exemplify this point. In addition, it is important to note that the use of a facilitator-directed structured approach is not in and of itself problematic, especially when applied in natural contexts to teach functional communication skills (see Remington, 1994). In fact, some individuals may require a large number of trials to learn a basic core of signs or symbols (e.g., Hodges & Schwethelm, 1984; Romski, Sevcik, & Pate, 1988). If this is the case, physical prompting or guidance techniques may be more efficient than less intrusive modeling procedures (Iacono & Parsons, 1986). Also, when an individual frequently communicates manual signs or symbols inaccurately, a structured approach may be preferable. If the individual requires corrective feedback on a regular basis during communication interactions, he or she may come to view communication as a negative experience. In such situations, the facilitator may use some structured teaching sessions to build a repertoire of accurate sign or symbol productions and may restrict corrections of inaccuracies to these times only. Carr and Kologinsky (1983) recommended such a "two-pronged approach" for teaching manual signs, with highly structured discrete-trial techniques to teach language forms and incidental instructional paradigms to teach the use of the forms. Similarly, Reichle, Sigafoos, and their colleagues have recommended and used a complementary blend of more and less structured techniques to teach a variety of pragmatic functions (e.g., requesting, rejecting, commenting) using manual signs or pictorial symbols (e.g., Reichle & Brown, 1986; Reichle, Rogers, & Barrett, 1984; Reichle, Sigafoos, & Piché, 1989; Sigafoos & Couzens, 1995; Sigafoos & Reichle, 1992). Indeed, most of the strategies for teaching choice making, requesting, rejecting, and conversational skills that we describe in Chapter 11 incorporate some structure to teach the target skills in a systematic fashion. In short, although highly artificial "language training programs" are clearly limited in the extent to which they result in generative language learning, structured, functional instruction in natural environments can teach basic semantic and pragmatic language forms.

Children learn language in dyads involving people with whom they have meaningful relationships. (Wetherby, 1989, p. 25)

Facilitator-directed, structured approaches have also been used to teach morphemic and syntactic language forms using AAC techniques (particularly, manual signs), with some success (e.g., Karlan et al., 1982; Remington, Watson, & Light, 1990; Romski & Ruder, 1984). For example, Iacono, Mirenda, and Beukelman (1993) used a structured discourse strategy to compare the use of speech plus unimodal (manual signs) versus multimodal (manual signs + a voice-output communication aid with PCS symbols) AAC interventions. The participants were two preschool children, and the target language forms included possessor + object possessed (e.g., *girl's napkin*), attribute + entity (e.g., *big banana*), action + object (e.g., *ride horse*), and entity + location (e.g., *ice cream* in *cup*). Intervention involved four specific steps to elicit the target structure using modeling, expansion, and verbal prompting with one or both AAC modalities plus speech. Both participants showed increases in their spontaneous production of two-word utterances, and one demonstrated more production in the multimodal condition. However, the authors noted that the facilitator-directed, structured contexts that were used to elicit the language forms might have contributed to the limited generalization evidenced in an unstructured play context. The problem with generalization is one of the major disadvantages of structured approaches to language intervention (Carr, 1982). From this study, it appears that at least some AAC users may require structured interventions to learn certain language forms, although additional research is needed to clarify the way in which this approach affects generalization across untrained examples of the form and across novel communicative contexts.

Milieu Teaching

Milieu teaching is a naturalistic strategy for teaching functional language skills (Kaiser, Yoder, & Keetz, 1992). Milieu teaching appears to be more effective than structured approaches in promoting early vocabulary learning and abstract symbol learning, although additional research is needed in this area (Yoder, Kaiser, & Alpert, 1991). Readers may refer to Chapter 11 for details about the teaching techniques that are subsumed under this rubric, including incidental teaching (Warren & Kaiser, 1986), mand-model procedures (Halle, 1982), and time delay (Halle, Marshall, & Spradlin, 1979). Kaiser et al. (1992) described the basic features of milieu teaching as follows:

- Teaching occurs following the child's lead or interest.
- Multiple, naturally occurring examples are used to teach simple, elaborated language forms.
- Child production of language is explicitly prompted.
- Consequences for child responding include those associated with the specific linguistic form and those that are natural to the context in which teaching occurs.
- To varying extents, the teaching episode is embedded in ongoing interactions between the instructor and the student.

Does milieu teaching promote language development when used in educational settings? Kaiser et al. (1992) conducted a comprehensive analysis of milieu teaching studies that involved, in total, 134 children and adolescents *who were able to speak.* The children included preschoolers from low socioeconomic backgrounds, preschoolers who were at risk, preschoolers with language delays, children with mild to severe cognitive disabilities, and children with autism. Kaiser (1993) and Kaiser et al. (1992) reported that

- Milieu teaching appears to be most effective with children at the early stages of language development who have limited speech and who are learning vocabulary or early semantic relationships.
- In the studies reviewed, milieu teaching consistently produced positive changes in the children's use of language in conversational settings in which the procedures were implemented.
- A range of language responses, including single words, adjectives, multiword phrases, compound sentences, and both specific and general requests in both vocal and nonvocal modes, have been taught through milieu teaching.
- There is limited evidence that milieu teaching positively affects children's global language development past the early stages.
- A great deal of variability exists in the research literature about the extent to which learned skills are generalized to novel encounters and contexts.
- The effectiveness of milieu teaching is largely a function of the fidelity, intensity, and duration of milieu teaching procedures. In other words, the better the teaching, the more positive the outcomes are likely to be!

In 1994, Kaiser and her colleagues reported the effects of what they called "enhanced milieu teaching" on language intervention with young children who have developmental delays (Hemmeter & Kaiser, 1994; Kaiser & Hester, 1994). This approach combines the principles of the Interactive Model (Tannock & Girolametto, 1992; see discussion later in this chapter), which emphasizes environmental arrangements and responsive interaction strategies to promote communication and milieu teaching. The results suggest that such a combined approach effectively overcomes the limited generalization reported in many milieu teaching studies and also promotes language development and use.

In general, other research reports on milieu teaching interventions with AAC users agree with the previous summary. Most reports of successful AAC interventions using milieu teaching have been confined to individuals at the early stages of language development who are learning functional, one-word communication skills (see examples in Chapter 11). Few reports have documented the efficacy of milieu teaching to develop more complex language with AAC techniques. In one such study, Iacono and Duncum (1995) applied milieu teaching principles within a child-directed play routine to compare the efficacy of speech plus either unimodal (manual sign) or multimodal (manual sign and DynaVox with DynaSyms) AAC techniques. They endeavored to elicit spontaneous words or word combinations from a preschooler with Down syndrome by using one or both AAC techniques. They found that the multimodal strategy was more successful in this regard, but milieu teaching procedures were also effective to a lesser degree in the unimodal condition. In addition, the participant, who produced only four different, spontaneous, single words during baseline testing, produced 31 different words, including 10 two-word and 2 three-word combinations, during and following intervention. This study suggests that milieu teaching can effectively promote language learning and use in individuals who use AAC techniques, but additional research is needed in this regard.

Interactive Model

Interventionists have established numerous parent training programs based on an interactive model over the years (e.g., the Hanen Early Language Parent Program, Manolson, 1985; Ecological Communication Organization, MacDonald, 1989). (See Chapter 10 for details about the underlying principles of these programs.) In a review of the empirical evidence related to outcomes, Tannock and Girolametto (1992) noted that there is evidence that, at least in the short term, parents trained within the Interactive Model learn to be more in tune with their child's abilities, more responsive to the child's focus and communicative attempts, and less controlling of the child's behavior and conversational topics. However, this review also concluded that both the short- and long-term treatment effects of standard Interactive Model interventions are usually restricted to increased use of existing competencies and do not include acquisition of new communication and/or language skills. The addition of focused stimulation techniques within the Interactive Model since the mid-1990s appears to hold more promise. Such techniques include 1) modeling specific target words frequently during a variety of activities; 2) selecting additional words for modeling, once the child acquires initial target words; and 3) modeling two-word combinations (e.g., agent and action, action and object) (Girolametto, Steig, Pearce, & Weitzman, 1996). The addition of focused stimulation techniques appears to result in greater child effects, including increased vocabulary, use of multiword phrases, and increased grammatical complexity (Girolametto et al., 1996). This is similar to the results of enhanced milieu teaching, which also incorporates responsiveness and more structured intervention techniques, as described previously (Hemmeter & Kaiser, 1994; Kaiser & Hester, 1994).

The focus of Interactive Model programs to date has been on young children with language delays who can speak. However, the results cited previously agree with those from a study in which the Hanen Parent Language Training Program (Manolson, 1985) was used to train the teacher of Faye, a 5-year-old girl who used gestures, speech, and manual signs to communicate (Lowe, 1995). After her facilitator employed the standard child-directed techniques from the Hanen program, Faye initiated more interactive turns and used more spoken words, gestures, and manual signs. It appeared, however, that many of the communicative forms were already in Faye's repertoire prior to training, and the Hanen training primarily changed the facilitator's behavior to allow Faye more opportunities to use the forms interactively. Nonetheless, it appears that Interactive Model programs, which are widely used in North America, can be applied successfully to at least increase communication opportunities for beginning AAC users. These programs are probably best considered to be one component of a multielement intervention strategy.

If a facilitator with competent communication skills cannot effectively communicate by using (a communication display), then we cannot reasonably expect the augmented speaker to develop communication competency with that (display). (Elder & Goossens', 1994, p. 164)

Aided Language Stimulation and the System for Augmenting Language (SAL)

Aided language stimulation (Elder & Goossens', 1994; Goossens' & Crain, 1986a; Goossens' et al., 1992) and SAL (Romski & Sevcik, 1992, 1993, 1996) were both designed specifically for AAC applications and are based on milieu teaching with several additional elements. They are both total-immersion approaches to teaching individuals to understand and use graphic symbols. Their purpose is to provide learners with models for combining symbols in a flexible manner and opportunities to do so. They are based on the premise that by observing graphic symbols being used extensively by others in natural interactions, "the [learner] can begin to establish a mental template of how symbols can be combined and recombined generatively to mediate communication during the activity" (Goossens' et al., 1995, p. 101). Because both techniques mimic the way natural speakers learn to comprehend language, they are intended to teach the AAC learner to use language in a very natural way that eliminates the need for more structured training interventions.

In aided language stimulation, a facilitator "highlights symbols on the user's communication display as he or she interacts and communicates verbally with the user" (Goossens' et al., 1992, p. 101). In this way, it is similar to the "total communication" approach used to teach manual signs to individuals with hearing or other impairments (Karlan, 1990). For example, the facilitator might say, "It's time to put the cookie mix in the bowl," while pointing to the symbols PUT, COOKIE, IN, and BOWL on an eye-gaze vest or board, electronic device, miniboard, or other type of display. Obviously, in order for this type of communication to occur, displays must be accessible to the facilitator, who should ensure in advance that they contain the necessary key vocabulary items for each activity in the learner's day. The facilitator should also provide numerous opportunities for interaction in the context of natural routines and activities. Table 12.1 details the steps of selecting vocabulary for aided language stimulation displays. See Figures 12.3 and 12.4 for examples of aided language communication displays that could be used in a preschool setting and a community setting, respectively.

Integral to aided language stimulation are a variety of unique instructional techniques that are used both to augment input (i.e., receptively) and to encourage the use

Table 12.1.   Aided language stimulation vocabulary selection

Example: Doll play

1. *Choose* an augmentative modality that incorporates pictorial symbols: This could be eye gaze, a communication board, or a voice-output device, for example.
2. *Delineate* a variety of doll play activity themes (e.g., cooking, doctor, kitchen, baby care).
3. *Delineate* subthemes associated with the activities (e.g., baby care—changing diapers, mealtime, dressing/undressing, grooming, bedtime).
4. *Select* vocabulary to reflect the interactions that can occur within each subtheme (e.g., baby care—changing diapers: stinky, wet, dry, change, pin, cry, no way, yucky, put on, take off, baby, mommy, wipe, bottom, powder, diaper, finished).
5. *Include* vocabulary commonly used across subthemes (e.g., more, yes, no, help).
6. *Develop* pictorial symbol displays for each subtheme, and post in the relevant activity area for easy access (e.g., in the doll play area of the classroom).
7. *Use* the pictorial symbols during interactions with the child, much as key word manual signing would be used. Encourage and support the child in attempts to use the symbols as one component of a multimodal communication system that might include speech/vocalizations or gestures, for example.

Adapted from Goossens' (1989) and Goossens' and Crain (1986a, 1986b).

of the communication display. The facilitator augments input by pointing to or highlighting symbols while he or she is talking, as described previously. Goossens' et al. (1992) noted that facilitators can accomplish this in several ways: 1) index finger pointing, 2) index finger pointing with a small squeaker concealed in the palm of the hand to

Figure 12.3.   Aided language stimulation display for a young child to use during a sand play activity. (From Goossens', C., Crain, S., & Elder, P. (1994). *Communication displays for engineered preschool environments: Books 1 and 2* (p. 128). Solana Beach, CA: Mayer-Johnson Co.; reprinted by permission.)

draw attention to the display, 3) pointing to each symbol with a small flashlight or squeeze light (this is called *shadow light cuing* in descriptions of aided language stimulation), and 4) using a "helping doll" with an elongated pointer (e.g., a small dowel) taped to one hand of the doll. Regardless of the technique used, the aim is to provide speech and symbol input during activities, in much the same way total communication is used to combine speech and manual signs.

Aided language stimulation also incorporates a variety of techniques for eliciting communication using symbols and other AAC modes. *Nonverbal juncture cues* are "nonverbal signals (achieved via facial expression, gesture, body posture) performed by the facilitator that precede the highlighting of a symbol on the communication display" (Goossens' et al., 1992, p. 111). The cues serve two functions: They code the target symbol in nonverbal form, and they help the individual to anticipate symbol selection by providing a brief time delay during which the individual might jump ahead of the facilitator and select the symbol spontaneously. For example, the facilitator might blow a bubble during a bubble game and then point to it in an exaggerated manner with wide eyes before pointing to the symbol BIG. Related to these are a series of *verbal and light cues* that are used to encourage use of the symbols. These are delivered in a least-to-most prompt hierarchy, as illustrated in the following script.

Figure 12.4. Aided language stimulation display for an adolescent or adult to use in a fast-food restaurant. (From Elder, P., & Goossens', C. (1996). *Communication overlays for engineering training environments: Overlays for adolescents and adults who are moderately/severely developmentally delayed* (p. 195). Solana Beach, CA: Mayer-Johnson Co.; reprinted by permission.)

Martha (M) is the facilitator, and George (G) is an adolescent with cerebral palsy who uses an eye-gaze display. They are baking cookies together. Martha points to each capitalized symbol on George's display while talking.

M: Let's get the COOKIE MIX and the BOWL. I'll put the COOKIE MIX IN the BOWL. [uses a *sabotage routine* by putting the box in the bowl without opening it, thus providing a *contextual cue* to elicit George's use of the symbol OPEN]

G: [laughs but does not eye gaze to OPEN]

M: Uh-oh! I guess I did something wrong here! I wonder what the problem is? [pauses for 5 seconds to give George time to look at the OPEN symbol *(indirect verbal cue)*]

G: [vocalizes agreement that something is wrong but does not look at the symbol]

M: [uses a *search light cue* by scanning her small flashlight across all the symbols on George's display, and then pauses for another 5 seconds]

G: [watches but does not respond]

M: I forgot to do something with the cookie mix box. [*direct verbal cue* and 5-second pause]

G: [still does not look at the OPEN symbol]

M: [provides a *momentary light cue* by flashing her light directly on the OPEN symbol for 2–3 seconds]

G: [still does not respond]

M: [provides a *constant or flashing light cue* by shining her light directly on the OPEN symbol until George looks at it to select it]

G: [looks at the OPEN symbol]

M: Oh! Right! I need to OPEN the COOKIE MIX before I PUT it IN the BOWL! Thank you, George! [opens box]

Of course, the prompt hierarchy would only be used in the above interaction up to the point at which George looks at the target symbol. The hierarchy used in this example is really an adaptation of the hierarchy used in traditional milieu teaching (especially incidental teaching; see Chapter 11).

Because aided language stimulation requires that, as much as possible, communication displays be available for each activity in the child's school and/or home setting, this intervention can be very labor intensive. The Mayer-Johnson Co., however, offers books of communication displays for 100 activities in preschool classrooms (e.g., snacktime, bubble play, Mr. Potato Head) (Goossens', Crain, & Elder, 1994) and 63 activities for adolescents and adults in community settings (Elder & Goossens', 1996).

The SAL approach is quite similar to aided language stimulation, with two notable exceptions: The use of an electronic voice-output communication device is considered a critical component of the intervention (Romski & Sevcik, 1992, 1993, 1996), and SAL techniques are much simpler than the elaborate procedures for augmented input and elicitation used in aided language stimulation. In SAL, communication displays using graphic symbols with a printed word gloss are constructed for the learner's voice-output device, and communication partners learn to activate symbols on the device to augment their speech input in naturally occurring communication interactions. Partners encourage but do not require learners to use the device throughout the day. Because SAL, like aided language stimulation, relies heavily on partners' cooperation and use of the technique on an ongoing basis, a variety of strategies are also included in SAL to ensure that partners' perceptions and experiences with the technique remain positive.

Do aided language stimulation and/or SAL work to promote language development in AAC users across the range of age and ability? Aside from numerous case studies and anecdotal reports of the effectiveness of interventions that incorporated aided language stimulation (e.g., Basil & Soro-Camats, 1996; Goossens', 1989; Heine, Wilkerson, & Kennedy, 1996; Lowe, 1995), no empirical evidence addresses this question. Fortunately, that is not the case for SAL. Romski and Sevcik (1992) conducted a 2-year longitudinal study of SAL and its outcomes with 13 students with mental retardation requiring limited or extensive support and severe expressive communication impairments who lived in Clayton County, Georgia. All of the students were in primary or secondary school classrooms, had 10-word or smaller spoken vocabularies, and were ambulatory. Experimenters provided each of them with portable voice-output communication devices in integrated home and school settings. Words were represented on devices with abstract lexigrams accompanied by their printed English equivalents. Facilitators learned to operate the devices and to use them in accordance with the basic principles of SAL, as described previously. For example, a teacher might say, "Johnny, let's go outside and play," while pointing to the symbols OUTSIDE and PLAY on his device. Thus, Johnny would see the teacher model the use of the symbols OUTSIDE and PLAY at the same time that he hears both the teacher and the voice-output device say the words. Aside from this, "communicative use of the device was not taught in the traditional sense. . . . Loosely structured naturalistic communicative experiences were provided to encourage, but not require, the children to use symbols when natural communicative opportunities arose" (Romski & Sevcik, 1992, p. 119).

The results of the SAL project are quite impressive. All of the students learned to use lexigraphic symbols in combination with gestures and vocalizations to request items, assistance, and information; to make comments; and to answer questions, among other functions (Romski & Sevcik, 1996). In addition, meaningful and functional symbol combinations *spontaneously emerged* in the repertoires of 10 of the 13 participants (Wilkinson, Romski, & Sevcik, 1994). These included, for example, symbol combinations for verb + noun (e.g., WANT + JUICE) as well as those for descriptor + noun (e.g., HOT DOG + GOOD, MORE + BASEBALL) and noun + social regulator (e.g., JUICE + PLEASE). In addition, the participants learned to recognize, at minimum, 60% of the printed words displayed on their communication devices, even though they received no direct instruction related to either symbol- or referent-word associations. Another important outcome was a general increase in the quantity and quality of the participants' intelligible spoken word productions. Finally, and perhaps most important, all of the participants showed evidence of generalized use of their communication devices with both familiar and unfamiliar adults as well as with peers without disabilities in a variety of environments.

The SAL project clearly demonstrates that a naturalistic, total-immersion approach can effectively facilitate communication and language skills in AAC users. Romski and Sevcik have extended their work to apply SAL techniques to toddlers (Romski, Sevcik,

& Cress, 1996) and continue to implement SAL with school-age youth with mental retardation requiring limited to extensive supports through Project FACTT (Facilitating Augmentative Communication Through Technology). Because of the many similarities between SAL and aided language stimulation, the outcome data for SAL are likely to have some application to aided language stimulation interventions.

Because language learning and development issues for AAC users are so critically important, additional research on aided language stimulation, SAL, and similar approaches is sorely needed to identify the critical factors that contribute to their success. For example, the extent to which the voice-output component of SAL contributes to successful intervention is not clear (Romski & Sevcik, 1993). In addition, the research on fast mapping as a strategy for learning new words has implications for both aided language stimulation and SAL (see the section on semantics earlier in this chapter). Hunt-Berg's (1996) research suggested that simply pointing to a graphic symbol while speaking the word may *not* be sufficient for AAC users to fast map the graphic symbol. For this process to occur, it appears that facilitators need to explicitly point from the symbol to its referent. Of course, Hunt-Berg's research only investigated fast mapping for nouns, not for verbs, adjectives, or other grammatical structures with which referential pointing would be more difficult. Additional research is needed to clarify how facilitators can best promote fast mapping through approaches such as aided language stimulation and SAL.

13

Literacy Development of AAC Users

with Janet Sturm

Literacy is used as an umbrella term, encompassing both reading and writing. (Koppenhaver & Yoder, 1993)

Reading is the process of constructing meaning from written texts. It is a complex skill requiring the coordination of interrelated sources of information. (Anderson, Hiebert, Scott, & Wilkinson, 1985, p. 6)

Writing is a holistic and authentic communication process that is generated through the meaningful construction of composed text. Writing is best understood as a set of distinctive thinking processes that writers orchestrate during the act of composing (Flower & Hayes, 1981). When composing, expert writers pay conscious attention to handwriting, spelling, punctuation, word choice, syntax, textual connections, purpose, organization, clarity, rhythm, euphony, and reader characteristics (Scardamalia, 1981). As writers develop, they pay increasing attention to this range of complicated processes.

Most individuals consider the ability to read, write, and spell to be a valued component of participation in society. These skills allow individuals to use literacy as a tool for communication, critical thinking, and the attainment of social and cultural power (Bishop, Rankin, & Mirenda, 1994). For AAC users with severe communication impairments, literacy skills at multiple levels facilitate successful participation in a variety of environments—home, work, school, and social settings. At a communicative level, literacy skills improve their ability to participate successfully in face-to-face interactions by providing them with access to language (Koppenhaver, Coleman, Kalman, & Yoder, 1991). Literacy skills for these individuals allow for more than conventional reading and writing by providing access to a means of self-expression in order to communicate thoughts and opinions and to foster personal independence (DeCoste, 1997b). Because of the range of potential communication devices, literacy skills provide augmentative and alternative communication (AAC) users with access to a greater number of AAC systems. Finally, literacy skills provide AAC users with access to a wide range of educational and vocational opportunities (Light & McNaughton, 1993). For individuals who use AAC systems, the development of reading and writing skills is a critical component for fostering communicative self-expression and independence.

Students who are unable to read and write successfully become increasingly disadvantaged as they progress though school. Individuals with severe speech and physical impairments (SSPIs) not only have motor impairments that limit their access to books and writing tools but may also have language and cognitive impairments that further complicate the literacy learning process. Limited research has described the literacy learning process and the elements of instructional strategies that are likely to help these students. It is clear, however, that professionals must consider individuals' needs, instructional strategies, educational adaptations, and assistive writing technology in order to make educational decisions that will provide individuals with SSPIs with both access to and opportunities for literacy development. In this chapter, we review literacy development from preschool through the school years and present special instructional and technical considerations for individuals with impairments that affect literacy.

WHO REQUIRES AAC SUPPORT FOR LITERACY?

The individuals who may require AAC support for literacy possess an array of strengths and weaknesses. They may have physical, fine motor, language, learning, cognitive, or visual impairments—or any combination of these simultaneously! When developing literacy programs for individuals who have multiple disabilities, it is important to address both their physical and sensory impairments as well as any learning, sensory, or cognitive impairments that they may also have by providing alternative access to literacy materials. In addition, assistive technology and/or assistive software often supports the literacy and language-learning needs of students whose primary impairments include learning disabilities, speech-language impairments, cognitive impairments, or visual impairments. In the following section, we describe the types of individuals and needs that should be considered when developing literacy curricula. Although the identified needs of the individuals we describe may differ in severity or occur as multiple problems, the primary principles of literacy instruction, which a later section of this chapter addresses, remain similar.

Primary Motor Impairments/
Severe Speech and Physical Impairments

A large number of individuals experience severe communication disabilities as a result of primary motor impairments that limit their ability to speak and write. This group includes individuals with congenital impairments such as cerebral palsy and arthrogryposis, as well as people with acquired impairments (e.g., spinal cord injuries). Typically, individuals with primary motor impairments do not experience significant primary cognitive or learning problems that contribute to their communication difficulties. At a minimum, they must receive appropriate alternative access to literacy curricula.

Most individuals with primary motor impairments are likely to have problems generating written communication at some point because their motor impairments make handwriting or even typing difficult. However, individuals with cerebral palsy who have insufficient speech for functional communication often also experience serious difficulties learning to read and write for a variety of other reasons.

A number of researchers have documented literacy learning difficulties experienced by many people with SSPIs, especially cerebral palsy. Approximately 50% of children in this group with measured IQ scores in the average range appear to demonstrate reading skills significantly below grade-level expectations (Berninger & Gans, 1986b; Koppenhaver & Yoder, 1992a). Even when they can read, these individuals often experience difficulties producing written communication into adolescence and adulthood. Analysis of the writing samples of young children with cerebral palsy consistently indicated incorrect usage of grammatical forms and errors in spelling performance (e.g., Kelford Smith, Thurston, Light, Parnes, & O'Keefe, 1989). Smith (1992) noted that many individual factors influence literacy learning for these individuals. These include

- Physical difficulties
- Limited world knowledge and vocabulary
- Language impairments
- Perceptual difficulties (e.g., visual, auditory)
- Discrepancies between reading achievement, receptive language, and IQ score
- Poor self-esteem
- Passive learning patterns

Individuals with SSPIs often learn to write slowly and with great difficulty. Typically, they experience an uneven profile of strengths and weaknesses that persists into adulthood. In an assessment of the reading skills of individuals with severe cerebral palsy, Berninger and Gans (1986b) reported that these individuals' reading scores were disproportionately low compared with their measured IQ scores and discourse-level receptive language abilities. For students with SSPIs, the greatest barrier to literacy learning may be limited access to formal instruction and lack of exposure to the general curriculum.

Handwriting/Fine Motor Impairments

It's not like I could read it and nobody else could, not even the creator could control it! (Ken, a 12-year-old boy with fine motor impairments, describing his illegible handwriting, personal communication, 1995)

Some students have fine motor control problems that inhibit the mechanics of producing words on paper. This difficulty with handwriting, often referred to as dysgraphia, may be related to underlying fine motor control or eye–hand coordination problems, visuospatial impairments, or attention deficits (Lerner, 1988). Although these students' difficulties producing legible handwriting and fluent text limits their writing effectiveness and enjoyment, their motor control impairments are not as severe as the ones that individuals with primary motor impairments experience. Students who struggle with handwriting often produce considerably shorter written products than their peers. Some just complain when they have reached their physical limits, whereas others simply stop writing (or refuse to write), regardless of whether they have completed their tasks.

Many students with fine motor impairments also experience learning disabilities, specific language impairments, and/or cognitive impairments. For example, in a study of 21 fourth-, fifth-, and sixth-grade students identified as having written language needs, 9 had information written in their individual education programs that was specifically related to the mechanics of handwriting (Sturm, Rankin, & Beukelman, 1994). Examples of the difficulties described for these students include the following:

- "Difficulty putting ideas on paper. Poor motor skills and letter formation"
- "Physical act of writing laborious and difficult"
- "Easily frustrated with writing assignments, has difficulty reading own work"
- "Extreme difficulty with handwriting (cannot be deciphered). Must be allowed to print"

It is interesting to note that these symptoms resemble those often experienced by writers with learning disabilities.

Individuals whose progress with handwriting instruction has not matched their writing needs or who write very slowly may benefit tremendously from using word processing programs controlled through standard keyboards or alternative access devices. As with individuals with primary motor impairments, educators and AAC teams can assist the development of these individuals' literacy skills by providing access to computers and minimizing the physical requirements for producing written products. It simply does not make sense to deprive children or adults of the enjoyment of writing because they have poor or illegible handwriting. Thus, educators and interventionists should address concerns about computers as supports for students with fine motor needs as early as prekindergarten. Unfortunately, many professionals are reluctant to allow access to computer support for young children in particular, possibly because they fear that the computer will become a permanent "crutch" and that handwriting will not develop as a result. As with all such decisions, this one need not be made on an either/or basis (see Chapter 8 for a related discussion). AAC teams may continue to address handwriting skills as part of these students' writing curricula; however, concurrent access to emergent literacy and basic word processing software for most writing tasks may also provide these students with a means to maintain academic performance. AAC teams should make decisions about how best to support young students with fine motor impairments in conjunction with teachers and educational support staff (to examine classroom writing requirements and evaluate the students' emergent literacy skills), an occupational therapist (to document the extent of fine motor needs and provide a prognosis for the development of functional handwriting), and a speech-language pathologist (to evaluate expressive and receptive language skills).

James made quite a scene during the open house prior to the beginning of his first-grade year. He refused to sign his name in the classroom guest book. When pressed by his parents, he sat on the floor and pouted. It soon became apparent to James's teacher that he experienced such severe fine motor control problems that he could not write or draw legibly. Although his reading comprehension scores were at the third-grade level, he refused to write or draw in class and would act out when pressed to do so. Within weeks, his performance began to lag behind that of his classmates.

Using a Macintosh computer with Kidsworks II software as a word processing and drawing program, James's teacher allowed him to complete his art and writing assignments using assistive technology. When the other students wrote by hand, he did so using the computer system. This eliminated his resistance to writing and drawing almost completely. To encourage the development of his handwriting skills, he received special instruction from the occupational therapist. In time, he agreed to hand write a first draft of his written work and produce final drafts with his computer.

Specific Language Impairment

Considerable attention has focused on describing a heterogeneous group of children who have considerable difficulty with spoken receptive and expressive language (e.g., Lahey, 1990; Leonard, 1991; McCauley & Demetras, 1990). The terms *specific language impairment, childhood aphasia, developmental aphasia, dysphasia,* and *language disability,* among others, have been used interchangeably to refer to the problems that children experience (Leonard, 1982). Specific language impairment is considered to be a primary, rather than a secondary, disorder in that it is not the result of mental retardation, autism, or other etiologies. Prevalence estimates for specific language impairment range from just above 3% (Leske, 1981) to 5.7% of preschool-age children (Stevenson & Richman, 1976). This figure declines to about 1% in the school-age population (Leske, 1981), probably because educators assign different labels, such as "learning" or "language-learning disabled," to children with specific language impairment who enter elementary school (Snyder, 1984).

Specific language impairment is considered to be an impairment in language expression, comprehension, or both, in the absence of apparent neurological damage or hearing impairment. Children with specific language impairment often demonstrate age-level performance on nonverbal tests or subtests of intelligence, even when their verbal scores are significantly below the norm (Leonard, 1991; Stark & Tallal, 1981). This does not mean, however, that the children's cognitive abilities are unaffected; in fact, areas such as symbolic functioning and cognitive processing are frequently impaired as well (Johnston, 1991a). Children with specific language impairment experience not only delays in language development but also long-standing language limitations, at least in the absence of remediation. Development of language is uneven, and specific language impairment typically affects the use of grammatical morphemes and function words more than other language subskills (Johnston, 1991b; Leonard, 1991). Some authors have described individuals with specific language impairment as "hearing but not understanding" (Bloom & Lahey, 1978, p. 510), referring to their relatively poor auditory processing skills, including difficulty with short-term auditory memory, temporal sequencing, and repetition of auditory patterns (Eisenson & Ingram, 1972). In his review of the specific language impairment research literature, Leonard (1982) noted that the symptoms experienced by this heterogeneous population can range from mild to severe and may encompass a wide range of communication difficulties that affect listening, speaking, reading, and writing. Thus, people with specific language impairment may also qualify for services under the category of learning disabilities, depending on the specific criteria used for identification in their locales. As individual needs are examined, it is important to remember that children with primary motor impairments may also have specific language impairment (or learning disabilities).

Learning Disabilities

My teacher's sole mission in life was to improve my spelling. I had to stay in the classroom during recess to write out, 50 times each, all the words I had misspelled. Because this had no noticeable effect on my spelling, she then had me write them out 100 times each. This took my entire lunch hour every day. I had to eat my sandwiches while writing. Eventually, I was writing the same misspelled words 500 times each. I had to use my free time at school because there wasn't enough time. (Russell Genet, an adult with dyslexia, recalling his fifth-grade experience in school, in Genet, 1995, p. 57)

Yesterday, our 7-year-old daughter was reading a book and asked her father to help her with a word. He grew red in the face, ran out of the room, and I found him crying. He admitted the truth. He can't read. He told me that he just can't recognize letters and words. (Letter sent to a reading problems clinic, in Lerner, 1988, p. 350)

As with other impairments discussed in this chapter, educators and AAC teams call learning disabilities by a variety of names, including *language-learning disabilities, dyslexia, minimal brain dysfunction,* and *specific reading disabilities,* among others (Wallach & Liebergott, 1984). The National Joint Committee on Learning Disabilities uses the following definition:

> Learning disabilities is a general term that refers to a heterogeneous group of disorders manifested by significant difficulties in the acquisition and use of listening, speaking, reading, writing, reasoning, or mathematical abilities. These disorders are intrinsic to the individual, presumed to be due to a central nervous system dysfunction, and may occur across the life span. Problems in self-regulatory behaviors, social perception, and social interaction may exist with learning disabilities but do not by themselves constitute a learning disability. Although learning disabilities may occur concomitantly with other handicapping conditions . . . or with extrinsic influences . . . they are not the result of those conditions or influences. (1991, p. 19)

Students who have learning disabilities have demonstrated a wide array of language problems including gaps in vocabulary as well as weak word, phrase, sentence, and discourse structures (Ehren, 1994). These language difficulties have a strong influence on children's success in school. Students with learning disabilities commonly demonstrate difficulty with several features of the writing process, including handwriting, the use of conventions, sentence structure, goal setting, content generation, organization and cohesion, and evaluation and revision of their writing (MacArthur, Schwartz, & Graham, 1991; Scott, 1989).

Cognitive Impairments

So is he ready for me to get out some books? (A response made by a skeptical mother of a 3-year-old child with moderate cognitive impairments who was told by the classroom teacher that her son really enjoyed looking at picture books)

Individuals with cognitive impairments (including mental retardation) are people whose intellectual abilities lag behind their same-age peers. The severity of cognitive impairment may vary widely across individuals and is usually established in terms of an individual's scores on both norm-referenced intelligence tests and adaptive behavior scales (Luckasson et al., 1992). (See Chapter 9 for a more complete description of this type of impairment.)

Because of these individuals' cognitive limitations, educators may not consider literacy learning as an educational goal. As a result, individuals with cognitive impairments are at risk of being held to reduced expectations and lacking exposure to literacy materials, both at home and at school. If educators believe that reading does not begin until individuals possess certain prerequisite skills, and if educators think of literacy as an "all or none" ability, they will not consider the potential for varying degrees of literacy learning by individuals with cognitive impairments. In truth, individuals with cognitive impairments can and should engage in the same emergent literacy activities as their peers without disabilities (e.g., listening repeatedly to stories, having access to writing tools). We cannot overemphasize the importance of intensive exposure to literacy materials in the early years.

When professionals make decisions about literacy instruction for individuals with cognitive impairments, they should consider not only the impairment itself but also any additional learning needs that might be present. For example, many individuals may experience difficulty understanding and expressing language, maintaining attention, and interpreting perceptual patterns. Thus, they may require additional scaffolding or educational adaptations to literacy materials to achieve success. Light and McNaughton (1993) emphasized the need for parents and teachers to understand their children's changing reading and writing skills, as well as to identify their children's strengths and needs, to set realistic goals, and to strive toward those goals on a continuous basis. With the appropriate instructional support, many individuals with cognitive impairments may experience the same rewards from literacy experiences (e.g., composing personal letters to a friend or relative) as their classmates without disabilities.

A full account of literacy development must consider not only the child's cognitive processes for acquiring literacy skills, but also the support systems provided by the family and social community for learning these skills. (Blackstone, 1989d, p. 1)

Visual Impairments

Estimates of the prevalence of school-age individuals with visual impairments of sufficient magnitude to interfere with the learning process range from 1 in 2,000 students (Scholl, 1986) to 2 in 1,000 (National Society to Prevent Blindness, 1980). It is important to note that the vast majority of these individuals are not totally blind. It is estimated that 80% of all individuals classified as legally blind have residual vision that is sufficient for use as a primary learning channel for reading, writing, and other school activities (Barraga, 1983).

The rate of visual impairment is much higher among people with multiple disabilities than in the general population (Brett, 1983; Schorr, 1983). Approximately 50%–60% of school-age individuals with visual impairments have additional impairments, with physical and/or cognitive disabilities occurring most often (Gates, 1985; Sacks & Silberman, 1998; Sadowsky, 1985). Approximately 46% of people with cerebral palsy have concurrent visual problems that may include eye muscle imbalances (e.g., strabismus), visual field cuts, visual-perceptual problems, and/or loss of visual acuity, any of which can significantly affect literacy learning (Batshaw, 1997). In addition, research has suggested that as many as 75%–90% of individuals with severe or profound cognitive disabilities also have visual impairments (Cress et al., 1981).

Given the high incidence of visual impairments in people with special needs, professionals should consider the degree and type of the individual's visual problem when providing access to reading and writing. Assessment of an individual's visual status involves specialized vision tests that evaluate a number of components including visual acuity, visual field magnitude, oculomotor functioning, light and color sensitivity, and visual stability (see Chapter 7 for more complete descriptions of these components). From a literacy perspective, it is important to use information about an individual's visual needs to determine the appropriate educational adaptations. Some adaptations may include 1) use of enlarged keyboards, print, and/or word processing text; 2) individualized location of the computer monitor; 3) attention to the visual glare on liquid crystal displays; and 4) use of braille as an alternative symbol set.

It is important to note that an individual may have one or multiple needs. Most children who have SSPIs have one or more disabilities and have special learning needs (Blackstone, 1989e). Literacy instruction for individuals who use AAC cannot focus solely on providing meaningful reading and writing opportunities. Instructors must also juggle factors such as the individual's need to repair message breakdowns; the challenge of including the individual in classroom interactions; and the selection of literacy tasks that are sensitive to vocabulary, time, and physical constraints (Koppenhaver & Yoder, 1993). In order to make the appropriate educational decisions for reading and writing support as well as other types of instruction, it is important to consider all of the individual's learning needs as part of a "package."

DEVELOPING LANGUAGE SKILLS: THE LANGUAGE AND LITERACY RELATIONSHIP

In order for individuals with augmented conversational systems to succeed in school, they must have a well-developed language knowledge and skill base by the time they enter the elementary grades. As we discuss in Chapter 12, these individuals must accomplish language learning (both incidental and formal) using AAC approaches. Thus, parents and preschool professionals must adapt AAC approaches to support the language-learning process. If children who use AAC are to be academically involved or competitive, it is essential that they master considerable language knowledge before entering the elementary grades.

> What the child who is least ready for systematic reading instruction needs most is ample experience with oral and printed language, and early opportunities to begin to write. (Anderson et al., 1985, p. 29)

Emergent Literacy and Literacy Development

What does it take for young children to learn to read? Fortunately, we have a considerable amount of information to answer this question, and we also know that, often, children with severe communication impairments lack exposure to key early literacy experiences.

Early Literacy Experiences of Typically Developing Children

The home environment plays an important role in laying the foundation for success in literacy. Literacy learning is thought by many to begin at birth, as writing, reading, speaking, and listening skills develop simultaneously (Adams, 1990). Thus, literacy learning is viewed as a continuous process that adults can support by providing literacy models and informal instruction. Many home activities provide the child with exposure to meaningful literacy experiences (Adams, 1990; Pierce & McWilliam, 1993):

- Actively reading stories aloud with a parent
- Engaging in multiple readings of favorite stories
- Examining and talking about printed media with encouragement from a parent
- Connecting ideas in a book with one's own experiences
- Playing with reading and writing materials in literacy-rich environments
- Watching adults use written materials (e.g., read newspapers)
- Enjoying books and talking about the content and structure of stories

A large part of becoming literate is learning the functions of literacy (Adams, 1990). By simply having exposure to favorite books, children learn a host of literacy concepts—story schema, plot structure, anticipation of events, memories from previous readings, and ways in which story language creates emotions such as surprise and humor (Clay, 1991). Through authentic literacy activities in their homes, children can also observe the ways in which adults use print. As adults read newspapers, magazines, books, and signs and as they write notes, grocery lists, checks, and letters, children are exposed to the functions of literacy. They learn that print occurs in a variety of forms, that it holds information, and that anyone can produce it (Adams, 1990).

The typical American child enjoys many hundreds of hours of storybook reading and several thousand hours of overall literacy support during her or his preschool years. (Adams, 1990, p. 336)

Early Literacy Experiences of Children with Severe Communication Impairments

Research suggests that substantial differences exist between the experiences of children who do and do not have disabilities in learning to read. One survey found that although parents of preschoolers without disabilities reported that they read to their children daily, parents of children with SSPIs read to their children, on average, two to three times per week (Light & Kelford Smith, 1993). Two thirds of the parents of children without disabilities reported that they typically asked their children to label pictures during story reading (e.g., "What's this?"), compared with only half of the parents of children with disabilities. Almost 80% of the parents of children with disabilities typically asked their children to point to pictures (e.g., "Where's the [object]?"), compared with only half of the parents of children without disabilities. The result was that the children with SSPIs received fewer opportunities to practice their expressive language skills, compared with their peers without disabilities. In addition, preschoolers with disabilities seemed to have much less access to writing and drawing materials than did preschoolers without disabilities (Light & Kelford Smith, 1993). Finally, parents of children with AAC systems focused their priorities on communication and on meeting the children's physical needs. In contrast, parents of typically developing children placed the highest priorities on communication, making friends, and literacy activities.

Martine Smith (1992) described two children with severe speech impairments due to cerebral palsy who had reading abilities within the typical range. She suggested that important factors contributing to their success in reading were relative strength in language competence, support for reading at home, physical independence, and motivation for reading.

Pierce and McWilliam (1993) summarized the factors that influence literacy development in children with severe communication impairments. These children often have difficulty manipulating and playing with literacy materials (e.g., selecting books, turning pages of books, playing with pencils and crayons) because of their motor impairments. Language and cognitive factors affect the development of play skills related to literacy (e.g., pretending to read), and parent modeling of literacy opportunities may be less frequent because the child is less mobile. Positioning and seating difficulties paired with visual impairments may make it difficult for these children to see illustrations while their parents or teachers read to them; this, in turn, influences the quality of the interactions during story reading activities. Overall, the nature and quality of interactions during literacy activities changes, as parents dominate to compensate for the children's inability to participate. The result is that the children are often unable to ask questions or make comments and, without access to adequate messages on an AAC system, are also restricted in their ability to respond to parent questions. Finally, the children may also be unable to provide their parents with feedback related to their level of understanding and their preferences.

The single most important activity for building the knowledge required for eventual success in reading is reading aloud to children. (Anderson et al., 1985, p. 23)

In an effort to identify factors that may contribute to the early development of literacy skills, Koppenhaver, Evans, and Yoder (1991) examined the early reading and writing experiences of 22 literate AAC users with cerebral palsy, ranging in age from 16 to 55 years. These individuals reported that when they were in school, they participated regularly in a variety of reading experiences that included 1) reading and listening to taped stories; 2) reading the same texts repeatedly; 3) reading texts to answer questions proposed by their teachers or in textbooks; 4) visiting classroom and school libraries; and 5) participating in independent, silent reading sessions. Many of them indicated that teachers gave them new vocabulary words before reading stories. Some individuals also noted that their teachers spent time reading aloud to them, and many emphasized the critical role of family members in facilitating their literacy learning. Two particularly important experiences included family members reading aloud to them while they viewed the text and family members providing them with opportunities for social interaction and attention by discussing the stories read. These literate AAC users recalled that they had access to a variety of different types of printed materials as children through visits to libraries and bookstores. They also had regular opportunities to choose their own reading materials and to observe others reading. The respondents suggested that the most significant factors contributing to their successful acquisition of literacy skills were the support and high expectations of their parents, in addition to their own talents and persistence. It is important to note that the early literacy experiences of these literate adults with SSPIs match the emergent literacy and literacy experiences of young children without disabilities. With a few adaptations, all classrooms can foster such experiences for children with SSPIs.

Many children with severe communication impairments also experience serious writing difficulties. Kelford Smith et al. (1989) analyzed written output produced in home environments by six adolescents and young adults with severe communication and congenital physical impairments. Although these individuals exhibited speech production impairments, utilized telegraphic output in their spoken communications, and had limited access to technology and literacy instruction until the later years of their educational programs, they all demonstrated basic levels of proficiency in producing and reading written text. The individuals and their caregivers suggested that several factors contributed to this acquisition of literacy skills, including 1) involvement in an integrated educational program at some point in their school careers, 2) access to computers for word processing, 3) the support of a specific teacher, and 4) previous use of Blissymbolics for face-to-face communication.

Reflecting on the positive literacy opportunities experienced by children with severe disabilities when integrated into general education classrooms, Erickson and Koppenhaver observed that children with disabilities were

> Participating members in a community of readers and writers. They are surrounded by models of literacy use and learning in an environment where teachers are held accountable for academic goals, where it is expected that children will learn to read and write. (1995, p. 683)

RELATIONSHIP BETWEEN LANGUAGE KNOWLEDGE AND LITERACY LEARNING

Because it is generally inappropriate to make assumptions about young children's future reading, writing, and spelling potentials, it is important to include literacy activities from a young age for all children. Although it is beyond the scope of this chapter to provide detailed strategies in this area, we present a summary of early childhood literacy approaches in this section.

Early Literacy Support

As described previously, communicative interactions centered around early literacy activities take on a variety of forms. Parents provide models, facilitate interactions, and guide children in their experiences with reading and writing materials. Research in the area of emergent literacy has shown that successful readers have had exposure to a wide array of literacy experiences in the home and arrive in school with a solid foundation for reading. In a review of research on children who learn to read before entering school, Ollila and Mayfield (1992) reported that these children's home environments have many books and offer easy access to printed materials and numerous writing materials for creating print.

A vast amount of literature describes the features of useful emergent literacy activities in the home (e.g., Adams, 1990; Anderson et al., 1985; Clay, 1991; Cunningham, 1995; Harris & Sipay, 1990; Harste, Burke, & Woodward, 1994; Ollila & Mayfield, 1992; Sulzby, 1994; Sulzby & Teale, 1991).Three main principles of child learning should guide activities: 1) activities should be *child directed* and *interactive,* with the parent following the child's lead; 2) parents should consider learning to be a *constructive process* in which the child participates actively and is supported to map previous knowledge onto new experiences; and 3) literacy tasks should be *meaningful, goal directed,* and embedded in *purposeful* activities. The following sections present reading and writing activities that utilize these emergent literacy principles and also provide illustrations of unique considerations for children who use AAC.

Reading and Storytelling

Blackstone (1989e) identified dozens of strategies that family members, teachers, and others can use to encourage the development of literacy skills. For example, parents and teachers should read age-appropriate stories aloud frequently and repeatedly because young children enjoy hearing the same story over and over. This repetitive reading helps children to see that all stories contain a predictable structure (pattern). This knowledge of story structure becomes important later in formal literacy instruction.

Children should be positioned on the lap of or next to the person who is reading so that they can see the pictures and words on a page. As children become familiar with a story, the reader can encourage them to indicate key pictures, fill in the blanks of a refrain vocally, or participate in other ways that help tell the story. Similarly, talking switches (e.g., the BIGmack) that activate single repetitive phrases (e.g., "I'll huff and I'll puff and blow your house down," "Brown bear, brown bear, what do you see?") can allow children who use microswitches to participate in storytelling. Once children are interested in this aspect of reading, it is important to indicate key words to them by pointing to the words or using other cuing techniques. Many children also enjoy learning the meaning of logos for places or activities, and many children learn to read the names of fast-food restaurants and cereals long before they enter kindergarten!

Another way to encourage a child's literacy development is through involvement in storytimes such as those sponsored by many libraries, as well as by visiting the library with the child to borrow books from an early age (Koppenhaver, Evans, & Yoder, 1991). Relatives and friends may need reminders to purchase books and other printed materials for young children with disabilities; otherwise they may forget that without such early stimulation, it will be difficult for children to develop a later interest in literacy. Seventy-one percent of the adult AAC users surveyed by Koppenhaver et al. (1991) reported that people read to them as children at least two to three times per week, and an even greater number reported receiving books as gifts for their personal libraries.

Musselwhite and King-DeBaun wrote a book entitled *Emerging Literacy Success: Merging Whole Language and Technology for Students with Disabilities* (1997) that is available from Creative Communicating in Utah. The book contains hundreds of illustrations and mini case examples to illustrate activities designed to support emerging literacy in students with disabilities of all ages.

In addition, AAC users need integrated communication and literacy activities that allow them to engage in active, meaningful interactions about texts. For example, one educational strategy for addressing literacy learning incorporates thematic curricula in which all activities center around a central topic that can also relate to literacy activities (e.g., the topic of bears with stories such as "Goldilocks and the Three Bears" and "Brown Bear, Brown Bear" [Martin, 1967]). Access to integrated literacy experiences requires creativity and planning on the part of the support staff and parents as they select relevant vocabulary words for discussing book content, making comments, predicting events, making inferences, and playing with the sounds of language. They will need to create communication boards to address book reading in general (see Figure 13.1) or to target specific books. Table 13.1 provides a list of resources that parents, educators, and support staff can use as guides for providing access to emergent literacy materials. Most of these resources also provide ideas for adapting curricular materials for AAC users in school environments.

Figure 13.1. General book reading overlays. (Courtesy of Caroline Musselwhite, 1997. Picture Communication Symbols copyright © 1994 by the Mayer-Johnson Co.)

Writing and Drawing

Children also need opportunities to learn writing, drawing, and other composition skills that involve the use of output tools. Many children, even those with severe physical disabilities, are highly motivated to try to manipulate crayons, paint brushes, and the other drawing and writing aids that they see their peers use, and they should have opportunities to do so whenever possible. Occupational therapists or other motor specialists may recommend adaptations to standard drawing or writing tools. Parents and professionals should encourage children to compose and produce drawn and written materials such as art projects (to be posted on the refrigerator at home or on school bulletin boards, of course!) and letters to Santa Claus so that they learn to enjoy artistic and written expression. Generally, it is not appropriate to emphasize that young children obey composition and spelling rules.

To relax and wait for "maturation" when it is experience that is lacking would appear to be deliberately depriving the child of opportunities to learn. (Clay, 1991, p. 22)

Table 13.1. Literacy resources for augmentative and alternative communication (AAC) users

Burkhart, L. (1993). *Total augmentative communication in the early childhood classroom.* Solana Beach, CA: Mayer-Johnson Co.

Goossens', C., Crain, S., & Elder, P. (1994). *Communication displays for engineered preschool environments: Books 1 and 2.* Solana Beach, CA: Mayer-Johnson Co.

Graham, T. (1982). *Let loose on Mother Goose: Activities to teach math, science, art, music, life skills, and language development.* Nashville, TN: Incentive Publications.

Kelly, J., & Friend, T. (1993). *Hands-on reading.* Solana Beach, CA: Mayer-Johnson Co.

Kelly, J., & Friend, T. (1995). *More hands-on reading.* Solana Beach, CA: Mayer-Johnson Co.

King-DeBaun, P. (1991). *Storytime: Stories, symbols, and emergent literacy activities for young, special needs children.* Park City, UT: Creative Communicating.

King-DeBaun, P. (1993). *Storytime just for fun: Stories, symbols, and emergent literacy activities for young, special needs children.* Park City, UT: Creative Communicating.

McNairn, P., & Shioleno, C. (1993). *Quick tech readable, repeatable stories and activities.* Wauconda, IL: Don Johnston, Inc.

McNairn, P., & Shioleno, C. (1995). *Quick tech magic: Music-based literacy activities.* Wauconda, IL: Don Johnston, Inc.

Musselwhite, C.R. (1993). *RAPS: Reading activities project for older students.* Phoenix, AZ: Southwest Human Development.

Raines, S.C., & Canady, R.J. (1989). *Story S-T-R-E-T-C-H-E-R-S: Activities to expand children's favorite books.* Beltsville, MD: Gryphon House.

Raines, S.C., & Canady, R.J. (1991). *More story S-T-R-E-T-C-H-E-R-S: Activities to expand children's favorite books.* Beltsville, MD: Gryphon House.

Simmons, T., & Young, C. (1994). *Tools for literacy and communication.* Solana Beach, CA: Mayer-Johnson Co.

Augmented Reading and Writing

For children with SSPIs, limited access to both reading and writing has acted as a great barrier to the development of literacy skills. While reading, these individuals have difficulty selecting books, turning pages, and reading aloud. While writing, many are unable to use a pencil to compose text.

Thanks to increased awareness of the potential of computer technology, access to emergent literacy software for children with SSPIs is greater than it has ever been. Because computer keyboards or other alternative access modes may eventually become primary vehicles for text composition in the primary grades, software programs should allow children with motor needs to develop mouse control skills and a basic understanding of computer operations (e.g., opening a file, saving, shutting down). If the child's goal is to develop mouse control skills, software games (e.g., Edmark Corporation's Early Learning Series) can serve as one portion of the child's literacy curriculum. If the child has not yet mastered mouse operations, he or she may operate many programs using a single switch, and many other programs can be set up for switch operation. Educators can use basic keyboarding programs to target children's early keyboarding skills (traditional or alternative access) as one part of an overall writing program. Talking software programs allow facilitators to enter books manually or with text scanning technology to allow AAC users to engage in independent story reading using a single switch.

A number of emergent literacy computer programs for young children are available to teach language and preliteracy skills to young children (see the Barkley AAC Center's World Wide Web site [http://aac.unl.edu] for descriptions of such programs). These programs provide AAC users with access to materials that foster critical reading skills (e.g., grapheme-phoneme awareness). Emergent reading software offers 1) opportunities to develop skills in visual discrimination, letter naming, letter recognition and recall, sight word recognition, spelling, and phonics (e.g., letter–sound combinations); 2) access to basic decoding and writing functions, such as sounding out words, inventing word spellings, and engaging in early writing that is legible (e.g., writing names of family members, writing familiar environmental print such as *Stop* or *Exit*); and 3) access to drawing tools or picture dictionaries to produce story illustrations.

In a research study conducted by Hess and McGarvey (1987), experimenters placed computers paired with emergent literacy software in kindergarten classrooms for several months. Results showed that the use of early literacy software significantly facilitated school readiness and reading readiness. One class of students in this study also received a computer in their home, and this class experienced even greater academic gains. Research examining the use of computers during the preschool and early elementary years shows that computers act as effective tools for facilitating school readiness (Hess & McGarvey, 1987; Murphy & Appel, 1984; Swigger & Campbell, 1981).

The positive effects of emergent literacy software on reading readiness are especially promising for children who are at risk of developing literacy problems due to motoric limitations. Access to emergent literacy software, starting in the home environment, may ensure that these students have positive literacy experiences and literacy skills that will allow them to be academically competitive during formal education. However, it is important to remember that these technology-driven activities should not replace the nontechnological preliteracy activities shown to be critical to emergent literacy. It is important for parents and teachers to build a solid literacy foundation by frequently exposing their children to reading and writing materials, modeling literacy activities, and encouraging active processing of literacy materials. Additional ideas for supporting access to generative writing will be addressed in the section on school-age augmented writing support.

Emergent Literacy Principles Applied: A Preschool Program for Children with Special Needs

The following description illustrates a practical application of the emergent literacy principles that we explain previously. The Munroe-Meyer Institute of Genetics and Rehabilitation, University of Nebraska Medical Center, conducts a preschool program for children with severe expressive communication needs (West, Bilyeu, & Brune, 1996). The principle "reading is for everybody" guides this model preschool program. Operating with this language-based philosophy, the program provides an excellent example of early intervention that targets the development of language and emergent literacy skills. Symbolization, literacy learning, and their shared relationship are woven into all aspects of the preschool curriculum. The children (and their parents) who participate in this program have a range of cognitive, social, and motor skills, and their individual needs are blended into the program from both a communication and participation perspective. The children and their parents attend this program for 1½ hours each week.

Although this program shares features common to most preschool classrooms (e.g., snacktime, music, calendar time, art), a unique feature of the program is its integration of classic children's literature and AAC. For each language-based literacy unit, the instructor selects a classic piece of children's literature (e.g., "The Gingerbread Man") that guides a central theme over the course of 10 weeks. The instructors in the preschool program take a selected book and, in advance, simplify the text by adding repeated lines and stronger repetitive patterns. When simplifying the text, however, they keep the content recognizable. For example, the concept of *gingerbread man* may be more difficult for some children to understand, but if the instructor were to use the words *cookie man*, the overall meaning of the text would change.

Also, during every large-group oral reading activity, the instructor selects and uses dynamic props (e.g., sunflower seeds planted in a shoe box of sand) that parallel activities in the book. The props assist in meeting the range of needs in the group and facilitate the learning of story structure concepts. For example, when a story announces "and then the man stepped in the mud!" the teacher presents a bag of mud for the children to manipulate. Some children will connect the relationship between the text (*in the mud*) and the bag of mud. For others, the bag of mud provides a sensory experience that occurs each time at that point in the story. Still other students may have difficulty attending to story reading in large groups. Props help these individuals to maintain attention and participate as they hold the props and "help" the teacher use them appropriately. The props help all of the children understand the concept of story structure by providing a concrete representation of the concepts in the storyline.

Communication displays of varying levels of complexity enable the participation of all students (see Figure 13.2 for examples of 9- and 36-location displays). During story reading, the teacher uses a consistent sequence to model the symbols on the displays and to encourage independent use. The sequence occurs as follows: An adult 1) turns a page of the book, 2) shows each child the page and models the vocabulary for that page on the AAC display, and 3) presents the story prop. Then, each child independently requests a turn with the prop using the vocabulary on the display. As some children combine symbols to make self-generated requests such as "I want my dolly," peer-to-peer modeling also occurs. In this case, the props provide a bridge between the symbols and story text. Multimodal communication—employing oral reading, manual signs, gestures, story props, and communication displays—facilitates language comprehension of the story text. The presence of the display in front of each student serves as a visual reminder about what will happen next in the story. Through the displays, students have access to symbols that require recognition memory rather than recall memory and that allow them to participate actively in the reading of the story. When the children engage in their own retelling of the story, the displays also facilitate language expression and allow some to retell quite elaborate renditions of the original story! Using theme-based early learning principles, the teacher can conduct follow-up activities (e.g., art, drama, music) that are consistent with the theme of the story and can reinforce vocabulary and concepts from the story.

A final feature of the Munroe-Meyer preschool program is that it provides independent access to literacy materials through the use of the IntelliPics software program (Intellitools, Inc.). The instructor can recreate each page of the book on a Macintosh computer using IntelliPics software. Prior to or just following the story reading sessions, each child can activate a single switch that takes him or her through an independent reading of the entire book. After the child hits a single switch, the computer turns a page on the screen, speaks the text, and a story illustration moves on the screen (e.g., a sled slides down a mountain). This reading activity not only provides independent access but also allows for repeated readings.

This preschool program also provides parents with literacy learning tools. Prior to the start of a unit, each parent receives a list of related book titles and a communication overlay that his or her child can use at home. One mother purchased a book before a reading unit started and read the book aloud at home with her son. When she arrived

at the preschool that week, she explained that her son did not seem to enjoy the book for this unit. However, after watching the preschool story reading session, this mother obtained ideas about how to adapt the text and provide interactive activities. She then used these literacy techniques at home with her son, and the book became one of his favorites. In fact, his name happened to be the same as the boy featured in the story, and he took great delight each time he heard his name read aloud!

The Munroe-Meyer preschool program illustrates the importance of literacy learning for all children and shows the successful integration of literacy activities for a group of children who have a range of needs. In a naturally occurring preschool environment, these children not only learn concepts related to the printed medium but can also come to understand the relationship between their symbol-based primary communication systems and text. As these children enter kindergarten, the concepts they have learned about reading, writing, and language will provide them with a base that can aid them in continued success with literacy learning.

SYMBOLIZATION AND LITERACY LEARNING

As we have seen, both language development and literacy development in young children are greatly influenced by early learning experiences. Just imagine how many words a typical child hears and sees before saying (or reading) that precious first word! For that matter, think about how many manual signs the deaf child of deaf parents sees before making that first sign! Now think about young AAC users who communicate using symbols: How many of those symbols do they see others using before *they* are expected to use them to send messages, read, spell, and write? Did you say, "Zero?" Often, sadly, that is the case—we expect young children with disabilities to use AAC symbols after they have had *almost no experience* seeing others do so! This is but one example of the potential impact graphic symbols have on the language and literacy learning processes. We discuss this issue further in the following sections.

Graphic Symbols and Language Development

Most young children with SSPIs who cannot speak are also unable to read and spell in order to prepare their messages. Obviously, these young AAC users must have some means to interact conversationally, and they must not wait until they are able to spell in order to do this. Therefore, interventionists must teach them some type of AAC symbol system that may itself have significant learning requirements. For example, a child must have systematic instruction and experience in order to learn to use the Blissymbolics system or iconic encoding (e.g., Minspeak). At the same time, many of these children are attempting to learn the orthographic form of their language. Because young AAC users may need to accomplish both of these learning tasks while they are enrolled in general elementary school classrooms, the tasks may place considerable, competing demands on the students' learning time. There is no simple solution to this dilemma. AAC specialists face the important task of learning more about how to assist young AAC users with primary motor impairments in achieving communicative competence while allowing them to participate successfully as competitive students. As many of these students must focus on the simultaneous acquisition of three modes of communication—speech, graphic symbols, and orthography—it is important that instructors consider overlapping features of the three modes and utilize instructional time as a means to foster integration of concepts across modes (Erickson & Baker, 1996).

Graphic Symbols and Literacy Development

Bishop, Rankin, and Mirenda noted that

Print awareness is knowledge about the forms and functions of print.

Phonologic awareness is the explicit awareness of the sound structure of language. Phonologic awareness can be present at three levels: 1) knowledge that words are separate units, 2) knowledge of syllables in words, and 3) knowledge that words can be segmented into phonemes.

Word recognition is the ability to associate a printed word with its spoken counterpart. (1994, p. 114)

AAC specialists have been investigating the relationship between graphic symbols and literacy learning. A central question in this area is whether individuals can transfer the processes and abilities developed through the use of graphic symbols to the tasks of reading (and writing) (Bishop et al., 1994). Unfortunately, as of 1998, no research existed that could help us to better understand this relationship. Nonetheless, interventionists routinely use the graphic symbols with which some AAC users communicate as a means to foster these individual's literacy development.

It is clear that use of graphic symbols serves as a primary vehicle for language learning. In the process of developing language, AAC users utilize their symbols for dual purposes: to communicate and to make inferences about how their world is perceived and constructed (Sevcik, Romski, & Wilkinson, 1991). Thus, graphic symbols provide AAC users with a way to learn about and depict their world. Word knowledge plays an integral role in an individual's ability to gain meaning from text and facilitates both reading acquisition and comprehension. The greater a person's vocabulary, the greater the likelihood that he or she will attain higher levels of comprehension.

The following sections address the relationship between graphic symbols and literacy learning for both reading acquisition and comprehension. We illustrate concepts about print that the use of graphic symbols may or may not facilitate. Those who are interested may refer to several published articles that provide a more thorough review of symbolization and its relationship to reading acquisition and comprehension (e.g., Bishop et al., 1994; Blischak, 1994; Foley, 1993; McNaughton, 1993a; McNaughton & Lindsay, 1995; Nelson, 1992; Rankin, Harwood, & Mirenda, 1994).

Graphic Symbols and Reading Acquisition

Researchers agree that good readers use their knowledge of spoken language and its sound segments (e.g., syllables, phonemes) to decode and interpret text (Adams, 1990). They also consider this knowledge of grapheme–phoneme correspondence to be critical to skilled reading. Because graphic symbols map spoken language at a morphemic or word level, their use may encourage the development of some of the basic skills and processes that individuals use when engaging in meaningful reading and writing (Bishop et al., 1994). When researchers have considered phonemic (i.e., print-to-speech) mapping, they have asked the following question: Can graphic symbols and word labels support the acquisition of skilled reading and writing?

In order to provide some insight into this relationship, Bishop et al. (1994) reviewed the literature relative to the development of early reading acquisition. They used Strickland and Cullinan's (1990) six concepts about print as a basis for interpretation. Through exposure to print, children learn 1) that print conveys meaning; 2) that there is directionality to the way we read; 3) a basic understanding of the concepts of words, letters, and sounds; 4) that the words we speak are mapped onto print and there are certain patterns in speech-to-print correspondence; 5) that each letter has a shape and a name; and 6) that letters can represent sounds. Bishop et al. (1994) speculated that exposure to graphic symbols with word labels potentially facilitates acquisition of the first three of these skills.

Print Conveys Meaning

When learning AAC symbols, children develop the knowledge that symbols convey meaning, and they may be able to transfer this concept to understand that print also conveys meaning. When they use graphic symbols for meaningful interactive communication, they establish associations between symbols' content and their communicative functions. Because speaking and writing both require the ability to make associations and because both acts can constitute meaningful communication, the skills AAC users acquire when using graphic symbols relate to those required to understand that print can also convey meaning.

Directionality of Print

When communication displays support left-to-right progressions, children may also learn the concept of print directionality. At an emergent literacy level, facilitators can help children integrate the relationship between graphic symbols and literacy by using symbol books or by making books that use the child's symbol set (Blackstone, 1989e). A subject-verb-object display arrangement may further facilitate directionality as the AAC user constructs sentences by selecting graphic symbols in a left-to-right order.

Words, Letters, and Sounds

When symbols are paired with traditional orthography, AAC users are exposed to the concept of words. In order to emphasize this concept, as well as to draw attention to the concept of letters, facilitators can teach AAC users to relate the words on their communication displays with written text (e.g., by asking "Is there a word/symbol on your board that sounds the same as the word you are trying to spell?" [Blackstone, 1989e, p. 3]). Word awareness also encompasses the concept that print represents sound. The AAC user may learn this concept more easily if his or her symbol system utilizes sound–symbol mapping rules. For example, the rebus symbol for the word *in* can take on a variety of forms depending on the initial consonant, consonant blend, or digraph paired with it (Bishop et al., 1994). DynaSyms may also be semiphonic in that the user can combine these symbols with morphemes and automatically transform them into new words (e.g., plurals and past tense forms).

Bishop et al. (1994) also speculated that graphic symbols may not support three basic literacy concepts: 1) speech matches printed words, 2) letters have different shapes, and 3) letters can represent sounds. Understanding the speech-to-print match requires knowing that we can map the words we speak onto print and that patterns govern how this occurs. Some research suggests that repeated exposure to graphic symbols paired with words may facilitate this understanding so that some individuals eventually learn to read words without their associated symbols (Romski & Sevcik, 1996). However, in a review of the research examining print awareness, Bishop et al. (1994) reported that prereaders do not typically recognize words out of context and that they do not learn to discriminate individual letters through paired associative learning. In the end, fluent reading requires understanding at the letter-phoneme level, rather than at the whole-word level. Other studies suggest that children do not automatically learn letter–phoneme connections and that children who are able to deduce the meanings of novel symbol combinations at the word level may still be unable to deduce their meanings at the phonemic level. Thus, AAC users, whose literacy exposure may be limited to graphic symbol–word associations, must have exposure to activities that teach letter–phoneme associations and facilitate speech-to-print matching.

Finally, graphic symbols are unlikely to teach AAC users that letters have shapes and names and that letters can represent sounds because the symbols are not orthographic in nature (Bishop et al., 1994). Graphic symbol use will teach these concepts only if the AAC user communicates with the symbol set in combination with traditional orthography and if the facilitator directs the user's attention toward the sound system of language. To facilitate alphabetic awareness, the facilitator should incorporate letter shapes, names, and sounds into the AAC user's communication displays and encourage him or her to use them during both interactive communication and literacy activities.

Rankin, Harwood, and Mirenda noted that *reading comprehension* is "the meaningful interpretation of print" (1994, p. 270).

The individual can achieve three *levels of comprehension,* lower, middle, and final, during the act of reading. Lower levels of comprehension consist of basic and factual interpretation of text. The middle level involves the ability to apply the information, interpret what it means, or make inferences about what was read. At the final level, the reader is able to appreciate what was read, while simultaneously creating, solving problems, and/or generalizing the information to new situations. These levels are of importance to AAC users because this population has diverse needs. Teachers or facilitators who design the individual's reading instruction should consider his or her cognitive ability, language skills, and need to gain information from text.

Word knowledge refers to "an individual's reading, listening, speaking, and writing vocabulary and is a critical aspect of understanding text" (p. 271).

When applied to reading comprehension, *metalinguistic awareness* refers to "the ability to perform mental operations on what is produced by the mental mechanisms involved in sentence comprehension" (p. 274).

Syntactic awareness refers to knowledge of the rules of morphology, word order, sentence organization, and the relationships between words and sentences. During the act of reading, syntactic awareness "allows a reader to 'chunk' units of text into manageable units in order to obtain meaning" (pp. 4, 277).

Graphic Symbols and Reading Comprehension

We cannot overemphasize the relationship between language knowledge and reading comprehension. In order for individuals to arrive at a meaningful understanding of printed text, they

Must understand the printed code of graphic symbols, have a functional use of the necessary language abilities and processes, have the cognitive ability to process information, and have the background knowledge necessary to make sense of the content of the message conveyed through text. (Rankin et al., 1994, p. 270)

AAC users who have had limited early language experiences may have language difficulties that severely restrict their ability to comprehend text. Rankin et al. (1994) described several important skills related to the influence of language abilities on reading comprehension. These critical variables include 1) phonologic processing skills, 2) word recognition abilities, 3) problem-solving skills, 4) lexical processing abilities, 5) syntactic awareness, 6) semantic knowledge, and 7) narrative discourse processing skills. Difficulty with any one of these skills may have an impact on the individual's ability to comprehend text. The sections that follow discuss briefly the phonologic, semantic, syntactic, and pragmatic skills related to reading comprehension.

Phonologic Processing Skills

We addressed phonologic processing skills previously in the section on skills for basic literacy acquisition. However, when considered as a feature of reading comprehension, phonologic awareness also plays a role in facilitating word recognition and thus supports the ability to understand text. When readers can identify words rapidly, they can allocate greater cognitive resources to the higher level processes involved in comprehension (Rankin et al., 1994).

Word Knowledge

For AAC users, word knowledge directly relates to the availability of symbols to communicate—the more symbols an AAC user has, the more vocabulary words he or she can manipulate and use. Vocabulary is also a critical factor in reading comprehension—the more word meanings a person knows, the more language he or she can understand, either aurally or visually (Harris & Sipay, 1990). Thus, word knowledge provides a foundation for reading comprehension, and vocabulary size provides an indicator of what written material an individual will be able to comprehend. Because children typically acquire vocabulary through communicative interactions, the degree to which AAC systems support language interactions with others will have a significant impact on AAC users' word knowledge. Furthermore, AAC users' regular exposure to word labels via graphic symbols may put them at an advantage for reading words (McNaughton, 1993a).

Syntactic Awareness

Researchers have hypothesized that graphic symbols support literacy learning by providing learners with information about the structural aspects of language. Rankin et al. (1994) suggested that graphic symbols play a role in supporting syntactic awareness and competence if facilitators or teachers teach the AAC user to integrate symbols into sentence sequences. In addition, AAC users may become adept at constructing meaningful messages using grammatical structures if their communication displays are organized according to the rules of syntax, as discussed previously. McNaughton (1993a) provided a series of questions that assessors can ask to evaluate the capacity of a symbol system to foster an AAC user's development of syntactic awareness.

Pragmatic Awareness

Pragmatic awareness is the ability to recognize relationships between groups of sentences, create an overall representation of the sentences, and use prior knowledge to gain the full meaning of a passage (Rankin et al., 1994). Skilled readers apply their pragmatic awareness to grasp the overall meaning of the text at the paragraph level. Because this skill develops through experience with written paragraphs, the influence of graphic symbols on comprehension at this level is unclear. To facilitate pragmatic awareness, the AAC system must allow the user to draw inferences, use metaphors and similes, and foster audience awareness. Many of these higher-level processes are difficult to facilitate through the graphic symbol sets typically used in AAC, with the possible exceptions of Blissymbolics and iconic encoding systems such as Minspeak.

In summary, it appears that frequent exposure to graphic symbols and orthography may not automatically give AAC users an "upper hand" in the early stages of literacy. Graphic symbols appear to influence emergent literacy primarily because they facilitate the development of linguistic and metalinguistic skills. The extent to which graphic symbols promote the development of basic reading skills appears to depend on how students are taught the spoken-to-written symbol relationship. The primary power of graphic symbols may lie in their power to increase communication with others (Bishop et al., 1994).

CLASSROOM LITERACY EXPERIENCES OF AAC USERS

In 1982, Harris discussed a number of factors that affect the discourse patterns of individuals who use AAC systems and their communication partners. Similarly, Pierce and McWilliam (1993) provided a summary of factors that influence the literacy participation of children with severe communication impairments. This summary shows that both communicative and physical constraints affect the nature and quality of literacy interactions. In this section, we summarize relevant research on the relationship between participation and literacy.

Mike conducted an unpublished ethnographic study of the nature of literacy instruction provided to five children with cerebral palsy (ages 10–14 years) in self-contained classrooms (cited in Koppenhaver & Yoder, 1993). Classroom activities were observed over a 17-week period for 2 hours at a time, for a total of 120 hours. The results indicated that the students received direct instruction in reading for an average of 15 minutes per day and that they seldom interacted with one another. Similarly, Koppenhaver (Koppenhaver & Yoder, 1993) observed and videotaped three boys (ages 10–14 years) with SSPIs and their teachers during literacy instruction in three different self-contained classrooms. Experimenters examined the type of teacher activities performed, the function of the instruction provided, and the instructional groupings used; and they calculated the percentage of actual instructional time. Results of the study showed that across teachers, less than 2% of the time was devoted to literacy tasks, and only 55%–63% of the total school time was allocated for actual teaching. Student variables studied during literacy instruction included the type of activity, mode of participation, and level of text used. Students engaged in transitional activities during 34%–38% of the classroom time, in reading activities during 23%–29% of the time, in listening activities during 15%–20% of the time, in writing activities during 10%–16% of the time, and in AAC intervention during 5%–9% of the total classroom time. The majority of literacy instruction focused on reading or writing words and sentences in isolation, completing fill-in-the-blank exercises, and performing spelling drills. These two studies provide insight into the type and amount of participation students with SSPIs typically have for literacy instruction. Overall, students with severe disabilities receive less literacy instruction than their classmates without disabilities.

In a related study, Wasson and Keeler (cited in Koppenhaver & Yoder, 1993) conducted an observation of the daily instruction provided to a set of 6-year-old twin girls.

One twin had severe disabilities and was placed in a special education classroom; the other did not have disabilities and was placed in a general classroom. Both children demonstrated typical IQ scores and had similar home experiences. Shortly after starting first grade, the twin with severe disabilities began to fall behind her sister in literacy learning. The results indicated that the child with severe disabilities received 30 minutes of instruction to every 60 that her sister received. In addition, the twin with disabilities received one fifth the number of opportunities to communicate (i.e., to ask and answer questions and to make comments). This occurred despite the fact that the child with severe disabilities had the benefit of a more favorable student-to-teacher ratio (8:3) than did her sister. Koppenhaver and Yoder (1992b) identified similar conditions in two additional classroom studies of individuals who used AAC systems. They also noted that in a follow-up intervention for the twin with severe disabilities, her AAC team made numerous educational adaptations such as cutting up workbook activities and placing the response choices in quadrants, and facilitating eye pointing during practice activities. Her communication response opportunities more than tripled as a result of these adaptations. The intervention portion of this study provides an example of the importance of assessing and manipulating contextual variables as part of an overall literacy intervention.

PARTICIPATION OF AAC USERS IN LITERACY INSTRUCTION: PROMOTING DEVELOPMENT OF READING AND WRITING SKILLS

So far in this chapter, we have painted a somewhat negative picture of the challenges AAC users face in learning to read, write, and spell. This is not meant to depress or discourage you—rather, it is meant to inspire you to act in support of increased literacy instruction for AAC users of all ages and abilities! The good news is that it is now possible to use computer technology to augment the reading, referencing, and writing skills of individuals both with and without disabilities. We discuss these instructional supports in the remainder of this chapter.

"We aren't going to spend time diagramming sentences or learning to spell in this class," (said the college night course instructor) with a smile. "What we *are* going to do is see if you have anything to say, if you can put your thoughts into words." We could bring dictionaries to class. We could have friends check our spelling and grammar. Like the bird that suddenly discovered it could sing, I discovered I could write and that I had something interesting to say. . . . I still can't spell so my computer's spell checker always gets a good workout. . . . And I've come to believe that real education is mainly acquired by reading, thinking, and talking with others. (Russell Genet, a man with dyslexia, in Genet, 1995, p. 58)

Augmented Reading and Referencing

Instructional Techniques

Educators rely on many instructional approaches to teach reading skills to all children. These methods include various phonics approaches, direct instruction tactics (DISTAR), language experience techniques, "whole language" approaches, the Orton-Gillingham method, and many, many others. In addition, teachers can choose from a wide array of remedial teaching strategies such as diagnostic teaching (Walker, 1996) and holistic approaches (Rhodes & Dudley-Marling, 1988), which they can often pair with instructional techniques such as explicit teaching, prereading graphic organization strategies, and directed reading-thinking activities (DRTA). Educators utilize these techniques to provide a "scaffold" of language and literacy experiences for students who struggle with the reading process and to foster their independence and success. It is far beyond the scope of this chapter to review the many remedial literacy strategies in use, and readers may refer to other texts for this information (e.g., Cunningham, 1995; Engelmann & Bruner, 1984; Gillingham & Stillman, 1970; Kamhi & Catts, 1989; Rhodes & Dudley-Marling, 1988; Stauffer, 1980; Walker, 1996; Weaver, 1994). However, we review briefly some of the most prevalent techniques and computer features used in augmented (e.g., computer-supported) literacy instruction with individuals who have learning disabilities. These techniques also may be useful with a broader range of individuals with communicative impairments because the literacy problems associated with learning disabilities may co-occur with other types of disabilities (e.g., primary motor impairments such as cerebral palsy). We also address alternative access to computer supported reading for individuals with primary motor impairments.

Andrea is a 16-year-old girl with spastic cerebral palsy who uses a DynaVox as her primary form of communication. Her impairments include mild to moderate cognitive disabilities, attention difficulties, and legal blindness in one eye. Her primary educational placement is in a resource classroom, and several of her academic courses take place in general classrooms. The other students in her resource class have a range of identified disabilities and also complete a portion of their coursework in general classrooms. Andrea has a great interest in politics (and actively participates in local election campaigns), but there is a large gap between her higher-level understanding of politics and her ability to read text. She has excellent visual word recognition of familiar concepts as well as the names of friends, classmates, and family members. Prior to intervention, however, she was unable to read beyond a first-grade text. Andrea wanted to be able to read during her leisure time, but she did not have the literacy skills or a mode for accessing text. In addition, her attention difficulties made single modality exposure to literacy materials (e.g., auditory only via books on tape) a less-than-optimum experience.

Computer-Supported Reading

Computers cannot and should not take the place of books for teaching reading, but computer technology can expand instructional possibilities. Computer-based options that employ word processing software to host reading materials are widely available in many schools (Wolverton, Beukelman, Haynes, & Sesow, 1992). Such computer applications, along with alternative access and screen reader options (via speech synthesis), allow students to choose and load text, display it on a computer monitor, and advance through the text independently, using commands such as page up, page down, and go to. Similarly, students can use a speech synthesizer that reads words, lines, or entire screens of text. Screen readers may also provide additional supports to AAC users through multimodal exposure to text information (i.e., visual and auditory). Many talking word processors (and communication software products) highlight text as the device speaks it aloud. AAC users can also use talking word processors as reading/ speaking tools, to participate in oral reports with their classmates.

Technology-assisted reading generally requires the creation of computer files containing the text to be read. Facilitators can accomplish this by entering text into a standard word processing program and saving it to the computer hard drive or to a floppy disk, or by using an optical text scanner. The optical scanner reads (i.e., scans) standard printed materials and translates the written characters into computer text that can be saved. This option, which is much less time consuming than entering text by hand, has become more widely used due to improved optical scanning technology.

Augmented referencing systems that incorporate compact discs, a computer network, and alternative access options may also facilitate literate students' abilities to access and read library resources. Basically, augmented referencing systems allow students to read magazines, encyclopedias, dictionaries, atlases, and other multivolume reference materials through a computer. Shell, Horn, and Bruning (1989) have implemented such a system for university students who have difficulty reading printed material due to a visual, linguistic, and/or physical inability to manage books. As of 1998, augmented referencing was still a new practice that could benefit from further research and development. (See the Barkley AAC Center's World Wide Web site [http://aac.unl.edu] for a summary of some of the commercial options that are available in this area [e.g., text scanners and readers, assistive software, reference CD Roms)].

Both Andrea's classroom teacher and her speech-language pathologist decided that she could gain access to reading with the software program Speaking Dynamically (Mayer-Johnson Co.). In order to select the reading content, Andrea reviewed political magazines (e.g., *U.S. News and World Report*) and selected stories that interested her. A facilitator then entered these articles into Speaking Dynamically, and Andrea could independently open them, highlight the text, and have the computer read them out loud. Seeing the text on the screen while the device simultaneously highlighted and spoke it allowed Andrea to use both her visual and auditory modalities and helped her to attend to the reading more closely. Occasionally, this reading activity also served as an academic (rather than leisure) task when she had to complete comprehension questions. Accessing articles with Speaking Dynamically offered Andrea a method for engaging in independent leisure reading.

Alternative Access

Many people with primary motor impairments have a great need to hold the text, turn its pages, and otherwise access printed materials in order to support the development of reading skills and to learn academic content. It is important, however, for intervention teams to put this need in perspective and determine if independent access should always be the AAC user's primary goal. Although student independence is certainly a worthwhile goal, it is also clear that this goal must be balanced with considerations of how to best use valuable instructional time. It might be more efficient to have a classmate without disabilities or a paraprofessional provide assistance with some printed materials or to use one of the many available low-tech options. Figure 13.3 illustrates several homemade devices for holding books or pages. In addition, the Barkley AAC Center's World Wide Web site (http://aac.unl.edu) contains a listing of additional, non-technical fine motor supports (e.g., splints with pencil attachments, ring splints that provide finger support and reduce hypermobilization of fingers, reading stands, book holders) and low-tech reading access systems (e.g., talking switches, loop tapes, page turners).

AAC users can choose from a variety of alternative access methods to operate computer hardware and software for reading and writing. At a basic level, both IBM-compatible and Macintosh computers have control options that allow changes to be made to the standard mouse, such as adjustments to the sensitivity and timing of mouse movements. Other adjustments allow AAC users to type capital letters (usually a process that requires two fingers) through a single finger operation (see Chapter 15). Other options for access include commercially available trackballs that have a variety of sizes and operational sensitivities. Alternatively, some individuals with physical impairments who cannot control a standard mouse may be able to operate a computer with trackpads. The trackpad is a flat, rectangular pad located on the keyboard that performs the same functions as a traditional mouse. By lifting and dragging a finger (or stylus) across the trackpad, the AAC user can move the computer cursor to access all computer operations.

Many AAC users may need specialized equipment to obtain alternative access to computers. Some of this equipment may include switches, standard keyboards with enlarged keys, large membrane keyboards, on-screen keyboards, scanning arrays, touch screens, light pointers, head-controlled access devices, and voice-recognition software. When determining alternative methods of computer access, it is important to consider not only the individual's physical access constraints but also his or her purposes for reading, writing, and communicating. (See the Barkley AAC Center's World Wide Web site [http://aac.unl.edu] for a detailed listing of commercially available alternative access methods.)

Figure 13.3.   Display of homemade devices for holding books and pages. (From *Teaching individuals with physical and multiple disabilities* by Bigge, © 1991. Reprinted by permission of Prentice-Hall, Inc., Upper Saddle River, NJ.)

After seeing Andrea working at the computer, other students in the classroom wanted to access their own stories and articles via Speaking Dynamically. These students had greater literacy needs than Andrea and were all considered to be nonreaders. As a result of their request, articles containing a wide array of student interests (ranging from political pieces on Bill Clinton to teen interest pieces on the characters from the television sitcom *Saved by the Bell*) were entered and saved in a master reading file. An interesting carryover of this reading activity was that students in the class organized a leisure reading time in which everyone listened to stories as a small group. The students took turns deciding whose article was to be read for that day and they held discussions about the article immediately following the reading. What began as a problem-solving process that provided Andrea with access to reading materials resulted in an innovative program in which students made decisions about curriculum content, formed their own reading group, engaged in independent reading of a wide variety of text, held active discussions about the content, and expanded their knowledge base by listening to articles that were in other areas of interest. (Courtesy of Denise Bilyeu, Munroe-Meyer Institute of Genetics and Rehabilitation, University of Nebraska Medical Center)

Technology-Supported Writing

We cannot emphasize enough that "supporting the writing process through computer technology" does not mean that educators can eliminate basic writing instruction from a child's curriculum! Computers cannot and should not replace sound, systematic instruction in writing skills. What they *can* do is make it easier and more enjoyable for a student with disabilities to participate in writing activities. Thus, the same instructional techniques that can be used successfully to teach students without disabilities to write are central to the learning process for students who use technology, as discussed in the section that follows.

Instructional Techniques

The current philosophy about writing development emphasizes that students learn to write by writing (Atwell, 1987; Calkins, 1994; Graves, 1994; Reif, 1992). Written language is a powerful vehicle for learning, and, for AAC users, it is also a powerful vehicle for communicating. Calkins reminded us that "writers live their lives differently because they write" (1994, p. 7).

In order to learn to write well, students need regular and frequent time for writing and opportunities to write about topics that are meaningful to them (Atwell, 1987; Reif, 1992). When they are learning to write, children need to know that writing involves composing a message using their own words to communicate with other people. Children need the freedom and flexibility to express their thoughts without being constrained by requirements for correct spelling or "neat" handwriting. A teacher's role is to help students write and to keep them writing by providing models, strategies, support, tools, and conditions that are conducive to writing (Graves, 1994).

As teachers make curricular decisions about writing instruction, they must take into account the specialized needs of students. Teachers should still apply the principles of good instruction with all students, regardless of their abilities or disabilities.

Current learning models view writing as a process in which students engage in prewriting (planning), writing (composing a draft), and rewriting (editing and revising) activities (Pressley & McCormick, 1995). This learning model, which is known as *process writing,* emphasizes some of the positive aspects of writing described previously, including daily, meaningful experiences composing text; student collaboration; and also learning. The principles of process writing focus on student responsibility for learning and place a strong emphasis on informal methods for learning. Students with learning difficulties who lack strategies for approaching all phases of the writing process may require additional supports of a more formal nature because the minimal guidance that teachers provide in process writing approaches may not be sufficient to help students with learning disabilities to acquire the skills they need to write successfully (Graham & Harris, 1997). These students need a balanced approach that allows for frequent writing time, collaboration, individual student learning, and explicit skill instruction.

Strategy Instruction

Students who struggle with writing have difficulty with both low-level (e.g., conventions and mechanics) and high-level aspects of the composition process (e.g., organization and generation of content). AAC users, who usually have extremely slow writing rates, may have a restricted ability to monitor these complex cognitive demands, and the form of their written language may be influenced by this constraint (Blackstone, 1989d). Given the slow writing rates of many AAC users, it is even more important to implement strategies to support all phases of the writing process. By using one method of explicit skill instruction, known as *strategy instruction,* teachers can aid beginning writers in developing problem-solving skills for approaching academic tasks. The goal of writing strategy instruction is to assist students in developing skills for planning and monitoring their own writing so that they can shift their cognitive resources to the higher-level processes needed for writing. This type of writing instruction involves goal setting, self-regulation, and performance evaluation.

Students who participate in strategy instruction interventions in which teachers convey information about good writing and model it appear to gain greater awareness of the writing task, learn strategies for approaching writing, and are able to generalize these skills to other writing tasks (Seidenberg, 1988). Strategy instruction, with which educators have taught students with learning disabilities successfully (Graham & Harris, 1989, 1993; Graham, MacArthur, Schwartz, & Page-Voth, 1992; MacArthur, Harris, & Graham, 1994), may also assist educators in determining educational goals and selecting literacy scaffolds for AAC users. If the primary educational goal for AAC users is to have opportunities to engage in independent written communication, teachers should implement strategies that teach them "what good writers do." (For additional information about strategy instruction, see Harris & Graham, 1996, and Pressley, Woloshyn, & Associates, 1995.)

One of the most important advances for children who are nonspeaking is the ability to produce their own words by spelling them. . . .Given enough time, a literate person using a letter board can produce any possible message. (Nelson, 1993, p. 11)

Augmented Writing

Koppenhaver and Yoder (1992b) noted that literacy instruction for children with disabilities places great emphasis on reading yet nearly always excludes writing. For many AAC users in particular, writing is a slow and laborious process, even with the aid of adaptive equipment. Nonetheless, it is essential that these individuals have ample opportunities to compose continuous, written text, and not merely write single words in isolation as part of workbook exercises (Koppenhaver & Yoder, 1990). Allowing students to get their thoughts down on paper is much more important than emphasizing correct grammar, spelling, and punctuation, at least initially. Consistent with both the whole language and the process writing approaches, AAC users should have frequent opportunities to "create literacy events by dictating stories; labeling; creating charts or bulletin boards; writing journals, stories, and poems; and by producing their own books" (Chaney, 1990, p. 245).

Providing access to meaningful writing activities while simultaneously considering the multiple learning needs of children who use AAC can be especially challenging. It may be helpful to think of a literacy scaffolding when addressing access to writing for these children. It is important that teachers utilize assistive technology to foster meaningful literacy learning and provide access to classroom writing curricula. Educational activities that focus on purposeful writing experiences rather than on writing subskills such as handwriting or spelling will facilitate the student's awareness that writing is meaningful, communicative, and enjoyable.

Individualized literacy supports, both technological and instructional, address individual student needs by providing varying levels of assistance and graduated independence. With the greatest degree of scaffolding, the student selects graphic symbols on a membrane keyboard that attaches to a computer, and the device enters words or entire sentences into the document. Through the direct selection of symbols, the student can generate a complete, illustrated story with text. In this early phase, assistive technology fosters the integration of symbols and traditional orthography by producing written text with the child's symbol set. As the student writes with symbols, he or she sees how the computer helps to generate a story, and the student can create entire stories to read together with classmates at a later date (see Figure 13.4 for a sample story). Students who use membrane keyboards can write stories based on classic literature, ideas generated as a class, or classroom experiences such as a trip to the zoo.

In the next phases of literacy scaffolding, the student begins to use alternative modes of writing access and/or engage in greater degrees of independent writing. For example, he or she may use an on-screen keyboard to generate writing through graphic symbols. When the student can manage words without symbols, a teacher can adapt the device to offer writing choices as text only with the graphic symbols removed. At the next level, the student can use the keyboard to copy these on-screen choices instead of relying on the device to insert the text into the document automatically. In the final phase of scaffolding, the student can engage in independent letter-by-letter message construction using alternative modes of access (e.g., alternative or on-screen keyboards). At this point, teachers may also consider implementing assistive features that provide access options for rate enhancement (e.g., word prediction). Although the scaffolding sequence we describe appears to be ordered in terms of increasing degrees of independence, the supports are not completely hierarchical. That is, the assistive support we describe does not have to occur in a sequence with one phase leading directly to the next. Students may require technical and instructional supports in different sequences and with different degrees of assistance.

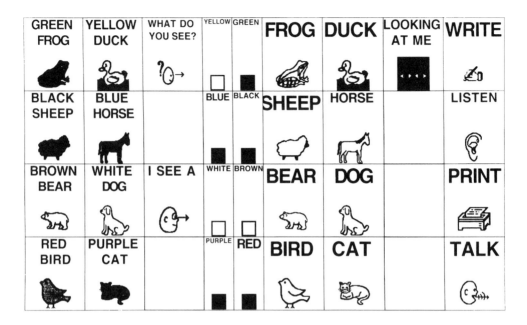

Figure 13.4.   Book overlay based on the story *Brown Bear, Brown Bear, What Do You See?* (Martin, 1967). (Courtesy of Denise Bilyeu (1995). Created with the Discover Create program from Don Johnston, Inc.)

When teachers provide writing scaffolding, they should remember to remove the scaffolding eventually (Nelson, 1993). In the early phase of literacy instruction, an alternative keyboard can provide significant support by allowing students to develop story content with preprogrammed words or sentences and generate complete stories quickly and efficiently. Through these experiences, students gain vocabulary and syntactic skills and develop a sense of story structure. If possible, the future writing goals for these students should include independent, spontaneous message construction. In addition, when using technology as a literacy scaffold, parents and teachers should remember to embed these activities in the principles of writing instruction that we previously describe. Students who use AAC should participate in frequent, meaningful writing experiences and should receive opportunities to engage in independent writing.

Sean is a 12-year-old boy with athetoid cerebral palsy. He has mild cognitive impairments and is considered to be academically competitive. Through scanning, Sean uses Speaking Dynamically software both as his primary form of communication and to meet his academic writing requirements.

As Sean entered junior high school, his educational team noted that one of his classroom teachers had placed all classroom worksheets into a Claris Works word processing document in which each student kept his or her own set of worksheets and entered the answers onto the blanks. Unfortunately, the Speaking Dynamically software could not interact with the Claris Works format and Sean's educational team needed to devise an alternative mode of access. In order to keep Sean academically competitive, they set up a Ke:nx QWERTY keyboard scanning array to run in conjunction with the Claris Works software. Sean is now able to complete all worksheets by "mousing" to each blank on the screen and using the scanning array to type in his responses. Sean is also able to use a single switch to independently complete all computer operations (e.g., turning the computer on/off), and he now uses the computer to complete all his writing assignments using word processing and other educational software. It is important to note that he can manipulate both his communication and his literacy technology with complete independence. (Courtesy of Denise Bilyeu, Munroe-Meyer Institute of Genetics and Rehabilitation, University of Nebraska Medical Center)

Alternative Access

Most children without disabilities enter elementary school with the ability to hold and manipulate pencils and other writing implements. Educators then take responsibility for developing the motor and language skills the children need for writing. When students with primary motor impairments enter school without any way to write, they cannot gain access to most written literacy experiences. Thus, they need to enter school with alternative ways to write so that they can benefit from typical classroom instruction and avoid the need for personalized literacy curricula. These students also need a way to produce printed output so that their work can be reviewed by their peers and corrected by the teacher in a manner similar to that of their classmates.

Rosenthal and Rosenthal (1989) suggested that school personnel utilize a "backwards elimination" approach to determine the writing adaptations needed by an individual student. Using this approach, the teacher simply works backward from the standard materials and procedures that students without disabilities use. Thus, initial adaptations might involve modifications of worksheets or textbooks. For example, the teacher might standardize workbook pages by changing fill-in-the-blank questions to those that require multiple-choice or matching responses. Then, the teacher can code answer options with a letter or number so that the student can respond by writing, typing, or pointing to a single character. In some cases, simply enlarging a worksheet by photocopying may be sufficient to allow a student with a motor disability to use a pencil to write in answers. Alternatively, shortening the length of assignments or modifying the overall workload may be appropriate strategies that allow the teacher to evaluate the quality of a student's work without lowering academic standards.

If simple solutions to participation prove ineffective, the backwards elimination approach requires that the teacher then try low-tech adaptive equipment or materials as solutions. For example, headsticks; splints with pencil attachments; modified pencil holders; or large pencils, crayons, and markers may be useful. Figure 13.5 illustrates examples of these adaptations.

Art is an affable, persistent university student with arthrogryposis. He received no AAC assistance when he was growing up; thus, he developed his own method of writing. He lies on his stomach on the floor, in front of a computer keyboard, and types with his tongue. No mouthstick, no headstick—just his tongue! He types in this manner, error-free, at a rate of 200 keystrokes a minute!

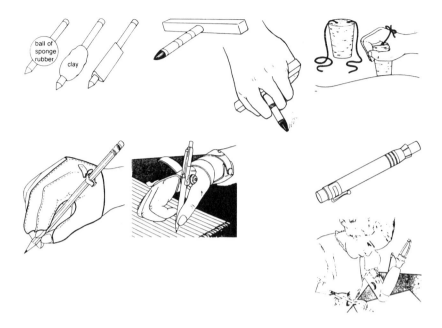

Figure 13.5. Example of adaptations for pencils and crayons. (From *Teaching individuals with physical and multiple disabilities* by Bigge, © 1991. Reprinted by permission of Prentice-Hall, Inc., Upper Saddle River, NJ.)

If simple writing adaptations prove ineffective or if the student experiences undue fatigue when writing with such equipment, the teacher should investigate electronic alternative access methods (see the section in this chapter on alternative access to reading). The process of writing for students with primary motor impairments is often time consuming and slow, even if electronic alternate access methods are used. For example, Kelford Smith et al. (1989) analyzed the writing samples of six individuals with primary motor impairments and reported mean typing rates of 1.5 words per minute. To enhance the speed of alternative access rates, the individual often requires rate enhancement techniques such as encoding or linguistic prediction (see Chapter 3 for a discussion of this issue). The following section presents software that provides augmented writing.

Computer-Supported Writing: Assistive Software Features

The following summary of basic word processors and software with assistive writing tools provides a more specific description of the potential role of computers during the prewriting, composing, and revising phases of the writing process. We provide this detailed information in order to illustrate some of the specific scaffolding tools available to support writing and in order to describe the relationship of these tools to the writing process.

Educators may use computer-supported writing applications that offer features beyond those of common word processors to provide additional writing support to students who struggle in this area (Hunt-Berg, Rankin, & Beukelman, 1994). Word processors with assistive features may support student writing but should not serve as the ultimate solutions to writing deficits. For example, a word processor with spelling assistance is not a long-term solution to poor spelling. Rather, the spelling assistance becomes a way to scaffold performance while students gain writing skills so that they can participate with their peers in the classroom.

Spelling Support

A range of available software tools provide spelling support. The most common spelling checkers operate following completion of the composition process. The checkers flag misspelled words and offer alternative spellings to the student. Other programs may flag misspellings by providing auditory feedback (e.g., a beep) immediately after the student mistypes a word. Word-prompt programs are another form of spelling support. They provide a list of words (e.g., words that begin with *b*) at the bottom of the screen and allow the writer to copy the desired word or automatically insert it into a document. Talking word processors may also provide students with spelling assistance in the form of an auditory presentation of his or her written product. This auditory feedback can occur immediately after a writing task is completed (e.g., at the end of a letter, word, or sentence) or following completion of the entire text (e.g., at the end of entire paragraphs or documents).

Content or Vocabulary Support

Students who have limited expressive vocabularies or who have difficulty finding the right word to express meanings may benefit from software that supports content and/or vocabulary generation. Word-prompt programs that provide lists of suggested words at the bottom of the screen may be useful to such students. This type of software may also support students' vocabulary selection and spelling during the composition process by encouraging students to use more challenging word choices. For example, a student who chooses the word *scared* when writing because she knows how to spell *scared* may attempt to use a word such as *terrified* if assistive software provides her with the word's spelling.

Grammar Support

Computer supports that provide assistance to students who have difficulty with the form and grammar of written work typically analyze completed documents for punctuation, word usage, spelling, and grammar. When selecting software support for grammatical and syntactic needs, it is important to compare the severity of students' grammatical and syntactic needs against the "grammar checking" function of the software packages. Most grammar-checking programs do not check only one feature of writing at a time. Rather, they focus on multiple issues at once. If the student's grammar and syntax needs are severe, grammar-checking software may frustrate the student because the software flags every error.

Organizational Support

Many students who struggle with writing have difficulty conceptualizing the overall organization of their written compositions. For example, some students may omit elements that are important to the structure of the type of text they are composing (e.g., the salutation in a letter), or they may forget to identify clearly one or more elements of a narrative, such as the setting or the main characters. Some software packages help writers to organize specific types of written structures by providing written prompts (i.e., questions) for students during composition. Several software programs foster the planning process by allowing teachers to enter a series of questions to prompt idea generation and attention to text structure (MacArthur, 1993). Other organizational software, such as Inspiration (Inspiration Software, Inc.) may help students organize their ideas in the prewriting phase by providing tools for creating semantic maps and webs. Finally, certain software packages also support the social construction of writing through collaborative writing projects. One of these programs, Aspects (Group Logic,

Inc.), allows students to work in teams and share their work in progress while they compose the same document from different computers.

Editing Support

Many students who struggle with writing avoid the editing process altogether. They may find writing a first draft difficult enough, or they may lack the skills needed to improve their written work. Educators can implement computer assistance during the editing phase in a variety of ways. The most obvious supports are the spell-checking and grammar-checking programs we describe above. Two other computer support options in this regard include the auditory feedback that talking word processors provide and the edit function available in the Process Writer (Scholastic, Inc.) program. Talking word processors assist students in the editing phase by providing them with auditory feedback for misspellings, missing elements in sentences, incorrect word forms, or missing terminal punctuation. Process Writer can support the peer editing strategy common in many process writing classrooms. In a stepwise manner, the Process Writer program provides an evaluation sequence for peer reviewers to constructively critique their colleagues' compositions.

Drawing and Publication Support

Students may benefit from illustration and publication software that allows them to produce aesthetically pleasing illustrations and that encourage writing for a range of audiences (MacArthur, 1993). This type of software may be especially useful for students in primary classrooms who have motor difficulties and need to produce writing products that are paired with illustrations. Some programs allow students to cut and paste color pictures from a dictionary menu into a word processing document; and others allow students to select picture backgrounds (i.e., settings) for their stories. For the student who has difficulty generating writing topics, picture dictionaries and backgrounds may provide a quite motivating source of ideas from which the student can draw. Software programs that provide publishing tools also support the concept of writing for an audience (MacArthur, 1993).

Visual Support

Specialized reading supports can be employed by individuals who are academically competitive and who experience various degrees of visual impairment. These supports include large-print text, braille text, low-vision devices, computers, optical character recognition devices, speech systems, or some combination of these. The expressive communication and writing systems used by individuals with visual impairments may include braille, typewriting, handwriting, audio recordings, and computers. Individual preferences for particular supports generally depend on a variety of factors, including the person's visual status and functional needs as well as the subject matter. (See the Barkley AAC Center's World Wide Web site [http://aac.unl.edu] for additional descriptions of reading and writing techniques for individuals with visual impairments.)

14

Educational Inclusion of AAC Users

with Janet Sturm

Education is a specialized form of communication. Human beings have developed particular times and places in which the scripts of their cultures are to be communicated from one generation to the next. We have come to call the set of practices by which this communication of cultural scripts is accomplished "education." The communication that occurs in educational contexts happens in oral, written, verbal, and nonverbal modes. . . . (Our) role is to facilitate the communication, thus the education, that occurs in the classroom. (Hoskins, 1990, p. 29)

The occasional inclusion of people with severe communication disorders into general educational environments has occurred for many years, as documented in autobiographies such as those by Christopher Nolan (1987) and Bill Rush (1986). Nevertheless, these unique personal accounts also serve to emphasize that inclusion of individuals with disabilities has been the exception to the rule rather than routine educational practice. In response to multiple societal and legal pressures, the educational environments considered to be appropriate for children with severe disabilities are rapidly changing. As this chapter shows, parents and school personnel must learn to work collaboratively in order for these efforts to be cohesive and successful. It is beyond the scope of this book to describe in detail the range of inclusion strategies now in place in many parts of North America. (See Stainback and Stainback, 1996, for a more comprehensive discussion of these issues.)

Because participation in the general classroom requires many kinds of extensive communication, effective augmentative and alternative (AAC) systems that are age- and context-appropriate serve as critical tools for academic success. This applies to students across the ability range who use AAC, regardless of their communication disorders. Unfortunately, it is not uncommon for children with severe communication disorders to attend kindergarten and then enter first grade without having access to the writing and drawing tools, the reading tools, or the conversational tools available to their fellow students. These students cannot hold pencils or crayons, yet they may not have access to augmented writing systems. Although they cannot hold books, turn pages, or use their voices to practice phonics, they are not given adapted reading equipment or computers. Although they may have difficulty answering questions in class and participating in social conversations, they are not provided with AAC systems for interaction. Thus, it is not at all surprising that many of these students fail to participate successfully in general classrooms because their communication skills and the resources with which they have been provided place them at a distinct disadvantage for both academic and social learning. When participation failure occurs, these students are often labeled as "nonacademically oriented" and are then assigned to either segregated classrooms, resource rooms, or other separate settings. In time, the students find themselves increasingly isolated from general classrooms and placed with typical students only during nonacademic classes such as music, art, or physical education. Until the mid-1980s, it was only under exceptional circumstances that any of these students were retained in general classrooms and provided with the adaptive devices and supports that enabled them to be successful.

As placement of students with severe communication disorders in general classrooms becomes more common, there is a critical need for policies, practices, and strategies to replace the prevailing "management by exception" approach. This chapter presents a framework for delivering inclusive communication and educational services within general classrooms to children who require AAC systems across the ability range.

Principle 1: Begin early to prepare the AAC user for the general classroom experience.

PREPARING AAC USERS FOR THE CLASSROOM

Students with severe communication disorders often enter early elementary grades without communication systems that permit them to participate in typical curricular activities. Needless to say, the educational experiences of these students are quite different from those of their peers. For example, these students are unable to write or speak in class at times when the teacher expects other students to do so. Instead, they must either passively observe other students or communicate through an aide or paraprofessional. Students with severe communication disorders often spend months and even the first years of school performing assessment and instructional activities related to AAC system use. These activities may conflict with regular classroom activities, causing them to fall further behind classmates as they must forfeit "academic time" in favor of "communication time."

A clear solution to this dilemma is to begin providing AAC services to children with severe communication disorders during their preschool years. Early attention allows children to develop linguistic, operational, and social competencies necessary to support participation in elementary school. In the United States, the Individuals with

Disabilities Education Act Amendments of 1997 (PL 105-17) mandates publicly funded preschool education for children with disabilities older than the age of 3 years and provides the legal basis for early AAC interventions. AAC teams must design such interventions to meet the conversational and interactional needs of young children—communication for today—as well as the academic and social needs of the general classroom—communication for tomorrow. Thus, AAC team members involved with preschool students must have a solid understanding of the participation requirements of elementary school programs in order to adequately prepare children for these environments.

Transition to Elementary School

The ultimate goal of communication and other interventions for young children is to facilitate their entry into general education environments (Brown et al., 1989; Salisbury & Vincent, 1990; Vincent et al., 1980). Early interventionists have focused increased attention on developing support mechanisms so that children who are not academically competitive by kindergarten age can enter and benefit from general classes with other children of the same age (e.g., Ford et al., 1989; Sailor et al., 1989; Stainback & Stainback, 1990). Several federally funded projects (e.g., Project TEEM in Vermont) have demonstrated successfully that educators can accomplish this at the kindergarten level, to the benefit of children and to the satisfaction of their parents (Conn-Powers, Ross-Allen, & Holburn, 1990; Hamblin-Wilson & Thurman, 1990).

Early intervention specialists have described some of the components that are necessary to facilitate transitions into general kindergarten environments (e.g., Conn-Powers et al., 1990; Salisbury & Vincent, 1990). For a communication professional, one of the most important elements of such inclusion efforts is ensuring that the child receives comprehensive services from a young age, so that he or she has a foundation for communication before beginning elementary school. It is also important to ensure that by the time the child reaches first grade, he or she has the tools necessary for academic participation and instruction. These tools may include an augmented writing system (either electronic or nonelectronic) in addition to whichever spoken communication system the child uses. The tools that a child needs may also include computer or software technology necessary for formal augmented reading instruction (see Blackstone, 1989e). Alternatively, the child may need tools to ensure that he or she participates to some degree in the educational activities of the general classroom. Whatever the case, it is important to start planning for the child's kindergarten placement approximately 2 years before the end of preschool so that interventionists can institute the necessary adaptations and arrangements. If placement in a general classroom is not an option for the child, preparation time is equally important for the next environment, whatever it is.

One way for interventionists to facilitate a smooth transition to kindergarten is to visit the target classroom well before the beginning of the school year in order to gather information about the participation patterns of typical children in that setting. Some kindergarten settings are quite structured and academically oriented, whereas others emphasize building concepts through play, exploration, and cooperative learning. The nature and expectations of the kindergarten environment greatly influence the interactive requirements placed on the child, which will, in turn, influence the direction of intervention planning in the preschool years. Certain early interventionists have developed "kindergarten survival skills" curricula in response to what will be expected of the child (e.g., Rule, Fiechtl, & Innocenti, 1990; Vincent et al., 1980).

Pretransition visits also facilitate dialogue between the kindergarten teacher and professional staff concerning the child's needs and abilities as well as the supports necessary for accommodation. For example, the school may need to make architectural modifications to facilitate physical accessibility or may need to hire a part-time paraprofessional to assist the teacher in optimizing the student's classroom participation. The speech-language pathologist and motor specialists in the new school may want to establish a plan for learning to use whatever communication equipment is in place or for sharing the day-to-day management of the communication program. Family involvement in the transition and planning process is also critical because family members are likely to be the only people with whom the child has regular contact until the transition is complete (Hamblin-Wilson & Thurman, 1990). Thus, family members often play a crucial role in the transfer of information about technology, interaction, and other components of the child's communication program (Berry, 1987). The specific transition-planning process depends on the school district and the individuals involved; however, during the first several months after transition, the educators and staff in the new school need to pay careful attention to the child's needs in order to avoid "reinventing the wheel" by providing redundant or unnecessary interventions.

What do you think?

We received a computer-generated card announcing Maria's graduation from middle school. It was her way of saying thanks and caused us to remember her as a preschool child with few good ways to communicate. Because of her cerebral palsy, she could not speak, walk, or eat independently. She had very expressive eyes, an infectious laugh, and a temper. In just a few years, she made the transition from a home-based program, to a special education preschool, to kindergarten, to first grade. She arrived in first grade with an electronic AAC system and a powered wheelchair. She had not mastered using either, but she had the tools. With the help of her school district personnel and parents, she has been a competitive student who always performs at grade level and never needs to repeat a grade. Along the way, she participated in several summer sessions to enhance her reading, writing, and communication interaction skills. Would she have been this successful if she hadn't received her communication and mobility equipment until entering fourth grade? *What do you think?*

Interventionists and educators must manage transitions between kindergarten and elementary school with care and systematic planning. First, the AAC team should not modify the AAC system unnecessarily during the first year of school. If a child has been prepared well for school, drastic changes to the communication system should not be necessary. If the AAC team makes substantive changes, the child is at risk for falling behind the other students academically while he or she learns to use the revised system. If AAC preparation prior to entry into elementary school has been inadequate, the elementary school AAC team faces a difficult problem and may need to intervene during the first grade, although this timing is not optimal.

Second, the AAC team in the elementary school should have the knowledge and skills to facilitate communication efforts of young AAC users. If team members must learn about an unfamiliar AAC system over the course of the school year, the student's ability to participate in the classroom will probably be affected adversely. We have found that one way to avoid this problem is for a paraprofessional to follow the student from preschool, to kindergarten, to elementary school, especially if his or her AAC system has sophisticated technical requirements. When this is not possible, providing facilitator training for the elementary school staff *prior to the beginning of the academic year* should be a primary goal of transition planning.

Principle 2: Whenever possible, keep the student in the general curriculum.

INVOLVING STUDENTS IN THE GENERAL CURRICULUM

The primary reason for including students with severe communication disabilities in general curricular activities is to expose them to the educational and social benefits of the general classroom. Several negative consequences may result if inclusion does not occur.

First, when students are excluded from the curriculum, teachers (often special educators) must develop personalized educational plans to meet their needs. They deliver this instruction either in a segregated setting (e.g., a resource room, a special education classroom) or in the general classroom during activities that are parallel to, but not the same as, those for other students. Early academic failure often results in a student receiving a totally personalized curriculum for the duration of his or her public school experience. Although a personalized curriculum may not appear problematic in theory, the reality is that such a curriculum often lacks continuity because its content depends on the preferences and philosophies of individual educational staff. Therefore, the individual's curriculum may change dramatically with the arrival of each new teacher or speech-language pathologist. Furthermore, inadequate longitudinal management of a totally personalized curriculum over the years usually results in a splintered educational program that is replete with gaps, redundancies, and oversights. In contrast, the general curriculum provides an overall program structure for educational staff that, at a minimum, encourages a cohesive scope and sequence of instruction.

Second, failure to be involved in the general curriculum appears to reduce available peer pressure and support. For example, in the early elementary school years, there is considerable peer pressure related to learning to read and write. Children with disabilities in general classroom environments are subject to this pressure as much as their classmates without disabilities, and they often respond with the desire to learn what their peers are learning. Peer pressure also encourages children with disabilities to learn at a similar rate to that of other students so that they don't stand out from their peers. A personalized curriculum in which no other students participate eliminates such opportunities for peer pressure and support.

Third, failure to be involved in the general curriculum diminishes opportunities for peer interaction and instruction. Even if a student with disabilities is physically present in a general classroom, opportunities for social and academic involvement with other students are reduced if he or she has a personalized curriculum. In addition, a personalized curriculum eliminates almost all opportunities for peer instruction in either direction (i.e., a child with disabilities tutoring a peer without disabilities or vice versa).

Fourth, lack of participation in the general curriculum may shape students' perceptions of themselves negatively and may also foster negative impressions of the students in the eyes of their classmates, teachers, and family members. If, however, students participate successfully in typical curricular experiences, they learn to see themselves as academically able and active in the same arena as their peers without disabilities.

In order to foster change in regular education, special educators need to reduce their current emphasis on classifying, labeling, and offering "special" programs for students who do not fit within the present regular education structure. Instead, they should put more emphasis on joining with regular educators to work for a reorganization of or modifications in the structure of regular education itself so that the needs of a wider range of students can be met within the mainstream of regular education. (Stainback, Stainback, Courtnage, & Jaben, 1985, p. 148)

THE PARTICIPATION MODEL

We use the Participation Model (see Figure 6.1) as a framework for making decisions associated with including AAC users in general educational programs. The following sections discuss and illustrate applications of the model to meet the needs of AAC users in general classrooms.

Identify Participation Patterns

In the past, students who were not academically competitive were usually excluded from general classrooms. Since the mid-1980s, inclusion has become more widespread in North America, although various levels of participation still exist in inclusive classrooms. We propose four variables that interventionists can manipulate to achieve a participation pattern that is appropriate to the needs and capabilities of an individual student. These include three levels of integration, four levels of academic participation, four levels of social participation, and three levels of independence, which Figure 14.1 depicts.

Integration

The term *integration* refers to the physical presence of a student with disabilities in a general classroom attended by same-age peers. Table 14.1 shows the three basic levels of integration: full, selective, and none.

An increasing number of students with AAC needs are *fully integrated* in general classroom environments, which means that they are physically present in the same classrooms attended by their same-age peers during a significant part of the school day. Thus, they, their classmates, and the teacher all consider them as part of the class. Physical integration may be all that is needed for social and academic advantages to accrue, but the mere physical presence of students with AAC needs in general classrooms usually is not enough to ensure social and academic participation. Thus, integration as we have defined it is *necessary but not sufficient* to ensure classroom participation and full inclusion (i.e., physical integration *and* academic and social participation).

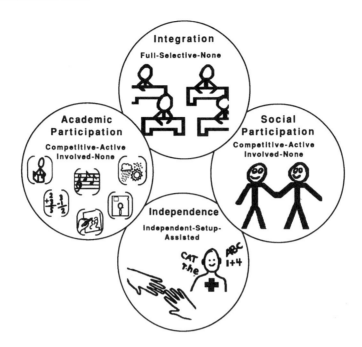

Figure 14.1. Four variables that can be manipulated to achieve a participation pattern for an individual student.

Lindsey is a 10-year-old student with severe, multiple disabilities who is included in a general classroom. Basic technology along with the support of school personnel and classmates who view her as a full-fledged member of the class help her to participate actively during classroom activities such as the following:

- A classmate records the weekly spelling words on an audiotape, and on Fridays Lindsey activates the tape recorder to announce each word and a sentence that includes the word. After about 8 seconds the Powerlink (AbleNet, Inc.) automatically turns off the tape until Lindsey activates the switch again to announce a subsequent word and sentence.
- In physical education class, also called "Sweating with Lindsey," the students must exercise as long as the music plays, and, of course, Lindsey controls the switch. At the end of the class, the students spontaneously line up and file by her wheelchair to give her "high fives" for a job well done.
- Lindsey uses a switch to activate an audiotape player to "read aloud" to her peers during storytime. A fellow student holds up the book to show pictures and illustrations.
- Lindsey uses a digital AAC device to announce her choices during snacktime and breaktime.
- When the teacher asks a question in class, Lindsey selects the student who is to respond. She activates a slide projector with a carousel containing two slides of each student, one with a serious and one with a silly pose. By changing the order of the slides occasionally, the students cannot predict when they will be called on to respond to a question. Also, anticipating the silly photo keeps the students attentive, as well as entertained. (Locke & Piché, 1994)

Selective integration in general classrooms may be an appropriate option in some situations, depending on a student's individual academic or social needs. For example, we know of high school students with severe disabilities who choose to spend one or two periods of their school day receiving remedial literacy instruction in a resource room environment rather than attending study hall, music, art, or other elective classes. Parents may also prefer the option of selective integration so that their child can receive specialized remediation services. We know at least one adolescent girl with physical disabilities whose parents prefer that she receive physical therapy in a separate room because they are uncomfortable having her therapy administered in physical education class while her friends without disabilities play basketball or do aerobics. Some students may spend considerable amounts of school time in community environments receiving vocational, recreational, or other instruction appropriate to their long-term needs. These selectively integrated students participate at various levels in the general school curriculum for the remainder of the school day.

Students may be selectively integrated as part of the process of moving from no integration to full integration. For example, it is not uncommon for students with mental retardation to spend most of their school day in a school or classroom separate from their peers, with the exception of one or two periods. These classes often include the nonacademic activities mentioned previously, such as art class, music class, library time, lunchtime, or recess. Although this type of selective integration may be a laudable first step toward full integration, it is rarely sufficient to offset the negative consequences to the student of falling out of the curriculum that we mention previously.

Some students with AAC systems may attend *no* general classes during one or more years of their school programs. As noted previously, a variety of social, legal, and educational mandates are rapidly reducing this segregation in many parts of the world. Special circumstances, however, may exist in which AAC and educational services provided in separate settings benefit the children involved. For example, we know of separate classrooms in the United States in which children with severe multiple disabilities receive intensive *short-term* instruction from AAC specialists with extensive technical and educational expertise. The explicit goals of these specialized classrooms are to 1) provide the children with suitable alternative access methods, 2) teach them to use their AAC systems efficiently, 3) provide extensive literacy instruction, and 4) integrate the students into general classrooms eventually. When professional expertise and the commitment to long-term academic and AAC gains are not available in inclusive settings, separate educational programming for these students may be a *short-term* solution.

Table 14.1. Levels of general classroom integration

Level	Definition
Full	Physically present in age-appropriate general education settings for the entire school day. At times, activity patterns may vary from those of peers.
Selective	Physically present in age-appropriate general education settings during some, but not all, of the school day. Receives educational services in separate classroom, resource room, community, or other settings during the remainder of the school day.
None (excluded)	Physically excluded from age-appropriate general education settings during all of the school day. There may be access to hallways or other settings used by peers without disabilities but at times separate from peers without disabilities.

Academic Participation

Table 14.2 shows the four levels of academic participation, listed from the highest to lowest level of participation.

Competitive

Competitive academic participation requires that a student with AAC needs meet the academic standards expected of peers who do not use AAC. Nevertheless, this does not necessarily mean that the student with disabilities completes all of the activities that his or her peers complete. For example, students with AAC systems often cannot write as rapidly as their peers, and, therefore, teachers may expect them to complete a reduced amount of written classwork, as long as they meet the same academic standards as their classmates. Some students may choose to reduce their total academic workloads in order to fulfill the requirements of classes in which they are competitive. For example, it is not uncommon for students with severe disabilities at the postsecondary level to enroll in only one or two classes each semester so that they can succeed academically and still have time to participate in the social opportunities available on a college campus. It is also important to note that students may be competitive in one, several, or all areas of the curriculum. Thus, an elementary school student may be competitive in math, reading, music, and art, while meeting somewhat lower expectations in other areas. Educators should determine each student's level of academic participation on an individual basis.

Competitive academic participation requires that families, teachers, and specialists coordinate efforts so that the student can work with maximal efficiency. The expectations of competitive academic participation do not allow for an adapted or remedial curriculum, taught by specialists, which is different from that of the general classroom. If educational specialists expect competitive participation, they must act as consultants to general classroom teachers so that all school activities contribute to the student's overall educational goal. In short, during competitive participation, educators should expect that the student will meet competitive standards and should modify activities and workloads as appropriate; educators should not, however, modify their standards and expect the student to complete the same quantity of work as his or her peers.

Active

Not all students with AAC systems can be academically competitive in all areas. Nevertheless, many students can be *academically active* and participate in the general curriculum, although they may not be able to meet the same academic standards as their

Table 14.2. Levels of academic participation

Level	Definition
Competitive	Academic expectations are the same as for peers, although the workload may be adjusted. Academic progress is evaluated in the same way as peer performance.
Active	Academic expectations are less than for peers, although similar content is taught. The workload may be adjusted. Academic progress is evaluated according to individualized standards.
Involved	Academic expectations are minimal. Student is included in classroom activities to the extent possible, with alternative activities available when needed. Progress is evaluated according to individualized standards.
None	No academic participation expectations at all. Student is passive during most learning activities in the general classroom. Progress may not be evaluated at all.

peers. Maintaining these students as active participants in general classrooms allows them to experience many of the benefits of inclusion, such as exposure to a structured educational sequence, peer social contact, and peer instruction. Meanwhile, agreements among educational staff and parents regarding the students' academic activity can reduce the pressures of competitive expectations and the negative experiences that might result from unrealistic expectations. Calculator and Jorgensen (1991) and Mirenda and Calculator (1993) described several curricular design strategies that educators can use to help AAC users to be active learners in the general classroom.

What do you think?

In 1986, all of the children who used AAC systems in Lincoln, Nebraska, public schools attended four schools. Many of the children went to special classrooms, although some went to general classrooms for parts of the day. AAC teams were present in each of the schools. Twelve years later, children who use AAC systems attended every school in the district—about 43 different schools! This arrangement allows children to have an inclusive education; however, it has become much more complicated to deliver assistive technology services. Is the tradeoff worth it—the benefits of community-based education versus the difficulties of decentralized assistive technology services?   *What do you think?*

Many students with AAC systems will be competitive in some academic areas and active in others. Alternatively, some students may be active in all areas and competitive in none; educators expect them to participate in the curriculum at some level, be involved with and learn at least part of the same academic content as other students, and be evaluated according to their individual goals. An active student may receive supplementary instruction to develop particular skills in certain areas such as math or reading. Depending on the academic expectations, the focus of the curriculum may shift from academic to functional goals as the students progress through school.

Involved

Some students, together with their educational teams and parents, may decide that participation in certain academic areas will be limited to *academic involvement,* rather than competitive or active participation. In this case, the student attends general class activities along with peer students but participates less actively in the general curriculum. For example, some students who are unable to speak or sing may enjoy being involved in the school choir. Because of their disabilities, they are not expected to be competitive or active on a routine basis; however, they like music and enjoy being around the music teacher and thus benefit in a number of ways from the experience and the positive social atmosphere of the choir.

Educators should not limit students' involvement to elective areas such as music and art. By modifying or adapting class activities, a teacher can involve a student who uses AAC in the general curriculum in many ways that meet the student's educational or social goals (Calculator & Jorgensen, 1991; Mirenda & Calculator, 1993). For example, we know of one selectively integrated junior high school student with severe disabilities who was involved one school year in general social studies, English, shop (e.g., woodworking), and health classes and who also received instruction in a variety of community environments. Some of the classes were of special interest to him (e.g., woodworking, health), whereas his team recommended others because the teachers were known to be accepting of students with AAC needs, regardless of their level of participation. In all of the classes, teachers made modifications so that he could work on relevant educational goals, and in none of these classes was he merely a passive observer with no involvement whatsoever. Again, students who use AAC may be involved in some areas, active in others, and competitive in still others.

None

The level of *no academic participation* is never acceptable or defensible, although it occurs far too often. In this case, the student is physically present in a general classroom for a particular lesson or activity but is passive and uninvolved for the majority of time. This may occur for a number of reasons, often because the student does not have the AAC tools needed for participation. Even fully integrated students may have no academic participation in one or more classroom activities, and this undesirable option requires prompt remediation.

It is wise to choose a school that your neighborhood friends attend. I was no surprise to the majority of my classmates; they had known me and how I did things for many years before I became a fellow classmate. They also were able to explain about me to any new students who had never met me or had any exposure to a person with disabilities. (Victor Valentic, a fully integrated, competitive AAC user, in Valentic, 1991, p. 9)

Social Participation

School involves more than just academic learning because all curricular and extracurricular activities occur within social contexts. Parents of typical students show their awareness of this aspect of school when they request that their child be assigned to the same classroom as a friend or to a specific teacher who encourages social development. The participation patterns of students with disabilities can also be described by four levels of social participation (see Table 14.3), similar to the four levels of academic participation discussed previously.

Competitive

Socially competitive students are active participants in a social group of peers. They are involved in the activities of the group, at least by choosing whether to engage in activities, and exert influence over group decisions. For example, a socially competitive student might initiate activities such as birthday or slumber parties on occasion and, in turn, is invited to similar activities by other group members. The student who is socially competitive typically plays, visits, "hangs out," or otherwise interacts with his or her classmates after school hours (e.g., weekends, evenings).

Active

Not all students with or without disabilities are socially competitive, but many are *socially active*. They make choices about and are involved in social activities, although

Table 14.3.   Levels of social participation

Level	Definition
Competitive	Chooses whether to be involved in social contexts with peers. Actively participates in social interactions. Actively influences the activities of the social group.
Active	Chooses whether to be involved in social contexts with peers. Actively participates in social interactions. Usually does not directly influence the activities of the group.
Involved	Chooses whether to be involved in social contexts with peers. Participation may be passive. Does not directly influence the activities of the group.
None	Is not involved in social interactions with peers.

they may not exert much influence over the social climate of a group and its interaction patterns. Some readers may have been able to apply this designation to themselves when they were children because they were "shy" or "studious" individuals who were not necessarily socially isolated but who also did not have a wide circle of friends. Socially active students with AAC needs may spend more time alone after school than do socially competitive students, although they may have some opportunities for interaction with peers who do not have disabilities. As with levels of academic participation, students may be socially active in some areas and competitive or involved in others.

Involved

Students who are *socially involved* attend class with their peers who do not have disabilities and may be involved in some extracurricular activities. Socially involved students, however, do not influence social situations and often are passive observers in social activities. Students who are socially involved in school rarely maintain contact with their peers after school hours. Thus, they may spend their evenings and weekends engaged in activities primarily with family members rather than with friends.

None

Students who have *no social participation* have limited access to their peers during school hours and thus have no opportunities to form friendships or make acquaintances. They are not members of a social group during school or nonschool hours. As is the case with academic participation, no social participation is generally undesirable and requires remediation.

Social participation patterns coexist with the patterns of inclusion and academic participation described previously. For example, when students with disabilities are at least selectively integrated in general classrooms, they have opportunities for social inclusion at some level, regardless of whether they are academically competitive, active, or involved. The extent of inclusion and social involvement for students with AAC needs depends on many factors. Students may be integrated—that is, physically present in general classrooms—as a result of school policy. Nevertheless, educational staff and family members still need to encourage the active social involvement of these students. An active or competitive level of social participation requires that students who use AAC form mutual friendships with some peers. (Chapter 10 contains descriptions of approaches for encouraging and facilitating mutual friendships, such as the Circles of Friends process.) Because the peer group plays such an important role in determining the level of social participation, educational personnel and family members can directly influence this component only to a limited extent.

Independence

School personnel must also plan for the level of independence expected in each academic area. Table 14.4 shows three levels of independence that serve as useful descriptions for students who are included in general classrooms.

As can be seen from this table, some students may be *completely independent* in at least some activities. Many AAC students, however, require appropriate environmental and technical assistance at the outset of an activity to set up their work environments or change position in the classroom. When these setup activities are completed, the students can function independently. Some other students need to be assisted in order to participate in general classrooms. The teacher is not the only available source of ongoing human assistance, and perhaps the primary (and most underutilized) source of assistance is the general classroom peer group.

Ideally, all students who use AAC systems should have opportunities to function independently (either with or without initial setup assistance) during some, but not necessarily all, of each school day. In early grades, AAC teams can easily facilitate such independence during language arts activities because students tend to work in small reading groups with other students at a similar academic level. It is important that students who use AAC participate independently at least some of the time because it communicates to the students themselves and to their classmates that they are legitimate members of the class in both academic and social areas. Independence also requires well-coordinated support efforts from the AAC team. For example, if a student is unable to independently participate in a subject area for several days, it is often a sign that the AAC team is not fulfilling its responsibilities by keeping the vocabulary in the AAC system current or by maintaining the device. Selective independent participation frees the educational staff from the expectation that the child must be independent throughout the entire school day in order to be included in a general classroom. We cannot emphasize enough that neither independence nor academic competitiveness are appropriate prerequisites to general classroom inclusion.

We can, whenever and wherever we choose, successfully teach all children whose schooling is of interest to us. We already know more than we need in order to do this. Whether we do it must finally depend on how we feel about the fact that we haven't done it so far. (Edmonds, 1979, p. 29)

Individual Participation Patterns

The discussion of patterns of participation in general classrooms is meant to serve as both a conceptual and a practical tool. We intend for the AAC team, which includes the student who uses AAC and his or her family, to address the various levels of integration, academic and social participation, and independence when making decisions about the desired participation profile prior to the beginning of each school year. This approach contrasts with a less systematic approach to inclusion that basically involves placing the student in a general classroom and then "seeing what happens." We have found that for many students with AAC needs, the latter approach almost guarantees confusion, frustration, and often failure. In order to facilitate systematic planning, we

Table 14.4.   Levels of independence

Level	Definition
Independent	Able to participate in an activity without assistance.
Independent with setup	Independent in an activity with assistance to set up, for example, educational materials, AAC or other equipment, or physical position.
Assisted	Able to participate in an activity with physical or verbal assistance from a teacher, paraprofessional, or peer student.

have provided a matrix in Figure 14.2 that the AAC team can use to discuss and make decisions about inclusion, academic and social participation, and independence.

The first decision concerns the integration pattern: Will the student attend a general classroom full time, selectively, or not at all? If integration is to be selective, in which specific curricular or extracurricular activities will it occur? Numerous factors influence these decisions, not the least of which may be the policies or practices of the school district, and the AAC team may need to address these before further planning can occur. Although our bias is toward full integration or nearly full integration with very few specialized classes, some families may choose a less inclusive participation pattern for their children for a variety of reasons. The family, AAC user, and the rest of the AAC team will need to arrive at consensus concerning the individual's level of integration.

Instructions: List school subjects and activities in the boxes that correspond with the individual's level of integration and participation. Then, using the following labels, indicate his or her level of independence in each activity: I = independent; Is = independent with setup; As = assisted.

Integration		Participation			
		Competitive	Active	Involved	None
Full	A				
	S				
Selective	A				
	S				
None	A				
	S				

Figure 14.2.   Inclusion, academic and social participation, and independence matrix. (Key: A = academic areas; S = social areas.)

Assuming that some level of integration is desirable and feasible, the next set of decisions relates to academic and social participation. For each area targeted for inclusion, what is the desired level of academic participation for the student? That is, is the student expected to be competitive, active, or involved? The AAC team can enter this information in Figure 14.2 for each academic (*A*) subject. Then, they can make similar decisions for the desired level of social (*S*) participation in each area of inclusion, using the corresponding line in the table to record decisions. Decisions regarding the desired level of independence in each area can be coded according to the scheme in Figure 14.2. We designed this matrix to facilitate team decision making in these areas so that AAC professionals will not approach inclusion haphazardly or, in the worst case, not at all. Two brief examples of the application of this multidimensional matrix follow.

Chad

Table 14.5 illustrates the participation profile that an AAC team targeted for Chad, a 13-year-old student. The AAC team in Chad's school began planning to include him in general classes when he entered junior high. Prior to this, he received all of his instruction in a separate special education classroom for students with severe physical disabilities and mental retardation requiring extensive support. He operated an electronic scanning device with a headswitch to communicate in social situations, and he was able to access a standard computer via a special cable that connected the device to the computer. The first decision made by Chad, his parents, and the rest of the education team was to aim for selective integration for the next school year. The team identified the following learning priorities for Chad: 1) literacy skills, 2) music (an activity that he enjoyed), 3) functional math skills, 4) computer skills, 5) physical therapy, and 6) community-based vocational instruction. The team included social studies as an additional learning priority because the teacher was a supportive facilitator of social interactions between students with and without disabilities. Thus, the team decided that Chad would be selectively integrated in general social studies, music, and beginning

Table 14.5.   Integration/academic and social participation/independence matrix for Chad

Integration		Participation			
		Competitive	Active	Involved	None
Full	A				
	S				
Selective	A		As: **computer class**, reading, math, physical therapy, vocational	As: **social studies** Is: **music**	
	S		active/involved in all integrated classes		
None	A				
	S				

A = academic areas; S = social areas; I = independent; Is = independent with setup; As = assisted; bold type = general classes.

computer classes and that he would receive his physical therapy, literacy (e.g., reading), functional math, and vocational instruction in specialized classes. The team planned an involved level of academic participation for social studies and music, whereas they chose an active level of academic participation for the remaining subject areas. Chad, his family, and the rest of the team wanted him to be socially active or involved as much as possible. Finally, they agreed that Chad would need assistance in order to participate at the desired levels in all areas except music.

Heather

Table 14.6 depicts the desired participation profile for Heather, a young student with severe athetoid cerebral palsy. Planning for integration into first grade began for Heather at the end of kindergarten. During her kindergarten year, she received an electronic direct-selection AAC device with a small, portable printer that was mounted on her powered wheelchair. The AAC team determined that Heather should be fully integrated in the first grade, and, after negotiation, the school district agreed to this goal. Furthermore, the team felt that Heather should be expected to be competitive in all academic areas, active in elective areas such as art and music, and involved in physical education. In addition, the AAC team and her family recommended that Heather should receive specialized instruction in the use of her AAC device three times per week, while her classmates engaged in free reading. Everyone agreed that she could be socially competitive or active in all areas. Heather's team targeted a combination of total independence and independence with setup as well as assisted independence in some areas to facilitate this high level of participation.

These two examples of Chad and Heather illustrate that although students with severe communication disorders may not be able to participate independently and competitively in all aspects of school life, they can participate to some degree. Careful, thoughtful planning and decision making in both academic and social areas allows for flexibility in an educational program, which permits a mix of competitive, active, and involved participation. Careful planning also allows parents and school staff to tailor academic and social expectations to the specific needs and abilities of the child, thus allowing clarification and evaluation of the responsibilities of each team member.

Once the decision about my education was made by myself and my parents, plans for how to manage that education were soon under way, and still are today as I complete high school and head for college. We have a formula; as problems present themselves, solutions are sought, and, at times, we have learned that you never give up, just keep on trying. (Victor Valentic, a fully integrated, competitive AAC user, in Valentic, 1991, p. 9)

Activity/Standards Inventory and Barrier Assessment

When the team has established the desired level of general class participation, they can implement intervention strategies by following the preliminary steps of the Participation Model (see Figure 6.1). The first step is completing an activity/standards inventory in the classroom at the beginning of the school year using the form in Figure 6.3. This inventory involves a detailed list of all activities that typical students are expected to

Table 14.6. Integration/academic and social participation/independence matrix for Heather

Integration		Participation			
		Competitive	Active	Involved	None
Full (except no silent reading time 3 times per week; replace with AAC instruction)	A	I or Is: **reading, writing, spelling, math, science, health, social studies**	Is or As: **music, art**	As: **physical education**	
	S	competitive or active in all areas			
Selective	A				
	S				
None	A				
	S				

A = academic areas; S = social areas; I = independent; Is = independent with setup; As = assisted; bold type = general classes.

complete during the school day, along with expected levels of academic participation. (Note that the levels of independence listed in Figure 6.3 are more specific than those in Figure 14.2. This is because actual implementation requires a more precise breakdown of the levels of assistance according to the types of assistance [e.g., verbal, physical] that educators need to provide.)

Next, the team should complete a similar analysis of the actual participation of the AAC user in the general classroom for activities identified as inclusion targets. Again, it is important to conduct this analysis as early in the school year as possible so that team members can identify and remedy discrepancies from the expected participation for peers, the target student's current level of participation, and the desired level of participation. Following that, the team makes observations about the types of barriers preventing participation.

As an example, Table 14.7 displays part of the activity/standards inventory completed for Heather. It became clear as team members completed the activity/standards inventory in the first month of school that most of Heather's peers were independent learners after setup. The team had agreed that this was a reasonable goal for Heather as well. The activity/standards inventory revealed that she was unable to participate at this level of support and was falling rapidly behind her classmates as a result. The AAC team thought this was the result of an opportunity barrier rather than a problem with access because she had the necessary AAC equipment at school to participate in math activities. The math curriculum used in her classroom, however, required her to work with manipulable items in various configurations, but she could not because of her physical impairments. She was also unable to complete work on the chalkboard because of her physical impairments and could not complete her homework because she was not allowed to take her school-owned AAC device home after school. In order to overcome the first two barriers, the team assigned a paraprofessional to provide Heather with assistance during math. Her parents agreed to assist her with homework and ask her to solve problems for which they wrote down the answers. Because the

Table 14.7. Activity/standards inventory for Heather

Directions:
1. List the *primary and secondary activities* in which peers without disabilities are expected to participate across the school day.
2. Select one or more peers without disabilities who are typical in terms of their ability to achieve the expected standards. After observing one of the peers in each of the activities listed, indicate the *level of peer participation* achieved by entering a *P* in the appropriate standards category for each activity.
3. After observing the target individual in each activity, indicate the *level of participation* achieved by entering a *T* in the appropriate standards category.
4. In the Discrepancy column, indicate *yes* if a participation gap exists for the target individual as compared with the peers, and *no* if a participation gap does not exist.
5. Based on your observations and impressions, indicate whether the barrier to participation appears to be related to opportunity barriers, access barriers, or both.

Activity	Level of peer participation					Discrepancy		Type(s) of barrier(s)	
	Independent	Independent with setup	Verbal assistance	Physical assistance	Unable to participate	Yes	No	Opportunity	Access
Math									
1. Complete worksheets from book.		P, T					X		
2. Answer questions in class.			P, T				X		
3. Do work on board.		P			T	X		X	
4. Work with manipulable items: count, sort.		P			T	X		X	
5. Complete homework.		P	P	P	T	X		X	

AAC team identified these obstacles early in the year, Heather quickly regained much of the ground she had lost.

As this example demonstrates, the activity/standards inventory process is critical in order to translate inclusion planning and desired levels of academic participation into realities. In situations in which several educational staff are involved in an instructional activity, completing this inventory can help the educational team reach a consensus.

It should be emphasized that saying it can be done is not the same as saying it will be easy. (Stainback & Stainback, 1990, p. 7)

Assess Opportunity Barriers

As the previous discussion about Heather shows, both opportunity and access barriers can account for discrepancies between the participation patterns of AAC users and those of their peers. Both types of barriers can limit academic or social participation. Because the AAC team's ability to overcome these barriers often makes the difference between successful and failed inclusion efforts, we discuss them in this section and following sections. First, we consider a variety of *opportunity barriers* that may interfere with inclusion efforts.

It is often helpful to identify opportunity barriers during a team meeting among representatives of the family, educational staff, and educational administrators. A thorough assessment of opportunity issues using a format similar to that in Figure 6.4 (Opportunity Assessment) is likely to reveal that each party is responsible for contributing to one or more barriers. Acknowledging this shared responsibility tends to diminish unnecessary blame laying or finger pointing among team members. For example, Table 14.8 contains a portion of the assessment of opportunity barriers that Heather's family and educational team completed.

Table 14.8 reveals that the school district policy prohibiting children from taking school-owned AAC devices home with them limited Heather's ability to complete homework and interact socially. Unfortunately, the team's inability to resolve this policy barrier meant that Heather's family had to obtain funding to purchase equipment for Heather to use at home.

In addition, it was a long-standing practice in Heather's school for young elementary school–age students to receive motor specialty services such as physical and occupational therapy in the morning, whereas the older elementary students received these services in the afternoon. This practice interfered with Heather's ability to participate in both math and language arts activities, which occurred every morning in her first-grade class. Furthermore, the speech-language pathologist did not employ a curriculum-based approach to service delivery. Pull-out speech therapy began to compete for academic time with curricular activities. Heather's team resolved these problems through an agreement with Heather's parents that she would receive motor specialty services during the regularly scheduled physical education class each morning instead of during math and language arts. In addition, the speech-language pathologist agreed

Table 14.8. Assessment of opportunity barriers for Heather

Directions:
1. List the activities for which potential opportunity barriers have been identified for the target student.
2. Indicate the nature of the opportunity barrier (e.g., policy, practice, attitude, knowledge, skill).
3. Briefly describe the intervention plan and those responsible for its implementation.

Activity	Opportunity barrier					Intervention plan and person(s) responsible
	Policy	Practice	Attitude	Knowledge	Skill	
1. Math, work on board, and work with manipulables		X				Hire a paraprofessional to provide assistance.
2. All homework, social interactions after school hours	X					Family will need to purchase AAC equipment with private funds.
3. Math, language arts conflicts with PT, OT, SLP schedule		X				Schedule PT during PE activities; SLP to offer direct services in the first grade during language arts
4. All curricular areas: lack of familiarity with first-grade curriculum, SpEd teacher not interested in learning content			X, SpEd	X, SLP, para., OT, PT		Education and familiarization of all specialty staff regarding first-grade curriculum; education regarding consultant role of special educator
5. Operating and programming the AAC device				X, all but SLP, para.	X	Orientation to first graders and teacher by SLP; paraprofessional to assume primary role for programming and maintenance until others are adept
6. Paraprofessional assignment and role		X		X		Assign para. to Heather and other AAC student in another first grade, meet biweekly to see if this works, adjust as needed, write district job description for para. by end of year

to discontinue pull-out speech therapy, and instead, she worked with Heather during her regularly scheduled language arts class to help her develop and use her speech in her reading group.

Another identified barrier pertained to the attitude of the special education teacher. She was experienced in planning individualized education programs for students with disabilities but had no experience acting as a consultant to a general classroom teacher in the context of an established curriculum. Moreover, she was not interested in taking the time to familiarize herself with the curriculum used in the first grade. Clearly, in order to integrate students while offering appropriate supports to general education staff, cooperative, not antagonistic or competitive, attitudes must prevail. Unfortunately, Heather's first-grade teacher did not receive appropriate educational supports from the special education teacher, although the paraprofessional, Heather's parents, and the speech-language pathologist all helped to fill in the major gaps.

The educators and support staff at Heather's school had many knowledge and skill barriers. Although the speech-language pathologist and the paraprofessional were both able to operate and program Heather's AAC device, the other school personnel—the general education teacher, special education teacher, and students—were largely unfamiliar with the equipment. In addition, as with the special education teacher, the paraprofessional and other staff were unfamiliar with the first-grade curriculum, although they were willing to familiarize themselves with its content. Because Heather was the first AAC user in the district to be fully included, her school's administrator had no experience or knowledge base concerning the role of the paraprofessional assigned to the first-grade classroom. Table 14.8 shows that much of the planning related to these knowledge and skill barriers required careful, ongoing attention at many levels. This is not unusual and should be expected, especially during the pioneering phase of inclusion efforts within a school or district. What is important is that team members view opportunity barriers as just that—as *barriers that can be overcome*—not as reasons to abandon the inclusion plan for either an individual student or for the district as a whole.

The removal of opportunity barriers is sometimes sufficient to allow a student to achieve the desired pattern of participation. Nevertheless, students who require AAC assistance may face access barriers to consider as well.

When education happens, it happens in the mind of the student. (Anonymous)

Assess Barriers to Access

Chapters 6 and 7 contain detailed discussions of assessment procedures to identify access barriers and strategies for instituting access-related interventions. Generic interventions such as those related to natural abilities, environmental adaptations, and AAC systems or devices are identified in the Participation Model (see Figure 6.1) because they apply to individuals of all ages and disabilities. In addition, a number of intervention issues, which the following sections discuss, require special attention for students in classroom environments.

Assess the Communication Patterns and Vocabulary Requirements of the Classroom

Within a typical classroom, several different types of learning contexts occur throughout the day, each with different inherent communication patterns. Some of these contexts are teacher-directed whereas others are primarily student-directed. Teacher-directed learning contexts include those related to whole-group instruction, in which the teacher interacts with the entire class, and those related to small-group learning, in which the teacher interacts with small groups for specialized instruction or sharing time. Student-directed activities include cooperative learning groups and some one-to-one interactions. Each of these has different implications for students who use AAC.

Teacher-Directed Large-Group Instruction

Sturm and Nelson (1997) studied communication patterns in first-, third-, and fifth-grade general classrooms. They identified 10 unofficial "rules" that guide most teacher-directed large-group instructional activities:

1. Teachers mostly talk and students mostly listen, except when the teacher grants permission to talk.
2. Teachers give cues about when to listen closely.
3. Teachers convey content about things and procedures about how to do things.
4. Teacher talk gets more complex in the upper grades.
5. Teachers ask questions and expect specific responses.
6. Teachers give hints about what is correct and what is important to them.
7. Student talk should be brief and to the point.
8. Students should ask few questions and keep them short.
9. Students talk to teachers, not to other students.
10. Students can make a limited number of spontaneous comments, but only about the process or content of the lesson.

Together, these 10 unofficial rules have implications for AAC students who participate in teacher-led group instructional activities. First, teachers expect students to be brief and provide relevant information. Second, teachers tend to ask questions about information that they think is important. Thus, teachers of large groups control most interactions and are likely to be very effective informants regarding AAC vocabulary issues because they already have an established agenda about the information that they expect students to know. Once the AAC team has identified important words and messages, they can "pool" the words for all students as part of the educational presentation on flipcharts, blackboards, and so forth so that the AAC user and his or her classmates have ready access to them. Alternatively, the AAC team can program the words individually into a student's AAC system.

Teacher-Directed Small-Group Instruction

Usually, the purpose of small-group instruction is to develop language, literacy, and thinking skills, with an emphasis on comprehension of text material and verbal expression (Anderson, Evertson, & Brophy, 1980; Tharpe & Gallimore, 1988). Small-group interactions tend to be topical but conversationally based, with considerable teacher-initiated questions and student responses. Individual students may interact by competing for turns or by being called on either randomly or sequentially. At times, the teacher encourages whole-group discussion. Because the teacher again tends to control both the topics discussed and the questions asked in small-group instruction, he or she can act as an informant to guide the advance preparation of AAC materials for students who need them.

Sharing Time

Teachers usually employ a sharing format for current events presentations, reports, and show-and-tell activities. According to Duchan (1995), people use language sharing contexts primarily to describe events in a logical and temporal sequence, usually in past tense (e.g., "Last weekend, we went to visit my grandmother. We drove there in a car. We stopped for lunch at Happy Holly's. When we got there. . . ."). Often, the teacher will comment following the completion of a student's narration and perhaps ask questions to expand or clarify the content. At times, the teacher encourages other students to ask questions. Thus, sharing time interactions are very much like the storytelling contexts described in Chapter 2, and AAC teams can design sharing time messages as we describe in that chapter.

Cooperative Group Instruction

Researchers have a poor understanding of the interactions that occur in the context of cooperative learning. In a cooperative learning group, there is often no designated leader. Thus, communication patterns among students in such groups appear to resemble more closely those that occur in peer conversational interactions than those that occur during teacher-led group instruction. Without the direction of an adult interaction facilitator, one might expect that cooperative learning groups might present communication difficulties for children using AAC systems because the group interactions often have little structure or predictability. However, one study demonstrated that educators can use such groups successfully as contexts for communication instruction. Hunt, Staub, Alwell, and Goetz (1994) described the involvement of three elementary school–age students with severe, multiple disabilities in cooperative learning activities within general classrooms. Experimenters selected target communication and motor responses in advance for the children and instructed peers without disabilities to provide appropriate cues, prompts, and consequences to teach these responses. The authors reported that by the end of the intervention all of the children with severe disabilities demonstrated the target communication and motor responses without prompting or assistance from their peers.

Seth was unable to speak and communicated with an AAC system. He was assigned to a collaborative learning group to prepare a class report on tornadoes. Each member of the group was responsible for a different aspect of the report. With the help of his paraeducator, he entered the report in his AAC system. He gave the presentation, releasing the report one sentence at a time, and participated in a panel discussion by asking questions of the other members in his group. Occasionally, he was able to answer a question from his classmates.

One-to-One Interactions

Simpson (1996) videotaped a series of students who used AAC systems in general classrooms. He observed that communication patterns varied considerably from one student to another. Although some of the students communicated primarily with their teacher, others distributed their interactions quite equally among the teacher, the paraeducator, and their peers. Other students interacted almost exclusively with their paraeducators in one-to-one teaching contexts. Assessment of the interaction patterns of the AAC student with the paraeducator, general classroom teacher, and peers may provide information about the unique vocabulary-use patterns of the classroom environment. Obviously, the AAC user will need specific vocabulary words related to educational activities as well as vocabulary to manage conversational interactions that occur on a one-to-one basis.

Pulling It All Together

As is apparent from the previous sections, the ultimate goal is to support students who use AAC so that they can be active learners, both academically and socially, in general classroom environments. We have found that to accomplish this goal, teachers must support students' communication in ways that match the requirements of a range of instructional situations. In order to be active learners, students must be able to participate in the classroom by having appropriate access to communication vocabulary items. Because of the rapidly changing content of classroom communication, however, it is difficult to provide all of the necessary vocabulary in a child's AAC system. Rather, teachers must "engineer the classroom" to provide all the children in the class with the communication supports that the AAC user needs (Goossens' & Crain, 1992).

With teacher-directed large- and small-group instruction, teachers are usually aware in advance of the information that they expect students to know. Thus, with some coaching, most teachers can learn to manage these instructional contexts so that they can make the necessary communication supports available to AAC students and their peers within the classroom environment. However, during sharing time, cooperative learning, and one-to-one activities, the communication expectations may be considerably less predictable and more interactive in nature. We find that, whenever possible, educators should add the messages needed to support instruction in such classroom contexts directly to students' AAC systems. These collaborative activities often provide excellent contexts for the development of skills related to linguistic and social competence.

As an AAC team we were uncomfortable that Julie was not getting sufficient conversational practice with her AAC system. We had worked so hard to support her as a successful student that most of our efforts focused on communication for academic participation. AAC support was directed toward the messages that allowed her to answer her teacher's questions, prepare her assignments, and develop her language skills. She was a successful student and performed at grade level.

To provide more opportunities for conversational interaction, her teacher agreed to increase collaborative learning experiences in the classroom. Julie's speech-language pathologist arranged her schedule so that she was in Julie's classroom during some of these times. She worked with Julie to develop the messages that would support conversational interactions with her peers and to coach her to use small talk, storytelling, turn taking, attention getting, and other pragmatic skills.

Assess Teacher Style

In order to include an AAC student successfully in a general classroom, it is useful to observe the classroom teacher as she or he teaches a class of typical students. A profile of the teacher's interaction patterns can be used by the AAC team to identify instructional strategies that will support the AAC student, those that with slight modification will provide support, and those that will be problematic. It is particularly useful to observe how the teacher 1) augments students' comprehension, 2) maps new language forms onto old or familiar information, 3) pools students' response options (i.e., choices), and 4) expects students to bid for opportunities to respond to teacher-directed questions (Wood, Lasker, Siegel-Causey, Beukelman, & Ball, 1997).

Augmenting Comprehension

All teachers support or augment students' comprehension of new information in some way. For example, teachers augment comprehension by using tangible items, photographs, illustrations, videotapes, and so forth. During assessment, it is useful to determine whether the specific augmented comprehension strategies used by a teacher will be useful to the particular AAC student who may be placed in that classroom. If so, the AAC team can encourage the teacher to continue to use the strategies and assure him or her that they are likely to be as successful with the AAC student as they are with typical students. If the specific strategies a teacher uses appear not to be useful to the AAC user, the team may need to coach the teacher to modify or expand his or her repertoire of augmented comprehension strategies so that they will meet the student's needs.

Mapping Language

Teachers at nearly all academic levels visually map new language forms as they teach. For example, as they provide verbal information to students, they may write key words or even an entire text on the blackboard, on overheads, or on a flipchart. During classroom assessment, AAC teams need to address the question of *how often* a teacher maps language and the strategies that he or she uses to do so. Teachers who frequently map language through writing on the blackboard are often willing to map (or display) the symbol system of an AAC user at the same time. Teachers who do not map frequently or who do so with slides or other short-duration strategies may need additional support to learn to map language successfully for an AAC user.

Pooling Responses

Teachers vary widely in the strategies they use to pool potential responses for their students by providing multiple response options. As mentioned previously, some teachers augment comprehension regularly with tangible objects, photos, or illustrations. These same teachers will often pool potential response options by leaving the tangible items on display so that students can use them as memory aids or point to them in response to teachers' questions. Such teachers often find it rather easy to include AAC users when asking questions during large- and small-group instruction because these strategies apply to them as well. However, other teachers tend to remove all tangible items and have the students respond only through writing or speech. These teachers may need help to learn to use more effective response pools that do not require AAC students to rely almost entirely on their memories and the vocabulary items available in their AAC systems.

Bidding for Response Opportunities

Finally, teachers vary considerably in the ways they expect their students to bid for response opportunities in the classroom. Some may call on specific children and prefer to have one child respond at a time. Others may expect the children who know the answer to bid for a turn by raising their hands; the teacher then selects a student to respond.

Teachers who find it rather easy to include AAC students tend to develop ways for the entire class to respond without being disruptive. For example, the teacher might say, "If you think that the correct answer is 24, look at me; otherwise look at the ceiling" or "If you think that blood is pumped by the heart, sit up really straight." Such response strategies allow the teacher to check the understanding of *all* of the children, including those who use AAC systems. From the AAC user's perspective, this is vastly preferable to the use of competitive response strategies that reward children who can raise their hands quickly and speak well.

Culp and Effinger (1996) wrote a book called *ChalkTalk: Augmentative Communication in the Classroom,* which describes a process that gives school teams a place to start when developing communication programs for students who use AAC systems. This manual provides observational protocols that help a team profile the communication patterns and needs of students in school settings. Additional activities guide the development of action plans that include the actions to be taken, the person or people responsible, the time of completion, and the procedures to be used.

Plan Interventions for Today and Tomorrow

Adapt the Educational Environment

Teachers may need to make adjustments to the physical environment in order to enhance access in a classroom. For example, it is not uncommon for teachers to position students who use wheelchairs off to the side or at the back of a room because their chairs make it difficult for others to get around them. Creating wider aisles between student desks and classroom furnishings is a preferable solution to this problem because this allows the AAC user to stay with the group instead of being physically marginalized. Wider doors adapted with special *open* buttons or electric eyes allow easy entrance into the classroom and other areas of the building, such as the music room, gymnasium, and cafeteria. Teachers should position student working surfaces (ideally, adjustable desks and tables) at appropriate heights for comfort and efficiency. Cutout desktops may be necessary so that students have a suitable distance between their wheelchairs and their working surfaces. Chalkboards placed at lower-than-usual levels and extended slightly out from walls allow students in wheelchairs to position themselves appropriately for writing activities. Teachers can also lower other items such as doorknobs, pencil sharpeners, coat racks, and light switches to heights accessible to all. Finally, classroom assignments should be made after taking into consideration the mobility needs of students, because some classrooms are more accessible than others.

Managing the Academic Workload

Educational specialists can increase the academic workload of a student with disabilities unnecessarily without realizing it. For example, Jason, a middle school student who requires AAC, received some resource room assistance to increase his literacy skills. He was learning to use a Macintosh computer with a standard word processing program and Co:Writer (Don Johnston, Inc.), a writing program with rate enhancement features. Early in his augmented writing program, Jason's resource room teacher gave him writing assignments without considering the many written assignments that his general education teachers required. It soon became apparent that Jason, who wrote very slowly anyway, was being asked to manage a workload that was far beyond his capabilities. Through collaborative efforts, the general and special education teachers began to coordinate their writing assignments so that Jason had sufficient writing practice and was still able to complete his general classroom assignments. For example, his English teacher agreed to accept the letters and stories that Jason wrote in the resource room as fulfilling his language arts requirements. In addition, the resource room teacher agreed to design assignments to relate to the subject matter covered in the general classes.

Assisting Students to Be Active Learners

Because the communication content in general classrooms changes so rapidly, it may be difficult to keep the vocabulary in the AAC system current. This leads to a tendency to provide AAC students with communication systems that are solely designed to address wants/needs and social interaction functions rather than the information-sharing functions that are integral to classroom participation. If this happens, AAC users are often forced to be passive learners: They cannot ask or answer questions in class, deliver topical reports, or otherwise participate in subject-oriented discussions because they do not have the vocabularies to do so. It is critical that the AAC support team aggressively attempt to translate the curriculum into communication units that will allow the AAC user to participate in these classroom interactions. This is particularly crucial during the early elementary years before students are able to spell well enough to compose their own messages. In this case, the demands on the AAC support team will be reduced if the AAC student has access to adequate rate enhancement techniques. Support staff, however, will still need to institute strategies that help students manage the time constraints of the general classroom.

Assisting Students to Manage Time Constraints

Students with severe communication and motor impairments often find it difficult to keep up with the pace of a general classroom because they have difficulty manipulating educational materials such as books and worksheets. Without accommodations to these difficulties, students may experience academic failure because they cannot complete their work, although they have mastered the content. Educators often use one of several approaches to accommodate the time constraints of students with disabilities.

Advance Preparation

It may be necessary for AAC teams to work with general education staff to preview upcoming assignments, topic areas, and class projects, so that they have ample time to create related adaptations. For example, if the AAC support team knows that upcoming science units will include planets, rocks, and dinosaurs over the next 2 months, they can begin to construct related communication displays or plan how to program the needed vocabulary words into an electronic AAC device.

In addition, teachers can encourage students who use AAC to prepare questions in advance or compose their answers to assigned questions at home in order to compensate for their reduced communication rates. For example, in her Teen Living class (a health and personal responsibility class), Ginger was involved in a unit on sex education. Although she was not able to grasp all of the class material, she clearly understood at least some of the discussion related to dating etiquette. She managed to convey to her inclusion support teacher that she had some questions about this subject. Prior to class, the teacher recorded Ginger's questions on a cassette tape, which Ginger activated in class using a single switch. The teacher also used this technique when Ginger was assigned class reports in a cooperative learning group. She worked with her classmates after school to prepare the report, and they recorded it on tape. Ginger was then responsible for playing the taped report the next day in class. Such advance-preparation strategies allow students with AAC systems to participate actively in general classes without requiring teachers and peers to wait while they compose messages or questions.

Use of Peer Instruction

The use of cooperative or peer instruction is increasing in general education (Gartner & Lipsky, 1990; Sapon-Shevin, 1990). Applying cooperative or peer instruction approaches to students who use AAC systems can be very effective in helping them meet classroom time demands. In addition, when teachers include students with disabilities in small cooperative learning or informal peer-instruction groups, the students are often able to participate more effectively than they can in large classroom situations.

In junior high, senior high, and college or university classes, educators can also enlist peer students to take notes in class for students with disabilities. They can insert carbon paper between pages of their notebooks so that a copy is made automatically, or

---

It is important to create a socially supportive environment for students with severe disabilities who are included in general classrooms. Hunt, Alwell, Farron-Davis, and Goetz (1996) provided a detailed discussion of their efforts to include students with multiple disabilities. They summarized their experiences as follows:

1. **Information provision and friendship programs:** Ongoing information on the ways in which the focus students communicated and the adaptive equipment they used was provided to schoolmates in the context of interactions between the student and a classmate. Further information was provided to schoolmates through participation in "clubs": a "support circle" for Isaac, a "sign club" for Todd, and a "recess club" for Daniel.
2. **Identification and utilization of a variety of media for interactive exchanges:** The various interactive media utilized fell into three categories: a) multimodal communication systems; b) interactive computer activities; and c) toys, games, and cooperative educational activities.
3. **Third-party facilitation through buddy systems, arrangement of interactive activities, and prompting to promote interactions:** A buddy system was established in which each focus student had a peer partner for the day who sat by him in class and accompanied him to recess, the cafeteria, and other school activities. Paraprofessionals received information during training meetings and feedback periods on facilitation strategies that included a) arranging classroom and other school contexts to ensure that the focus student was involved in an activity and that a peer partner, communication devices, and adaptive equipment were available, b) prompting interactions between the focus student and classmates, c) prompting the focus student to use a variety of communicative means, and d) interpreting the communicative behaviors of the focus student for classmates. (Hunt et al., 1996, p. 58)

the notes can be photocopied. At the University of Nebraska, we initially paid peers a small wage to take notes for students with disabilities, but we found that they were more cooperative and reliable when they were enlisted as volunteers rather than as paid employees. We have also found that regardless of grade level, students with AAC systems should be encouraged to at least outline their class notes whenever possible, in order to stay mentally involved in the subject matter of the class. Alternatively, many students prefer to tape classroom lectures and use the tapes to clarify information from the peer notes. Some tape recorders have a feature that allows the user to press a button to mark specific sections while recording. Then, as they review the tapes with the notes, they can fast forward to the marked sections rather quickly. This reduces their listening time and encourages students to stay involved in the class so that they can mark important segments on the tape.

Adapting Academic Testing

Competitive students with disabilities usually have difficulty completing academic tests in the same amount of time as their peers without disabilities. If adjustments in time limits are not made, these students are either penalized for their disabilities or must rely on the assistance of a paraprofessional to complete tests in the time allotted. Penalization is clearly unacceptable, and student reliance on a paraprofessional often leaves the teacher wondering who is really taking the test, the student or the paraprofessional.

One solution is to provide an adapted environment in which students can take tests under close supervision. For example, the University of Nebraska has a policy that students with disabilities may take their academic tests at the Center for Students with Disabilities. The staff at the Center monitor all test taking to confirm that students have completed their own work. They remove time limits, however, and all tests thus become instruments for evaluating competence rather than speed. The faculty members at the university have no choice but to cooperate if students choose to use the Center. Many junior high and senior high schools provide similar options to students with disabilities through the assistance of resource teachers.

Reduced Workloads

Students who are expected to participate at a competitive level (i.e., held to the same standards as their peers without disabilities) do not necessarily have to complete the same amount of work as their peers. If a teacher is willing to allow a student to discontinue an assignment once he or she has demonstrated mastery of a concept or a process, the student and teacher save precious time. In many cases, if the teacher does not allow this to occur, all involved may experience frustration. For example, it is not uncommon to hear parents report how upsetting it is to watch their child work long hours to complete several pages of math problems when it is clear that he or she understands the concepts by the end of the first page.

Some students and families favor the selective participation strategy of not enrolling in classes that are not required or for which the student can meet the requirements in a different way. For example, some students who are unable to participate as involved students in a physical education program may choose to meet this requirement through physical therapy after school hours. This way, they can use the physical education period to complete other academic work. As another example, a competitive student may wish to be exempted from elective classes in order to complete required coursework. Obviously, when making such decisions, the student, family, and educational staff must consider the social as well as the educational consequences that might result.

Selective Retention

In the United States, children with disabilities are eligible to remain as public school students past the age of 18 when most of their peers graduate. This extra time for students who use AAC systems means that rather than rushing through an educational program at the same pace as their peers without disabilities, they and their families may opt for retention at a grade level in order to meet specific academic goals. Such retentions tend to occur at four different times. First, some students may not have the AAC equipment that they need to enter first grade. Their parents may choose to retain them in kindergarten for an additional year so that the AAC team has time to develop the appropriate communication supports. Second, we know of a number of parents who have elected to retain their children in the third or fourth grade. In particular, this option has been chosen by parents who had children with literacy skills not sufficiently developed to allow learning to occur. The additional work in reading and writing that these students completed was often sufficient to narrow the gap in this area. Third, some students may participate in junior high school for an additional year. In schools in the United States, much of the junior high curriculum consists of an enhanced version and review of the concepts and processes taught in earlier years to ensure that students are fluent in this material before they enter high school. Students who do not master this material in elementary school may benefit from an extra year in junior high for academic reasons. Finally, students may choose to extend the length of their high school programs in order to complete academic requirements.

Early in his elementary years, we discussed with Grant's parents the possibility of academic retention. For several years, Grant performed at grade level. However, by the end of sixth grade, he had begun to struggle with writing, spelling, and math. Grant enrolled in a 2-year junior high program. By the end of eighth grade, his academic difficulties remained, so his parents and teachers decided to retain him in junior high for an additional year. As of 1998, he was planning to graduate from high school. He has taken 5 years to complete a 4-year program and plans to enroll in a junior college the fall following his graduation.

Educators should retain a student only with the agreement of the student and his or her parents. If parents support this option, they will often encourage their child to make friends with students who are younger so that the social consequences of a possible retention are less drastic. Of course, in many cases the detrimental social impact of retention may outweigh any potentially positive academic benefits. In fact, it is primarily the social implications of selective voluntary retention that make this such a controversial topic. In addition, many general educators and administrators seem to believe that retaining typical students serves no constructive purpose, which may or may not be true. Regardless, applying the same logic to students with disabilities and rejecting selective retention for philosophical reasons only appear equally nonconstructive. To our knowledge, there is simply no reason not to consider this option for competitive or active students who experience academic difficulties because of their reduced communication efficiency.

Principle 3: When students with disabilities are not successful in high school and college, it may be because of their limited literacy skills and limited world knowledge.

Developing the Student's Knowledge Base

The development of adequate literacy skills, coupled with cultural and world knowledge, is increasingly viewed as an important factor for educational success. Those who assist students with disabilities at the postsecondary level suggest repeatedly that the primary source of most of these students' academic difficulties lies in deficiencies in these two related areas.

A student's knowledge base develops in many different ways. The family contributes to it, as does television, other media, and printed materials. The contributions of the family, community, and media are supplemented when educators provide students who have disabilities with extensive access to printed materials at school and involve these students in the general school curriculum. Even if they cannot read and write, elementary school–age students are able to learn a great deal about the world around them through experience and exposure. Nevertheless, as they progress through school, students increasingly are required to read in order to learn. Students who experience reading problems are at risk for missing out on much of the information and knowledge imparted in schools. This problem becomes even worse in high school and college. The result is that students who are unable to read often lag far behind their peers in world knowledge, not necessarily because they are unable to learn the information, but because they have limited access to it.

Initially, (eighth-grade) science was selected because the teacher was an enthusiastic individual who was very interested in involving all learners in the class. The team struggled with how science related to a functional, life space domain curriculum but went ahead with the plans to include the learner (with a severe disability) in the class anyway. After several weeks in the class, it became apparent that the student enjoyed the science subject area. His spoken vocabulary increased dramatically to include science jargon including . . . "rocks," "rivers," (and) "stars." (York & Vandercook, 1989, p. 16)

Another factor contributing to insufficient world knowledge for many students with disabilities is the amount of time they spend outside the general classroom. As of 1998, it is still not uncommon for students with AAC systems to be selectively integrated into general educational activities. This usually means that they participate in elective, resource room, or segregated classes for much of their school day, especially when their peers without disabilities are engaged in academic subjects. An obvious consequence of this arrangement is that students who are AAC users miss the classes in which students acquire world knowledge.

Education teams may decide to exclude students from academic classes because the students cannot be competitive with their classmates who do not have disabilities.

Nevertheless, as noted previously, educators should consider other valid levels of participation for the sake of building a student's world knowledge. For example, we know of a high school student with a severe learning disability who used an augmented software writing program to compensate for his spelling difficulties. He was enrolled primarily in vocational education courses, yet he was interested in history, government, and earth science and participated actively in these courses. He attempted to read the assignments, and he participated in class discussions. Because the continued development of his literacy skills was an important goal of his educational program, he wrote short essays to meet the class requirements rather than taking the tests required of the competitive students.

Teachers may include some students as involved, but not active, participants in academic classes in order to give these students access to world knowledge. For example, Felipe attended a junior high biology class that was considerably beyond his academic ability level. Nevertheless, he was involved in various plant experiments with his peer group, enjoyed learning to use a microscope to examine cells, participated in a presentation about ecology by collecting examples of recyclable materials, and listened to recorded portions of the textbook using a tape recorder and a single switch. Thus, he benefited both academically and socially from this opportunity for involvement.

It is important to emphasize that we are not advocating placing students in academic classes in which they are not able to participate nor in classes from which they cannot benefit. For example, placing Felipe in a junior high math class would have been quite pointless because he was not interested in or able to learn the material at all. If the student sits passively in the classroom, day after day, it is unlikely that he or she is absorbing much world knowledge or deriving much social benefit from the experience.

When I commented on Brannon's intense interest in the scientific terms that I entered into his AAC system, his father grinned and filled me in on the details. When Brannon was about 7 years old, his father and his grandfather built him a joystick-controlled go-cart that was small enough to maneuver on the trails through the woods near their home. His father would ride behind him on a motorcycle equipped with a remote stopping switch. Anytime that Brannon got into difficulty, his father could stop the motor of the go-cart and set the brake with the remote switch. Through the years, father and son had toured the woods learning about plants, birds, and animals. What a wonderful contribution to Brannon's world knowledge! (D. Beukelman, personal communication, May 1997)

Role of Parents and Caregivers

Parents, siblings, relatives, and caregivers can play an important role in assisting a student with disabilities to develop his or her knowledge base. These caregivers are often willing to take this role seriously once they are aware of the importance of this information to the student's ongoing educational development. For example, they can involve the student in their own hobbies, vocations, and daily chores and impart a wide range of information through direct experience and incidental teaching. As they watch television or videotapes, they can also interact with the student to provide background information and discuss the implications of the material presented. A parent or relative might wish to assume primary responsibility for teaching the student a specific content area. In one instance, a student's father taught her much of the school's science curriculum at home for several years. The school district supported their efforts by providing textbooks, workbooks, and videotapes. School personnel evaluated the student's performance and documented her progress. During her usual science period, the student attended the resource center to develop her writing skills. This unique arrangement allowed the student to master the content of the science curriculum, while receiving much needed remedial instruction in literacy.

Principle 4: Specialists must complement, not compete with, the academic program.

COLLABORATIVE TEAMING AND CONSENSUS BUILDING

In an inclusive educational program, the primary role of specialists such as speech-language pathologists, motor therapists, and special education teachers is to help the AAC student to participate successfully in the general classroom. This may involve the provision of direct AAC services, or it may involve direct skill instruction. The overriding responsibility of the specialist, however, is to serve as a consultant to the general teacher and to assist in adapting the educational environment and the curriculum. This may constitute a major shift in the specialist's role from direct to indirect instructional provider.

(Collaborative teaming is) an interactive process that enables teams of people with diverse expertise to generate creative solutions to mutually defined problems. The outcome is enhanced, altered, and produces solutions that are different from those that the individual team members would produce independently. (Idol, Paolucci-Whitcomb, & Nevin, 1986, p. 1)

Consensus Building

As we discuss in Chapter 5, collaborative efforts between AAC team members require the use of a variety of consensus-building strategies that allow team members to articulate their priorities, identify potential conflicts, and design proactive solutions to resolve these conflicts before they become problematic. In addition, successful collaborations often require creative solutions aimed at accomplishing multiple objectives within a single activity. Collaborative efforts also require careful deployment of personnel and adequate delineation of their roles and responsibilities (see Pugach & Johnson, 1990). Several examples illustrate the range of strategies that teachers and specialists may use to accomplish these goals.

Heather

As discussed previously, when Heather was in first grade, her math curriculum involved extensive use of manipulable objects (e.g., stones, beads, bottle caps). Her teacher used these to teach the children about basic mathematical concepts such as counting, grouping, and combining. Because of her cerebral palsy, Heather was unable to manipulate these items independently and required the assistance of a paraprofessional. When the school hired a paraprofessional, the question then became: What is her role? Should she become Heather's "hands" and simply manipulate objects for her? Or, should her role be that of a tutor for Heather, providing separate remedial math activities under the first-grade teacher's direction? Or should she be involved as part of the team to devise strategies so that Heather can participate in the standard math program as independently as possible? After much discussion, her AAC team decided that, in fact, their combined role should be to help Heather participate in the math program as independently as possible. Thus, they proceeded to work collaboratively to develop a math communication board that allowed Heather to interact with her classmates and participate in peer instructional activities. In addition, they developed an adapted "touch math" system that enabled Heather to use a modified number line to learn about numerous mathematical principles. The paraprofessional assumed a major role in this collaborative effort by modifying and updating the system, as well as by assisting Heather during regular math activities.

Ginger

During high school, Ginger was included in several nonacademic classes such as Teen Living, home economics, computers, and art. She also took part in a functional curriculum, in which she received vocational and community-referenced instruction. Ginger was unable to participate in the basic sewing unit of her home economics class because of her severe physical impairments. The motor specialists on the AAC team collaborated with the general teacher to devise a relay system that Ginger controlled with a single switch. With this, she could turn the sewing machine, electric scissors, and other sewing appliances on and off. She also used a simple sewing communication board devised by the speech-language pathologist to participate in making decisions about the fabrics, thread, buttons, and patterns to be used for class projects. For the duration of the sewing unit, Ginger's teacher paired her with a peer without disabilities, who was responsible for actually manipulating the appliances and fabrics. Thus, the collaborative efforts between the AAC specialists and the home economics teacher resulted in a solution that enhanced Ginger's participation, both academically and socially.

Lakota

Lakota was just beginning to learn to operate an electronic AAC device in kindergarten, and her speech-language pathologist and a paraprofessional were her primary instructors. Early in the spring, Lakota's kindergarten teacher planned to present a unit about plants, and the class would visit the Sunken Garden, a city park with an extensive floral display. The children would be accompanied on the field trip by a class of landscape architecture students from the local university who wanted to observe the interests and interaction patterns of young children in a public garden. In an effort to combine AAC device instruction with support for Lakota's participation in kindergarten activities, the specialist staff devised an AAC overlay that contained messages pertaining to the plant unit and subsequent field trip. During the field trip, the specialist mounted the AAC device on Lakota's wheelchair so that she could "talk" with the student observers and interact with her classmates.

Part III

Augmentative and Alternative Communication Interventions for Individuals with Acquired Disabilities

15

Adults with
Acquired Physical Disabilities

When I first realized that I would be unable to speak some day, I viewed it as losing my life. Communication was my life. Now I realize that was a little overly dramatic, but not much. (For me) speechlessness is not a loss of life, but a loss of access to life. I find it difficult to access my friends. They used to stop by to chat, and I wished sometimes that they would leave me alone. Now if they stop at all, they stay for just a few minutes. They have difficulty tolerating my reduced ability to communicate. I have lost access to them. Because of that, I do not have the opportunities to discuss, joke, and most of all argue. (A lawyer with amyotrophic lateral sclerosis (ALS), in Beukelman & Garrett, 1986, p. 5)

The mechanics of spoken communication are so automatic for natural speakers that the content of interactions, not the speaking processes involved, is the primary focus of communicative exchanges. It is almost impossible for those who have learned and continue to speak without difficulty to imagine what it would be like to be unable to speak due to an acquired disability. This chapter briefly summarizes assessment and intervention approaches to a number of such disabilities, including ALS, multiple sclerosis (MS), Parkinson's disease (PD), spinal cord injury (SCI), brain-stem stroke, and others. Subsequent chapters discuss information related to the acquired disabilities of traumatic brain injury (TBI) and aphasia secondary to stroke.

The Barkley AAC Center's World Wide Web site (http://aac.unl.edu) contains links to many excellent sites that provide a range of information on the neurological conditions and syndromes discussed in this chapter.

A MODEL FOR INTERVENTION

Augmentative and alternative communication (AAC) teams have employed a somewhat streamlined version of the Participation Model (see Figure 6.1) with adults who have severe acquired communication disorders. This model has been referred to as a matching model (Coleman, Cook, & Meyers, 1980) or a Communication Needs Model (Beukelman et al., 1985) and involves three simultaneous types of assessment, all of which are represented in Figure 6.1: 1) an identification of participation and communication needs, 2) an assessment of capabilities to determine available and appropriate communication options, and 3) an assessment of external constraints. In addition, strategies for evaluating the effectiveness of AAC interventions are important to this model. (See Chapters 6 and 7 for a detailed discussion of assessment.)

Identify Participation Patterns and Communication Needs

Participation Patterns

Individuals who experience acquired physical disabilities that are so severe that their ability to communicate is affected usually experience other dramatic changes in their lives. Depending on the progression of the condition or disease, these changes may occur gradually, as with a degenerative disease, or more abruptly, as with trauma or stroke. Individuals' physical disabilities as well as their personal lifestyle preferences determine their communication needs. For example, some people with severe degenerative disabilities, such as ALS, prefer to center their lives around their home environments. These individuals find that it is more efficient and less demanding on their families to establish their homes as their primary work and social setting, rather than to continue to participate extensively in the larger community. Thus, they may work at home if they are active vocationally. Friends can visit them at home, and they may travel only for health care services. Other individuals may adopt a different participation strategy and attempt to stay active in the community as long as they possibly can. These individuals may continue to work outside the home and to attend recreational activities, religious functions, and social events with friends and family.

Such decisions about patterns of participation substantially affect an individual's communication needs and preferences and the corresponding AAC options. For example, an individual who communicates primarily at home may need an AAC system that can be moved to various rooms on a cart or a computer stand with wheels, rather than an AAC device that attaches directly to a wheelchair. Individuals who participate actively in the community need communication systems that are self-contained, compact, and fully portable. During assessment and intervention, it is important to consider the individual opinions and preferences of adults with acquired disabilities regarding participation and lifestyle patterns.

Consensus Building

It is important to develop consensus among the AAC user and the people supporting him or her when developing a communication needs profile. One way to build consensus is to organize potential communication needs into specific and detailed components that the user and his or her facilitators can designate as *mandatory, desirable, unimportant,* or *may be mandatory in the future,* as displayed in Figure 15.1.

A detailed needs assessment has advantages for both the person with the disability and his or her family or support networks. For example, it is not uncommon for adults

Name: _____

Date: _____

Interviewer: _____

Responders: _____

Please indicate whether the needs listed are:
  M = Mandatory
  D = Desirable
  U = Unimportant
  F = May be mandatory in the future

Positioning
In bed
  While supine _____
  While lying prone _____
  While lying on side _____
  While in a Clinitron bed _____
  While in a Roto bed _____
  While sitting in bed _____
  While in arm restraints _____
  In a variety of positions _____
Related to mobility
  Carry the system while walking _____
  Independently position the system _____
  In a manually controlled wheelchair _____
  In an electric wheelchair _____
  With a lapboard _____
  While the chair is reclined _____
  Arm troughs _____
Other equipment
  With hand mitts _____
  With arterial lines _____
  Orally intubated _____
  While trached _____
  With oxygen mask _____
  With electric wheelchair controls _____
  Environmental control units _____
Other needs related to positioning _____

Communication Partners
  Someone who cannot read (e.g., child or nonreader) _____
  Someone with no familiarity with the system _____
  Someone who has poor vision _____
  Someone who has limited time or patience _____
  Someone who is across the room or in another room _____
  Someone who is not independently mobile _____
  Several people at a time _____
  Someone who is hearing impaired _____
  Other needs related to partners _____

Locations
  In one room only _____
  In multiple rooms in the same building _____
  In dimly lit rooms _____
  In bright rooms _____

(continued)

Figure 15.1. Communication needs assessment. (From Beukelman, D., Yorkston, K., & Dowden, P. (1985). *Communication augmentation: A casebook of clinical management* (pp. 209–211). Austin, TX: PRO-ED; reprinted by permission.)

Figure 15.1. (*continued*)

In noisy rooms _____
Outdoors _____
Traveling in a car or van _____
Moving from place to place within a building _____
At a desk or computer terminal _____
In more than two locations in a day _____
Other needs related to locations _____

Message Needs
Call attention _____
Signal emergencies _____
Provide unique information _____
Make requests _____
Carry on a conversation _____
Express emotion _____
Give opinions _____
Convey basic medical needs _____
Greet people _____
Prepare messages in advance _____
Edit texts prepared by the user _____
Make changes in diagrams _____
Compile lists (e.g., phone numbers) _____
Perform calculations _____
Take notes _____
Other needs related to messages _____

Modality of Communication
Prepare printed messages _____
Prepare auditory messages _____
Talk on the phone _____
Communicate with other equipment (e.g., environment control units) _____
Communicate privately _____
Switch from one modality to another during communication _____
Via several modalities at a time (e.g., taking notes while talking on the phone) _____
Communicate via an intercom _____
Via formal letters or reports _____
On pre-prepared worksheets _____
Other needs related to modality of communication _____

with acquired communication disorders to insist that their AAC systems return (or maintain) all of the functions of natural communication to them. This is quite natural because many people struggle to accept their disabilities and are often frustrated by their inability to communicate in the same way that was possible with natural speech. In the process of completing a communication needs inventory, such individuals are forced to go beyond the generic expectation of "being able to do everything that I could do before this happened" in order to identify *specific* communication needs and assign them priority.

In addition, it is not uncommon for family members and friends who surround a person with an acquired physical disability to have differences of opinion regarding the person's communication needs. There is no way to predict what these differences will be, but it is important to try to achieve some degree of consensus among these people about the individual's communication needs or, if that is impossible, to at least clarify their differences of opinion. If neither of these tasks is accomplished early in the assessment process, it is nearly impossible to institute a successful intervention because the chosen communication intervention may meet the needs perceived by one party but not the needs perceived by another.

Assess Specific Capabilities

As we discuss in Chapter 6, AAC teams usually conduct assessments of cognitive, motor, language, and sensory capabilities with people who have acquired physical disabilities. One particularly important aspect of the assessment process for these individuals involves predicting the natural course of various capabilities. People with degenerative diseases will gradually lose some capabilities while other capabilities remain stable. People in stable condition following brain-stem stroke or SCI may regain certain capabilities either naturally or with therapeutic intervention. Subsequent sections of this chapter discuss these issues in more detail.

Assess Constraints

A variety of external constraints may affect the AAC decisions that are made for a specific individual, and some of these constraints commonly affect people with acquired communication disorders. The attitudes of family members and friends about the communication disorder in general and the recommended AAC intervention in particular may influence decisions. For example, families of some older adults appear to have difficulty accepting the use of electronic communication techniques for a spouse or parent because they struggle with accepting their loved one's loss of speech or writing ability. Families of teenagers or young adults may resist low-tech options, even if these are the most appropriate techniques for the time being, because they believe that their child "deserves the very best" and mistakenly equate sophisticated equipment with the best intervention choice.

Another constraint involves the availability of facilitators to learn about the operation and use of an electronic AAC system in order to assist the user to learn and maintain it. In some locations, facilitators may not be able to obtain adequate support for certain types of communication options. Another important external constraint involves the availability of funding for equipment and instruction. Funding patterns for AAC systems vary dramatically in different parts of the world. Some countries, provinces, or states fund AAC systems for children who participate in educational programs but provide little financial support for adults. Other areas fund AAC systems for adults with acquired disabilities, although they fail to support adults with physical disabilities as a result of congenital disorders. Still other areas severely restrict AAC funding for older adults. It is impossible to outline in this book such funding constraints in detail. As is the case with children, successful AAC interventions require that the AAC team assess constraints and focus on the remediation of these limitations as vigorously as they focus on the individual's communication needs and capabilities.

Evaluate Intervention Outcomes

There are three primary reasons for measuring the outcomes of interventions with adults who have acquired physical disabilities. The first reason is to identify the communication needs that have and have not been met. When an intervention approach succeeds in meeting certain communication needs, the AAC team should document these for the sake of the individual and his or her family. If an initial intervention does not meet certain communication needs, the team should refine the approach and intervene in ways that will facilitate meeting communication needs over time. The second reason for measuring intervention effectiveness is to document the effectiveness of the AAC program that is providing services. Agencies that provide funding for AAC interventions with adults usually demand this documentation for continued funding. The third reason for measuring intervention effectiveness is to document the overall AAC efforts of a particular center or agency. If interventionists document the effectiveness of AAC interventions for specific users, administrative support for AAC efforts will probably increase.

The following sections of this chapter discusses AAC approaches that apply to specific impairments and syndromes. We cannot provide a complete clinical description of these conditions here, so we highlight only those aspects of the disease process that most directly influence AAC interventions.

AMYOTROPHIC LATERAL SCLEROSIS

ALS is a progressive degenerative disease of unknown etiology involving the motor neurons of the brain and spinal cord. Because 75% of people with ALS are unable to speak by the time of their death (Saunders, Walsh, & Smith, 1981), these individuals need extensive AAC services.

Emery and Holloway (1982) defined the mean age of onset for ALS as 56 years of age. The most common early symptom is weakness, with approximately one third of those affected reporting initial upper-extremity (arm and hand) weakness, one third reporting leg weakness, and one quarter presenting with bulbar (brain-stem) weakness manifested by dysarthria and dysphagia. Extraocular muscle movements are usually spared, as is sphincter control. As the disease progresses, motor weakness may become pervasive, leaving the individual dependent on others for personal care, mobility, and feeding. Of individuals with ALS, 14%–39% survive for 5 years, about 10% live for up to 10 years, and a few may live 20 years after onset. Individuals with primarily bulbar symptoms tend to have a more rapid course, with a median survival of 2.2 years after the appearance of initial symptoms (Tandan & Bradley, 1985).

The average worldwide incidence of ALS ranges between 0.4 and 1.8 cases per 100,000 of the population, and the prevalence rates range from 4 to 6 cases per 100,000 of the population (Tandan & Bradley, 1985). The male-to-female ratio is 2:1 (Emery & Holloway, 1982).

Communication Symptoms

People with ALS usually do not experience language impairments as a result of their disease; however, dysarthria, a motor speech disorder, results from the weakness and spasticity inherent in the disease. Dysarthria of the mixed flaccid-spastic type is almost niversally present at some point during the course of ALS (Darley, Aronson, & Brown,

1975; Dworkin, Aronson, & Mulder, 1980; Yorkston, Beukelman, & Bell, 1988). People with predominantly bulbar involvement experience this speech disorder early in the disease process, and their speech and swallowing functions may deteriorate rapidly. Such individuals may be able to walk and even to drive, although they are unable to speak. Individuals with predominantly spinal involvement, however, may retain normal or mildly dysarthric speech for a considerable period of time, even as they experience extensive motor impairments in their extremities.

Although the progression of speech symptoms may differ from individual to individual, most people with ALS experience a severe communication disorder during the last months or years of their lives. In a retrospective study of 100 hospice patients with ALS, 28% were anarthric (unable to speak) and 47% were severely dysarthric at the time of their deaths. Only 25% could speak understandably during the terminal stage of the illness (Saunders et al., 1981). In a related study of the use of AAC devices by 40 individuals with ALS, Sitver and Kraat (1982) reported that individuals required AAC systems, on the average, within 3 years after initial diagnosis, with a range from 6 months to 10 or more years.

Identify Participation Patterns and Communication Needs

As noted previously, people with ALS tend to adopt one of two lifestyle patterns. Some, such as Stephen Hawking, the Nobel Prize–winning physicist, continue to participate outside the home in work and community affairs. These individuals require durable, portable AAC systems and, in some cases, powered mobility. Others tend to develop their homes as their social centers and work, socialize, and conduct their affairs within this stable and customized environment. For home-centered individuals, either movable (i.e., mounted on a table or cart) or portable AAC systems may meet their communication needs. These individuals may also use AAC systems that require extensive facilitator support (e.g., eye pointing, lip reading) because they rarely need to function as independently as do their counterparts who participate actively in the community.

The (communication) system allowed Mark to communicate specific words and phrases when I could not understand him. This was especially good when he wanted to ask doctors a specific question or describe a specific symptom. The system was a good conversation piece. Mark enjoyed demonstrating the system to his friends. This often helped to ease their discomfort with his terminal disease. . . . Many friends were more willing to come by after they saw this system demonstrated. They felt it made Mark more comfortable because he was able to communicate with them. In short, it helped remove the isolation factor when one has no speech. . . . (The communication system) gave Mark something to do. He was actively involved—no longer just a spectator. . . . He could write out notes and messages to the kids and to me at his leisure. . . . (However, the scanning approach was) not a comfortable mode of communication. Mark would get nervous after concentrating so hard. (Mark's wife, after Mark died from ALS, in Beukelman et al., 1985, p. 108)

Assess Specific Capabilities

Cognitive/Linguistic Skills

The individual usually retains cognitive and linguistic functions as ALS progresses, although there are some reports of dementia in a small percentage (5%) of cases (Yorkston, Beukelman, et al., 1988); however, researchers doubt that this is directly related to ALS itself. The incidence of depression in individuals with ALS does not differ from that in other individuals with ongoing illnesses, nor is the suicide rate unusually high. Thus, people with ALS are able to understand and relate to the world around them and formulate messages much like other adults.

Sensory/Perceptual Skills

Minimal evidence suggests that ALS is associated with changes in sensory function that interfere with the operation of AAC devices. Impairment of motor control, however, is usually more extensive than impairment of perceptual skills.

Motor Skills

The pattern of motor control capability greatly affects the selection of an AAC system for an individual with ALS. These capabilities generally differ markedly from individual to individual, depending on whether the person first experiences bulbar or spinal symptoms.

Bulbar (Brain-Stem) ALS

People with predominantly bulbar symptoms are usually able to control, for some time, AAC devices that they can operate via direct selection using their hands or fingers. For example, Yorkston (1989) described an individual with ALS who pointed to letters on an alphabet board in order to communicate messages and supplement her distorted natural speech. During the initial stages of the disease, she was able to write longer messages. Because she did not consider telephone communication as a pressing need, this individual decided to defer a decision regarding the use of a speech-output device until her disease progressed. Another man with ALS communicated with an alphabet board and a small portable typewriter. As his disease progressed, he continued to type using a single finger, and he moved his arm and hand with the assistance of a mobile arm support (Beukelman et al., 1985).

Spinal ALS

People with ALS who exhibit predominantly spinal symptoms usually experience extensive motor impairments of their trunks and limbs at the same time as they are unable to meet their communication needs through speech. For these individuals, the need for an augmented writing system often precedes the need for a conversational system.

Individuals with severe impairments related to limb control usually require a scanning system of some type. For example, Beukelman et al. (1985) described a man who was unable to move his upper or lower limbs, and using a direct selection optical pointer became too fatiguing after less than 1 minute. However, he demonstrated the ability to activate, release, and reactivate a switch that was mounted on a pillow beside his head when he was seated in a large easy chair. Because he had the head rotation capability needed for this and because he could generate accurate as well as nonfatiguing movement, he used this motor pattern to operate an automated scanner until his death.

The motor control site for alternative access may need to be changed several times during the progression of the individual's disease. For example, one AAC user we know controlled her system initially with a single switch operated by either hand. In time, her AAC team modified the switch so that she could control it with minimal movement of a single finger. Finally, her team mounted a P-switch on her forehead, as depicted in Figure 15.2. She operated this switch by wrinkling her forehead slightly as she raised her eyebrows.

Assess Constraints

Although not specifically mentioned in the Participation Model (see Figure 6.1), certain constraints that are discussed in the following sections apply to people with ALS and their support systems.

Operational Competence

People with ALS, like most AAC users, require time and instruction in order to gain communicative competence with their AAC systems. Because ALS is predictably degenerative, these individuals are in the unique position of being able to select their AAC systems and learn to operate them while they can still use natural speech to meet at least their most basic communication needs. In fact, if an AAC system is selected and implemented after an individual is no longer able to speak, the AAC experience often becomes extremely frustrating for all involved.

This raises the question of how to predict when a person with ALS will need to use an AAC system. Yorkston, Smith, Miller, and Hillel (1991) explored this issue in a retrospective survey of 77 people with ALS. Their results indicated that, for the group as a whole, there was little or no relationship between the severity of the speech disorder and the length of time since diagnosis. For example, five individuals had functional

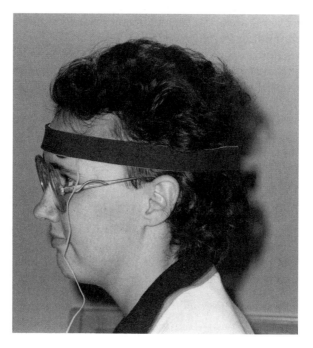

Figure 15.2.   A P-switch worn on the forehead.

speech 5 years postdiagnosis, whereas others spoke so poorly within 1 year of diagnosis that they required AAC systems. The authors of the survey suggested the following guidelines for clinical practice:

> Although rapid decline of speech function [in ALS] is certainly not inevitable, it occurs frequently enough so that sound clinical management dictates early preparedness. In our clinic, exploration of augmentative options begins *when speech has slowed and intelligibility is inconsistent in adverse listening situations.* (Yorkston et al., 1991, p. 10, emphasis added)

Facilitator Support

People with ALS require ongoing support from facilitators in order to use their AAC systems. This support may include instruction in technical or other skills that enable the individual to operate the device efficiently and accurately. Individuals may also need facilitator support to select and modify messages stored in the system. In addition, as the individual's capabilities change with progression of the disease, facilitators may need to change the motor control options and the positioning of the system. Facilitators may also have to give instruction in the social use of the AAC system.

Because people with severe ALS often find it difficult to travel, they generally require locally available professional facilitator support. Several regional AAC centers have developed networks of professional service providers within their states or areas to meet the needs of people with degenerative diseases. The regional center trains and supports network personnel concerning the needs of an individual AAC user.

Equipment Availability

Several features of ALS make the procurement of AAC equipment difficult. First, some people experience very rapid deterioration of natural speech abilities, and their need for AAC equipment becomes extremely urgent. Thus, delays in obtaining AAC services due to long waiting lists at regional centers, lack of funding for assessment services, and lack of funding for purchasing AAC devices can greatly impede the success of an intervention process. Second, because some people with ALS will use their AAC systems for only very brief periods of time prior to death, funding agencies may be reluctant to purchase systems for them. In order to counteract these and other equipment-related problems, an increasing number of regional programs for people with neurological diseases have established lending libraries of AAC equipment. As individuals' capabilities change, the libraries provide different AAC devices for as long as necessary, thus avoiding the need to purchase new devices for each limited-use period.

Intervention Staging

For many years the University of Washington Medical Center in Seattle has operated a multidisciplinary clinic program for people with ALS, which addresses the areas of communication, nutrition, and swallowing. Yorkston, Miller, and Strand (1995) described the multistage system they have developed in this program.

Stage 1: No Detectable Speech Disorder

In this early stage of the disease, examiners can detect no (or minimal) changes in speech. This stage may be very short for people with primarily bulbar symptoms and may be extended for people with primarily spinal symptoms. The purpose of intervention at this stage is to confirm that speech is still normal and to answer questions. Early in a degenerative disease, individuals and their families require some time to accept the diagnosis and grieve for their loss. Then, families often go through an educational phase in which they attempt to learn as much as possible about the disease and its impact on the individual and family. During this phase, individuals with ALS and their families usually welcome general information about communication impairment and AAC as well as information about the AAC service options that are available. AAC teams and medical personnel should take care at this stage not to be too graphic or detailed about the later communication difficulties that individuals may experience.

Stage 2: Obvious Speech Disorder with Intelligible Speech

In the second stage of the disease, changes in speech are noticed by unfamiliar listeners, especially when the speaker is fatigued. Intervention in this stage should focus on learning to minimize environmental interference by muting sound on the television, arranging conversations in quiet settings, choosing quiet restaurants, finding a quiet place to talk with friends at church, and so forth. During this stage, most people with ALS begin to reduce their speaking rates to minimize their speech disturbance and maintain speech intelligibility. When the speaking rate has slowed to 50% of typical, which is approximately 95 words per minute on a sentence reading task, such as the Sentence Intelligibility Test (Yorkston, Beukelman, & Tice, 1996) or a paragraph reading task, such as Pacer/Tally (Yorkston, Beukelman, & Tice, 1997), AAC teams should initiate assessment and intervention. Speakers learn strategies for establishing conversational topics and confirming that their listeners are aware of the topics. Interventionists should encourage frequent listeners to have their hearing checked, if there is any possibility of hearing impairment. Finally, speakers with ALS are taught strategies for coping with conversation in groups, such as learning to use and accept voice amplification.

Stage 3: Reduction in Speech Intelligibility

At the third stage, speakers with reduced speech intelligibility will find that listeners ask them to repeat messages with increasing frequency. If they have not already slowed their speaking rate to compensate for reduced speech intelligibility, the speech-language pathologist will encourage them to do so at this time. Also, they need to learn to reduce their breath group length (the number of words spoken on a single breath) in order to conserve energy. If speakers are leaking considerable air through their nasal cavities during speech and their speech articulation is still quite precise, they may be fitted with a palatal lift to position their weak soft palate more appropriately (Yorkston, Beukelman, et al., 1988). They should learn breakdown resolution strategies, such as rephrasing messages before repeating them. Finally, for many speakers, the AAC assessment and intervention started in Stage 2 should be completed early in this stage so that the individuals have AAC systems available to resolve communication breakdowns when needed.

It is often helpful to provide people with ALS and their caregivers with information about how other people with the disease have used their AAC systems. For example, Beukelman and Lasker (1998) reported data on the AAC use patterns of 11 people with ALS from the work of Mathy and Brune at the Munroe-Meyer Institute of Genetics and Rehabilitation (see Figure 15.3). All of the individuals in their survey were multimodal AAC users; that is, they used a variety of low- and high-tech options to meet their varied communication needs. These individuals used their electronic AAC de-

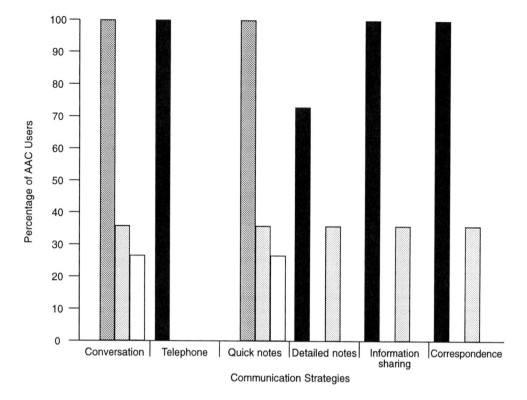

Figure 15.3. AAC use patterns in 11 individuals with amyotrophic lateral sclerosis (ALS). (Key: ■ = high-tech strategy; ■ = low-tech strategy; ■ = handwriting; □ = no-tech strategy.) (From Beukelman, D., & Lasker, J. (1998). Augmentative and alternative communication for persons with neurologic impairment. In R.B. Lazar (Ed.), *Principles of neurologic rehabilitation* (p. 486). New York: McGraw-Hill; reprinted by permission.)

vices to talk on the telephone; write messages and letters; convey detailed, complicated messages; and communicate with strangers. However, they used low-tech or unaided communication options to provide brief instructions and to converse face-to-face with family and familiar caregivers. If the service provider makes such information available, families can be protected somewhat from having unrealistic expectations of the AAC user and the technological supports that are available at the time.

> Efficiency of communication becomes more critical as the amount of energy for John to respond increases and his endurance fades. His will to live depends on his ability to communicate. Communication is the last great love of his life available to him. (C. Brahne and V. Hall, writing about a man with ALS, in Brahne & Hall, 1995, p. 10)

Stage 4: Residual Natural Speech and AAC

During the fourth stage, AAC moves from being a secondary to a primary communication system for most individuals with ALS. For a time, they may use alphabet supplementation (Beukelman & Yorkston, 1977), during which they point to the first letter of a word as they speak the word using their residual natural speech. Of course, facilitators will need to help the individuals change their communication modes for different communication situations. For example, individuals will probably need an electronic communication system for speaking on the telephone, writing, and conversing with strangers.

Stage 5: Loss of Useful Speech

During the fifth stage, individuals lose functional natural speech and must rely on AAC. It is important that people with ALS and their caregivers develop adequate yes/no communication systems to use during meals, in bed, and during emergencies. Eye-pointing systems are also helpful at this stage as an alternative to electronic communication systems in many contexts. Of course, individuals may also require high-tech AAC systems for many communication functions. During this phase, some individuals will choose ventilator support to compensate for their respiratory problems. If this occurs, special communication training to deal with ventilator care will also be required.

For a time, the only way I could communicate was to spell out words letter by letter, by raising my eyebrows when someone pointed to the right letter on a spelling card. It is pretty difficult to carry on a conversation like that, let alone write a scientific paper. However, a computer expert in California . . . heard of my plight. He sent me a computer program he had written, called Equalizer. This allowed me to select words from a series of menus on the screen, by pressing a switch in my hand. . . . When I have built up what I want to say, I can send it to a speech synthesizer. . . . I can manage up to 15 words a minute. . . . Using this system, I have written a book and many scientific papers. I have also given many scientific and popular talks. (Stephen Hawking, describing the communication system he uses as a result of ALS, in Hawking, 1995)

MULTIPLE SCLEROSIS

MS is a degenerative disease of the white matter of the central nervous system. The lesions of MS are multiple plaques that cause destruction of the myelin sheath of central nerve axons, although the axon itself is preserved except in very chronic cases.

In the northern part of the United States, the prevalence of MS is about 1 in 1,000; and in the southern states, the prevalence is about one third to one half of this figure. Approximately 95% of all cases begin between the ages of 10 and 50 years, with a median onset age of 27 years of age. Although MS is considered to be a disease of young people, it is not uncommon for an initial diagnosis to occur between 50 and 60 years of age. The female-to-male ratio of occurrence is 3:2 (Arnason, 1982).

The natural course of MS differs greatly from person to person. Poser (1984) has divided the clinical course of MS into five classes:

1. **Relapsing and remitting:** About 70% of young people with MS fall into this category. They experience virtually full recovery from the neurological signs and symptoms after each episode of relapse.
2. **Chronic progressive:** This is most commonly present in individuals who are older adults at the onset of the disease. The motor and neurological symptoms gradually worsen over time, with no intermittent remissions.
3. **Combined relapsing/remitting with chronic progression:** The majority of individuals reach this stage of the disease, which results in a gradual deterioration of capabilities over time, although individuals experience periods of relative remission.
4. **Benign:** About 20% of all individuals with MS have a normal life span with relatively normal functioning and little or no progression of the disease.
5. **Malignant:** A small percentage (5%–10%) of (predominantly) young people with MS show rapid and extensive involvement of cognitive, cerebellar, and pyramidal systems, which leads to death in a relatively short time.

The average life expectancy of young males with MS is about 35 years following the onset of the disease. The prognosis is worse 1) in males than in females; 2) if the age at onset is greater than 35 years; 3) if a chronic, progressive pattern appears at onset; or 4) if cerebellar symptoms occur at initial presentation (Poser, 1984).

Communication Symptoms

Dysarthria is the most common communication problem associated with MS, but the study of large groups of individuals with MS has shown that dysarthria is not a universal characteristic of this disease. Ivers and Goldstein (1963) reported in a study of 144 individuals with MS that dysarthria was present in 19% of the participants. Darley, Brown, and Goldstein (1972) reported that 41% of their MS sample demonstrated overall speech performance that was not "essentially normal" in terms of its impact on listeners. Nevertheless, when researchers utilized a self-reporting technique, only 23% of these individuals reported a "speech and/or communication disorder"; thus, a large percentage of this sample appeared to be unaware of the severity of their speech problems. Overall, a survey of studies related to the prevalence of dysarthria in MS revealed a range of occurrence of 19%–41%, depending on who made the assessment and how they sampled the population.

Although a number of individuals with MS demonstrate speech impairments, most do not require AAC systems. Beukelman, Kraft, and Freal (1985) reported that 4% of 656 survey respondents with MS indicated that their communication was so severely impaired that strangers were unable to understand them.

One evening . . . I had gone to the bathroom for a shower. . . . All was well as I entered the bathroom and showered. Then I began to wheel myself to the bedroom after I had finished. I tried to say something to my wife as I neared the door, but the words would not come and all I could manage was a babbling as I tried to express myself. My wife said to me, "What did you do, flush your voice down the drain?" Now this is not a real funny line. However, under those circumstances, it sounded hilarious. We both burst into laughter. . . . My voice control did not return for a few days . . . (but it) did return. (A man with MS, in Michael, 1981, p. 27)

Identify Participation Patterns and Communication Needs

Because the onset of MS occurs relatively early in life, individuals with MS are usually in educational programs or employed when they first experience symptoms. The intermittent and gradual onset of symptoms usually does not require people with MS to modify their lifestyles immediately, although some people with visual problems, which are quite common in MS, may require technological assistance to read computer screens or detailed printed materials. In time, however, impairments that are unrelated to verbal communication often prevent these individuals from attending school or working. For example, Kraft (1981) reported that arm and leg spasticity is an important reason why many people with MS drop out of the employment market. Loss of balance, loss of normal bladder control, and fatigue also interfere. In addition, a combination of weakness, spasticity, ataxia, and tremor may interfere with walking and necessitate the use of a wheelchair for mobility.

Because most people with MS whose speech is so impaired that they require AAC systems are no longer able to attend school or work, they rarely have communication needs related to these domains. Furthermore, some individuals with severe speech impairments require personal care assistance beyond what their families can offer; and they may live in residential or nursing centers, which may limit their communication needs even further. Thus, the primary communication needs of many people with MS are conversational, although individuals may require assistance with writing as well.

Assess Specific Capabilities

Cognitive Skills

The cognitive limitations of individuals with MS have been poorly documented, but more than half of these individuals seem to display definite evidence of cognitive impairment. Neuropsychological testing most often reveals impaired abstract conceptualization and short-term memory impairments (Poser, 1984). Although cognitive impairment in most individuals is unlikely to interfere with AAC intervention, the AAC team should consider the possibility and undertake appropriate assessments. In particular, short-term memory impairments may make new learning difficult, and teams are more likely to have success with AAC approaches that build on old skills.

Language Skills

Although dysarthria is the most common communication problem associated with MS, aphasia has also been reported. Several large studies of individuals with MS have noted no occurrence of aphasia (Olmos-Lau, Ginsberg, & Geller, 1977). Beukelman et al. (1985), however, noted that other researchers reported the incidence of aphasia as ranging from 1% to 3% of people with MS.

Sensory/Perceptual Skills

Vision limitations are common in MS; 16%–30% of people with MS experience optic neuritis, the acute or subacute loss of central vision in one eye with peripheral vision spared, as their first symptom. Optic neuritis is often manifested initially by an inability to see text on a computer screen or to read small print in general. The visual limitations of MS cause particular problems in the context of AAC interventions because many of these techniques require extensive visual capabilities. Many of these individuals cannot use complicated visual scanning arrays; instead, they may require auditory scanning systems such as the one described in the following section. Large-print text is a common requirement of people with MS, as is synthetic speech feedback that echoes the letters and words selected in typing or from a communication display. For example, an AAC system designed for a 30-year-old woman with MS consisted of an expanded keyboard with 1-inch square keys and speech feedback (Honsinger, 1989).

(Here) is my list of lists: Long-term projects and obligations . . . daily tasks, projects, and obligations; spring cleaning tasks; items to be taken on overnight outings and trips, . . . personal care schedule; phone numbers; books on loan from the National Library Service for the Blind and Physically Handicapped and from Recordings for the Blind, Inc.; two lists of physical therapy exercises; names and phone numbers of friends and former clients; names and addresses of out-often friends and family; calendar; medical and surgical supplies that must be stocked; and fears and questions I have concerning life with a progressive disease. Some of my lists are on large sheets of braille paper, others are in a looseleaf binder. All are on cassette tapes. (Denise Karuth, a young woman who is blind as a result of MS, describing the lists she keeps as memory aids, in Karuth, 1985, p. 27)

Motor Skills

Individuals' motor control capabilities in MS vary considerably, and, therefore, careful motor assessment is an important aspect of all AAC interventions. Intention tremor, which occurs during or is exaggerated by voluntary movement, is a prevalent motor control problem. The tremor often disrupts an individual's attempts to access a keyboard or activate a switch. AAC teams can sometimes identify a way to stabilize sufficiently the body part involved in access so that the individual can make voluntary movements without excessive tremor. At other times, AAC teams may need to attach a switch to an individual's limb or hand so that the switch can move with the body part during tremor but still remain in position to be activated by a finger. Often, the motor control and visual impairments of MS combine to limit AAC options severely. For example, Porter (1989) described an AAC intervention that occurred near the end of a person's life. The individual's visual and motor control limitations were quite extensive, but he learned to control a simple call buzzer and auditory scanning system using a pressure switch that attached to a pillow beside his head.

Assess Constraints

Several characteristics of MS complicate AAC interventions. First, symptom patterns vary considerably across individuals. Although the clinical course of MS follows five general patterns of progression, individual manifestations can be complex and vary over time. Obviously, changes in an AAC system may be needed to accommodate this variability. Second, as noted previously, visual impairments are quite common in MS and can make AAC interventions particularly challenging. Third, AAC interventions usually occur in conjunction with other efforts to compensate for the multiple impairments experienced by people with MS. Therefore, AAC teams must coordinate their interventions with other interventions in the context of changing symptom patterns.

Intervention Staging

As with ALS, interventions for MS can be described using a five-stage model.

Stage 1: No Detectable Speech Disorder

Early in the disease process, no (or minimal) changes in speech can be detected. In fact, many people with MS may not experience speech symptoms for an extended period of time. After confirmation of the diagnosis, many people with MS and their families engage in an educational phase in which they attempt to learn as much as possible about the disease and its impact. Individuals and their families often request general information about communication impairment and MS. Service providers should take care to explain the variable patterns of motor speech disturbance.

Stage 2: Detectable Speech Disorder

At the second stage, unfamiliar listeners notice changes in speech. Speech symptoms worsen and lessen slightly during exacerbations and remissions of the MS. Although phonation may be unstable, individuals usually do not experience reductions in speech loudness, although they may have difficulty maintaining appropriate volume levels in restaurants and at public meetings. AAC teams usually do not recommend speech intervention in this stage.

Stage 3: Obvious Speech Disturbances with Intelligible Speech

At the third stage, speakers with MS experience dysarthria that is severe enough to be apparent to anyone who speaks with them. Even at this stage, many may not receive intervention for speech, depending on how limited their participation patterns are due to other impairments (e.g., problems with fatigue, mobility, balance). Facilitators should teach them breakdown resolution strategies, such as rephrasing messages before repeating them.

Stage 4: Reduction in Speech Intelligibility

During the fourth stage, speakers with MS will experience reductions in speech intelligibility. By taking care to establish the topic they are discussing and speaking in optimal listening conditions, their speech is likely to remain comprehensible to familiar listeners. Toward the end of this stage, some choose to use alphabet supplementation (Beukelman & Yorkston, 1977), in which they point to the first letter of a word as they speak in order to remain comprehensible. They often use the alphabet board to resolve communication breakdowns as well.

Stage 5: Loss of Most Useful Speech

During the fifth stage, individuals have very limited functional natural speech, and the speaker must rely on AAC. It is important that people with MS and their caregivers develop adequate yes/no communication systems to use during meals, in bed, and during emergencies. Some people with MS have sufficient visual and motor ability to operate an electronic communication system. Individuals with severe visual impairments must rely on auditory scanning. A relatively small percentage of individuals with MS require a multipurpose AAC system. Given the range of motor control, visual, sensory, and cognitive impairments experienced in MS, interventions should be very individualized.

Huntington Disease

Huntington disease (HD) is an inherited autosomal dominant degenerative disease whose symptoms typically appear in the fourth decade, with death occurring 15–20 years after onset. HD is often associated with personality changes and gradually progresses to cognitive changes and memory losses. The speech impairment associated with HD varies considerably from person to person. For some, abnormal motor movements may be restricted primarily to the lower extremities without obvious speech disorder. For others, speech is so impaired that AAC strategies are required (Yorkston, Miller, & Strand, 1995).

A review of the literature reveals limited successful use of high-technology AAC systems for people with HD. Low-tech AAC strategies that focus primarily on choice making and scheduling should be introduced early in the course of the disease so that people with HD can learn to use them before their cognitive impairments make new learning difficult. Communication partners also require careful training so that they can cue and prompt the individual to use the AAC system in consistent ways.

GUILLAIN-BARRÉ SYNDROME

Guillain-Barré syndrome (GBS) results from the progressive destruction and regeneration of the myelin sheath of peripheral nerve axons. Paralysis progresses from the lower extremities upward, and maximal paralysis usually occurs within 1–3 weeks of onset. As the myelin sheath slowly regenerates, nerve function and associated muscle strength gradually return. Typically, motor recovery begins with the structures of the head and face and progresses inferiorly. About 85% of people with GBS recover completely with no residual impairments.

Guillain-Barré syndrome . . . occurs in about 1.7 cases per 100,000 people (or about 3,500 cases per year in North America) and is among the most common neurologic causes of admission to the ICU. (It is) characterized by the acute onset of a symmetrical descending paralysis that extends from the legs to the trunk, arms, and cranial nerves. . . . Treatment includes ventilation in about one third of all cases. . . . If respiratory failure occurs, the average period on a ventilator is 50 days, with a 108-day period of hospitalization. (Fried-Oken, Howard, & Stewart, 1991, pp. 45–46)

Communication Disorders

The weakness associated with GBS causes flaccid dysarthria and in many cases anarthria (complete loss of speech). In addition, severe weakness often requires ventilator support through oral intubation or tracheotomy. Language and cognition are usually unaffected.

Intervention Stages

The stages of progression of GBS require different types of AAC support, as described in the following sections.

Stage 1: Deterioration Phase

As noted previously, people with GBS experience maximal paralysis within 1–3 weeks of onset. Because weakness progresses upward from the lower extremities, the diagnosis usually is made before speech becomes impaired. Little time usually passes, however, between diagnosis and onset of severe speech impairment. Typically, individuals with GBS are hospitalized following their diagnosis so that medical personnel can monitor their symptom progression and provide appropriate supports and intervention. As part of this effort, medical teams should monitor these individuals' communication impairment so that AAC intervention can be provided at an appropriate time.

Stage 2: Loss of Speech

During this stage, the progress of symptoms stabilizes. Those people who require AAC intervention are usually unable to speak by this stage and receive respiratory support from a ventilator. Initially, AAC intervention consists of low-technology options, with emphasis on the establishment of a reliable yes/no system, followed by the development of an eye-pointing or eye-linking technique. AAC teams should develop communication boards that will support the individual's needs through dependent (i.e., partner-assisted) visual and auditory scanning, yes/no responses, and eye pointing. Usually, these communication boards will include social messages, health-related messages, and letters and numbers for message construction.

Stage 3: Prolonged Speechlessness

The period of time during which people with GBS are unable to speak varies from individual to individual. Some people, however, experience weeks or months of dependence on AAC systems to communicate with family, friends, and health care staff. Typically, the individual continues to use the low-tech strategies introduced in Stage 2; however, a high-tech option may also be appropriate to allow the individual greater independence and less need to rely on knowledgeable, well-trained listeners. Usually, the extensive motor impairments of these individuals require them to use scanning AAC systems, often with a switch controlled by eyelid or head movement. Given the temporary nature of these individuals' AAC use, most learn to communicate with letter-by-letter spelling and retrieval of a limited number of alphabetically encoded messages. Typically, these people do not use systems that require them to memorize extensive codes.

Stage 4: Spontaneous Recovery of Speech

During the fourth phase, the individual with GBS makes the transition from speechlessness to normal speech. Often, this transition takes several weeks or months. As muscle strength returns to the oral mechanism, the individual may still depend on a ventilator and a tracheostomy tube. Some speakers find an oral-type electrolarynx (see Chapter 18) very helpful at this point. By controlling the sound sources of the electrolarynx with a head switch, the sound can be turned on when the person wishes to speak and turned off when she or he wishes to listen or rest. While the muscles of the oral cavity are still weak, the individual may have imprecise articulation and reduced speech intelligibility. Some individuals find it helpful to first establish the communicative topic or context with their AAC system, then attempt to use their residual speech, and finally resolve communication breakdowns with their AAC system. As recovery progresses, medical personnel will remove ventilator support and the individual will again be able to speak independently. Usually, the individual requires no ongoing natural speech interventions.

Stage 5: Long-Term Residual Motor Speech Disorder

As mentioned previously, 85% of people with GBS experience complete recovery of motor control. The remaining 15% experience residual weakness. Of this residual group, just a few experience long-term motor speech disorders (i.e., dysarthria). For them, speech interventions to maximize the effectiveness of their natural speech are appropriate. We do not know of any individual with GBS who required long-term AAC support.

Botulism (a form of food poisoning) clinically resembles Guillain-Barré syndrome. . . . (It) is an infection of the nervous system caused by the organism *Clostridium botulinum*, which when ingested produces widespread muscle weakness. The disease often occurs when someone eats uncooked canned food that has not been sterilized properly. (Fried-Oken et al., 1991, p. 46)

PARKINSON'S DISEASE

PD is a syndrome composed of a cluster of motor symptoms that include tremor at rest, rigidity, paucity (i.e., reduction in movement), and impaired postural reflexes. PD results from a loss of dopaminergic neurons in the basal ganglia (especially the substantia nigra) and the brain stem. The onset is typically insidious; in retrospect, many individuals recall stiffness and muscle aches, which they first attributed to normal aging. The symptom that often initiates the first visit to a physician is tremor in a resting position.

Medical treatment since the 1970s has greatly altered the natural course of PD. Prior to the availability of the pharmacological agent levodopa (L-dopa), about one fourth of all individuals with PD died within the first 5 years following diagnosis, and 80% died after 10–14 years (Yorkston, Beukelman, & Bell, 1988). Although the changes in mortality rate due to L-dopa are not yet clear, this treatment has altered the lifestyles of people with PD dramatically. Individuals with PD are able to move much more freely and manage their lives much more independently with L-dopa than without it.

The average annual incidence of parkinsonism (excluding drug-induced cases) is 18.2 cases per 100,000 people. The prevalence is estimated to be between 66 and 187 cases per 100,000. There is no significant difference of incidence between males and females. The incidence increases sharply above the age of 64, and peak incidence is between 75 and 84 years of age. There is a trend toward increased age at the time of diagnosis. (Yorkston, Beukelman, & Bell, 1988)

Although pharmocological treatment dramatically improves the performance of many people with PD, some side effects of the medication can interfere with the use of AAC approaches. There may be individual fluctuations in response (also known as *on-off response*), probably due to differences in medication absorption and dopamine receptor responsiveness. With long-term therapy, some people also experience involuntary movements that interfere with functional activities. These involuntary movements may cause emotional distress as well.

Communication Symptoms

The prevalence of speech disorders among people with PD is quite high. Of 65 individuals with PD studied by Buck and Cooper (1956), 37% had normal speech, 22% had a moderate degree of speech involvement, and 29% had severe speech impairments. Researchers have not determined the percentage of individuals with impaired speech due to PD who might benefit from AAC techniques.

Probably the most complete overview of parkinsonian speech characteristics comes from the work of Darley, Aronson, and Brown (1969a, 1969b, 1975), who studied 32 people with dysarthria due to PD. They noted that the speech of this group was characterized by

> Reduced variability in pitch, loudness, reduced loudness level overall, and decreased use of all vocal parameters for achieving stress and emphasis. Markedly imprecise articulation is generated at variable rates in short bursts of speech punctuated by illogical pauses and often by inappropriate silences. Voice quality is sometimes harsh, sometimes breathy. (Darley et al., 1975, p. 175)

Nevertheless, speech disorders among people with PD are not uniform. Some speakers are difficult to understand, primarily because they speak excessively fast. Their speaking rates may exceed those of normal speakers or exceed those that are optimal for people with motor control disorders. Other speakers are difficult to understand because they speak with reduced intensity or loudness. Still others speak with such limited movement of their articulators that they have difficulty producing precise speech sounds. As PD progresses, many speakers demonstrate combinations of these speech disorders.

Researchers have not documented the natural course of symptoms in people with PD who have communication disorders. Clinical observations reveal a gradual process, with speech becoming increasingly difficult to understand. Most people with PD communicate with natural speech to a greater or lesser extent. Therefore, when they use AAC techniques, the techniques make up part of a multimodal communication system that includes natural speech.

Identify Participation Patterns and Communication Needs

The communication needs of people with PD depend on two primary factors. Many people with PD are older adults, and most are retired. Therefore, their communication needs reflect, first of all, the social environments of their retirement. In addition, the range of physical impairments in PD varies greatly from person to person. Some people have such severe physical limitations that they require extensive physical assistance from attendants or family members. The level of dependence greatly influences each individual's communication needs.

Assess Specific Capabilities

Cognitive/Linguistic Skills

People with PD acquire their disability late in life, so they usually have developed typical language skills. Therefore, they can spell and read at levels necessary to support most AAC interventions.

Controversy exists as to whether dementia is a feature of PD (Bayles et al., 1996). During tests, examiners have found that some individuals have specific memory impairments, and some individuals complain of slowness in problem solving. The AAC team must consider whether such cognitive limitations are likely to interfere with AAC interventions. The team may provide additional instruction and practice in order to help the person compensate for learning or memory difficulties.

Sensory/Perceptual Skills

Disturbances in sensory function usually do not interfere with AAC interventions for people with PD.

Motor Skills

Clinical reports describe people who have successfully used direct selection AAC techniques such as alphabet boards, as discussed previously. Because researchers have reported few AAC interventions with PD speakers, however, the motor control problems that may influence such AAC interventions are not well documented. Thus, AAC teams may need to consider several motor control problems. Many individuals have reduced range and speed of movement due to the rigidity associated with PD. The AAC team will need to reduce the size of the selection display (e.g., on an alphabet board) for these individuals. Other individuals experience extensive tremors that are usually worse when they are at rest. Many can dampen the tremors if they can stabilize their hands on the surface of a communication board or device. A keyguard is often helpful with devices that have keyboards. Some people experience hyperkinesia (excessive movement) as a side effect of the medication that controls their parkinsonian symptoms. These excessive movements may interfere with the fine motor control required for some AAC options.

Assess Constraints

Two types of constraints are usually associated with AAC interventions for people with PD. First, because most people with PD are able to speak to some extent, they may display some resistance toward the need for an AAC intervention. Some will blame their listeners for their communication failures, even if this is not the case. Communication partners need to actively encourage these individuals to use AAC techniques. Second, many people with PD are older adults and have spouses and friends in the same age group. Therefore, the hearing limitations of their listeners may act as a significant barrier to effective communication.

Intervention Stages

Again, we use a five-stage model of support to describe potential AAC interventions for individuals with PD.

Stage 1: No Detectable Speech Disorder

Early in the disease, people with PD have received a diagnosis but do not yet exhibit speech symptoms. As with other degenerative diseases, individuals and their families often engage in an educational phase after a time of acceptance and grief. During this phase, they will often ask about communication disorders. During Stage 1, intervention involves the confirmation that speech is now normal and the provision of information about the types of available supports, should the individual need and desire them.

Stage 2: Obvious Speech Disorder

Usually, the presenting symptom that signals the beginning of the second stage is a reduction in speech loudness (Logemann, Fisher, Boshes, & Blonsky, 1978). Speech intervention is recommended during this stage and usually follows the guidelines provided by Ramig and Scherer (1992) that include intensive instruction and practice to speak with increased loudness, respiratory support, effort, and flexibility. It is beyond the scope of this book to discuss this intervention program. However, Ramig and Scherer's (1992) research strongly supports the implementation of such a speech intervention program early in the disease when speech symptoms begin to appear so that speech intelligibility disorders can be delayed or prevented.

Because many people with PD speak with reduced voice loudness, portable speech amplification systems may improve communication interactions effectively during this stage. Small, portable voice amplifiers such as the one illustrated in Figure 15.4 are most effective when speakers produce consistent phonation (i.e., voicing) during speech, although voice loudness may be severely reduced. In addition, many telephone adaptations are available to people with PD and other disorders who have difficulty using the telephone because of communication impairments (see Blackstone, 1991). If the individual whispers, however, amplification usually does not improve intelligibility.

Figure 15.4.   A portable voice amplifier.

Stage 3: Reduction in Speech Intelligibility

During the third stage, reduction in speech intelligibility becomes apparent due to imprecise consonant sound production, reduced speech loudness, and voice breathiness. For some speakers with PD, alterations in the speaking rate also occur; these may include rushes of excessively rapid speech, difficulty initiating speech, and excessive overall speaking rates. Intervention includes speaking rate control and/or voice amplification, depending on the speaker.

Individuals who speak too rapidly often benefit considerably from interventions designed to slow their speech rate. Several AAC techniques may help slow the speech rate, thereby often helping to increase speech intelligibility. Beukelman and Yorkston (1978) introduced alphabet board supplementation, which was among the first of such interventions documented in the literature. This procedure requires the speaker to point to the first letter of each word on an alphabet board or other type of AAC device as he or she utters the word. This not only forces speakers to slow their speaking rates but also provides their communication partners with extra information in the form of the first letters of words. For some speakers, the slowed speaking rate alone appears to be the major factor contributing to improved intelligibility. For others, the communication partner's knowledge of the first letter of the spoken word also contributes to more effective communication. In addition, when communication breakdowns do occur, speakers can use their alphabet boards to spell messages.

The intelligibility of poorly articulated speech usually improves considerably when the communication partner is aware of the topic of conversation. Thus, people

Mary's family complained that they were no longer able to understand her. She had difficulty initiating speech, as she seemed to freeze on the first word of some utterances. Once started, she spoke with bursts of excessive speech rates. Due to a lack of movement related to her PD, Mary showed no facial expression. Thus, during speech, her articulators barely moved. Mary learned to use a small alphabet board and point to the first letter of each word as she spoke. With this technique, she reduced her overall speaking rate to about 35–40 words per minute and eliminated the rushes of excessive speech rates. Her speech was quite understandable even when her listeners did not observe the communication board to determine the first letter of each word. When people had difficulties understanding her, she spelled her message with her board. Although Mary had success with this approach, she was reluctant to use it. She felt that it looked strange. It also required more effort than speaking her messages. However, with encouragement from her family, she used the alphabet supplementation approach for several years. Toward the end of Mary's life, her motor control deteriorated to the point where she was unable to point efficiently. Her facilitators abandoned the alphabet board and helped her use a dependent scanning approach until her death.

with PD may be encouraged to provide their listeners with the topic of a message or a conversation before beginning to speak. At times, the individual can communicate the topic successfully through natural speech, but he or she may also need to identify the topic using an AAC device such as a topic display. Topic displays often appear on the same communication boards used for alphabet supplementation of rate-reduced speech. Figure 15.5 illustrates this combination.

Small Talk	Sports	Shopping	Weather
Family	Food	Church	Computers
Personal Care	A B C D E F	Yes	Please repeat each word I say, so I know you understand.
	G H I J K L	No	
Transportation	M N O P Q R	Maybe	
	S T U V W X	I don't know.	You misunderstood! Start over.
Trips	Y Z	Forget it.	
Appointments	I will spell the word. I will say the word.	I have something to say.	This is important! Wait a minute!

Figure 15.5. Alphabet-topic board.

It is important that people with PD and their frequent communication partners act as informants and identify relevant topics to be included on the board. Some people with PD may also find it useful to employ a "remnant book," as described in Chapter 11. Individuals may use remnants such as theater tickets, napkins from restaurants, traffic tickets, bank statements, programs from plays, church bulletins, and racing forms to communicate topics as well as to clarify the details of an experience.

Stage 4: Natural Speech Supplemented with AAC

In the fourth stage of PD, the individual does not have functional natural speech. AAC interventions may include the use of pace-setting boards or alphabet supplementation to control speaking rate and increase the comprehensibility of residual natural speech. Some individuals prefer to use portable typing systems to prepare written messages because their handwriting is illegible.

Stage 5: Loss of Useful Speech

A very small percentage of people with PD lose all functional speech during the fifth stage of the disease. Clearly, when an individual has such a severe speech disorder, he or she requires AAC intervention. Given the overall motor control impairment and relatively frequent cognitive impairments late in the disease, AAC interventions are often difficult to institute and are very individualized.

Alzheimer's Disease

Bourgeois (1991) provided an excellent research review of the communication treatment of people with dementia including Alzheimer's disease (AD). The communication symptoms of people with AD are many and varied. Word-finding impairments often result in vague and empty speech. Individuals with AD commonly produce verbal perseverations, which include the repetition of ideas. Pragmatic skills including turn taking and topic maintenance become disordered. Late in the disease, mutism, echolalia, and bizarre nonsensical utterances often predominate. Many of these symptoms appear to result from memory impairments.

Intervention efforts usually involve strategies to structure the living environments of people with AD and provide external memory aids such as memory books, calendars, signs, and timers. In addition, AAC teams must train communication partners to provide a reinforcing and stimulating environment. A number of authors have provided additional information regarding communication and dementia including Bayles (1984), Bourgeois (1992), Clark and Witte (1995), and Molloy and Lubinsky (1995).

SPINAL CORD INJURY

SCI occurs when the cord is bruised, crushed, or torn by a bone fracture, a dislocation (caused by disruption of the ligaments between individual vertebrae), or both. A person with SCI progresses through several stages. During spinal shock, which occurs immediately following the injury, the individual may experience paralysis, sensory loss, and loss of reflexes in parts of the body below the site of injury. Spinal shock lasts from several days to several weeks, after which time the reflexes return. Donovan noted that

> If reflexes return before voluntary function is present, it [is] likely that voluntary function will never develop and the lesion is complete. In such an instance, the SCI interrupted all tracts to and from the brain. Frequently, however, a lesion will be referred to as being incomplete. (1981, p. 66)

Incomplete lesions may involve a localized portion of the spinal cord that is totally unable to transmit messages, whereas the remainder of the cord retains near-normal functioning. Alternatively, an incomplete lesion may involve diffuse injury to the cord; in this case, certain nerve tracts still function, but they do so abnormally.

Recovery from SCI varies from person to person. Individuals with complete lesions usually do not experience long-term recovery of neurological function, whereas people with incomplete lesions may recover neurological function. In both cases, most people learn to compensate for their disabilities, at least to some extent, through active rehabilitation efforts.

The incidence of SCI is 25–30 injuries per 1,000,000 people per year. Automobile accidents account for 35% of all SCIs, falls add another 15%, gunshot wounds contribute 10%, and diving accidents cause 6%. The remaining 34% of SCIs are the result of a variety of other conditions. The mean age of a person with an SCI is about 30, and the median age (the age at which half of those injured are older and half are younger) is 25. The age group most represented is 18- to 21-year-olds (Donovan, 1981).

Communication Symptoms

Spinal cord lesions in the cervical region usually interfere with handwriting. Keyboard control is also limited because reduced finger control and strength occur with low cervical and high thoracic injuries and because arm and hand paralysis occurs with middle and high cervical injuries. Table 15.1 summarizes the physiological functions that are affected when various spinal motor root segments are injured.

If the spinal lesion occurs at or above the nuclei of the phrenic nerve (usually at the first or second cervical vertebra), the individual will depend on a ventilator due to a loss of innervation of the diaphragm. Most individuals who depend on a ventilator permanently learn to speak by venting air past their tracheostomy tube and through the larynx as the ventilator forces air into the lungs. For a more complete description of procedures in this area, readers may refer to Dowden, Honsinger, and Beukelman (1986) and Honsinger, Yorkston, and Dowden (1987).

Keith was 25 years old when he sustained a neck injury at the level of the fourth cervical vertebra. His complete SCI left him unable to move his body, but he is able to speak. Prior to his injury, Keith was a civil engineer. Using a sip-and-puff switch, Keith learned to send Morse code that an emulator device translated, providing alternative access to an IBM desktop computer. This system was integrated into the mainframe computer of Keith's employer. With practice, Keith was able to write error-free at a rate of 25–30 words per minute. For the past 8 years, Keith has worked full time, writing engineering reports by using the resources of both his desktop computer and the mainframe computer of the engineering firm. (Beukelman et al., 1985)

Identify Participation Patterns and Communication Needs

Since the 1970s, the opportunities available to people with even the most severe SCIs have increased dramatically. Powered mobility, portable respiratory ventilation systems, modified public and private transportation, computer technology, and AAC interventions allow children with cervical spinal injuries to attend general elementary

Table 15.1.   Muscles supplied and functions served by spinal nerve motor roots

Root segment	Representative muscles	Function served
C1 and C2	High neck muscles	Aid in head control
C3 and C4	Diaphragm	Inspiration (breathing in)
C5 and C6	Deltoid	Shoulder flexion, abduction (arm forward, out to side)
	Biceps	Elbow flexion (elbow bent)
C6 and C7	Extensor carpi radialis	Wrist dorsiflexion (back of hand up)
	Pronator teres	Wrist pronation (palm down)
C7 and C8	Triceps	Elbow extension (elbow straight)
	Extensor digitorum communis	Finger extension ("knuckles" straight)
C8 and T1	Flexor digitorum superficialis	Finger flexion (fist clenched)
	Opponens pollicis	Thumb opposition (thumb brought to little finger)
	Interossei (intrinsics)	Spreading and closing the fingers
T2–T6	Intercostals	Forced inspiration (breathing in)
		Expiration (breathing out, coughing)
T6–T12	Intercostals	Forced inspiration (breathing in)
	Abdominals	Aid in expiration (coughing)
		Aid in trunk flexion (sitting up)
L1, L2, and L3	Iliopsoas	Hip flexion (thigh to chest)
	Adductors	Hip adduction (thigh to midline, legs together)
L3 and L4	Quadriceps	Knee extension (knee straight)
L4, L5, and S1	Gluteus medius	Hip abduction (thigh out to side, legs apart)
	Tibialis anterior	Foot dorsiflexion (foot up, walk on heels)
L5, S1, and S2	Gluteus maximus	Hip extension (thigh in line with trunk, hips straight, e.g., standing)
	Gastrocnemius	Foot plantarflexion (foot down, walk on toes)
S2, S3, and S4	Anal sphincter	Bowel function (fecal continence)
	Urethral sphincter	Bladder control (urinary continence)

From Beukelman, D., and Garrett, K. (1988). Augmentative and alternative communication for adults with acquired severe communication disorders. *Augmentative and Alternative Communication, 4,* 111; reprinted by permission.

schools, young adults to attend colleges, and adults to hold typical jobs. Increasingly, people who depend on ventilators are able to participate in fully integrated educational and vocational environments. These extensive opportunities greatly expand the communication needs for people with SCI. AAC teams need to analyze these needs, especially communication needs in employment settings, in order to develop appropriate AAC interventions.

Assess Specific Capabilities

Cognitive/Linguistic Skills

People with SCI usually retain their preinjury language and cognitive skills. Therefore, because most people are injured as adolescents or young adults, they are able to spell messages and learn to operate complicated AAC systems. Because SCI may occur as the result of abnormal displacement of the head during an accident, TBI may co-occur with SCI. When identifying AAC interventions for individuals with both impairments, AAC teams must consider the learning and memory impairments associated with TBI.

Sensory/Perceptual Skills

SCI does not result in hearing and vision impairments. Nevertheless, tactile and position impairments below the spinal cord lesion should be expected with complete lesions and may or may not be present with incomplete lesions.

Motor Skills

Because motor control is the primary problem resulting from SCI, the goal of intervention is to provide efficiently alternative computer keyboard access that minimizes fatigue. Beukelman and Garrett (1988) suggested dividing individuals with SCI into three groups, depending on their alternative access needs: 1) those individuals who have typical or near-typical hand control, 2) those with limited hand function who can perform single-finger typing with one or both hands, and 3) those who have little or no upper-extremity control but who demonstrate normal or near-normal control of their facial and neck muscles. In the following sections, we discuss potential AAC interventions for each group of individuals.

Typical Hand Function

Individuals with typical hand function can usually operate a typewriter or computer keyboard, without modifications, provided that these devices are efficiently positioned in the individual's work space. An occupational therapist, vocational specialist, or rehabilitation engineer with a knowledge of workplace modifications and workstation development may need to help facilitate such interventions.

Limited Hand Function

Individuals who can type with a single finger usually require several types of adaptive assistance in order to do so efficiently. Some individuals with limited hand function may benefit from the assistance of a universal cuff, such as the one illustrated in Figure 15.6, or will need to activate the keyboard with a stick or pencil. People who can use only one hand will require keyboard assistance so that simultaneous double or triple key activations can be managed (e.g., shift key + letter key for uppercase letters). A number of standard computers contain a "sticky key" function that allows users to execute such multiple simultaneous keystroke commands by activating one key at a time.

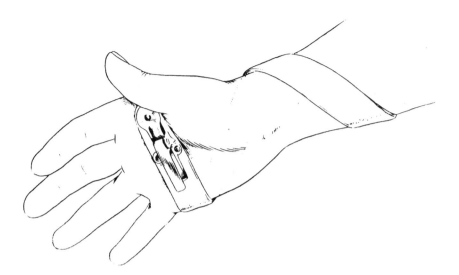

Figure 15.6.   A universal cuff for typing. (From Kottke, F., & Lehman, J. (Eds.). (1990). *Krusen's handbook of physical medicine and rehabilitation* (4th ed., p. 582). Philadelphia: W.B. Saunders; reprinted by permission.)

Alternatively, individuals may choose from a number of adaptive software programs, such as EZKeys (Words+, Inc.).

Most single-finger typists prefer to use some type of rate enhancement technique to increase their communication speed and to reduce fatigue. As discussed in Chapter 3, these techniques include various encoding strategies that permit retrieval of entire words, messages, or even paragraphs. People who could read prior to their accidents generally select an alpha or alpha-numeric encoding strategy.

Communication rate enhancement software packages that people with SCI may find useful include Productivity Plus (Productivity Software International, Inc.), EZKeys (Words+, Inc.), Handikey (Microsystems Software, Inc.) and Co:Writer (Don Johnston, Inc.).

Individuals with limited hand function who have extensive writing needs may find that single-finger typing is still too slow and laborious, even with rate enhancement techniques. These individuals may employ more rapid access approaches using Morse code or voice recognition, described later in this chapter.

No Functional Hand or Arm Control

Individuals who have no functional hand or arm control can operate computer and other AAC equipment through a variety of alternative access options. The most appropriate approach depends on the needs, capabilities, and preferences of the AAC user; the restrictions imposed by an educational agency, employer, and computer system; the abilities of facilitators; and the availability of funding. Generally, AAC teams can choose from four options.

Individuals with SCI have used *mouthsticks* and *headsticks* for decades to operate typewriters, computers, tape recorders, and telephones. Mouthsticks and headsticks are appropriate for some applications, but this approach is often too slow and fatiguing for use during full-time employment or education. Fatigue occurs because keyboard activation requires precise backward and forward movements of the head, neck, and sometimes trunk.

Efforts to reduce fatigue and muscle strain have led AAC specialists to develop other options that the individual can control with his or her head. These include a variety of *head-pointing options* that utilize light or sound and can be used with most standard desktop computer systems (see Chapter 4). Usually, the AAC team mounts a light beam or transmitter of some type on the user's head and positions a receiving unit beside or on top of the computer monitor. The person then moves his or her head to direct the transmitter at a keyboard displayed on the screen in order to type. The receiving unit translates the head movements into cursor movements that the user can then accept either with a remote switch (usually a mouth control switch, as shown in Figure 15.7) or by maintaining the transmitter at the desired location for a specific time. The user may enhance communication rates achieved with such head-pointing systems by utilizing rate enhancement software programs, as described previously.

People with SCI have also used *Morse code* in their AAC devices. Morse code emulators that translate the dots and dashes of Morse code into standard orthography or computer commands are available for most desktop computer systems. (See Chapter 3 for more extensive discussion of this technique.)

Figure 15.7.   Using a Headmaster with mouth control switch to operate a Macintosh computer.

Some Morse code emulators commonly used in AAC include Ke:nx for Macintosh computers and PC A.I.D. and PC Serial A.I.D. for IBM-compatible computers (distributed by Don Johnston, Inc.); WSKE Morse Code (Words+, Inc.); and HandiCODE (Microsystems Software, Inc.).

Voice-recognition technology offers people with SCI an exciting alternative access option. Because most individuals with SCI are able to speak, they can operate voice-recognition systems just as well as individuals without disabilities can. Although this technology has provoked interest in the AAC field, the number of messages that the early voice-recognition systems could recognize *accurately* was quite limited (e.g., Coleman & Meyers, 1991). In the 1990s, voice-recognition systems with larger vocabulary capacities became commercially available at a cost that is reasonable for individual AAC users. Undoubtedly, people with SCI as well as people without disabilities will use such systems more and more. (See Chapter 4 for additional information.)

BRAIN-STEM STROKE

Strokes (i.e., cerebrovascular accidents) that disrupt the circulation serving the lower brain stem often cause severe dysarthria or anarthria (i.e., an inability to produce speech). Because the brain stem contains the nuclei of all the cranial nerves that activate the muscles of the face, mouth, and larynx, damage to this area of the brain may result in an inability or a reduced ability to control these muscles voluntarily or reflexively. The nerve tracts that activate the trunk and limbs via the spinal nerves also pass through the brain stem. Therefore, severe damage to the brain stem may impair motor control of the limbs as well as motor control of the face and mouth.

Communication Symptoms

Communication symptoms associated with brain-stem stroke vary considerably with the level and extent of damage to the brain stem. Some people are dysarthric but can communicate partial or complete messages through speech. These individuals usually experience dysarthria of the predominantly flaccid type due to damage to the nerve nuclei of the cranial nerves. Other individuals may display a marked spastic component in addition to flaccidity. Many people with brain-stem stroke are unable to speak because of the severity of their impairments.

Identify Participation Patterns and Communication Needs

Medical and lifestyle issues influence the communication needs of people who experience brain-stem stroke, as does the extent of their communication disorders. Following brain-stem stroke, an individual may require extensive personal and medical care, depending on the severity of the stroke and subsequent health conditions. People who survive a brain-stem stroke are usually unable to work. Some can be cared for at home, whereas others may live in settings that range from independent living to nursing care centers. Individuals who experience brain-stem strokes are usually aware of the world around them and are able to exchange information and achieve social closeness through their message formulations. Thus, they may have extensive communication needs.

Ruby was 44 years of age when a severe brain-stem stroke left her unable to speak or swallow. When we first met her on the rehabilitation unit, she was able to communicate by answering yes/no questions and by using a dependent scanning approach. She communicated *no* by closing her eyes and *yes* by leaving them open and raising her eyebrows slightly. The dependent scanning approach included a small chalkboard with the letters of the alphabet positioned vertically on the left and right sides. To communicate a message, Ruby's communication partner pointed to each column of letters (A–L on the left side and M–Z on the right side). Ruby raised her eyebrows to signal the desired column of letters. Then her partner scanned down the column until Ruby signaled the preferred letter. In order to remember the letters that had already been chosen, the partner wrote each letter on the chalkboard. Ruby's partners were encouraged to guess the remainder of a word or message when enough of a message had been communicated.

With proper positioning and head support, Ruby was able to move her head voluntarily to some degree, and she began to practice controlling a headlight pointer that was mounted on a headband and positioned over her right ear. In time, she was able to point to the letters on the chalkboard; with this technique, her communication rate was three times faster than with dependent scanning. Finally, Ruby learned to access an electronic AAC device using an optical head-pointing strategy. In time, the AAC device was mounted on her wheelchair and could also be transferred to her bed when needed. Ruby used this system for about 8 years. (Beukelman et al., 1985)

Assess Specific Capabilities

Cognitive Skills

No accompanying cognitive limitations are expected if the stroke involves only the brain stem. If the stroke extends higher into the brain or is associated with a more extensive medical episode that interfered with the supply of oxygen to the brain, a wide variety of cognitive impairments may exist. These need to be assessed on an individual basis.

Language Skills

If brain-stem stroke does not affect the cortical or subcortical structures associated with language functioning, language skills should not be impaired. Thus, the skills of people with brain-stem stroke usually reflect their prestroke linguistic performances.

Sensory/Perceptual Skills

A high brain-stem stroke may affect the cranial nerve nuclei that control muscles for eye and eyelid movement, whereas a middle or low brain-stem stroke probably will not impair these muscles. Thus, visual functioning may or may not be impaired. In all cases, brain-stem stroke generally leaves hearing unimpaired but often damages tactile and position senses.

Motor Skills

People with severe dysarthria or anarthria following a brain-stem stroke usually experience motor control problems of their limbs as well as of their speech mechanisms. AAC specialists have reported interventions that employ eye or head pointing as the alternative access mode for these individuals who experience motor control problems. For example, Beukelman et al. (1985) reported case studies of two people with brain-stem strokes who successfully used electronic AAC systems via optical pointers mounted on their eyeglasses. Both individuals were required to spend much time in bed for medical reasons and learned to operate their AAC systems while in their wheelchairs and also while lying supine. AAC teams designed special mounting systems to support their devices in bed.

Intervention Stages

Throughout the years, a number of individuals with severe brain-stem strokes have received AAC services. The pattern of these interventions is quite similar and is outlined in the following sections.

Stage 1: No Useful Speech

The initial goal during Stage 1 is to provide an early communication system so that those people who are unable to speak due to brain-stem stroke can respond to yes/no questions. These individuals frequently report that they were well aware of their situation and were able to comprehend spoken information long before those around them realized it. Given the severe impairment of motor control that accompanies brain-stem stroke, yes/no responses usually involve slight head or eye movements. Once an AAC team has identified a response mode for the individual, the team will often need to train communication partners to formulate communication interactions in a yes/no format.

> I remember one of the nurses giving me a bed bath and saying to the respiratory therapist, "She used to be a filmmaker." As if I wasn't there, as if I couldn't hear, as if my life was over. I wanted to shake them and say, "Don't talk about me like I'm dead!" But I couldn't shout or shake anyone or even explain it to Michael on the stupid letter board. I remember my finger wobbling around, not able to reach the right letter. I remember the blur of the board in my double vision. I remember the letter board getting lost, over and over again. Why the hell didn't they have an extra one? (Bonnie Sherr Klein, writing of her experiences after a brain-stem stroke, 1997, p. 138)

For those individuals who stabilize at Stage 1 and never regain functional speech, AAC teams usually implement a three-phase intervention sequence.

Phase 1: Initial Choice Making

Those who are unable to recover natural speech will need to develop progressively more complex AAC systems. In time, some of these individuals may be able to respond to visual and/or auditory dependent scanning techniques to support the formulation of messages. Once AAC teams have developed a yes/no response strategy, communication intervention usually focuses on choice-making responses signaled with the eyes. Teams use two strategies most often—eye pointing and eye linking. Eye pointing (see Chapter 4) involves teaching the individual to look directly at the item of choice. During eye linking, the choices are displayed on a transparent board; however, in this case, the AAC user is instructed to look at the item of choice while the partner looks at the user's eyes. The communication partner then moves the transparent board until their eyes "link" (i.e., meet) across the symbol of choice. This strategy is preferable when the AAC user's eye gaze is difficult to "read."

Phase 2: Pointing

In time, some individuals with brain-stem stroke are able to move their heads sufficiently to direct a light beam at items of choice (e.g., letters, symbols). Depending on the recovery of motor control, some may also be able to point to messages with their fingers or hands.

Phase 3: Use of a Multipurpose Electronic AAC Device

After progressing through Phases 1 and 2, some people with brain-stem stroke are able to learn to control a high-tech AAC device. Usually, the individual manages alternative access by head pointing (with either a light or sonar pointer); however, due to lack of motor control or fatigue, some individuals require a scanning system all or some of the time.

Stage 2: Reestablish Subsystem Control for Speech

During this stage, people unable to speak because of brain-stem stroke work systematically to develop voluntary control of their respiratory, phonatory (vocal), velopharyngeal, and articulatory subsystems while they continue to use their AAC systems for communication interaction. Because weakness is such a predominant symptom of brain-stem stroke, intervention at this stage involves strengthening the muscles of the subsystem and coordinating actions of the subsystems during speech-like and speech behaviors. Early in this stage, the AAC system will support the majority of communication interactions; however, late in this stage individuals will convey an increasing percentage of messages through natural speech. (For a complete description of these intervention strategies, see Yorkston, Beukelman, & Bell, 1988.)

Stage 3: Independent Use of Natural Speech

During this stage, speech intervention focuses on speech intelligibility, with the goal of meeting all communication needs through natural speech. We have worked with several speakers who used alphabet supplementation early in this stage. In time, they used AAC only to resolve communication breakdowns, and finally, AAC became unnecessary for communication interaction, although writing was still difficult or required the use of AAC.

Stage 4: Maximizing Speech Naturalness and Efficiency

By this stage, the person with brain-stem stroke will no longer need to use an AAC system. The goal is for the individual to speak as naturally as possible by learning to use appropriate breath groups and stress patterns.

Stage 5: No Detectable Speech Disorder
Few individuals who have sustained a brain-stem stroke achieve typical speech patterns.

Locked-in Syndrome

Locked-in syndrome (LIS, also known as ventral pontine syndrome) results in a conscious quadriplegic state that limits the individual's voluntary movement to vertical eye movements and perhaps eye blinks. The usual cause is a basilar artery stroke (occlusion or hemorrhage), a tumor, or trauma that results in damage to the upper pons or occasionally the midbrain. Culp and Ladtkow (1992) followed 16 people with LIS for at least 1 year. Fifteen of these individuals experienced LIS following stroke, and one experienced LIS following a blow to the occipital region. All remained nonambulatory, and nearly half of them experienced sufficient visual difficulties to interfere with their AAC interventions. Eight eventually developed adequate vision and motor skills for direct selection access, and nine relied on scanning access. Thirteen of the 16 individuals chose high-technology AAC systems.

In 1997, Jean-Dominique Bauby, a French man with LIS, completed a book entitled *Scaphandre et le Papillon (The Diving Bell and the Butterfly)*. After a stroke in 1995, Bauby required ventilator assistance to breathe and was fed via a gastric tube; he was unable to move, except for blinking his eyes. He wrote the book with the help of an assistant, who repeatedly recited the alphabet arranged according to the frequency of letter use in the French language. Bauby used eye blinks to indicate to his assistant which letters to use to spell out words. At the end of the book, Bauby asked, "Is there a key out in the cosmos that can unlock my bubble? A currency valuable enough to buy my freedom? I have to look elsewhere. I'm going there." Bauby died less than 72 hours later.

CONCLUSIONS

Numerous factors influence AAC interventions for people with severe communication disabilities due to acquired physical impairments. First, the diseases, conditions, and syndromes associated with the physical impairments usually require close medical monitoring. Therefore, frequent, detailed, and accurate communication with medical personnel is necessary.

Second, the medical and physical status of individuals with acquired physical impairments can affect their capability levels. Because fatigue is common for people with physical impairments, interventionists should take care to provide these individuals with AAC systems that they can control even when tired. In addition, these individuals' responses to medication can vary. For example, people with PD may experience a range of physical abilities, depending on their medication regimens. Those with physical impairments may be susceptible to health problems such as infections and respiratory disorders, both of which limit physical endurance.

Third, people with severe communication disabilities due to acquired physical impairments often experience additional disabilities in areas such as mobility, object manipulation, eating, and swallowing. Their communication needs are usually influenced by the nature and severity of these associated disabilities. In order to obtain appropriate services, they must request assistance, instruct caregivers and attendants, and interact with professional personnel regarding the range of their disabilities. Thus, AAC teams must plan their interventions to accommodate other assistive technologies, such as powered wheelchairs, electronically controlled beds, and respiratory support equipment.

Electronic communication options, such as e-mail, electronic chat rooms, closed list servers, and World Wide Web sites, provide people who use high-tech AAC systems important additional communication options. Several characteristics make these electronic communication options quite comfortable for people who communicate using AAC. For example, off-line preparation of messages allows people with slow message preparation rates to take as much time during the process as they need. Also, individuals can access electronic communication options according to their personal schedules.

16

Adults with Severe Aphasia

with Kathryn L. Garrett

I did comprehend somewhat vaguely what was said to me, but I could not answer except in gestures or by neologisms (made-up words). I knew the language I used was not correct but I was quite unable to select the appropriate words. I recollect trying to read the headlines of the *Chicago Tribune*, but they didn't make any sense to me at all. I didn't have any difficulty focusing; it was simply that the words, individually or in combination, didn't have meaning. (Scott Moss, recalling the first days following his stroke, in Moss, 1972, p. 4)

Aphasia is the impairment of an individual's ability to interpret and formulate language as a result of brain injury. Most individuals acquire aphasia as a result of a cerebral vascular accident, commonly known as a stroke. Other etiologies for aphasia include brain injury related to accidents, brain tumors, and other neurological illnesses. Most people acquire aphasia when they are 60 or 70 years of age or older, after a lifetime of communicating typically. However, people of all ages can experience aphasia. Usually without warning, aphasia leaves individuals with impaired language and communication skills. Depending on the severity of the aphasia, some individuals are unable to meet their communication needs for a short time only, but many may never again communicate easily and effectively.

Each year, 400,000 individuals have strokes, and 80,000 of these people experience aphasia as a result. Approximately 1 million people, or 1 out of every 275 adults in the United States, have aphasia. The incidence of aphasia is equal for males and females; people of all ethnicities and educational and socioeconomic backgrounds experience aphasia. Despite speech-language therapy, 72% of all individuals with aphasia who responded to a 1987 National Aphasia Association survey could not return to work. Approximately 70% of those surveyed felt that people avoided contact with them because of difficulty with communication.

Recovery patterns of people with aphasia secondary to stroke vary considerably. Most motor recovery takes place within 3–6 weeks, although upper-extremity functioning may continue to improve over 6 months. Language functioning may slowly return over a much longer period of time. Some individuals with aphasia experience a nearly complete recovery of their language capabilities. Others demonstrate mild or moderate language impairments that reduce the efficiency of their communication. This chapter focuses primarily on the significant number of people with aphasia who experience permanent severe communication disorders. Individuals in this group can sometimes use an augmentative and alternative communication (AAC) intervention.

COMMUNICATION DISORDERS

Aphasia is not restricted to a single language process; rather, people with aphasia usually have reduced abilities in all language and communication modalities, including speaking, auditory comprehension, reading, writing, and communicating through gestures or pantomime. The degree of impairment in each modality may differ, which creates distinct patterns of impairment. For example, some people experience an auditory comprehension impairment that is relatively severe when compared with their other language impairments. Others have only mild comprehension problems but experience considerable difficulty expressing themselves, particularly in producing the correct names of people, objects, or places. Others comprehend messages well and are able to produce important words but have difficulty producing grammatically complete messages. Still other individuals have profound communication impairments in all modalities. These and other patterns of language disorders in aphasia have been widely described. A detailed discussion of the various types of aphasia is beyond the scope of this text. (See Johns, 1985, and Rosenbek et al., 1989, for extensive descriptions of the classic aphasia taxonomy and neurological aspects of the disorder.)

PARTICIPATION MODEL

AAC teams have traditionally used a standard classification system of the types of aphasia (e.g., Broca's, Wernicke's, conduction) to diagnose and plan interventions for people with mild and moderate impairments. The Participation Model (see Figure 6.1) may be a more effective framework for organizing AAC interventions for people with severe aphasia. This model approaches the communication difficulties these individuals experience from an integrative perspective that encourages the use of both natural communication modalities, such as residual speech as well as writing, and AAC techniques as appropriate. Because Chapters 6 and 7 contain detailed discussions of this model, this chapter provides only a brief review of the application of the model to aphasia.

Participation Patterns

The participation patterns and the communication needs of adults with acquired severe communication disorders depend on two factors: the individual's lifestyle and communication capabilities. We discuss lifestyle issues first and address capability issues in the section of this chapter concerning assessment. The lifestyles of people with aphasia are determined by factors such as their living environments, their friendships, and their family networks, as well as by their lifelong interaction styles.

People with aphasia due to strokes live in a variety of different environments. Some continue to live in their homes, with a spouse, and have opportunities to interact with neighbors, friends, and relatives. Other individuals are no longer able to live in their homes and may live in retirement centers, in nursing centers, or in the homes of children or relatives. Many people with severe aphasia who were employed prior to their strokes have to retire because of residual impairments. Some individuals with aphasia continue to participate quite actively in community activities, whereas others decrease the frequency of their contact with others significantly. Thus, the participation patterns of individuals with aphasia are often quite different after a stroke than before. It is important for AAC teams to identify and customize intervention strategies to match poststroke participation patterns and also to envision the activities in which people with aphasia could participate if they were given access to AAC.

COMMUNICATION INTERACTION FUNCTIONS

As we mention in Chapter 1, Light (1988) suggested that communication interaction functions can be divided into four general categories: expression of basic wants and needs, information transfer, social closeness, and social etiquette. Figure 16.1 depicts

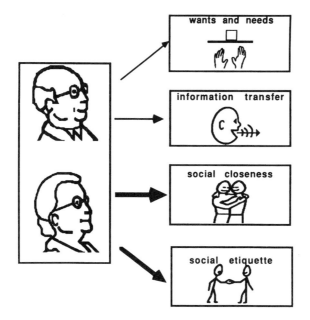

Figure 16.1.   Prestroke communication needs of older adults (the width of each arrow indicates the degree of importance). (Picture Communication Symbols copyright © 1994 by Mayer-Johnson Company; adapted by permission.)

these communication interaction functions, and the width of the arrows indicates each functions' degree of importance for older adults in general. Interventionists can, with careful planning, incorporate these interaction functions into AAC strategies for adults with aphasia.

Before a severe stroke, many older adults are able to care for their own wants and needs. They can prepare their own food, manage their own clothing, and transport themselves from place to place. They may require occasional assistance with household chores, property maintenance, or transportation, but, in general, they request minimal assistance with their wants and needs. Following a stroke, the proportion of time they spend on communicating wants and needs may increase somewhat because they need to request items for comfort and environmental access more frequently.

In addition to the brief, precise communication of basic needs and wants, most older adults strive for social closeness in their interactions. They spend much time interacting with their relatives, acquaintances, and friends. As they become older, their immediate families may play a more limited role in their lives, especially if they live far away, and they will turn more often to their social networks for interaction. As time passes, their relatives and friends may die or experience disabilities that limit social contact, so older adults must add to their network of friends and acquaintances. Thus, for an older adult, the ability to communicate for social closeness is a very important interaction function. Some AAC strategies can meet this need for social closeness, both in the content of the messages and in the interactional structure of the strategy.

In addition to interaction to support social closeness, the ability to transfer information remains important for older adults. The purpose of information transfer, however, often changes as people get older. When people raise a family and hold a job, they generally need to transfer information primarily related to daily and upcoming activities and events. As people enter their 70s and 80s, however, information transfer increasingly reflects their cultural roles as "tellers" of the past. In such roles, they often reiterate the oral histories of their families, recount past events, and attempt to interpret present experiences in terms of their past (Stuart, 1991). It is important for designers of AAC system for older adults to have an awareness of these individuals' roles in the information transfer process. For example, AAC teams should develop systems that will facilitate efficient communication of the narratives that older adults enjoy retelling (Fried-Oken, 1995). AAC strategies should also allow people to participate in favorite activities that require precise transmission of information, such as playing cards or conducting business at the bank.

Most older adults also continue participating in the social etiquette routines of their cultures. For example, they often appreciate being able to thank other individuals for assisting them, and they may become unhappy or frustrated when they are unable to interact using proper etiquette. Fortunately, most people who have aphasia retain their awareness of what is proper etiquette unless they experience significant cognitive deterioration.

She (the nurse) apparently gave Scott the phone and he uttered a sound but that's all that it was; I could not make head or tail out of what he was trying to say to me. I remember feeling that I had just fallen down to China. My heart just dropped! And there he was just babbling something over the phone to me, but nothing that I could understand. At this juncture I knew that something was very wrong and I simply said to him, "Well, let's hang up the phone and I'll be there in a few minutes." I got over there as quickly as I could and when I saw him he could say absolutely nothing to me. He just looked at me. Apparently he understood me but he couldn't say anything back. (Scott Moss's wife, recalling the first verbal interaction she had with her husband after his stroke, in Moss, 1972, p. 21)

A NEW COMMUNICATION CLASSIFICATION SYSTEM

Garrett and Beukelman introduced a new classification system for individuals with severe aphasia to aid in planning AAC interventions: "As we focus on enhancing the current communicative performance of persons with aphasia and their listeners, new descriptive classifications are necessary to guide clinical intervention" (1992, p. 251). We base the following categories of people with aphasia on the severity of the communication impairments that affect individual abilities to meet current needs and to participate in communication exchanges. The groups are distinctive, and AAC teams should use different intervention approaches when working with individuals from each group.

Basic-Choice Communicator

The *basic-choice communicator* has a profound cognitive-linguistic disorder across modalities. These individuals thus have extreme difficulties initiating basic communication and responding to conversational input. They frequently do not respond even with nonverbal signals such as pointing or nodding, particularly when the partner communicates by speaking only. Often, these people fail to respond to the physician's or speech-language pathologist's initial screening questions in the acute medical care environment. They are frequently discharged to long-term care facilities after minimal or no rehabilitation.

Basic-choice communicators may benefit from modifications to the typical linguistic treatment programs used in aphasia rehabilitation. For example, instead of asking the individual a series of unrelated yes/no questions in a stimulation-type therapy session, the clinician could identify opportunities for the individual to communicate choices and to develop shared-reference and turn-taking skills during everyday routines. During morning dressing, the therapist or caregiver could point to the calendar, discuss the season or weather, and then indicate several items of clothing. After ensuring that the basic-choice communicator has visually attended to the clothing items, the partner could verbally present the choices at a slow pace, encouraging the individual to choose or show preference by nodding, vocalizing, reaching, or showing changes in facial expression. To encourage participation in familiar social activities such as picking gift items for a family member, the therapist, caregiver, or family member could first show pictures of the individual who will receive the gift and discuss the occasion using props (e.g., a calendar and a birthday card for the selection of a birthday present). Then, prior to asking multiple-choice questions, the facilitator could encourage the person with severe aphasia to look at pictures of gift choices presented in a simplified catalog (i.e., a few pictures cut apart, pasted on blank paper, and taped inside a notebook) and could ask the person to turn pages, if appropriate. After the individual chooses or shows preference for a gift, the facilitator can ask him or her to make other decisions regarding cost or color of the item, if appropriate.

The goals of AAC interventions with basic-choice communicators are to increase their participation in meaningful adult communication activities, provide them with a very simple system for communicating basic messages, and prepare them for more advanced types of communication strategies if they continue to improve medically. Although many individuals with aphasia function as basic-choice communicators shortly after their strokes, people with persistent global aphasia and severe neurological impairments may remain basic-choice communicators for an extended period of time.

Controlled-Situation Communicator

Controlled-situation communicators convey messages more capably than basic-choice communicators because they can indicate their needs by spontaneously pointing to objects and items. Controlled-situation communicators are aware of daily routines and can participate in conversations structured by a skilled communication partner. Nevertheless, controlled-situation communicators do not have the linguistic ability to initiate communication acts consistently. Thus, these individuals may be quite isolated socially. With assistance, however, they can participate in controlled, predictable exchanges (e.g., introductions in a group) or in routine conversations when their communication partners provide written or pictorial choices. Many individuals with persistent severe aphasia, Broca's aphasia, or Wernicke's aphasia may function as controlled-situation communicators for the short or long term.

Daughter:	How are you, Mom?
Mother with aphasia:	(nods head up and down, then side to side)
Daughter:	Have you been keeping busy?
Mother:	(nods head up and down, then side to side)
Daughter:	I left the kids at home today.
Mother:	(points to daughter's purse)
Daughter:	Is there something you want?
Mother:	(pulls purse toward herself, opens it, and finds wallet)
Daughter:	Oh, you want to see how much money I have?
Mother:	(shakes head *no*)
Daughter:	Oh, do you want to see the new school pictures?
Mother:	(nods head *yes*)
Daughter:	I'm glad we figured that out. Let me show you.

When implementing AAC interventions for controlled-situation communicators, team members attempt to provide the necessary communication tools and techniques so that these people can engage in specific communication activities. Because these individuals often become confused if a variety of different communication activities are combined, team members should select simple and familiar contexts. These might include, for example, watching a baseball game, eating a meal, and celebrating a birthday party.

To facilitate choice making, partners must learn to manage several communication-related tasks. First, when facilitating communication with an individual who cannot initiate interactions, the partner needs to be able to identify the basic topic of interest.

He or she can often determine this intuitively by examining the context of the interaction and taking cues from the individual's daily routine. For example, if the individual becomes agitated while watching a political debate on television, chances are fairly good that he or she wants to communicate something about politics or the candidates. It may often be useful for the facilitator to provide symbols of some type that reflect frequently occurring topics so that the individual can choose from the options.

A primary communication technique that facilitators may use with controlled-situation communicators is *written-choice communication* (Garrett & Beukelman, 1992). This technique requires the facilitator to generate word choices pertinent to a conversational topic (see Figure 16.2). The person with severe aphasia participates by pointing to the choices in order to make his or her opinions and preferences known. The clinician's role is to instruct the facilitators and assist them to prepare notebooks containing choices to support interactions. The clinician often places an instruction card (see Figure 16.3) on the cover of the notebook to briefly explain the procedure to communication partners.

During an AAC assessment, the communication team should determine the types of symbols appropriate for conversational use. Many controlled-situation communicators can recognize and comprehend written words, especially when they are generated within the context of a conversation and spoken aloud by the partner. Lasker, Hux, Garrett, Moncrief, and Eischeid (1997) also determined that some individuals can respond to written choices that the partner does not supplement with spoken output, whereas others can answer verbal choice questions without the accompanying written words. Still other individuals comprehend photographs or line drawings best, particularly if they had literacy difficulties before the stroke.

Friend (F):   Can you give me advice on what to make for the school bake sale tomorrow?
Person with aphasia (P):   (nods *yes*)
F: Should I take an angel food cake, brownies, or cookies? (writes choices vertically in notebook)
   • ANGEL FOOD CAKE
   • BROWNIES
   • COOKIES
P: (points to brownies)
F: Yes, those always sell fast (circles BROWNIES). Should I make them from scratch or get a box mix? (writes choices)
   • SCRATCH
   • BOX MIX
P: (laughs and points to BOX MIX)
F: (laughs and circles BOX MIX) Yeah, it's hard to make them as good as Betty Crocker! (pause) What do you think about the kids' elementary school? Do you think they're getting a good education or a so-so one? (writes a rating scale on the page)

P: (hesitates, points to 4)
F: (circles 4) Yeah, we're pretty happy with the school district. Too bad the classes are so big, though!
P: (nods *yes*)

Figure 16.2.   Sample of written-choice conversation.

I HAVE HAD A STROKE. I WOULD LIKE TO TALK TO YOU, BUT I CANNOT SPEAK.

WE *CAN* CONVERSE IF YOU ASK ME A QUESTION AND OFFER ME WRITTEN CHOICES TO POINT TO. HERE'S HOW:

1. THINK OF A QUESTION YOU WOULD HAVE ASKED ME BEFORE MY STROKE. TRY TO FIND OUT MY OPINION, GET MY ADVICE, OR FIND OUT MY PREFERENCE.

    Example:
    "What crops have you gotten out of your garden so far?"
    "Who's going to win the football game Saturday?"
    "What do you think of the new tax law?"

2. ONCE YOU'VE ASKED THE QUESTION, THINK OF POSSIBLE ANSWERS OR CHOICES. WRITE THEM IN THIS NOTEBOOK. USE A DARK PEN OR MARKER. USE LARGE CAPITAL LETTERS. PUT A DOT IN FRONT OF EACH CHOICE. USE A SCALE FOR "HOW MUCH" QUESTIONS.

    Example:
    *   TOMATOES
    *   CUCUMBERS
    *   BEANS

    ---

    *   NEBRASKA
    *   PENN STATE

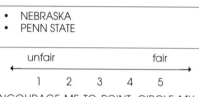

3. ENCOURAGE ME TO POINT. CIRCLE MY ANSWER. ASK PLENTY OF FOLLOW-UP QUESTIONS—I ENJOY CONVERSING!

Figure 16.3. Written-choice notebook cover card. (From *Augmentative communication in the medical setting.* Copyright © 1992 by Communication Skill Builders, a division of The Psychological Corporation. Reproduced by permission. All rights reserved.)

Comprehensive Communicator

The *comprehensive communicator* retains a variety of communication skills following a stroke, but these skills are often too fragmented or inconsistent for effective communication to occur without support. Due to their typically independent lifestyles, these individuals usually wish to participate in various types of conversational exchanges that occur in many environments. The comprehensive communicator often has a range of preserved skills that may include drawing, gestures, first-letter-of-word spelling, and pointing to words or symbols, in addition to limited speaking abilities. Many successful comprehensive communicators have Broca's aphasia. We also know a woman with conduction aphasia who was an outstanding comprehensive communicator (Garrett & Beukelman, 1992). She was able to manage the social aspects of communication quite well but required extensive support when asked to communicate specific information to her friends, her lawyer, her doctor, and the bus driver.

I . . . provided (Betty) with an identification paper on which was typed all the information necessary to help her through any of the emergency situations that might occur. . . . I felt that it was about as much protection as I could give her, as a driving aphasic. She was to carry it in her purse always. (In addition to basic identification, the paper contained messages such as *My car will not start*, and *I have a flat tire*.). . . . Betty had driven to the dry cleaner's with some clothes and when she came out the car would not start. She consulted her identification paper and decided to walk the two blocks to the nearest gas station. While walking she repeated over and over the words from the instruction sheet, "My car will not start," so she would not have to be embarrassed by pointing to the written sentence. The attendant understood her and drove her back to . . . (the place where) her car was standing. . . . Next she telephoned my office to ask me to pick her up, making use of the instruction sheet for the phone number. (David Knox, writing about his wife, Betty, after her stroke, in Knox, 1971, pp. 65–66)

AAC interventions for the comprehensive communicator are quite complex. In addition to identifying anticipated participation patterns, clarifying communication needs, and identifying topics of interest, the AAC specialist must teach the individual to manage a variety of AAC techniques. For example, Beukelman et al. (1985) described a man with Broca's aphasia who used a series of AAC approaches as he progressed through various phases of recovery. Initially, he communicated with a simple communication book that contained photographs of familiar people, places, and activities, and his family provided picture albums identifying family members, interests, and experiences. In time, this man used portfolios of his work as an interior designer to augment his conversational efforts, and this helped him to establish a topic and provided pictorial support for specific words and ideas. Eventually, his team developed a multimodal AAC system for him that included an electronic communication device with voice output, limited natural speech, gestures, a communication book, portfolios, books, and blueprints on the walls of the design studio in his home. A design assistant also served as a facilitator.

An often overlooked but critical aspect of AAC interventions for comprehensive communicators is their need for substantial instruction and guided practice to teach them *when* to use the various AAC techniques provided. Garrett, Beukelman, and Low-Morrow (1989) described this process with a comprehensive communicator whose AAC system contained many different components, as outlined in Table 16.1.

This man required 3–4 months to learn ways to decide when to use a specific AAC technique and to become proficient in choosing the correct technique. He used the instructional sequence summarized in Table 16.2 to guide his decision making in intervention sessions. He first attempted to say a message using his natural speech. If he experienced a communication breakdown, he then attempted to gesture, write, or repeat the spoken message. If he was still unsuccessful, he used the word notebook, alphabet card, or new information pocket. Finally, he directed his listener to the clues or control phrases.

Unfortunately, it is not uncommon in clinical practice to slight this training phase in multimodal intervention. Other common reasons that comprehensive communicators often fail to use their AAC systems effectively include the following: 1) The vocabulary and content of the AAC materials provided are inappropriate, 2) important communication partners are not willing or encouraged to accept augmented modes of communication, and 3) teaching and training in naturalistic situations does not occur.

Augmented-Input Communicator

Augmented-input communicators have auditory processing difficulties that interfere with their ability to understand language, especially language that is complex or that shifts

Table 16.1.   Components of an AAC system for a comprehensive communicator with Broca's aphasia

Communication component	Purpose	Comments
Word dictionary	To talk about frequently occurring topics of interest in conversations	Easier to use when words were organized topically rather than alphabetically
Alphabet card	To communicate unique information or to resolve communication breakdowns	Included first-letter-of-word cuing that allowed partner to deduce semi-intelligible spoken words
New information pocket	To communicate about current or recent events in conversations	Included newspaper clippings and remnants from the race track, for example
Breakdown resolution "clues"	To help resolve communication breakdowns	Included phrases to guide the partner through a structured form of 20 questions: "It's a (place/person/event/thing/time)."
Conversational control phrases	To enhance conversational control and to prevent or resolve breakdowns from rapid, unannounced topic shifts	Included phrases such as "I'm changing the topic now" and "Ask me questions."
Natural communication modalities	To enhance conversational efficiency	Included gestures, natural speech, drawing, and writing

Adapted from Garrett, Beukelman, and Low-Morrow (1989).

the conversational topic. These individuals often nod their heads but in fact are often "holding their place" in the conversation instead of signaling true comprehension (i.e., indicating that they are listening rather than comprehending). Thus, they often experience significant confusion and communication breakdowns as a conversation progresses.

To avoid communication breakdowns, communication partners need to supplement verbal input for augmented communicators through gestures or visual symbols. To provide augmented input, communication partners write or show photographs, drawings, or other symbols representing key words and topics as they speak. Individuals with receptive aphasia can then use these visual representations to help them un-

Table 16.2.   Instructional sequence for a comprehensive communicator with Broca's aphasia

Step 1: Natural speech
    Try to say it
Step 2: Other natural modalities
    Use a gesture *or*
    Write it *or*
    Try to say it again
Step 3: Augmented techniques
    Use the word dictionary *or*
    Use the alphabet card *or*
    Use the new information pocket
Step 4: Breakdown strategies
    Use a clue phrase *or*
    Use a control phrase

derstand the conversational information. Individuals with aphasia can also point to these same visual representations to identify aspects of the interaction that they have not understood or about which they want additional information.

Individuals with aphasia often employ this augmented-input strategy in conjunction with the written-choice conversation technique (Garrett & Beukelman, 1992) described previously. Similar to written-choice conversation, the technique of augmented input is completely partner dependent, which means that communication partners must learn to resolve communication breakdowns by initiating the technique. The clinician can assist with this process by demonstrating the technique, by providing a notebook with instructions on the cover to partners, and by teaching the person with aphasia to signal when he or she is experiencing comprehension difficulties.

Although a variety of individuals with severe aphasia may benefit from augmented-input techniques at some point in their recovery, people with Wernicke's aphasia often require augmented input permanently. Other individuals with aphasia who demonstrate intermittent auditory processing problems may also benefit from this technique.

Partner:	And so we went to the arboretum to see which trees grow best around here, and then we went to the nursery to pick out some varieties. . . .
Charles:	(raises hand to stop interaction, shakes head *no*)
Partner:	Oh, I'm sorry—I was going too fast again. Here (writes *arboretum*, draws a picture of a tree). We went to the arboretum (points to word and pauses to check for comprehension). . .then we went to the nursery to get some plants (writes *nursery* and draws arrow from previous message) and then we took them home to plant them (sketches house with plants by sidewalk). Did I make sense?
Charles:	(nods *yes*)

Specific-Need Communicator

The specific-need communicator needs communication support in situations that require specificity, clarity, or efficiency. For example, an individual with aphasia might want to communicate on the telephone, place bets at the racetrack, follow recipes, or write memos. Any individual with aphasia could have such well-defined, specific communication needs. Individuals who live in settings that demand some independence generally need support when communicating specific needs.

AAC interventions for specific-need communicators are usually limited in scope because these individuals can often manage much of their communication through gestures and limited speech. When planning an intervention, it is first necessary to analyze the requirements of the specific communication task and to consider the person's current capabilities in light of the task. For example, an individual may need help setting up a system to allow verbal communication over the telephone. The individual might employ a tape recorder system in which a pre-recorded message requests, PLEASE ASK ME QUESTIONS THAT I CAN ANSWER YES OR NO. Individuals with aphasia often need to communicate specific messages in a noisy place such as a cafeteria or bank. Often, a facilitator can prepare a small communication card with a restricted set of the messages that the individual will need in the situation. One woman with mild expressive aphasia and severe agraphia tearfully expressed her need to go to the grocery store and recall the items she wanted to purchase. Because she could not easily write a list before shopping, she had to rely on her memory and frequently forgot important items. A facilitator created a grocery list adaptation (see Figure 16.4) for her so that she could circle items instead of writing them.

    To address the specific need of writing personal letters, some individuals with severe aphasia and agraphia have used a scaffolded letter-writing format (Garrett, Staab, & Agocs, 1996). In this approach, some people who have difficulty writing a letter without assistance can choose phrases from a list and copy them into the partially completed sentences on a form letter (see Figure 16.5 and Figure 16.6). The successful completion and mailing of a letter also illustrates how the Participation Model can be applied to all types of communication activities for people with aphasia.

    Many people with aphasia require interventions in the area of specific needs, particularly as they begin to deal with a lifetime of communication disability. The AAC team must make a careful analysis of specific, individual communication needs to complete the AAC intervention package.

ASSESSMENT CONSIDERATIONS

Assess Communication Needs in Natural Contexts

It is important to be sensitive to the communication opportunities provided in specific contexts when assessing the ability of an individual with severe aphasia to participate in communication interactions. A common mistake is to provide an individual with an

---

Date _____
We need to buy:

FOOD

Basic Foods
Bread
Cheese
Margarine
Ketchup
Mustard
Mayonnaise
Salt
Pepper
Lettuce
Potatoes
Rice
Macaroni
Spaghetti
 • Sauce
 • Noodles
 • Mushrooms

Meats
Hamburger
Chicken breast
Bacon
Tuna
Rib eye
Delmonico steak

DRINKS
Milk
Coffee
Tea
Juice
 • OJ
 • Grapefruit
Pop
 • Pepsi
 • Coke
 • 7Up

CLEANING SUPPLIES
Bath soap
Soft soap
Toilet paper
Ajax
Bleach
Scouring pads
Paper towels

COSMETICS
Shampoo
Deodorant
Band-Aids
Shaving cream
Razors

Figure 16.4. Grocery list.

AAC system that has been set up for the wrong context. For example, it is not uncommon that people are discharged from rehabilitation programs with AAC supports that allow them to communicate quite effectively—as long as they are in rehabilitation settings! Such systems will probably be quite useless once the individual is at home or in an extended care facility, where the communication opportunities and related needs are much different. Periodically, it may be useful to conduct a communication needs assessment (Beukelman et al., 1985; see Figure 15.1) to confirm that interventions are truly appropriate for individuals with aphasia in their immediate contexts.

Families and friends of people with severe aphasia play a vital role in determining communication opportunities. If families and friends do not attempt to include the individual, both physically and socially, in communicative interactions, this individual will have difficulty participating successfully. It is also important to remember that the communication patterns of the family before the stroke will eventually prevail. Thus, if the person with aphasia was not particularly social or talkative in the family prior to the stroke, it is unlikely that the family's interaction patterns will suddenly change to encourage much communication.

Assess Specific Capabilities

Aphasia interventions have traditionally emphasized the restoration of communication and linguistic processes. In keeping with this emphasis, AAC teams designed assessment procedures to identify the cognitive and linguistic impairments of an individual with aphasia and created interventions to reduce these impairments.

This traditional approach has been inadequate for individuals whose communication disorders are so severe that they are unable to meet their daily communication needs. The traditional approach has meant that, in many cases, people have lived with-

1.	Jan		Feb			March			April			May				June
	July		Aug			Sept			Oct			Nov				Dec
	1	2	3	4	5	6	7	8	9	10	11	12	13	14	15	16
	17	18	19	20	21	22	23	24	25	26	27	28	29	30	31	

2. (write in names of possible letter recipients here)

3. Hello!   Hi!   Howdy!   Greetings!

4. . . . are you?   . . . is it going?   . . . is your family?

5. fine   OK   pretty good   terrific   a little tired

6. stayed at home   visited the family   worked around the yard
   vacationed in _____   had the grandkids for a week

7. had a great time   enjoyed ourselves   were glad for fall

8. your vacation   your family   school   your job   your friends

9. fine   keeping busy   taking it easy   enjoying your grandkids

10. write soon   call me sometime   come visit   take care

11. Sincerely,   Fondly,   With best wishes,   Love,

Figure 16.5. Multiple-choice letter format.

1. _____ _____, 199__

Dear 2. _____

3. _____ ! How 4. _____ ?

I am 5. _____. This month we

6. _____. We really

7. _____.

So, tell me about 8. _____.

I hope you are 9. _____.

Please 10. _____.

11. _____,

_____

Figure 16.6.   Blank form letter.

out the ability to communicate adequately with their spouses, children, grandchildren, friends, and others. Thus, interventionists have changed their methods gradually to provide AAC supports of various types to people with aphasia. These AAC approaches typically capitalize on an individual's residual capabilities. Garrett and Beukelman (1992) identified several such residual skills, which are discussed in the following sections.

We all use flowery adjectives to describe our opinion or rating of. . . experiences, but not Betty. She has adopted a short cut that is quite descriptive and effective, as well as being widely applicable. When asked how she likes the food in a restaurant, she may reply, "B." That is all, just "B." This means that it is almost tops, but not quite. A "C" rating is pretty bad. The same system is used for movies, purchased items, perishable foods, television programs, art objects, etc. (David Knox, writing about his wife, Betty, after her stroke, in Knox, 1971, pp. 117–118)

Linguistic Skills

Although people with aphasia may demonstrate extensive limitations in their linguistic systems, they usually have not forgotten the words and structures with which they struggle. Rather, they may not be immediately available for efficient communication. Some individuals with aphasia use telegraphic speech to communicate because they have difficulty accessing the grammatical aspects of language efficiently. Other individuals may retain a great deal of information about grammar but have difficulty retrieving the content—that is, the specific words—that pertains to their communication. Some individuals can write portions of words or key letters to signal their intent. Many people with aphasia have some ability to read, particularly if the written words appear in context.

Although a person with aphasia can use his or her residual linguistic skills for communication at times, his or her linguistic performance is often highly erratic. Thus, an individual may be able to communicate a message at one point in time and may have difficulty conveying the same message later or in a different context.

Two months after the stroke I wanted to get a new head for my electric razor. I spent twenty minutes with the Yellow Pages and finally, in a sweat, asked (my wife) Jane to look up the store. I was within three pages but couldn't find it. After I had purchased the razor head, I couldn't install it because the directions were mildly complex. I was directed to: "Remove the head, first pushing the blades to the down position and to the left, and insert new blades from the right, keeping them in the proper numerical order." Clearly this was not written with an aphasic in mind. (Dr. Charles Clay Dahlberg, writing of his experiences after a stroke, in Dahlberg & Jaffe, 1977, p. 55)

Functional Communication Skills

To avoid underestimating the functional capabilities of individuals with aphasia, it is critical to be sensitive to the variable skills these individuals demonstrate when administering formal tests of language. Most tests are designed to be administered *acontextually* in order to measure linguistic processing capabilities without the influence of contextual supports, such as predictable conversational topics. Nevertheless, communication usually does not occur out of context, and many individuals with aphasia find it very difficult to perform communicatively in such abstract, nonfunctional situations. Therefore, it may be necessary to supplement standard aphasia tests with assessments of the person's language performance in natural environments and with familiar people.

An additional screening tool may assist the clinician in making AAC decisions for people with aphasia. Garrett and Beukelman's (1992) categorical assessment form (see Figure 16.7) provides the clinician with a means of checking for present or emerging communication competencies. This process may help the clinician to make overall decisions about the primary AAC intervention based on the category in which the individual best fits at the time of the initial assessment.

The second screening tool, the Multimodal Screening Task for Aphasia (see Figure 16.8a–g), allows the clinician to determine how a potential communicator gains access to information. The clinician assembles a booklet that contains 1) concrete concepts that are easily represented with pictures and words (e.g., *shoes, bed*; see Figure 16.8a), 2) slightly more abstract concepts that can be combined with other items to represent complex meanings (e.g., *open, close, children, money*; see Figure 16.8b–c), 3) written words and phrases organized by topic or environment (see Figure 16.8d), 4) an outline map of the country in which the person lives to represent locations of children's homes or favorite vacations (see Figure 16.8e), and 5) an alphabet board for the person with

Directions: Assess the patient with a "minimal-criterion" approach; if the patient demonstrates the skill at least once, give credit and mark it with +. If the skill is partially evident, mark it with +/−. If the patient cannot demonstrate the skill, mark it with −. If you judge that the patient would be able to demonstrate the skill given augmentative techniques and/or additional training, rate the patient's potential in the last column (G = good, F = fair, P = poor). Observe the skill in the context of functional activities or augmentative activities where possible. Readminister this checklist if it appears that the patient's capabilities, needs, or setting have changed.

Determine the patient's basic communicator type by observing in which section clusters of + and +/− ratings occur and by comparing this with the results of formal testing and clinical observation. (For example, a patient who demonstrates auditory comprehension breakdowns and has some initial success with skills listed in the augmented input section may be an augmented-input communicator). While most communicator types are fairly easy to differentiate, some individuals may have needs in more than one area (in particular, the comprehensive and the augmented-input communicators). Other patients may not fit any of these profiles.

Name: Setting: Date:

Communicator Type	Communication Skill	Skill Present (+, +/−, −)	Potential with Tx[a] (G, F, P)
Basic-Choice Communicator	Points to clothing items given choice during morning dressing routine		
	Points to photos in catalog to answer "favorite outfit" question		
	Looks up when greeted		
	Takes objects, returns them		
	Other skills:		
Controlled-Situation Communicator	Attends to print		
	Points to photos or picture symbols of needs (n = 2) to answer questions		
	Can confirm or select topics of interest		
	Can point to or look at written choices to answer conversational questions		
	Aware of daily routine (example: gets glasses before therapy)		
	Other skills:		
Comprehensive Communicator	Speaks some words		
	Writes some words or word fragments		
	Can communicate by drawing schematics, maps, objects		
	Can locate items by category (structured task OK)		
	Can communicate a specific word by pointing to first letter		
	Gestures		
	Pantomimes		
	Recognizes own errors		

(continued)

Figure 16.7.   Categorical assessment form. (From *Augmentative communication in the medical setting.* Copyright © 1992 by Communication Skill Builders, a division of The Psychological Corporation. Reproduced by permission. All rights reserved.) ([a]Tx = treatment.)

Figure 16.7. (*continued*)

Name:	Setting:	Date:	
Communicator Type	Communication Skill	Skill Present (+, +/−, −)	Potential with Tx (G, F, P)
	Recognizes communication breakdowns Demonstrates some pragmatic competence in discourse Knows which communication modality to use and when Wants to communicate in more than one setting with more than one partner Initiates questions and comments Other skills:		
Specific-Need Communicator	Has indicated need to perform specific communication task more efficiently: • talking on the phone • writing letters • saying prayers • saying names of family members • signing name • making purchases • making lists • making memos • communicating destination on public transportation system • calling for assistance Demonstrates most skills from other communicator types Other skills:		
Augmented-Input Communicator	Attends to print Attends to gestures Written key words appear to enhance comprehension Partner gestures appear to enhance comprehension Signals lack of understanding/ breakdowns Other skills:		

aphasia to communicate highly specific names (e.g., names of towns, names of restaurants; see Figure 16.8f) by spelling or pointing to the first letter.

The clinician first asks the person with aphasia to point to items by name. In the first trial, items are located on a single page; in subsequent trials other pages contain the same items. The clinician records whether the person with aphasia can identify items from a set of choices and search for the same items on other pages or levels (see Figure 16.8g). Next, the clinician asks the person with aphasia to match abstract items with a related word or picture (e.g., by asking "Which one would help you communi-

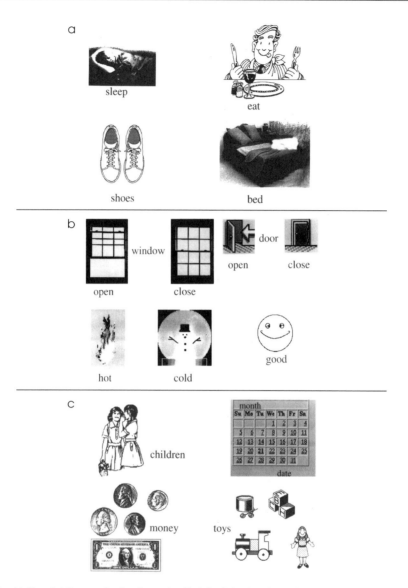

Figure 16.8. Multimodal Communication Screening Task for Aphasia: a) needs, b) descriptors, c) combinatorial concepts, d) environmental phrases, e) map of the United States, f) spelling card, and g) scoresheet. (Copyright © 1997 by Kathryn L. Garrett.)

cate that you would like to go for a walk outside?" and offering *shoes* and *door* as choices). In the next task, the clinician asks the person to locate written messages in response to questions about a specific situation (e.g., "How would you let me know you wanted your hair cut and then permed?"). Then the clinician asks the person with aphasia to identify the homes of family members or favorite vacation spots on the outline map. The next task involves pointing to the first letter of or spelling the name of a family member's town, a favorite restaurant, or a favorite sports team. Finally, the person with aphasia is asked to communicate a complex message (e.g., "By pointing to a sequence of pictures, words, letters, or locations on the map, communicate that your grandchildren are going to Disney World next month if they have enough money"). Us-d **AT THE DRUGSTORE**

I NEED MORE:
- Aspirin
- Toothpaste
- Hair products
  - Shampoo
  - Hairspray
  - Conditioner
- Deodorant
- _____

PLEASE FILL MY PRESCRIPTION
- × 1
- × 2
- When do I take my pills?

WRITE DOWN YOUR INSTRUCTIONS FOR ME

GRANDCHILDREN

TELL ME ABOUT SCHOOL
- How are your grades?
- Your friends?
- How's soccer?
  - football?
  - basketball?
  - tennis?
- Do you do your homework?
- What are your favorite classes?

WHAT DO YOU WANT FOR . . .
- Your birthday?
- Chanukah?
- Christmas?
- $?
- a gift?
- a hug?

I LOVE YOU!

e

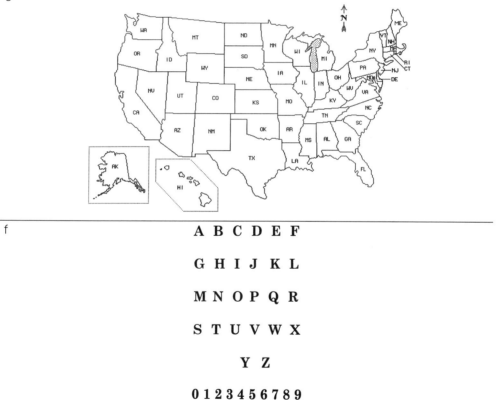

f

A B C D E F

G H I J K L

M N O P Q R

S T U V W X

Y Z

0 1 2 3 4 5 6 7 8 9

(continued)

ing this simple assessment task, the clinician can better identify the level of informational complexity that a potential communicator can successfully use and comprehend. In addition, observing this diagnostic activity may help some family members to better understand why a clinician may suggest low-tech instead of high-tech communication options for the individual with aphasia.

484

Figure 16.8g. *(continued)*

CLIENT NAME: _____

DATE: _____

EVALUATOR: _____

INSTRUCTIONS: Show the person with aphasia the booklet containing the symbolized choices. Explain that the pictures, letters, sentences and map locations can all be used to communicate ideas. Provide examples if necessary. For each item, ask individual "How would you communicate _____?" You can use this book or any other way you have to communicate." Mark + if all concepts were communicated, +/− if some were communicated, and − if no items were communicated. Circle concepts that were successfully conveyed. Record cues if provided. Substitute alternate concepts as appropriate.

	Target Symbols	Abstract Meaning?	Multiple page search needed	+/−	Cues	Comments
A. Identification of nouns by name						
1. *Shoes*	Pic/word	no	no			
2. *Open Door*	Pic/word	no	yes (2)			
3. *Grandchild*	Pic/word	yes	yes (3)			
4. Need to *buy* something	Pic/word	yes	yes (3)			
5. *State* of residence ("Nebraska")	Map or first letter	no	yes (5)			
B. Two-symbol combinations						
6. I've been *walking* a lot and I'm *tired.*	Pic/word	yes	no			
7. *Open the window;* it's too *hot.*	Pic/word	no	yes (2)			
8. I'm *glad* my *grandkids* are visiting.	Pic/word	yes	yes (3)			
C. Three-symbol combinations						
9. I want to *buy* some *toys* for my *grandchildren.*	Pic/word	yes	yes (3)			
10. The *kids* are coming *next week* from *(name of state or city).*	Pic/word, map, or first letter	yes	yes (6)			
11. I want *to eat* an *expensive* meal at *name of favorite restaurant* tonight.	Pic/word, map, or first letter	yes	yes (6)			

D. Phrase lists

"Pretend you're at the drugstore with your grandkids. Find the page that will help you do this. Then, tell me how you'd say . . . "

12.	I need more aspirin and shampoo.	Phrase list	no	no
13.	Please fill my prescription for 2 refills and write down your instructions for me.	Phrase list	no	no
14.	Tell me about school. How is your _____?	Phrase list	no	no
15.	Do you do your homework? Are your grades good?	Phrase list	yes	yes (2)

Summary and Interpretation: Can this person intentionally locate info on multiple pages? Combine concepts? Use symbols abstractly? Use written words, maps, or the first letter of a word? Use other modalities? Answer and initiate questions? _____

_____

_____

_____

_____

_____

_____

_____

_____

Nonverbal Communication Skills

Many individuals with severe aphasia retain a considerable repertoire of nonverbal communication skills, such as gestures, facial expressions, pantomime, and vocalizations. Such skills allow some of these individuals to communicate extensive information. Other individuals are impaired in their ability to produce nonverbal communication either consistently or efficiently. Instruction and practice are necessary for them to use this mode.

Motor Skills

Individuals with aphasia following a stroke usually retain the ability to control their limbs on at least one side of the body (usually the left). Therefore, they may be able to gesture, turn pages, or point to communication choices via direct selection. However, they may experience difficulties when asked to complete a complex sequence of motor movements (e.g., locating words on multiple pages of a book or electronic communication device) because of limb apraxia. They may also have some difficulty physically carrying heavy communication devices or manipulating the on/off buttons of those systems. The AAC team may want to consult with an occupational or physical therapist when deciding on a portable communication device or system.

Sensory Skills

The individual's visual system may be spared entirely following a stroke. Frequently, however, he or she may experience a visual field cut, usually on the right side. This means that the person is unable to see images with the right side of both eyes. Thus, the individual will not be able to see AAC or other materials that are positioned in the right visual field. A person's ability to scan the visual field or the extent of field cut should be determined. In addition, it is important to assess the individual's residual visual capabilities and identify any visual deterioration that has occurred naturally with age, as well as any new impairments. The clinician may find it useful to conduct a brief word cancellation/scanning task (see Figure 16.9) in which the person with aphasia must read line by line and circle each occurrence of the target word.

Perceptual Skills

People with aphasia often understand many of the visual images with which people represent the world. For example, they recognize various icons of geography, such as maps, and icons of events, such as logos and signs. They also usually retain the ability to identify photographs and drawings that relate to people and places. Many people with aphasia retain knowledge about the relative relationships of size, shape, goodness, and importance among objects and experiences. For example, an individual with aphasia may refer to another adult by gesturing to indicate that this adult is taller than a child.

Individuals with aphasia may retain some ability to draw and can communicate messages through this modality (Lyon & Helm-Estabrooks, 1987). Although these individuals may never have considered themselves artists before the onset of aphasia, they can often depict ideas clearly enough through drawing that knowledgeable communication partners can understand their messages. Individuals with aphasia may often retain a memory of the chronology of events in their lives. For example, a person may indicate that a certain event, such as military service, occurred after high school but before marriage. An individual may also refer to important events in terms of their

Name: _____

Date: _____

Circle the word *good* each time you see it. Read left to right.

breath	good	take	moth	home	good
bye	one	good	good	bee	shine
good	good	baby	house	shirt	good
see	nose	good	good	hope	fine
good	show	tired	pies	seem	good

good	table	shine	carpet	good	good	team
paste	good	glue	time	girl	gone	good
good	born	shout	socks	pick	tone	glow
glow	good	point	there	see	good	pass

good	table	shine	carpet	good	good	team
paste	good	glue	time	girl	gone	good
good	born	shout	socks	pick	tone	glow
glow	good	point	there	see	good	pass

Figure 16.9.   Word scanning/cancellation task for vision screening.

proximity to the birth dates of his or her children. AAC teams can assess these skills informally.

Pragmatic Skills

In addition to the generic skills that the Participation Model (see Figure 6.1) identifies, specific skill areas are particularly helpful to individuals with aphasia, such as pragmatic skills or the knowledge of how communication works. Because most individuals with aphasia have communicated using natural speech and writing for most of their lives, they are quite familiar with how communication works. That is, they are aware of the turn-taking skills, speaker/listener roles, and topic coordination that communication requires. They can also recognize and attempt to clarify ambiguous communicative messages. Thus, when compared with individuals who have had few or no normal communication experiences, individuals with aphasia are relatively aware of the structure and rules of conversational interaction.

Experiential Skills

It is particularly helpful that people with aphasia usually have an experiential skill base underlying communication. Most individuals with aphasia have lived for a considerable period of time and have experienced relatively typical, routine lifestyles, so their knowledge about the world is extensive. They have participated many times in the basic interactive routines of life. Therefore, although they may not retain a strong linguistic base for communication after the onset of aphasia, they are very aware of the settings in which communication normally occurs. To gather "fuel" for upcoming AAC interactions, it may be helpful for the AAC team to informally assess interests, topics, and autobiographical information through interviews with family members prior to beginning an AAC intervention (see Figures 16.10a and 16.10b).

Assess Constraints

Partner Skills

Because communication partners are so important in communication interactions with people who have severe aphasia, it is useful to assess the partners' capabilities as well. AAC teams usually cannot conduct this assessment formally, so they obtain information about the communication skills of partners from observing interactions with the individual with aphasia. It is also important to determine whether the partner is able to learn or is interested in learning new ways of communicating with the person with severe aphasia. The clinician should also formally evaluate potential communication partners in basic areas that include speaking style and understandability, handwriting legibility, reading skills, hearing, and vision.

It is also important to assess how communication partners have adjusted to the behavior of a spouse, parent, or loved one following a stroke. Figure 16.11 depicts the screening tool that Garrett and Beukelman (1991) developed to assess partner adjustment.

Cognitive-Linguistic Demands of Potential AAC Strategies

People with aphasia face significant challenges when communicating through alternative modes. They must first acknowledge that their efforts to communicate by speaking or writing may not be effective and then identify a more appropriate method. They

Biographical Information Sketch

Directions: Fill in as much information as you know. Add comments and stories in the margins when you think they will help us get to know your family member better. Think of things that have always been interesting to discuss together. Leave blanks if the question is not relevant, or change the wording of the question. Thanks!

My name is _____

My nickname is _____ . I live in _____

in the state of _____ . I was born in _____ in the year

_____ . I mostly grew up in the city, town, or area of _____ .

I had _____ brothers and _____ sisters. My maiden name was _____

_____ . My ancestry is _____ .

Some of the things that happened to me in my childhood included

_____

_____

_____

_____

_____

I went to school for _____ years. I was good at _____ in school.

My first job was _____ .

After school I also _____ .

I started dating when I was _____ years old. I met my husband/wife at _____

_____ . My husband/wife's name is _____ .

We got married on _____ . We lived in _____ after we

were married. We moved to _____ .

We *bought/rented* (please circle) our first house. We built our house in _____ .

We had _____ children. Some of the stories I remember from when they were little include

_____

_____

_____

_____

The following is a list of important information about my children:

Name	_____	_____	_____
Age	_____	_____	_____
Spouse	_____	_____	_____
Lives in	_____	_____	_____
Job	_____	_____	_____
Accomplishments	_____	_____	_____
Grandchildren	_____	_____	_____

My religious background is _____ . I now attend religious services

at _____ .

I worked for most of my life as a _____

in the town of _____ . Several things that I remember most from

my working years include _____

_____

_____ . I retired in _____ .

_____

(*continued*)

Figure 16.10a. Blank assessment form for interests and autobiographical information. (From *Augmentative communication in the medical setting.* Copyright © 1992 by Communication Skill Builders, a division of The Psychological Corporation. Reproduced by permission. All rights reserved.)

Figure 16.10a.   (*continued*)

I served in the military from _____ to _____ . I was in the _____
(branch). Most of my time was spent in _____ (location).
I have always been interested in _____ .
Some community activities that I participate in are _____
_____ .
Some of my best friends are _____
_____ .
Places I have traveled include _____ .
Some day I really want to _____ .

Additional information I feel would be interesting for the staff to know:

_____
_____
_____
_____
_____

must attempt to map language to ideas, even if that language is fragmented and difficult to retrieve and sequence. They must demonstrate the initiative and tenacity to convey a message to a partner despite frequent communication breakdowns.

AAC strategies and technologies may also add several cognitive and linguistic demands to this scenario. If a strategy requires writing, pointing, or gaining access to electronic buttons, the individual with aphasia must have appropriate alternative access, typically with the nondominant limb. Locating written or picture messages in a book or electronic device requires the individual to translate symbols that are much more novel than natural speech. They must learn the meanings and internal representations of unfamiliar symbols such as line drawings or Blissymbols. When communicating with multiple symbols, people with aphasia must also learn to search an array, search multiple arrays or levels, and possibly combine symbols to represent complex meanings. If the individual uses a message encoding strategy, such as numeric encoding (e.g., N1 = *I need the bathroom*), then he or she must recall these encoded representations. Even spelling, a more natural communication skill, is a type of encoding that requires selection and sequencing of arbitrary symbols to represent sounds and meanings. Because successful spelling requires many repetitions of this procedure, spelling is often extremely difficult for people with aphasia. Therefore, it may be more frustrating than therapeutic for people with aphasia to communicate with a typewriter or computer keyboard.

People with aphasia who communicate with an AAC device that stores a number of messages on one or more levels must also demonstrate sufficient working memory to complete the steps involved in accessing the messages before forgetting their intent or losing their partner's interest. In addition, if they use an AAC device, they may have to learn new operational skills such as turning the device on/off, comprehending synthesized or digitized speech, locating messages stored on invisible levels, using flowchart operational menus, keyboarding, and recharging the device (if it operates on batteries).

Finally, individuals with aphasia must also have the metacognitive skills to introduce their novel communication strategies to unfamiliar partners. They also have to know how to use their strategies in a dynamic manner so that, for example, they speak

---

Inventory of Topics

Instructions to Clinician: Inventory favorite communication topics by having the patient, family, and friends complete the following form. To adapt the form for the person with aphasia, present topics on separate cards; embellish with pictures, if necessary. Have the patient indicate preferred topics by (1) pointing, (2) sorting cards into a "favorite" pile, (3) rating topics presented one at a time by pointing to a number on a rating scale such as the following. Provide a model as needed.

```
        ←─────────────────────────→
           1    2    3    4    5
        don't like    so-so    favorite
```

- -

Instructions: Circle favorite topics you talked about with _____ .

Family	List special family events: _____
	Other info: _____
	_____
Sports	List favorite teams: _____
	List memorable games: _____
Gardening	List specialties: _____
Hobbies/Interests	List: _____
Current Events/Local	List recent events or gossip: _____
	_____
Current Events:	_____
National/International	List events of interest: _____
	_____
Military Service	List branch: _____
	List years: _____
Politics	List party: _____
	List favorite presidents, political figures: _____
	_____
Job/Career	List notable achievements: _____
	_____
Crafts	List: _____
Pets	List names, type: _____
Farming	Briefly describe type of operation: _____
Other	_____
	_____

Figure 16.10b. Blank assessment form of communication topics. (From *Augmentative communication in the medical setting.* Copyright © 1992 by Communication Skill Builders, a division of The Psychological Corporation. Reproduced by permission. All rights reserved.)

and write as much as they can and then shift to an AAC strategy when they experience communication breakdowns.

By definition, aphasia affects each of these processing skills that AAC systems demand. For example, communicators with primarily Broca's expressive aphasia typically exhibit difficulties with syntactic encoding. Therefore, communication strategies that require symbol combinations may frustrate these individuals. Placing messages or symbols in multilevel communication systems may impose significant cognitive processing challenges for many people with aphasia who demonstrate word-retrieval or short-term recall problems. Complex visual displays may also affect people who have visual field cuts. An individual with hemiplegia may have difficulties carrying, holding, or accessing a system with his or her nondominant hand.

We do not intend for this review of the challenges that users encounter when using AAC strategies and devices to warn clinicians away from implementing AAC with communicators who have aphasia. Instead, our message is that it is critical to match

Patient _____
Partner _____
Date _____

Circle the number that best describes your feelings.

		Disagree				Agree
1.	My family member/friend has changed since his or her stroke.	1	2	3	4	5
2.	My family member/friend doesn't understand what's going on.	1	2	3	4	5
3.	My family member/friend compensates well for his or her communication problems.	1	2	3	4	5
4.	I think I have adjusted well to his or her disability.	1	2	3	4	5
5.	We participate in as many activities as we used to.	1	2	3	4	5
6.	We communicate as well as we did before the stroke.	1	2	3	4	5
7.	I think my family member/friend should be more active than he or she is right now.	1	2	3	4	5
8.	Our family has accepted the disability.	1	2	3	4	5
9.	People don't understand what is wrong with my family member/friend.	1	2	3	4	5
10.	I communicate with my family member/friend as often as I used to.	1	2	3	4	5
11.	We have received enough information about stroke and aphasia.	1	2	3	4	5
12.	I need to communicate better with my family member/friend.	1	2	3	4	5
13.	My family member/friend respects himself or herself as much as before the stroke.	1	2	3	4	5
14.	My family member/friend is frustrated.	1	2	3	4	5

Figure 16.11.   Screening tool to assess communication partner attitude. (From *Augmentative communication in the medical setting.* Copyright © 1992 by Communication Skill Builders, a division of The Psychological Corporation. Reproduced by permission. All rights reserved.)

strategies to the individual's needs and skills. For example, if an individual shows only basic environmental awareness, it would be inappropriate to select a high-technology system that requires sequential cognitive operations (e.g., spelling, combining words). This individual might best fit into the category of basic-choice communicator, and the therapy program could instead target the individual's ability to demonstrate preferences and shared reference in contextual routines. People who cannot independently retrieve or combine words or symbols to convey their meaning might benefit more from the partner-initiated written-choice conversation strategy. In this strategy, because the partner retrieves the specific words related to the topic, the person with aphasia simply has to recognize the appropriate answers from a limited set of choices. Although comprehensive communicators may be able to handle more complex message storage systems, they may require restricted message sets, a constantly visible display, or highly relevant symbols or words. Some people with expressive aphasia who fall into the comprehensive communicator category prefer communication notebooks rather than communication devices. When questioned, they state that they prefer the portability of the low-tech system. They also have been observed to search physically for messages on tangible paper pages more effectively than when locating messages on invisible levels in an electronic system.

Conduct Strategy Trials

To ensure that communication strategies match the skills and needs of the person with aphasia, it is useful to allow the person with aphasia to try out the strategy in a simulated or real communication situation. It is important for AAC teams to determine whether controlled-situation and augmented-input communicators can participate successfully in several conversations and to verify that their responses are accurate. It is also important to teach communication partners, both family and caregivers, to facilitate AAC strategies. When working with comprehensive communicators, AAC teams should inventory vocabulary for a particular situation (e.g., a visit to the beauty shop), represent and store the messages, model use of the system, and then see how well the person with aphasia communicates with the system in a simulated interaction. Only in the context of real-life communication trials can the individual display his or her competencies and future training needs.

TEACHING FUNCTIONAL USE OF AAC STRATEGIES

Both people with aphasia and their communication partners will require training and support if communication is to be accurate, efficient, and nonfatiguing. We describe such instructional strategies in the sections that follow.

Instructional Strategies for the Person with Aphasia

Basic-Choice Communicator

People who are basic-choice communicators may learn to initiate some actions within contextual routines and to express their choices or preferences. Clinicians may prefer to conduct treatment sessions with the individual in environments that are conducive to setting up contextual routines, for example, in the dining room or kitchen. To facilitate increased initiations, the clinician can offer the individual multiple opportunities to participate in the same routine, while simultaneously decreasing cues.

Controlled-Situation Communicator

Controlled-situation communicators who participate in written-choice conversations may require the facilitator to provide some initial modeling and hand-over-hand assistance to understand that they must point to the written symbols to communicate. Frequently, this requires only a session or two. Sometimes it is useful to begin with a few simple choices (e.g., favorite restaurants) before progressing to multiple, abstract conversational choices (e.g., political viewpoints). Other times, people with aphasia can begin discussing complex topics almost immediately.

Clinicians may find it helpful to begin a written-choice notebook for the controlled-situation communicator. The individual can take this notebook to other therapy sessions in the rehabilitation environment or to other activities in the long-term care or home environment. Therapists can then observe what the individual communicates in other situations as well. This strategy may also allow the individual with aphasia to begin searching the notebook for information that he or she has previously discussed; this process is a steppingstone to more independent information access. Clinicians can also try to encourage individuals in this category to communicate more independently by asking them to find it in their notebooks. Another teaching strategy to promote spontaneously initiated communication is to store one or more messages on a digitized voice-output communication system. The clinician can simulate a communication opportunity such as greeting or commenting and then model use of the system. Next, the person with aphasia can try to activate the message independently during reenactments of the communication activity. Some individuals have learned to develop the skills necessary to become comprehensive communicators by first locating information in their written-choice notebooks, then learning to initiate greetings or comments on a voice-output system, and finally locating and selecting multiple messages to participate in lengthier interactions. At times, the clinician may wish to create a written script for the individual to follow until he or she can anticipate and access the upcoming messages without assistance.

Comprehensive Communicator

Comprehensive communicators may benefit from training offered in three stages: 1) completion of a comprehensive message inventory; 2) training in use of specific strategies such as first-letter supplemental spelling, drawing, or prestored message access; and 3) training in selection of appropriate strategies to match real-life communication demands. In the first stage, it may be useful for AAC specialists to work with family members and the person with aphasia to list potential communication environments, such as the beauty shop, store, physician's office, or their children's homes. Then family members can generate phrases or the person with aphasia can choose ones that reflect the possible sequence of messages in the specific situation. The AAC team should then store the messages in the communication device (low- or high-tech). Sometimes it is appropriate to store all of the messages that an individual will use in a particular situation on a single level or page. At other times, it is useful to store them by category (e.g., restaurant names, family names). Other types of information are best represented as a graphic image, such as state names on a map or family relationships on a family tree.

For some comprehensive communicators, the inclusion of a "life story" section in their AAC system has been successful. By depicting the important events and details of their lives (e.g., birth, information about parents and siblings, school years, military service, marriage, jobs, children, hobbies, retirement, stroke, rehabilitation), they can communicate a great deal about themselves in a narrative form that is popular with older people. In addition the life story can serve as a chronological order of events for those who have trouble recalling the numerical dates of events. Finally, some find the chronological order of the life story to be a relatively efficient way to retrieve specific information about people, places, and activities.

After the AAC team stores messages in the system that can be anticipated in advance, it is then important to identify modalities that the person with aphasia can use successfully to convey novel messages. Writing, drawing, spelling, first-letter spelling, speaking, and gesturing may all be appropriate methods for the individual to talk about topics that the basic AAC system does not contain. The clinician should make sure that the system includes the tangible materials that the individual will need, such as a first-letter spelling card and/or paper for writing.

Next, it is important to teach the comprehensive communicator to become as expert as possible in the use of each component strategy. For example, if the individual has difficulty locating phrases quickly, the AAC team should emphasize teaching him or her to find phrases rapidly in response to situational questions such as "What would you say if you wanted to know how your grandchild is doing at school?" Likewise, if the person with aphasia cannot initially point to the first letters of words to supplement partially intelligible speech, it may be useful to teach him or her first how to find the letter cue (e.g., *B, P*) in response to a clinician's question such as "Do you think the Pirates or the Braves will win the pennant this year?" The clinician can provide additional assistance, if necessary, by indicating the first-letter choices. The AAC team can conduct similar teaching activities for all of the individual strategies that compose the comprehensive augmented communication system. It may be helpful to design a chart for the individual that lists each possible strategy and the situations for which he or she may be most useful.

Lyon (1995) has written extensively about the use of drawing as a communication aid for people with severe aphasia. Many people who experience aphasia following stroke are no longer able to write with their preferred hand. However, some are still able to draw well enough with their nonpreferred hand to support conversational interaction with a trained communication partner who is willing to interact with them using a multimodal approach that includes speech, drawings, and gestures (Lyon, 1995). Bauer and Kaiser (1995), Cubelli (1995), Rao (1995), and Ward-Lonergan and Nicholas (1995) all provide case reports of people with aphasia who successfully used drawing to support their communication interactions. In addition, an entire issue of *Aphasiology* was devoted to drawing by people with aphasia (see *Aphasiology, 8*(1), 1995).

After the comprehensive communicator has shown functional competence with individual component strategies, the AAC team should set up simulated communication situations for the individual to practice strategies in a more dynamic manner that resembles natural interaction. Some individuals benefit from a written script that details the message and modality on a step-by-step basis. It may also be useful for clinicians to use a volunteer or student as a confederate communication partner while they coach or cue the comprehensive communicator through each communication opportunity. The clinician can offer suggestions regarding the most appropriate modality or can provide more specific verbal cues or choices. Providing multiple opportunities for interaction with a gradual reduction in cues may allow the communicator to refine his or her skills and develop independence in actual communication situations. Some individuals may even develop the ability to communicate in highly demanding situations with impatient or difficult communication partners if they have the opportunity to practice in both simulated and realistic situations.

Augmented-Input Communicator

The augmented-input communicator must first learn to signal when he or she does not comprehend the speaker. This may be a difficult skill to learn for several reasons. First, some individuals may have such significant comprehension or cognitive difficulties that they do not know when they are processing information inaccurately. Second, and quite common, people with aphasia may not wish to signal that they have not understood because of their desire to maintain social etiquette and not injure the feelings of the speaker. It is important to reassure the augmented-input communicator that signaling a communication breakdown is actually quite helpful to the conversational partner. Some ways of signaling that may be effective as well as socially appropriate include raising a finger or hand, displaying a quizzical look, or stating "What?" or "No."

The augmented-input communicator may then benefit from practicing how to provide the communication partner with a notebook or paper pad that bears instructions on the cover (Garrett & Beukelman, 1992). This instructional card states that communication partners should write key words or gesture whenever they perceive that the person with aphasia cannot comprehend them.

Specific-Need Communicator

The specific-need communicator will use a variety of strategies, depending on the particular communication situation that requires augmenting. These individuals may also benefit from situational training similar to that described above. If, for example, the person with aphasia needs to use a voice-output device for telephone communication, he or she may benefit from multiple opportunities to role-play the situation or use a written script containing possible phrases. If the specific-need communicator wants to use a form letter, he or she may need to draft a few letters in a therapy session so the clinician can provide some initial cues before the individual completes the activity independently. Some individuals may even be able to increase the amount of spontaneous writing they generate without a script once they have repeatedly practiced writing. It is critical that instructional strategies for this category of communicators match the needs of the individual in the specific communication environment.

Instructional Strategies for Communication Partners

In general, communication partners of people with aphasia need to learn the following skills: 1) how to wait for a response or an initiation, 2) how to provide opportunities for communication, 3) how to offer choices, and 4) how to inventory messages and add them to communication systems. The following sections detail more specific teaching suggestions for partners of each of the communicator types.

Basic-Choice Communicator

Communication partners who are unfamiliar with the communication difficulties of people with aphasia often tend to use a 20-questions (i.e., yes/no) format for communicating basic messages. This strategy is often ineffective, however, because the individual becomes confused and has difficulty managing this linguistic form. Instead, communication partners should learn to provide simple choices from a limited number of options.

Probably the most important skill that partners can learn is to pause *without talking* for some time after offering a choice, to allow the individual to respond or to indicate that none of the choices are appropriate. This is quite important, as many basic-choice communicators need considerable processing time in a quiet, nondistracting environment in order to formulate a message. After the individual with aphasia has made a choice, the partner then needs to learn to affirm it with a brief verbalization before proceeding (e.g., "Oh, you want the red shirt?"). Obviously, if the individual attempts to speak in response, this effort should be accepted and encouraged. The individual with aphasia may, however, use other means for affirmation or negation at this point. For instance, some individuals may use a prolonged eye gaze toward the item they desire to affirm their response. Others may simply reach for the item as a form of affirmation or push it away as a form of negation. Still others will nod their heads for affirmation and do nothing to indicate rejection. It is important for facilitators to become familiar with the individual's acceptance/rejection signals so that they do not expect complex or sophisticated signals. Often, basic-choice communicators will indicate a choice and then become confused when their communication partners engage in prolonged yes/no questioning or prodding to confirm the choice.

It also is important to provide appropriate encouragement and instruction to those who facilitate communication for basic-choice communicators. Facilitators must learn to analyze situations and predict appropriate communication choices, which are two skills that are initially unfamiliar and often sources of frustration to them. AAC teams should not rush facilitators who are older adults through training, and these facilitators should have ample time to observe someone else engaging in basic-choice communication with their spouse or friend. AAC teams should also teach younger facilitators, such as children and grandchildren (who often present choices too rapidly), to be deliberate, to pause without talking so the person can respond, and to be patient and calm during communication interactions.

Controlled-Situation Communicator

Because the primary communication strategy for controlled-situation communicators—written-choice communication—is a completely partner-dependent process, it is well worth the time for AAC teams to provide thorough partner instruction. Partners must learn how to offer symbolized choices to start the conversation, provide interesting topic choices, ask open-ended rather than yes/no questions, ask questions that they don't already know the answers to, and continue a conversational sequence of questions. The speech-language pathologist should model the technique and then encourage potential communication partners to try these strategies with the person who has aphasia during a teaching session.

Comprehensive Communicators

Most of all, it is important for the partners of comprehensive communicators to give the individual the time and opportunity to communicate through an alternative modality. People with aphasia frequently complain that their partners interrupt them and finish their sentences before they can construct their messages in an alternative manner. It may be helpful for AAC teams to set up role-play situations involving both the person with aphasia and the communication partner and coach both people on their respective communication roles and responsibilities.

AAC teams should try to involve communication partners from the beginning of the message inventory process. Team members can do this by obtaining lists of potential communication situations and messages from communication partners early in the treatment process. Communication partners can also play a role in editing message pages or overlays and can provide feedback on the communicator's effectiveness in a particular situation at home or in the community.

Augmented-Input Communicator

Partners of augmented-input communicators must develop an awareness of current or impending communication breakdowns. They must learn to tell when the individual truly comprehends their messages and when he or she signals comprehension without really understanding. Partners must learn to index, or mark, what they are talking about by pointing to the item, gesturing, or writing down key words. Above all, the individual must be able to resolve communication breakdowns on an ongoing basis. AAC teams may find that it is helpful to engage both partners and communicators in conversation during the therapy session and coach partners to use augmented-input strategies at opportune moments.

Specific-Need Communicator

Partners of specific-need communicators can contribute significantly by identifying situations at home or in the community that will require highly precise communication on the part of the person with aphasia. Their continued participation in the message inventory process and role-playing activities is also very beneficial.

Ongoing Partner Involvement

As the individual's recovery of natural speech stabilizes, the nature of the AAC system often stabilizes as well so that the specific communication techniques no longer require modification. Nevertheless, it is essential that the *content* of an AAC system remain dynamic. As changes occur in the situations and contexts of an individual's life, the AAC system must reflect these changes because otherwise the individual's motivation and interest in using the system will quickly diminish. Continual modification of the content of an AAC system requires that one or more facilitators, usually family members or caregivers, learn to monitor and adjust the AAC system. Facilitators must also be able to train new people who enter the life of the person with aphasia (e.g., a son- or daughter-in-law, a new neighbor) so that they, too, can become effective communication partners. Failure to identify and adequately prepare facilitators is a common reason for AAC intervention failures among people with severe aphasia.

CONCLUSIONS

Interest in applying AAC principles to people with severe aphasia is increasing. With functional communication as the primary goal, people with aphasia increasingly are receiving AAC options soon after their strokes. During rehabilitation, therapy to promote the recovery of natural speech is encouraged, and AAC systems are modified to support functional communication that cannot be managed through natural speech.

As the application of AAC principles and methodologies to aphasia becomes better understood, it will be important to investigate the following issues in more detail:

- Which strategies are most successfully used by different types of communicators?
- What is the impact of different types of training procedures on communicative competence?
- How does the communication of people with aphasia who have access to AAC strategies differ from their prestroke communication patterns and from the communication of individuals who have never participated in AAC interventions?
- What are the cognitive-linguistic prerequisites for various AAC strategies and how do we assess these skills?
- What are the differences in functional outcomes (e.g., activity level, quality of life, communication successfulness, wellness, acceptance of disability) when people with aphasia participate in AAC interventions?
- How do AAC interventions affect the well-being and lifestyles of communication partners?

Clearly, the successful integration of AAC interventions depends also on flexibility and continuity of service delivery as the individual with aphasia makes transitions from setting to setting. Professionals, family members, and people with aphasia may have to team together to create better solutions for management of long-term aphasia. Options include increasing the emphasis on training partners to use immediate communication strategies early in the individual's recovery, with more intensive involvement of the speech-language pathologist later in the rehabilitation process. It may be useful to schedule individuals with aphasia for routine follow-up visits each year when they receive their annual therapy visit allotment from their insurer. Some people with aphasia may benefit from weekly group therapy sessions rather than individual treatment sessions only. Still others may benefit from home visits by the speech-language pathologist as well as other health care professionals for only there are the true communication challenges visible. With careful planning, AAC interventions can enrich the communication options for individuals and their communication partners at all stages of their adjustment to life with aphasia.

17

Individuals with
Traumatic Brain Injury

Augmentative and alternative communication (AAC) interventions for people who have experienced traumatic brain injury (TBI) have changed dramatically. Until the mid-1990s, AAC teams initiated interventions primarily with individuals who experienced severe, persistent anarthria or dysarthria following TBI. It was not uncommon for teams to delay AAC interventions until the individual's associated communication disorders "stabilized"; consequently, many people with TBI were unable to speak functionally for months or even years after their accidents. The justification for this conservative approach had three bases. First, cognitive limitations during early stages of recovery make it difficult for many people with TBI to operate complex AAC techniques. Second, because the cognitive and motor performance of a person with TBI changes, an appropriate long-term AAC system is difficult to select. Third, clinical observations indicated that some individuals with TBI do recover functional speech and, therefore, do not require long-term AAC systems. With this view, AAC teams felt that the most conservative approach was the "safest" when recommending an intervention.

The goal of an AAC team working with an individual with TBI is to provide communication assistance so that he or she is able to participate effectively in a rehabilitation program and is able to communicate ongoing needs. Thus, the focus of intervention has shifted from providing a single AAC system for long-term use to providing a series of AAC systems designed to meet short-term communication needs while continuing efforts to reestablish natural speech. For example, the changing AAC intervention goals over a 3-year period for Ann, an adolescent with TBI, are illustrated in Table 17.1 (Light et al., 1988).

This chapter outlines the general approaches to AAC intervention for individuals with TBI. However, because individuals with brain injuries recover over an extended period of time, it is beyond the scope of this book to detail the extensive AAC intervention concepts, techniques, and strategies developed for these individuals. DeRuyter and Kennedy (1991) and Ladtkow and Culp (1992) have written two in-depth presentations of such information.

Table 17.1.   Principal goals of intervention with Ann over a 3-year period

Phase One: 6–9 months post-trauma
1. To establish consistent and reliable yes/no responses
2. To develop a preliminary communication display as a means to indicate basic needs and wants

Phase Two: 13–16 months post-trauma
1. To provide a means to request attention
2. To encourage more explicit "yes" responses
3. To develop a communication display as a means to share information and express needs and wants

Phase Three: 22–23 months post-trauma
1. To provide access to a microcomputer for written communication
2. To establish more explicit "no" responses for unfamiliar listeners
3. To develop strategies to share information and generate novel vocabulary

Phase Four: 36 months post-trauma
1. To develop breath control, articulation skills, and voicing
2. To develop strategies to interact effectively with unfamiliar partners and in group activities
3. To develop conversation skills around a range of topics
4. To enhance the rate of written expression

Phase Five: 40–44 months post-trauma
1. To continue to develop breath control, articulation skills, and voicing
2. To recognize breakdowns in communication
3. To use clarification strategies to repair communication

From Light, J., Beesley, M., and Collier, B. (1988). Transition through multiple augmentative and alternative communication systems: A three-year case study of a head-injured adolescent. *Augmentative and Alternative Communication, 4*, 3; reprinted by permission.

PREVALENCE AND ETIOLOGY

Injuries to the head that result in temporary or permanent brain damage are quite common. It is difficult to estimate the number of these injuries that occur each year because many go unreported. Individuals who do not lose consciousness or do so only briefly are rarely admitted to the hospital and may not even go to an emergency room. The incidence of traumatic brain injury as reported by emergency room records is approximately 200 per 100,000 people. Of the 500,000 individuals who sustain TBI in the United States each year, approximately 50,000–100,000 survive with impairments that are so severe that they interfere with independent living. An additional 200,000 or more experience continuing sequelae that interfere with their ability to perform daily living skills (Gualtieri, 1988; Jennett, Snoek, Bond, & Brooks, 1981; Kalsbeek, McLauren, Harris, & Miller, 1981; Kraus, 1978; Olsen & Henig, 1983).

Individuals with TBI do not represent a random sample of the total population. More than twice as many males as females are injured. The risk of TBI is also greater among children from 4 to 5 years of age, males from 15 to 24 years of age, older adults (especially those over 75 years of age), and individuals who have had previous TBI (Beukelman & Yorkston, 1991).

The causes of TBI are varied. Motor vehicle accidents are the most common cause, and falls of various types are second. Among students, recreational- and sports-related injuries such as those that occur from bicycling, skating, and horseback riding are common. Among adolescents and young adults, assaults are a common cause of TBI. The high incidence of TBI among young adults is the result of an increased frequency of motor vehicle accidents in this age group since the mid-1980s.

Severe brain injuries dramatically affect the lives of survivors and their families. In 1988, most survivors of severe TBI

> Lived with their families, did not work or attend school, and were dependent on others for skills, finances, and services outside the home. Due to the lack of available programs, families most frequently assumed the major responsibility for the survivor's long-term care despite no training in the area. (Jacobs, 1988, p. 425)

As people with TBI recover, they usually progress through a continuum of care that begins in a trauma unit. Through hours, days, months, and years, these individuals recover abilities and functions at different rates. These complex but individual patterns of change affect nearly all aspects of their lives.

CLASSIFICATION SYSTEMS

Several categorical scales have been developed in an effort to describe people with severe TBI. The Levels of Cognitive Functioning scale (Hagen, 1984), which describes cognitive and associated language behaviors that occur during recovery, is presented in Table 17.2. AAC teams use scales such as this to design AAC and other interventions appropriate to each stage.

COMMUNICATION DISORDERS

Communication disorders associated with TBI can be classified into three areas of impairment. First, some of the language characteristics of people with TBI are a consequence of *cognitive impairments,* as we summarize in Table 17.2. The level of linguistic performance can vary depending on the individual's cognitive level. Second, language disorders may occur because of *damage to specific language processing areas* of the brain. Sarno, Buonaguvro, and Levita (1986) evaluated 125 individuals with TBI using the Battery of Language Test and reported that 29% of the individuals exhibited classic symptoms associated with acquired aphasia. An additional 36% exhibited *subclinical aphasia,* which the researchers defined as "linguistic processing deficits on testing in the absence of clinical manifestations of linguistic impairment" (p. 106).

Third, some communication disorders in TBI are caused by *damage to the motor control networks and pathways* of the brain that occurred at the time of injury. No researchers have completed a detailed study of the incidence of dysarthria following TBI. Rusk, Block, and Lowman (1969) reported that approximately one third of a group of 96 people with TBI demonstrated dysarthria during their "acute illness." Several different types of dysarthria have been observed following TBI, in particular ataxic dysarthria (Simmons, 1983; Yorkston & Beukelman, 1981; Yorkston, Beukelman, Minifie, & Sapir, 1984). In addition, Netsell and Daniel (1979) described flaccid dysarthria in a man with TBI. Yorkston and Beukelman (1981) also described mixed spastic-flaccid and mixed spastic-ataxic dysarthria.

Table 17.2.   Levels of cognitive functioning and associated language behaviors

General behaviors	Language behaviors
I. No Response Patient appears to be in a deep sleep and is completely unresponsive to any stimuli.	Receptive and expressive: No evidence of processing or verbal or gestural expression.
II. Generalized Response Patient reacts inconsistently and non-purposefully to stimuli in a nonspecific manner. Responses are limited and often the same, regardless of stimulus presented. Responses may be physiologic changes, gross body movements, or vocalization.	Receptive and expressive: No evidence of processing or verbal or gestural expression.
III. Localized Response Patient reacts specifically, but inconsistently, to stimuli. Responses are directly related to the type of stimulus presented. May follow simple commands such as "Close your eyes" or "Squeeze my hand" in an inconsistent, delayed manner.	Language begins to emerge. Receptively: Patient progresses from localizing to processing and following simple commands that elicit automatic responses in a delayed and inconsistent manner. Limited reading emerges. Expressively: Automatic verbal and gestural responses emerge in response to direct elicitation. Negative head nods emerge before positive head nods. Utterances are single words serving as "holophrastic" responses.
IV. Confused-Agitated Behavior is bizarre and nonpurposeful relative to immediate environment. Does not discriminate among persons or objects; is unable to cooperate directly with treatment efforts; verbalizations are frequently incoherent or inappropriate to the environment; confabulation may be present. Gross attention to environment is very short, and selective attention is often nonexistent. Patient lacks short-term recall.	Severe disruption of frontal–temporal lobes, with the resultant confusion apparent. Receptively: Marked disruption in auditory and visual processing, including inability to order phonemic events, monitor rate, and attend to, retain, categorize, and associate stimuli. Disinhibition interferes with comprehension and ability to inhibit responses to self-generated mental activity. Expressively: Marked disruption of phonologic, semantic, syntactic, and suprasegmental features. Output is bizarre, unrelated to environment, and incoherent. Literal, verbal, and neologistic paraphasias appear with disturbance of logicosequential features and incompleteness of thought. Monitoring of pitch, rate, intensity, and suprasegmentals is severely impaired.
V. Confused, Inappropriate, Nonagitated Patient is able to respond to simple commands fairly consistently. However, with increased complexity of commands or lack of any external structure, responses are nonpurposeful, random, or fragmented. Has gross attention to the environment but is highly distractible and lacks ability to focus attention on a specific task; with structure, may be able to converse on a social-automatic level for short periods; verbalization is often inappropriate and confabulatory; memory is severely impaired; often shows inappropriate use of subjects; individual may perform previously learned tasks with structure but is unable to learn new information.	Linguistic fluctuations are in accordance with the degree of external structure and familiarity-predictability of linguistic events. Receptively: Processing has improved, with increased ability to retain temporal order of phonemic events, but semantic and syntactic confusions persist. Only phrases or short sentences are retained. Rate, accuracy, and quality remain significantly reduced. Expressively: Persistence of phonologic, semantic, syntactic and prosodic processes. Disturbances in logicosequential features result in irrelevances, incompleteness, tangents, circumlocutions, and confabulations. Literal paraphasias subside, while neologisms and verbal paraphasias

(continued)

Table 17.2.   *(continued)*

General behaviors	Language behaviors
	continue. Utterances may be expansive or telegraphic, depending on inhibition–disinhibition factors. Responses are stimulus bound. Word retrieval deficits are characterized by delays, generalizations, descriptions, semantic associations, or circumlocutions. Disruptions in syntactic features are present beyond concrete levels of expression or with increased length of output. Written output is severely limited. Gestures are incomplete.
VI. Confused-Appropriate Patient shows goal-directed behavior but depends on external input for direction; follows simple directions consistently and shows carryover for relearned tasks with little or no carryover for new tasks; responses may be incorrect due to memory problems but appropriate to the situation; past memories show more depth and detail than recent memory.	Receptively: Processing remains delayed, with difficulty in retaining, analyzing, and synthesizing. Auditory processing is present for compound sentences, while reading comprehension is present for simple sentences. Self-monitoring capacity emerges. Expressively: Internal confusion-disorganization is reflected in expression, but appropriateness is maintained. Language is confused relative to impaired new learning and displaced temporal and situational contexts, but confabulation is no longer present. Social–automatic conversation is intact but remains stimulus bound. Tangential and irrelevant responses are present only in open-ended situations requiring referential language. Neologisms are extinguished, with literal paraphasias present only in conjunction with an apraxia. Word retrieval errors occur in conversation but seldom in confrontation naming. Length of utterance reflects inhibitory–initiation mechanisms. Written and gestural expression increases. Prosodic features reflect the "voice of confusion," characterized by monopitch, monostress, and monoloudness.
VII. Automatic-Appropriate Patient appears appropriate and oriented within hospital and home settings, goes through daily routine automatically, but is frequently robotlike with minimal-to-absent confusion; has shallow recall of activities; shows carryover for new learning but at a decreased rate; with structure, is able to initiate social or recreational activities; judgment remains impaired.	Linguistic behaviors appear "normal" within familiar, predictable, structured settings, but deficits emerge in open-ended communication and less structured settings. Receptively: Reductions persist in auditory processing and reading comprehension relative to length, complexity, and presence of competing stimuli. Retention has improved to short paragraphs but without the abilities to identify salient features, organize, integrate input, order, and retain detail. Expressively: Automatic level of language is apparent in referential communication. Reasoning is concrete and self-oriented. Expression becomes tangential and irrelevant when abstract linguistic concepts are attempted. Word retrieval errors are minimal. Length of utterance and gestures approximately normal. Writing is disorganized and simple at a paragraph level. Prosodic features may remain aberrant. Pragmatic features of ritualizing and referencing are present, while other components remain disrupted.
VIII. Purposeful and Appropriate Patient is able to recall and integrate past and recent events and is aware of and responsive to the environment,	Language capacities may fall within normal limits. Otherwise, problems persist in competitive

(continued)

Table 17.2.   (continued)

General behaviors	Language behaviors
shows carryover for new learning and needs no supervision once activities are learned; may continue to show a decreased ability relative to premorbid abilities in language, abstract reasoning, tolerance for stress, and judgment in emergencies or unusual circumstances.	situations and in response to fatigue, stress, and emotionality, characterized in reduced effectiveness, efficiency, and quality of performance. Receptively: Rate of processing remains reduced but unremarkable on testing. Retention span remains limited at paragraph level but improved with use of retrieval–organization strategies. Analysis, organization, and integration are reduced in rate and quality. Expressively: Syntactic and semantic features fall within normal limits, while verbal reasoning and abstraction remain reduced. Written expression may fall below premorbid level. Prosodic features are essentially normal. Pragmatic features of referencing, presuppositions, topic maintenance, turn taking, and use of paralinguistic features in context remain impaired.

From Hagen, C. (1984). Language disorders in head trauma. In A. Holland (Ed.), *Language disorders in adults* (pp. 257–258). Austin, TX: PRO-ED; reprinted by permission.

RECOVERY FROM SEVERE COMMUNICATION DISORDERS

Communication disorders of individuals with TBI can change dramatically over the course of their recovery. Limited longitudinal research describes the patterns of these changes; however, some authors have provided insight about the course of recovery.

Ladtkow and Culp (1992) followed 138 people with TBI over an 18-month period. They reported that 29 of these individuals (21%) were judged to be nonspeaking at some point in their recovery. Of these 29, 16 individuals (55%) regained functional speech during the middle stage of recovery (i.e., Levels IV and V in Table 17.2). Thirteen individuals (45%) did not regain functional speech; unfortunately, the description of the cognitive recovery of those who did not regain functional speech is incomplete. The authors merely indicated that only three people (10%) reached the late stage of recovery, corresponding to Levels VI, VII, and VIII.

In a related study, Dongilli, Hakel, and Beukelman (1992) investigated the recovery of 27 people who were unable to speak on admission to inpatient rehabilitation following TBI. Of these, 16 individuals (59%) became functional natural speakers during inpatient rehabilitation, whereas the other 11 (41%) did not. All individuals who became functional speakers did so at Level V or VI. Of the 11 individuals who left inpatient rehabilitation unable to speak, one achieved functional natural speech almost 24 months postinjury, and another was making substantial progress toward becoming a functional speaker 48 months postinjury.

As the Dongilli et al. (1992) study shows, people with TBI may experience severe communication disorders for cognitive- as well as motor-related reasons. Jordan and Murdoch (1990) described a 7-year-old girl who was mute for 10 months subsequent to coma. Following her mutism, the girl demonstrated rapid and unexpected recovery of functional communication skills, although she continued to experience higher-level language impairments.

Adding to this limited information base regarding recovery from communication disorders are two interesting case studies. In one, Workinger and Netsell (1988) described a man who recovered intelligible speech 13 years following injury and used various AAC systems during the intervening years. In addition, Light et al. (1988) described the transitions of an adolescent girl with TBI through approximately 3 years of multiple AAC systems before she became a functional natural speaker (see Table 17.1).

(Judy) tried to talk several times during the day. Much of it sounded unintelligible, but occasionally we heard a "Where am I?" or other words we could understand. We could not tell if she knew us, or understood anything we said. Then a few days later . . . Judy started trying to answer. . . . We spent the rest of the day hanging over her bed admiring her, as you might hang over the crib of a newborn baby. . . . The next day she responded less. This turned out to be a pattern. Nearly every day on which she showed definite improvement was followed by one of passivity or even apparent regression. It kept us on an emotional roller coaster. (D. Thatch, recounting the first few days in the hospital after her daughter Judy's severe TBI, in Weiss, Thatch, & Thatch, 1987, p. 17)

Enderby and Crow (1990), who followed four people with severe bulbar dysfunction due to TBI, reported similar outcomes. They reported that although the individuals made few gains within the first 18 months after injury, they made substantial improvements as long as 48 months postinjury.

NATURAL ABILITY INTERVENTIONS RELATED TO SPEECH

As noted in the previous discussion, some individuals with TBI recover natural speech following injury, whereas others do not. As of 1998, the communication disorders field does not have enough information to predict the likelihood of natural speech recovery. Therefore, individuals who experience TBI, their families, and their rehabilitation teams must address natural speech recovery on an individual basis. Some individuals may be able to produce a number of intelligible words, although they may not develop completely functional speech in all situations. Family members, friends, and team members should encourage the use and improvement of these words if that allows the individuals to manage certain aspects of communication interaction.

Most individuals with TBI use multiple modes of communication at every stage of recovery. Thus, AAC systems must be integrated with reemerging natural speech. Rehabilitation that emphasizes reestablishing natural speech only or AAC only may not meet all the communication needs of a person with TBI.

Augmenting the Intelligibility of Natural Speech

Some people with dysarthria following TBI can say many words, but their words may be unintelligible because of their impaired motor control. They may call on AAC techniques to augment the intelligibility of natural speech.

Topic Identification

If a person's speech is marginally intelligible, his or her message can often be understood if the listener is aware of the semantic context or topic. Hammen, Yorkston, and Dowden (1991) reported that the improvement in speech intelligibility associated with contextual knowledge for a heterogeneous group of dysarthric speakers was 1) 18.2% for the group with profound dysarthria (less than 35% intelligible without context), 2) 40.2% for the group with severe dysarthria (35%–50% intelligible without context), and 3) 29% for the group with moderate dysarthria (greater than 50% intelligible without context). Communication boards containing lists of frequently occurring topics can be used to establish context at the beginning of an interaction and to lessen the likelihood of a communication breakdown. Dongilli's (1994) research generally supported these results. For people with TBI who cannot indicate the topic about which they wish to talk, identification of a location that is topic related (e.g., home, school, church) may help the listener comprehend a spoken message.

Supplemented Speech

Beukelman and Yorkston (1977) reported that a supplemented speech strategy substantially improved the speech intelligibility of dysarthric speakers. In supplemented speech, the speaker identifies the first letter of each word on an alphabet board or other type of AAC display while saying the word. This procedure provides listeners with information that allows them to restrict their word retrieval to words that begin with the letter indicated. In the same study, Beukelman and Yorkston described the impact of supplemented speech on the speech of two dysarthric speakers, one of whom had sustained a TBI. When this young man spoke without AAC support, his sentence intelligibility was 33%, compared with 66% when he used supplemented speech.

Portable Voice Amplification

Some people with dysarthria following TBI speak so quietly that their speech is difficult to hear, especially in groups of people or noisy environments. These individuals may find it useful to increase the loudness of their speech with a portable speech amplifier (see Chapter 18 for more extensive discussion of this approach).

ACCESS ASSESSMENT AND INTERVENTION

AAC teams should base their intervention approaches with people who have TBI on individual levels of cognitive recovery (DeRuyter & Kennedy, 1991; Ladtkow & Culp, 1992). AAC approaches have been described for three general stages of recovery: 1) the *early stage*, which involves Levels I, II, and III (Table 17.2); 2) the *middle stage*, which includes Levels IV and V; and 3) the *late stage*, which includes Levels VI, VII, and VIII. Assessment and intervention goals and techniques differ considerably in these three stages (see Blackstone, 1989a, for a summary).

Early Stage (Levels I, II, and III)

Assessment

It is almost impossible in the early stage of recovery to assess cognitive, language, or motor control capabilities because the individual may be unable to stay awake or pay attention for any significant amount of time. Thus, AAC teams should attempt very little formal assessment. Instead, team members should document systematic observations to identify changes in the individual's response patterns and to identify functional movements that the individual may use in a subsequent AAC program. Family members, friends, and other communication partners can also observe and chart such information if they spend a large amount of time with the individual. Because they know the person well, they are in a good position to document changes and responses.

As individuals with TBI become more alert, they are gradually able to differentiate between two or more people or objects. This is a positive sign, as it is often a precursor to the development of a yes/no response. The response mode for differentiation varies from person to person and may include eye pointing, moving a body part, or activating a beeper. The stimuli to which people recovering from TBI are able to respond must be presented in a careful and controlled manner. Family members and communication partners can usually be trained in this approach. They can also provide information about the interests and preinjury activities of the individual with TBI so that medical and rehabilitation personnel can provide the person with interesting and meaningful stimulation.

Keenan and Barnhart (1993) documented the return of yes/no responses in 82 individuals with severe TBI: 49% signaled yes/no with head nods, 26% with motor responses of upper and lower extremities, 15% with eye gaze, and 9% with speech. Individuals with primarily cognitive or hemiplegic impairments developed yes/no responses earlier than those with flexor withdrawal or high or low muscle tone. Twenty-nine percent of the individuals regained yes/no responses within 3 months of onset, 66% within 6 months, and 84% within 9 months.

AAC Intervention

During the early stages of recovery, people with TBI are unable to speak functionally because of cognitive impairments. Some people may have language or motor control impairments that further contribute to their communication disorder. Ladtkow and Culp suggested that "the primary treatment goal of early stage TBI recovery is for the person to emerge from coma and to begin to respond consistently to simple commands" (1992, p. 154). Given this goal, the purpose of implementing AAC techniques during this stage is to stimulate the individual and to facilitate consistent, purposeful responses.

AAC techniques used at this point vary considerably depending on the individual's overall neurological involvement. For example, consider the individual who is functioning in the range of Levels I–III and who also has considerable motor control impairment. This individual might be unable to respond to stimuli consistently not only because of cognitive problems but also because of his or her motor weakness, spasticity, or lack of coordination. An AAC intervention for such a person might provide an alternative access mode, such as a single switch (Garrett, Schutz-Muehling, & Morrow, 1990). Then, as the individual begins to respond to various stimuli by making purposeful movements, facilitators can encourage contingency awareness (i.e., cause and effect). For example, facilitators might encourage the individual to operate a tape recorder with a single switch to play favorite music or listen to recorded letters from family members or friends. In addition, a single switch with a control unit can be used to activate electrical appliances such as fans, radios, and lamps. As the individual becomes more purposeful, he or she may activate single message tapes containing basic greetings and other social phrases with a single switch and tape recorder (see Chapter 13 for additional suggestions). Then, if motor control permits, facilitators can connect two or more switches to different tape recorders so the individual can choose from among different musical selections or letters. During the early stage of recovery, a limited number of symbols (e.g., one to four) might represent choices. Symbols should be brightly colored or exaggerated (Fried-Oken & Doyle, 1992). AAC teams should take care to understand the visual capabilities of AAC users following TBI, as impairments can range from double vision to cortical blindness.

Middle Stage (Levels IV and V)

Assessment

In the middle stage of recovery, the individual may respond consistently to stimuli while still showing evidence of considerable performance and communication impairments due to attention and memory impairments. Individuals who do not have specific language impairments or severe motor control impairments usually begin to speak functionally during these stages, although they may produce somewhat confused messages (Dongilli et al., 1992; Ladtkow & Culp, 1992). In addition, people with TBI generally begin to indicate their basic needs at this point. These may include comfort messages related to being hot/cold, hurt, or hungry. Individuals may also be able to communicate messages related to their location, time of day, and other personal information. Family members and friends can assist with the selection of topics that are particularly important to people in the middle stages of recovery.

Early in the middle phase of recovery, people with TBI often experience agitation and poor awareness of their communication deficits. Therefore, they may initially have difficulty accepting AAC interventions. This may be reflected in limited willingness to participate in some aspects of AAC assessment.

The aim of assessment in the middle stage is to identify residual capabilities that the individual with TBI can utilize to achieve the specific communication goals mentioned previously. Most of the procedures for this assessment are nonstandardized and informal. The initial assessment often focuses on seating and postural issues, which team members should coordinate with AAC concerns. Proper seating and positioning help to minimize reflex activity, excessive tone, and other movements that may interfere with verbal communication or AAC system usage (DeRuyter & Kennedy, 1991). Specifically, "the overall seating and positioning goals during [this] stage should be to provide for a structurally appropriate and functional position in which minimal or no pain is encountered" (DeRuyter & Kennedy, 1991, p. 342).

Assessment of motor control capability is important to determine the individual's direct selection or scanning options. As we discuss in Chapter 6, assessors should consider various access sites in terms of accuracy, efficiency, reliability, and endurance. This assessment may be difficult in some cases because people with TBI may require orthopedic surgical procedures that interfere, either temporarily or permanently, with their ability to use specific motor access sites (DeRuyter & Kennedy, 1991). Thus, it is important for AAC specialists to coordinate communication interventions with medical procedures by working closely with the medical team responsible for the individual's overall care. Assessment should also focus on the memory and attention capabilities of people with TBI. Complex scanning patterns (row–column or group–item) may be too demanding, so AAC teams should limit the individual's early scanning experiences to circular or linear scanning.

People with TBI often experience visual-perceptual and visual acuity disturbances, and these should also be considered in AAC assessment. At lower cognitive levels, assessors can usually determine visual functioning by observing the individual's ocular response to threat, gross focus movements of the eyes, and the individual's ability to follow a bright object or familiar face (DeRuyter & Kennedy, 1991). At higher cognitive levels, many visual disturbances can be detected through standard ophthalmological examinations. A member of the AAC team should accompany the individual to such assessments to encourage the examiner to consider AAC-related issues, such as the optimum size for symbols and the array and the optimum distance between the user and the display.

AAC Intervention

Depending on the nature of the brain injury, AAC teams should choose one or two major communication goals for the middle stages of recovery. The goal may be to help the person compensate for attentional and memory impairments. This is particularly relevant for individuals with TBI who begin to speak during this stage because they often need communication techniques to help them remember, for example, the names of important people and their schedule of activities.

A second goal of intervention in the middle stage applies specifically to individuals who have sustained damage to language or motor control areas of the brain. These individuals probably will not develop natural speech at this point in their recovery. Thus, AAC interventions should seek to provide these individuals with techniques that support conversational interaction. In Levels IV and V, messages that relate to wants/needs and information sharing are more important to most individuals than are messages that support social closeness and social etiquette (DeRuyter & Kennedy, 1991).

Most AAC interventions during the middle stages of recovery are nonelectronic and include alphabet boards, pictures, word boards, yes/no techniques, and dependent scanning, among others. In an effort to reduce the complexity of communication, AAC teams may elect to use context-specific activity displays (miniboards) at this stage. For example, specific boards might facilitate participation in cognitive rehabilitation activities, recreational events, or daily living routines. Depending on the linguistic capabilities of the individual, photographs, line drawings, or printed words and phrases may symbolize the messages on the activity displays. Interventionists should remember that people in this stage of recovery may experience difficulty visually discriminating similar symbols or symbols with several elements. Individuals might use alphabetic displays, but encoding is almost always too difficult at this stage of recovery (Fried-Oken & Doyle, 1992). To control the complexity of the AAC system, teams may choose small activity displays with specific content, rather than large, complex boards containing multiple areas of content. For those with extensive attention and memory limitations, interventionists might consider written choice strategies (see Chapter 16).

DeRuyter and Donoghue (1989) described in detail the AAC interventions over a 28-week period for a young man who was unable to speak functionally due to TBI. During the first weeks of intervention (8 months postinjury), he established a reliable yes/no response by nodding his head, and he began to learn the visual-perceptual and upper-extremity skills necessary for eventual use of a communication board. In addition, his AAC team initiated interventions designed to encourage the development of natural speech during this time. By the 10th week of intervention, he was able to use a simple alphabet board, 12" × 18", with approximately 2-inch letters. Initially, he exhibited "extreme frustration" (1989, p. 52) with the board because of his motor planning deficits. By the 26th week of intervention, however, this young man exhibited "no hesitation in using his alphabet board when he was unable to communicate effectively verbally or gesturally" (1989, p. 53). His team introduced an electronic AAC device with voice output. With very little training on the device, he was able to communicate at a rate of up to eight words per minute. At the time of his discharge from the inpatient rehabilitation facility, he communicated via limited speech, a sophisticated gesturing system, an alphabet board, and an AAC device with an expanded membrane keyboard.

During the middle stage, the individual may use single switches to activate call buzzers or appliances or to run tape recorders (see Chapter 18 for suggestions about these applications). Depending on the physical capabilities of the individual, such switch control activities may serve as training for the operation of a long-term environmental control device.

Communication partners play an important role in structuring communication interactions during the middle stage. For example, partners may need to introduce topics for conversation, suggest the augmentative mode that can be used most productively at a particular time, assist with resolving communication breakdowns, and create motivating communication opportunities. Communication partners should actively help to structure interactions, but they should also be very patient and allow ample time for people with TBI to prepare, clarify, and repair their messages. Perhaps one of the most common partner errors is to rush or offer excessive encouragement during this stage by offering multiple suggestions of how to formulate or complete a message. This can be very distracting and frustrating to the individual with TBI who must concentrate very hard in order to think, plan, compose, and finally produce a communicative utterance. At times, partners will also need to learn to provide systematic cuing in order for the person in middle stages to use his or her communication system effectively. In time, individuals with TBI should attempt to phase out partner cuing.

Late Stage (Levels VI, VII, and VIII)

Assessment

By the latest stage in recovery, most individuals have regained the cognitive capability to become natural speakers, and those who remain unable to speak usually experience severe specific language or motor control disorders. AAC teams can implement the

Participation Model (Figure 6.1) at this point for particularly effective assessment and intervention planning.

Analysis of the *participation patterns* of individuals with TBI and their families forms a particularly important part of this process. When people with TBI move from acute rehabilitation, to outpatient rehabilitation, to independent living, to employment, their patterns and expectations of participation change dramatically. These expectations greatly affect the nature and extent of their communication needs. It is also important to *assess opportunity barriers,* in much the same manner as is discussed in Chapter 6. For people with TBI in late-stage recovery, AAC teams often identify communication needs, assess specific capabilities and constraints, and match these to AAC system/device interventions (DeRuyter & Kennedy, 1991; Ladtkow & Culp, 1992).

AAC Intervention

In the late stage of recovery, individuals with TBI are generally oriented and able to demonstrate goal-directed, socially appropriate behavior. They may still have difficulties learning new information, however, due to residual cognitive impairments. Some individuals may become natural speakers during Level VI, but by Levels VII and VIII, most individuals who are likely to become natural speakers without extensive intervention have already done so (Dongilli et al., 1992). Thus, by the late stage of recovery, many people with TBI can interact and converse with their families and friends through natural speech. Nevertheless, even those individuals who regain speech may require augmented writing systems for an extended period. In addition, people with residual language and motor control impairments will continue to require long-term communication systems to meet their specific interaction needs. Individuals have many interaction needs at this point, including those related to communicating wants/needs, sharing information, achieving social closeness, and participating in social routines (DeRuyter & Kennedy, 1991).

During the late stage of cognitive recovery, traditional AAC techniques that resemble those used with other individuals who experience physical and cognitive impairments are often appropriate. Although people with TBI who cannot speak usually experience a high incidence of physical problems, approximately 78% of those in one study were able to successfully utilize direct selection AAC techniques (DeRuyter & Lafontaine, 1987). Almost 75% of the direct selection users in DeRuyter and Lafontaine's database operated their devices with their fingers or hands, whereas the remainder used eye pointing, headlight pointing, or chin pointing; 16% utilized dependent or independent scanning, and the remainder used other or no AAC techniques.

It might be assumed that due to the cognitive impairments associated with TBI, individuals will require AAC systems that contain pictorial or other nonorthographic

As social support for health care and rehabilitation decreases in some countries, people with TBI are spending less and less time in intensive rehabilitation programs where AAC services may be available. It is important that people with TBI and their families educate themselves early in the recovery process about available AAC services and how to gain access to such services when they are needed.

symbols. This, however, is often not the case. It is important to remember that even late in the recovery process, cognitive impairments may mask considerable residual skills. One of the most important skills that people with TBI retain is the ability to read and spell. Thus, many individuals with TBI can utilize AAC systems that employ orthographic symbols, including letters, words, and sentences (Fried-Oken & Doyle, 1992). AAC teams should take care when introducing encoding strategies, as some people, even in the late stage of recovery, may have difficulty learning and implementing these strategies efficiently.

Those who assist people with TBI during the recovery process may be well aware that new learning can be difficult and require considerable time and practice. This is an important consideration for those individuals who require long-term communication systems because some AAC approaches require extensive training for operation. Examples of such methods are those that are technically complex to operate or that require the user to learn a large number of messages using sequences of alphabetic or iconic codes. The AAC team should exercise caution when introducing such techniques and should be careful not to make frequent changes in a system once the individual has learned it.

18

AAC in Intensive
and Acute Care Settings

When I was in the ICU (intensive care unit), I couldn't move my arms, and I had a halo (a brace to stabilize the neck) on my head, and I had a trach (tracheostomy tube) down my throat, and my eyes were swollen shut for 4 or 5 days. So, I couldn't communicate with anybody. I couldn't tell them when I hurt and where I hurt. So, I had mascara in my eyes for 9 days, and my eyes watered and watered for 9 days, until a nurse finally asked me enough pointed questions so that I could explain my eyes were hurting. (An ICU patient after her discharge from the unit, in Mitsuda, Baarslag-Benson, Hazel, & Therriault, 1992, p. 6)

Most hospitals contain intensive care units (ICUs) that serve a wide range of individuals who are unable to communicate, either temporarily or permanently. Such communication problems occur as a result of primary medical conditions, such as traumatic brain injury (TBI), stroke, and Guillain-Barré syndrome (GBS), or as a side effect of medical interventions such as intubation and tracheostomy. Providing augmentative and alternative communication (AAC) services in intensive and acute medical care settings is increasingly common.

Although many individuals in medical settings need AAC services, it is difficult for many AAC specialists to imagine initiating interventions for several reasons. First, few AAC professionals have experience caring for individuals in an ICU, and most have probably never been in one, except to visit a family member or friend briefly. Therefore, most AAC professionals have experiences limited to visiting hours or to indirect contact with an ICU environment through television documentaries. As a result, these people tend to imagine that the individual in an ICU is very passive. It may seem as if individuals are "having things done to them" constantly and that they are passive regarding their own care. This perception logically leads to the belief that because people in intensive care are so ill and so passive, they do not need to communicate. This is not at all the case, with the exception of people who are unconscious. Most people in intensive care need to communicate regularly with hospital staff in order to participate in their own care, and these people may feel an urgent need to communicate with family members at this uncertain and frightening time in their lives.

You don't really know what's going on very much from the doctors because they don't try and talk to you directly. But the good things that were in the ICU was I had a lot of family support, so I had family there every day. . . . So I always knew I had somebody there that could help me, because you can't communicate with the nurses. It's like your family can understand you better for some reason. The nurses, they just give you the medicine and go about their business, but they don't really try and communicate at all in any way. So it's kind of a scary thing because you don't know exactly what's going on, and you don't know how bad you are. You just know that you are in a lot of pain and you are in bad shape. You don't know exactly what has happened even. (An ICU patient with a spinal cord injury, in Mitsuda et al., 1992, p. 7)

In an ICU, communication also allows individuals to provide medical information to caregivers and serves as a critical link between the person and his or her support system, which includes family, friends, and others. Depending on length of stay in an ICU, it may also be necessary to communicate about family finances, the operation of a business, the care of dependent children, and other personal matters.

CAUSES OF COMMUNICATION DISORDERS IN ICU AND ACUTE CARE SETTINGS

Communication disorders in the ICU can occur as a result of both primary causes (i.e., those directly related to the individual's illness or condition) and secondary causes (i.e., those related to the individual's need for temporary respiratory support). These are discussed in the sections that follow.

Primary Causes

Many individuals in an ICU are unable to speak because of their primary illness or condition. These include individuals with Parkinson's disease, stroke, TBI, and amyotrophic lateral sclerosis (ALS). Some of these conditions, such as stroke, occur abruptly and without warning, and the people affected are usually completely unfamiliar with AAC approaches, as are their families and friends. Other primary conditions, such as ALS, are progressive, resulting in gradual physical deterioration. Many of these individuals will have used AAC systems prior to entering the hospital, and both they and their families may be familiar with a wide range of AAC approaches. Hospital staff, however, are unlikely to be as knowledgeable about AAC options and will need to learn about the individual's system quickly. (See Chapters 16 and 17 for extensive discussion of these primary medical conditions and the AAC approaches typically used with them.)

Secondary Causes

Individuals with a number of medical conditions may require respiratory support, either temporarily or permanently. These include, for example, people with GBS, botulism, cardiopulmonary insufficiency, and extensive surgical interventions. Such respiratory support often interferes with communication processes and a person's ability to speak. This is particularly true if endotracheal intubation or tracheostomy is required.

Endotracheal Intubation

An endotracheal tube (Figure 18.1) is designed to transport air from a ventilator to an individual's respiratory system. Endotracheal tubes are usually passed in emergency situations through the individual's mouth, pharynx, and larynx into the trachea (i.e., the airway below the larynx). This oral intubation interferes with communication in several ways. First, because the endotracheal tube passes through the oral cavity, it is impossible to articulate speech accurately. Second, because the endotracheal tube passes between the vocal folds, which are located in the larynx, it is impossible to produce sound (i.e., phonation). Thus, people who are orally intubated are unable to communicate using natural speech.

An endotracheal tube may also pass through the nasal cavity into the trachea. Although in this case the tube does not interfere with articulation as occurs when it passes through the mouth, the endotracheal tube does pass between the vocal folds. Therefore, an individual is unable to produce vocal sounds and efforts to communicate are limited to mouthing messages with the lips.

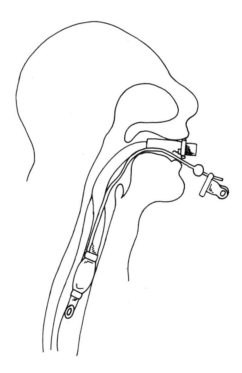

Figure 18.1. An endotracheal tube in place.

Tracheostomy

A tracheostomy is another way to transport air from a ventilator to an individual's respiratory system. It is a surgical opening from the front wall of the lower neck into the trachea (i.e., the airway below the larynx). Tracheostomies are usually performed at the level of the second or third tracheal ring. Generally, the opening of the tracheostomy is maintained by inserting a tube or button through the neck wall into the trachea. As illustrated in Figure 18.2, the tracheostomy tube curves to extend down into the trachea to keep it open for the movement of air. The ventilator attaches to the portion of the tube that extends anterior to the neck. An individual with a tracheostomy tube who depends on a ventilator has limited natural speech because air passes from the ventilator through the tube, rather than through the oral cavity and past the vocal folds.

Tracheostomy tubes remain in place when the individual no longer needs ventilator support to maintain an open airway or to permit suction of respiratory secretions. Nonetheless, air passes in and out of the trachea via the tracheostomy tube, bypassing the vocal folds. Thus, no phonation is possible, and messages must be mouthed. However, depending on the respiratory problem, some individuals who do not breathe with ventilator assistance are able to inhale through the tracheostomy tube, then occlude the tube with their fingers or an external valve and exhale through the larynx and the oral cavity. In this way, air moves past the vocal folds on exhalation, and they are able to produce sound and speak naturally. In other cases, individuals who can breathe on their own may be fitted with a tracheal button that maintains the tracheostomy through the neck wall. These individuals can inhale through the button and then occlude the button with their finger or a valve to direct air past the vocal folds and produce speech.

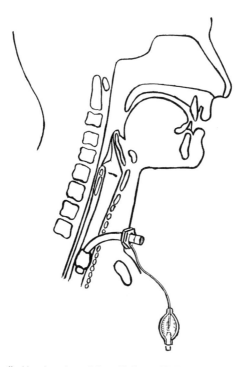

Figure 18.2.   Lateral view of a cuffed tracheostomy tube with the cuff inflated. (From Logemann, J. (1983). *Evaluation and treatment of swallowing disorders* (p. 105). Austin TX: PRO-ED; reprinted by permission.)

AAC SERVICE DELIVERY IN ICU AND ACUTE CARE SETTINGS

Because ICUs are so organizationally complex, on-site professionals usually provide the most effective ongoing AAC services. It is much more difficult for a consultant to come intermittently to a hospital to provide AAC services because the individual may be unavailable, too ill, resting, or receiving other medical treatments that take priority at the time of the consultant's visit. The core AAC team generally includes a speech-language pathologist, a physical therapist, and an occupational therapist who are employed by the hospital. In addition to their roles on the AAC team, these professionals may be responsible for other therapy needs of individuals in the ICU. They may consult with personnel from a regional AAC center or with a local AAC specialist in the area.

The delivery of AAC services in ICU or acute care settings is structured differently from typical rehabilitation or educational settings. A successful AAC program in an ICU or acute care setting must accommodate factors specific to these settings in order to be accepted and used by patients and medical personnel.

When they put the tubes in, you get to the point of being helpless and you feel a need to communicate and talk to someone. You can't move. And you can't talk. And you want to say things. And you think, "Now I'd like to ask some more questions. You explained to me what's going on. But no, I want to know more now. What's going to happen?" And all you can really do is just lay there. That's when you really, really get spooked the most. (Mike S., a 46-year-old man who had GBS, in Fried-Oken et al., 1991, p. 43)

Patient Issues

Individuals in acute medical settings have serious medical needs that are critical to their survival. The delivery of AAC services simply cannot interfere with the delivery of medical care. Such services must be integrated into the overall care plan for the individual.

The intensity of medical care in an ICU affects the AAC program in a variety of ways. Medical staff are responsible for establishing and delivering an overall medical plan of which communication intervention may be a small part. Thus, the AAC staff cannot provide services without a request or referral from the medical team. The AAC team must clearly communicate the types of services they can deliver. They must consult with the medical team before and during AAC interventions to ensure that efforts coordinate well with the overall medical plan. If communication specialists do not follow these guidelines, they may fail to meet individuals' AAC needs.

Because individuals in an ICU receive such extensive medical support, it is not uncommon for as many as 10–25 different professionals as well as visiting family members and friends to have contact with each person during a 24-hour period. Thus, a variety of individuals must be able to understand AAC interventions. Signs on the walls, written messages, or verbal instructions must provide instructions for all these people. AAC interventions in ICUs must be minimally complex and require minimal training and learning to be successful.

I think the staff should be trained separately from initial contact with the patient. I think they should already know how. At least the basic tools. . . . And they should have a separate kind of training so that whenever a patient comes in, any staff member can go up and say "Here. Now let's use this here. A speech therapist will be down later. But right now, this is a basic method. And you can count on any nurse here knowing exactly how to use this and you can communicate with any of us." We should have had at least that. Staff needs to be trained. (Alec K., a 35-year-old man who had GBS, in Fried-Oken et al., 1991, pp. 49–50)

Medical Team Issues

Because *nursing personnel* are generally responsible for carrying out most day-to-day activities in the medical care plan, they have extensive contact with both individuals in the ICU and their family members. Thus, nurses are in an excellent position to assist the AAC team by monitoring an individual's status, coordinating AAC interventions with the medical care plan, documenting the individual's communication needs, and keeping family members informed of changes in the communication plan. The nursing coordinator in the ICU often assumes the role of patient advocate during communication intervention and actively encourages physicians to request AAC services.

Respiratory therapists deal with a high proportion of the people in ICU and acute care units. Respiratory therapists are generally responsible for day-to-day management of individuals' respiratory status, including people with endotracheal or tracheostomy tubes. The AAC team must cooperate closely with respiratory therapists for successful intervention. Ongoing physician education is also important, especially in training hospitals where the staff consists of interns and residents as well as senior medical personnel. The AAC team may be invited to present their plan directly to the medical team in the ICU. Instruction about AAC services, however, usually occurs in the context of ongoing service delivery in the ICU.

(The scanning device) was a useless tool to me. There were two problems. First. . . it took too much effort to learn to hit the switch right. And once you did, you needed other words anyway. With so many things sitting around your bed, you need something that is always there, easily accessible, reasonably easy to understand and use. The machines don't fit that bill at all. (Alec K., a 35-year-old man who had GBS, in Fried-Oken et al., 1991, p. 47)

ESTABLISHING AN AAC PROGRAM IN AN ICU

It is beyond the scope of this chapter to provide an extensive discussion regarding how to develop an AAC program in an intensive or acute care medical setting (see Mitsuda et al., 1992, for a detailed description of this process). Mitsuda et al. (1992) noted that AAC teams should pay careful attention to individuals' equipment needs in ICUs as well as to administrative, organizational, and personnel training issues. They suggested that the following equipment and materials form the basis for many AAC interventions in ICU settings: 1) a lightweight neck-type electrolarynx (i.e., one that is positioned against the neck and vibrates the air column within the vocal tract); 2) an oral-type electrolarynx (i.e., one that delivers sound into the oral cavity through a tube); 3) materials to construct alphabet boards, word boards, and picture boards; 4) several magic slates (these are generally sold as toys and consist of a sheet of plastic over a piece of coated board that can be written on; when the plastic is lifted, written messages disappear); and 5) a portable mounting system on wheels to hold cardboard message boards or eye-pointing displays. These minimal equipment needs reflect the previously stated philosophy of simplifying AAC interventions in this area and are echoed by Dowden, Beukelman, and Lossing:

> Clinicians with very few communication augmentation systems can nonetheless serve ICU patients quite well. . . . The majority of our patients were served with electrolarynges or . . . modified natural speech approaches. With additional access to the least expensive communication systems (Plexiglas boards for eye-gaze . . . paper and pencil [and a few small typing systems]), we were able to serve all but a few of our patients. This means that even the smallest clinical program should consider serving patients in intensive care units. (1986, p. 43)

More extensive electronic AAC devices may be necessary for people who require a long-term communication intervention (e.g., people with high spinal cord injuries who need writing systems, people with aphasia secondary to stroke). Because of the complexity of these systems and their learning requirements for both individuals in the ICU and staff, AAC teams usually do not initiate these interventions in the ICU. Rather, they introduce them either during inpatient rehabilitation or after the individual is discharged from the hospital.

AAC INTERVENTION MODEL

Communication specialists have not utilized the Participation Model (Figure 6.1), which is described in detail in Chapters 6–8, for individuals in the ICU setting. Instead, a Communication Needs Model, similar to the model described in Chapter 15, has been used (Dowden, Honsinger, & Beukelman, 1986; Mitsuda et al., 1992). Nevertheless, the Participation Model can be used quite effectively in intensive care settings as the basis for an overall AAC program.

IDENTIFY PARTICIPATION PATTERNS AND COMMUNICATION NEEDS

The Participation Model supports the overall delivery of AAC services to people in intensive care environments. Interventionists can expect restricted participation patterns because individuals limited to essentially one communication environment (the ICU) have limited contact with people in their social networks and are not working. Thus, most individuals in the ICU have quite limited communication needs. A communication needs assessment checklist for intensive and acute care units is depicted in Figure 18.3 (Dowden, Honsinger, & Beukelman, 1986).

This checklist resembles the assessment presented in Figure 15.1, but it contains a variety of options that are specific to ICU settings. Assessors should designate each of the needs listed as "mandatory," "desirable," or "unimportant." The AAC team should

Re: Environment   Indicate: Mandatory, Desirable, Unimportant

Does individual need to:

  move from room to room   _____

  move within a room   _____

  communicate in w/c   _____

    manual chair

    electric w/c

      (controls: _____)

    other w/c (specify: _____)

Does individual need to communicate:

  while lying supine

  while lying prone

  while side-lying

  in several positions
    (specify: _____)

  in a regular bed

  in a Roto-bed

  in a Clinitron bed

  while sitting in bed

  while in a regular bed

  at standing table

  while on floor mat

  while standing

  with arterial lines in place

  with hand mitts

  while restrained

  while orally intubated

  while nasally intubated

  while trached

  with oxygen mask on

  with NG tube in place

  with a halo in place

  while walking

  in bathroom

  in other locations
    (specify: _____)

  outdoors

  in van, car, bus—no w/c

  in bright room

  in dim room

  in noisy room

  in quiet room

Re: Partners

Does individual need to communicate:

  with anyone visually impaired

  with anyone hearing impaired

  with anyone who cannot read

  with speakers of another language
    (specify: _____)

(continued)

Figure 18.3.   Assessment of communication needs in an ICU setting. (From Dowden, P., Honsinger, M., & Beukelman D. (1986). Serving non-speaking people in acute care settings. *Augmentative and Alternative Communication, 2,* 31–32; reprinted by permission.)

Figure 18.3.   *(continued)*

Re: Partners	Indicate: Mandatory, Desirable, Unimportant
with anyone across the room	_____
with more than one listener	_____
with anyone with limited time	_____
with anyone untrained on system	_____
with anyone who cannot always look at display	_____
with general public	
(specify where: _____)	_____

Re: Messages

In room, does individual need to:

call attention	_____
signal emergencies	_____
answer yes/no questions	_____
answer other questions	_____
ask questions	_____
provide unique information	_____
make requests	_____
carry on a conversation	_____
express emotion	_____
give his/her opinion	_____
convey basic medical needs	_____
greet people	_____
leave messages/notes	_____
prepare messages in advance	_____

Re: Modes

Does individual need to:

produce printed copy	
take notes for self	_____
leave notes for others	_____
produce speech	
produce quiet speech	_____
produce loud speech	_____
use telephone	
talk on the telephone	_____
take notes while on phone	_____
access phone independently	_____
switch from one mode to another	
between print and speech	_____
between print and telephone	_____
switch tasks within one mode	
during message preparation	_____
during text preparation	_____

complete the checklist with input from nursing personnel, family members (if they are available), and the patient (if he or she is able to participate).

ASSESS OPPORTUNITY BARRIERS

Individuals in the ICU deserve to have access to AAC services to meet even their restricted communication needs, and a lack of availability of AAC services can be considered to be an opportunity barrier. Few hospitals appear to have actual policies against AAC services; even so, AAC teams must deal with a number of practice or knowledge barriers. These barriers may include 1) medical teams that do not refer individuals for

AAC services, 2) nursing personnel who prefer not to be burdened with additional work in an already busy (and, perhaps, understaffed) ICU, and 3) speech-language pathologists and other professionals who are not familiar with conducting AAC interventions in ICU settings.

(While I was in the ICU), I wanted to communicate a friend's place where he works so they could tell him that I had been injured, and I had to blink the alphabet. But it took a while for them to figure out that I was blinking the alphabet because I was blinking so many times. Because first they wanted the phone number, and I kept telling them no there was no phone number because he didn't have a phone. He had just moved. So, then they finally realized, because I had blinked so many times because the first letter was an "R," they figured out that it was the alphabet so I could tell them the place that he worked through blinking the alphabet. (An ICU patient with a spinal cord injury, in Mitsuda et al., 1992, p. 7)

ASSESS BARRIERS TO ACCESS

As with other AAC assessments, those that occur in the ICU require considerations of specific capabilities and constraints, such as access barriers.

Assess Specific Capabilities: Preliminary Screening

Many individuals in the ICU are unable to participate in extensive assessment procedures. The AAC team should conduct a preliminary screening as the first step of an assessment to determine whether the individual is an appropriate candidate for a more complete evaluation (Dowden, Honsinger, & Beukelman, 1986). Tasks in the initial screening are shown in Figure 18.4. In order to respond to these tasks, the individual must be able to follow simple directions and have some way of indicating *yes* and *no*. This is often the first type of communication that develops between individuals and their staff or family members. Sometimes the first step in assessment is to isolate or identify a yes/no response. Medical teams rarely refer individuals for evaluation unless they can respond in this way.

Dowden, Honsinger, and Beukelman described the use of the screening tasks in Figure 18.4 as follows:

> Patients are eliminated immediately if they are functional speakers or if they do not respond to either touch or their spoken name. Of those who are responsive, some may fail to pass the initial screening procedure, and are eliminated as too confused, agitated, or disoriented to cooperate with the communication augmentation intervention. (1986, p. 25)

These authors reported that of the 42 individuals who completed six or more of the screening tasks, 9% were provided with "limited switch approaches" (i.e., electronic scanning devices) that met communication needs, 53%–68% used oral or direct selection approaches that met their needs, and 70%–82% used several approaches simultaneously to meet their needs. Of eight individuals in their study who completed fewer than six tasks accurately, three did not receive AAC services because they died or were transferred to another hospital. The remaining five underwent further assessment, but

Attending behaviors:

Attends to spoken name?   yes   no

Attends to "Look at me"?   yes   no

Orientation questions:

"Is your name (_____)?"   yes   no

"Is the current year (_____)?"   yes   no

"Is (_____) your home town?"   yes   no

"Are you married?"   yes   no

Single-step commands:

"Close your eyes."   yes   no

"Open your mouth."   yes   no

Figure 18.4.   Initial cognitive-linguistic screening tasks for ICU assessment. (From Dowden, P., Honsinger, M., & Beukelman, D. (1986). Serving non-speaking people in acute care settings. *Augmentative and Alternative Communication, 2,* 31; reprinted by permission.)

the AAC team was completely unsuccessful in providing them with AAC techniques to meet their communication needs. Dowden, Beukelman, and Lossing drew two conclusions from these findings:

> First, it appears that the percentage of needs met may be related to the patient's cognitive status, as measured grossly by the cognitive screening tasks because on the average, more communication needs were met for Group 2 patients [i.e., those who passed six or more items] than Group 1 patients [i.e., those who passed fewer than six items]. Second, within Group 2, the percentage of needs met appears to change with the type of intervention. For example, it appears that serving patients with multiple systems meets, on the average, more communication needs than serving the patient with a single system. (1986, p. 43)

Assess Specific Capabilities and Intervene Accordingly

Inidividuals who successfully complete preliminary screening tasks undergo a more extensive assessment of their capabilities. Mitsuda et al. (1992) provided a flowchart to guide the decision-making process, which we have modified and present in Figure 18.5. Discussion of an extended capability assessment and related interventions follows.

People with Sufficient Oral-Motor Control for Speech

Many individuals in an ICU have sufficient motor control for speech, provided that they have an adequate sound source for voicing. Thus, the first step in evaluating someone in an ICU should be assessment of oral-motor capabilities. If these are ade-

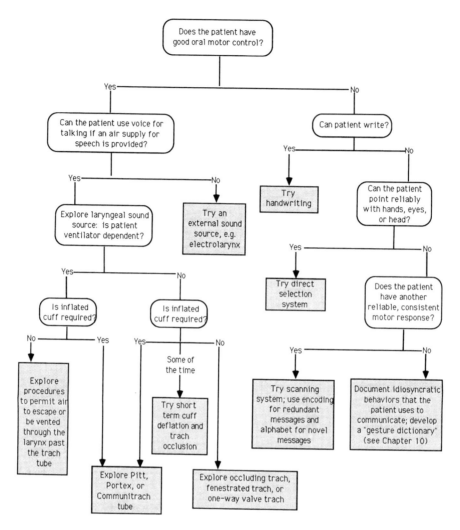

Figure 18.5.   AAC intervention planning flowchart for intensive care unit applications. (Adapted from Mitsuda, Baarslag-Benson, Hazel, & Therriault, 1992.)

quate to support speech, assessors should explore oral communication options. If oral-motor control is inadequate, assessors must explore other communication options.

Voicing Capabilities

Many individuals who have adequate oral-motor control for speech are unable to produce sound (i.e., voice) for one of several reasons. Some lack airflow past their vocal folds because of a tracheostomy but are able to produce vocal sounds if this airflow can be reestablished temporarily. Other individuals may experience severe respiratory problems or require ventilator supports that preclude any airflow past the vocal folds. We discuss interventions related to these two options later in this chapter.

Still other people may not have the motor control necessary to produce voicing. For these individuals, one of two types of electrolarynges often serves as an effective intervention device. A "neck-type" electrolarynx (Figure 18.6) is positioned against the exterior neck wall and vibrates the air column within the vocal tract. "Mouth-

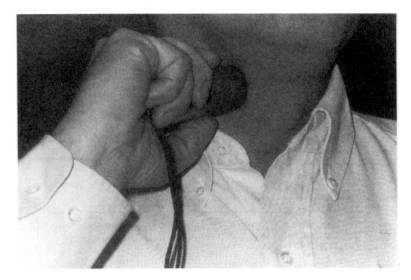

Figure 18.6.   A neck-type (Romet) electrolarynx.

ing words" then produces audible speech. The second, an oral-type electrolarynx (Figure 18.7), delivers sound into the oral cavity through a tube or a catheter. The oral-type electrolarynx is useful for individuals who cannot use a neck-type electrolarynx due to extensive tissue damage, swelling, or surgical tenderness in the neck area or because they must wear cervical collars that obscure their necks.

Figure 18.7.   Using an oral-type (CooperRand) electrolarynx.

Reestablishing the Airflow for Voicing

The first step in initiating an intervention to reestablish the flow of air past the vocal folds is to determine if the individual requires a cuffed tracheostomy tube and whether the cuff must be inflated. (A cuffed tracheostomy tube is shown in Figure 18.2.) The air supply for respiration passes through the cuffed tube into the lungs. The cuff around the tube inflates against the wall of the trachea to prevent air from escaping from the ventilator and lungs through the mouth and to prevent food or liquid from moving through the mouth and pharynx into the respiratory system. Many individuals require the cuff to be inflated at all times. Some devices, however, allow the airflow to be directed through the vocal folds on exhalation although the cuffed tracheostomy tube is in place. An external valve that directs the air stream usually operates these "talking tracheostomy" products. Individuals who can tolerate the deflation of their tracheostomy cuffs for brief periods may achieve phonation by allowing air to escape from the respiratory system past the deflated cuff and vocal folds. They are able to produce natural speech in this way.

Another option is to use a tracheostomy tube that does not involve a cuff. This option may be appropriate for someone who requires a tracheostomy to maintain an open airway because of swelling or trauma to the neck area but who does not depend on a ventilator. In this case, the individual can direct air past the vocal folds by 1) learning to occlude the tube with a finger during exhalation, 2) utilizing a fenestrated tracheostomy tube that has an opening on the top in the trachea, or 3) using a one-way valve that permits inhalation through the tube and exhalation through the vocal tract.

I think that board (a magic slate) was my preference over everything. You could communicate quickly and say what you wanted to say. You can write your letters and separate your words, like in normal writing. And it was much quicker and easier to understand by other people. I think they probably like it the best, too. So the Magic board was the best one, once I could start using my hands again. When I was unable to use my hands, of course the alphabet board (for dependent scanning) was the best, assuming that the other person understood how to use it, which many didn't. (Alec K., a 35-year-old man who had GBS, in Fried-Oken et al., 1991, p. 47)

Individuals with Insufficient Oral-Motor Control for Speech

The flowchart assessment (see Figure 18.5) may reveal insufficient oral-motor control for speech. If this is the case, individuals may require communication systems that use writing, direct selection, and/or scanning, as discussed in the following sections.

Writing Options

Handwriting can serve as an effective communication mode in an ICU because many people are comfortable and familiar with this mode of communication. Some individuals prefer to use a pencil and tablet so that as they write and save messages, they can begin to construct their own communication book. Then, rather than writing the same message again and again, they can simply refer to a question or a comment they have communicated previously. Others prefer to use a magic slate so that they can erase messages when they are finished and thus maintain privacy.

Options for People Who Cannot Write

Some individuals are unable to write by hand, but they can point accurately with their hands, eyes, or head. AAC teams generally encourage these individuals to use a direct selection communication system. This direct selection system can be as simple as an alphabet board with some words or phrases on it. Other individuals may prefer a small typing system. Usually, individuals in an ICU do not have the time or motivation to use an encoding strategy. Therefore, some prefer to type their messages. If available, voice output may be preferred by some individuals. Small portable digitized voice systems that contain 30–60 easily accessible messages are convenient. If the individual has insufficient hand or arm control to use these options, he or she may use a headlight pointer to indicate words or letters on a wall or ceiling chart or on a communication board placed on a mounting stand.

Some individuals may be limited to eye pointing in one of two forms. The first form is conventional eye pointing, in which the individual selects and gazes at a message on a display that is mounted on a transparent plastic board. The communication partner then interprets the direction of the individual's eye gaze and reads the related message. The second form, a technique known as "eye linking," may be used. In eye linking, the individual looks at the desired message, and the partner (who is positioned opposite the individual on the other side of the transparent communication board) moves the board until his or her eyes are "linked" directly across from the individual's. At that point, the message that the individual wants to convey lies between the two people. Many individuals find this to be easier than eye pointing.

Options for People Who Cannot Use Direct Selection

Some individuals do not have the motor capability to engage in direct selection communication. If they have other reliable, consistent motor responses, individuals may be able to successfully use a scanning communication option. Many families can learn to use dependent scanning, in which an array of letters or messages is displayed on a communication board. The communication partner points to various message options, and the individual sends a YES signal when a desired message is reached by making a gesture or eye blink or by activating a beeper with a switch. Independent (i.e., electronic) scanning is more difficult to implement in an ICU setting, and, as noted previously, this difficulty may cause a low rate of success with this option (Dowden, Beukelman, & Lossing, 1986). Most individuals generally are unfamiliar with this type of communication, and the learning requirements for scanning may be too great for effective application of this option in an ICU environment.

Assess Constraints

The two most common constraints that affect AAC interventions in the ICU are related to funding and listener instruction. We discuss these briefly in the following sections.

Funding

Individuals encounter different constraints in ICU settings than those experienced by individuals in other environments. For example, although adults generally have a problem procuring AAC funding, this is not usually the case in the ICU. The same sources that are responsible for hospitalization fees usually fund all medical-related services, including AAC services.

Instruction of Listeners

The ICU environment imposes quite extensive learning constraints. First, the individuals are very ill and under a considerable amount of stress. Many individuals in an ICU demonstrate little ability or tolerance for learning. Second, many professionals and others interact with these individuals over the course of their hospital stay. Thus, the most effective AAC interventions are those that require minimal listener training. As noted previously, individuals and their medical teams do not use complicated AAC systems in ICU environments.

References

Adams, M.J. (1990). *Beginning to read: Thinking and learning about print*. Cambridge: The MIT Press.

Adamson, L., & Dunbar, B. (1991). Communication development of young children with tracheostomies. *Augmentative and Alternative Communication, 7*, 275–283.

Alant, E. (1993). *Towards community-based communication intervention for severely handicapped children*. Pretoria, South Africa: Human Sciences Research Council.

Alant, E. (1996). Augmentative and alternative communication in developing countries: Challenge of the future. *Augmentative and Alternative Communication, 12*, 1–12.

Alant, E., & Emmett, T. (1995). *Breaking the silence: Communication and education for children with severe handicaps*. Pretoria, South Africa: Human Sciences Research Council.

Alm, N., & Parnes, P. (1995). Augmentative and alternative communication: Past, present, and future. *Folia Phoniatrica et Logopaedica, 47*, 165–192.

Alwell, M., Hunt, P., Goetz, L., & Sailor, W. (1989). Teaching generalized communicative behaviors within interrupted behavior chain contexts. *Journal of The Association for Persons with Severe Handicaps, 14*, 91–100.

American Psychiatric Association. (1994). *Diagnostic and statistical manual of mental disorders* (4th ed.). Washington, DC: Author.

American Speech-Language-Hearing Association (ASHA). (1989). Competencies for speech-language pathologists providing services in augmentative communication. *Asha, 31*, 107–110.

American Speech-Language-Hearing Association. (1991). Report: Augmentative and alternative communication. *Asha, 33*(Suppl. 5), 9–12.

Americans with Disabilities Act (ADA) of 1990, PL 101-336, 42 U.S.C. §§ 12101 *et seq.*

Anderson, L.M., Evertson, C.M., & Brophy, J.E. (1980). An examination of classroom context: Effects of lesson format and teacher training on patterns of teacher-assisted contacts during small group instruction. *Journal of Classroom Interaction, 15*(2), 21–26.

Anderson, R.C., Hiebert, E.H., Scott, J.A., & Wilkinson, I.A.G. (1985). *Becoming a Nation of Readers: The report of the commission on reading*. Washington, DC: The National Institute of Education.

Angelo, D., Jones, S., & Kokoska, S. (1995). Family perspective on augmentative and alternative communication: Families of young children. *Augmentative and Alternative Communication, 11*, 193–201.

Angelo, D., Kokoska, S., & Jones, S. (1996). Family perspective on augmentative and alternative communication: Families of adolescents and young adults. *Augmentative and Alternative Communication, 12*, 13–22.

Angelo, J. (1987). *A comparison of three coding methods for abbreviation expansion in acceleration vocabularies*. Unpublished doctoral dissertation, University of Wisconsin–Madison.

Anthony, D. (1971). *Seeing Essential English* (Vols. 1–2). Anaheim, CA: Educational Services Division, Anaheim Union School District.

Aram, D., & Nation, J. (1982). *Child language*. St. Louis: Mosby.

Arnason, B.G.W. (1982). Multiple sclerosis: Current concepts and management. *Hospital Practice, 17*, 81–89.

Arwood, E.L. (1983). *Pragmaticism: Theory and application*. Rockville, MD: Aspen Publishers.

Atwell, N. (1987). *In the middle: Writing, reading, and learning with adolescents*. Portsmouth, NH: Boynton/Cook.

Bailey, B., & Downing, J. (1994). Using visual accents to enhance attending to communication symbols for students with severe multiple disabilities. *RE:view, 26*(3), 101–118.

Bailey, D., Buysse, V., Edmondson, R., & Smith, T. (1992). Creating family-centered services in early intervention: Perceptions in four states. *Exceptional Children, 58,* 298–309.

Baker, B. (1982, September). Minspeak: A semantic compaction system that makes self-expression easier for communicatively disabled individuals. *Byte, 7,* 186–202.

Baker, B. (1986). Using images to generate speech. *Byte, 11,* 160–168.

Ball, L., Marvin, C., Beukelman, D., Lasker, J., & Rupp, D. (1997). *"Generic small talk" use by preschool children.* Manuscript submitted for publication, University of Nebraska–Lincoln.

Bambara, L., Spiegel-McGill, P., Shores, R., & Fox, J. (1984). A comparison of reactive and nonreactive toys on severely handicapped children's manipulative play. *Journal of The Association for Persons with Severe Handicaps, 9,* 142–149.

Baron-Cohen, S., Allen, J., & Gillberg, C. (1992). Can autism be detected at 18 months? *British Journal of Psychiatry, 161,* 839–843.

Barraga, N. (1983). *Visual handicaps and learning* (Rev. ed.). Austin, TX: Exceptional Resources.

Barrera, R., Lobato-Barrera, D., & Sulzer-Azaroff, B. (1980). A simultaneous treatment comparison of three expressive language training programs with a mute autistic child. *Journal of Autism and Developmental Disorders, 10,* 21–38.

Barritt, L., & Kroll, B. (1978). Some implications of cognitive developmental psychology for research in composing. In C. Cooper & L. Odell (Eds.), *Research on composing: Points of departure* (pp. 49–57). Urbana, IL: National Council of Teachers of English.

Bashir, A., Grahamjones, F., & Bostwick, R. (1984). A touch-cue method of therapy for developmental verbal apraxia. *Seminars in Speech and Language, 5*(2), 127–128.

Basil, C. (1992). Social interaction and learned helplessness in severely disabled children. *Augmentative and Alternative Communication, 8,* 188–199.

Basil, C., & Soro-Camats, E. (1996). Supporting graphic language acquisition by a girl with multiple impairments. In S. von Tetzchner & M. Jensen (Eds.), *Augmentative and alternative communication: European perspectives* (pp. 270–291). London: Whurr Publishers.

Batshaw, M.L. (1997). *Children with disabilities* (4th ed.). Baltimore: Paul H. Brookes Publishing Co.

Bauby, J.-D. (1997). *The diving bell and the butterfly* (Jeremy Leggatt, Trans.). New York: Alfred A. Knopf.

Bauer, A., & Kaiser, G. (1995, January–February). Drawings on drawings. *Aphasiology, 9*(1), 68–78.

Baumgart, D., Johnson, J., & Helmstetter, E. (1990). *Augmentative and alternative communication systems for persons with moderate and severe disabilities.* Baltimore: Paul H. Brookes Publishing Co.

Bayles, K., Tomoeda, C., Wood, J., Montgomery, E., Cruz, R., Azuma, T., & McGeagh, A. (1996). Changes in cognitive function in idiopathic Parkinson's disease. *Archives of Neurology, 53,* 1140–1146.

Bayles, K.A. (1984). Language and dementia. In A. Holland (Ed.), *Language disorders in adults* (pp. 209–244). San Diego: College-Hill Press.

Beattie, W., Booth, L., Newell, A., & Arnott, J. (1990). The role of predictive computer programs in special education. *Augmentative and Alternative Communication, 6,* 89–90.

Beck, A., & Dennis, M. (1996). Attitudes of children toward a similar-aged child who uses augmentative communication. *Augmentative and Alternative Communication, 12,* 78–87.

Beckman, P., & Kohl, F. (1984). The effects of social and isolated toys on the interactions and play of integrated and nonintegrated groups of preschoolers. *Education and Training of the Mentally Retarded, 19,* 169–174.

Bedrosian, J. (1997). Language acquisition in young AAC system users: Issues and directions for future research. *Augmentative and Alternative Communication, 13,* 179–185.

Bedrosian, J., Hoag, L., Calculator, S., & Molineux, B. (1992). Variables influencing perceptions of the communicative competence of an adult augmentative and alternative communication system user. *Journal of Speech and Hearing Research, 35,* 1105–1113.

Bellugi, U., & Fischer, S. (1972). A comparison of sign language and spoken language. *Cognition, 1,* 173–200.

Berlin, C., & Hood, L. (1987). Auditory brainstem response and middle ear assessment in children. In F. Martin (Ed.), *Hearing disorders in children* (pp. 151–167). Austin, TX: PRO-ED.

Berlowitz, C. (1991, January 13). Ana begins to speak. *This World,* 16.

Berninger, V., & Gans, B. (1986a). Assessing word processing capability of the nonvocal, nonwriting. *Augmentative and Alternative Communication, 2,* 56–63.

Berninger, V., & Gans, B. (1986b). Language profiles in nonspeaking individuals of normal intelligence with severe cerebral palsy. *Augmentative and Alternative Communication, 2,* 45–50.

Bernthal, J., & Bankson, N. (1988). *Articulation and phonological disorders* (2nd ed.). Upper Saddle River, NJ: Prentice Hall.

Berry, J. (1987). Strategies for involving parents in programs for young children using augmentative and alternative communication. *Augmentative and Alternative Communication, 3*, 90–93.

Besio, S., & Chinato, M. (1996). A semiotic analysis of the possibilities and limitations of Blissymbols. In S. von Tetzchner & M. Jensen (Eds.), *Augmentative and alternative communication: European perspectives* (pp. 182–194). London: Whurr Publishers.

Beukelman, D. (1987). When you have a hammer, everything looks like a nail. *Augmentative and Alternative Communication, 3*, 94–95.

Beukelman, D. (1990). AAC in the 1990s: A clinical perspective. In *Proceedings of the Visions Conference: Augmentative and alternative communication in the next decade* (pp. 109–113). Wilmington, DE: Alfred I. DuPont Institute.

Beukelman, D. (1991). Magic and cost of communicative competence. *Augmentative and Alternative Communication, 7*, 2–10.

Beukelman, D., & Ansel, B. (1995). Research priorities in augmentative and alternative communication. *Augmentative and Alternative Communication, 11*, 131–134.

Beukelman, D., & Garrett, K. (1986). Personnel preparation in augmentative communication. *Nebraska Speech, Language, and Hearing Journal, 24*, 5–8.

Beukelman, D., & Garrett, K. (1988). Augmentative and alternative communication for adults with acquired severe communication disorders. *Augmentative and Alternative Communication, 4*, 104–121.

Beukelman, D., Jones, R., & Rowan, M. (1989). Frequency of word usage by nondisabled peers in integrated preschool classrooms. *Augmentative and Alternative Communication, 5*, 243–248.

Beukelman, D., Kraft, G., & Freal, J. (1985). Expressive communication disorders in persons with multiple sclerosis: A survey. *Archives of Physical Medicine and Rehabilitation, 66*, 675–677.

Beukelman, D., & Lasker, J. (1998). Augmentative and alternative communication for persons with neurologic impairment. In R.B. Lazar (Ed.), *Principles of neurologic rehabilitation* (pp. 483–489). New York: McGraw-Hill.

Beukelman, D., & Mirenda, P. (1988). Communication options for persons who cannot speak: Assessment and evaluation. In C.A. Coston (Ed.), *Proceedings of the National Planners Conference on Assistive Device Service Delivery* (pp. 151–165). Washington, DC: Association for the Advancement of Rehabilitation Technology.

Beukelman, D., & Yorkston, K. (1977). A communication system for the severely dysarthric speaker with an intact language system. *Journal of Speech and Hearing Disorders, 42*, 265–270.

Beukelman, D., & Yorkston, K. (1978). A series of communication options for individuals with brain stem lesions. *Archives of Physical Medicine and Rehabilitation, 59*, 337–342.

Beukelman, D., & Yorkston, K. (1979). The relationship between information transfer and speech intelligibility of dysarthric speakers. *Journal of Communication Disorders, 12*, 189–196.

Beukelman, D., & Yorkston, K. (1984). Computer enhancement of message formulation and presentation for communication augmentation system users. *Seminars in Speech and Language, 5*, 1–10.

Beukelman, D., & Yorkston, K. (1989). Augmentative and alternative communication application for persons with severe acquired communication disorders: An introduction. *Augmentative and Alternative Communication, 5*, 42–48.

Beukelman, D., & Yorkston, K. (1991). Traumatic brain injury changes the way we live. In D. Beukelman & K. Yorkston (Eds.), *Communication disorders following traumatic brain injury: Management of cognitive, language, and motor impairments* (pp. 1–14). Austin, TX: PRO-ED.

Beukelman, D., Yorkston, K., & Dowden, P. (1985). *Communication augmentation: A casebook of clinical management.* Austin, TX: PRO-ED.

Beukelman, D., Yorkston, K., Poblete, M., & Naranjo, C. (1984). Frequency of word occurrence in communication samples produced by adult communication aid users. *Journal of Speech and Hearing Disorders, 49*, 360–367.

Beukelman, D., Yorkston, K., & Smith, K. (1985). Third-party payer response to requests for purchase of communication augmentation systems: A study of Washington state. *Augmentative and Alternative Communication, 1*, 5–9.

Bigge, J. (1991). *Teaching individuals with physical and multiple disabilities* (3rd ed.). Columbus, OH: Charles E. Merrill.

Biklen, D. (1990). Communication unbound: Autism and praxis. *Harvard Educational Review, 60*, 291–314.

Biklen, D. (1992). *Schooling without labels*. Philadelphia: Temple University Press.

Biklen, D. (1993). *Communication unbound*. New York: Teachers College Press.

Biklen, D. (1996). No time for silence. *TASH Newsletter, 22*(12), 20–23.

Biklen, D., & Cardinal, D. (1997). *Contested words, contested science: Unraveling the facilitated communication controversy*. New York: Teachers College Press.

Bird, F., Dores, P., Moniz, D., & Robinson, J. (1989). Reducing severe aggressive and self-injurious behaviors with functional communication training. *American Journal on Mental Retardation, 94,* 37–48.

Bishop, D.V.M., Byers Brown, B., & Robson, J. (1990). The relationship between phoneme discrimination, speech production, and language comprehension in cerebral-palsied individuals. *Journal of Speech and Hearing Research, 33,* 210–219.

Bishop, D.V.M., & Robson, J. (1989a). Accurate non-word spelling despite congenital inability to speak: Phoneme-grapheme conversion does not require subvocal articulation. *British Journal of Psychology, 80,* 1–13.

Bishop, D.V.M., & Robson, J. (1989b). Unimpaired short-term memory and rhyme judgment in congenitally speechless individuals: Implications for the notion of "articulatory coding." *Quarterly Journal of Experimental Psychology, 40A,* 123–140.

Bishop, K., Rankin, J., & Mirenda, P. (1994). Impact of graphic symbol use on reading acquisition. *Augmentative and Alternative Communication, 10,* 113–125.

Blackburn, D., Bonvillian, J., & Ashby, R. (1984). Manual communication as an alternative mode of language instruction for children with severe reading disabilities. *Language, Speech, and Hearing Services in Schools, 15,* 22–31.

Blackman, J. (1983). *Medical aspects of developmental disabilities in children from birth to three*. Iowa City: University of Iowa Press.

Blackstone, S. (1988a). Auditory scanning (AS) techniques. *Augmentative Communication News, 1*(5), 4–5, 8.

Blackstone, S. (1988b). Light pointing: Abandoned too soon? *Augmentative Communication News, 1*(2), 1–7.

Blackstone, S. (1989a). For consumers: Societal rehabilitation. *Augmentative Communication News, 2*(3), 1–3.

Blackstone, S. (1989b). Individuals with developmental apraxia of speech (DAS). *Augmentative Communication News, 2*(2), 1–4, 6.

Blackstone, S. (1989c). M & Ms: Meaningful, manageable measurement. *Augmentative Communication News, 2*(3), 3–5.

Blackstone, S. (1989d). The 3 R's: Reading, writing, and reasoning. *Augmentative Communication News, 2*(1), 1–6, 8.

Blackstone, S. (1989e). Visual scanning: What's it all about? and training approaches. *Augmentative Communication News, 2*(4), 1–5.

Blackstone, S. (1990). Populations and practices in AAC. *Augmentative Communication News, 3*(4), 1–3.

Blackstone, S. (1991). Telecommunication technologies. *Augmentative Communication News, 4*(4), 3–8.

Blackstone, S. (1993). Cultural sensitivity and AAC services. *Augmentative Communication News, 6*(2), 3–5.

Blackstone, S. (1994a). Auditory scanning. *Augmentative Communication News, 7*(2), 6–7.

Blackstone, S. (1994b). Equipment loan programs: A rationale. *Augmentative Communication News, 7*(1), 4.

Blackstone, S. (1997). Time study and caseload allocation: Three examples. *Augmentative Communication News, 9*(5), 1–8.

Blackstone, S., & Pressman, H. (1995). *Outcomes in AAC conference report: Alliance '95*. Monterey, CA: Augmentative Communication.

Blackstone, S.W., Cassatt-James, E.L., & Bruskin, D. (Eds.). (1988). *Augmentative communication: Implementation strategies*. Rockville, MD: American Speech-Language-Hearing Association.

Blackstone, S.W., & Painter, M.J. (1985). Speech problems in multihandicapped children. In J.K. Darby (Ed.), *Speech and language evaluation in neurology: Childhood disorders* (pp. 219–242). New York: Grune & Stratton.

Blischak, D. (1994). Phonologic awareness: Implications for individuals with little or no functional speech. *Augmentative and Alternative Communication, 10,* 245–254.

Bliss, C. (1965). *Semantography*. Sydney, Australia: Semantography Publications.

Blissymbolics Communication International. (1984). *Picture your Blissymbols*. Toronto, Ontario, Canada: Author.

Blockberger, S. (1995). AAC intervention and early conceptual and lexical development. *Journal of Speech-Language Pathology & Audiology, 19,* 221–232.

Blockberger, S. (1996, November). *The acquisition of grammatical morphology in children with severe speech impairments.* Paper presented at the annual convention of the American Speech-Language-Hearing Association, Seattle.

Blockberger, S. (1997). *The acquisition of grammatical morphology by children who are unable to speak.* Unpublished doctoral dissertation, University of British Columbia, Vancouver, Canada.

Blockberger, S., Armstrong, R., O'Connor, A., & Freeman, R. (1990, August). *Children's attitudes toward a nonspeaking child using various augmentative and alternative communication techniques.* Paper presented at the fourth conference of the International Society for Augmentative and Alternative Communication (ISAAC), Stockholm.

Blockberger, S., & Johnston, J. (1997, May). *Children who are unable to speak versus typical children: A comparison of acquisition of grammatical morphology.* Paper presented at the Symposium on Research in Child Language Disorders, Madison, WI.

Blockberger, S., & Kamp, L. (1990). The use of voice output communication aids (VOCAs) by ambulatory children. *Augmentative and Alternative Communication, 6,* 127–128.

Bloom, L., & Lahey, M. (1978). *Language development and language disorders.* New York: John Wiley & Sons.

Bloomberg, K. (1990). Computer pictographs for communication. *Communication Outlook, 12*(1), 17–18.

Bloomberg, K., & Johnson, H. (1990). A statewide demographic survey of people with severe communication impairments. *Augmentative and Alternative Communication, 6,* 50–60.

Bloomberg, K., Karlan, G., & Lloyd, L. (1990). The comparative translucency of initial lexical items represented by five graphic symbol systems and sets. *Journal of Speech and Hearing Research, 33,* 717–725.

Boden, D., & Bielby, D. (1983). The way it was: Topical organization in elderly conversation. *Language and Communication, 6*(1/2), 73–79.

Boehm, A. (1986). *Boehm Test of Basic Concepts–Revised* (Boehm–R). San Antonio, TX: The Psychological Corporation.

Bogdan, R., & Taylor, S. (1994). *The social meaning of mental retardation: Two life stories.* New York: Teachers College Press.

Bolton, S., & Dashiell, S. (1984). *INCH: Interaction Checklist for Augmentative Communication.* Wauconda, IL: Don Johnston, Inc.

Bondy, A., & Frost, L. (1995). Educational approaches in preschool: Behavior techniques in a public school setting. In E. Schopler & G. Mesibov (Eds.), *Learning and cognition in autism* (pp. 311–333). New York: Plenum.

Bonvillian, J., & Friedman, R. (1978). Language development in another mode: The acquisition of signs by a brain-damaged adult. *Sign Language Studies, 19,* 111–120.

Bonvillian, J., & Nelson, K. (1978). Development of sign language in autistic children and other language-handicapped individuals. In P. Siple (Ed.), *Understanding language through sign language research* (pp. 187–209). New York: Academic Press.

Boardmaker [Computer software]. (1995). Solana Beach, CA: Mayer-Johnson Co.

Borden, P., Lubich, J., & Vanderheiden, G. (1995). *Trace Resourcebook: Assistive technologies for communication, control, and computer access (1996–97 Edition).* Madison, WI: Trace Research and Development Center.

Bornstein, H. (1990). Signed English. In H. Bornstein (Ed.), *Manual communication: Implications for education* (pp. 128–138). Washington, DC: Gallaudet University Press.

Bornstein, H., Saulnier, L., & Hamilton, L. (1983). *The comprehensive Signed English dictionary.* Washington, DC: Gallaudet University Press.

Boubekker, M., Foulds, R., & Norman, C. (1986). Human quality synthetic speech based upon concatenated diphones. In *Proceedings of the ninth annual conference of RESNA* (pp. 405–407). Washington, DC: The Association for the Advancement of Rehabilitation Technology.

Bourgeois, M.S. (1991). Communication treatment for adults with dementia. *Journal of Speech and Hearing Research, 34,* 831–844.

Bourgeois, M.S. (1992). Evaluating memory wallets in conversation with persons with dementia. *Journal of Speech and Hearing Research, 35*(6), 1344–1357.

Bracken, B. (1984). *Bracken Basic Concept Scale (BBCS).* San Antonio, TX: The Psychological Corporation.

Brady, D., & Smouse, A. (1978). A simultaneous comparison of three methods for language training with an autistic child: An experimental single case analysis. *Journal of Autism and Childhood Schizophrenia, 8,* 271–279.

Brahne, C., & Hall, V. (1995). One life to live. *Communication Outlook, 17*(1), 9–10.

Brandenberg, S., & Vanderheiden, G. (1988). Communication board design and vocabulary selection. In L. Bernstein (Ed.), *The vocally impaired: Clinical practice and research* (3rd ed., pp. 84–135). Needham Heights, MA: Allyn & Bacon.

Braun, U., & Stuckenschneider-Braun, M. (1990). Adapting "Words Strategy" to the German culture and language. *Augmentative and Alternative Communication, 6,* 115.

Brett, E.M. (1983). The blind retarded child. In K. Wybar & D. Taylor (Eds.), *Pediatric ophthalmology: Current aspects* (pp. 113–122). New York: Marcel Dekker.

Bricker, D. (1993). Then, now, and the path between: A brief history of language intervention. In A.P. Kaiser & D.B. Gray (Eds.), *Communication and language intervention series: Vol. 2. Enhancing children's communication: Research foundations for intervention* (pp. 11–31). Baltimore: Paul H. Brookes Publishing Co.

Bridges Freeman, S. (1990). *Children's attitudes toward synthesized speech varying in quality.* Unpublished doctoral dissertation, Michigan State University, East Lansing.

Brigance, A.H. (1981). *BRIGANCE® Comprehensive Inventory of Basic Skills.* North Billerica, MA: Curriculum Associates.

Bristow, D., & Fristoe, M. (1984). *Systematic evaluation of the nonspeaking child.* Miniseminar presented at the annual convention of the American Speech-Language-Hearing Association, San Francisco.

Bristow, D., & Fristoe, M. (1987). *Effects of test adaptations on test performance.* Paper presented at the annual convention of the American Speech-Language-Hearing Association, New Orleans.

Bristow, D., & Fristoe, M. (1988). Effects of test adaptations on test performance. *Augmentative and Alternative Communication, 4,* 171.

Brodin, J. (1991). *To interpret children's signals: Play and communication in profoundly mentally retarded and multiply handicapped children.* Unpublished doctoral dissertation, University of Stockholm, Sweden.

Brophy-Arnott, M., & Campbell-Sutherland, C. (1992). Social communication: Using a computer-based AAC system. *Communicating Together, 14*(2), 7–11.

Bross, R. (1992). An application of structural linguistics to intelligibility measurement of impaired speakers of English. In R. Kent (Ed.), *Speech intelligibility in speech disorders: Theory, measurement, and management* (pp. 35–65). Amsterdam: John Benjamins.

Brothers, S. (1991). Let's talk! *Asha, 33,* 59–60.

Brown, C. (1954). *My left foot.* London: Secker & Warburg.

Brown, F. (1991). Creative daily scheduling: A nonintrusive approach to challenging behaviors in community residences. *Journal of The Association for Persons with Severe Handicaps, 16,* 75–84.

Brown, L., Long, E., Udvari-Solner, A., Davis, L., VanDeventer, P., Ahlgren, C., Johnson, F., Gruenewald, L., & Jorgensen, J. (1989). The home school: Why students with severe intellectual disabilities must attend the schools of their brothers, sisters, friends, and neighbors. *Journal of The Association for Persons with Severe Handicaps, 14,* 1–7.

Brown, L., Sherbenou, R.J., & Johnsen, S.K. (1990). *Test of Nonverbal Intelligence (TONI-2): A Language-Free Measure of Cognitive Ability* (2nd ed.). Circle Pines, MN: American Guidance Service.

Brown, R. (1977, May–June). *Why are signed languages easier to learn than spoken languages?* Keynote address at the National Association of the Deaf Symposium on Sign Language Research and Teaching, Chicago.

Bruno, J. (1989). Customizing a Minspeak system for a preliterate child: A case example. *Augmentative and Alternative Communication, 5,* 89–100.

Bryen, D., Goldman, A., & Quinlisk-Gill, S. (1988). Sign language with students with severe/profound mental retardation: How effective is it? *Education and Training in Mental Retardation, 23,* 129–137.

Bryen, D., & Joyce, D. (1985). Language intervention with the severely handicapped: A decade of research. *Journal of Special Education, 19,* 7–39.

Bryen, D., & McGinley, V. (1991). Sign language input to community residents with mental retardation. *Education and Training in Mental Retardation, 26,* 207–213.

Bryen, D.N., Slesaransky, G., & Baker, D.B. (1995). Augmentative communication and empowerment supports: A look at outcomes. *Augmentative and Alternative Communication, 11,* 79–88.

Buck, J., & Cooper, I. (1956). Speech problems in Parkinsonian patients undergoing anterior choroidal artery occlusion or chemopallidectomy. *Journal of the American Geriatric Society, 4,* 1285–1290.

Burgemeister, B. (1973). *Columbia Mental Maturity Scale, Levels A–H* (3rd ed.). San Antonio, TX: The Pscyhological Corporation.

Burkhart, L. (1980). *Homemade battery powered toys and educational devices for severely handicapped children.* (Available by writing L. Burkhart, 8503 Rhode Island Avenue, College Park, MD 20740.)

Burkhart, L. (1982). *More homemade battery devices for severely handicapped children with suggested activities.* (Available by writing L. Burkhart, 8503 Rhode Island Avenue, College Park, MD 20740.)

Burkhart, L. (1993). *Total augmentative communication in the early childhood classroom.* Solana Beach, CA: Mayer-Johnson Co.

Burkhart, L. (1994, October). *Organizing vocabulary on dynamic display devices: Practical ideas and strategies.* Paper presented at the sixth biennial conference of the International Society for Augmentative and Alternative Communication, Maastricht, the Netherlands.

Burkhart, L.J. (1988). *Using computers and speech synthesis to facilitate communicative interaction with young and/or severely handicapped children.* Wauconda, IL: Don Johnston, Inc.

Burroughs, J., Albritton, E., Eaton, B., & Montague, J. (1990). A comparative study of language delayed preschool children's ability to recall symbols from two symbol systems. *Augmentative and Alternative Communication, 6,* 202–206.

Buzolich, M., King, J., & Baroody, S. (1991). Acquisition of the commenting function among system users. *Augmentative and Alternative Communication, 7,* 88–99.

Buzolich, M., & Lunger, J. (1995). Empowering system users in peer training. *Augmentative and Alternative Communication, 11,* 37–48.

Calculator, S. (1988a). Evaluating the effectiveness of AAC programs for persons with severe handicaps. *Augmentative and Alternative Communication, 4,* 177–179.

Calculator, S. (1988b). Promoting the acquisition and generalization of conversational skills by individuals with severe handicaps. *Augmentative and Alternative Communication, 4,* 94–103.

Calculator, S. (1997). AAC and individuals with severe to profound disabilities. In S.L. Glennen & D. DeCoste (Eds.), *Handbook of augmentative and alternative conmmunication* (pp. 445–471). San Diego: Singular Publishing Group.

Calculator, S., & Bedrosian, J. (1988). *Communication assessment and intervention for adults with mental retardation.* San Diego: College-Hill Press.

Calculator, S., & Jorgensen, C. (1991). Integrating AAC instruction into regular education settings: Expounding on best practices. *Augmentative and Alternative Communication, 7,* 204–214.

Calculator, S., & Jorgensen, C. (1994). *Including students with severe disabilities in schools: Fostering communication, interaction, and participation.* San Diego: Singular Publishing Group.

Calculator, S., & Luchko, C. (1983). Evaluating the effectiveness of a communication board training program. *Journal of Speech and Hearing Disorders, 48,* 185–191.

Calkins, L.M. (1994). *The art of teaching writing* (2nd ed.). Portsmouth, NH: Heinemann.

Campbell, P.H. (1989). Dysfunction in posture and movement in individuals with profound disabilities: Issues and practices. In F. Brown & D.H. Lehr (Eds.), *Persons with profound disabilities: Issues and practices* (pp. 163–189). Baltimore: Paul H. Brookes Publishing Co.

Campbell, R., & Lutzker, J. (1993). Using functional equivalence training to reduce severe challenging behavior: A case study. *Journal of Developmental and Physical Disabilities, 5,* 203–216.

Canfield, H., & Locke, P. (1997). *A book of possibilities: Activities using simple technology.* Minneapolis, MN: AbleNet.

Cardinal, D., Hanson, D., & Wakeham, J. (1996). An investigation of authorship in facilitated communication. *Mental Retardation, 34,* 231–242.

Carey, S. (1978). The child as word learner. In M. Halle, J. Bresnan, & G. Miller (Eds.), *Linguistic theory and psychological reality* (pp. 264–293). Cambridge: The MIT Press.

Carey, S., & Bartlett, E. (1978). Acquiring a single new word. *Papers and Reports on Child Language Development, 15,* 17–29.

Carlsen, K., Hux, K., & Beukelman, D. (1994). Comprehension of synthetic speech by individuals with aphasia. *Journal of Medical Speech-Language Pathology, 2,* 105–111.

Carlson, F. (1981). A format for selecting vocabulary for the nonspeaking child. *Language, Speech, and Hearing Services in Schools, 12,* 140–145.

Carlson, F. (1985). *Picsyms categorical dictionary.* Lawrence, KS: Baggeboda Press.

Carlson, F., Hough, S., Lippert, E., & Young, C. (1988). Facilitating interaction during mealtime. In S. Blackstone, E. Cassatt-James, & D. Bruskin (Eds.), *Augmentative communication: Implementation strategies* (pp. 5.8-10–5.8-20). Rockville, MD: American Speech-Language-Hearing Association.

Carr, E. (1982). Sign language. In R. Koegel, A. Rincover, & A. Egel (Eds.), *Educating and understanding autistic children* (pp. 142–157). San Diego: College-Hill Press.

Carr, E., Binkoff, J., Kologinsky, E., & Eddy, M. (1978). Acquisition of sign language by autistic children: I. Expressive labeling. *Journal of Applied Behavior Analysis, 11,* 459–501.

Carr, E., & Dores, P. (1981). Patterns of language acquisition following simultaneous communication with autistic children. *Analysis and Intervention in Developmental Disabilities, 1,* 1–15.

Carr, E., & Kologinsky, E. (1983). Acquisition of sign language by autistic children: II. Spontaneity and generalization. *Journal of Applied Behavior Analysis, 16,* 297–314.

Carr, E., Pridal, C., & Dores, P. (1984). Speech versus sign comprehension in autistic children: Analysis and prediction. *Journal of Experimental Child Psychology, 37,* 587–597.

Carr, E., Robinson, S., & Palumbo, L. (1990). The wrong issue: Aversive versus nonaversive treatment; The right issue: Functional versus nonfunctional treatment. In A. Repp & N. Singh (Eds.), *Perspectives on the use of nonaversive and aversive interventions for persons with developmental disabilities* (pp. 361–380). Sycamore, IL: Sycamore Publishing.

Carr, E.G., Levin, L., McConnachie, G., Carlson, J.I., Kemp, D.C., & Smith, C.E. (1994). *Communication-based intervention for problem behavior: A user's guide for producing positive change.* Baltimore: Paul H. Brookes Publishing Co.

Carrow-Woolfolk, E. (1985). *Test for Auditory Comprehension of Language–Revised (TACL–R).* San Antonio, TX: The Psychological Corporation.

Carter, M., Hotchkis, G., & Cassar, M. (1996). Spontaneity of augmentative and alternative communication in persons with intellectual disabilities: A critical review. *Augmentative and Alternative Communication, 12,* 97–109.

Casey, L. (1978). Development of communicative behavior in autistic children: A parent program using manual signs. *Journal of Autism and Childhood Schizophrenia, 8,* 45–59.

Census Bureau. (1996). *Disability status of persons (SIPP).* Washington, DC: U.S. Government Printing Office.

Chadsey, C., & Wentworth, H. (1974). *The Grosset Webster Dictionary.* New York: Grosset & Dunlap.

Chadsey-Rusch, J., Drasgow, E., Reinoehl, B., Halle, J., & Collet-Klingenberg, L. (1993). Using general-case instruction to teach spontaneous and generalized requests for assistance to learners with severe disabilities. *Journal of The Association for Persons with Severe Handicaps, 18,* 177–187.

Chadsey-Rusch, J., & Halle, J. (1992). The application of general-case instruction to the requesting repertoires of learners with severe disabilities. *Journal of The Association for Persons with Severe Handicaps, 17,* 121–132.

Chaney, C. (1990). Evaluating the whole language approach to language arts: The pros and cons. *Language, Speech, and Hearing Services in Schools, 21,* 244–249.

Chapman, R., Kay-Raining Bird, E., & Schwartz, S. (1990). Fast mapping in event contexts by children with Down syndrome. *Journal of Speech and Hearing Disorders, 55,* 761–770.

Clark, C., Davies, C., & Woodcock, R. (1974). *Standard rebus glossary.* Circle Pines, MN: American Guidance Service.

Clark, J., & Pellerin, N. (1996). The life of Justin Clark. *Communicating Together, 13*(1), 7–8.

Clark, L.W., & Witte, K. (1995). Nature and efficacy of communication management in Alzheimer's disease. In R. Lubinsky (Ed.), *Dementia and communication* (pp. 238–256). San Diego: Singular Publishing Group.

Clay, M. (1991). *Becoming literate: The construction of inner control.* Portsmouth, NH: Heinemann

Cline, D., Hofstetter, H., & Griffin, J. (1980). *Dictionary of visual science* (3rd ed.). Radnor, PA: Chilton Book Co.

Cohen, C., & Palin, M. (1986). Speech syntheses and speech recognition devices. In M. Grossfeld & C. Grossfeld (Eds.), *Microcomputer applications in rehabilitation of communication disorders* (pp. 183–211). Rockville, MD: Aspen Publishers.

Cohen, D.J., & Donnellan, A.M. (Eds.). (1987). *Handbook of autism and pervasive developmental disorders.* New York: John Wiley & Sons.

Coleman, C., Cook, A., & Meyers, L. (1980). Assessing the non-oral client for assistive communication devices. *Journal of Speech and Hearing Disorders, 45,* 515–526.

Coleman, C., & Meyers, L. (1991). Computer recognition of the speech of adults with cerebral palsy and dysarthria. *Augmentative and Alternative Communication, 7,* 34–43.

Collier, B. (1997). *See what we say: Vocabulary and tips for adults who use augmentative and alternative communication.* North York, Ontario, Canada: William Bobek Productions.

Conn-Powers, M., Ross-Allen, J., & Holburn, S. (1990). Transition of young children into the elementary education mainstream. *Topics in Early Childhood Special Education, 9*(4), 91–105.

Cook, A. (1994). Guest editorial: The more things change. *Canadian Journal of Rehabilitation, 8,* 73–78.

Cook, A.M., & Hussey, S.M. (1995). *Assistive technologies: Principles and practice.* St. Louis: Mosby.

Costello, J., & Shane, H. (1994, November). *Augmentative communication assessment and the feature matching process.* Miniseminar presented at the annual convention of the American Speech-Language-Hearing Association, New Orleans.

Crabtree, M., Mirenda, P., & Beukelman, D. (1990). Age and gender preferences for synthetic and natural speech. *Augmentative and Alternative Communication, 6,* 256–261.

Crais, E. (1992). Fast mapping: A new look at word learning. In R. Chapman (Ed.), *Processes in language acquisition and disorders* (pp. 159–185). St. Louis: Mosby.

Crary, M. (1987). *A neurolinguistic model of articulatory/phonological disorders.* Paper presented at the Boy's Town Institute Communication Series, Omaha, NE.

Creech, R. (1981). Attitude as a misfortune. *Asha, 23,* 550–551.

Creech, R. (1993). A "first" for AAC users. *Communicating Together, 11*(3), 3–5.

Creech, R., Kissick, L., Koski, M., & Musselwhite, C. (1988). Paravocal communicators speak out: Strategies for encouraging communication aid use. *Augmentative and Alternative Communication, 4,* 168.

Creedon, M. (1973). *Language development in nonverbal autistic children using a simultaneous communication system.* Paper presented at the meeting of the Society for Research in Child Development, Philadelphia.

Cregan, A. (1989a). *Sigsymbol dictionary.* (Available by writing A. Cregan, The End House, 76 Wood Close, Hatfield, Herts, AL10 8TX, England.)

Cregan, A., (1989b). *Sigsymbolit.* (Translated by S. Häkkinen). Helsinki, Finland: Samfundet Folkhälsan.

Cregan, A. (1993). Sigsymbol system in a multimodal approach to speech elicitation: Classroom project involving an adolescent with severe mental retardation. *Augmentative and Alternative Communication, 9,* 146–160.

Cregan, A., & Lloyd, L. (1990). *Sigsymbols (American edition).* Wauconda, IL: Don Johnston, Inc.

Cress, P. (1987). Visual assessment. In M. Bullis (Ed.), *Communication development in young children with deaf-blindness: Literature review* (pp. 33–44). Monmouth, OR: Teaching Research.

Cress, P., Spellman, C., DeBriere, T., Sizemore, A., Northam, J., & Johnson, J. (1981). Vision screening for persons with severe handicaps. *Journal of The Association for Persons with Severe Handicaps, 6*(3), 41–50.

Crossley, R. (1988). *Unexpected communication attainment by persons diagnosed as autistic and intellectually impaired.* Paper presented at the third biennial conference of the International Society for Augmentative and Alternative Communication, Anaheim, CA.

Crossley, R. (1990, September). *Communication training involving facilitated communication.* Paper presented to the Australian Association of Special Education, Canberra, Australia.

Crossley, R. (1991). Communication training involving facilitated communication. *Communicating Together, 9*(2), 19–22.

Crossley, R., & McDonald, A. (1984). *Annie's coming out.* New York: Viking Penguin.

Crystal, D. (1987). Teaching vocabulary: The case for a semantic curriculum. *Child Language Teaching and Therapy, 3,* 40–56.

Cubelli, R. (1995). More on drawing in aphasia therapy. *Aphasiology, 9,* 78–83.

Culp, D. (1987). Outcome measurement: The impact of communication augmentation. *Seminars in Speech and Language, 8,* 169–181.

Culp, D. (1989). Developmental apraxia and augmentative or alternative communication: A case example. *Augmentative and Alternative Communication, 5,* 27–34.

Culp, D., & Carlisle, M. (1988). *PACT: Partners in augmentative communication training.* Tucson, AZ: Communication Skill Builders.

Culp, D., & Effinger, J. (1996). *ChalkTalk: Augmentative communication in the classroom.* Anchorage: The Assistive Technology Library of Alaska.

Culp, D., & Ladtkow, M. (1992). Locked-in syndrome and augmentative communication. In K. Yorkston (Ed.), *Augmentative communication in the medical setting* (pp. 59–138). San Antonio, TX: The Psychological Corporation.

Cumley, G. (1991). *AAC facilitator roles and responsibilities.* Unpublished manuscript, University of Nebraska–Lincoln.

Cumley, G. (1997). *Introduction of augmentative and alternative modality: Effects on the quality and quantity of communication interactions of children with severe phonological disorders.* Unpublished doctoral dissertation, University of Nebraska–Lincoln.

Cumley, G., & Swanson, S. (1997). *Case studies: Augmentative and alternative communication options for children with developmental apraxia of speech.* Manuscript submitted for publication.

Cunningham, P.M. (1995). *Phonics they use: Words for reading and writing* (2nd ed.). New York: HarperCollins.

Curcio, F. (1978). Sensorimotor functioning and communication in mute autistic children. *Journal of Autism and Childhood Schizophrenia, 8,* 181–189.

Dahlberg, C., & Jaffe, J. (1977). *Stroke: A doctor's personal story of his recovery.* New York: W.W. Norton.

Dahle, A., & Goldman, R. (1990, November). *Perception of synthetic speech by normal and developmentally disabled children.* Paper presented at the annual convention of the American Speech-Language-Hearing Association, Seattle.

Dahlgren Sandberg, A., & Hjelmquist, E. (1996). Phonologic awareness and literacy abilities in nonspeaking preschool children with cerebral palsy. *Augmentative and Alternative Communication, 12,* 138–154.

Daniloff, J., Lloyd, L., & Fristoe, M. (1983). Amer-Ind transparency. *Journal of Speech and Hearing Disorders, 48,* 103–110.

Daniloff, J., Noll, J., Fristoe, M., & Lloyd, L. (1982). Gesture recognition in patients with aphasia. *Journal of Speech and Hearing Disorders, 47,* 43–56.

Daniloff, J., & Shafer, A. (1981). A gestural communication program for severely-profoundly handicapped children. *Language, Speech, and Hearing Services in Schools, 12,* 258–268.

Daniloff, J., & Vergara, D. (1984). Comparison between the motoric constraints for Amer-Ind and ASL sign formation. *Journal of Speech and Hearing Research, 27,* 76–88.

Darley, F., Aronson, A., & Brown, J. (1969a). Cluster of deviant speech dimensions in the dysarthrias. *Journal of Speech and Hearing Research, 12,* 462–496.

Darley, F., Aronson, A., & Brown, J. (1969b). Differential diagnostic patterns of dysarthria. *Journal of Speech and Hearing Research, 12,* 246–269.

Darley, F., Aronson, A., & Brown, J. (1975). *Motor speech disorders.* Philadelphia: W.B. Saunders.

Darley, F., Brown, J., & Goldstein, N. (1972). Dysarthria in multiple sclerosis. *Journal of Speech and Hearing Research, 15,* 229–245.

Dattilo, J., & Camarata, S. (1991). Facilitating conversation through self-initiated augmentative communication treatment. *Journal of Applied Behavior Analysis, 24,* 369–378.

Dawson, G., & Osterling, J. (1997). Early intervention in autism. In M.J. Guralnick (Ed.), *The effectiveness of early intervention* (pp. 307–326). Baltimore: Paul H. Brookes Publishing Co.

Day, H.M., Horner, R., & O'Neill, R. (1994). Multiple functions of problem behaviors: Assessment and intervention. *Journal of Applied Behavior Analysis, 27,* 279–290.

DeCoste, D.C. (1997a). Augmentative and alternative communication assessment strategies: Motor access and visual considerations. In S.L. Glennen & D.C. DeCoste (Eds.), *The handbook of augmentative and alternative communication* (pp. 243–282). San Diego: Singular Publishing Group.

DeCoste, D.C. (1997b). The role of literacy in augmentative and alternative communication. In S.L. Glennen & D.C. DeCoste (Eds.), *The handbook of augmentative and alternative communication* (pp. 283–333). San Diego: Singular Publishing Group.

Deegan, S. (1993, June). Minspeak: A powerful encoding technique. *Communicating Together, 11*(2), 22–23.

Delsandro, E. (1997). AAC for adults with developmental disabilities. In S.L. Glennen & D. DeCoste (Eds.), *Handbook of augmentative and alternative communication* (pp. 637-673). San Diego: Singular Publishing Group.

Dennis, R., Reichle, J., Williams, W., & Vogelsberg, R.T. (1982). Motoric factors influencing the selection of vocabulary for sign production programs. *Journal of The Association for Persons with Severe Handicaps, 7*(1), 20–32.

DeRuyter, F. (1992). The importance of outcomes and cost benefit analysis in AAC. *Consensus Validation Conference: Resource Papers.* Washington, DC: The National Institute on Disability and Rehabilitation Research.

DeRuyter, F. (1995). Only the lead dog sees the scenery? In S. Blackstone & H. Pressman (Eds.), *Outcomes in AAC conference report: Alliance '95* (pp. 13–14). Monterey, CA: Augmentative Communication.

DeRuyter, F., & Donoghue, K. (1989). Communication and traumatic brain injury: A case study. *Augmentative and Alternative Communication, 5*, 49–54.

DeRuyter, F., & Kennedy, M. (1991). Augmentative communication following traumatic brain injury. In D. Beukelman & K. Yorkston (Eds.), *Communication disorders following traumatic brain injury: Management of cognitive, language, and motor impairments* (pp. 317–365). Austin, TX: PRO-ED.

DeRuyter, F., & Lafontaine, L. (1987). The nonspeaking brain injured: A clinical and demographic database report. *Augmentative and Alternative Communication, 3*, 18–25.

Deshler, K., & Schumaker, J. (1988). An instructional model for teaching students how to learn. In J. Graden, J. Zins, & M. Curtis (Eds.), *Alternative educational delivery systems: Enhancing instructional options for all students* (pp. 391–411). Washington, DC: National Association of School Psychologists.

Dixon, L.S. (1981). A functional analysis of photo-object matching skills of severely retarded adolescents. *Journal of Applied Behavior Analysis, 14*, 465–478.

Doherty, J. (1985). The effects of sign characteristics on sign acquisition and retention: An integrative review of the literature. *Augmentative and Alternative Communication, 1*, 108–121.

Doherty, J., Daniloff, J., & Lloyd, L. (1985). The effect of categorical presentation on Amer-Ind transparency. *Augmentative and Alternative Communication, 1*, 10–16.

Doherty, J., Karlan, G., & Lloyd, L. (1982). Establishing the transparency of two gestural systems by mentally retarded adults. *Asha, 24*, 834.

Dollaghan, C. (1987) Fast mapping in normal and language impaired children. *Journal of Speech and Hearing Disorders, 52*, 218–222.

Dongilli, P., Hakel, M., & Beukelman, D. (1992). Recovery of functional speech following traumatic brain injury. *Journal of Head Trauma Rehabilitation, 7*, 91–101.

Dongilli, P.A., Jr. (1994). Semantic context and speech intelligibility. In J.A. Till, K.M. Yorkston, & D.R. Beukelman (Eds.), *Motor speech disorders: Advances in assessment and treatment* (pp. 175–192). Baltimore: Paul H. Brookes Publishing Co.

Donnellan, A. (1984). The criterion of the least dangerous assumption. *Behavior Disorders, 9*, 141–150.

Donnellan, A., Mirenda, P., Mesaros, R., & Fassbender, L. (1984). Analyzing the communicative functions of aberrant behavior. *Journal of The Association for Persons with Severe Handicaps, 9*, 201–212.

Donovan, W. (1981). Spinal cord injury. In W. Stolov & M. Clowers (Eds.), *Handbook of severe disability* (pp. 65–82). Washington, DC: U.S. Government Printing Office.

Dowden, P. (1997). Augmentative and alternative communication decision making for children with severely unintelligible speech. *Augmentative and Alternative Communication, 13*, 48–58.

Dowden, P., Beukelman, D., & Lossing, C. (1986). Serving non-speaking patients in acute care settings: Intervention outcomes. *Augmentative and Alternative Communication, 2*, 38–44.

Dowden, P., Honsinger, M., & Beukelman, D. (1986). Serving non-speaking patients in acute care settings: An intervention approach. *Augmentative and Alternative Communication, 2*, 25–32.

Duchan, J. (1987). Perspectives for understanding children with communicative disorders. In P. Knoblock (Ed.), *Understanding exceptional children and youth* (pp. 163–199). Boston: Little, Brown.

Duchan, J. (1995). *Supporting language learning in everyday life.* San Diego: Singular Publishing Group.

Duffy, L. (1977). *An innovative approach to the development of communication skills for severely speech handicapped cerebral palsied children.* Unpublished master's thesis, University of Nevada, Las Vegas.

Dunham, J. (1989). The transparency of manual signs in a linguistic and an environmental non-linguistic context. *Augmentative and Alternative Communication, 5*, 214–225.

Dunn, L.M., & Dunn, L.M. (1981). *Peabody Picture Vocabulary Test–Revised.* Circle Pines, MN: American Guidance Service.

Dunn, M. (1982). *Pre–sign language motor skills.* Tucson, AZ: Communication Skill Builders.

Durand, V.M. (1990). *Severe behavior problems.* New York: Guilford Press.

Durand, V.M. (1993). Functional communication training using assistive devices: Effects on challenging behavior. *Augmentative and Alternative Communication, 9*, 168–176.

Durand, V.M., & Kishi, G. (1987). Reducing severe behavior problems among persons with dual sensory impairments: An evaluation of a technical assistance model. *Journal of The Association for Persons with Severe Handicaps, 12*, 2–10.

Dworkin, J., Aronson, A., & Mulder, D. (1980). Tongue force in normals and in dysarthric patients with amyotrophic lateral sclerosis. *Journal of Speech and Hearing Research, 23*, 828–837.

Dybwad, G., & Bersani, H. (1996). *New voices: Self-advocacy by people with disabilities.* Cambridge, MA: Brookline Books.

Easton, J. (1989). Oh, the frustration! *Communication Outlook, 10*(3), 16–17.

Ecklund, S., & Reichle, J. (1987). A comparison of normal children's ability to recall symbols from two logographic systems. *Language, Speech, and Hearing Services in Schools, 18,* 34–40.

Edman, P. (1991). Relief Bliss: A low tech technique. *Communicating Together, 9*(1), 21–22.

Edmonds, R. (1979). Some schools work and more can. *Social Policy, 9*(5), 25–29.

Egof, D. (1988). *Coding communication devices: The effects of symbol set selection and code origin on the recall of utterances.* Paper presented at the third annual Council for Exceptional Children conference, Baltimore.

Ehren, B.J. (1994). New directions for meeting the academic needs of adolescents with language learning disabilities. In G.P. Wallach & K. Butler (Eds.), *Language learning disabilities in school age children: Some principles and applications* (pp. 393–417). New York: Macmillan.

Eisenson, J., & Ingram, D. (1972). Childhood aphasia: An updated concept based on recent research. *Acta Symbolica, 3,* 108–116.

Ekman, P. (1976). Movements with precise meanings. *Journal of Communication, 26,* 14–26.

Ekman, P., & Friesen, W. (1969). The repertoire of nonverbal behavior: Categories, origin, usage, and coding. *Semiotica, 1,* 49–98.

Elder, P., & Goossens', C. (1994). *Engineering training environments for interactive augmentative communication: Strategies for adolescents and adults who are moderately/severely developmentally delayed.* Birmingham, AL: Southeast Augmentative Communication Conference Publications.

Elder, P., & Goossens', C. (1996). *Communication overlays for engineering training environments: Overlays for adolescents and adults who are moderately/severely developmentally delayed.* Solana Beach, CA: Mayer-Johnson Co.

Elder, P., Goossens', C., & Bray, N. (1989). *Semantic compaction proficiency profile* (Experimental edition). Birmingham, AL: Southeast Augmentative Communication Conference Publications.

Emery, A., & Holloway, S. (1982). Familial motor neuron diseases. In L. Rowland (Ed.), *Human motor neuron diseases.* New York: Raven Press.

Enderby, P., & Crow, E. (1990). Long-term recovery patterns of severe dysarthria following head injury. *British Journal of Disorders of Communication, 25,* 341–354.

Enderby, P., & Philipp, R. (1986). Speech and language handicap: Towards knowing the size of the problem. *British Journal of Disorders of Communication, 27,* 159–173.

Engelmann, S., & Bruner, E. (1984). *Reading mastery program: DISTAR.* Chicago: Science Research Associates.

Erickson, K., & Baker, B. (1996, August). *Language, literacy, and semantic compaction.* Paper presented at the seventh biennial conference of the International Society for Augmentative and Alternative Communication, Vancouver, British Columbia, Canada.

Erickson, K.A., & Koppenhaver, D.A. (1995). Developing a literacy program for children with severe disabilities. *The Reading Teacher, 48*(8), 676–684.

Eulenberg, J. (1987). Yan Sheinfeld's new song. *Communication Outlook, 9*(2), 9–13.

Evans, I.M. (1991). Testing and diagnosis: A review and evaluation. In L.H. Meyer, C.A. Peck, & L. Brown (Eds.), *Critical issues in the lives of people with severe disabilities* (pp. 25–44). Baltimore: Paul H. Brookes Publishing Co.

Falvey, M.A. (1986). *Community-based curriculum: Instructional strategies for students with severe handicaps.* Baltimore: Paul H. Brookes Publishing Co.

Falvey, M.A. (1995). *Inclusive and heterogeneous schooling: Assessment, curriculum, and instruction.* Baltimore: Paul H. Brookes Publishing Co.

Farrier, L., Yorkston, K., Marriner, N., & Beukelman, D. (1985). Conversational control in nonimpaired speakers using an augmentative communication system. *Augmentative and Alternative Communication, 1,* 65–73.

Fay, L. (1993). An account of the search of a woman who is verbally impaired for augmentative devices to end her silence. In M. Willmuth & L. Holcomb (Eds.), *Women with disabilities: Found voices* (pp. 105–115). Binghamton, NY: The Haworth Press.

Fay, W., & Schuler, A. (1980). *Emerging language in autistic children.* Baltimore: University Park Press.

Fell, A., Lynn, E., & Morrison, K. (1984). *Non-oral communication assessment.* Ann Arbor, MI: Alternatives to Speech.

Fenson, L., Dale, P., Reznick, S., Thal, D., Bates, E., Hartung, J., Pethick, S., & Reilly, J. (1993). *MacArthur Communicative Development Inventory: Words and Sentences.* San Antonio, TX: The Psychological Corporation.

Ferrier, L., Shane, H., Ballard, H., Carpenter, T., & Benoit, A. (1995). Dysarthric speakers' intelligibility and speech characteristics in relation to computer speech recognition. *Augmentative and Alternative Communication, 11,* 165–174.

Fiocca, G. (1981). *Generally understood gestures: An approach to communication for persons with severe language impairments.* Unpublished master's thesis, University of Illinois at Urbana, Champaign.

Fisher, R., Ury, W., & Patton, B. (1991). *Getting to yes: Negotiating agreement without giving in.* New York: Penguin Books USA.

Fisher, W., Piazza, C., Cataldo, M., Harrell, R., Jefferson, G., & Conner, R. (1993). Functional communication training with and without extinction and punishment. *Journal of Applied Behavior Analysis, 26,* 23–36.

Fishman, I. (1987). *Electronic communication aids.* San Diego: College-Hill Press.

Flannery, B., & Horner, R. (1994). The relationship between predictability and problem behavior for students with severe disabilities. *Journal of Behavioral Education, 4,* 157–176.

Flower, L.S., & Hayes, J.R. (1981). A cognitive process theory of writing. *College Composition, 32,* 365–387.

Foley, B.E. (1993). The development of literacy in individuals with severe congenital speech and motor impairments. *Topics in Language Disorders, 13*(2), 16–32.

Ford, A., & Mirenda, P. (1984). Community instruction: A natural cues and corrections decision model. *Journal of The Association for Persons with Severe Handicaps, 9,* 79–87.

Ford, A., Schnorr, R., Meyer, L., Davern, L., Black, J., & Dempsey, P. (Eds.). (1989). *The Syracuse community-referenced curriculum guide for students with moderate and severe disabilities.* Baltimore: Paul H. Brookes Publishing Co.

Foulds, R. (1980). Communication rates of nonspeech expression as a function in manual tasks and linguistic constraints. In *Proceedings of the International Conference on Rehabilitation Engineering* (pp. 83–87). Toronto, Ontario, Canada: RESNA Press.

Foulds, R. (1985). Observations on interfacing in nonvocal communication. In C. Barry & M. Byrne (Eds.), *Proceedings of the fourth international Conference on Communication Through Technology for the Physically Disabled* (pp. 46–51). London: The International Cerebral Palsy Association.

Foulds, R. (1987). Guest editorial. *Augmentative and Alternative Communication, 3,* 169.

Francis, W., Nail, B., & Lloyd, L. (1990, November). *Mentally retarded adults' perception of emotions represented by pictographic symbols.* Paper presented at the annual convention of the American Speech-Language-Hearing Association, Seattle.

Franklin, N.K., Mirenda, P., & Phillips, G. (1994). Comparisons of five symbol assessment protocols with nondisabled preschoolers and learners with severe intellectual disabilities. *Augmentative and Alternative Communication, 12,* 73–77.

Fraser, B.A., Hensinger, R.N., & Phelps, J.A. (1990). *Physical management of multiple handicaps: A professional's guide* (2nd ed.). Baltimore: Paul H. Brookes Publishing Co.

Freeman, B.J. (1993a). *Diagnosis of the syndrome of autism: Questions parents ask.* Unpublished manuscript, University of California–Los Angeles.

Freeman, B.J. (1993b). The syndrome of autism: Update and guidelines for diagnosis. *Infants and Young Children, 6,* 1–11.

Freeman, B.J. (1997). Guidelines for evaluating intervention programs for children with autism. *Journal of Autism and Developmental Disorders, 27*(6), 641–651.

Freeman, B.J., & Ritvo, E. (1984). The syndrome of autism: Establishing the diagnosis and principles of management. *Pediatric Annals, 13,* 37–44.

Fried-Oken, M. (1989). *Sentence recognition for auditory and visual scanning techniques in electronic augmentative communication devices.* Paper presented at the Rehabilitation Engineering and Assistive Technology Association (RESNA)/United States Society for Augmentative and Alternative Communication annual conference, New Orleans.

Fried-Oken, M. (1995). Story telling as an augmentative communication approach for a man with severe apraxia of speech and expressive aphasia. *Augmentative and Alternative Communication (American Speech-Language-Hearing Association Special Interest Division #12 Newsletter), 4,* 3–4.

Fried-Oken, M., & Doyle, M. (1992). Language representation for the augmentative and alternative communication of adults with traumatic brain injury. *Journal of Head Trauma Rehabilitation, 7*(3), 59–69.

Fried-Oken, M., Howard, J., & Prillwitz, D. (1988). Establishing initial communicative control with a loop-tape system. In S.W. Blackstone, E.L. Cassatt-James, & D. Bruskin (Eds.), *Augmen-

tative communication: Implementation strategies (pp. 5.1-45–5.1-51). Rockville, MD: American Speech-Language-Hearing Association.

Fried-Oken, M., Howard, J., & Stewart, S. (1991). Feedback on AAC intervention from adults who are temporarily unable to speak. *Augmentative and Alternative Communication, 7,* 43–50.

Fried-Oken, M., & More, L. (1992). An initial vocabulary for nonspeaking preschool children based on developmental and environmental language sources. *Augmentative and Alternative Communication, 8,* 41–56.

Frith, U. (1989). *Autism: Explaining an enigma.* St. Louis: Blackwell Mosby.

Frost, L., & Bondy, A. (1994). *PECS: The Picture Exchange Communication System Training Manual.* Cherry Hill, NJ: Pyramid Educational Consultants.

Fucci, D., Reynolds, M., Bettagere, R., & Gonzales, M. (1995). Synthetic speech intelligibility under several experimental conditions. *Augmentative and Alternative Communication, 11*(2), 113–117.

Fuller, D., & Lloyd, L. (1991). Toward a common usage of iconicity terminology. *Augmentative and Alternative Communication, 7,* 215–220.

Fuller, D., Lloyd, L., & Schlosser, R. (1992). Further development of an augmentative and alternative communication symbol taxonomy. *Augmentative and Alternative Communication, 8,* 67–74.

Fuller, D., Lloyd, L., & Stratton, M. (1997). Aided AAC symbols. In L. Lloyd, D. Fuller, & H. Arvidson (Eds.), *Augmentative and alternative communication: Principles and practice* (pp. 48–79). Needham Heights, MA: Allyn & Bacon.

Garrett, K., & Beukelman, D. (1992). Augmentative communication approaches for persons with severe aphasia. In K. Yorkston (Ed.), *Augmentative communication in the medical setting* (pp. 245–338). Tucson, AZ: Communication Skill Builders.

Garrett, K., Beukelman D., & Low-Morrow, D. (1989). A comprehensive augmentative communication system for an adult with Broca's aphasia. *Augmentative and Alternative Communication, 5,* 55–61.

Garrett, K., Schutz-Muehling, L., & Morrow, D. (1990). Low level head injury: A novel AAC approach. *Augmentative and Alternative Communication, 6,* 124.

Garrett, K., Staab, L., & Agocs, L. (1996, November). *Perceptions of scaffolded letters generated by a person with aphasia.* Paper presented at the annual convention of the American Speech-Language-Hearing Association, Seattle.

Garrett, S. (1986). A case study in tactile Blissymbols. *Communicating Together, 4*(2), 16.

Gartner, A., & Lipsky, D.K. (1990). Students as instructional agents. In W. Stainback & S. Stainback (Eds.), *Support networks for inclusive schooling: Interdependent integrated education* (pp. 81–93). Baltimore: Paul H. Brookes Publishing Co.

Gates, C. (1985). Survey of multiply handicapped visually impaired children in the Rocky Mountain/Great Plains region. *Journal of Visual Impairment and Blindness, 79,* 385–391.

Gee, K., Graham, N., Goetz, L., Oshima, G., & Yoshioka, K. (1991). Teaching students to request the continuation of routine activities by using time delay and decreasing physical assistance in the context of chain interruption. *Journal of The Association for Persons with Severe Handicaps, 16,* 154–167.

Genet, R. (1995). You just can't keep a good person down! *Asha, 37,* 57–58.

Gerra, L., Dorfman, S., Plaue, E., Schlackman, S., & Workman, D. (1995). Functional communication as a means of decreasing self-injurious behavior: A case study. *Journal of Visual Impairment and Blindness, 89,* 343–347.

Giangreco, M.F. (1996a). Choosing options and accommodations for children (COACH): Curriculum planning for students with disabilities in general education. In S. Stainback & W. Stainback (Eds.), *Inclusion: A guide for educators* (pp. 237–254). Baltimore: Paul H. Brookes Publishing Co.

Giangreco, M.F. (1996b). *VISTA: Vermont interdependent services team approach. A guide to coordinating support services.* Baltimore: Paul H. Brookes Publishing Co.

Giangreco, M.F., Cloninger, C.J., & Iverson, V.S. (1998). *Choosing outcomes and accommodations for children (COACH): A guide to educational planning for students with disabilities* (2nd ed.). Baltimore: Paul H. Brookes Publishing Co.

Gillingham, A., & Stillman, B. (1970). *Remedial training for children with specific difficulty in reading, spelling, and penmanship.* Cambridge, MA: Educators Publishing Service.

Girolametto, L. (1988). Improving the social-conversational skills of developmentally delayed children: An intervention study. *Journal of Speech and Hearing Disorders, 53,* 156–167.

Girolametto, L., Greenberg, J., & Manolson, A. (1986). Developing dialogue skills: The Hanen Early Language Parent Program. *Seminars in Speech and Language, 7*, 367–382.

Girolametto, L., Steig Pearce, P., & Weitzman, E. (1996). Interactive focused stimulation for toddlers with expressive language delays. *Journal of Speech and Hearing Research, 39*, 1274–1283.

Glennen, S. (1997). Augmentative and alternative communication assessment strategies. In S.L. Glennen & D. DeCoste (Eds.), *The handbook of augmentative and alternative communication* (pp. 149–192). San Diego: Singular Publishing Group.

Glennen, S., & Calculator, S. (1985). Training functional communication board use: A pragmatic approach. *Augmentative and Alternative Communication, 1*, 134–142.

Glennen, S.L., & DeCoste, D. (1997). *The handbook of augmentative and alternative communication.* San Diego: Singular Publishing Group.

Gleser, G., Gottschalk, L., & John, W. (1959). The relationship of sex and intelligence to choice words: A normative study of verbal behavior. *Journal of Clinical Psychology, 15*, 182–191.

Gloeckler, T., & Simpson, C. (1988). *Exceptional students in regular classrooms: Challenges, services, and methods.* Mountain View, CA: Mayfield Publishing.

Goetz, L., Gee, K., & Sailor, W. (1983). Crossmodal transfer of stimulus control: Preparing students with severe multiple disabilities for audiological assessment. *Journal of The Association for Persons with Severe Handicaps, 8*, 3–13.

Goetz, L., Gee, K., & Sailor, W. (1985). Using a behavior chain interruption strategy to teach communication skills to learners with severe disabilities. *Journal of The Association for Persons with Severe Handicaps, 10*, 21–30.

Goldman-Eisler, F. (1986). *Cycle linguistics: Experiments in spontaneous speech.* New York: Academic Press.

Goodenough-Trepagnier, C., Tarry, E., & Prather, P. (1982). Derivation of an efficient nonvocal communication system. *Human Factors, 24*, 163–172.

Goodman, J., & Remington, B. (1993). Acquisition of expressive signing: Comparison of reinforcement strategies. *Augmentative and Alternative Communication, 9*, 26–35.

Goossens', C. (1989). Aided communication intervention before assessment: A case study of a child with cerebral palsy. *Augmentative and Alternative Communication, 5*, 14–26.

Goossens', C., & Crain, S. (1986a). *Augmentative communication assessment resource.* Wauconda, IL: Don Johnston, Inc.

Goossens', C., & Crain, S. (1986b). *Augmentative communication intervention resource.* Wauconda, IL: Don Johnston, Inc.

Goossens', C., & Crain, S. (1987). Overview of nonelectronic eye-gaze communication devices. *Augmentative and Alternative Communication, 3*, 77–89.

Goossens', C., & Crain, S. (1992). *Utilizing switch interfaces with children who are severely physically challenged.* Austin, TX: PRO-ED.

Goossens', C., Crain, S., & Elder, P. (1992). *Engineering the preschool environment for interactive, symbolic communication.* Birmingham, AL: Southeast Augmentative Communication Conference Publications.

Goossens', C., Crain, S., & Elder, P. (1994). *Communication displays for engineered preschool environments: Books 1 and 2.* Solana Beach, CA: Mayer-Johnson Co.

Goossens', C., Heine, K., Crain, S., & Burke, C. (1987). *Modifying Piagetian tasks for use with physically-challenged individuals.* Birmingham: University of Alabama, Sparks Center for Developmental and Learning Disorders.

Gorenflo, C., & Gorenflo, D. (1991). The effects of information and augmentative communication technique on attitudes toward nonspeaking individuals. *Journal of Speech and Hearing Research, 34*, 19–26.

Gorenflo, C., Gorenflo, D., & Santer, S. (1994). Effects of synthetic voice output on attitudes toward the augmented communicator. *Journal of Speech and Hearing Research, 37*, 64–68.

Graham, S., & Harris, K.R. (1989). A component analysis of cognitive strategy instruction: Effects of LD students' compositions and self-efficacy. *Journal of Educational Psychology, 81*(3), 353–361.

Graham, S., & Harris, K.R. (1993). Self-regulated strategy development: Helping students with learning problems develop as writers. *The Elementary School Journal, 94*(2), 169–181.

Graham, S., & Harris, K.R. (1997). Whole language and process writing: Does one approach fit all? In J. Lloyd, E. Kameenui, & D. Chard (Eds.), *Issues in educating students with disabilities* (pp. 239–258). Mahwah, NJ: Lawrence Erlbaum Associates.

Graham, S., MacArthur, C., Schwartz, S., & Page-Voth, V. (1992). Improving the compositions of students with learning disabilities using a strategy involving product and process goal setting. *Exceptional Children, 58*(4), 322–334.

Graham, T. (1982). *Let loose on Mother Goose: Activities to teach math, science, art, music, life skills, and language development.* Nashville, TN: Incentive Publications.

Grandin, T., & Scariano, M. (1986). *Emergence: Labeled autistic.* Novato, CA: Arena Press.

Granlund, M. (1995). "Whose goal is it, anyway," Swedish researcher asks. In S. Blackstone & H. Pressman (Eds.), *Outcomes in AAC conference report: Alliance '95* (pp. 31–32). Monterey, CA: Augmentative Communication.

Granlund, M., Björck-Åkesson, E., Brodin, J., & Olsson, C. (1995). Communication intervention for persons with profound disabilities: A Swedish perspective. *Augmentative and Alternative Communication, 11,* 49–59.

Granlund, M., & Olsson, C. (1987). *Talspråksalternativ kommunikation och begåvningshandikapp [Alternative communication and mental retardation].* Stockholm, Sweden: Stiftelsen ALA.

Granlund, M., Ström, E., & Olsson, C. (1989). Iconicity and productive recall of a selected sample of signs from Signed Swedish. *Augmentative and Alternative Communication, 5,* 173–182.

Granlund, M., Terneby, J., & Olsson, C. (1992a). Creating communicative opportunities through a combined inservice training/supervision package. *European Journal of Special Needs Education, 7,* 229–252.

Granlund, M., Terneby, J., & Olsson, C. (1992b). Subject characteristics and the communicative environment of profoundly retarded adults. *Scandinavian Journal of Educational Research, 36,* 323–338.

Graves, D.H. (1994). *A fresh look at writing.* Portsmouth, NH: Heinemann.

Green, G., & Shane, H. (1994). Science, reason, and facilitated communication. *Journal of The Association for Persons with Severe Handicaps, 19,* 151–172.

Gregory, C., & McNaughton, S. (1993, September). Language! Welcoming a parent's perspective. *Communicating Together, 11*(3), 21–23.

Grove, N., & Walker, M. (1990). The Makaton Vocabulary: Using manual signs and graphic symbols to develop interpersonal communication. *Augmentative and Alternative Communication, 6,* 15–28.

Gualtieri, C. (1988). Pharmacotherapy and the neurobehavioral sequelae of traumatic brain injury. *Brain Injury, 2,* 101–129.

Guralnick, M. (1990). Social competence and early intervention. *Journal of Early Intervention, 14,* 3–14.

Gustason, G. (1990). Signing Exact English. In H. Bornstein (Ed.), *Manual communication: Implications for education* (pp. 108–127). Washington, DC: Gallaudet University Press.

Gustason, G., Pfetzing, D., & Zawolkow, E. (1980). *Signing Exact English* (3rd ed.). Los Alamitos, CA: Modern Signs Press.

Guy, T. (1995). Communication. *Communicating Together, 12*(1), 8.

Guyette, T., & Diedrich, W. (1981). A critical review of developmental apraxia of speech. In N. Lass (Ed.), *Speech and language advances in basic research and practice* (Vol. 5). New York: Academic Press.

Haaf, R. (1994). Technology in transition: Colin. *Communicating Together, 12*(3), 11–13.

Haaf, R., Millin, N., & Verberg, G. (1994). Sheila. *Communicating Together, 12*(2), 4–6.

Hagberg, B., Hagberg, G., & Zetterstrom, R. (1989). Decreasing perinatal mortality: Increase in cerebral palsy morbidity. *Acta Paediatrica Scandinavica, 78,* 664–670.

Hagen, C. (1984). Language disorders in head trauma. In A. Holland (Ed.), *Language disorders in adults* (pp. 245-281). Austin, TX: PRO-ED.

Hall, P. (1992). At the center of controversy: Developmental apraxia. *American Journal of Speech-Language Pathology, 1,* 23–25.

Hall, P., Jordan, L., & Robin, D. (1992). *Developmental apraxia of speech: Theory and clinical practice.* Austin, TX: PRO-ED.

Halle, J. (1987). Teaching language in the natural environment: An analysis of spontaneity. *Journal of The Association for Persons with Severe Handicaps, 12,* 28–37.

Halle, J., Baer, D., & Spradlin, J. (1981). Teachers' generalized use of delay as a stimulus control procedure to increase language use by handicapped children. *Journal of Applied Behavior Analysis, 14,* 389–409.

Halle, J., Marshall, A., & Spradlin, J. (1979). Time delay: A technique to increase language use and facilitate generalization in retarded children. *Journal of Applied Behavior Analysis, 12,* 431–439.

Halle, J.W. (1982). Teaching functional language to the handicapped: An integrative model of natural environment teaching techniques. *Journal of The Association for Persons with Severe Handicaps, 7,* 29–37.

Hamblin-Wilson, C., & Thurman, S. (1990). The transition from early intervention to kindergarten: Parental satisfaction and involvement. *Journal of Early Intervention, 14,* 55–61.

Hamilton, B., & Snell, M. (1993). Using the milieu approach to increase spontaneous communication book use across environments by an adolescent with autism. *Augmentative and Alternative Communication, 9,* 259–272.

Hammen, V.L., Yorkston, K.M., & Dowden, P. (1991). Index of contextual intelligibility: Impact of semantic context on dysarthria. In C.A. Moore, K.M. Yorkston, & D.R. Beukelman (Eds.), *Dysarthria and apraxia of speech: Perspectives on management* (pp. 43–53). Baltimore: Paul H. Brookes Publishing Co.

Hamre-Nietupski, S., Stoll, A., Holtz, K., Fullerton, P., Ryan-Flottum, M., & Brown, L. (1977). Curricular strategies for teaching selected nonverbal communication skills to nonverbal and verbal severely handicapped students. In L. Brown, J. Nietupski, S. Lyon, S. Hamre-Nietupski, T. Crowner, & L. Gruenewald (Eds.), *Curricular strategies for teaching functional object use, nonverbal communication, problem solving, and mealtime skills to severely handicapped students: Part I* (Vol. 7, pp. 94–250). Madison: University of Wisconsin–Madison and Madison Metropolitan School District.

Hanson, M.J., & Hanline, M.F. (1989). Integration options for the very young child. In R. Gaylord-Ross (Ed.), *Integration strategies for students with handicaps* (pp. 177–193). Baltimore: Paul H. Brookes Publishing Co.

Happé, F. (1994). *Autism: An introduction to psychological theory.* London: UCL Press.

Hardy, J. (1983). *Cerebral palsy.* Upper Saddle River, NJ: Prentice Hall.

Haring, T., Neetz, J., Lovinger, L., Peck, C., & Semmel, M. (1987). Effects of four modified incidental teaching procedures to create opportunities for communication. *Journal of The Association for Persons with Severe Handicaps, 12,* 218–226.

Harrington, D. (1976). *The visual fields: A textbook and atlas of clinical perimetry* (4th ed.). St. Louis: Mosby.

Harrington, K. (1988). A letter from Annie. *Communicating Together, 6*(4), 5–7.

Harris, A.J., & Sipay, E.R. (1990). *How to increase reading ability* (9th ed.). White Plains, NY: Longman.

Harris, D. (1982). Communication interaction processes involving nonvocal physically handicapped children. *Topics in Language Disorders, 2*(2), 21–37.

Harris, K.R., & Graham, S. (1996). *Making the writing process work: Strategies for composition and self-regulation.* Cambridge, MA: Brookline Books.

Harste, J.C., Burke, C.L., & Woodward, V.A. (1994). Children's language and world: Initial encounters with print. In R.B. Ruddell, M.R. Ruddell, & H. Singer (Eds.), *Theoretical models and processes of reading* (4th ed., pp. 48–69). Newark, DE: International Reading Association.

Hart, B., & Risley, T. (1975). Incidental teaching of language in the preschool. *Journal of Applied Behavior Analysis, 8,* 411–420.

Hart, V. (1977). The use of many disciplines with the severely and profoundly handicapped. In E. Sontag, J. Smith, & N. Certo (Eds.), *Educational programming for the severely and profoundly handicapped* (pp. 391–396). Reston, VA: Council for Exceptional Children.

Hawking, S. (1995). *Professor Stephen Hawking* [On-line]. Available: http://www.damtp.cam.ac.uk/user/hawking/disability.html.

Hayden, D., & Square, P. (1994). Motor speech treatment hierarchy: A systems approach. *Clinics in Communication Disorders, 4,* 162–174.

Haynes, S. (1985). Developmental apraxia of speech: Symptoms and treatment. In D.F. Johns (Ed.), *Clinical management of neurogenic communicative disorders* (pp. 259–266). Boston: Little, Brown.

Health and Welfare Canada. (1988). *1991 HALS Adults in Households Microdata File, User Codebook.* [On-line]. Available: http://www.datalib.ubc.ca/datalib/gen/files_unixg/health_act_lim/codebook_1991.html.

Heaton, E., Beliveau, C., & Blois, T. (1995). Outcomes in assistive technology. *Journal of Speech-Language Pathology and Audiology, 19,* 233–240.

Hedrick, D., Prather, E., & Tobin, A. (1984). *Sequenced Inventory of Communication Development* (Rev. ed.). Seattle: University of Washington Press.

Heine, K., Wilkerson, R., & Kennedy, T. (1996). *Unity now and later: Equipping a two-year-old now, while preparing in the future.* Paper presented at the 1996 Minspeak conference, Wooster, OH.

Helfrich-Miller, K. (1994). A clinical perspective: Melodic intonation therapy for developmental apraxia. *Clinics in Communication Disorders, 4,* 175–182.

Heller, K., Allgood, M., Ware, S., Arnold, S., & Castelle, M. (1996). Initiating requests during community-based vocational training by students with mental retardation and sensory impairments. *Research in Developmental Disabilities, 17,* 173–184.

Heller, K., Ware, S., Allgood, M., & Castelle, M. (1994). Use of dual communication boards with students who are deaf-blind. *Journal of Visual Impairment and Blindness, 88,* 368–376.

Hemmeter, M., & Kaiser, A. (1994). Enhanced milieu teaching: Effects of parent-implemented language intervention. *Journal of Early Intervention, 18,* 269–289.

Hess, R., & McGarvey, L. (1987). School-relevant effects of educational uses of microcomputers in kindergarten classrooms and homes. *Journal of Educational Computer Research, 3,* 269–287.

Hetzroni, R., & Harris, O. (1996). Cultural aspects in the development of AAC users. *Augmentative and Alternative Communication, 12,* 52–58.

Higginbotham, D. (1989). The interplay of communication device output mode and interaction style between nonspeaking persons and their speaking partners. *Journal of Speech and Hearing Disorders, 54,* 320–333.

Higginbotham, D., Mathy-Laikko, P., & Yoder, D. (1988). Studying conversations of augmentative communication system users. In L.E. Bernstein (Ed.), *The vocally impaired: Clinical practice and research* (pp. 265–294). New York: Grune & Stratton.

Higginbotham, D.J. (1992). Evaluation of keystroke savings across five assistive communication technologies. *Augmentative and Alternative Communication, 8,* 258–272.

Higginbotham, D.J. (1994). What an unlikely couple! The marriage of semantic compaction and word prediction. *Communicating Together, 12*(2), 9–11.

Higginbotham, D.J., Bak, C., Drazek, A., Kelly, C., & White, K. (1992). Word prediction in MS DOS Land: Part 2. Performance and ease of use evaluation. *Communicating Together, 10*(2), 9–10.

Higginbotham, D.J., Drazek, A.L., Kowarsky, K., Scally, C., & Segal, E. (1994). Discourse comprehension of synthetic speech delivered at normal and slow presentation rates. *Augmentative and Alternative Communication, 10,* 191–202.

Higginbotham, D.J., Scally, C., Lundy, D., & Kowarsky, K. (1995). Discourse comprehension of synthetic speech across three augmentative and alternative communication (AAC) output methods. *Journal of Speech and Hearing Research, 38*(3), 889–901.

Hirdes, J., Ellis-Hale, K., & Pearson Hirdes, B. (1993). Prevalence and policy implications of communication disabilities among adults. *Augmentative and Alternative Communication, 9,* 273–280.

Hoag, L., & Bedrosian, J. (1992). The effects of speech output type, message length, and reauditorization on perceptions of communicative competence of an adult AAC user. *Journal of Speech and Hearing Research, 35,* 1363–1366.

Hoag, L., Bedrosian, J., Johnson, D., & Molineux, B. (1994). Variables affecting perceptions of social aspects of the communicative competence of an adult AAC user. *Augmentative and Alternative Communication, 10,* 129–137.

Hodgdon, L. (1996). *Visual strategies for improving communication.* Troy, MI: QuirkRoberts Publishing.

Hodges, P., & Schwethelm, B. (1984). A comparison of the effectiveness of graphic symbol and manual sign training with profoundly retarded children. *Applied Psycholinguistics, 5,* 223–253.

Hodson, B. (1986). *The assessment of phonological processes* (Rev. ed.). Austin. TX: PRO-ED.

Hodson, B., & Paden, E. (1991). *A phonological approach to remediation: Targeting intelligible speech* (2nd ed.). Austin, TX: PRO-ED.

Hoffmeister, R. (1990). ASL and its implications for education. In H. Bornstein (Ed.), *Manual communication: Implications for education* (pp. 81–107). Washington, DC: Gallaudet University Press.

Honsinger, M. (1989). Midcourse intervention in multiple sclerosis: An inpatient model. *Augmentative and Alternative Communication, 5,* 71–73.

Honsinger, M., Yorkston, K., & Dowden, P. (1987, May–June). Communication options for intubated patients. *Respiratory Management,* 45–52.

Hooper, J., Connell, T., & Flett, P. (1987). Blissymbols and manual signs: A multimodal approach to intervention in a case of multiple disability. *Augmentative and Alternative Communication, 3,* 68–76.

Horn, E., & Jones, H. (1996). Comparison of two selection techniques used in augmentative and alternative communication. *Augmentative and Alternative Communication, 12,* 23–31.

Horner, R., & Budd, C. (1985). Acquisition of manual sign use: Collateral reduction of maladaptive behavior and factors limiting generalization. *Education and Training of the Mentally Retarded, 20*, 39–47.

Horner, R.H., McDonnell, J.J., & Bellamy, G.T. (1986). Teaching generalized skills: Instruction in simulation and community settings. In R.H. Horner, L.H. Meyer, & H.D.B. Fredericks (Eds.), *Education of learners with severe handicaps: Exemplary service strategies* (pp. 289–314). Baltimore: Paul H. Brookes Publishing Co.

Hoskins, B. (1990). Collaborative consultation: Designing the role of the speech-language pathologist in a new educational context. In W. Secord (Ed.), *Best practices in school speech-language pathology* (pp. 29–38). San Antonio, TX: The Psychological Corporation.

Houghton, J., Bronicki, B., & Guess, D. (1987). Opportunities to express preferences and make choices among students with severe disabilities in classroom settings. *Journal of The Association for Persons with Severe Handicaps, 11*, 255–265.

House, L., & Rogerson, B. (1984). *Comprehensive screening tool for determining optimal communication mode.* East Aurora, NY: United Educational Services.

Huebner, K. (1986). Curricula adaptations. In G.T. Scholl (Ed.), *Foundations of education for blind and visually handicapped children and youth: Theory and practice* (pp. 363–404). New York: American Foundation for the Blind.

Huer, M. (1983). *The Non-Speech Test.* Wauconda, IL: Don Johnston, Inc.

Huer, M. (1987). White's gestural system for the lower extremities. *Communicating Together, 5*, 3–4.

Huer, M., & Lloyd, L. (1988). Perspectives of AAC users. *Communication Outlook, 9*(2), 10–18.

Huer, M., & Lloyd, L. (1990). AAC users' perspectives on augmentative and alternative communication. *Augmentative and Alternative Communication, 6*, 242–250.

Humes, L., Nelson, K., & Pisoni, D. (1991). Recognition of synthetic speech by hearing impaired elderly listeners. *Journal of Speech and Hearing, 34*, 1180–1184.

Hunnicutt, S., Rosengren, E., & Baker, B. (1990). Development of the Swedish language Minspeak Words Strategy. *Augmentative and Alternative Communication, 6*, 115–116.

Hunt, P., Alwell, M., Farron-Davis, F., & Goetz, L. (1996). Creating socially supportive environments for fully included students who experience multiple disabilities. *Journal of The Association for Persons with Severe Handicaps, 21*, 53–71.

Hunt, P., Alwell, M., & Goetz, L. (1988). Acquisition of conversation skills and the reduction of inappropriate social interaction behaviors. *Journal of The Association for Persons with Severe Handicaps, 13*, 20–27.

Hunt, P., Alwell, M., & Goetz, L. (1990). *Teaching conversation skills to individuals with severe disabilities with a communication book adaptation.* (Available by writing P. Hunt, San Francisco State University, 14 Tapia Street, San Francisco, CA 94132.)

Hunt, P., Alwell, M., & Goetz, L. (1991a). Establishing conversational exchanges with family and friends: Moving from training to meaningful communication. *Journal of Special Education, 25*, 305–319.

Hunt, P., Alwell, M., & Goetz, L. (1991b). Interacting with peers through conversation turntaking with a communication book adaptation. *Augmentative and Alternative Communication, 7*, 117–126.

Hunt, P., & Goetz, L. (1988a). Teaching spontaneous communication in natural settings through interrupted behavior chains. *Topics in Language Disorders, 9*(1), 58–71.

Hunt, P., & Goetz, L. (1988b). *Using an interrupted behavior chain strategy to teach generalized communication responses.* Unpublished handbook. (Available by writing P. Hunt, San Francisco State University, 14 Tapia Street, San Francisco, CA 94132.)

Hunt, P., Goetz, L., Alwell, M., & Sailor, W. (1986). Using an interrupted behavior chain strategy to teach generalized communication responses. *Journal of The Association for Persons with Severe Handicaps, 11*, 196–204.

Hunt, P., Staub, D., Alwell, M., & Goetz, L. (1994). Achievement by all students within the context of cooperative learning groups. *Journal of The Association for Persons with Severe Handicaps, 19*, 290–301.

Hunt-Berg, M. (1996). *Learning graphic symbols: The roles of visual cues in interaction.* Unpublished doctoral dissertation, University of Nebraska–Lincoln.

Hunt-Berg, M., Rankin, J., & Beukelman, D. (1994). Ponder the possibilities: Computer supported writing for struggling writers. *Learning Disabilities Research and Practice, 9*(3), 169–178.

Hurlbut, B., Iwata, B., & Green, J. (1982). Nonvocal language acquisition in adolescents with severe physical disabilities: Blissymbol versus iconic stimulus formats. *Journal of Applied Behavior Analysis, 15,* 241–258.

Hustad, K., Kent, R., & Beukelman, D. (in press). DECTalk and MacinTalk speech synthesizers: Intelligibility differences for listeners with three levels of experience. *Journal of Speech and Hearing Research.*

Hymes, D. (1972). On communicative competence. In J.B. Pride & J. Holmes (Eds.), *Sociolinguistics* (pp. 269–293). London: Penguin Books, Ltd.

Iacono, T., & Duncum, J. (1995). Comparisons of sign alone and in combination with an electronic communication device in early language intervention: A case study. *Augmentative and Alternative Communication, 11,* 249–259.

Iacono, T., Mirenda, P., & Beukelman, D. (1993). Comparison of unimodal and multimodal AAC techniques for children with intellectual disabilities. *Augmentative and Alternative Communication, 9,* 83–94.

Iacono, T., & Parsons, C. (1986). A survey of the use of signing with the intellectually disabled. *Australian Communication Quarterly, 2,* 21–25.

Iacono, T., & Waring, R. (1996, August). *A case study of a parent-implemented AAC language intervention comparing signs versus sign+aid.* Paper presented at the seventh biennial conference of the International Society for Augmentative and Alternative Communication, Vancouver, British Columbia, Canada.

Idol, L., Paolucci-Whitcomb, P., & Nevin, A. (1986). *Collaborative consultation.* Rockville, MD: Aspen Publishers.

Individuals with Disabilities Education Act (IDEA) of 1990, PL 101-476, 20 U.S.C. §§ 1400 *et seq.*

Individuals with Disabilities Education Act Amendments of 1997, PL 105-17, 20 U.S.C. §§ 1400 *et seq.*

Ivers, R., & Goldstein, N. (1963). Multiple sclerosis: A current appraisal of symptoms and signs. *Proceedings of the Staff Meetings of the Mayo Clinic, 38,* 457–466.

Jacobs, H. (1988). The Los Angeles head injury survey: Procedures and initial findings. *Archives of Physical Medicine and Rehabilitation, 69,* 425–431.

Jennett, B., Snoek, J., Bond, M., & Brooks, N. (1981). Disability after severe head injury: Observations on use of the Glasgow Outcome Scale. *Journal of Neurology, Neurosurgery, and Psychiatry, 44,* 285–293.

Jennische, M. (1993, June). There are still reasons for concern. *Communicating Together, 11*(2), 21–22.

Jensema, C. (1982). Communication methods and devices for deaf-blind persons. *Directions, 3,* 60–69.

Jinks, A., & Sinteff, B. (1994). Consumer response to AAC devices: Acquisition, training, use, and satisfaction. *Augmentative and Alternative Communication, 10,* 184–190.

Johns, D. (1985). *Clinical management of neurogenic communication disorders.* Austin, TX: PRO-ED.

Johnson, D., & Johnson, R. (1987a). *Joining together: Group theory and skills* (2nd ed.). Upper Saddle River, NJ: Prentice Hall.

Johnson, D., & Johnson, R. (1987b). *Learning together and alone: Cooperation, competition, and individualization* (2nd ed.). Upper Saddle River, NJ: Prentice Hall.

Johnson, D., Johnson, R., Holubec, E., & Roy, P. (1984). *Circles of learning.* Arlington, VA: Association for Supervision and Curriculum Development.

Johnson, J. (1986). *Self-talk: Communication boards for children and adults.* Tucson, AZ: Communication Skill Builders.

Johnson, J. (1988). *Self-talk stickers: Pictures and words for augmentative communication boards.* Tucson, AZ: Communication Skill Builders.

Johnson, J.M., Baumgart, D., Helmstetter, E., & Curry, C.A. (1996). *Augmenting basic communication in natural contexts.* Baltimore: Paul H. Brookes Publishing Co.

Johnson, R. (1994). *The Picture Communication Symbols Combination.* Solana Beach, CA: Mayer-Johnson Co.

Johnson-Martin, N., Wolters, P., & Sowers, S. (1987). Psychological assessment of the nonvocal, physically handicapped child. *Physical and Occupational Therapy in Pediatrics, 7*(2), 23–38.

Johnston, J. (1991a). The continuing relevance of cause: A reply to Leonard's "Specific Language Impairment as a Clinical Category." *Language, Speech, and Hearing Services in Schools, 22,* 75–79.

Johnston, J. (1991b). Questions about cognition in children with specific language impairment. In J. Miller (Ed.), *Research on child language disorders: A decade of progress* (pp. 299–308). Austin, TX: PRO-ED.

Jolly, A., Test, D., & Spooner, F. (1993). Using badges to increase initiations of children with severe disabilities in a play setting. *Journal of The Association for Persons with Severe Handicaps, 18,* 46–51.

Jordan, F., & Murdoch, B. (1990). Unexpected recovery of functional communication following a prolonged period of mutism post-head injury. *Brain Injury, 4,* 101–108.

Jose, R.T. (Ed.). (1983). *Understanding low vision.* New York: American Foundation for the Blind.

Joseph, D. (1986). The morning. *Communication Outlook, 8*(2), 8.

Joyce, M. (1993, Fall). Public speaking with a computer. *Communication Outlook, 15*(3), 5–13.

Jung, J. (1989). *Genetic syndromes in communication disorders.* Austin, TX: PRO-ED.

Kaiser, A. (1993). Functional language. In M. Snell (Ed.), *Instruction of students with severe disabilities* (4th ed., pp. 347–379). Columbus, OH: Charles E. Merrill.

Kaiser, A., & Hester, P. (1994). Generalized effects of enhanced milieu teaching. *Journal of Speech and Hearing Research, 37,* 1320–1340.

Kaiser, A., Ostrosky, M., & Alpert, C. (1993). Training teachers to use environment arrangement and milieu teaching with nonvocal preschool children. *Journal of The Association for Persons with Severe Handicaps, 18,* 188–199.

Kaiser, A.P., Yoder, P.J., & Keetz, A. (1992). Evaluating milieu teaching. In S.F. Warren & J. Reichle (Eds.), *Communication and language intervention series: Vol. 1. Causes and effects in communication and language intervention* (pp. 9–47). Baltimore: Paul H. Brookes Publishing Co.

Kalman, S., & Pajor, A. (1996). Some psychological and psychosocial aspects of introducing augmentative and alternative communication in Hungary: Tales, facts, and numbers. In S. von Tetzchner & M.H. Jensen (Eds.), *Augmentative and alternative communication: European perspectives* (pp. 355–372). London: Whurr Publishers.

Kalsbeek, W., McLauren, R., Harris, B., & Miller, J. (1981). The national head and spinal cord injury survey: Major findings. *Journal of Neurosurgery, 53,* 519–536.

Kamhi, A., & Catts, H. (1989). *Reading disabilities: A developmental language perspective.* Boston: Little, Brown.

Kangas, K., & Lloyd, L. (1988). Early cognitive skills as prerequisites to augmentative and alternative communication use: What are we waiting for? *Augmentative and Alternative Communication, 4,* 211–221.

Karlan, G. (1990). Manual communication with those who can hear. In H. Bornstein (Ed.), *Manual communication: Implications for education* (pp. 151–185). Washington, DC: Gallaudet University Press.

Karlan, G., Brenn-White, B., Lentz, A., Hodur, P., Egger, D., & Frankoff, D. (1982). Establishing generalized verb-noun phrase usage in a manual language system with moderately handicapped children. *Journal of Speech and Hearing Disorders, 47,* 31–42.

Karuth, D. (1985). If I were a car, I'd be a lemon. In A. Brightman (Ed.), *Ordinary moments: The disabled experience* (pp. 9–31). Syracuse, NY: Human Policy Press.

Kates, B., & McNaughton, S. (1975). *The first application of Blissymbolics as a communication medium for nonspeaking children: History and development, 1971–1974.* Don Mills, Ontario, Canada: Easter Seals Communication Institute.

Kaul, S. (1990). Sounds of silence. *Communication Outlook, 11*(3), 6–9.

Kearns, T. (1990). Training families as effective sign communication partners and teachers. *Augmentative and Alternative Communication, 6,* 103.

Keenan, J., & Barnhart, K. (1993). Development of yes/no systems in individuals with severe traumatic brain injuries. *Augmentative and Alternative Communication, 9,* 184–190.

Kelford Smith, A., Thurston, S., Light, J., Parnes, P., & O'Keefe, B. (1989). The form and use of written communication produced by physically disabled individuals using microcomputers. *Augmentative and Alternative Communication, 5,* 115–124.

Kelly, J., & Friend, T. (1993). *Hands-on reading.* Solana Beach, CA: Mayer-Johnson Co.

Kelly, J., & Friend, T. (1995). *More hands-on reading.* Solana Beach, CA: Mayer-Johnson Co.

Kemper, S. (1988). Geriatric psycholinguistics: Syntactic limitations of oral and written language. In L. Light & D. Burke (Eds.), *Language, memory, and aging* (pp. 58–76). Cambridge, England: Cambridge University Press.

Kennedy, M., & Shoultz, B. (1997). Thoughts about self-advocacy. *TASH Newsletter, 23*(3), 7–8.

Kent, R., Miolo, G., & Bloedel, S. (1992, November). *Measuring and assessing the intelligibility of children's speech.* Miniseminar presented at the annual convention of the American Speech-Language-Hearing Association, San Antonio, TX.

Kent, R., Miolo, G., & Bloedel, S. (1994). The intelligibility of children's speech: A review of evaluation procedures. *American Journal of Speech-Language Pathology, 3,* 81–95.

Keogh, W., & Reichle, J. (1985). Communication intervention for the "difficult-to-teach" severely handicapped. In S.F. Warren & A.K. Rogers-Warren (Eds.), *Teaching functional language* (pp. 157–194). Austin, TX: PRO-ED.

Kiernan, C. (1983). The use of nonvocal communication techniques with autistic individuals. *Journal of Child Psychology and Psychiatry, 24,* 339–375.

Kiernan, C., Reid, B., & Jones, M. (1982). *Signs and symbols: Use of non-vocal communication systems.* Portsmouth, NH: Heinemann.

King, J., Spoeneman, T., Stuart, S., & Beukelman, D. (1995). Small talk in adult conversations. *Augmentative and Alternative Communication, 11,* 244–248.

King-DeBaun, P. (1991). *Storytime: Stories, symbols, and emergent literacy activities for young, special needs children.* Park City, UT: Creative Communicating.

King-DeBaun, P. (1993). *Storytime just for fun: Stories, symbols, and emergent literacy activities for young, special needs children.* Park City, UT: Creative Communicating.

Kipila, E., & Williams-Scott, B. (1990). Cued speech. In H. Bornstein (Ed.), *Manual communication: Implications for education* (pp. 139–150). Washington, DC: Gallaudet University Press.

Kirk, S.A., McCarthy, J.J., & Kirk, W.D. (1968). *Illinois Test of Psycholinguistic Abilities.* Urbana: University of Illinois Press.

Kirstein, I. (1981). *Oakland Schools Picture Dictionary.* Wauconda, IL: Don Johnston, Inc.

Klein, B.S. (1997). *Slow dance: A story of stroke, love, and disability.* Toronto, Ontario, Canada: Knopf Canada.

Klein, M. (1988). *Pre–sign language motor skills.* San Antonio, TX: The Psychological Corporation.

Klick, S. (1985). Adapted cuing technique for use in treatment of dyspraxia. *Language, Speech, and Hearing Services in Schools, 16,* 256–259.

Klick, S. (1994). Adapted cuing technique: Facilitating sequential phoneme production. *Clinics in Communication Disorders, 4,* 183–189.

Kliewer, C., & Biklen, D. (1996). Labeling: Who wants to be called retarded? In W. Stainback & S. Stainback (Eds.), *Controversial issues in special education* (pp. 83–95). Needham Heights, MA: Allyn & Bacon.

Knapp, M. (1980). *Essentials of nonverbal communication.* New York: Holt, Rinehart & Winston.

Knox, D. (1971). *Portrait of aphasia.* Detroit: Wayne State University Press.

Koegel, L.K., Koegel, R.L., & Dunlap, G. (1996). *Positive behavioral support: Including people with difficult behavior in the community.* Baltimore: Paul H. Brookes Publishing Co.

Koehler, L., Lloyd, L., & Swanson, L. (1994). Visual similarity between manual and printed alphabet letters. *Augmentative and Alternative Communication, 10,* 87–95.

Koester, H., & Levine, S. (1996). Effect of a word prediction feature on user performance. *Augmentative and Alternative Communication, 12,* 155–168.

Konstantareas, M. (1984). Sign language as a communication prosthesis with language-impaired children. *Journal of Autism and Developmental Disorders, 14,* 9–23.

Koppenhaver, D., Evans, D., & Yoder, D. (1991). Childhood reading and writing experiences of literate adults with severe speech and motor impairments. *Augmentative and Alternative Communication, 7,* 20–33.

Koppenhaver, D., & Yoder, D. (1990, July–August). *A descriptive analysis of classroom reading and writing instruction for adolescents with severe speech and physical impairments.* Paper presented at the International Special Education Conference, Cardiff, Wales.

Koppenhaver, D., & Yoder, D. (1992a). Literacy issues in persons with severe physical and speech impairments. In R. Gaylord-Ross (Ed.), *Issues and research in special education* (Vol. 2, pp. 156–201). New York: Teachers College Press.

Koppenhaver, D., & Yoder, D. (1992b). Literacy learning of children with severe speech and physical impairments in school settings. *Seminars in Speech and Language, 13*(2), 143–153.

Koppenhaver, D., & Yoder, D. (1993). Classroom literacy instruction for children with severe speech and physical impairments (SSPI): What is and what might be. *Topics in Language Disorders, 13*(2), 1–15.

Koppenhaver, D.A., Coleman, P.P., Kalman, S.L., & Yoder, D.E. (1991). The implications of emergent literacy research for children with developmental disabilities. *American Journal of Speech-Language Pathology, 1*(1), 38–44.

Kottke, F., & Lehman, J. (Eds.). (1990). *Krusen's handbook of physical medicine and rehabilitation* (4th ed.). Philadelphia: W.B. Saunders.

Koul, R., & Allen, G. (1993). Segmental intelligibility and speech interference thresholds of high-quality synthetic speech in the presence of noise. *Journal of Speech and Hearing Research, 36,* 790–798.

Koul, R., & Hanners, J. (1997). Word identification and sentence verification of two synthetic speech systems by individuals with mental retardation. *Augmentative and Alternative Communication, 13,* 99–107.

Kouri, T. (1989). How manual sign acquisition relates to the development of spoken language: A case study. *Language, Speech, and Hearing Services in Schools, 20,* 50–62.

Kozleski, E. (1991). Expectant delay procedure for teaching requests. *Augmentative and Alternative Communication, 7,* 11–19.

Kraat, A. (1985). *Communication interaction between aided and natural speakers: A state of the art report.* Toronto, Ontario, Canada: Canadian Rehabilitation Council for the Disabled.

Kraft, G. (1981). Multiple sclerosis. In W. Stolov & M. Clowers (Eds.), *Handbook of severe disability* (pp. 111–118). Washington, DC: U.S. Department of Education.

Kraus, J. (1978). Epidemiologic features of head and spinal cord injury. *Advances in Neurology, 19,* 261–279.

Kravitz, E., & Littman, S. (1990). A communication system for a nonspeaking person with hearing and cognitive impairments. *Augmentative and Alternative Communication, 6,* 100.

Kynette, D., & Kemper, S. (1986). Aging and loss of grammatical forms: A cross-sectional study of language performance. *Language and Communication, 6*(1/2), 65–72.

Ladtkow, M., & Culp, D. (1992). Augmentative communication with the traumatically brain injured population. In K. Yorkston (Ed.), *Augmentative communication in the medical setting* (pp. 139–243). Tucson, AZ: Communication Skill Builders.

Lafontaine, L., & DeRuyter, F. (1987). The nonspeaking cerebral palsied: A clinical and demographic database report. *Augmentative and Alternative Communication, 3,* 153–162.

Lahey, M. (1990). Who shall be called language disordered? Some reflections and one perspective. *Journal of Speech and Hearing Research, 55,* 612–620.

Lahey, M., & Bloom, L. (1977). Planning a first lexicon: Which words to teach first. *Journal of Speech and Hearing Disorders, 42,* 340–349.

Lalli, J., Browder, D., Mace, C., & Brown, D. (1993). Teacher use of descriptive analysis data to implement interventions to decrease students' problem behaviors. *Journal of Applied Behavior Analysis, 25,* 227–238.

Lalli, J., Casey, S., & Kates, K. (1995). Reducing escape behavior and increasing task completion with functional communication training, extinction, and response chaining. *Journal of Applied Behavior Analysis, 28,* 261–268.

Landman, C., & Schaeffler, C. (1986). Object communication boards. *Communication Outlook, 8*(1), 7–8.

Langley, B. (1980). *Functional vision inventory for the multiply and severely handicapped.* Chicago: C.H. Stoelting.

Lasker, J., Ball, L., Bringewatt, J., Stuart, S., & Marvin, C. (1996, November). *Small talk across the lifespan: AAC vocabulary selection.* Paper presented at the annual convention of the American Speech-Language-Hearing Association, Seattle.

Lasker, J., Hux, K., Garrett, K., Moncrief, E., & Eischeid, T. (1997). Variations on the written choice communication strategy for individuals with severe aphasia. *Augmentative and Alternative Communication, 13,* 108–116.

Lee, K., & Thomas, D. (1990). *Control of computer-based technology for people with physical disabilities: An assessment manual.* Toronto, Ontario, Canada: University of Toronto Press.

Leese, B., Wright, K., Hennessy, S., Tolley, K., Chamberlain, M.A., Stowe, J., & Rowley, C. (1993). How do communication aid centres provide services to their clients? *European Journal of Disorders of Communication, 28,* 263–272.

Leiter, R. (1969). *Leiter International Performance Scale.* Chicago, IL: C.H. Stoelting.

Leonard, L. (1982). The nature of specific language impairment in children. In S. Rosenberg (Ed.), *Handbook of applied psycholinguistics: Major thrusts of research and theory* (pp. 295–328). Mahwah, NJ: Lawrence Erlbaum Associates.

Leonard, L. (1991). Specific language impairment as a clinical category. *Language, Speech, and Hearing Services in Schools, 22,* 66–68.

Leonhart, W., & Maharaj, S. (1979). *A comparison of initial recognition and rate of acquisition of Pictogram Ideogram Communication (PIC) and Bliss symbols with institutionalized severely retarded adults.* Unpublished manuscript, Pictogram Centre, Saskatoon, Saskatchewan, Canada.

Lerner, J. (1988). *Learning disabilities: Theories, diagnosis, and teaching strategies.* Boston: Houghton Mifflin.

Leske, M.C. (1981). Speech prevalence estimates of communicative disorders in the U.S. *Asha, 23,* 229–237.

Letto, M., Bedrosian, J., & Skarakis-Doyle, E. (1994). Application of Vygotskian developmental theory to language acquisition in a young child with cerebral palsy. *Augmentative and Alternative Communication, 10,* 151–160.

Levin, J., & Scherfenberg, L. (1988). *Selection and use of simple technology in home, school, work, and community settings.* Wauconda, IL: Don Johnston, Inc.

Light, J. (1988). Interaction involving individuals using augmentative and alternative communication systems: State of the art and future directions. *Augmentative and Alternative Communication, 4,* 66–82.

Light, J. (1989a). *Encoding techniques for augmentative communication systems: An investigation of the recall performance of nonspeaking physically disabled adults.* Unpublished doctoral dissertation, University of Toronto, Ontario, Canada.

Light, J. (1989b). Toward a definition of communicative competence for individuals using augmentative and alternative communication systems. *Augmentative and Alternative Communication, 5,* 137–144.

Light, J. (1993). Teaching automatic linear scanning for computer access: A case study of a preschooler with severe physical and communication disabilities. *Journal of Special Education Technology, 2,* 125–134.

Light, J. (1996). *Exemplary practices to develop the communicative competence of students who use augmentative and alternative communication: Final grant report.* University Park: The Pennsylvania State University.

Light, J., Adkins, D., Ahmon, C., Jordan, J., Moulton, J., & Seich, A. (1998). *The effect of nonverbal feedback on the communicative competence of individuals who use AAC.* Manuscript in preparation.

Light, J., Beer, D., Buchert, L., Casey, E., DiMarco, R., & Dolan, K. (1995, December). *The effect of grammatical completeness on the communicative competence of AAC users.* Poster presented at the national convention of the American Speech-Language-Hearing Association, Orlando, FL.

Light, J., Beesley, M., & Collier, B. (1988). Transition through multiple augmentative and alternative communication systems: A three-year case study of a head-injured adolescent. *Augmentative and Alternative Communication, 4,* 2–14.

Light, J., & Binger, C. (1998a). *Building communicative competence with individuals who use augmentative and alternative communication.* Baltimore: Paul H. Brookes Publishing Co.

Light, J., & Binger, C. (1998b). *Teaching the use of an introduction strategy to enhance the communicative competence of individuals who use AAC.* Manuscript in preparation, The Pennsylvania State University.

Light, J., Binger, C., Agate, T., Corbett, M., Gullipalli, G., Lepowski, S., & Ramsay, K. (1996, August). *Use of partner-focused questions to enhance communicative competence.* Paper presented at the seventh biennial conference of the International Society for Augmentative and Alternative Communication, Vancouver, British Columbia, Canada.

Light, J., Binger, C., Agate, T., & Ramsay, K. (in press). *Teaching partner-focused questions to enhance the communicative competence of individuals who use AAC.* Journal of Speech Language Hearing Research.

Light, J., Binger, C., Bailey, M., & Millar, D. (1997). *Teaching the use of nonobligatory turns to enhance the communicative competence of individuals who use AAC.* Manuscript submitted for publication, The Pennsylvania State University.

Light, J., Binger, C., Dilg, H., & Livelsberger, B. (1996, August). *Use of an introduction strategy to enhance communication competence.* Paper presented at the seventh biennial conference of the International Society for Augmentative and Alternative Communication, Vancouver, British Columbia, Canada.

Light, J., Collier, B., & Parnes, P. (1985a). Communication interaction between young nonspeaking physically disabled children and their primary caregivers: Part I. Discourse patterns. *Augmentative and Alternative Communication, 1,* 74–83.

Light, J., Collier, B., & Parnes, P. (1985b). Communication interaction between young nonspeaking physically disabled children and their primary caregivers: Part II. Communicative functions. *Augmentative and Alternative Communication, 1,* 98–107.

Light, J., Collier, B., & Parnes, P. (1985c). Communication interaction between young nonspeaking physically disabled children and their primary caregivers: Part III. Modes of communication. *Augmentative and Alternative Communication, 1,* 125–133.

Light, J., Dattilo, J., English, J., Gutierrez, L., & Hartz, J. (1992). Instructing facilitators to support the communication of people who use augmentative communication systems. *Journal of Speech and Hearing Research, 35,* 865–875.

Light, J., & Kelford Smith, A. (1993). The home literacy experiences of preschoolers who use augmentative communication systems and their nondisabled peers. *Augmentative and Alternative Communication, 9,* 10–25.

Light, J., & Lindsay, P. (1992). Message-encoding techniques for augmentative communication systems: The recall performances of adults with severe speech impairments. *Journal of Speech and Hearing Research, 35,* 853–864.

Light, J., Lindsay, P., Siegel, L., & Parnes, P. (1990). The effects of message and coding techniques on recall by literate adults using AAC systems. *Augmentative and Alternative Communication, 6,* 184–201.

Light, J., & McNaughton, D. (1993). Literacy and augmentative and alternative communication (AAC): The expectations and priorities of parents and teachers. *Topics in Language Disorders, 13*(2), 33–46.

Light, J., McNaughton, D., & Parnes, P. (1986). *A protocol for the assessment of the communicative interaction skills of nonspeaking severely handicapped adults and their facilitators.* Toronto, Ontario, Canada: Augmentative Communication Service, Hugh MacMillan Medical Centre.

Lindsay, P., Cambria, R., McNaughton, S., & Warrick, A. (1986). *The educational needs of nonspeaking students and their teachers.* Paper presented at the second biennial conference of the International Society for Augmentative and Alternative Communication, Cardiff, Wales.

Linfoot, K. (Ed.). (1994). *Communication strategies for people with developmental disabilities: Issues from theory to practice.* Baltimore: Paul H. Brookes Publishing Co.

Lippman, O. (1971). *Lippman HOTV.* Forest Park, IL: Good-Lite.

Lloyd, L., & Blischak, D. (1992). AAC terminology policy and issues update. *Augmentative and Alternative Communication, 8,* 104–109.

Lloyd, L., & Fuller, D. (1986). Toward an augmentative and alternative communication symbol taxonomy: A proposed superordinate classification. *Augmentative and Alternative Communication, 2,* 165–171.

Lloyd, L., & Karlan, G. (1984). Nonspeech communication symbols and systems: Where have we been and where are we going? *Journal of Mental Deficiency Research, 38,* 3–20.

Locke, P., & Mirenda, P. (1988). A computer-supported communication approach for a nonspeaking child with severe visual and cognitive impairments: A case study. *Augmentative and Alternative Communication, 4,* 15–22.

Locke, P., & Mirenda, P. (1992). Roles and responsibilities of special education teachers serving on teams delivering AAC services. *Augmentative and Alternative Communication, 8,* 200–214.

Locke, P., & Piché, L. (1994). Inclusion + technology = friendships. *Communication Outlook, 16*(4), 5–8.

Loeding, B., Zangari, C., & Lloyd, L. (1990). A "working party" approach to planning inservice training in manual signs for an entire public school staff. *Augmentative and Alternative Communication, 6,* 38–49.

Logemann, J. (1983). *Evaluation and treatment of swallowing disorders.* Austin, TX: PRO-ED.

Logemann, J.A., Fisher, H.B., Boshes, B., & Blonsky, E. (1978). Frequency and cooccurrence of vocal tract dysfunction in the speech of a large sample of Parkinson patients. *Journal of Speech and Hearing Disorders, 43,* 47–57.

Lovaas, O.I. (1987). Behavioral treatment and normal educational and intellectual functioning in young autistic children. *Journal of Consulting and Clinical Psychology, 55,* 3–9.

Lowe, S. (1995). *Communication in the classroom: A single case study examining the effect of a facilitator's use of language on the communicative performance of a functionally nonspeaking child.* Unpublished master's thesis, National Hospitals College of Speech Sciences, London University, London.

Luckasson, R., Coulter, D.L., Polloway, E.A., Reiss, S., Schalock, R.L., Snell, M.E., Spitalnik, D.M., & Stark, J.A. (1992). *Mental retardation: Definition, classification, and systems of support* (9th ed.). Washington, DC: American Association on Mental Retardation.

Luftig, R. (1984). An analysis of initial sign lexicons as a function of eight learnability variables. *Journal of The Association for Persons with Severe Handicaps, 9,* 193–200.

Lyon, J. (1995). Drawing: Its value as a communication aid for adults with aphasia. *Aphasiology, 9,* 33–94.

Lyon, J., & Helm-Estabrooks, N. (1987). Drawing: Its communicative significance for expressively restricted aphasic adults. *Topics in Language Disorders, 8,* 61–71.

MacArthur, C., Harris, K., & Graham, S. (1994). Improving students' planning process through cognitive strategy instruction. *Advances in Cognition and Educational Practice, 2,* 173–198.

MacArthur, C., Schwartz, S.S., & Graham, S. (1991). A model for writing instruction into a process approach to writing. *Learning Disabilities Practice, 6,* 230–236.

MacArthur, C.A. (1993). Beyond word processing: Computer support for writing processes. *LD Forum, 19*(1), 22–27.

MacDonald, J. (1989). *Becoming partners with children.* San Antonio, TX: Special Press.

MacDonald, J., & Carroll, J. (1992). Communicating with young children: An ecological model for clinicians, parents, and collaborative professionals. *American Journal of Speech-Language Pathology, 1,* 39–48.

MacDonald, J., & Gillette, Y. (1986). *Ecological communication system (ECO).* Columbus: Ohio State University, Nisonger Center.

MacGinitie, W. (1980). *Gates-MacGinitie Reading Tests* (Canadian edition). Scarborough, Ontario, Canada: ITP Nelson Canada.

MacGinitie, W., & MacGinitie, K. (1980). *Gates-MacGinitie Reading Tests* (3rd ed.). Chicago: Riverside.

Maharaj, S. (1980). *Pictogram ideogram communication.* Regina, Saskatchewan, Canada: The George Reed Foundation for the Handicapped.

Mahoney, G., & Powell, A. (1986). *Transactional intervention program: Teacher's guide.* Farmington: Pediatric Research and Training Center, University of Connecticut Health Center.

Manolson, A. (1985). *It takes two to talk: A Hanen early language parent book.* Toronto, Ontario, Canada: Hanen Early Language Resource Centre.

Manolson, A., Ward, B., & Dodington, N. (1995). *You make the difference in helping your child learn.* Toronto, Ontario, Canada: Hanen Early Language Resource Centre.

Markwardt, F. (1989). *Peabody Individual Achievement Test–Revised.* Circle Pines, MN: American Guidance Service.

Marquardt, T., Dunn, C., & Davis, B. (1985). Apraxia of speech in children. In J. Darby (Ed.), *Speech and language evaluation in neurology: Childhood disorders* (pp. 113–132). New York: Grune & Stratton.

Marriner, N. (1993, December). *The Picture Exchange Communication System (PECS).* Workshop presented in Richmond, British Columbia, Canada.

Marriner, N., Beukelman, D., Wilson, W., & Ross, A. (1989). *Implementing Morse Code in an augmentative communication system for ten nonspeaking individuals.* Unpublished manuscript, University of Washington, Seattle.

Marshall, P. (1994, December). Greetings, ISAAC friends! *Communicating Together, 12*(4), 4–7.

Martin, B., Jr. (1967). *Brown bear, brown bear, what do you see?* New York: Henry Holt & Co.

Marvin, C., & Privratsky, A. (1996, November). *After school talk: The effects of materials sent home with preschool children.* Paper presented at the annual convention of the American Speech-Language-Hearing Association, Seattle.

Marvin, C.A., Beukelman, D.R., & Bilyeu, D. (1994). Vocabulary-use patterns in preschool children: Effects of context and time sampling. *Augmentative and Alternative Communication, 10,* 224–236.

Massey, H. (1988). Language-impaired children's comprehension of synthetic speech. *Language, Speech, and Hearing Services in Schools, 19,* 401–409.

Matas, J., & Beukelman, D. (1989). *Teaching Morse Code as an augmentative communication technique: Learner and instructor performance.* Unpublished manuscript, University of Washington–Seattle.

Matas, J., Mathy-Laikko, P., Beukelman, D., & Legresley, K. (1985). Identifying the nonspeaking population: A demographic study. *Augmentative and Alternative Communication, 1,* 17–31.

Mathy-Laikko, P., & Coxson, L. (1984). *Listener reactions to augmentative communication system output mode.* Paper presented at the annual convention of the American Speech-Language-Hearing Association, San Francisco.

Mathy-Laikko, P., Iacono, T., Ratcliff, A., Villarruel, F., Yoder, D., & Vanderheiden, G. (1989). Teaching a child with multiple disabilities to use a tactile augmentative communication device. *Augmentative and Alternative Communication, 5,* 249–256.

Mathy-Laikko, P., Ratcliff, A.E., Villarruel, F., & Yoder, D.E. (1987). Augmentative communication systems. In M. Bullis (Ed.), *Communication development in young children with deaf-blindness: III. Literature review* (pp. 205–241). Monmouth: Communication Skills Center for

Young Children with Deaf-Blindness, Teaching Research Division, Oregon State System of Higher Education.

McCauley, R., & Demetras, M. (1990). The identification of language impairment in the selection of specifically language-impaired subjects. *Journal of Speech and Hearing Research, 55,* 468–475.

McDonald, A. (1994). Readers write. *Communicating Together, 12*(4), 15.

McDonald, E., & Schultz, A. (1973). Communication boards for cerebral palsied children. *Journal of Speech and Hearing Disorders, 38,* 73–88.

McDonald, E.T. (1987). Cerebral palsy: Its nature, pathogenesis, and management. In E.T. McDonald (Ed.), *Treating cerebral palsy: For clinicians by clinicians* (pp. 1–20). Austin, TX: PRO-ED.

McDonald, J., Schwejda, P., Marriner, N., Wilson, W., & Ross, A. (1982). Advantages of Morse Code as a computer input for school-aged children with physical disability. In *Computers and the handicapped* (pp. 95–106). Ottawa, Ontario, Canada: National Research Council of Canada.

McEachin, J., Smith, T., & Lovaas, O.I. (1993). Long-term outcome for children with autism who received early intensive behavioral treatment. *American Journal on Mental Retardation, 97,* 359–372.

McEwen, I., & Lloyd, L.L. (1990). Positioning students with cerebral palsy to use augmentative and alternative communication. *Language, Speech, and Hearing Services in Schools, 21,* 15–21.

McGinnis, J. (1991). *Development of two source lists for vocabulary selection in augmentative communication: Documentation of the spoken and written vocabulary of third grade students.* Unpublished doctoral dissertation, University of Nebraska–Lincoln.

McGregor, G., Young, J., Gerak, J., Thomas, B., & Vogelsberg, T. (1992). Increasing functional use of an assistive communication device by a student with severe disabilities. *Augmentative and Alternative Communication, 8,* 243–250.

McLean, J., McLean, L., Brady, N., & Etter, R. (1991). Communication profiles of two types of gestures using nonverbal persons with severe to profound mental retardation. *Journal of Speech and Hearing Research, 34,* 294–308.

McNairn, P., & Shioleno, C. (1993). *Quick tech readable, repeatable stories and activities.* Wauconda, IL: Don Johnston, Inc.

McNairn, P., & Shioleno, C. (1995). *Quick tech magic: Music-based literacy activities.* Wauconda, IL: Don Johnston, Inc.

McNaughton, D., Fallon, K., Tod, J., Weiner, F., & Neisworth, J. (1994). Effect of repeated listening experiences on the intelligibility of synthesized speech. *Augmentative and Alternative Communication, 10*(3), 161–168.

McNaughton, D., & Light, J. (1989). Teaching facilitators to support the communication skills of an adult with severe cognitive disabilities: A case study. *Augmentative and Alternative Communication, 5,* 35–41.

McNaughton, S. (1990a). Introducing AccessBliss. *Communicating Together, 8*(2), 12–13.

McNaughton, S. (1990b). StoryBliss. *Communicating Together, 8*(1), 12–13.

McNaughton, S. (1993a). Graphic representational systems and literacy learning. *Topics in Language Disorders, 13*(2), 58–75.

McNaughton, S. (1993b). Language! Welcoming a parent's perspective. *Communicating Together, 11*(3), 21–23.

McNaughton, S. (1995). Responding to "What is your latest thinking on Bliss?" *Communicating Together, 12*(4), 22–23.

McNaughton, S., & Jennische, M. (1992, December). Language! Just what do we mean? *Communicating Together, 10*(4), 21–23.

McNaughton, S., & Lindsay, P. (1995). Approaching literacy with AAC graphics. *Augmentative and Alternative Communication, 11,* 212–228.

Medhat, M.A., & Hobson, D. (1992). *Standardization of terminology and descriptive methods for specialized seating: A reference manual.* Washington, DC: RESNA Press.

Mergler, N., & Goldstein, M. (1983). Why are there old people? *Human Development, 26,* 130–143.

Meyer, L.H., Peck, C.A., & Brown, L. (Eds.). (1991). *Critical issues in the lives of people with severe disabilities.* Baltimore: Paul H. Brookes Publishing Co.

Michael, P. (1981). *Multiple sclerosis: A dragon with a hundred heads.* Port Washington, NY: Ashley Books.

Millin, N. (1995). Developing our own voices. *Communicating Together, 12*(1), 2–4.

Mills, J., & Higgins, J. (1983). *Non-oral communication assessment and training guide.* Encinitas, CA: Authors.

Mirenda, P. (1985). Designing pictorial communication systems for physically able-bodied students with severe handicaps. *Augmentative and Alternative Communication, 1,* 58–64.

Mirenda, P. (1993). AAC: Bonding the uncertain mosaic. *Augmentative and Alternative Communication, 9*, 3–9.

Mirenda, P. (1997). Supporting individuals with challenging behaviour through functional communication training and AAC: A research review. *Augmentative and Alternative Communication, 13*, 207–225.

Mirenda, P., & Beukelman, D. (1987). A comparison of speech synthesis intelligibility with listeners from three age groups. *Augmentative and Alternative Communication, 3*, 120–128.

Mirenda, P., & Calculator, S. (1993). Enhancing curricula design. *Clinics in Communication Disorders, 3*(2), 43–58.

Mirenda, P., & Dattilo, J. (1987). Instructional techniques in alternative communication for learners with severe intellectual disabilities. *Augmentative and Alternative Communication, 3*, 143–152.

Mirenda, P., Eicher, D., & Beukelman, D. (1989). Synthetic and natural speech preferences of male and female listeners in four age groups. *Journal of Speech and Hearing Research, 32*, 175–183, 703.

Mirenda, P., Iacono, T., & Williams, R. (1990). Communication options for persons with severe and profound disabilities: State of the art and future directions. *Journal of The Association for Persons with Severe Handicaps, 15*, 3–21.

Mirenda, P., & Locke, P. (1989). A comparison of symbol transparency in nonspeaking persons with intellectual disabilities. *Journal of Speech and Hearing Disorders, 54*, 131–140.

Mirenda, P., Malette, P., & McGregor, T. (1994, October). *Multicomponent, integrated communication systems for persons with severe intellectual disabilities.* Paper presented at the sixth biennial conference of the International Society for Augmentative and Alternative Communication, Maastricht, the Netherlands.

Mirenda, P., & Mathy-Laikko, P. (1989). Augmentative and alternative communication applications for persons with severe congenital communication disorders: An introduction. *Augmentative and Alternative Communication, 5*, 3–13.

Mirenda, P., & Santogrossi, J. (1985). A prompt-free strategy to teach pictorial communication system use. *Augmentative and Alternative Communication, 1*, 143–150.

Mirenda, P., & Schuler, A. (1988). Teaching individuals with autism and related disorders to use visual-spatial symbols to communicate. In S. Blackstone, E. Cassatt-James, & D. Bruskin (Eds.), *Augmentative communication: Intervention strategies* (pp. 5.1-17–5.1-25). Rockville, MD: American Speech-Language-Hearing Association.

Mirenda, P., & Schuler, A. (1989). Augmenting communication for persons with autism: Issues and strategies. *Topics in Language Disorders, 9*, 24–43.

Mitsuda, P., Baarslag-Benson, R., Hazel, K., & Therriault, T. (1992). Augmentative communication in intensive and acute care settings. In K. Yorkston (Ed.), *Augmentative communication in the medical setting* (pp. 5–58). Tucson, AZ: Communication Skill Builders.

Mizuko, M. (1987). Transparency and ease of learning of symbols represented by Blissymbols, PCS, and Picsyms. *Augmentative and Alternative Communication, 3*, 129–136.

Mizuko, M., & Esser, J. (1991). The effect of direct selection and circular scanning on visual sequential recall. *Journal of Speech and Hearing Research, 34*, 43–48.

Mizuko, M., & Reichle, J. (1989). Transparency and recall of symbols among intellectually handicapped adults. *Journal of Speech and Hearing Disorders, 54*, 627–633.

Mizuko, M., Reichle, J., Ratcliff, A., & Esser, J. (1994). Effects of selection techniques and array sizes on short-term visual memory. *Augmentative and Alternative Communication, 10*, 237–244.

Molloy, D.W., & Lubinsky, R. (1995). Dementia: Impact and clinical perspectives. In R. Lubinsky (Ed.), *Dementia and communication* (pp. 2–21). San Diego: Singular Publishing Group.

Montgomery, J. (1987). Augmentative communication: Selecting successful interventions. *Seminars in Speech and Hearing, 8*, 187–197.

Morris, S. (1995). The Preschool Speech Intelligibility Measure. *American Journal of Speech-Language Pathology, 4*, 22–28.

Morrow, D., Beukelman, D., Mirenda, P., & Yorkston, K. (1993). *Vocabulary selection for augmentative communication systems: A comparison of three techniques.* Unpublished manuscript, University of Nebraska–Lincoln.

Moss, C.S. (1972). *Recovery with aphasia: The aftermath of my stroke.* Champaign: University of Illinois Press.

Mount, B. (1994). Benefits and limitations of Personal Futures Planning. In V.J. Bradley, J.W. Ashbaugh, & B.C. Blaney (Eds.), *Creating individual supports for people with developmental disabilities: A mandate for change at many levels* (pp. 97–108). Baltimore: Paul H. Brookes Publishing Co.

Mount, B., & Zwernik, K. (1988). *It's never too early, it's never too late* (Pub. No. 421-88-109). St. Paul, MN: Metropolitan Council.

Mullen, E. (1985). *Psychological S–R Evaluation for Severely Multihandicapped Children (PSR)*. East Providence, RI: Meeting Street School.

Murphy, A. (1994). Celebrating the life of Andrew Murphy. *Communicating Together, 12*(3), 4–9.

Murphy, J., Marková, I., Collins, S., & Moodie, E. (1996). AAC systems: Obstacles to effective use. *European Journal of Disorders of Communication, 31,* 31–44.

Murphy, J., Marková, I., Moodie, E., Scott, J., & Boa, S. (1996). Augmentative and alternative communication systems used by people with cerebral palsy in Scotland: Demographic survey. *Augmentative and Alternative Communication, 11,* 26–36.

Murphy, R.T., & Appel, L.R. (1984). *Evaluation of Writing to Read*. Princeton, NJ: Educational Testing Service.

Murray-Branch, J., Udvari-Solner, A., & Bailey, B. (1991). Textured communication systems for individuals with severe intellectual and dual sensory impairments. *Language, Speech, and Hearing Services in Schools, 22,* 260–268.

Musselwhite, C. (1985). *Songbook: Signs and symbols for children*. Wauconda, IL: Don Johnston, Inc.

Musselwhite, C. (1986a). *Adaptive play for special needs children: Strategies to enhance communication and learning*. San Diego: Singular Publishing Group.

Musselwhite, C. (1986b). Introducing augmentative communication: Interactive training strategies. *NSSLHA Journal, 14,* 68–82.

Musselwhite, C. (1990, August). *Topic setting: Generic and specific strategies*. Paper presented at the fourth biennial conference of the International Society for Augmentative and Alternative Communication, Stockholm.

Musselwhite, C. & King-DeBaun, P. (1997). *Emerging literacy success: Merging whole language and technology for students with disabilities*. Park City, UT: Creative Communicating.

Musselwhite, C., & Ruscello, D. (1984). Transparency of three symbol communication systems. *Journal of Speech and Hearing Research, 27,* 436–443.

Musselwhite, C., & St. Louis, K. (1988). *Communication programming for persons with severe handicaps* (2nd ed.). Austin, TX: PRO-ED.

Musselwhite, C.R. (1993). *RAPS: Reading activities project for older students*. Phoenix, AZ: Southwest Human Development.

Nagi, S. (1991). Disability concepts revisited: Implications for prevention. In A. Pope & A. Tarlov (Eds.), *Disability in America: Toward a national agenda for prevention* (pp. 309–327). Washington, DC: National Academy Press.

Nakamura, K., Arima, M., Sakamoto, A., & Toyota, R. (1993). Telephoning with a voice output device: Listener reactions. *Augmentative and Alternative Communication, 9*(4), 251–258.

National Aphasia Association. (1987). *The impact of aphasia on patient and family: Results of a needs survey*. New York: Author.

National Joint Committee for the Communicative Needs of Persons with Severe Disabilities. (1992). Guidelines for meeting the communication needs of persons with severe disabilities. *Asha, 34*(Suppl. 7), 1–8.

National Joint Committee on Learning Disabilities. (1991). Learning disabilities: Issues on definition. *Asha, 33*(Suppl. 5), 18–20.

National Society to Prevent Blindness. (1980). *Vision problems in the U.S.* New York: Author.

Nelson, N. (1992). Performance is the prize: Language competence and performance among AAC users. *Augmentative and Alternative Communication, 8,* 3–18.

Nelson, N.W. (1993). *Childhood language disorders in context: Infancy through adolescence*. New York: Macmillan.

Netsell, R., & Daniel, B. (1979). Dysarthria in adults: Physiologic approach to rehabilitation. *Archives of Physical Medicine and Rehabilitation, 60,* 502–508.

New York Association for the Blind. (n.d.). *Lighthouse flashcard test*. New York: Author.

Newell, A. (1992). Social communication: Chattering, nattering, and cheek. *Communication Outlook, 14*(1), 6–8.

Newell, A., Arnott, J., Booth, L., Beattie, W., Brophy, B., & Ricketts, I. (1992). Effects of the "PAL" word prediction system on the quality and quantity of text generation. *Augmentative and Alternative Communication, 8,* 304–311.

Nolan, C. (1981). *Dam-burst of dreams*. New York: St. Martin's Press.

Nolan, C. (1987). *Under the eye of the clock*. New York: St. Martin's Press.

Norris, L., & Belair, B. (1988). The client's role on the AAC assessment team. *Augmentative and Alternative Communication, 4,* 168–169.

Northup, J., Wacker, D., Berg, W., Kelly, L., Sasso, G., & DeRaad, A. (1994). The treatment of severe behavior problems in school settings using a technical assistance model. *Journal of Applied Behavior Analysis, 27,* 33–48.

Noyes, J., & Frankish, C. (1992). Speech recognition technology for individuals with disabilities. *Augmentative and Alternative Communication, 8,* 297–303.

Nurss, J., & McGauvran, M. (1986). *Metropolitan Reading Readiness Test* (6th ed.). San Antonio, TX: The Psychological Corporation.

Nyberg, E. (1993, March). Some notes on Minspeak, language, and language development. *Communicating Together, 11*(1), 19–22.

O'Brien, J., & Lyle, C. (1987). *Framework for accomplishment.* Decatur, GA: Responsive Systems Associates.

O'Keefe, B., & Dattilo, J. (1992). Teaching the response-recode form to adults with mental retardation using AAC systems. *Augmentative and Alternative Communication, 8,* 224–233.

Oliver, C., & Halle, J. (1982). Language training in the everyday environment: Teaching functional language use to a retarded child. *Journal of The Association for Persons with Severe Handicaps, 8,* 50–63.

Ollila, L.O., & Mayfield, M.I. (1992). Home and school together: Helping beginning readers to succeed. In S.J. Samuals & A.E. Farstrup (Eds.), *What research has to say about reading instruction* (2nd ed., pp. 17–45). Newark, DE: International Reading Association.

Olmos-Lau, N., Ginsberg, M., & Geller, J. (1977). Aphasia in multiple sclerosis. *Neurology, 27,* 623–626.

Olsen, D., & Henig, E. (1983). *A manual of behavioral management strategies for traumatically brain injured adults.* Chicago: Rehabilitation Institute of Chicago.

O'Neill, R., Horner, R., Albin, R., Sprague, J., Storey, K., & Newton, S. (1997). *Functional assessment and program development for problem behavior: A practical handbook* (2nd ed.). Pacific Grove, CA: Brooks/Cole.

Oregon Research Institute. (1989). *Getting in touch: Communicating with a child who is deaf-blind* [Film]. Champaign, IL: Research Press.

Orelove, F.P., & Sobsey, D. (1996). *Educating children with multiple disabilities: A transdisciplinary approach* (3rd ed.). Baltimore: Paul H. Brookes Publishing Co.

Osberger, M. (1992). Speech intelligibility in the hearing impaired: Research and clinical implications. In R. Kent (Ed.), *Speech intelligibility in speech disorders: Theory, measurement, and management* (pp. 233–264). Amsterdam: John Benjamins.

Osborn, A. (1963). *Applied imagination: Principles and procedures of creative problem-solving.* New York: Charles Scribner's Sons.

Osterling, J., & Dawson, G. (1994). Early recognition of children with autism: A study of first birthday home videotapes. *Journal of Autism and Developmental Disorders, 24,* 247–257.

Otos, M. (1983). *Nonverbal prelinguistic communication: A guide to communication levels in prelinguistic handicapped children.* Salem: Oregon Department of Education.

Ourand, P., & Gray, S. (1997). Funding and legal issues in augmentative and alternative communication. In S.L. Glennen & D. DeCoste (Eds.), *The handbook of augmentative and alternative communication* (pp. 335–360). San Diego: Singular Publishing Group.

Paget, R., Gorman, P., & Paget, G. (1976). *The Paget Gorman Sign System* (6th ed.). London: Association for Experiments in Deaf Education.

Pamplin, B. (1996a). How the family changes. *Communicating Together, 313*(2), 18.

Pamplin, B. (1996b). What do I know? I am just the patient! *Communicating Together, 13*(1), 16.

Paneth, N., & Kiely, J. (1984). The frequency of cerebral palsy: A review of population studies in industrialized nations since 1950. *Clinics in Developmental Medicine, 87,* 46–56.

Park, C.C. (1982). *The siege.* Boston: Little, Brown.

Parnes, P. (1995). "Oh, Wow Days are gone forever," Canadian administrator reports. In S. Blackstone & H. Pressman (Eds.), *Outcomes in AAC conference report: Alliance '95* (pp. 21–22). Monterey, CA: Augmentative Communication.

Parnes, S. (1985). *A facilitating style of leadership.* Buffalo, NY: The Creative Education Foundation.

Parnes, S. (1988). *Visioning: State-of-the-art process for encouraging innovative excellence.* East Aurora, NY: DOK Publishers.

Pearpoint, J., Forest, M., & O'Brien, J. (1996). MAPs, Circles of Friends, and PATH: Powerful tools to help build caring communities. In S. Stainback & W. Stainback (Eds.), *Inclusion: A guide for educators* (pp. 67–86). Baltimore: Paul H. Brookes Publishing Co.

Pearpoint, J., O'Brien, J., & Forest, M. (1993). *PATH*. Toronto, Ontario, Canada: Inclusion Press.

Peck, C., & Cooke, T. (1983). Benefits of mainstreaming at the early childhood level: How much can we expect? *Analysis and Intervention in Developmental Disabilities, 3,* 1–22.

Peck, C.A. (1985). Increasing opportunities for social control by children with autism and severe handicaps: Effects on learner behavior and perceived classroom climate. *Journal of The Association for Persons with Severe Handicaps, 10,* 183–193.

Peck, S., Wacker, D., Berg, W., Cooper, L., Brown, K., Richman, D., McComas, J., Frischmeyer, P., & Millard, T. (1996). Choice-making treatment of young children's severe behavior problems. *Journal of Applied Behavior Analysis, 29,* 263–290.

Pecyna, P. (1988). Rebus symbol communication training with a severely handicapped preschool child: A case study. *Language, Speech, and Hearing Services in Schools, 19,* 128–143.

Perske, R., & Perske, M. (1988). *Circles of friends.* Nashville, TN: Abingdon.

Pierce, P., Steelman, J., Koppenhaver, D., & Yoder, D. (1993, March). Linking symbols with language. *Communicating Together, 11*(1), 18–19.

Pierce, P.L., & McWilliam, P.J. (1993). Emerging literacy and children with severe speech and physical impairments (SSPI): Issues and possible intervention strategies. *Topics in Language Disorders, 13*(2), 47–57.

Pinker, S. (1994). *The language instinct: How the mind creates language.* New York: William Morrow.

Poole, M. (1979). Social class, sex, and linguistic coding. *Language and Speech, 22,* 49–67.

Porter, P. (1989). Intervention in end stage of multiple sclerosis. *Augmentative and Alternative Communication, 5,* 125–127.

Poser, C.M. (Ed.). (1984). *The diagnosis of multiple sclerosis.* New York: Thieme-Stratton.

Premack, D. (1970). A functional analysis of language. *Journal of the Experimental Analysis of Behavior, 14,* 107–125.

Pressley, M., & McCormick, C. (1995). *Advanced educational psychology: For educators, researchers, and policy makers.* New York: HarperCollins.

Pressley, M., Woloshyn, V., & Associates. (1995). *Cognitive strategy instruction that really improves academic performance* (2nd ed.). Cambridge, MA: Brookline Books.

Prizant, B. (1983). Language and communicative behavior in autism: Toward an understanding of the "whole" of it. *Journal of Speech and Hearing Disorders, 46,* 241–249.

Pugach, M.C., & Johnson, L.J. (1990). Meeting diverse needs through professional peer collaboration. In W. Stainback & S. Stainback (Eds.), *Support networks for inclusive schooling: Interdependent integrated education* (pp. 123–137). Baltimore: Paul H. Brookes Publishing Co.

Pulli, T., & Jaroma, M. (1990). Exploring novel solutions for motivating simplified signing, pictorializing, and vocalizing. *Augmentative and Alternative Communication, 6,* 103.

Radell, U. (1997). Augmentative and alternative communication assessment strategies: Seating and positioning. In S.L. Glennen & D. DeCoste (Eds.), *The handbook of augmentative and alternative communication* (pp. 193–242). San Diego: Singular Publishing Group.

Raghavendra, P., & Fristoe, M. (1990). "A spinach with a V on it": What 3-year-olds see in standard and enhanced Blissymbolics. *Journal of Speech and Hearing Disorders, 55,* 149–159.

Raghavendra, P., & Fristoe, M. (1995). "No shoes; they walked away?": Effects of using enhancements on learning and using Blissymbols by normal 3-year-old children. *Journal of Speech and Hearing Research, 38,* 174–188.

Raines, S.C., & Canady, R.J. (1989). *Story S-T-R-E-T-C-H-E-R-S: Activities to expand children's favorite books.* Beltsville, MD: Gryphon House.

Raines, S.C., & Canady, R.J. (1991). *More story S-T-R-E-T-C-H-E-R-S: Activities to expand children's favorite books.* Beltsville, MD: Gryphon House.

Ramig, L., & Scherer, R. (1992). Speech therapy for neurological disorders of the larynx. In A. Blitzer, M. Brin, C. Sasaki, S. Fahn, & K. Harris (Eds.), *Neurological disorders of the larynx* (pp. 163–181). New York: Thieme Medical Publishers.

Rankin, J.L., Harwood, K., & Mirenda, P. (1994). Influence of graphic symbol use on reading comprehension. *Augmentative and Alternative Communication, 10,* 269–281.

Rao, P. (1994). Introducing a communication board for child-to-child conversations. *Communication Outlook, 16*(2), 10–12.

Rao, P. (1995). Drawing and gesture as communication options in a person with severe aphasia. *Topics in Stroke Rehabilitation, 2,* 49–56.

Ratcliff, A. (1994). Comparison of relative demands implicated in direct selection and scanning: Considerations from normal children. *Augmentative and Alternative Communication, 10,* 67–74.

Reed, C., Delhorne, L., Durlach, N., & Fischer, S. (1990). A study of the tactual and visual reception of fingerspelling. *Journal of Speech and Hearing Research, 33,* 786–797.

Reed, C., Delhorne, L., Durlach, N., & Fischer, S. (1995). A study of the tactual reception of sign language. *Journal of Speech and Hearing Research, 38*, 477–489.

Reed, C., Rabinowitz, W., Durlach, N., Delhorne, L., Braida, L., Pemberton, J., Mulcahey, B., & Washington, D. (1992). Analytic study of the Tadoma method: Improving performance through the use of supplementary tactual displays. *Journal of Speech and Hearing Research, 35*, 450–465.

Rees, N. (1982). Language intervention with children. In J. Miller, D. Yoder, & R. Schiefelbusch (Eds.), *Contemporary issues in language intervention* (American Speech-Language Hearing Association Report No. 12, pp. 309–316). Rockville, MD: American Speech-Language-Hearing Association.

Rehabilitation Act Amendments of 1992, PL 102-569, 29 U.S.C. §§ 701 *et seq.*

Reichle, J., & Brown, L. (1986). Teaching the use of a multipage direct selection communication board to an adult with autism. *Journal of The Association for Persons with Severe Handicaps, 11*, 68–73.

Reichle, J., & Karlan, G. (1985). The selection of an augmentative system of communication intervention: A critique of decision rules. *Journal of The Association for Persons with Severe Handicaps, 10*, 146–156.

Reichle, J., Rogers, N., & Barrett, C. (1984). Establishing pragmatic discrimination among the communicative functions of requesting, rejecting, and commenting in an adolescent. *Journal of The Association for Persons with Severe Handicaps, 9*, 31–36.

Reichle, J., Sigafoos, J., & Piché, L. (1989). Teaching an adolescent with blindness and severe disabilities: A correspondence between requesting and selecting preferred objects. *Journal of The Association for Persons with Severe Handicaps, 14*, 75–80.

Reichle, J., & Wacker, D.P. (Eds.). (1993). *Communication and language intervention series: Vol. 3. Communicative alternatives to challenging behavior: Integrating functional assessment and intervention strategies.* Baltimore: Paul H. Brookes Publishing Co.

Reichle, J., & Ward, M. (1985). Teaching the discriminative use of an encoding electronic communication device and Signing Exact English to a moderately handicapped child. *Language, Speech, and Hearing Services in Schools, 16*, 58–63.

Reichle, J., & Yoder, D. (1985). Communication board use in severely handicapped learners. *Language, Speech, and Hearing Services in Schools, 16*, 146–157.

Reichle, J., York, J., & Sigafoos, J. (1991). *Implementing augmentative and alternative communication: Strategies for learners with severe disabilities.* Baltimore: Paul H. Brookes Publishing Co.

Reif, L. (1992). *Seeking diversity: Language arts with adolescents.* Portsmouth, NH: Heinemann.

Remington, B. (1994). Augmentative and alternative communication and behavior analysis: A productive partnership? *Augmentative and Alternative Communication, 10*, 3–13.

Remington, B., & Clarke, S. (1993a). Simultaneous communication and speech comprehension: Part I. Comparison of two methods of teaching expressive signing and speech comprehension skills. *Augmentative and Alternative Communication, 9*, 36–48.

Remington, B., & Clarke, S. (1993b). Simultaneous communication and speech comprehension: Part II. Comparison of two methods overcoming selective attention during expressive sign training. *Augmentative and Alternative Communication, 9*, 49–60.

Remington, B., Watson, J., & Light, J. (1990). Beyond the single sign: A matrix-based approach to teaching productive sign combinations. *Mental Handicap Research, 3*, 33–50.

Reynolds, M., Bond, Z., & Fucci, D. (1996). Synthetic speech intelligibility: Comparison of native and non-native speakers of English. *Augmentative and Alternative Communication, 12*, 32–36.

Rhodes, L.K., & Dudley-Marling, C. (1988). *Readers and writers with a difference: A holistic approach to teaching learning disabled and remedial students.* Portsmouth, NH: Heinemann.

Ritvo, E., Freeman, B.J., Mason-Brothers, A., & Ritvo, A. (1993). Clinical characteristics of mild autism in adults. *Comprehensive Psychiatry, 35*, 149–156.

Roach, E.G., & Kephart, N.C. (1966). *Purdue Perceptual-Motor Survey.* Columbus, OH: Charles E. Merrill.

Robin, D. (1992). Developmental apraxia of speech: Just another motor problem. *American Journal of Speech-Language Pathology, 1*, 19–22.

Robinson, C., Bataillon, K., Fieber, N., Jackson, B., & Rasmussen, J. (1985). *Sensorimotor assessment form.* Omaha, NE: Meyer Rehabilitation Center.

Romski, M., & Sevcik, R. (1988a). Augmentative and alternative communication systems: Considerations for individuals with severe intellectual disabilities. *Augmentative and Alternative Communication, 4*, 83–93.

Romski, M., & Sevcik, R. (1988b). *Speech output communication systems: Acquisition/use by youngsters with retardation.* Miniseminar presented at the annual convention of the American Speech-Language-Hearing Association, Boston.

Romski, M., Sevcik, R., & Pate, J. (1988). Establishment of symbolic communication in persons with severe retardation. *Journal of Speech and Hearing Disorders, 53*, 94–107.

Romski, M., White, R., Millen, C., & Rumbaugh, D. (1984). Effects of computer keyboard teaching on symbolic communication of severely retarded persons: Five case studies. *The Psychological Record, 34*, 39–54.

Romski, M.A., & Ruder, K. (1984). Effects of speech and speech and sign instruction on oral language learning and generalization of object + action combinations by Down's syndrome children. *Journal of Speech and Hearing Disorders, 49*, 293–302.

Romski, M.A., Sevcik, R., & Cress, C. (1996, August). *Research in augmentative communication development for toddlers: Considerations for practice.* Paper presented at the seventh biennial conference of the International Society for Augmentative and Alternative Communication, Vancouver, British Columbia, Canada.

Romski, M.A., Sevcik, R., Robinson, B., Mervis, C., & Bertrand, J. (1995). Mapping the meanings of novel visual symbols by youth with moderate or severe mental retardation. *American Journal on Mental Retardation, 100*, 391–402.

Romski, M.A., & Sevcik, R.A. (1992). Developing augmented language in children with severe mental retardation. In S.F. Warren & J. Reichle (Eds.), *Communication and language intervention series: Vol. 1. Causes and effects in communication and language intervention* (pp. 113–130). Baltimore: Paul H. Brookes Publishing Co.

Romski, M.A., & Sevcik, R.A. (1993). Language learning through augmented means: The process and its products. In A.P. Kaiser & D.B. Gray (Eds.), *Communication and language intervention series: Vol. 2. Enhancing children's communication: Research foundations for intervention* (pp. 85–104). Baltimore: Paul H. Brookes Publishing Co.

Romski, M.A., & Sevcik, R.A. (1996). *Breaking the speech barrier: Language development through augmented means.* Baltimore: Paul H. Brookes Publishing Co.

Rosen, M., & Goodenough-Trepagnier, C. (1981). Factors affecting communication rate in nonvocal communication systems. In *Proceedings of the Fourth Annual Conference on Rehabilitation Engineering* (pp. 194–195). Washington, DC: RESNA Press.

Rosenbek, J., LaPointe, L., & Wertz, R. (1989). *Aphasia: A clinical approach.* Austin, TX: PRO-ED.

Rosenberg, S., & Beukelman, D. (1987). The participation model. In C.A. Coston (Ed.), *Proceedings of the national planners conference on assistive device service delivery* (pp. 159–161). Washington, DC: The Association for the Advancement of Rehabilitation Technology.

Rosenthal, R., & Rosenthal, K. (1989). *A model for mainstreaming handicapped kids: Handicapped kids are regular kids, too!* Lincoln, NE: Meadowlane Elementary School.

Rossi, P. (1986). Mathematics. In G.T. Scholl (Ed.), *Foundations of education for blind and visually handicapped children and youth: Theory and practice* (pp. 367–374). New York: American Foundation for the Blind.

Roth, F., & Cassatt-James, E. (1989). The language assessment process: Clinical implications for individuals with severe speech impairments. *Augmentative and Alternative Communication, 5*, 165–172.

Rotholz, D., Berkowitz, S., & Burberry, J. (1989). Functionality of two modes of communication in the community by students with developmental disabilities: A comparison of signing and communication books. *Journal of The Association for Persons with Severe Handicaps, 14*, 227–233.

Rounsefell, S., Zucker, S., & Roberts, M. (1993). Effects of listener training on intelligibility of augmentative and alternative speech in the secondary classroom. *Education and Training in Mental Retardation, 28*, 296–308.

Rowland, C. (1990). Communication in the classroom for children with dual sensory impairments: Studies of teacher and child behavior. *Augmentative and Alternative Communication, 6*, 262–274.

Rowland, C. (1996). *Communication matrix.* Portland: Oregon Health Sciences University, Portland Projects.

Rowland, C., & Schweigert, P. (1989). Tangible symbols: Symbolic communication for individuals with multisensory impairments. *Augmentative and Alternative Communication, 5*, 226–234.

Rowland, C., & Schweigert, P. (1990). *Tangible symbol systems: Symbolic communication for individuals with multisensory impairments.* Tucson, AZ: Communication Skill Builders

Rowland, C., & Schweigert, P. (1991). *The early communication process using microswitch technology.* Tucson, AZ: Communication Skill Builders.

Rowland, C., & Schweigert, P. (1992). Early communication and microtechnology: Instructional sequence and case studies of children with severe multiple disabilities. *Augmentative and Alternative Communication, 8*, 273–286.

Rowland, C., & Schweigert, P. (1993). Analyzing the communication environment to increase functional communication. *Journal of The Association for Persons with Severe Handicaps, 18,* 161–176.

Rowland, C., & Schweigert, P. (1996). *Tangible symbol systems* (Rev. ed.) [Videotape]. San Antonio, TX: The Psychological Corporation.

Rule, S., Fiechtl, B., & Innocenti, M. (1990). Preschool environments: Development of a survival skills curriculum. *Topics in Early Childhood Special Education, 9*(4), 78–90.

Rumbaugh, D. (1977). *Language learning by a chimpanzee: The LANA project.* New York: Academic Press.

Rupprecht, S., Beukelman, D., & Vrtiska, H. (1995). Comparative intelligibility of five synthesized voices. *Augmentative and Alternative Communication, 11,* 244–248.

Rush, W. (1986). *Journey out of silence.* Lincoln, NE: Media Publishing and Marketing.

Rusk, H., Block, J., & Lowman, E. (1969). Habilitation of the brain-injured patient: A report of 157 cases with long-term followup of 118. In E. Walker, W. Caveness, & M. Critchley (Eds.), *The effect of head injury.* Springfield, IL: Charles C Thomas.

Sacks, S.Z., & Silberman, R.K. (1998). *Educating students who have visual impairments with other disabilities.* Baltimore: Paul H. Brookes Publishing Co.

Sadowsky, A. (1985). Visual impairment among developmentally disabled clients in California regional centers. *Journal of Visual Impairment and Blindness, 79,* 199–202.

Sailor, W., Anderson, J.L., Halvorsen, A.T., Doering, K., Filler, J., & Goetz, L. (1989). *The comprehensive local school: Regular education for all students with disabilities.* Baltimore: Paul H. Brookes Publishing Co.

Sailor, W., Utley, B., Goetz, L., Gee, K., & Baldwin, M. (1982). *Vision assessment and program manual for severely handicapped and/or deaf-blind students.* San Francisco: San Francisco State University, Bay Area Severely Handicapped/Deaf-Blind Project.

Salisbury, C., & Vincent, L. (1990). Criterion of the next environment and best practices: Mainstreaming and integration 10 years later. *Topics in Early Childhood Special Education, 10*(2), 78–89.

Sapon-Shevin, M. (1990). Student support through cooperative learning. In W. Stainback & S. Stainback (Eds.), *Support networks for inclusive schooling: Interdependent integrated education* (pp. 65–79). Baltimore: Paul H. Brookes Publishing Co.

Sarno, M., Buonaguvro, A., & Levita, E. (1986). Characteristics of verbal impairment in closed head injured patients. *Archives of Physical Medicine & Rehabilitation, 67,* 400–405.

Saunders, C., Walsh, T., & Smith, M. (1981). Hospice care in the motor neuron diseases. In C. Saunders & J. Teller (Eds.), *Hospice: The living idea.* London: Edward Arnold.

Savage-Rumbaugh, E. (1984). Verbal behavior at a procedural level by a chimpanzee. *Journal of the Experimental Analysis of Behavior, 41,* 223–250.

Scardamalia, M. (1981). How children cope with the cognitive demands of writing. In C.H. Frederickson, M.F. Whiteman, & J.F. Dominic (Eds.), *Writing: The nature of development and teaching of written communication* (Vol. 2, pp. 81–103). Mahwah, NJ: Lawrence Erlbaum Associates.

Schaeffer, B. (1980). Spontaneous language through signed speech. In R. Schiefelbusch (Ed.), *Nonspeech language and communication* (pp. 421–446). Baltimore: University Park Press.

Schank, R. (1990). *Tell me a story: A new look at real and artificial memory.* New York: Charles Scribner's Sons.

Schlosser, R., Belfiore, P., Nigam, R., Blischak, D., & Hetzroni, O. (1995). The effects of speech output technology on the learning of graphic symbols. *Journal of Applied Behavior Analysis, 28,* 537–549.

Schlosser, R., & Lloyd, L. (1993). Effects of initial element teaching in a story-telling context on Blissymbol acquisition and generalization. *Journal of Speech and Hearing Research, 36,* 979–995.

Schlosser, R., Lloyd, L., & McNaughton, S. (1996). *Graphic symbol selection in research and practice: Making the case for a goal-driven process.* Paper presented at the fourth International Society for Augmentative and Alternative Communication Symposium on Research in Augmentative and Alternative Communication, Vancouver, British Columbia, Canada.

Scholl, G. (1986). What does it mean to be blind? Definitions, terminology, and prevalence. In G. Scholl (Ed.), *Foundations of education for blind and visually handicapped children and youth: Theory and practice* (pp. 23–35). New York: American Foundation for the Blind.

Schorr, G. (1983). Visual impairment. In J. Blackman (Ed.), *Medical aspects of developmental disabilities in children birth to three* (pp. 227–231). Iowa City: The University of Iowa.

Schuler, A., & Prizant, B. (1987). Facilitating communication: Pre-language approaches. In D. Cohen & A. Donnellan (Eds.), *Handbook of autism and pervasive developmental disorders* (pp. 301–315). New York: John Wiley & Sons.

Scott, C. (1989). Problem writers: Nature, assessment, and intervention. In A.G. Kamhi & H.W. Catts (Eds.), *Reading disabilities: A developmental language perspective* (pp. 303–344). Needham Heights, MA: Allyn & Bacon.

Seidenberg, P.L. (1988). Cognitive and academic instructional intervention for learning-disabled adolescents. *Topics in Language Disorders, 8*(3), 56–71.

Seligman, M. (1975). *Helplessness: On depression, development, and death.* San Francisco: W.H. Freeman.

Semel, E., Wiig, E., & Secord, W. (1995). *Clinical Evaluation of Language Fundamentals–Third Edition (CELF–3).* San Antonio, TX: The Psychological Corporation.

Sergiovanni, T. (1990). *Value-added leadership: How to get extraordinary performance in schools.* San Diego: Harcourt Brace Jovanovich.

Sevcik, R., & Romski, M. (1986). Representational matching skills of persons with severe retardation. *Augmentative and Alternative Communication, 2,* 160–164.

Sevcik, R., Romski, M.A., & Wilkinson, K. (1991). Roles of graphic symbols in the language acquisition process for persons with severe cognitive disabilities. *Augmentative and Alternative Communication, 7,* 161–170.

Shakespeare, W.T., & Muir, C.K. (Eds.). (1982). *Troilus and Cressida.* New York: Oxford University Press.

Shane, H., & Bashir, A. (1980). Election criteria for the adoption of an augmentative communication system: Preliminary considerations. *Journal of Speech and Hearing Disorders, 45,* 408–414.

Shane, H., & Cohen, C. (1981). A discussion of communicative strategies and patterns by nonspeaking persons. *Language, Speech, and Hearing Services in Schools, 12,* 205–210.

Sheehan, C., & Matuozzi, R. (1996). Validation of facilitated communication. *Mental Retardation, 34,* 94–107.

Shell, D., Horn, C., & Bruning, R. (1989, October–November). Technologies for the information age: Enhancing disabled persons' access and use of text based information. *Closing the Gap,* 24–27.

Shelton, I., & Garves, M. (1985). Use of visual techniques in therapy for developmental apraxia of speech. *Language, Speech, and Hearing Services in Schools, 16,* 129–131.

Shriberg, L. (1994). Five subtypes of developmental phonological disorders. *Clinics in Communication Disorders, 4,* 38–53.

Shriberg, L., Aram, D., & Kwiatowksi, J. (1997a). Developmental apraxia of speech: I. Descriptive and theoretical perspectives. *Journal of Speech, Language, and Hearing Research, 40,* 273–285.

Shriberg, L., Aram, D., & Kwiatowksi, J. (1997b). Developmental apraxia of speech: II. Toward a diagnostic marker. *Journal of Speech, Language, and Hearing Research, 40,* 286–312.

Shriberg, L., Aram, D., & Kwiatowksi, J. (1997c). Developmental apraxia of speech: III. A subtype marked by inappropriate stress. *Journal of Speech, Language, and Hearing Research, 40,* 313–337.

Siegel-Causey, E., & Downing, J. (1987). Nonsymbolic communication development: Theoretical concepts and educational strategies. In L. Goetz, D. Guess, & K. Stremel-Campbell (Eds.), *Innovative program design for individuals with dual sensory impairments* (pp. 15–48). Baltimore: Paul H. Brookes Publishing Co.

Siegel-Causey, E., & Guess, D. (1988). *Enhancing interactions between service providers and individuals who are severely multiply disabled: Strategies for developing nonsymbolic communication.* Monmouth, OR: Teaching Research. (Available by contacting Teaching Research at 345 North Monmouth Avenue, Monmouth, OR 97361.)

Siegel-Causey, E., & Guess, D. (1989). *Enhancing nonsymbolic communication interactions among students with severe disabilities.* Baltimore: Paul H. Brookes Publishing Co.

Sienkiewicz-Mercer, R., & Kaplan, S. (1989). *I raise my eyes to say yes.* Boston: Houghton Mifflin.

Sigafoos, J., & Couzens, D. (1995). Teaching functional use of an eye gaze communication board to a child with multiple disabilities. *British Journal of Developmental Disabilities, 16,* 114–125.

Sigafoos, J., & Dempsey, R. (1992). Assessing choice making among children with multiple disabilities. *Journal of Applied Behavior Analysis, 25,* 747–755.

Sigafoos, J., Kerr, M., Roberts, D., & Couzens, D. (1994). Increasing opportunities for requesting in classrooms serving children with developmental disabilities. *Journal of Autism and Developmental Disabilities, 24,* 631–645.

Sigafoos, J., Laurie, S., & Pennell, D. (1995). Preliminary assessment of choice making among children with Rett syndrome. *Journal of The Association for Persons with Severe Handicaps, 20,* 175–184.

Sigafoos, J., Laurie, S., & Pennell, D. (1996). Teaching children with Rett syndrome to request preferred objects using aided communication: Two preliminary studies. *Augmentative and Alternative Communication, 12,* 88–96.

Sigafoos, J., & Meikle, B. (1996). Functional communication training for the treatment of multiply determined challenging behavior in two boys with autism. *Behavior Modification, 20,* 60–84.

Sigafoos, J., & Reichle, J. (1992). Comparing explicit to generalized requesting in an augmentative communication mode. *Journal of Developmental and Physical Disabilities, 4,* 167–188.

Sigafoos, J., Roberts, D., Couzens, D., & Kerr, M. (1993). Providing opportunities for choice-making and turn-taking to adults with multiple disabilities. *Journal of Developmental and Physical Disabilities, 5,* 297–310.

Sigafoos, J., Roberts, D., Kerr, M., Couzens, D., & Baglioni, A. (1994). Opportunities for communication in classrooms serving children with developmental disabilities. *Journal of Autism and Developmental Disabilities, 24,* 259–279.

Silverman, F. (1995). *Communication for the speechless* (3rd ed.). Needham Heights, MA: Allyn & Bacon.

Silverstein, S. (1974). *Where the sidewalk ends.* New York: Harper & Row.

Simeonsson, R., Olley, J., & Rosenthal, S. (1987). Early intervention for children with autism. In M. Guralnick & F. Bennett (Eds.), *The effectiveness of early intervention for at-risk and handicapped children* (pp. 275–293). New York: Academic Press.

Simmons, N. (1983). Acoustic analysis of ataxic dysarthria: An approach to monitoring treatment. In W. Berry (Ed.), *Clinical dysarthria.* Austin, TX: PRO-ED.

Simmons, T., & Young, C. (1994). *Tools for literacy and communication.* Solana Beach, CA: Mayer-Johnson Co.

Simpson, K. (1996). *Interaction patterns of four students with severe expressive communication impairments in regular classroom settings.* Unpublished doctoral dissertation, University of Nebraska–Lincoln.

Simpson, S. (1988). If only I could tell them. . .!! *Communication Outlook, 9*(4), 9–11.

Sitver, M., & Kraat, A. (1982). Augmentative communication for the person with amyotrophic lateral sclerosis (ALS). *Asha, 24,* 783.

Skelly, M. (1979). *Amer-Ind gestural code based on universal American Indian hand talk.* Amsterdam: Elsevier/North Holland.

Skelly, M., Schinsky, L., Smith, R., Donaldson, R., & Griffin, P. (1975). American Indian sign: A gestural communication for the speechless. *Archives of Physical and Rehabilitation Medicine, 56,* 156–160.

Skelly, M., Schinsky, L., Smith, R., & Fust, R. (1974). American Indian sign (Amer-Ind) as a facilitator of verbalization in the oral apraxic. *Journal of Speech and Hearing Disorders, 39,* 445–456.

Smebye, H. (1990, August). *A theoretical basis for early communication intervention.* Paper presented at the fifth biennial conference of the International Society for Augmentative and Alternative Communication, Stockholm.

Smith, A., Thurston, S., Light, J., Parnes, P., & O'Keefe, B. (1989). The form and use of written communication produced by physically disabled individuals using microcomputers. *Augmentative and Alternative Communication, 5,* 115–124.

Smith, M. (1992). Reading abilities of nonspeaking students: Two case studies. *Augmentative and Alternative Communication, 8,* 57–66.

Smith, M. (1996). The medium or the message: A study of speaking children using communication boards. In S. von Tetzchner & M. Jensen (Eds.), *Augmentative and alternative communication: European perspectives* (pp. 119–136). London: Whurr Publishers.

Smith-Lewis, M., & Ford, A. (1987). A user's perspective on augmentative communication. *Augmentative and Alternative Communication, 3,* 12–17.

Snow, J., & Forest, M. (1987). Circles. In M. Forest (Ed.), *More education integration.* Downsview, Ontario, Canada: G. Allan Roeher.

Snyder, L. (1984). Developmental language disorders: Elementary school age. In A. Holland (Ed.), *Language disorders in children* (pp. 129–158). San Diego: College-Hill Press.

Snyder-McLean, L., Solomonson, B., McLean, J., & Sack, S. (1984). Structuring joint action routines: A strategy for facilitating language and communication development in the classroom. *Seminars in Speech and Language, 5,* 213–228.

Sobsey, D., & Wolf-Schein, E. (1996). Children with sensory impairments. In F.P. Orelove & D. Sobsey (Eds.), *Educating children with multiple disabilities: A transdisciplinary approach* (3rd ed., pp. 411–450). Baltimore: Paul H. Brookes Publishing Co.

Soto, G. (1996, August). *Multi-unit utterances and syntax in graphic symbol communication.* Paper presented at the fourth biennial research symposium of the International Society for Augmentative and Alternative Communication, Vancouver, British Columbia, Canada.

Soto, G., & Toro-Zambrana, W. (1995). Investigation of Blissymbol use from a language research paradigm. *Augmentative and Alternative Communication, 11,* 118–130.

Spellman, C.R., De Briere, T.J., & Cress, P.J. (1989). *Parsons Visual Acuity Test.* South Bend, IN: Bernell Corporation.

Spiegel, B., Benjamin, B., & Spiegel, S. (1993). One method to increase spontaneous use of an assistive communication device: A case study. *Augmentative and Alternative Communication, 9,* 111–118.

Spragale, D., & Micucci, S. (1990). Signs of the week: A functional approach to manual sign training. *Augmentative and Alternative Communication, 6,* 29–37.

Stainback, S., & Stainback, W. (1996). *Inclusion: A guide for educators.* Baltimore: Paul H. Brookes Publishing Co.

Stainback, W., & Stainback, S. (1990). *Support networks for inclusive schooling: Interdependent integrated education.* Baltimore: Paul H. Brookes Publishing Co.

Stainback, W., Stainback, S., Courtnage, L., & Jaben, T. (1985). Facilitating mainstreaming by modifying the mainstream. *Exceptional Children, 52,* 144–152.

Stark, R., & Tallal, P. (1981). Perceptual and motor deficits in language impaired children. In R. Keith (Ed.), *Central auditory and language disorders in children* (pp. 121–144). San Diego: College-Hill Press.

Stauffer, R. (1980). *The language experience approach to the teaching of reading.* New York: Harper & Row.

Stedt, J., & Moores, D. (1990). Manual codes on English and American Sign Language: Historical perspectives and current realities. In H. Bornstein (Ed.), *Manual communication: Implications for education* (pp. 1–20). Washington, DC: Gallaudet University Press.

Steege, M., Wacker, D., Cigrand, K., Berg, W., Novak, C., Reimers, T., Sasso, G., & DeRaad, A. (1990). Use of negative reinforcement in the treatment of self-injurious behavior. *Journal of Applied Behavior Analysis, 23,* 459–468.

Stephenson, J., & Linfoot, K. (1995). Choice-making as a natural context for teaching early communication board use to a ten year old boy with no spoken language and severe intellectual disability. *Australia and New Zealand Journal of Developmental Disabilities, 20,* 263–286.

Stephenson, J., & Linfoot, K. (1996). Pictures as communication symbols for students with severe intellectual disability. *Augmentative and Alternative Communication, 12,* 244–256.

Sternberg, L. (1982). Communication instruction. In L. Sternberg & G. Adams (Eds.), *Educating severely and profoundly handicapped students* (pp. 209–241). Rockville, MD: Aspen Publishers.

Stevenson, J., & Richman, M. (1976). The prevalence of language delay in a population of three-year-old children and its association with general retardation. *Developmental Medicine and Child Neurology, 18,* 431–441.

Stillman, R., & Battle, C. (1984). Developing prelanguage communication in the severely handicapped: An interpretation of the Van Dijk method. *Seminars in Speech and Language, 5,* 159–170.

Stillman, R., & Battle, C. (1985). *The Callier-Azusa Scales for the Assessment of Communicative Abilities.* Dallas: University of Texas, Callier Center.

Storey, K., & Provost, O. (1996). The effect of communication skills instruction on the integration of workers with severe disabilities in supported employment settings. *Education and Training in Mental Retardation and Developmental Disabilities, 31,* 123–141.

Strickland, D., & Cullinan, B. (1990). Afterword. In M. Adams (Ed.), *Beginning to read: Thinking and learning about print* (pp. 425–433). Cambridge: The MIT Press.

Stromswold, K. (1994, January). *Language comprehension without production: Implications for theories of language acquisition.* Paper presented at the Boston University Conference on Language Development, Boston.

Stuart, S. (1988). Expanding sequencing, turn-taking and timing skills through play acting. In S. Blackstone, E. Cassatt-James, & D. Bruskin (Eds.), *Augmentative communication: Implementation strategies* (pp. 5.8-21–5.8-26). Rockville, MD: American Speech-Language-Hearing Association.

Stuart, S. (1991). *Topic and vocabulary use patterns of elderly men and women in two age cohorts.* Unpublished doctoral dissertation, University of Nebraska–Lincoln.

Stuart, S., Vanderhoof, D., & Beukelman, D. (1993). Topic and vocabulary use patterns of elderly women. *Augmentative and Alternative Communication, 9,* 95–110.

Sturm, J., & Nelson, N. (1997). Formal classroom lessons: New perspectives on a familiar discourse event. *Language, Speech, and Hearing Services in Schools, 28,* 255–273.

Sturm, J.M., Rankin, J.L., & Beukelman, D.R. (1994, November). *Using word-prompt computer programs with learning disabled student writers.* Poster session presented at the annual convention of the American Speech-Language-Hearing Association, New Orleans.

Sulzby, E. (1994). Children's emergent reading of favorite story books: A developmental study. In R.B. Ruddell, M.R. Ruddell, & H. Singer (Eds.), *Theoretical models and processes of reading* (4th ed., pp. 244–280). Newark, DE: International Reading Association.

Sulzby, E., & Teale, W.H. (1991). Emergent literacy. In R. Barr, M.L. Kamil, P. Mosenthal, & P.D. Pearson (Eds.), *Handbook of reading research* (Vol. 2, pp. 727–757). While Plains, NY: Longman.

Sundberg, M. (1993). Selecting a response form for nonverbal persons: Facilitated communication, pointing systems, or sign language. *Analysis of Verbal Behavior, 11,* 99–116.

Sunny Hill Health Centre for Children, Ministry of Health, and Ministry Responsible for Seniors. (1992). *A conceptual model of practice for school system therapists.* Vancouver, British Columbia, Canada: Author.

Sutton, A. (1989). The social-verbal competence of AAC users. *Augmentative and Alternative Communication, 5,* 150–164.

Sutton, A. (1996, August). *Language acquisition theory and research: Implications for AAC.* Paper presented at the fourth International Society for Augmentative and Alternative Communication Symposium on Research in Augmentative and Alternative Communication, Vancouver, British Columbia, Canada.

Sutton, A., & Gallagher, T. (1993). Verb class distinctions and AAC language-encoding limitations. *Journal of Speech and Hearing Research, 36,* 1216–1226.

Sutton, A., & Morford, J. (1995, December). *Picture board use in speaking children: The role of modality.* Poster presented at the annual convention of the American-Speech-Language-Hearing Association, Orlando, FL.

Sutton, B., King, J., Hux, K., & Beukelman, D. (1995). Younger and older adults' rate performance when listening to synthetic speech. *Augmentative and Alternative Communication, 11,* 147–153.

Sweeney, L., & Finkley, E. (1989). Early manual communication skills assessment. In S.W. Blackstone, E.L. Cassatt-James, & D. Bruskin (Eds.), *Augmentative communication: Intervention resource* (pp. 3-159–3-168). Rockville, MD: American Speech-Language-Hearing Association.

Swengel, K., & Marquette, J. (1997). Service delivery in AAC. In S.L. Glennen & D. DeCoste (Eds.), *The handbook of augmentative and alternative communication* (pp. 21–58). San Diego: Singular Publishing Group.

Swiffin, A., Arnott, J., Pickering, J., & Newell, A. (1987). Adaptive and predictive techniques in a communication prosthesis. *Augmentative and Alternative Communication, 3,* 181–191.

Swigger, K., & Campbell, J. (1981). Computers and the nursery school. In D. Harris & L. Nelson-Heern (Eds.), *Proceedings of the National Educational Computing Conference* (pp. 264–268). Iowa City: National Educational Computing Conference.

Szeto, A., Allen, E., & Littrell, M. (1993). Comparison of speed and accuracy for selected electronic communication devices and input methods. *Augmentative and Alternative Communication, 9,* 229–242.

Talking symbols [Computer software]. (1990). Solana Beach, CA: Mayer-Johnson Co.

Tandan, R., & Bradley, W. (1985). Amyotrophic lateral sclerosis: Part 1. Clinical features, pathology, and ethical issues in management. *Annals of Neurology, 18,* 271–280.

Tannock, R., & Girolametto, L. (1992). Reassessing parent-focused language intervention programs. In S.F. Warren & J. Reichle (Eds.), *Communication and language intervention series: Vol. 1. Causes and effects in communication and language intervention* (pp. 49–79). Baltimore: Paul H. Brookes Publishing Co.

Technology-Related Assistance for Individuals with Disabilities Act of 1988, PL 100-407, 29 U.S.C. §§ 2201 *et seq.*

Teller, D.Y., McDonald, M.A., Preston, K., Sebris, S.L., & Dobson, V. (1986). *Teller acuity cards.* Dayton, OH: Vistech Corporation.

Tharpe, R., & Gallimore, R. (1988). *Rousing minds to life: Teaching, learning, and schooling in social context.* New York: Cambridge University Press.

Thousand, J.S., & Villa, R.A. (1992). Collaborative teams: A powerful tool in school restructuring. In R.A. Villa, J.S. Thousand, W. Stainback, & S. Stainback (Eds.), *Restructuring for caring and effective education: An administrative guide to creating heterogeneous schools* (pp. 73–108). Baltimore: Paul H. Brookes Publishing Co.

Tirosh, E., & Canby, J. (1993). Autism with hyperlexia: A distinct syndrome? *American Journal on Mental Retardation, 98,* 84–92.

Todman, J., Elder, L., & Alm, N. (1995). Evaluation of the content of computer-aided conversations. *Augmentative and Alternative Communication, 11,* 229–234.

Turnell, R., & Carter, M. (1994). Establishing a repertoire of requesting for a student with severe and multiple disabilities using tangible symbols and naturalistic time delay. *Australia and New Zealand Journal of Developmental Disabilities, 19,* 193–207.

Turner, E., Barrett, C., Cutshall, A., Lacy, B.K., Keiningham, J., & Webster, M.K. (1995). The user's perspective of assistive technology. In K.F. Flippo, K.J. Inge, & J.M. Barcus (Eds.), *Assistive technology: A resource for school, work, and community* (pp. 283–290). Baltimore: Paul H. Brookes Publishing Co.

Udwin, O., & Yule, W. (1990). Augmentative communication systems taught to cerebral palsied children: A longitudinal study: I. The acquisition of signs and symbols, and syntactic aspects of their use over time. *British Journal of Disorders of Communication, 25,* 295–309.

Udwin, O., & Yule, W. (1991a). Augmentative communication systems taught to cerebral palsied children: A longitudinal study: II. Pragmatic features of sign and symbol use. *British Journal of Disorders of Communication, 26,* 137–148.

Udwin, O., & Yule, W. (1991b). Augmentative communication systems taught to cerebral palsied children: A longitudinal study: III. Teaching practices and exposure to sign and symbol use in schools and homes. *British Journal of Disorders of Communication, 26,* 149–162.

Ulatowska, H., Cannito, M., Hayashi, M., & Fleming, S. (1985). *The aging brain: Communication in the elderly.* San Diego: College-Hill Press.

Valentic, V. (1991). Successful integration from a student's perspective. *Communicating Together, 9*(2), 9.

van Balkom, H., & Welle Donker-Gimbrère, M. (1996). A psycholinguistic approach to graphic language use. In S. von Tetzchner & M. Jensen (Eds.), *Augmentative and alternative communication: European perspectives* (pp. 153–170). London: Whurr Publishers.

Vandercook, T., York, J., & Forest, M. (1989). The McGill action planning system (MAPS): A strategy for building the vision. *Journal of The Association for Persons with Severe Handicaps, 14,* 205–215.

Vanderheiden, G. (1988). A unified quantitative modeling approach for selection-based augmentative communication systems. In L. Bernstein (Ed.), *The vocally impaired: Clinical practice and research* (pp. 40–83). New York: Grune & Stratton.

Vanderheiden, G., & Kelso, D. (1987). Comparative analysis of fixed-vocabulary communication acceleration techniques. *Augmentative and Alternative Communication, 3,* 196–206.

Vanderheiden, G., & Yoder, D. (1986). Overview. In S. Blackstone (Ed.), *Augmentative communication: An introduction* (pp. 1–28). Rockville, MD: American Speech-Language-Hearing Association.

Vanderheiden, G.C., & Lloyd, L. (1986). Communication systems and their components. In S. Blackstone (Ed.), *Augmentative communication: An introduction* (pp. 49–162). Rockville, MD: American Speech-Language-Hearing Association.

Van Dijk, J. (1966). The first steps of the deaf-blind child towards language. *International Journal for the Education of the Blind, 15*(4), 112–114.

Van Oosterum, J., & Devereux, K. (1985). *Learning with rebuses.* Black Hill, Ely, Cambridgeshire, England: EARO, The Resource Centre.

Van Tatenhove, G. (1996). *Field of dreams: Sowing language and reaping communication.* Paper presented at the 1996 Minspeak conference, Wooster, OH.

Vaughn, B., & Horner, R. (1995). Effects of concrete versus verbal choice systems on problem behavior. *Augmentative and Alternative Communication, 11,* 89–92.

Venkatagiri, H. (1993). Efficiency of lexical prediction as a communication acceleration technique. *Augmentative and Alternative Communication, 12,* 161–167.

Venkatagiri, H. (1994). Window size in lexical prediction. *Augmentative and Alternative Communication, 10,* 105–112.

Venkatagiri, H. (1995). Techniques for enhancing communication productivity in AAC: A review of research. *American Journal of Speech-Language Pathology, 4,* 36–45.

Venkatagiri, H., & Ramabadran, T. (1995). Digital speech synthesis: A tutorial. *Augmentative and Alternative Communication, 11,* 14–25.

Vicker, B. (1996). *Using tangible symbols for communication purposes: An optional step in building the two-way communication process.* Bloomington: Indiana University, Indiana Resource Center for Autism.

Viggiano, J. (1981). Ignorance as handicap. *Asha, 23,* 551–552.

Villa, R.A., Thousand, J.S., Stainback, W., & Stainback, S. (Eds.). (1992). *Restructuring for caring and effective education: An administrative guide to creating heterogeneous schools*. Baltimore: Paul H. Brookes Publishing Co.

Vincent, L.J., Salisbury, C., Walter, G., Brown, P., Gruenewald, L.J., & Powers, M. (1980). Program evaluation and curriculum development in early childhood/special education: Criteria of the next environment. In W. Sailor, B. Wilcox, & L. Brown (Eds.), *Methods of instruction for severely handicapped students* (pp. 303–328). Baltimore: Paul H. Brookes Publishing Co.

von Tetzchner, S., & Jensen, M.H. (1996). *Augmentative and alternative communication: European perspectives*. London: Whurr Publishers.

von Tetzchner, S., & Martinsen, H. (1992). *Introduction to symbolic and augmentative communication*. London: Whurr Publishers.

Wacker, D., Steege, M., Northup, J., Sasso, G., Berg, W., Reimers, T., Cooper, L., Cigrand, K., & Donn, L. (1990). A component analysis of functional communication training across three topographies of severe behavior problems. *Journal of Applied Behavior Analysis, 23*, 417–429.

Wacker, D., Wiggins, B., Fowler, M., & Berg, W. (1988). Training students with profound or multiple handicaps to make requests via microswitches. *Journal of Applied Behavior Analysis, 18*, 331–343.

Walker, B.J. (1996). *Diagnostic teaching of reading: Techniques for instruction and assessment* (3rd ed.). Upper Saddle River, NJ: Prentice Hall.

Walker, M. (1987, March). *The Makaton Vocabulary: Uses and effectiveness*. Paper presented at the first international AFASIC Symposium, University of Reading, England.

Walker, M., Parsons, F., Cousins, S., Henderson, R., & Carpenter, B. (1985). *Symbols for Makaton*. Camberley, England: Makaton Vocabulary Development Project.

Wallace, J.F. (1995). Creative financing of assistive technology. In K.F. Flippo, K.J. Inge, & J.M. Barcus (Eds.), *Assistive technology: A resource for school, work, and community* (pp. 245–268). Baltimore: Paul H. Brookes Publishing Co.

Wallach, G., & Liebergott, J. (1984). Who shall be called "learning disabled?": Some new directions. In G. Wallach & K. Butler (Eds.), *Language learning disabilities in school-age children* (pp. 1–14). Baltimore: Williams & Wilkins.

Ward-Lonergan, J., & Nicholas, M. (1995). Drawing to communication: A case report of an adult with global aphasia. *European Journal of Disorders of Communication, 30*, 475–491.

Warren, S., & Kaiser, A. (1986). Incidental language teaching: A critical review. *Journal of Speech and Hearing Disorders, 51*, 291–299.

Wasson, P., Tynan, T., & Gardiner, P. (1982). *Test adaptations for the handicapped*. San Antonio, TX: Educational Service Center.

Weaver, C. (1994). *Reading processes and practice: From socio-linguistics to whole language*. Portsmouth, NH: Heinemann.

Webb, A. (1984). Dustin–3: Augmented communication for a preschool child. *Communication Outlook, 6*(2), 4–5.

Weiss, L., Thatch, D., & Thatch, J. (1987). *I wasn't finished with life*. Dallas, TX: E-Heart Press.

Weiss, M., Wagner, S., & Bauman, M. (1996). A case of validated facilitated communication. *Mental Retardation, 34*, 220–230.

Welle-Donker Gimbrère, M., & van Balkom, H. (1995). *Grafische symbolen in ondersteunde communicatie [Graphic symbols in augmentative communication]*. Baarn, the Netherlands: INTRO.

Weller, E., & Mahoney, G. (1983). A comparison of oral and total communication modalities on the language training of young mentally handicapped children. *Education and Training of the Mentally Retarded, 18*, 103–110.

West, C.M., Bilyeu, D.D., & Brune, P.J. (1996, November). *AAC strategies for the preschool classroom: Developing communication and literacy*. Short course presented at the annual convention of the American Speech-Language-Hearing Association, Seattle.

Westby, C. (1985). Learning to talk—talking to learn: Oral-literate language differences. In C. Simon (Ed.), *Communication skills and classroom success: Therapy methodologies for language-learning disabled students* (pp. 181–213). San Diego: College-Hill Press.

Wetherby, A. (1989). Language intervention for autistic children: A look at where we have come in the past 25 years. *Journal of Speech-Language Pathology and Audiology, 13*(4), 15–28.

Wetherby, A., & Prizant, B. (1993). *Communication and Symbolic Behavior Scales (CSBS)*. Chicago: Riverside.

Wetherby, A., & Prutting, C. (1984). Profiles of communicative and cognitive-social abilities in autistic children. *Journal of Speech and Hearing Research, 27*, 364–377.

Wiig, E.H., Secord, W., & Semel, E. (1992). *Clinical Evaluation of Language Fundamentals–Preschool (CELF–Preschool)*. San Antonio, TX: The Psychological Corporation.

Wilkinson, G. (1993). *Wide Range Achievement Test–Third Revision (WRAT–3)*. Wilmington, DE: Jastak Associates.

Wilkinson, K., Romski, M.A., & Sevcik, R. (1994). Emergence of visual-graphic symbol combinations by youth with moderate or severe mental retardation. *Journal of Speech and Hearing Research, 37*, 883–985.

Williams, D. (1994). *Somebody somewhere*. Toronto, Ontario, Canada: Doubleday Canada, Ltd.

Williams, D. (1996). *Autism: An inside out approach*. London: Jessica Kingsley Publishers.

Williams, M. (1992). Empowerment and self advocacy. *Communicating Together, 10*(3), 19.

Williams, M. (1995a). Excerpts from "Thoughts on the Future." In S. Blackstone & H. Pressman (Eds.), *Outcomes in AAC conference report: Alliance '95* (pp. 29–30). Monterey, CA: Augmentative Communication.

Williams, M. (1995b, March). Whose outcome is it anyway? *Alternatively Speaking, 2*(1), 1–2, 6.

Williams, M. (1996, November). Words+ outstanding consumer lecture presented at ISAAC '96. *The ISAAC Bulletin, 45*, 1–8.

Williams, R. (1989). *In a struggling voice*. Seattle: The Association for Persons with Severe Handicaps. (Available by writing The Association for Persons with Severe Handicaps, 29 West Susquehanna Avenue, Suite 210, Baltimore, MD 21204.)

Wilson, R., Teague, G., & Teague, M. (1984). The use of signing and fingerspelling to improve spelling performance with hearing children. *Reading Psychology, 5*, 267–273.

Windsor, J., & Fristoe, M. (1989). Key word signing: Listeners' classification of signed and spoken narratives. *Journal of Speech and Hearing Disorders, 54*, 374–382.

Windsor, J., & Fristoe, M. (1991). Key word signing: Perceived and acoustic differences between signed and spoken narratives. *Journal of Speech and Hearing Research, 34*, 260–268.

Wing, L. (1996). *The autistic spectrum: A guide for parents and professionals*. London: Constable.

Wing, L., & Atwood, T. (1987). Syndromes of autism and atypical development. In D. Cohen & A. Donnellan (Eds.), *Handbook of autism and pervasive developmental disorders* (pp. 3–19). New York: John Wiley & Sons.

Wolverton, R., Beukelman, D., Haynes, R., & Sesow, D. (1992). Strategies in augmented literacy using microcomputer-based approaches. *Seminars in Speech and Language, 13*(2), 154–165.

Wood, C., Storr, J., & Reich, P. (1992). *The complete Blissymbol reference guide*. Toronto, Ontario, Canada: Blissymbolics Communication International.

Wood, L., Lasker, J., Siegel-Causey, E., Beukelman, D., & Ball, L. (1997). *Using an augmented comprehension framework: Concepts and practices*. Manuscript in preparation, University of Nebraska–Lincoln.

Woodcock, R. (1987). *Woodcock Reading Mastery Tests–Revised*. Circle Pines, MN: American Guidance Service.

Woodcock, R., Clark, C., & Davies, C. (1968). *Peabody Rebus Reading Program*. Circle Pines, MN: American Guidance Service.

Woodward, J. (1990). Sign English in the education of deaf students. In H. Bornstein (Ed.), *Manual communication: Implications for education* (pp. 67–80). Washington, DC: Gallaudet University Press.

Workinger, M., & Netsell, R. (1988). *Restoration of intelligible speech 13 years post-head injury*. Unpublished manuscript, Boys Town National Communication Institute, Omaha, NE.

World Health Organization. (1992). *International statistical classification of diseases and related health problems* (10th ed.). Geneva: Author.

Wright, C., & Nomura, M. (1987). *From toys to computers: Access for the physically disabled child*. Wauconda, IL: Don Johnston, Inc.

Writer, J. (1987). A movement-based approach to the education of students who are sensory impaired/multihandicapped. In L. Goetz, D. Guess, & K. Stremel-Campbell (Eds.), *Innovative program design for individuals with dual sensory impairments* (pp. 191–223). Baltimore: Paul H. Brookes Publishing Co.

Yoder, P., Kaiser, A., & Alpert, C. (1991). An exploratory study of the interaction between language teaching methods and child characteristics. *Journal of Speech and Hearing Research, 34*, 155–167.

Yoder, D., & Kraat, A. (1983). Intervention issues in nonspeech communication. In J. Miller, D. Yoder, & R.L. Schiefelbusch (Eds.), *Contemporary issues in language intervention. ASHA Reports, 12*, 27–51. Rockville, MD: American Speech-Language-Hearing Association.

York, J., Nietupski, J., & Hamre-Nietupski, S. (1985). A decision-making process for using microswitches. *Journal of The Association for Persons with Severe Handicaps, 10,* 214–223.

York, J., & Vandercook, T. (1989). Strategies for achieving an integrated education for middle school aged learners with severe disabilities. In J. York, T. Vandercook, C. MacDonald, & S. Wolff (Eds.), *Strategies for full inclusion* (pp. 1–20). Minneapolis: University of Minnesota, Institute on Community Integration.

York, J., & Weimann, G. (1991). Accommodating severe physical disabilities. In J. Reichle, J. York, & J. Sigafoos (Eds.), *Implementing augmentative and alternative communication: Strategies for learners with severe disabilities* (pp. 239–256). Baltimore: Paul H. Brookes Publishing Co.

Yorkston, K. (1989). Early intervention in amyotrophic lateral sclerosis: A case presentation. *Augmentative and Alternative Communication, 5,* 67–70.

Yorkston, K., & Beukelman, D. (1981). Ataxic dysarthria: Treatment sequences based on intelligibility and prosodic considerations. *Journal of Speech and Hearing Disorders, 46,* 398–404.

Yorkston, K., Beukelman, D., & Bell, K. (1988). *Clinical management of dysarthric speakers.* San Diego: College-Hill Press.

Yorkston, K., Beukelman, D., Minifie, F., & Sapir, S. (1984). Assessment of stress patterning in dysarthric speakers. In M. McNeil, A. Aronson, & J. Rosenbek (Eds.), *The dysarthrias: Physiology, acoustics, perception, management* (pp. 131–162). San Diego: College-Hill Press.

Yorkston, K., Beukelman, D., & Tice, R. (1996). *Sentence Intelligibility Test (Version 1.0)* [Software]. Lincoln, NE: Communication Disorders Software.

Yorkston, K., Beukelman, D., & Tice, R. (1997). *Pacer/Tally.* Lincoln, NE: Tice Technology Services.

Yorkston, K., Fried-Oken, M., & Beukelman, D. (1988). Single word vocabulary needs: Studies from various nonspeaking populations. *Augmentative and Alternative Communication, 4,* 149.

Yorkston, K., & Karlan, G. (1986). Assessment procedures. In S. Blackstone (Ed.), *Augmentative communication: An introduction* (pp. 163–196). Rockville, MD: American Speech-Language-Hearing Association.

Yorkston, K., Smith, K., & Beukelman, D. (1990). Extended communication samples of augmented communicators: I. A comparison of individualized versus standard vocabularies. *Journal of Speech and Hearing Disorders, 55,* 217–224.

Yorkston, K., Smith, K., Miller, R., & Hillel, A. (1991). *Augmentative and alternative communication in amyotrophic lateral sclerosis.* Unpublished manuscript, University of Washington–Seattle.

Yorkston, K., Strand, E., & Kennedy, M. (1996). Comprehensibility of dysarthric speech: Implications for assessment and treatment planning. *American Journal of Speech-Language Pathology, 5,* 55–66.

Yorkston, K.M., Miller, R.M., & Strand, E.A. (1995). *Management of speech and swallowing disorders in degenerative disease.* San Antonio, TX: The Psychological Corporation.

Yoss, K., & Darley, F. (1974). Therapy in developmental apraxia of speech. *Language, Speech, and Hearing Services in Schools, 5,* 23–31.

Zagare, F. (1984). *Game theory: Concepts and applications.* Thousand Oaks, CA: Sage Publications.

Zangari, C., Lloyd, L., & Vicker, B. (1994). Augmentative and alternative communication: An historic perspective. *Augmentative and Alternative Communication, 10,* 27–59.

Zimmerman, I., Steiner, V., & Evatt-Pond, R. (1992). *The Preschool Language Scale–Third Edition (PLS–3).* San Antonio, TX: The Psychological Corporation.

Appendix

Resource List

Ability OnLine Support Network, 919 Alness Street, North York, Ontario M3J 2J1, Canada (416-650-6207; fax: 416-650-5073; modem: 416-650-5411; Internet e-mail address: ability.online@ablelink.org; World Wide Web site: http://www.ablelink.org).

AbleNet, Inc., 1081 10th Avenue, SE, Minneapolis, MN 55414-1312 (800-322-0956; World Wide Web site: http://www.ablenetinc.com).

American Guidance Service, 4201 Woodland Road, Post Office Box 99, Circle Pines, MN 55014-1796 (800-328-2560; fax: 612-786-9077; Internet e-mail address: agsmail@agsnet.com; World Wide Web site: http://www.agsnet.com).

Assistive Technology, Inc., 850 Boylston Street, Chestnut Hill, MA 02167 (800-793-9927; 617-731-4900; fax: 617-731-5201; Internet e-mail address: customercare@assistivetech.com; World Wide Web site: http://www.assistivetech.com).

Assistive Technology Center, World Wide Web site: http://www.asel.udel.edu/at-online/programs/tech_act.

Association de Paralysie Cérébral du Québec, Inc., Centre de Ressources Bliss [Bliss Resource Center], 525 boulevard Wilfrid-Hamel est, Suite A-50, Québec, Québec G1M 2S8, Canada (418-529-3347).

Attainment Company, Inc., Post Office Box 930160, Verona, WI 53593-1060 (800-327-4269; Internet e-mail address: attain@waun.tds.net).

Augmentative Communication Online User's Group; Internet e-mail address to subscribe: acolug-request@vm.temple.edu.

Aurora Systems, Inc., 2647 Kingsway, Vancouver, British Columbia V5R 5H5, Canada (800-361-8255).

Barkley Augmentative and Alternative Communication Center; World Wide Web site: http://aac.unl.edu/aac.html.

Bernell Corporation, 750 Lincolnway, East, Post Office Box 4637, South Bend, IN 46634 (219-234-3200).

Betacom-Bridges, 2999 King Street, West, Inglewood, Ontario L0N 1K0, Canada (800-465-0142; 905-838-1411; fax: 905-838-1487).

Blissymbolics Communication International, 1630 Lawrence Avenue, West, Suite 104, Toronto, Ontario M6L 1C6, Canada (416-242-9114; fax: 416-244-6543; World Wide Web site: http://home.istar.ca:80/~bci/index.htm/).

Communication Skill Builders, 55 Horner Avenue, Toronto, Ontario M8Z 4X6, Canada (800-387-7278); or c/o The Psychological Corporation, 555 Academic Court, San Antonio, TX 78204-2498 (800-228-0752).

COMPIC, Post Office Box 1233, Camberwell 3124, Victoria, Australia (01-61-3-9804-0130; 01-61-3-9804-0139; fax: 01-61-3-9804-0157; Internet e-mail address: info@compic.com).

Creative Communicating, Post Office Box 3358, Park City, UT 84060 (801-645-7737).

Crestwood Company, 6625 North Sidney Place, Milwaukee, WI 53209 (414-352-5678; fax: 414-352-5679; World Wide Web site: http://www.communicationaids.com).

Don Johnston, Inc., 1000 North Rand Road, Building 115, Post Office Box 639, Wauconda, IL 60084 (800-999-4660; World Wide Web site: http://www.donjohnston.com).

Edmark Corporation, Post Office Box 97021, Redmond, WA 98073-9721 (425-556-8400; Internet e-mail address: edmarkteam@edmark.com; World Wide Web site: http://www.edmark.com).

Functional Communication Outreach Service, Yooralla Society of Victoria, 244 Flinders Street, Melbourne 3000, Victoria, Australia.

Gallaudet University Press, 800 Florida Avenue, NE, Washington, DC 20002-3695 (800-451-1073).

Good-Lite Company, 1540 Hannah Avenue, Forest Park, IL 60130-2693 (708-366-3860).

Great Talking Box Company, 2211 B Fortune Drive, San Jose, CA 95131 (408-456-0133).

Group Logic, Inc., 1408 North Fillmore Street, Suite 10, Arlington, VA 22201 (800-476-8781; 703-528-1555; fax: 703-528-3296; Internet e-mail address: info@grouplogic.com; World Wide Web site: http://www.grouplogic.com).

Harmony Place Support Services, 132 Railside Road, Unit 6, North York, Ontario M3A 1A3, Canada (416-510-3351; fax: 416-510-0824).

Imaginart Communication Products, 307 Arizona Street, Bisbee, AZ 85603 (520-432-5471).

Inclusion Press International, 24 Thome Crescent, Toronto, Ontario M6H 2S5, Canada (416-658-5363; fax: 416-658-5067).

Indiana Resource Center for Autism, Indiana University, 2853 East 10th Street, Bloomington, IN 47408-2601 (812-855-6508).

Innocomp, 26210 Emery Road, Suite 301, Warrensville Heights, OH 44128 (800-382-8622; fax: 216-464-3638; Internet e-mail address: innocomp@aol.com).

Inspiration Software, Inc., 7412 Southwest Beaverton Hillsdale Highway, Suite 102, Portland, OR 97225-2167 (800-877-4292; 503-297-3004; fax: 503-297-4676; World Wide Web site: http://www.inspiration.com).

Institute on Disabilities, Temple University, Philadelphia, PA 19122 (telephone and TTY: 215-204-1356; fax: 215-204-6336; Internet e-mail address: uap@blue.ocis.temple.edu; World Wide Web site: http://www.temple.edu/inst_disabilities).

Intellitools, Inc., 55 Leveroni Court, Suite #9, Novato, CA 94949 (800-899-6687; 415-382-5959; fax: 415-382-5950; Internet e-mail address: info@intellitools.com; World Wide Web site: http://www.intellitools.com).

International Society for Augmentative and Alternative Communication, 49 The Donway, West, Suite 308, Toronto, Ontario M3C 3M9, Canada (416-385-0351; fax: 416-385-0352; Internet e-mail address: isaac_mail@mail.cepp.org).

Kompagne VOF, Winthontlaan 200-A1, Utrecht 3526 KV, the Netherlands.

Made by Mom Creations, 307 Louellen Street, New Westminster, British Columbia V3M 4G6, Canada (604-525-1012).

Makaton Vocabulary Development Project, 31 Firwood Drive, Camberley, Surrey GU15 3QD, United Kingdom (01-44-0-1276-61390; fax: 01-44-0-1276-681368; World Wide Web site: http://www.makaton.mta.ca/).

Mayer-Johnson Co., Post Office Box AD, Solana Beach, CA 92075-0838 (World Wide Web site: http://www.mayer-johnson.com).

Med Labs, Inc., 28 Vereda Cordillera, Goleta, CA 93117 (800-968-2486).

Microsystems Software, Inc., 600 Worcester Road, Framingham, MA 01701 (508-879-9000; World Wide Web site: http://www.handiware.com).

Modern Signs Press, Post Office Box 1181, Los Alamitos, CA 90720 (World Wide Web site: http://www.mbnet.mb.ca:80/~swuerz/mspage.html).

National Aphasia Association, 156 Fifth Avenue, New York, NY 10010 (800-922-4622).

National Cued Speech Association, Nazareth College of Rochester, 4245 East Avenue, Rochester, NY 14618 (Internet e-mail address: ncsa@naz.edu; World Wide Web site: http://web7.mit.edu/CuedSpeech/ncsainfo.html).

Nelson Canada, 1120 Birchmount Road, Scarborough, Ontario M1K 5G4, Canada (416-752-9448; fax: 416-752-8101; World Wide Web site: http://www.thomson.com/nelson).

New York Association for the Blind, 111 East 59th Street, New York, NY 10022.

Oregon Health Sciences University, Center for Self-Determination, 3608 Southeast Powell Boulevard, Portland, OR 97202 (fax: 503-232-6423).

Paul H. Brookes Publishing Co., Post Office Box 10624, Baltimore, MD 21285-0624 (800-638-3755; 410-337-9580; fax: 410-337-8539; Internet e-mail address: custserv@pbrookes.com; World Wide Web site: http://www.pbrookes.com).

Permanent Reflections, 206 Browning Avenue, Toronto, Ontario M4K 1X2, Canada (416-463-7415; Internet e-mail address: mikey@spectranet.ca).

Poppin and Company, Post Office Box 176, Unity, ME 04988 (207-437-2746; fax: 207-437-2404).

Prentke Romich Company, 1022 Heyl Road, Wooster, OH 44691 (800-262-1933; Internet e-mail address: info@prentrom.com; World Wide Web site: http://www.prentrom.com).

Productivity Software, International, Inc., 211 East 43rd Street, Suite 2202, New York, NY 10017-4707 (212-818-1144; fax: 212-818-1197).

The Psychological Corporation (U.S.), 555 Academic Court, San Antonio, TX 78204-9941 (800-211-8378; fax: 800-232-1223).

The Psychological Corporation (Canada), 55 Horner Avenue, Toronto, Ontario M8Z 4X6, Canada (800-387-7278; fax: 800-665-7307).

Rehabilitation Engineering Research Center, Applied Science and Engineering Laboratories, University of Delaware, Alfred I. DuPont Institute, 1600 Rockland Road, Post Office Box 269, Wilmington, DE 19899 (302-651-6830).

San Francisco State University, Bay Area Severely Handicapped/Deaf-Blind Project, San Francisco, CA 94132.

Scholastic, Inc., Post Office Box 7502, Jefferson City, MO 65102-9968 (800-724-6527; fax: 800-223-4011).

Scotlander Software, Ltd., 74 Victoria Crescent Road, Glasgow G12 9JN, United Kingdom (fax: 01-41-357-5034).

Self Advocates Becoming Empowered, Post Office Box 121211, Nashville, TN 37212-1211.

Semantic Compaction Systems, 1000 Killarney Drive, Pittsburgh, PA 15234 (412-885-8541; fax: 412-885-8548; Internet e-mail address: minspeak@sgi.net; World Wide Web site: http://128.2.110.35/scs/index.html).

Sentient Systems Technology, 2100 Wharton Street, Pittsburgh, PA 15203 (800-344-1778; World Wide Web site: http://www.sentient-sys.com:80).

Support Helps Others Use Technology, 1000 Killarney Avenue, Pittsburgh, PA 15234 (800-934-4391).

Southeast Augmentative Communication Publications, 2430 11th Avenue, North, Birmingham, AL 35234 (205-251-0165; fax: 205-226-9107).

Special Communications, 916 West Castillo Drive, Litchfield Park, AZ 85340.

Tash International, Inc., Unit 1-91, Station Street, Ajax, Ontario L1S 3H2, Canada (800-463-5685; 905-686-4129; fax: 905-686-6895; Internet e-mail address: tashcan@aol.com; World Wide Web site: http://www.tashusa.com).

Trace Research and Development Center, University of Wisconsin–Madison, S-151 Waisman Center, 1500 Highland Avenue, Madison, WI 53705-2280 (608-263-5776; 608-263-5910; fax: 608-263-0529; Internet e-mail address: webmaster@waisman.wisc.edu; World Wide Web site: http://trace.wisc.edu).

University of Dundee, Department of Applied Computing, Dundee DD1 4HN, United Kingdom (01-44-1382-344151; fax: 01-44-1382-345509; World Wide Web site: http://www.computing.dundee.ac.uk).

University of Illinois Press, 1325 South Oak Street, Champaign, IL 61820-6903 (217-333-0950).

Vistech Corporation, 4162 Little York Road, Dayton, OH 45414 (937-454-1399).

Widgit Software Ltd., 102 Radford Road, Leamington Spa, Warwickshire CV31 1LF, United Kingdom (01-44-0-1926-885303; fax: 01-44-0-1926-885293; Internet e-mail address: widgit@widgitsw.demon.co.uk; World Wide Web site: http://www.widgit.com).

Words+, Inc., 40015 Sierra Highway, Building B-145, Palmdale, CA 93550 (800-869-2521; fax: 805-255-8969; World Wide Web site: http://www.words-plus.com).

Wuerz Publishing, 895 McMillan Avenue, Winnipeg, Manitoba R3M 0T2, Canada (204-956-0308; fax: 204-956-5053; World Wide Web site: http://www.mbnet.mb.ca/~swuerz/).

ZYGO Industries, Inc., Post Office Box 1008, Portland, OR 97207-1008 (toll free for U.S. and Canada: 800-234-6006; 503-684-6006; fax: 503-684-6011; World Wide Web site: http://www.zygo-usa.com).

Index

Page numbers followed by "f" denote figures; those followed by "t" indicate tables.